FAITH SEEKING UNDERSTANDING

what is the difference between person
and work of christ?

person: christology
work: soteriology

FAITH SEEKING UNDERSTANDING

An Introduction to Christian Theology

• •

SECOND EDITION

Daniel L. Migliore

WILLIAM B. EERDMANS PUBLISHING COMPANY
GRAND RAPIDS, MICHIGAN / CAMBRIDGE, U.K.

© 1991, 2004 Wm. B. Eerdmans Publishing Co.

First edition 1991
Second edition 2004

Wm. B. Eerdmans Publishing Co.
255 Jefferson Ave. S.E., Grand Rapids, Michigan 49503 /
P.O. Box 163, Cambridge CB3 9PU U.K.

Printed in the United States of America

09 08 07 06 05   7 6 5 4 3 2

ISBN 0-8028-2787-X

www.eerdmans.com

Contents

CONTENTS

Contents

Contents

Acknowledgments

Many students, colleagues, and friends have assisted me in the writing of this book. I especially wish to thank those who read the manuscript in whole or in part and offered helpful comments: Cornelius Plantinga, Jr. (Professor of Systematic Theology, Calvin Theological Seminary), and several colleagues at Princeton Theological Seminary: George S. Hendry (Charles Hodge Professor Emeritus of Systematic Theology), Hugh T. Kerr (Benjamin B. Warfield Professor Emeritus of Systematic Theology), Nancy Duff (Assistant Professor of Ethics), and Kathleen D. Billman and Leanne Van Dyk (Ph.D. candidates).

I am also indebted to George Stroup (Professor of Systematic Theology, Columbia Theological Seminary), Michael Welker (Professor of Systematic Theology, University of Münster), and Sang Hyun Lee, Mark Kline Taylor, and David E. Willis-Watkins (Professors of Systematic Theology, Princeton Theological Seminary), with each of whom at various times I have team taught the basic course in theology at Princeton. Just how much their ideas have enriched my own would be embarrassing to relate in detail.

I am grateful to President Thomas Gillespie and the Trustees of Princeton Theological Seminary for a sabbatical leave in 1990-1991 that enabled me to complete the writing of this book. Joe Herman, a faculty assistant with extraordinary talents, helped with the typing and other details.

My gratitude to my wife Margaret for her love and support as well as for her wise editorial advice is far greater than I can say.

Finally, I want to express my thanks to the many first-year M.Div. students in THo1 who patiently listened to earlier versions of some of these chapters. Their questions, suggestions, and encouragement have been a continuous source of strength and joy to me. To all these students this book is gratefully dedicated.

Preface to the Second Edition

"Everything has changed." These words were heard again and again in the days after the attack on the World Trade Center in New York on September 11, 2001. Many things have indeed changed since that event. After the initial shock and sadness, the United States launched "counter-terrorist" wars first in Afghanistan and then in Iraq. Anxiety is widespread, security concerns are paramount, and the foundations of international order are shaking. At another level, however, everything has not changed. What has not changed is a world groaning in bondage to sin, death, and destruction, where strangers are feared, violence is a way of life, and the poor and vulnerable are forgotten. What has also not changed is the good news of the gospel of God's forgiving and transforming love, the promise and power of God's work of reconciliation in Jesus Christ, and the real but often unnoticed manifestations of a new world of hospitality, friendship, and peace born of the Spirit of Christ.

What the church needs at all times and especially in times of crisis is clarity of conviction and purpose. While signs will not be lacking in this second edition of *Faith Seeking Understanding* of my own wrestling with recent terrorist acts and wars against terrorism, my central concern has been to sharpen and expand the basic convictions informing this introduction to Christian theology: the understanding of God as triune, the centrality of Jesus Christ and his work of reconciliation, and the hope of fulfillment of life in communion with God and with all others by the power of the Holy Spirit.

I said in the preface to the first edition and repeat now that every theology must be *critical* reflection on the beliefs and practices of the faith community out of which it arises. In this way theology that speaks from and to the church also becomes public theology. Faith seeks understanding and does not pretend that it has arrived at its goal. More than a decade ago I worried about "the surge of fundamentalism in Christianity and Islam" and hoped that the cultured despisers of religion would not continue to underestimate the immense influence, for good or ill, of religious conviction on human life. I would now add only that when religious passion goes awry, it is the most dangerous and destructive passion of all. Religious communities have a continuing responsibility to search for what is central in their faith heritage and to examine all their doctrines and practices in that light. That is a crucial theological task both for times when it is claimed that "everything has changed" and for quieter times when no catastrophic event has occurred to show how important this self-critical responsibility of faith communities is.

Criticism needs, of course, a criterion. In the Christian church the criterion of critical and constructive theological work is the "the central Christian message," the gospel of Jesus Christ, the incarnate, crucified, and risen Word of God. This living Word is present here and now by the power of the Holy Spirit in the witness, life, and service of the church. The same Word and Spirit are also at work, if still more hidden, throughout the creation to bring God's reconciliation of the world to completion. My effort in this new edition has been to strengthen what I earlier called "the fullness of trinitarian faith" and its relational understanding of God, creation, reconciliation, and consummation.

I continue to hold that "the work of theology is inseparably bound to an identifiable faith community" and goes hand in hand with "participation in the common life of a community of faith, prayer, and service." As for the "Reformed theological heritage and orientation" that I said marked the first edition of the book, I hope that it continues to be evident in the new edition, provided that "Reformed" is not understood as an alternative to "catholic" or "ecumenical." I have no desire to do "denominational theology." Like every Christian theologian, I stand within a particular stream of the Christian theological tradition. But Christian theology is necessarily "catholic" in scope and "evangelical" in substance or it is not Christian theology at all.

In addition to rewriting, expanding, and updating all chapters, I have added two new chapters on "Confessing Jesus Christ in Context" and "The Finality of Jesus Christ and Religious Pluralism." I have also supplied a glossary of terms that I hope will be helpful to first readers in theology.

Once again, my indebtedness to students, colleagues, and friends is great. Thanks especially to Ph.D. candidates Rachel Baard, Matthew Flemming, Matthew Lundberg, Kevin Park, and Ruben Rosario Rodriguez, and to my colleagues, Professors Karlfried Froehlich and Mark K. Taylor. Each read parts of the revised text and suggested improvements. I am, of course, entirely responsible for the flaws that remain.

xii

Preface to the First Edition

The past few decades have been a time of remarkable ferment in Christian theology. Many new emphases, proposals, and movements have appeared — black theology, feminist theology, Latin American liberation theology, process theology, narrative theology, and metaphorical theology, to mention only the more prominent. It has been a time of unprecedented ecumenical dialogue, of intense reflection on theological method, of dramatic paradigm shifts, of insistence on the importance of praxis, and of many experiments in conversation between theology and other areas of inquiry. Some observers of this ferment have suggested that theology is in utter disarray; I do not share that pessimistic judgment.

Still, the present situation is not without its dangers, especially for the beginning student in theology. The exciting diversity of new theological proposals and programs can easily lead to confusion or thoughtless eclecticism. These dangers are heightened if certain perennial tasks of theology are neglected. One writer warns, for example, of the "abdication of responsibility" for constructive or systematic theological work in our time, due in part to a preoccupation with methodological issues. "There is a growing danger," he says, "that the work of theology is being replaced by the work of preparing to do theology."[1]

My purpose in writing this book is to offer an introduction to Christian theology that is both critically respectful of the classical theological tradition and critically open to the new voices and emphases of recent theology. I hope that the influence of the liberation theologies of our time — especially femi-

---

1. Theodore W. Jennings, Jr., *The Vocation of the Theologian* (Philadelphia: Fortress, 1985), 2-3.

nist, black, and Latin American — will be evident throughout the book. I am fairly certain that my Reformed theological heritage and orientation will not go unnoticed. I will consider my work successful if it helps to strengthen younger theologians in the conviction that a mutually critical and a mutually enriching interaction between liberation theologies and classical theological traditions is both possible and worth the effort.

Everyone who does theology today must be self-critically aware of his or her own social location and ecclesial context. While I am Protestant, North American, white, and male, my background and experience do not conform to the stereotypical WASP profile. My formative experience of Christian community was in a small Presbyterian congregation in Pittsburgh, Pennsylvania, of which my father was pastor. Almost all of the members of the church were struggling Italian immigrants and their families. Years before my encounter with the civil rights movement in the 1960s and with various liberation theologies in the 1970s, I learned some important lessons about the inseparability of faith and practice in that small congregation. Communication of the gospel in that context was always more than a theoretical affair, and concern for those at the margins of society was always a priority of Christian ministry.

While I do not pretend that my presentation of Christian doctrine will be adequate for all times and places, I hope that I have expressed a measure of the fullness of the faith of the worldwide Christian community. I further hope that readers will find that I have tried to listen to a large chorus of old and new voices and that I welcome the help and correction that comes from continuing dialogue with Christians whose experience and context are quite different from my own. I am grateful for the assistance I have received in this learning process from many students and colleagues, male and female, black and white, North and South American, European, African, and Asian.

The immediate context of my own theological work is a seminary of a "mainline" Protestant church in North America. While I am aware of the hazards of any attempt to write an outline of Christian doctrine at the present time, I am equally aware of the likely consequences of failing to make such an effort. In the context of North American schools of theology with which I am familiar, the absence of the risk of systematic reinterpretation of Christian doctrine results in the victory of unexamined orthodoxy or the triumph of nontheological professionalism.

Several convictions about the nature of theology inform this introduction. One is that Christian theology, or any other theology for that matter, arises out of, and remains importantly linked to, a *particular community of faith*. Whether theology is pursued in a seminary or in a university setting is not at issue here. The point is that theological inquiry does not arise in a vacuum. It is not built on amorphous religious experiences or on the pious imaginations of isolated individuals. On the contrary, the work of theology is inseparably bound to an identifiable faith community that worships God, attends to Scripture and its accounts of God's work and will, and engages in manifold ministries of education, reconciliation, and liberation. In short, theological inquiry requires continuing participation in the common life of a community of faith, prayer, and service. Apart from such participation, theology would soon become an empty exercise.

As I hope this book makes clear, I am also convinced that theology must be *critical reflection* on the community's faith and practice. Theology is not simply reiteration of what has been or is currently believed and practiced by a community of faith. It is a quest for truth, and that presupposes that the proclamation and practice of the community of faith are always in need of examination and reform. When this responsibility for critical reflection is neglected or relegated to a merely ornamental role, the faith of the community is invariably threatened by shallowness, arrogance, and ossification. The surge of fundamentalism in Christianity and Islam in recent years may yet persuade even the cultured despisers of religion that, for good or ill, religious commitment continues to exercise immense influence on human life. In our religiously pluralistic world the importance of *internal* critical reflection on the doctrines and practices of faith communities should not be overlooked.

Most decisively, critical reflection on the faith of the Christian community involves the deployment of a comprehensive theological vision, an interpretation of the *central Christian message* in interaction with the culture, experience, and need of a particular time and place. As we become increasingly aware today of our need for a thoroughgoing critique of domination in all spheres of life, systematic theology has the task of a consistent rethinking of God's power and presence in trinitarian terms, in which God is seen not as an all-controlling heavenly monarch but as the triune God who lives and acts in mutual self-giving and community-forming love. As the philosophy of individualism shows itself to be not only intellectually bankrupt but a contributor to ways of life that exploit the poor and ravage the environment, theology today is challenged to rethink the meaning of salvation along relational and communitarian lines, defining it not as a rescue of individual souls from the world but as the creation of a new and deeper freedom in community with God and solidarity with others. As mere theory and empty rhetoric come under fire because of their impotence in the face of the urgent crises of our time — racial injustice, political oppression, ecological deterioration, exploitation of women, the threat of nuclear holocaust — theology must understand itself not as abstract speculation but as concrete reflection that arises out of and is directed to the praxis of Christian faith, hope, and love. Thus a revised trinitarian theology, a corresponding relational understanding of creation, redemption, and consummation, and an orientation of theology to praxis are the major components of the theological vision that informs the following outline of Christian doctrine.

Finally, a word about the organization of the material. The order follows the classical loci of theology for the most part and is by intention trinitarian in both structure and content. The primary position given to the doctrine of the Trinity reflects my conviction concerning the central importance of this doctrine not only for classical Christian theology but for contemporary liberation faith and theology as well. After a lengthy period of Christological concentration in theology, we must reclaim for our time the fullness of trinitarian faith.[2]

The sole novelty in the presentation of topics is the inclusion of three imaginary dialogues of representative theologians and theological positions of the twentieth century. The dialogue form is, I think, not only pedagogically appealing, but often captures the vitality of theological inquiry and the open-endedness of theological discussions much better than more conventional expositions.

2. The constitution of the World Council of Churches states, "The World Council of Churches is a fellowship of churches which confess the Lord Jesus Christ as God and Savior according to the scriptures and therefore seek to fulfill together their common calling to the glory of the one God, Father, Son, and Holy Spirit."

Sources Frequently Cited

Karl Barth, *Church Dogmatics,* 13 vols. (Edinburgh: T&T Clark, 1936-1969).

The Book of Confessions, Presbyterian Church (U.S.A.) (Louisville: Office of the General Assembly, 1999).

John Calvin, *Institutes of the Christian Religion,* 2 vols., ed. John T. McNeill (Philadelphia: Westminster Press, 1960).

Luther's Works, 55 vols., gen. eds. Jaroslav Pelikan and Helmut T. Lehman (St. Louis: Concordia; Philadelphia: Fortress, 1955-1986).

Paul Tillich, *Systematic Theology,* 3 vols. (Chicago: University of Chicago Press, 1951-1963).

CHAPTER 1

The Task of Theology

Christian theology has many tasks. This is evident both from a reading of the history of theology and from the wide variety of current understandings of its nature and task. Some theologians today contend that the task of Christian theology is to provide a clear and comprehensive description of Christian doctrine. Other theologians emphasize the importance of translating Christian faith in terms that are intelligible to the wider culture. For others theology is defined broadly as thinking about important issues from the perspective of Christian faith. And still others insist that theology is reflection on the practice of Christian faith within an oppressed community.[1]

Underlying each of these understandings of the task of theology is the assumption that faith and inquiry are inseparable. Theology arises from the freedom and responsibility of the Christian community to inquire about its faith in God. In this chapter I propose to describe the work of theology as a continuing search for the fullness of the truth of God made known in Jesus Christ. Defining the theological task in this way emphasizes that theology is

1. For some representative discussions of the nature and task of theology, see Karl Barth, *Evangelical Theology* (New York: Doubleday Anchor Books, 1964), 1-10; Paul Tillich, *Systematic Theology* (Chicago: University of Chicago Press, 1951), vol. 1, 3-68; Gustavo Gutiérrez, *A Theology of Liberation*, rev. ed. (Maryknoll, N.Y.: Orbis Books, 1988), 3-12; David Tracy, *The Analogical Imagination: Christian Theology and the Culture of Pluralism* (New York: Crossroad, 1981), 3-98; *The Vocation of the Theologian*, ed. Theodore W. Jennings, Jr. (Philadelphia: Fortress, 1985); Anne E. Carr, "The New Vision of Feminist Theology," in *Freeing Theology: The Essentials of Theology in Feminist Perspective*, ed. Catherine Mowry Lacugna (San Francisco: Harper, 1993), 5-29; Wolfhart Pannenberg, *Systematic Theology* (Grand Rapids: Eerdmans, 1991), 1-61; Jürgen Moltmann, *Experiences in Theology: Ways and Forms of Christian Theology* (Minneapolis: Fortress, 2000), xiv-xxiv, 3-27, 43-63; Rowan Williams, *On Christian Theology* (Oxford: Blackwell, 2000), 3-15.

not mere repetition of traditional doctrines but a persistent search for the truth to which they point and which they only partially and brokenly express. As continuing inquiry, the spirit of theology is interrogative rather than doctrinaire; it presupposes a readiness to question and to be questioned. Like the search of a woman for her lost coin (Luke 15:8), the work of theology is strenuous but may bring great joy.

Theology as Faith Seeking Understanding

According to one classical definition, theology is "faith seeking understanding" (fides quaerens intellectum). This definition, with numerous variations, has a long and rich tradition. In the writings of Augustine it takes the form, "I believe in order that I may understand." According to Augustine, knowledge of God not only presupposes faith, but faith also restlessly seeks deeper understanding. Christians want to understand what they believe, what they can hope for, and what they ought to love.[2] Writing in a different era, Anselm, who is credited with coining the phrase "faith seeking understanding," agrees with Augustine that believers inquire "not for the sake of attaining to faith by means of reason but that they may be gladdened by understanding and meditating on those things that they believe." For Anselm, faith seeks understanding, and understanding brings joy. "I pray, O God, to know thee, to love thee, that I may rejoice in thee."[3] Standing in the tradition of Augustine and Anselm, Karl Barth contends that theology has the task of reconsidering the faith and practice of the community, "testing and rethinking it in the light of its enduring foundation, object, and content. . . . What distinguishes theology from blind assent is just its special character as 'faith seeking understanding.'"[4]

A common conviction of these theologians, and of the classical theological tradition generally, is that Christian faith prompts inquiry, searches for deeper understanding, dares to raise questions. How could we ever be finished with the quest for a deeper understanding of God? What would be the likely result if we lacked the courage to ask, Do I rightly know who God is and what God wills? According to Martin Luther, "That to which your heart clings

2. Augustine, Confessions and Enchiridion, ed. Albert C. Outler (Philadelphia: Westminster, 1955), 338.

3. St. Anselm: Proslogium; Monologium; An Appendix in Behalf of the Fool by Gaunilon; and Cur Deus Homo, trans. Sidney Norton Deane (La Salle, Ill.: Open Court Publishing Co., 1951), 178, 33.

4. Barth, Evangelical Theology, 36.

and entrusts itself is . . . really your God."[5] As Luther goes on to explain, our god may in fact be money, possessions, power, fame, family, or nation. What happens when those who say they believe in God stop asking whether what their heart really clings to is the one true God or an idol?

Christian faith is at bottom trust in and obedience to the free and gracious God made known in Jesus Christ. Christian theology is this same faith in the mode of asking questions and struggling to find at least provisional answers to these questions. Authentic faith is no sedative for world-weary souls, no satchel full of ready answers to the deepest questions of life. Instead, faith in God revealed in Jesus Christ sets an inquiry in motion, fights the inclination to accept things as they are, and continually calls in question unexamined assumptions about God, our world, and ourselves. Consequently, Christian faith has nothing in common with indifference to the search for truth, or fear of it, or the arrogant claim to possess it fully. True faith must be distinguished from fideism. Fideism says there comes a point where we must stop asking questions and must simply believe; faith keeps on seeking and asking.

Theology grows out of this dynamism of Christian faith that incites reflection, inquiry, and pursuit of the truth not yet possessed, or only partially possessed. There are at least two fundamental roots of this quest of faith for understanding that we call theology. The first has to do with the particular *object* of Christian faith. Faith is faith in the living God, and God is and remains a mystery beyond human comprehension. Although the "object" of our faith, God never ceases to be "subject." Faith is a relation to the living God and not to a dead, manipulable idol. In Jesus Christ the living, inexhaustibly rich God has been revealed as sovereign, holy love. To know God in this revelation is to acknowledge the infinite and incomprehensible depth of the mystery called God. Christians are confronted by mystery in all the central affirmations of their faith: the wonder of creation; the humility of God in Jesus Christ; the transforming power of the Holy Spirit; the miracle of forgiveness of sins; the gift of new life in communion; the call to the ministry of reconciliation; the promise of the consummation of God's reign. To the eyes of faith, the world is encompassed by the mystery of the free grace of God.

As Gabriel Marcel has explained, a mystery is very different from a problem. While a problem can be solved, a mystery is inexhaustible. A problem can be held at arm's length; a mystery encompasses us and will not let us keep a safe distance.[6] Christian faith prompts inquiry not least because it

---

5. Luther, "Large Catechism," in *The Book of Concord,* ed. Theodore G. Tappert (Philadelphia: Fortress, 1959), 365.

6. Marcel, *The Mystery of Being* (Chicago: Henry Regnery, 1960), 1: 260-61.

points to the shocking mystery that in the humble servant Jesus, his ministry, death, and resurrection, God is at work for our salvation. So while Christians affirm that God has decisively spoken in Jesus Christ (Heb. 1:1-2), there is much they do not understand. Perhaps there will come a time when no questions need be asked (John 16:23), but here and now faith sees only dimly, not face to face (1 Cor. 13:12), and the questions of faith abound.

The second root of the quest of faith for understanding is the *situation of faith*. Believers do not live in a vacuum. Like all people, they live in particular historical contexts that have their own distinctive problems and possibilities. The changing, ambiguous, and often precarious world poses ever new questions for faith, and many answers that sufficed yesterday are no longer compelling today.

Questions arise at the edges of what we can know and what we can do as human beings. They thrust themselves on us with special force in times and situations of crisis such as sickness, suffering, guilt, injustice, personal or social upheaval, and death. Believers are not immune to the questions that arise in these situations. Indeed, they may be more perplexed than others, because they have to relate their faith to what is happening in their lives and in the world. Precisely as believers they experience the frequent and disturbing incongruity between faith and lived reality. They believe in a sovereign and good God, but they live in a world where evil often seems triumphant. They believe in a living Lord, but more often than not they experience the absence rather than the presence of God. They believe in the transforming power of the Spirit of God, but they know all too well the weakness of the church and the frailty of their own faith. They know that they should obey God's will, but they find that it is often difficult to know what God's will is in regard to particular issues. And even when they know God's will, they frequently resist doing it. Christian faith asks questions, seeks understanding, both because God is always greater than our ideas of God, and because the public world that faith inhabits confronts it with challenges and contradictions that cannot be ignored. Edward Schillebeeckx puts the point succinctly: Christian faith "causes us to think."[7]

By emphasizing that faith, far from producing a closed or complacent attitude, awakens wonder, inquiry, and exploration, we underscore the humanity of the life of faith and of the discipline of theology. Human beings are open when they ask questions, when they keep seeking, when they are, as Augustine says, "ravished with love for the truth." To be human is to ask all sorts

---

7. Schillebeeckx, preface to *Interim Report on the Books Jesus and Christ* (New York: Crossroad, 1981).

of questions: Who are we? What is of highest value? Is there a God? What can we hope for? Can we rid ourselves of our flaws and improve our world? What should we do? When persons enter on the pilgrimage of faith, they do not suddenly stop being human; they do not stop asking questions. Becoming a Christian does not put an end to the human impulse to question and to seek for deeper understanding. On the contrary, being a pilgrim of faith intensifies and transforms many old questions and generates new and urgent questions: What is God like? How does Jesus Christ redefine true humanity? Is God present in the world today? What does it mean to be responsible disciples of the crucified and risen Lord? Those who have experienced something of the grace of God in Jesus Christ find themselves wanting to enter more fully into that mystery and to understand the world and every aspect of their lives in its light.

According to the philosopher Descartes, the only reliable starting point in the pursuit of truth is self-consciousness. *Cogito ergo sum,* "I think, therefore I am." The logic of Christian faith differs radically from this Cartesian logic in at least two respects. First, the starting point of inquiry for the Christian is not self-consciousness but awareness of the reality of God, who is creator and redeemer of all things. Not "I think, therefore I am," but "God is, therefore we are." As the psalmist writes, "O Lord, our Sovereign, how majestic is your name in all the earth. . . . When I look at your heavens, the work of your fingers, the moon and the stars that you have established; what are human beings that you are mindful of them, mortals that you care for them?" (Ps. 8:1, 3-4).

Second, for Christian faith and theology, inquiry is elicited by faith in God rather than being an attempt to arrive at certainty apart from God. Not "I seek certainty by doubting everything but my own existence," but "Because God has shown mercy to us, therefore we inquire." If we believe in God, we must expect that our old ways of thinking and living will be continually shaken to the foundations. If we believe in God, we will have to become seekers, pilgrims, pioneers with no permanent residence. We will no longer be satisfied with the unexamined beliefs and practices of our everyday lives. If we believe in God, we will necessarily question the gods of power, wealth, nationality, and race that clamor for our allegiance. Christian faith is not blind faith but "thinking faith"; Christian hope is not superficial optimism but "well-founded hope"; Christian love is not romantic naivete but "open-eyed love."[8]

---

8. See Douglas John Hall, *Thinking the Faith: Christian Theology in a North American Context* (Minneapolis: Augsburg, 1989); Hendrikus Berkhof, *Well-Founded Hope* (Richmond: John Knox, 1969); Jürgen Moltmann, *Experiences in Theology.*

As long as Christians remain pilgrims of faith, they will continue to raise questions — hard questions — for which they will not always find answers. Rather than having all the answers, believers often find that they have a new set of questions. This is surely the experience of the women and men in the Bible. The Bible is no easy answer book, although it is sometimes read that way. If we are ready to listen, the Bible has the power to shake us violently with its terrible questions: "Adam, where are you?" (Gen. 3:9). "Cain, where is your brother Abel?" (Gen. 4:9). To judge the cause of the poor and needy — "Is not this to know me? says the Lord" (Jer. 22:16). "Who do you say that I am?" (Mark 8:29). "My God, my God, why have you forsaken me?" (Mark 15:34). When faith no longer frees people to ask hard questions, it becomes inhuman and dangerous. Unquestioning faith soon slips into ideology, superstition, fanaticism, self-indulgence, and idolatry. Faith seeks understanding passionately and relentlessly, or it languishes and eventually dies. If faith raises ever new questions, then the theological task of the Christian community is to pursue these questions, to keep them alive, to prevent them from being forgotten or suppressed. Human life ceases to be human not when we do not have all the answers, but when we no longer have the courage to ask the really important questions. By insisting that these questions be raised, theology serves not only the community of faith but also the wider purpose of God "to make and to keep human life human" in the world.[9]

Theological inquiry of the sort I have been describing continually meets resistance from our fears. While we may be accustomed to raising questions in other areas of life, we are inclined to fear disturbance in matters of faith. We fear questions that might lead us down roads we have not traveled before. We fear the disruption in our thinking, believing, and living that might come from inquiring too deeply into God and God's purposes. We fear that if we do not find answers to our questions we will be left in utter despair. As a result of these fears, we imprison our faith, allow it to become boring and stultifying, rather than releasing it to seek deeper understanding.[10]

Only trust in the perfect love of God is able to overcome our persistent fears (1 John 4:18) and give us the courage to engage in free theological work. Theology can then become a process of seeking, contending, wrestling, like Jacob with the angel, wanting to be blessed and limping away from the struggle (Gen. 32:24ff.). Theology as faith seeking understanding offers many moments of delight in the beauty of the free grace and resurrection power of

---

9. Paul Lehmann, *Ethics in a Christian Context* (New York: Harper & Row, 1963), 112.

10. For an illuminating discussion of the role of fear in theological learning, see F. LeRon Shults, *Reforming Theological Anthropology* (Grand Rapids: Eerdmans, 2003), 70-76.

God. Yet it is also able to look into the abyss. It would cease to be responsible theology if it forgot for a moment the cross of Jesus Christ and the experiences of human life in the shadow of the cross where God seems absent and hell triumphant. This is the meaning of Luther's arresting declaration of what it takes to be a theologian: "It is by living, no — more — by dying and being damned to hell that one becomes a theologian, not by knowing, reading, or speculating."[11]

The Questionableness of Theology

If Christian faith causes us to think, this is not to say that being Christian is exhausted in thinking, even in thinking about the doctrines of the church. Christian faith causes us to do more than think. Faith sings, confesses, rejoices, suffers, prays, and acts. When faith and theology are exhausted in thinking, they become utterly questionable. This is because the understanding that is sought by faith is not speculative knowledge but the wisdom that illumines life and practice. As John Calvin explains, genuine knowledge of God is inseparable from worship and service.[12] Faith seeks the truth of God that wants not only to be known by the mind but also to be enjoyed and practiced by the whole person. Theology as thoughtful faith comes from and returns to the service of God and neighbor.

No doubt there is such a thing as too much theology — or, more precisely, there is such a thing as unfruitful, abstract theology that gets lost in a labyrinth of academic trivialities. When this happens, theology comes under judgment. In a paraphrase of the prophet Amos, Karl Barth humorously expresses the likely judgment of God on theology that has become pointless and endless talk: "I hate, I despise your lectures and seminars, your sermons, addresses and Bible studies. . . . When you display your hermeneutic, dogmatic, ethical and pastoral bits of wisdom before one another and before me, I have no pleasure in them. . . . Take away from me your . . . thick books and . . . your dissertations . . . your theological magazines, monthlies and quarterlies."[13]

Simple Christian piety has always objected to speculative and useless theology that frivolously asks how many angels can dance on the head of a pin or presumptuously deals with the mystery of God as with a problem in al-

---

11. *Luthers Werke* (Weimar), 5.163.28, quoted by Jürgen Moltmann, *Experiences in Theology*, 23-24.

12. Calvin, *Institutes of the Christian Religion*, 1.2.1. Note also that for Calvin the gospel is not "a doctrine of the tongue but of life" (3.6.4).

13. Barth, *Evangelical Theology*, 120.

gebra. It is entirely understandable why some Christians find such theological activity completely questionable. In their frustration, they say, "Away with theology and all its clever distinctions and wearisome debates. What we need is not more theology but simple faith, not more elegant arguments but transformed hearts, unadorned commitment to Christ, unqualified acceptance of what the Bible teaches, and uncompromising trust in the Holy Spirit."

While this criticism of theology in the name of simple piety is important and stands as a constant warning against detached, insensitive, and overly intellectualized theology, it cannot itself go unchallenged without serious injury to the life of individual Christians and the well-being of the Christian community. Christian faith is indeed simple, but it is not simplistic. Loyalty to and heartfelt trust in Christ are indeed basic and necessary, but Christians are enjoined to bring their whole life and their every thought into captivity to Christ (2 Cor. 10:5), and this is always an arduous process. While the church is indeed to stand under the authority of the biblical witness, it must avoid bibliolatry and read Scripture with sensitivity to its particular historical contexts and its diverse literary forms. While Christians are certainly to rely on the power of the Holy Spirit, they are also commanded to test the spirits to see whether they are from God (1 John 4:1). The grace of God is indeed a mystery in which men and women are invited to participate rather than an intellectual puzzle that they are to solve. But to speak of God as a mystery is one thing; to revel in mystification and obscurantism is quite another. "Theology," Karl Barth writes, "means taking rational trouble over the mystery. . . . If we are unwilling to take the trouble, neither shall we know what we mean when we say that we are dealing with the mystery of God."[14] An appeal to the Bible or the Holy Spirit should not be considered an alternative to serious reflection. Christian faith must not be reduced to a euphoric feeling or to a religious cliché. Christ is indeed the answer, but what was the question? And who is Christ? Christian faith is no authoritarian, uncritical, unreflective set of answers to the human predicament. Genuine faith does not suppress any questions; it may give people a lot more questions than they had before. Thus the anxiety of simple piety is misplaced. The sort of thinking that Christian faith sets in motion does not replace trust in God but acts as a critical ingredient that helps to distinguish faith from mere illusion or pious evasion.

The attack on theology as a questionable pursuit, however, comes from another quarter as well. It is launched by the representatives of practical faith who find theology, at least as it is often done, useless and even pernicious.

14. Barth, *Church Dogmatics*, 1/1: 423.

Charging that most theology is a mere intellectual game that leads to paralysis rather than action, these critics say, "Christians should stop all this barren theorizing and get on with doing something for Christ's sake. Did not the apostle Paul say that the kingdom of God is not talk but power (1 Cor. 4:20)? Surely faith is more than thinking correctly (a notion that might be called the heresy of orthodoxy). Faith is a matter of transformation — personal, social, and world transformation. It is being willing to put your life on the line for the sake of Christ and his gospel." Here again, there is some truth in this line of criticism. When theology becomes mere theory divorced from Christian life and practice, it is indeed questionable. But the criticism is one-sided. If theory without practice is empty, practice without theory is blind. How are Christians to know whether this or that action is "for the sake of Christ and the coming kingdom of God" if they impatiently shrug off important questions: Who is Christ? What is his kingdom? Mindless leaps into action are no more Christian than thinking for thinking's sake. God's call to faithfulness can sometimes be a summons to be still and wait. There is a creative waiting as well as a creative acting. Christian faith causes us to think, to raise questions, to be suspicious of the bandwagons, the movements that are intolerant of questions, the generals on the right or the left who demand unquestioning allegiance and simply bark, "Forward, march!"

But the critics of theology may go further and charge that it is not only speculative and impractical but that it often assumes a quite sinister and despicable form. It often serves to give religious justification to the rule of the powerful and to conditions of injustice. Since the doctrines of the church have often been invoked in defense of the way things are, it should come as no surprise that Karl Marx concluded that the critique of religion and theology must be the first step in the critique of social and economic injustice. The suspicion of the "mystifying" function of much religion and theology is by no means original to Marxism. We find it at work in the judgments of the Old Testament prophets and in the teaching of Jesus. They knew very well the extent to which religion and its official custodians can stand in opposition to God's intentions for human life. Theology indeed becomes questionable when it ceases to ask itself what powers it is in fact serving and whose interests it may be promoting. It is clear that much Christian theology has not yet learned to take these questions with the seriousness that they deserve.

Theology, I have been contending, is the continuous process of inquiry that is prompted both by the surprising grace of God and by the distance between the promise of God's coming reign on the one hand and our experience of the brokenness of human life on the other. If the task of theology is properly understood, it will not be seen as an activity that can be abandoned to a cadre of professional theologians in the church. It is an activity in which all members of the community of faith participate in appropriate ways. In the life of faith "no one is excused the task of asking questions or the more difficult one of providing and assessing answers."[15] If theology has been put to uses that make it questionable and even contemptible, all members of the community of faith must ask themselves to what extent they have contributed to this misuse by their own surrender of theological responsibility. To be sure, faith and theology are not identical. An advanced degree in theology is no more a guarantee of a living faith than a life of faith is deficient because of the absence of a theological degree. Still, faith and theological inquiry are closely related. If faith is the direct response to the hearing of God's word of grace and judgment, theology is the subsequent but necessary reflection of the church on its language and practice of faith. And this reflection happens at many levels and in many different life contexts.

The Questions of Theology

While Christian theology can be pursued in different social contexts, it has a special relationship to the life of the church. Theology serves the church by offering both guidance and criticism. Theological reflection plays an important role in the life of the church because the church must be self-critical. It must be willing to examine its proclamation and practices to determine their faithfulness to the gospel of Jesus Christ that is the basis and norm of the church's life and mission.

Up to this point, I have been speaking of the process of inquiry called Christian theology in a somewhat undifferentiated way. There are in fact several branches of theology, and it is important to see how they relate to each other.[16] *Biblical theology* studies in detail the canonical writings of the Old and New Testaments that are acknowledged by the church as the primary witnesses to the work and word of God. *Historical theology* traces the many ways in which Christian faith and life have come to expression in different times and places. *Philosophical theology* employs the resources of philosophical inquiry to examine the meaning and truth of Christian faith in the light of rea-

---

15. Barth, *Church Dogmatics*, 3/4: 498.

16. On the need for rethinking the nature and organization of theological studies, see Edward Farley, *Theologia: The Fragmentation and Unity of Theological Education* (Philadelphia: Fortress, 1983); Charles M. Wood, *Vision and Discernment: An Orientation in Theological Study* (Atlanta: Scholars Press, 1985); David H. Kelsey, *To Understand God Truly: What's Theological about a Theological School?* (Philadelphia: Westminster/John Knox, 1992).

son and experience. *Practical theology* explores the meaning and integrity of the basic practices of the church and the specific tasks of ministry such as preaching, educating, pastoral counseling, caring for the poor, and visiting the sick, the dying, and the bereaved.

In this book we take up that aspect of the larger theological task of the community of faith that is called *systematic theology* (also called doctrinal or constructive theology). Informed by and interacting with the other theological disciplines, its particular task is to venture a faithful, coherent, timely, and responsible articulation of Christian faith. This is a critical and creative activity, and it requires both courage and humility. Systematic theology is challenged to rethink and reinterpret the doctrines and practices of the church in the light of what the church itself avows to be of central importance — namely, the gospel of Jesus Christ that liberates and renews life. All Christians, and especially those who exercise leadership in the Christian community as pastors and teachers, participate in the task of systematic theology insofar as they are constrained to ask at least four basic questions that bear upon every phase of Christian life and ministry.

1. *Are the proclamation and practice of the community of faith true to the revelation of God in Jesus Christ as attested in Scripture?* All questions of theology are finally aspects of this question. What is the Christian gospel, the "good news" of God made known in Christ, and how is it to be distinguished from its many misrepresentations and distortions? On this question hang the very identity of the Christian community and the faithfulness of its proclamation and life.

The apostle Paul pursues this critical inquiry of theology when he argues in Galatians and Romans that trust in the grace and forgiveness of God is radically different from a religion based on achievements and merits. Paul is blunt and uncompromising. There is for him only one true gospel (Gal. 1:6ff.). False gospels are to be exposed and rejected. In later centuries, Irenaeus argued against the Gnostics, Athanasius against Arianism, Augustine against Pelagianism, Luther against a late medieval system of salvation by works, Barth against nineteenth-century liberal Protestantism that had become the domesticated religion of bourgeois culture. From time to time, a creed or confession has been hammered out — the creeds of Nicea and Chalcedon, the Augsburg Confession, the Heidelberg Catechism, the Barmen Declaration, to name a few — marking a time and place where the church has been compelled to state its faith in the midst of controversy, as unambiguously as possible, lest the gospel be obscured or even lost.

In our own time, there are all sorts of facsimiles of the gospel being proclaimed, from the seductive cults of self-fulfillment to the ugly arrogance of apartheid Christianity. Is what is purported to be Christian proclamation an appropriate representation of the gospel? No responsible member of the Christian community — certainly no leader of the community — can avoid asking this question. If the gospel is never simply identical with everything that is called Christian or that wraps itself in religious garb, theological vigilance is necessary. If the gospel resists identification with many things that we have gotten used to in our personal and social life, the community of faith cannot cease to ask itself whether it has rightly heard and properly understood what Scripture attests as the "gospel of God" (Rom. 1:1). Theology as a formal discipline exists to keep that question alive, to ask it over and over again.

2. *Do the proclamation and practice of the community of faith give adequate expression to the whole truth of the revelation of God in Jesus Christ?* This second question of systematic theology tests the wholeness and coherence of the affirmations of the Christian community.

Many people are suspicious of "systematic" theology, and often with good reason. When theology undertakes to derive the whole of Christian doctrine from a single principle or group of principles, the "system" that is produced loses touch with the living Word of God. When theology adopts a rationalistic attitude that tries to master the revelation of God instead of faithfully following its lead, it becomes a "system" closed to the interruptions of God's grace and judgment. When theology thinks that the edifice that it builds is complete and permanent and will, like the Word of God, abide forever, it becomes a "system" devoid of faith. It is not the task of theology to build "systems" of thought in any of these senses. However brilliant and original such theological systems may be, they are at bottom efforts to control revelation, and they put real theological thinking to sleep.

Nevertheless, the effort of theology to be "systematic" should be affirmed insofar as it expresses trust in the unity and faithfulness of God in all of God's works. Because God is faithful, there are patterns and continuities in the acts of God attested in Scripture that give shape and coherence to theological reflection. Even in our "postmodern" era when, as David Tracy argues, "fragments" rather than "totalities" best describe the form of our knowledge of the world, of ourselves, and especially of God, a provisional "gathering of the fragments" is still possible and necessary.[17]

Just as Christian faith is not a smorgasbord of beliefs, so Christian theology is not a disparate bundle of symbols and doctrines from which one can

---

17. David Tracy, "Form and Fragment: The Recovery of the Hidden and Incomprehensible God," in *Reflections: Center of Theological Inquiry* 3 (Autumn 2000): 62-88.

select at will or organize into any pattern one pleases. The cross of Jesus Christ cannot be understood apart from his life and his resurrection, nor can either of these be properly understood apart from the cross. God's work of reconciliation cannot be rightly understood apart from the work of creation or the hope in the second coming of Christ and the consummation of all things. Christian doctrines form a coherent whole. They are deeply intertwined. They comprise a distinctive grammar. They tell a coherent story. Even expressions of faith that laudably aim to be "Christocentric" would be seriously defective if, for example, they neglected the goodness of creation or minimized the reality of evil in the world or marginalized Christian hope in the coming reign of God.

It is thus an inescapable part of the theological task to ask, What is the whole gospel that holds the church together in the bond of faith, hope, and love? If matters of race, gender, and ethnic heritage threaten the unity of the church, is that in part because our understandings of God, human beings created in the image of God, and the nature and purpose of the church are insufficiently formed by the gospel of Jesus Christ? If the church bears an uncertain witness on ecological issues, is that in part because the doctrine of creation has been badly neglected or is insufficiently integrated with other doctrines of the faith? If the church sets personal redemption against concern for social justice or concern for social justice against personal redemption, is that in part because its understanding of salvation is truncated? If the church is disturbed by the voices of the poor, women, blacks, Hispanics, the unemployed, the physically and mentally challenged, is this not because its quest for the whole truth of the gospel is arrested? When a deaf ear is turned to these disturbing voices, is it not because we assume that we are already in possession of the whole truth? In every age Christian theology must be strong and free enough to ask whether the church bears witness in its proclamation and life to the fullness and catholicity of the gospel of Jesus Christ. The church is always threatened by a false unity that does not allow for the inclusion of strangers and outcasts. Theology exists to keep alive the quest for the whole gospel that alone can bring unity without loss of enriching diversity, community without loss of personal or cultural integrity, peace without compromise of justice. Theology must not only ask, What is the true gospel? but also, What is the whole gospel? What is the breadth and length and height and depth of the love of God in Christ (Eph. 3:18-19)?

3. *Do the proclamation and practice of the community of faith represent the God of Jesus Christ as a living reality in the present context?* The Christian message must be interpreted again and again in new situations and in con-

cepts and images that are understandable to people in those situations. As Dietrich Bonhoeffer asked, Who is Christ for us *today?*[18]

The questions "What is the present gospel?" and "Who is Christ for us today?" may sound shocking at first. Is there a different gospel then and now, there and here? The answer is that there is indeed only one gospel of the triune God who created the world, who has acted redemptively for the world in Christ, and who is still renewing and transforming all things by the power of the Holy Spirit. Yet it is necessary to reinterpret the language of Christian faith — its stories, doctrines, and symbols — for our own time and place if we are faithfully to serve the gospel rather than uncritically to endorse the cultural forms in which it has been mediated to us.

Responsible theology is not an exercise in the repristination of an earlier culture. It is not a simple repetition of the faith of our fathers and mothers. To be sure, the task of theology requires us to listen to the past witness of the church. As Barth reminds us, "Augustine, Thomas Aquinas, Luther, Schleiermacher and all the rest are not dead, but living. They still speak and demand a hearing as living voices, as surely as we know that they and we belong together in the Church. They made in their time the same contribution to the task of the Church that is required of us today. As we make our contribution, they join in with theirs, and we cannot play our part today without allowing them to play theirs."[19] However, as Barth also emphasizes, we cannot discharge our own theological responsibility today by simply repeating the words of Augustine, Thomas Aquinas, or Luther. On the contrary, the work of theology involves our own thinking and deciding in our own time and place. It calls for our own faithfulness, creativity, and imagination. It is a *constructive* task. It involves the risk of re-presenting the Christian faith in new concepts and in new actions. It demands thinking through and living out the faith in relation to new experiences, new problems, and new possibilities. The Bible itself is a model of this process of dynamic re-presentation of the faith of the community in new times and situations. Bonhoeffer's question must not be avoided: Who is Jesus Christ for us *today?*

4. *Does the proclamation of the gospel of Jesus Christ by the community of faith lead to transforming practice in personal and social life?* This fourth basic question of systematic theology addresses the concrete and responsible embodiment of faith and discipleship in particular contexts. Christian faith calls people to freedom and responsibility in every sphere of life. Thus an indispensable task of theology is to ask how the gospel might reform and trans-

---

18. Dietrich Bonhoeffer, *Letters and Papers from Prison* (New York: Macmillan, 1972), 279.
19. Karl Barth, *Protestant Theology in the Nineteenth Century* (London: SCM, 2001), 17.

form human life in concrete ways in our own time and in our own situation. What bearing does the gospel have on the everyday decisions and actions of the community of faith and its individual members? What patterns of our own life, what institutional structures that we may have long taken for granted, must now be called in question by the gospel? What structures of evil must be named and challenged if the gospel is to have any concrete impact on human life in the present? Where can we discern the signs of new beginnings in a world marked by violence, terror, injustice, and apathy?

All these questions presuppose an inseparable bond between our trust in God's grace and our call to God's service. The gospel of Jesus Christ proclaims God's gift of forgiveness, reconciliation, freedom, and new life. But the gift of God enables and commands our free, glad, and courageous discipleship. Theology and ethics are thus conjoined. As James Cone writes, "Theological concepts have meaning only as they are translated into theological praxis, that is, the Church living in the world on the basis of what it proclaims."[20] True faith works through love (Gal. 5:6). We cannot seriously receive God's gift of new life without asking equally seriously what God commands us to do. Theology exists to remind us of God's gift *and* command, and thus to keep alive the question: What would it mean for us personally and corporately to bear a faithful and concrete witness to the crucified and risen Lord in our world today?

These four central questions of systematic theology must be asked not once but continuously. Theology never achieves more than partial success in answering them. However important it is to respect and learn from the answers given to these questions in the past, there is no guarantee that theology can simply build upon past answers. For this reason, theology must always have the freedom, wisdom, and courage to acknowledge its failures and to "begin again at the beginning."[21] Since such freedom, wisdom, and courage are gifts of the Spirit of God, prayer is the inseparable companion of theological inquiry. *Veni Creator Spiritus,* "Come, Creator Spirit!" Serious theological inquiry begins, continues, and ends in invocation.[22]

---

20. Cone, *God of the Oppressed* (New York: Seabury Press, 1975), 36.

21. Barth, *Evangelical Theology,* 146.

22. "Theological work must really and truly take place in the form of a liturgical act, as invocation of God, and as prayer" (Barth, *Evangelical Theology,* 145). For the significance of prayer for "honest theology," see also Rowan Williams, *On Christian Theology,* 3-15.

Methods of Asking Theological Questions

Theology not only asks questions but must be self-conscious about the way it does so. This is, in brief, the problem of theological method. While much has been written about theological method in recent years, we are far from any clear consensus. No doubt differences in theological method reflect fundamental differences in understandings of revelation and the mode of God's presence in the world. They also show the limitations of any single method to do all the tasks of theology.

An important factor affecting theological method is the primary social location in which a particular theology is pursued. The concrete situation of a theology helps to shape the questions that are raised and the priorities that are set. David Tracy contends that the present plurality of theologies can be understood as a result of their various primary locations in church, academy, or society. In each setting, different aims and criteria come into play. Each social location of theology imposes its own set of questions, its own relative criteria of truth and adequacy, and its own special emphases. Theology in the academic context naturally tends to be apologetically oriented; theology in the church is interested primarily in the clarification and interpretation of the church's message; theology in the wider society is concerned about the practical realization of God's new justice and peace.[23] With the help of Tracy's analysis, we can readily identify three important types of theological method, three different ways of asking theological questions.

1. One influential method of theology is Karl Barth's *Christocentric theology*, or the theology of the Word of God. Barth describes theology as a discipline of the church in which the church continuously tests itself and its proclamation by its own norm, which is Jesus Christ as attested in Scripture. For Barth, to say that theology is a discipline of the church is not to say that its task is simply to repeat church doctrines or traditions. Barth's *Church Dogmatics* is a thoroughly critical inquiry even if he claims that its method and norms are independent of other university disciplines. Theology for Barth is the process of subjecting the church and its proclamation to questioning and testing by reference to the living Word of God in Jesus Christ. The primary questions with which theology has to do are the questions the Word of God addresses to us here and now rather than the questions that arise out of our experience or situation. In spite of popular misrepresentations of his method, Barth does not say that we must suppress our own questions in the study of Scripture and in theological inquiry generally; nor does he argue that theol-

---

23. Tracy, *The Analogical Imagination*, 3-98.

ogy should work in isolation from philosophy, the social sciences, and other disciplines. His overriding emphasis, however, is that the questions of theology, no less than its answers, must be disciplined by theology's own subject matter and norm. In short, Barth's theological method underscores the priority of the Word of God and the unsettling questions that it continuously puts to all human life, but most especially to the church regarding the faithfulness of its proclamation and life.

2. A second very influential method of theology is the *method of correlation,* associated especially with the apologetic theology of Paul Tillich.[24] In this method, existential questions are formulated by an analysis of the human situation in a given period as seen in its philosophy, literature, art, science, and social institutions. These questions are then correlated with the "answers" of the Christian message. The aim is to create genuine conversation between human culture and revelation rather than driving a wedge between them. From Tillich's perspective, Barth's theological method is more of a soliloquy than a conversation. It moves only from revelation to culture and experience, rather than back and forth. Responding to critics of his method, Tillich contends that the method of correlation does not surrender the normativeness of revelation to general culture and human experience. Revelation is not normed *by* the situation but it must speak *to* it if it is to make sense, and this can happen only if theology attends to the actual questions raised within a particular situation. David Tracy's revisionary theology is a modification of Tillich's method of correlation. He stresses more fully and explicitly than Tillich that correlation involves mutual correction and mutual enrichment of the partners in the conversation. Only in this way, Tracy argues, is it possible to open theology to the important contributions of culture and to approach culture with genuine concern for the intelligibility and credibility of the truth claims of faith.

3. A third method of theology is the *praxis approach* of liberation theology. "Praxis" is a technical term designating a way to knowledge that binds together action, suffering, and reflection. The praxis method of theology is represented by African American, feminist, black South African, and many other Third World liberation theologians, most notably in Latin America. Gustavo Gutiérrez, a pioneer of Latin American liberation theology, recognizes that theology in the past has taken different forms and followed different paths. Among the most influential are the way of spiritual wisdom *(sapientia)* especially associated with the Augustinian tradition of theology, and the way of rational knowledge *(scientia)* represented by the Thomistic tradition. Gutiérrez allows that these ways of doing theology are "permanent and indispens-

---

24. See Tillich, *Systematic Theology,* especially 1: 3-68, 2: 13-16.

able functions of all theological thinking," but he defends the importance of a new form of theology as "critical reflection on Christian praxis in the light of the Word."[25] In this method of theology, real commitment to and struggle for justice come first. It is out of the real struggle for human freedom and justice in the world that the pertinent questions of theology are raised. A new way of reading and interpreting Scripture results when concrete praxis is taken as the point of departure for critical theological reflection. The first step is "real charity, action and commitment to the service of others. Theology is reflection, a critical attitude. Theology follows; it is the second step."[26] So understood, theology promotes justice rather than serving as an ideology that justifies a given social or ecclesiastical order. Beginning with participation in the struggle for change, theology helps to deepen and direct this struggle by recourse to the sources of revelation. Thus "the theology of liberation offers us not so much a new theme for reflection as a *new way* to do theology."[27] Liberation theologians are not satisfied with either Barth's *Church Dogmatics* or Tillich's *Systematic Theology*. Theology and the questions that it pursues must arise "from below," from the practice of solidarity with the poor and their struggle for justice and freedom.

It will become fairly obvious to the reader that the method and content of theology presented in the following chapters is considerably influenced by Karl Barth's approach to theology and by his creative reinterpretation of the Reformed theological tradition. At the same time, contributions from both the theologies of correlation and praxis will also be apparent. The ecumenical church has learned — and will no doubt continue to learn — from the methods of Christocentric and correlational theologies. It has, however, only begun to learn from the insights and methods of the contextual and liberation theologies. Writing from a prison cell, Bonhoeffer reflected on what theology and the church should have learned from having been compelled to live for ten years through the horrors and suffering of the Nazi regime: "There remains [for us] an experience of incomparable value. We have for once learnt to see the great events of world history from below, from the perspective of the outcast, the suspects, the maltreated, the powerless, the oppressed, the reviled — in short, from the perspective of those who suffer."[28]

Bonhoeffer tells us that he had to *learn* to view life and the gospel from below. And so, I suspect, do most of us in the church in North America. We

25. Gutiérrez, *A Theology of Liberation*, 11.
26. Gutiérrez, *A Theology of Liberation*, 9.
27. Gutiérrez, *A Theology of Liberation*, 12.
28. Bonhoeffer, *Letters and Papers from Prison*, 17.

are learning slowly that it makes a difference whether the Bible is read and the gospel is apprehended only from the standpoint of relatively well-to-do people or "from below," through the eyes of those who are weak and who don't count for much by the standards of successful people and institutions. As Gutiérrez has noted, much depends on whether the effort of theology is to help make the proclamation and practice of the gospel more understandable and credible to First World nonbelievers or to test itself against the situation of the forgotten ones of the Third World.

It would, of course, be a mistake for theology to take up one of these tasks and totally reject the other. The questions about Christian faith raised by the heirs of the Enlightenment deserve a hearing and a response, even if the presuppositions of these questions must be challenged more vigorously than has been the case in much modern theology. Yet it is equally true that theology has for too long ignored the questions raised by the weak and powerless of the earth. What is the true gospel? What is the whole gospel? What is the present gospel? What concrete practice of the gospel is called for today? These inescapable questions of faith and theology need to be asked also "from below," from the vantage point of what Bonhoeffer called "the incomparable experience" of solidarity with the afflicted. This should not be construed as a summons to anti-intellectualism or romanticism. It concerns finally the kind of theology one intends to pursue: a theology that accompanies those who cry "out of the depths" (Ps. 130:1) and that finds its center in the message of "Christ crucified" (1 Cor. 1:23), or a triumphalist theology that serves only the interests of the powerful.

To summarize these introductory reflections, I have contended that asking questions is part of what it means to be human, and that asking tough questions in the light of the grace of God in Jesus Christ is part of what it means to be Christian. What is theology? It is neither mere repetition of church doctrines nor grandiose system-building. It is faith asking questions, seeking understanding. It is disciplined yet bold reflection on Christian faith in the God of the gospel. It is the activity of "taking rational trouble over the mystery" of God revealed in Jesus Christ as attested by Scripture. It is inquiry yoked to prayer. When theology is neglected or becomes distracted, the community of faith may drift aimlessly, or be captured by spirits alien to its own. However difficult the theological task today, there is no escaping the questions about the truth, the wholeness, the intelligibility, and the concrete practice of the gospel. And there is no escaping the issue of whether all these questions of theology will be asked not only from the locations of church, academy, and society familiar to most North Americans but also "from below," from the "incomparable experience" of solidarity with a wounded humanity and a groaning creation.

CHAPTER 2

The Meaning of Revelation

Christian theology has to offer some account of the basis of the church's affirmations about God. It has to answer the question of the source of the knowledge believers claim to have of God and of all creatures in relation to God. Questions of this sort are not ordinarily addressed in the hymns, prayers, and creeds of the church. These primary expressions of faith do not attempt to give a reasoned account of the truth claims that they make. The most familiar and the most widely used of Christian creeds — the Apostles' and the Nicene — simply begin with the words, "I (or We) believe. . . ." Theological reflection on such confessions, however, is compelled to ask how the community of faith has come to know these things. What is the source of this knowledge of God? What kind of knowledge is it? What place do Scripture, the witness of the church, and human reason, experience, and imagination have in the knowledge of God? Such questions have usually been discussed in theology, especially in the modern period, under the topic of revelation.[1]

What Is Revelation?

Revelation literally means an "unveiling," "uncovering," or "disclosure" of something previously hidden. The word is used, of course, in many different contexts, some trivial, as when a new line of apparel is "revealed," others more serious, as when new knowledge suddenly comes to light in a scientific field or in a personal relationship and is called a "revelation" because it seems less a hard-won achievement than a surprising gift. A revelation of this sort may

---

1. See *Divine Revelation*, ed. Paul Avis (Grand Rapids: Eerdmans, 1997).

20

humble or elate us, disturb or even shock us. The effect of such revelatory experiences may be dramatic, possibly changing the way we think about the world or the way we live our lives.[2]

Flannery O'Connor depicts an event of "revelation" in a way that points to the deeper theological meaning of the term. She tells the story of Mrs. Turpin, a hard-working, upright, church-going farmer's wife, who is unexpectedly accosted by a mentally disturbed teenage girl in a doctor's office. After bearing Mrs. Turpin's superior attitude and demeaning remarks about white trash and blacks as long as she can, the girl suddenly throws a heavy book at Mrs. Turpin, begins to strangle her, and calls her a "wart hog from hell." When Mrs. Turpin returns to her farm, she cannot get the girl's words out of her mind. Standing beside her pigpen, she is outraged by being called a wart hog. She knows she is a good person, certainly far superior to white trash and blacks. She reminds God of that, as well as of all the work she does for the church. "What did you send me a message like that for?" she angrily asks God. But as she stares into the pig pen, she has a glimpse of "the very heart of mystery," and begins to absorb some "abysmal life-giving knowledge." She has a vision of a parade of souls marching to heaven, with white trash, blacks, lunatics, and other social outcasts up front, and respectable people like herself at the rear of the procession, the shocked expressions on their faces showing that all their virtues are being burned away. Mrs. Turpin returns to her house with the shouts of hallelujah from the heaven-bound saints in her ears.[3]

As O'Connor's story suggests, revelation is not something that confirms what we already know. Basically, it has to do with a knowledge of God and ourselves that is utterly surprising and disturbing. It is an event that shakes us to the core. Although it comes as a gift, offering us a glimpse of "the very heart of mystery," it is resisted because it is so threatening and frightening. The knowledge it conveys is an "abysmal life-giving knowledge," but it also demands a kind of death because it turns upside down the lives of people who receive it. Revelation compels momentous decisions about who God is and how we are to understand the world and ourselves.

Scripture is filled with accounts of the revelation of God breaking into human life as a surprising gift and an unsettling commission. Moses hears the voice of God from a burning bush instructing him to lead the people of Israel out of bondage in Egypt (Exod. 3); David becomes aware of the sin he has

2. See John Baillie, *The Idea of Revelation in Recent Thought* (New York: Columbia University Press, 1956), 19ff.; and John Macquarrie, *Principles of Christian Theology*, 2d ed. (New York: Scribner's, 1977), 84ff.

3. Flannery O'Connor, "Revelation," in *Everything That Rises Must Converge* (New York: Farrar, Straus and Giroux, 1965), 191-218.

committed when Nathan tells him the story of a rich man who robs and kills a poor man's only lamb (2 Sam. 12); Isaiah has a vision in which God summons him to service (Isa. 6:1-8); Paul experiences a revelation of Jesus Christ that changes him from a persecutor of the church to an apostle of the gospel to the Gentiles (Gal. 1:12); Peter has a dream that teaches him that God shows no partiality and intends the gospel message to be preached to Gentiles as well as Jews (Acts 10:9ff.). Revelation is the disclosure of the character and purpose of God, and when it is received, it radically changes the lives of its recipients.

The revelation of God is not just one more item of information in our store of knowledge, not just one of the many things we know or think we know. When God is revealed, everything is seen in a new light. William Abraham helpfully describes revelation as a "threshold" concept. It is like crossing the threshold of a house. While some features of a house can be seen from outside, much remains hidden. In crossing the threshold, "one enters into another world." This is the effect of the event that Christian faith and theology call revelation: "Once one acknowledges the revelation, then everything may have to be rethought and redescribed in the light of what has been discovered."[4]

God Hidden and Revealed

While the idea of revelation has been a centerpiece of much modern theology, some theologians argue that its importance has been greatly exaggerated.[5] They contend that this concept is actually quite peripheral in the Bible. One charge is that the notion of revelation tends to focus attention on the sorts of epistemological questions that are prominent in modern philosophy and science (Are our claims to knowledge well-grounded?), rather than on the question of salvation (Is there forgiveness of sins?). If we concentrate on the theme of revelation, do we not suggest that the basic human predicament is ignorance rather than sin? In the Bible people do not ask, "What must I know?" but "Who must I be and what must I do to be saved?" (see Mark 10:17; John 3:3).

There is some truth in this criticism. A doctrine of revelation throws both believers and unbelievers off track when it is presented as an effort to secure and defend a comprehensive *theory* of knowledge, including Christian

4. William J. Abraham, "The Offense of Revelation," *Harvard Theological Review* 95, no. 3 (July 2002): 259.

5. See F. Gerald Downing, *Has Christianity a Revelation?* (London: SCM, 1964); for a summary of the discussion, see George Stroup, *The Promise of Narrative Theology: Recovering the Gospel in the Church* (Richmond: John Knox, 1981), 51-59.

affirmations about God. Such efforts must inevitably fail. In all our knowing, and most certainly in our knowledge of God revealed decisively in Jesus Christ, there are truths that we know without being able fully to explain how we can possibly know them. The doctrine of revelation does not pretend to provide a full-blown theory of knowledge. Whenever the doctrine is understood in this way, it is not surprising that the question of whether or not it is possible to know God becomes more important than actually knowing God.[6]

The charge that revelation is an inflated concept in modern theology also gains credence if revelation is equated with a set of doctrines requiring unquestioning assent. According to Scripture, faith is primarily a matter of personal trust in and obedience to God rather than mere intellectual assent to a set of authoritative doctrines. But knowledge of God in the biblical tradition does not mean simply information about one of the myriad objects whose existence we may more or less indifferently acknowledge. Rather, revelation brings "saving knowledge," a knowledge that bears decisively on the meaning, wholeness, and fulfillment of our life in relationship to God and others. As we noted in the preceding chapter, Calvin speaks for the entire Christian tradition in insisting that the knowledge of God given in the gospel is far more than agreeing that God exists or assenting to whatever the church teaches. Properly speaking, God is known only where there is piety, where knowledge of the grace of God in Jesus Christ is fused with love of God and the desire to do God's will.[7]

But if it is a mistake to equate knowledge of God with mere information, it is also a mistake to think of faith as a desperate leap in the dark. Believers claim that what they affirm of God is true. How could we trust God if we did not have any knowledge of God's trustworthiness? How could we obey the will of God if we had no knowledge of what that will is? How could we rightly worship or pray or serve a God who is totally unknown and unknowable? How could there be any conviction or joy in proclaiming a God who is absolutely hidden? Christian faith and life are inseparable from reliable knowledge of the character and purpose of God. If we do not want to call the source of this knowledge revelation, then we will have to invent some other term to take its place.

There is another reason for criticism of the emphasis on revelation in modern theology. Talk of the self-revelation of God seems to suggest that we know all there is to know about God. The claim to total knowledge is emphatically rejected by postmodern philosophers and theologians, who believe all

---

6. See William J. Abraham, *Canon and Criterion in Christian Theology: From the Fathers to Feminism* (Oxford: Clarendon Press, 1988), 466-80.

7. Calvin, *Institutes of the Christian Religion*, 1.2.1.

such claims are inherently arrogant and inevitably lead to oppression of one sort or another. Human knowledge is fragmentary and incomplete. If this is true of our knowledge of ourselves and our world, it is surely true of our knowledge of God.

Confession that God has been revealed, however, is altogether different from the claim to know everything about God or to have God under our control. When God is revealed, God remains God and does not become a possession at our disposal. Whatever may be the case in other forms of knowledge, in the knowledge of God given in revelation, God does not become a prisoner of our categories and concepts. God remains free, ever mystery, ever "hidden." The paradoxical theme of God as revealed yet hidden is rooted in the scriptural witness and is basic to a Christian doctrine of revelation.

Scripture clearly declares that the holy, transcendent God of Israel, whose ways and thoughts are as high above us as the heavens are higher than the earth (Isa. 55:9), does not remain silent (Ps. 50:3). "Have you not known? Have you not heard? Has it not been told you from the beginning?" (Isa. 40:21). God has spoken and has done mighty deeds, and because of this, God is no longer unknown. In the Old Testament, God is reliably known in the history of the gracious covenant of Yahweh with the people of Israel. This history includes the promise of God to Abraham and Sarah (Gen. 17), the disclosure of the divine name to Moses (Exod. 3:14), the liberation of Israel from bondage in Egypt, the giving of the Torah, and the preaching of God's judgment and grace by the prophets.

Yet the witness of the Old Testament is also that *God remains, paradoxically, hidden in the event of revelation.* In God's self-revelation God has become identifiable, yet God is never fully comprehensible. Even in revelation — precisely in revelation — God never ceases to be a mystery, never ceases to be "more" than human beings can think or say. God remains ever free, and in this sense ever hidden in revelation. This is vividly expressed in many biblical narratives. At the burning bush, Moses is given the name of God, but it is the name of unfathomable mystery: "I am who I am," or "I will be who I will be" (Gen. 3:14).[8] Moses asks to see God but is permitted to see only God's back side (Exod. 33:12-23). Elijah hears the voice of God not in the wind, earthquake, or fire, but in a small voice (1 Kings 19:11ff.); Isaiah declares, "Truly, you are a God who hides himself, O God of Israel, the Savior" (Isa. 45:15).

---

8. For this translation, see Gerhard von Rad, *Old Testament Theology*, vol. 1 (New York: Harper & Row, 1962), 180. Von Rad adds, "The promise of Jahweh's efficacious presence remains at the same time . . . illusive and impalpable — this is Jahweh's freedom, which does not commit itself in detail."

According to the New Testament witness, the revelation of God is decisively embodied in Jesus Christ. He is God's light in a world of darkness. In him God has been reliably and definitively revealed. In his proclamation, ministry, death, and resurrection, and in the renewing work of the Holy Spirit, a new relationship between God and all humanity is established. While expressing the revelation of God in Christ in different ways, the New Testament authors agree on the uniqueness, normativity, and unsurpassability of this revelation. They confess that in Jesus Christ, God has spoken not only through a prophet but through a Son (Heb. 1:1-2), that the eternal divine Word has become incarnate in a singular human life (John 1:14), that the light of the glory of God has shone in the face of Jesus Christ (2 Cor. 4:6), that in him the Spirit-anointed liberator of all the oppressed has appeared (Luke 4:18ff.).

At the same time, for the New Testament witness as for the Old, *the revelation of God is, paradoxically, a hidden revelation.* The hiddenness of God in Jesus Christ is not simply that he is a finite, vulnerable, mortal creature like other human beings. Rather, God's self-disclosure is deeply hidden in the servant form of this person and above all in his crucifixion. As Paul recognizes, the message of God's act of revelation and reconciliation in a humble servant who suffers and is crucified for our sake is sheer scandal and folly to the wise and powerful of this world (1 Cor. 1:22-23).

Furthermore, for the New Testament community, becoming a Christian does not remove the hiddenness of God in revelation. A study of New Testament uses of the term "revelation" *(apokalypsis)* shows that it often refers to the future manifestation of Christ (e.g. 1 Cor. 1:7; 1 Pet. 1:13). Christians have seen God's glory (John 1:14), but they do not yet see God face to face (1 Cor. 13:12). There is a depth of riches in God that we do not now comprehend (Rom. 11:33). Our true life is hidden with Christ in God (Col. 3:3). We are God's children now, but what we will be when Christ comes again has not yet been revealed (1 John 3:2). In brief, while God's revelation in Jesus Christ is completely trustworthy, we cannot fully comprehend the being of God and God's gifts of creation, reconciliation, and redemption.

This emphasis on the freedom, mystery, and hiddenness of God in revelation should not be seen as merely an invention of Christian apologetics designed to appeal to the postmodern sensibility of the fragmentary character of all human knowledge. The mystery of God is a theme that is deeply rooted in the Christian theological tradition.[9] Augustine declares, "God is always

---

9. See Denys Turner, *The Darkness of God: Negativity in Christian Mysticism* (Cambridge: Cambridge University Press, 1995); also *Silence and the Word: Negative Theology and Incarnation,* ed. Oliver Davies and Denys Turner (Cambridge: Cambridge University Press, 2002).

greater *(Deus semper maior),* however much we may have grown."[10] The theologians of the Eastern church emphasize the darkness of God, by which they mean the hiddenness and incomprehensibility of the essence of God.[11] Thomas Aquinas frequently reminds us that God remains largely hidden to finite human reason: "No created intellect can comprehend God wholly."[12] The theme of God's hiddenness is very prominent in Luther's theology: "God has hidden himself in Christ."[13] According to Barth, all serious knowledge of God begins with the knowledge of the hiddenness of God, i.e. the inalienable freedom and surprising grace of God who is self-revealed in Jesus Christ. "God's hiddenness . . . meets us in Christ, and finally and supremely in the crucified Christ; for where is God so hidden as here, and where is the possibility of offense so great as here?"[14] Implicit or explicit in the many variations on the theme of the hiddenness of God in the Christian theological tradition is the confession that in Jesus Christ crucified and risen, God is truly revealed yet also, paradoxically, hidden.

Revelation as Objective and Subjective

How shall we speak of the event of revelation? Shall we think of it as an *objective occurrence* or as a *subjective experience?* Does it refer to something that really happens "out there" in the world or is it primarily an event "in here," an interior change of consciousness or a new way of seeing the world on the part of the believer? Some doctrines of revelation emphasize the objective and others the subjective aspects of revelation. Surely both sides of the event of revelation are important and must be held together. Revelation is God's free and gracious self-disclosure through particular events that are attested and interpreted by people of faith. In Paul Tillich's words, "Revelation is always a subjective and an objective event in strict interdependence."[15] Revelation refers both to the living Word of God speaking and acting through particular persons and events and to the inner working of God's Spirit enabling people

10. Augustine, *Expositions on the Psalms* (Psalm 63), in *Nicene-Post Nicene Fathers*, vol. 8, ed. Philip Schaff (Grand Rapids: Eerdmans, 1989), 262.

11. See Vladimir Lossky, *The Mystical Theology of the Eastern Church* (Cambridge: James Clarke, 1957), esp. chap. 2.

12. Thomas Aquinas, *Summa Theologica*, Pt. 1, q. 12, a. 8.

13. *Luther's Works*, 28: 126. See also Jürgen Moltmann, *The Crucified God* (New York: Harper & Row, 1974).

14. Karl Barth, *The Göttingen Dogmatics* (Grand Rapids: Eerdmans, 1991), 335.

15. Tillich, *Systematic Theology*, 1: 111.

to see, appropriate, and bear witness to this activity. God is the primary actor in the event of revelation, but human beings are also participants.

Probably the most frequently discussed issue in recent reflection on the doctrine of revelation is what part human reason and imagination play in the revelatory process. A number of theologians have noted that the experience of revelation as described in theology is similar to other experiences of fresh insight or "paradigm shifts," as in artistic creation or in scientific inquiry.[16] These theologians emphasize that the idea of revelation is distorted when it is seen as a supernatural substitute for the use of human reason and the play of human imagination. Revelation does not destroy or disable human capacities; to the contrary, the concrete love of God in Jesus Christ is powerfully attractive. It non-coercively captures the allegiance of the heart, brings new vision to human imagination, and provides new direction to human reason.

According to Garrett Green, the revelation of God in the history of Israel and supremely in the person of Jesus Christ takes effect in human life by releasing our powers of imagination from bondage to false idols. It provides us with a new paradigm of who God is and what it means to live according to God's will. Revelation and faith help us to see and thus to live differently; the whole of reality is reinterpreted in the light of the pattern of divine and human life embodied in the person of Christ.[17] This is the point of the apostle Paul's appeal to his readers to have the mind of Christ (Phil. 2:5) and to let their minds be transformed by the revelation of God in Christ rather than being conformed to ways of thinking and living characteristic of worldly powers (Rom. 12:2). In John Calvin's striking metaphor, the biblical witness to revelation is like a pair of spectacles that enable us to see God, the world, and ourselves in a radically new manner.[18]

Of course, reality can be seen and interpreted in many different ways. The revelation of God does not force itself on us. It frees us to see the world as created and reconciled by God, but this does not eliminate other possible ways of seeing. In the light of Christ as the true image of God (Col. 1:15), we are enabled to know and love God as holy and beneficent, one whose intentions toward us are gracious. We are not coerced but freed to understand ourselves as people created in God's image and destined for communion with God and each other. Believers are aware of other ways of seeing and interpret-

16. On the idea of "paradigm shift" in scientific inquiry, see Thomas Kuhn, *The Structure of Scientific Revolutions,* 2d ed. (Chicago: University of Chicago Press, 1970).

17. See Garrett Green, *Imagining God: Theology and the Religious Imagination* (San Francisco: Harper & Row, 1989).

18. Calvin, *Institutes,* 1.6.1.

ing reality and can even recognize the partial truth of these other interpretations. Nevertheless, they affirm that the revelation of the costly love of God in Jesus Christ is truth that can be counted on in life and in death (Rom. 8:38-39). He is not just *a* truth, but *the* truth that sets humanity free (John 8:32); not just *a* light, but *the* light that illumines all of life (John 8:12).

One of the most influential modern analyses of the meaning of revelation is that of H. Richard Niebuhr. He speaks of the event of revelation as being like a "luminous sentence" that we come across in a difficult book, "from which we can go forward and backward and so attain to some understanding of the whole."[19] It is like a "special occasion" (Alfred North Whitehead) in the life of a person or community that provides a central clue for the interpretation of all other occasions. "The special occasion to which we appeal in the Christian church is called Jesus Christ, in whom we see the righteousness of God, his power and wisdom," says Niebuhr. "But from that special occasion we also derive the concepts which make possible the elucidation of all the events in our history. Revelation means this intelligible event which makes all other events intelligible."[20]

We can summarize what has been said to this point about the meaning of the term "revelation" as used in Christian theology in the following theses:

First, revelation refers to *God's own self-disclosure.* Apart from this act, the character and purposes of God would remain a matter of sheer guesswork. To speak of revelation is to declare that *God* graciously takes the initiative and freely communicates with us. Revelation comes *to* us rather than *from* us. It is experienced as a gift we receive rather than as a discovery we make on our own about God, the world, and ourselves.

Second, the term "revelation" points to *particular events and particular people* through whom God has communicated God's identity and will. In Scripture, revelation means God's communication in word and deed with the people of Israel and above all, in the person and work, in the passion and resurrection of Jesus Christ. There is a "scandal of particularity," a relentless specificity and an inexpungible particularity about the reality Christians call revelation.

Third, the revelation of God is also, paradoxically, a *hiding of God.* If it is truly God who is revealed, God remains hidden, beyond our grasp, never our prisoner.[21] For the revealed God is the free and ever surprising God who re-

---

19. H. Richard Niebuhr, *The Meaning of Revelation* (New York: Macmillan, 1941), 93. See also Green, *Imagining God,* 61.

20. Niebuhr, *The Meaning of Revelation,* 93.

21. See Douglas John Hall, *Thinking the Faith: Christian Theology in a North American Context* (Minneapolis: Augsburg, 1989), 404-9.

sists our efforts to turn God into an idol. We know this to be true primarily because of God's revelation in Jesus Christ. In his person, revelation means the presence of God in the least expected place, in the midst of sinners, in the company of the poor, in the deep hiddenness of the cross. This feature of radical otherness, of the hidden and the unexpected — even of the outrageous — belongs to the revelation of God.

Fourth, the revelation of God calls for our *personal response and appropriation.* As God's personal approach to us, revelation seeks the response of our whole person. Stated differently, true knowledge of God is practical knowledge rather than merely theoretical knowledge. The goal of the event of revelation is not our possession of secret doctrines but a transformed life with new understanding of God and ourselves, new dispositions and affections, new sensibilities, new ways of seeing the world and our neighbors.

Fifth, the revelation of God is *always a disturbing, even shocking event.* It disrupts the way we have previously understood God, the world, and ourselves. Precisely for that reason, revelation often encounters resistance and rejection.

Sixth, revelation becomes the *new interpretative focus* for our understanding of God, the world, and ourselves. Far from narrowing our vision or limiting our search for understanding, revelation renews the mind and transforms the imagination. In the light of the "special occasion" called Jesus Christ, we see God and all things in a new light and seek to act in accordance with this new vision. Revelation is a radical paradigm change in our interpretation of reality, and as such it is an inexhaustible source of creative imagination and of transforming human action in the world.

General and Special Revelation

In the above summary of the meaning of revelation, I have emphasized the particularity and the radical "otherness" of the revelation of God as understood by Christian faith and theology. Does this emphasis deny the presence and activity of God in all of nature and history? Is not the Spirit of God the universal giver of life (Ps. 104:30), and is not the Word of God incarnate in Jesus Christ (John 1:14) also present and at work in all creation (John 1:9)? What then is the relationship between the biblical witness to the revelation of God that culminates in Christ and what has been revealed of God in the natural order and in universal history?

Christian theology has traditionally distinguished two media of the knowledge of God: general revelation and special revelation. The Bible teaches and experience confirms some revelation of God in the created order, in human conscience, and in the lives of people who do not possess the Mosaic law and have not heard the gospel message. "The heavens are telling the glory of God, and the firmament proclaims his handiwork," writes the psalmist (19:1). The apostle Paul contends that God's eternal power and deity have been clearly shown in the things that have been created (Rom. 1:20). When Paul speaks to the Athenians on the Areopagus, he proclaims to them the identity of the unknown God that they have been worshiping (Acts 17:22ff.).

Acknowledgment of the fact that the Bible teaches that some knowledge of God is available to all would seem to have distinct advantages. For one thing, it appears to provide a basis for presenting the Christian message with some assurance of common ground between Christians and non-Christians. It also clearly encourages Christians to be receptive to knowledge acquired by the human sciences and to be respectful of and open to the teachings of other religious traditions. On the other hand, a preoccupation with general revelation poses many dangers. It may lead to the conclusion that special revelation is superfluous, or at least that it lacks the critical significance that Christians have always attached to it.

Christian theologians have related general and special revelation in a variety of ways. At one end of the spectrum are philosophers and theologians who claim that religions based on allegedly special revelation are only different symbolic expressions of a universally available knowledge of God. At the other end of the spectrum is the argument that revelation in Christ alone provides true knowledge of God and that all other claims to know God are simply false. Somewhere in the middle range of the spectrum are those who insist on the importance of general revelation as providing a broad foundation for morality and religion, even if what is known on this basis is incomplete and in need of the fuller knowledge of God given in the special revelation attested in Scripture. According to the First Vatican Council (1870), for example, God's existence can be demonstrated and some things can be known of God by human reason apart from any appeal to special revelation. The relation between general and special revelation in this view is like the relationship between part and whole, the incomplete and the complete.

John Calvin's position on this issue, while not without some ambiguity, offers a distinctive emphasis. Insisting that there is a natural knowledge of God, Calvin readily speaks of a universal "sense of divinity" and a universally implanted "seed of religion." Not only do the liberal arts assist us in entering into the secrets of the divine wisdom, but even the uneducated are aware of the evidence of the divine workmanship in the creation. Hence Calvin concludes that "there is within the human mind and by natural instinct an awareness of divinity. This we take to be beyond controversy."[22]

All this sounds clear enough, but it is important to follow the whole course of Calvin's argument. Calvin contends that the universal "sense of divinity" is severely weakened by sin and is thus "insufficient," "confused," vague, and dim by comparison with the special revelation in Scripture. The relative dimness of the revelation in creation and in human conscience is, in Calvin's view, a source of real danger. What ordinarily follows from this indefinite and unstable knowledge of God is not what Vatican I optimistically depicts in its statement on what can be known of God by unaided human reason. Instead, Calvin emphasizes that the knowledge of God available to humanity in the world of nature and in the universal moral and religious awareness is regularly corrupted, often turned into something sinister and destructive. Calvin's contention, then, following the apostle Paul in Romans 1:18-23, is that while there is a universal revelation that renders all people responsible, the habit of sinful human beings is to turn this general knowledge of God into idolatry. Religion is often put to the service of evil human purposes.

Most Christian theologians today would be more generous than Calvin in finding truth and value in what can be known of God in the created order and in the different religions of humanity. As a renaissance scholar, Calvin honored the arts and sciences, but when assessing religions other than the Reformed faith, he tended to highlight only their distortions. By contrast, many Christian theologians today would emphasize that all religions must be approached with openness and respect, and some would acknowledge the presence of God's gracious initiative and faithful human responses in other religious traditions.

However, we should not allow Calvin's exaggerations to obscure the important point he is making — namely, that a vague and superficial religiosity, when it does not lead simply to indifference or despair, is continuously vulnerable to idolatrous manipulation.[23] One thinks of the ominous coupling of a shadowy religiosity with a militant nationalism or racism in such slogans as "God and Fatherland" or "God, family, and country." The ideology of too many German Christians during the Third Reich, the mixture of religion and apartheid in South Africa, and the vague but uniformly comforting references to God and religious values in chauvinistic movements in the United States

22. Calvin, *Institutes*, 1.3.1.

23. For some of the ideas in this paragraph, I am indebted to Prof. Michael Welker of Heidelberg University.

and other countries are vivid reminders of the essential correctness of Calvin's (and later, Barth's) warning that we are repeatedly inclined to control and manipulate the knowledge of God that goes under the name of general revelation.

According to some critics of special revelation, concentration on the particular and unique revelation of God attested in Scripture and centered above all in Jesus Christ must necessarily lead to a narrow and arrogant attitude. Narrowness and arrogance have, to be sure, all too frequently found a home in the church, and on this account the church needs to be called to repentance. It is a mistake, however, to lay the blame for this on the appeal to special revelation. On the contrary, provincialism and exclusivism are often the result of losing touch with what is specifically Christian rather than excessive loyalty to it. Hence the familiar criticism of an emphasis on the particularity of Christian revelation should be reversed. A plausible argument can be made that a vague and amorphous religious commitment is far more vulnerable to ideological manipulation than the specific witness of the biblical tradition to the revelation of God. Indeterminate religiosity is easily co-opted by self-interested individuals, groups, and nations. It offers unlimited potential for pretension and self-righteousness. Admittedly, the Bible has also been used for ideological purposes, as the appeal to certain biblical texts to legitimize slavery and the subordination of women makes clear enough. Still, the danger that resides in vague religiosity is especially acute because its resources for self-criticism are considerably weaker than in a community of faith that recognizes the authority of the prophetic tradition of the Bible.

A new capacity for criticism, including self-criticism, accompanies the Christian experience of revelation. Revelation and the critique of all forms of idolatry go hand in hand. We should not think of special revelation, then, as the mere denial of general revelation. Nor should we think of it, equally simplistically, as the tranquil continuation and completion of general ideas of divinity. Rather, special revelation repeatedly challenges, corrects, and transforms all of our earlier knowledge of God, from whatever source, as well as confirming what is good and true in it. The revelation of God in Jesus Christ is a continual disturbance to all religious life, including and beginning with the Christian religion.[24]

Prophetic criticism belongs necessarily to a revelation of God that calls for concern for the poor and needy (Jer. 22:16) and that summarizes the will of God as "to do justice, to love kindness, and to walk humbly before God"

---

24. See Niebuhr, *The Meaning of Revelation:* "Revelation is not a development of our religious ideas but their continuous conversion" (182).

(Mic. 6:8). In the New Testament the revelation of God finds supreme expression in one who takes up the cause of the poor, forgives sinners, teaches that the greatest of God's commandments is to love God above all else and to love one's neighbor as oneself (Mark 12:29-31), and at the end is crucified between two criminals. If we look to this crucified and risen Christ as God's decisive revelation, the knowledge of God will always be a disturbing and disruptive reality in our lives. We will not pretend that revelation merely confirms what we already know and how we presently live. We will not claim to have revelation in our possession and under our control. Revelation always means the surprising, unexpected, scandalous activity of God. The gospel of the crucified Lord constitutes a "permanent revolution" in our understanding of God, the world, and ourselves.[25]

In summary, while the distinction between general and special revelation has some validity, it can easily be misused. It can lead to the domestication or even replacement of special revelation. Or it can promote the compartmentalizing of our knowledge of God with the result that revelation and reason, Christ and culture, nature and history are seen as completely separate domains. Knowledge of God based on general revelation does not remain unchanged with the coming of special revelation. The surprising self-disclosure of God in the ministry and cross of Jesus calls for the transformation of our personal and interpersonal relations, our attitude toward nature, our cultural activity, and, most basically, our ways of imagining and relating to God.[26]

Models of Revelation

In a widely-read book, Avery Dulles identifies five models of revelation.[27] One of its values is the recognition that each model has both strengths and deficiencies. Because it provides a good foundation for further reflection on the doctrine of revelation, it is worth summarizing here.

According to Dulles's first model, revelation takes the form of authoritative doctrine. It is located in the infallible propositions of Scripture or the infallible doctrines of the church. The model of revelation as authoritative doctrines or revealed propositions was typical of pre–Vatican II Roman Catholic theology and is still prevalent in some Protestant fundamentalist theologies. While this model may have the laudable aim of wanting to defend the

25. Niebuhr, *The Meaning of Revelation*, 182.
26. See H. Richard Niebuhr, *Christ and Culture* (New York: Harper, 1951).
27. Avery Dulles, *Models of Revelation*, 2d ed. (Maryknoll, N.Y.: Orbis, 1992).

cognitive content of revelation, its view of the meaning of revelation is excessively rationalist. The revelation of God cannot be reduced to a set of authoritative propositions.

A second model identifies revelation with particular historical events. In this model revelation is not equated with the biblical text itself or with church teachings per se but is located in the momentous events recounted in Scripture. According to this view, the more we learn from historical research about events such as the exodus of Israel from Egypt or the resurrection of Jesus from the dead, the closer to revelation we come. The revelation of God refers to the "mighty acts of God" in history. Dulles thinks there is much to be said for this way of thinking about revelation, but contends that it rather too simplistically separates the acts of God from the interpretation that accompanies these acts in the scriptural witness and from the response of believers today to this witness.

According to Dulles's third model, revelation is seen as a special inner experience. It is essentially an inner feeling of communion with God. In this view, the locus of revelation is not the Bible or the doctrines of the church or the historical facts that purportedly lie behind the biblical witness. It is instead a present personal experience leading to a spiritual awakening and renewal. This model rightly calls attention to the personal and subjective side in the event of revelation but its view of experience is often narrow and individualistic. There is little sense here of the importance of the community of believers, its sacred texts, and its faith practices as bearers of the revelation of God.

Dulles calls his fourth model dialectical presence. In this model the emphasis is on a non-objectifiable encounter with the Word of God that is mediated by Scripture and church proclamation. God's Word cannot be identified with the word of its human witnesses, although it is mediated through them. When revelation occurs, it is the mysterious act of God's free grace. Dulles finds merit in this model's emphasis on the transcendence and freedom of God and the seriousness with which it takes the finitude and limitations of the media of revelation. Nevertheless, he thinks it is inadequately informed by the reality of the Incarnation. As a result, it fails to provide an intelligible bridge between God and creature.

The fifth model understands revelation as new awareness that leads to transformative action. Revelation is seen as a breakthrough in human consciousness that expresses itself in creative imagination and ethical action. In this understanding, revelation generates self and world transformation. The model of revelation as new awareness escapes the tendency of some of the other models to reduce the receiver of revelation to passivity before God and emphasizes the active role of the receiver. Dulles suggests, however, that the new consciousness model of revelation frequently downplays or even breaks completely free of the witness of Scripture and tradition.

As is evident from this summary, Dulles does not consider any of these five models to be entirely satisfactory. Although he does not offer another model, he is clearly open to one that would more adequately describe the revelation Christians find preeminently in Jesus Christ as attested in Scripture and confirmed by the power of the Holy Spirit at work in the life and practices of the church. He also reminds readers that the revelation of God cannot be confined to a past event or a present experience but also points to the final appearance of Christ at the Parousia (e.g., 1 Cor. 1:7; Col. 3:4). In other words, revelation is not finished, but an event whose completion Christians still await.

Revelation as God's Self-Disclosure Narrated in Scripture

Christian faith looks to the ministry, death, and resurrection of Jesus Christ as attested in Scripture as the supreme revelation of God and the basis of understanding all things in relation to God. While God is present and active in all of nature and history, for Christian faith and theology the fullness of revelation comes decisively in a personal life. Only revelation through a person can be fully intelligible to us, who are persons, and only personal revelation can adequately disclose the reality of God, who is supremely personal.[28] As Basil Mitchell notes, "The basic analogy involved in all talk of revelation is that of communication between persons."[29]

If we take interpersonal communication to be the most satisfactory analogy of what is meant by the revelation of God, there will be some elements in common with each of the models in Dulles's typology, but the focus will be different. Our reflection will center not on propositions (although propositions have their place), nor on historical facts (although they are important), nor on our experiences of conversion and renewal (although these are certainly part of the meaning of revelation), nor on the crisis of the human condition before God (although it is impossible to separate revelation and crisis), nor on our heightened awareness of freedom and responsibility (although revelation does include these). Instead, we will attempt to understand God's self-revelation as analogous to interpersonal knowledge. We

---

28. See William Temple, *Nature, Man and God* (London: Macmillan, 1956), 319.

29. Basil Mitchell, "Does Christianity Need a Revelation?" *Theology* 83 (1980): 105.

must emphasize that this is *only* an analogy, and analogy in theology means a similarity in great difference.

How are persons known?[30] If we assume that persons are embodied agents who disclose their identity and intentions in their words and actions, an analogy between knowledge of other persons and the personal self-disclosure of God to us can be developed in the following way.

First, our knowledge of persons requires *attention to persistent patterns* in their actions that manifest, as we might say, who they really are, what is in their heart, what their true character is. Not everything that we do reveals our identity and our deepest intentions and dispositions. We may notice that in times of crisis a certain person is always the first one at the side of someone in need, asking what she can do to help. By virtue of this consistent pattern of activity, we feel justified in describing her as a truly sensitive and caring person. What she is "really like" has been "revealed" to us by a persistent pattern of behavior.

By analogy, the revelation of God can be understood as God's self-disclosure through personal action that exhibits a particular pattern. For Christian believers, the character and intentions of God are not immediately evident in every event of nature or history. They are focused in the particular event named Jesus of Nazareth — and not just in every detail that might be mentioned about this person (height, hair color, taste in music) but in the persistent pattern of his dedication to God and his self-giving love to others, distilled in the gospel stories and climaxed in the passion narrative.

Second, a person's identity is freely disclosed. While not necessarily arbitrary, there is an element of spontaneity and unpredictability about the action of persons. A person is *free to do new and surprising things.* When a person is stereotyped or his actions are thought to be entirely predictable, violence is done to his personhood. We often depend on others to tell us what they intended by their actions, especially when what they do is unexpected.

Similarly, while never speaking of God's action as capricious, the Bible always respects God's freedom to do the unexpected. While the faithfulness of God can be counted on, the purpose of God is accomplished in ever new and surprising ways. To the extent that we neglect this freedom and inexhaustibility of God, we turn knowledge of God into something we can control and manipulate to serve our own interests. As often as Israel was called by the prophets to remember what God had done and commanded in the past, Israel was also summoned to be open to the new actions of God (see Isa. 43:18-19).

30. The argument presented in the following paragraphs is indebted to Thomas F. Tracy's *God, Action, and Embodiment* (Grand Rapids: Eerdmans, 1984).

Third, knowledge of persons involves a continuous *invitation to trust and to live in response to promises.* This is connected with the freedom of personal knowledge — freedom both on the side of the subject who is known and on the side of the knower. Because there is always the element of the new, the surprising, and the unpredictable in personal knowledge, promising is an important dimension of all personal relationships. We cannot promise our friend, nor can our friend promise us, to be absolutely the same tomorrow as today. But we can promise to be there for our friend, to be faithful in our care and love, even if this shows itself in a different and perhaps surprising way.

Here again the analogy proves useful in relation to the biblical description of God's self-disclosure. The revelation of God in the history of Israel and in the ministry, death, and resurrection of Jesus Christ is characterized by promises and calls to faithfulness.[31] "Your sins are forgiven" (Luke 7:48); "Blessed are you poor, for yours is the kingdom of God" (Luke 6:20); "Believe in me, and you will never thirst again" (John 4:14); "Those who want to save their life will lose it, and those who lose their life for my sake will save it" (Luke 9:24); "Take courage, I have conquered the world" (John 16:33); "Behold, I am with you always to the close of the age" (Matt. 28:20).

Finally, our identity as persons is often *rendered in narrative form.* If this is true of our self-disclosure to each other, by analogy it is also true of the self-disclosure of God. In Scripture God's revealed identity is rendered primarily by narrative.[32] As F. Michael McLain writes, "If God is an agent who acts in the world so as to disclose divine character and purpose, then narrative is the appropriate form in which to render God's identity."[33]

A number of contemporary theologians have explored the narrative form as a clue to understanding the meaning of revelation as God's personal self-disclosure.[34] Narrative is deemed an apt vehicle for identifying God because it can effectively convey the persistent patterns that define a person's character and purpose. It can depict personal action in its freedom, unpredictability, and promissory character. It is not surprising, then, that narrative

31. See Ronald F. Thiemann, *Revelation and Theology: The Gospel as Narrated Promise* (Notre Dame: University of Notre Dame Press, 1985).

32. See Richard Bauckham, "Jesus the Revelation of God," in *Divine Revelation,* ed. Paul Avis, 174-200.

33. F. Michael McLain, "Narrative Interpretation and the Problem of Double Agency," in *Divine Action,* ed. Brian Hebblethwaite and Edward Henderson (Edinburgh: T&T Clark, 1990), 143.

34. See Stroup, *The Promise of Narrative Theology;* also Stroup, "Revelation," in *Christian Theology: An Introduction to Its Traditions and Tasks,* rev. ed. (Philadelphia: Fortress, 1985), 114-40; and Thiemann, *Revelation and Theology.*

plays a special role in the biblical witness to the identity and purpose of God. In a recent work, Gabriel Fackre moves beyond Dulles's typology and develops an "encompassing view" of revelation set in a "narrative framework." According to Fackre, revelation must be understood within the context of the whole drama of God with the world from creation to consummation. Revelation embraces the entirety of the self-communicating activity of the triune God. The great drama of divine revelation attested in Scripture identifies God in multiple ways that include the activity of God in creation, reconciliation, and the final redemption of all things.[35]

Although I agree with those who say biblical narrative is of special importance in a Christian doctrine of revelation, I believe a few qualifications are necessary. One qualification is that for Christian faith it is *not just any* biblical narrative that is decisive in rendering God's identity. At the center of the Christian understanding of the self-revelation of God is Jesus Christ the crucified (Gal. 3:1; 1 Cor. 1:23). In him the identity, purpose, and power of God are made manifest as nowhere else. In the words of H. Richard Niebuhr, "How strangely we must revise in the light of Jesus Christ all our ideas of what is really strong in this powerful world. . . . We see the power of God over the strong of earth made evident not in the fact that he slays them, but in his making the spirit of the slain Jesus unconquerable."[36]

A second qualification of the narrative emphasis in a doctrine of revelation is that God's self-disclosure attested in Scripture is *not just* a narrative. The truth that Jesus Christ died and was raised for us takes narrative form, but Jesus Christ is not just a character in a story. Moreover, the narratives of Scripture are not simply interesting stories told to inform, entertain, or edify us. They aim to engage, liberate, convert, and transform us. Their purpose is to tell what God has done for us and to invite us to enter into the new freedom that is ours in Christ. They make truth claims about God and about the world in relation to God, and they call for our personal response. Only as these narratives of the activity of God intersect our own lives, personally and corporately, opening us to a new relationship to God, a new identity, a new life, and a new mission, do they become for us genuine media of the revelation of God.[37]

A final qualification is that the biblical narrative of God's self-disclosure is an *unfinished* narrative. It remains open, as Rowan Williams reminds us:

35. Gabriel Fackre, *The Doctrine of Revelation: A Narrative Interpretation* (Grand Rapids: Eerdmans, 1997).

36. Niebuhr, *The Meaning of Revelation*, 187.

37. For an illuminating discussion of the "collision" between the biblical narrative and our personal narratives, see Stroup, *The Promise of Narrative Theology*, 171-75.

"The narrative of Jesus is not finished, therefore not in any sense controlled, even by supposedly 'authorized' tellers of the story. . . . Jesus remains subject of his history."[38] To say that the biblical narrative of revelation is unfinished is to say that only God can complete it. We are not to try to bring the narrative under our control by closing it off ourselves and making it into a tidy system. To say that Jesus remains subject of his history is to say that he is alive, and that the self-revelation of God in him never becomes our possession. Recognition that the biblical narrative of revelation is unfinished will prompt us to attend to literary forms in the biblical witness other than narrative. These other forms articulate dimensions of God's self-revelation in God's history with Israel and in the person and work of Jesus Christ that might otherwise be neglected or ignored. In addition to narrative, Scripture contains prophetic oracles, proverbs, commands, hymns, cries, lamentations, and apocalyptic visions, and each is an important way of witnessing to the self-revelation of God who remains ever free and beyond our control.[39] While Scripture renders the identity and faithfulness of God capaciously in its grand narrative of God's actions from creation to consummation and decisively in God's act of reconciliation in Jesus Christ, Scripture also gives voice to the experience of the absence and silence of God, the times when believers do not experience God's presence and do not see how their lives are encompassed by the overarching narrative of God's mighty deeds. The forms of the scriptural witness to revelation are diverse and none should be neglected.

Revelation, Scripture, and Church

In Christian theology the word "revelation" refers first of all not to the Bible, or to a creed, or to a set of doctrines, or to some ecclesiastical authority. It refers to the whole of the triune God's activity in creation, redemption, and consummation that has its center in Jesus Christ. His life, death, and resurrection are the supreme manifestation of the nature and purpose of God. The free grace of God in Jesus Christ is the core of the Christian message and the focus of a Christian doctrine of revelation.

Yet we would know nothing of the good news of the reconciliation of the world with God through Christ (2 Cor. 5:19) apart from the witness of Scripture and the activity of God's Spirit. The Spirit of God leads us to a right

---

38. Rowan Williams, *On Christian Theology* (Oxford: Blackwell, 2000), 193.

39. See Paul Ricoeur, "Toward a Hermeneutic of the Idea of Revelation," in *Essays in Biblical Interpretation,* ed. L. S. Mudge (Philadelphia: Fortress, 1980), 73-118.

knowledge of God and ourselves by illuminating the message of Scripture and opening our minds and hearts to this message. Where either the Spirit-illumined witness of Scripture or its continuing proclamation by the church in the power of the Spirit is ignored or disparaged, the reality of revelation in the Christian sense is endangered.

In his doctrine of the three forms of the Word of God, Karl Barth clarifies the relationship between revelation and the concrete media through which it is received. As Barth explains, there are three forms of the Word of God: revealed, written, and proclaimed.[40] These distinct but inseparable forms of the one Word of God are related to each other like three concentric circles. The innermost circle is the revealed Word of God or the Word of God incarnate in Jesus Christ. We have access to this circle only through a second circle formed by the prophetic and apostolic witness of Scripture. This witness is in turn mediated to us by the proclamation of the church, the third, outer circle of the Word of God.

This description of the threefold structure of the Word of God makes it clear that God has chosen to give human beings an important part in the event of revelation. This is singularly true, of course, of the incarnation of God in the person and work of Jesus Christ. The Word became flesh (John 1:14). God is decisively revealed in the words and deeds of this particular human being. But Scripture and church proclamation, with all their limitations and flaws, are also forms of the Word of God and have an indispensable role in conveying God's self-revelation to us. The good news of God's reconciliation of the world in Christ comes to us not directly but indirectly, through the primary witness of Scripture and the secondary witness of church proclamation.

The light of God that shines in Jesus Christ is transmitted, first of all, through the prism of the biblical witnesses. As long as the church remains faithful to the self-communication of the triune God, it will acknowledge the priority and authority of the scriptural witness in its life and mission. At the same time, the real humanity of the biblical witnesses will also be recognized without apology or embarrassment. It is not a weakness but a strength of the Christian understanding of revelation that its original witnesses are unmistakably historically conditioned and remarkably diverse human beings. That we have the treasure of the gospel in clay jars (2 Cor. 4:7) is as true of Scripture as it is of all subsequent Christian witness based on Scripture. Hence not everything found in the Bible is to be taken as a direct word of God to us. Some texts of the Bible may stand in utmost tension with the revelation of the character and purpose of God as identified by the grand narrative of Scrip-

40. Barth, *Church Dogmatics*, 1/1 (2d ed., 1975): 88-124.

ture. We cannot deny, for example, that Scripture contains passages that describe God in patriarchal images or as issuing commands to slaughter enemies. Scripture witnesses to revelation but is not identical with it. Even Calvin acknowledged this, although not as boldly as Luther.[41] Today it is essential that a Christian doctrine of revelation distinguish clearly between Scripture's witness to the personal self-disclosure of God definitively in Jesus Christ and the historical contingencies and ambiguities of this witness.

But second, *the original witness of Scripture to God's revelation in Jesus Christ is itself mediated to us through the witness of the church.* We hear and understand the message of Scripture with the help of many interpreters. Like the Ethiopian official, we need guidance in the understanding of Scripture (Acts 8:30-31). If we were to cut ourselves off from the proclamation and life of the church as the medium through which we receive the biblical message, our understanding of the revelation of God would not be purer, as biblicists mistakenly imagine, but greatly impoverished. To be sure, the revelation of God places the church under judgment and calls it to repent of the ways in which it has obscured and distorted revelation. Nevertheless, the community of believers is the matrix of understanding, the indispensable context of interpretation of the revelation of God attested in Scripture.

Sensitive to the fallibility of church teaching and practice and aware of the need for continuous reform within the church, Protestant theology has tended to locate revelation in the biblical text alone, in isolation from the witness of the church past and present. But this is as barren as the attempt to set the church on the same level with or even above Scripture. While the Reformers were right in insisting that the central witness of Scripture is normative for the faith and life of the church, this witness does not exist in a vacuum. The truth is that neither "Scripture alone" nor "Scripture plus church tradition" is sufficient to communicate the gospel of Christ effectively. Only the Spirit of God who freely uses the witness of Scripture in the context of the witness and life of the church is able to create and nurture faith in and obedience to Christ as Savior and Lord.[42]

Although the relationship between revelation, Scripture, and the teachings and traditions of the church continues to be a point of contention between Protestant, Roman Catholic, and Eastern Orthodox theologies, all con-

41. On the one hand, Calvin speaks of God as the "author" of all of Scripture (*Institutes of the Christian Religion,* 1.3.4); on the other hand, he contends that it is only when Scripture "shows forth Christ" that it conveys the word of life (1.9.3).

42. See George S. Hendry, *The Holy Spirit in Christian Theology* (Philadelphia: Westminster, 1956): "Luther says the Word is the cradle in which Christ lies; we may also say that the church is the nursery in which the cradle lies" (95).

verge toward the recognition that Scripture and church doctrine are not two independent media of revelation. Church doctrines are what the church confesses and teaches on the basis of the revelation of God attested in Scripture.[43] Church teachings have a real but relative authority in the life of faith. Always subordinate to Scripture, the church's common creeds and contemporary confessions provide important hermeneutical keys to what is central in Scripture and give succinct summaries of the mighty acts of God. According to Calvin, ecumenical creeds such as the Apostles' Creed are to be highly valued because they "sum up in a few words the main points of our redemption."[44] Creeds and confessions play an important role in the life of the church as "primary commentaries" on Scripture, not as independent channels of revelation.[45]

Recognizing that there are flaws and distortions in all witnesses to revelation is disturbing to many Christians. But if we remember that God's grace and power are made perfect in human weakness (2 Cor. 12:9), we will have little difficulty in seeing the grace of God at work in the fact that fallible human beings are taken into the service of God's revelation. By communicating indirectly with us, God's revelation is accommodated to our creaturely condition. God respects our humanity and seeks our free response.[46] The light of revelation does not descend on us perpendicularly from above; it comes through worldly media by the power of God's Spirit, who enlists our participation in the process of responsible interpretation and critical appropriation.

Because all human witnesses to revelation are subject to ambiguity and distortion, it is necessary to understand the reception of revelation as a dialectical process. On the one hand, there can be no reception of the revelation of God in Christ apart from *attentive and trustful reading and hearing* of the witness of Scripture in company with other members of the people of God. Only in the context of the faith, prayer, proclamation, sacramental life, and service of the church does the transforming power of Jesus Christ attested by Scripture become effective for us.

43. Jaroslav Pelikan, *The Christian Tradition: A History of the Development of Doctrine,* vol. 1: *The Emergence of the Catholic Tradition, 100-600* (Chicago: University of Chicago Press, 1971). Pelikan defines Christian doctrine as "what the church of Jesus Christ believes, teaches, and confesses on the basis of the word of God" (1).

44. Calvin, *Institutes,* 2.16.18. Cf. the concise formulation of Nicholas Lash: "What the Scriptures say at length, the creed says briefly"; *Believing Three Ways in One God: A Reading of the Apostles' Creed* (London: SCM Press, 1992), 8.

45. On the place of the church's creeds and confessions in relation to Scripture, see Barth, *Church Dogmatics,* 1/2: 585-660.

46. On "indirect communication" as the necessary form of God's revelation, see Soren Kierkegaard, *Concluding Unscientific Postscript* (Princeton: Princeton University Press, 1941), 216ff.

On the other hand, there is always a need for *critical appropriation* of the revelation of God in Christ as mediated to us by Scripture and the proclamation and life of the church. Only as we enter into the new freedom in Christ that resists every form of bondage, including those that may be supported by certain elements of Scripture and church teaching, do we become active and responsible recipients of the revelation of God. Neither the witness of Scripture nor that of the church is more than a servant of the living and free God. They point beyond themselves to the living Word of God, to a judging and renewing reality at work in our midst but never under our control.

A doctrine of revelation will thus acknowledge that we are human beings, that our lives are shaped by the particular communities to which we belong and most especially by the community of faith, by the values it espouses, the stories it tells, the doctrines it teaches, the practices it engages in. Reception of the revelation of God and the reformation of human life in its light occur in a communal context. This does not mean that faithfulness to the revelation of God is simply a process of "socialization" into the beliefs and practices of the Christian community. Becoming Christian involves far more than appropriating and repeating a tradition. To respond in faith to the revelation of the living God mediated through Scripture and the witness of the church is to become a free and joyful witness of the truth of the good news one has received and to share responsibility for interpreting it and living it out.

An important conclusion to be drawn from these reflections is that the community of faith that is called to service by the revelation of God must never presume to have control of the revelation that it attests. If that were to happen, revelation would be replaced by ideology, and theology by idolatry. God's self-revelation is true and trustworthy but it is never controllable, never simply identical with a book, a system of doctrine, a particular tradition, or the special experience of an individual or group. It is God's free and gracious act of self-disclosure in Jesus Christ mediated through the polyphonic witness of Scripture and the living testimony of the community of faith by the power of the Holy Spirit. Revelation can never be considered our possession, something we can take for granted. It is an event for which the church must continually pray: "Come, Holy Spirit! Speak once again to your people through your Word." In acknowledging our dependence on God's self-revelation supremely given in Jesus Christ, the Christian community confesses that it is not its own master, that God alone is Lord, that this community is called to proclaim Jesus Christ and not itself (2 Cor. 4:5), and that it must expect to be addressed and reformed again and again by the living Word of God in the power of God's Spirit.

CHAPTER 3

The Authority of Scripture

S ince the beginning of the church, every Christian theology has implicitly or explicitly acknowledged the authority of Scripture. The serious question has never been *whether* Scripture is a primary authority for Christian faith and life, but *what sort of* authority it is.[1]

For the sixteenth-century Reformers, the authority of Scripture was rooted in its liberating message, in the good news of God's gracious acceptance of sinners offered in Jesus Christ. The Bible was experienced not as an arbitrary or despotic authority but as a source of renewal, freedom, and joy.

This is not the way everyone, or even every Christian, understands the meaning of scriptural authority today. Many people inside and outside the church equate the idea of the authority of the Bible with coercion rather than liberty, with terror rather than joy. They know all too well how the authority of the Bible has been invoked to suppress free inquiry and to legitimize such practices as slavery and patriarchy.

Thus a major task of theology today is to develop a liberative understanding of the authority of Scripture. Toward this end I will contend that the authority of Scripture has to be understood in relation to its central content and its particular function within the community of faith. Scripture is the unique and irreplaceable witness to the liberating and reconciling activity of God in the history of Israel and supremely in Jesus Christ. By the power of the Holy Spirit, Scripture serves the purpose of relating us to God and transforming our life.

---

1. Portions of this chapter are based on my earlier discussion of the authority of Scripture in Chapter One of *Called to Freedom: Liberation Theology and the Future of Christian Doctrine* (Philadelphia: Westminster, 1980).

The Problem of Authority in Modern Culture

The problem of the authority of Scripture is part of the wider crisis of authority in modern Western culture.[2] Since the Enlightenment, every claim to authority has had to justify itself before the bar of autonomous reason. In this process of critical examination, much that was previously considered authoritative is dismissed as arbitrary and groundless.

Kant's famous dictum "Dare to think for yourself" is the motto of Enlightenment mentality. In the name of autonomous reason and the freedom of the individual, every established "house of authority"[3] — whether of state, church, or society — is placed in question. As heirs of Enlightenment rationality, we have acquired a strong and persistent allergy to the notion of authority.

Applied in every field of inquiry, the modern critical mentality has undoubtedly enriched the meaning and task of being human. In all areas of modern culture, the summons to give up infantile dependencies and become mature people who think and decide for themselves continues to make its mark. The development of modern democratic systems of government, for example, owes much to Enlightenment philosophy. Christian faith and theology should honor the good that has accompanied this modern critical spirit as well as reject the pretensions. Christian faith is not nostalgia for a world undisturbed by the critical mentality; it is not a secret ally of the state authoritarianisms of Hitler, Stalin, Duvalier, and Marcos, nor of ecclesiastical authoritarianisms that refuse to allow any dissent whatever to their established teachings. While there are deep ambiguities in modern culture's critique of oppressive authority in the name of autonomous human reason that should be exposed, a simplistic rejection of the critical tradition of the Enlightenment would be a theological mistake. The gospel proclaims the gift of a new freedom from every bondage and arbitrary rule.

Many Christians are willing to accept the modern spirit of critical reason and its radical questioning of traditional authority up to the point of the study and interpretation of Scripture. Yet Scripture has no immunity from this wider cultural critique of authority. There is no turning back from the vigorous pursuit of critical methods of biblical study that have shattered many traditional ways of thinking and speaking of biblical authority. While it is true that the application of critical reason to the Bible has not been without

---

2. See Jeffrey Stout, *The Flight from Authority: Religion, Morality, and the Quest for Autonomy* (Notre Dame: University of Notre Dame Press, 1981).

3. See Edward Farley, *Ecclesial Reflection* (Philadelphia: Fortress, 1982).

its own distorting ideologies, the imperative that this places on theology is to be not *less* but *more* critical.

The basic question that a doctrine of Scripture must address is, What do we mean by the authority of Scripture? Does its authority reside in a coercive power capable of enforcing compliance or in its inviting power that calls for our free and glad trust in God? Is the authority of Scripture an arbitrary datum simply to be accepted by a sacrifice of the intellect, or is it inseparable from the scriptural proclamation of the liberating grace of God in Jesus Christ? Put differently, the question is whether the church has forgotten that its own scriptural tradition contains a powerful critique of arbitrary authority and a distinctive message of freedom.[4]

Within the biblical witness, there is relentless criticism of every authority that identifies itself with the ultimate authority of God. Jesus refused to ascribe ultimacy either to religious doctrines and traditions (Matt. 5:21ff.; Mark 11:28ff.) or to the claims of the state (Mark 12:13-17). The apostle Paul distinguished between written codes that kill and the Spirit that gives life (2 Cor. 3:6). This remarkable biblical heritage of freedom from all idolatry, including bibliolatry, was vigorously upheld by Martin Luther, who used the term "straw" to describe all scriptural texts that failed to express clearly the liberating message of Christ. John Calvin was not as bold as Luther in his doctrine of Scripture; nevertheless, in his own way, he also refused to separate the authority of Scripture from "that which shows forth Christ" and insisted that it is "the secret testimony of the Spirit" that finally persuades us of the truth of Scripture.[5] In short, the Reformers' view of the authority of Scripture was intimately bound to its proclamation of new life and freedom in Christ.

Occasioned by the modern crisis of authority, but under the primary impulse of the gospel, it has been a major effort of modern theologians to divest theology of authoritarian ways of thinking about God, the church — and Scripture. Gerhard Ebeling argues that there is a "deep, inner connection" between the historical-critical reading of Scripture and the Reformers' doctrine of justification by grace through faith in that both function to remove all false securities.[6]

4. For recent discussions of the authority of Scripture, see Terrence E. Fretheim and Karlfried Froehlich, *The Bible as Word of God in a Postmodern World* (Minneapolis: Fortress, 1998); Christopher Bryan, *And God Spoke: The Authority of the Bible for the Church Today* (Cambridge, Mass.: Cowley Publications, 2002).

5. Calvin, *Institutes of the Christian Religion*, 1.9.3; 1.7.4.

6. Ebeling, "The Significance of the Critical Historical Method for Church and Theology in Protestantism," in *Word and Faith* (Philadelphia: Fortress, 1963), 17-61.

Thus, while Christian theology takes issue with the Enlightenment assumption that the only true authority is that of the independent and isolated self (an assumption also under attack by postmodern philosophy), it nevertheless engages in its own critique of oppressive authority, including versions of such authority that appear in some doctrines of Scripture. In the God of the gospel attested in Scripture, Christian faith finds the authority of liberating love that creates new community rather than an authority that works by coercive power. The gracious reign of God manifest in Jesus Christ is characterized not by authoritarian rule but by the "authoring" of new life in Christ and the new freedom for which Christ has set us free.

Inadequate Approaches to the Authority of Scripture

Before developing further this understanding of the liberative function of Scripture in the life of the community of faith, it may be helpful to identify several inadequate approaches to scriptural authority.

1. In the biblicist view, the Bible is authoritative by virtue of its *supernatural origin* and the direct identity of its words with the Word of God. This view arose out of the church's efforts to defend its faith against the acids of modernity. Anxious to protect the insights of the Reformation, Protestant theologians became increasingly defensive and strident in their claims about the supernatural character of Scripture. They insisted that every book, every chapter, every verse, every word was directly inspired by God. Speaking of the Scriptures as inspired is, of course, an ancient doctrine of the Christian tradition. Basically, the doctrine affirms that God the Holy Spirit accompanied and guided the human writers of Scripture, respecting their humanity in all its limitations and its conditioning by historical, social, and cultural context, yet conveying God's Word through these human witnesses. Various theories about how this took place and with what effect have been advanced. But there has been little consensus even among those who consider the doctrine of inspiration to be of great importance.[7] One theory of inspiration often associated with the biblicist view is that God dictated the words of Scripture to the biblical writers, who acted as secretaries. This way of thinking about inspiration leads to two problematic conclusions.

First, in the biblicist view inspiration involves inspiredness. It refers to an inherent property of Scripture resulting from its supernatural origin. It re-

---

7. See the helpful discussion of William J. Abraham, *The Divine Inspiration of Holy Scripture* (Oxford: Oxford University Press, 1981).

fers to something set before us as a given, a sheer datum. The task of a doctrine of inspiration is thus reduced to the defense of certain theories of the miraculous origin of the Bible. Missing in this interpretation of inspiration as inspiredness is the awareness that the Word of God is not directly accessible, not a possession under our control. The Word of God is an act of God in which the God who has spoken speaks here and now, and will speak again through the witness of Scripture and its proclamation by the church. Thus the same Spirit of God who guided the prophets and apostles must again be active in the preaching and hearing of their witness if what is spoken and heard is to be received as the Word of God.

Second, in the biblicist view inspiration requires infallibility. Since God is considered the author of Scripture in a straightforward literal sense, it is said to be without error. Some Protestant apologists have pushed this assertion to extreme limits. Scripture is without error not only in what it teaches about God and human salvation but also in all matters of history and science of which it speaks. The defense of the Christian faith thus becomes the defense of the doctrine of infallibility. To the Roman Catholic dogma of the infallibility of the pope (1870), directed against the rising tide of modernity, there corresponds the Protestant doctrine of the infallibility of the Bible. The church that wants an absolute guarantee of its faith and proclamation finds it in the parallel doctrines of biblical and papal infallibility. But a church with an infallible teaching office or an infallible Bible no longer allows Scripture to work as liberating and life-giving Word in its own way. Insistence on the infallibility of the Bible obscures the true basis of Christian confidence.

This biblicist doctrine of the authority of Scripture is a perfect target of the critique of heteronomy characteristic of the modern period. According to the biblicist view, the Bible is to be taken as authority not because of *what* it tells us centrally about God and humanity, or because of the transforming *effect* its message can have on human life, or because of its constitutive *role* in the life of the Christian community, but simply because its words are identified without qualification with God's words. One result of this identification is that biblical texts tend to be leveled in importance. When this happens, the account of the command of God to utterly destroy the Amalekites, their men, women, children, infants, and animals (1 Sam. 15:3),[8] or the apostolic instructions that slaves should obey their masters (Eph. 6:5) and women should be silent in the church (1 Tim. 2:12) are vested with the same authority as the

8. On the problem of the holy war texts in the Bible, see John J. Collins, "The Zeal of Phinehas: The Bible and the Legitimation of Violence," *Journal of Biblical Literature* 122 (2003): 3-21.

proclamation that God was in Christ (2 Cor. 5:19) and that in him there is new and inclusive community (Gal. 3:28). In this way biblicism turns the life-giving authority of Scripture into a deadening authoritarianism.

2. With the rise of the modern historical consciousness, a new approach to Scripture was introduced. The Bible was read simply as a *historical source.* This has brought many gains to our understanding of Scripture. It has helped to break the chains of scholastic and dogmatic readings of Scripture. It has helped us to understand the biblical writings in their own historical contexts.

Yet alongside its achievements, the historical method also created a new potential for taking Scripture captive. The interest of the historian focused primarily on establishing "what really happened," what could be validated as "factual." What was authoritative was not the text in its received form but the "facts" behind the text as reconstructed by the historian.

A serious consequence of this historicist interpretation was "the eclipse of biblical narrative."[9] When attention focuses on the facts behind the text, the meaning of the Bible is separated from its literary form. What qualifies as factual is then necessarily set within a new interpretative framework provided by the modern biblical scholar. Thus the historicist approach allows the Bible to speak only within the limits of the assumptions about the nature of history brought by the interpreter to the texts.

3. Another approach to the authority of Scripture views it as a *religious classic.* Typically, Scripture is here described as great (or at least important) literature, and its authority is seen as analogous to that of "classics" in the literary tradition and other spheres of human culture. The approach to the Bible as literature is very popular in university courses in religion. Since there is so much sheer ignorance of the Bible in American culture today, it may seem inappropriate to say anything critical about this approach to the Bible. But though knowledge of the Bible as literature is a laudable goal, it cannot serve as a substitute for the unique function of the Bible in the community of faith. The Bible is not just great literature for the faith community. God is not just a character in a story, however captivating and well told. Jesus Christ is not just an impressive if somewhat puzzling literary figure. As James Barr notes, no one doubts that Jesus was raised from the dead in the gospel story; the question that really matters for faith is whether Jesus was really raised and is alive today.[10] The believing community approaches the Bible not only as literature,

---

9. See Hans Frei, *The Eclipse of Biblical Narrative* (New Haven: Yale University Press, 1974).

10. Barr, quoted by John Barton, in *People of the Book? The Authority of the Bible in Christianity* (Louisville: Westminster/John Knox, 1988), 49.

great or not so great, but as Scripture, as normative witness to the acts of the living God for our salvation.[11]

4. Still another approach to Scripture sees it as a *private devotional text* whose authority is located in the saving meaning it has for the individual. There is, of course, a legitimate concern that prompts this emphasis. Against the speculation of scholastic theology, the obsession with past facts in modern historicism, and the aestheticism of detached literary readings, piety concentrates on the meaning of the Bible for the individual's salvation. The Bible speaks to me and assures me of God's forgiveness and mercy in Jesus Christ. What is significant for faith is not the crucifixion of Jesus as a bare historical fact, but the message that Christ died for me.

While it is always important to read and hear the message of Scripture "for me," this emphasis becomes distorted when it is separated from the meaning of Scripture "for us" and "for the world." A reduction of Scripture occurs when it serves only to illumine my own experience and struggle as a pilgrim of faith. The individualistic interpretation of Scripture represents a retreat of the church and theology. The public realm is abandoned in favor of the private realm of life, where faith can be secure from attack.

The Indispensability of Scripture in Relating Us, by the Power of the Spirit, to the Living God Revealed in Jesus Christ

Beyond the dead letter of biblicism, the uncritical assumptions of historicism, the narrowness of bourgeois privatism, and the detachment of aestheticism lies the real authority of Scripture in the life of the community of faith. Christians do not believe *in* the Bible; they believe in the living God attested *by* the Bible. Scripture is indispensable in bringing us into a new relationship with the living God through Christ by the power of the Holy Spirit, and thus into new relationship with others and with the entire creation. To speak of the authority of the Bible rightly is to speak of its power by God's Spirit to help create and nourish this new life in relationship with God and with others.

The Bible is a unique witness to the sovereign grace of God at work in the history of Israel and above all in the life, death, and resurrection of Jesus. As witness, the Bible does not call attention to itself. "A real witness," Karl

---

11. See Krister Stendahl, "The Bible as a Classic and the Bible as Holy Scripture," *Journal of Biblical Literature* 103 (1984): 3-10.

Barth insisted, "is not identical with that to which it witnesses, but it sets it before us."[12] An authentic witness directs our attention to some other reality. Thus the Bible is the Word of God only in a derivative sense. The living Word of God is Jesus Christ, and it is with him that we are brought into relationship by the witness of Scripture. Scripture is thus authoritative not in itself but, as the Reformers insisted, as it "sets forth Christ," as it functions in the community of faith by the power of the Spirit to create a liberating and renewing relationship with God through Christ.

Barth was fond of describing the function of the scriptural witness as like that of the figure of John the Baptist in the Isenheim altarpiece by the painter Matthias Grünewald.[13] With his abnormally long index finger, John points to the crucified Lord. The inscription on the painting reads: "He must increase, but I must decrease."

The witness of Scripture accomplishes its purpose in a polyphonic rather than homophonic manner. Its faith discourse is extraordinarily rich. As Paul Ricoeur has argued, the literary genres of the scriptural witness are fittingly diverse ways of bringing us into relationship with God. The narrative form is required if God is to be identified as a living, personal agent who acts as creator, reconciler, and redeemer. Prophetic discourse is a fitting medium to call in question the complacency and arrogance of the people of God who recite and celebrate the great acts of God in the past but who do not live justly, love mercy, and walk humbly with God (Mic. 6:8). Wisdom literature aptly gives expression not only to the presence of God in everyday experience but also to the radical hiddenness of God in the experience of suffering and evil. In short, the various literary forms of the biblical witness are irreducible media of revelation and mutually complement and correct each other. The church should not ignore or collapse this literary diversity into an artificial unity any more than it should anxiously try to harmonize the theological differences in the scriptural witness between the Old and the New Testaments, between Paul and James, or between John and the Synoptics. The scriptural witness is extraordinarily rich and diverse.[14]

Yet there is a coherence in this diversity of the scriptural witness that is provided largely by its overall narrative framework. An extensive literature has developed in recent theology around this theme. As Charles Wood

12. Barth, *Church Dogmatics,* 1/2: 463.

13. See Barth, "Biblical Questions, Insights, and Vistas," in *The Word of God and the Word of Man* (New York: Harper, 1957), 65.

14. See Ricoeur, "Toward a Hermeneutic of the Idea of Revelation," in *Essays on Biblical Interpretation,* ed. L. S. Mudge (Philadelphia: Fortress, 1980), 73-118.

writes, "When one regards the biblical canon as a whole, the centrality to it of a narrative element is difficult to overlook: not only the chronological sweep of the whole, from creation to new creation . . . but also the way the large narrative portions interweave, and provide a context for the remaining materials so that they, too, have a place in the ongoing story, while these other materials — parables, hymns, prayers, summaries, theological exposi- tions — serve in different ways to enable readers to get hold of the story and to live their way into it."[15]

My central point is that biblical authority has a different basis and works in a different way from that described by traditional theories. Through the biblical witness, and especially through its narratives of God's gracious, liberating activity in Jesus Christ, God is newly identified for us and we are led into a new way of life in communion with God and with others. If our at- tention is focused on the larger pattern of the biblical story, with its climax in the life, death, and resurrection of the unsubstitutable person Jesus of Naza- reth, we shall have little doubt about the indispensability of the Bible to Christian faith and life.[16]

The Bible is a witness, and at its center it attests the sovereign, liberating grace of God in Christ. As described by the biblical narratives, God is always greater than we imagine. Scripture not only declares the coming of the Christ but tells the story of the crucified Christ; it not only praises the eternally rich God but proclaims that this God became one of the poor; it not only speaks of God's judgment and grace but declares that God stands on the side of the poor and the oppressed and judges the exalted and the powerful. This is the ever-disturbing, even revolutionary witness of the Bible.

Scripture witnesses to God's world-transforming activity. Of course, the coming reign of God inaugurated in Jesus Christ includes personal transfor- mation. The liberation of the individual from the egocentrism, isolation, apa- thy, and hopelessness of existence in bondage to sin and death is of funda- mental importance. Nevertheless, the "strange, new world of the Bible" (Barth) cannot be limited to the individual, nor to a private zone of life. It reaches out to all people and to the whole creation. It announces the begin-

---

15. Wood, *The Formation of Christian Understanding: An Essay in Theological Hermeneu- tics* (Philadelphia: Westminster, 1981), 100. See also *Scriptural Authority and Narrative Interpre- tation*, ed. Garrett Green (Philadelphia: Fortress, 1987); George Lindbeck, *The Nature of Doc- trine: Religion and Theology in a Postliberal Age* (Philadelphia: Westminster, 1984).

16. On the Bible as a means of grace by which we are brought into communion with God, see James Barr, *The Scope and Authority of the Bible* (Philadelphia: Westminster, 1980), especially Chapter Four. On the "unsubstitutable identity" of Jesus Christ as rendered by the gospel narra- tive, see Hans Frei, *The Identity of Jesus Christ* (Philadelphia: Fortress, 1975), 136.

ning of a new world, new relationships, new politics, in which justice prevails over injustice, friendship over hostility, mutual service over domination of some by others, and life over death.[17]

Principles of the Interpretation of Scripture

If the authority of Scripture is understood primarily in terms of its indispensable witness to the sovereign, liberating, and reconciling love of God in Jesus Christ, the following principles of interpretation may be proposed.

1. *Scripture should be interpreted with historical and literary sensitivity; yet Scripture's unique witness to the living God resists its imprisonment in the past or its reduction to pious fiction.* Interpretation of Scripture within the community of faith is not driven merely by antiquarian or aesthetic interests. Believers turn to Scripture to hear the Word of God and to hold to the promise of liberation and salvation in Christ. Historical and literary criticism, while not ends in themselves, can serve a better hearing of this Word.

Historical study of the Bible is important for many reasons. To begin with, it helps us to take seriously the particularity of God's actions. If God becomes known through events at particular times and places, then the historical study of the Bible is one way we respect the historical particularity of revelation. The Bible proclaims the liberating acts of God by naming particular places, events, and persons. Of course, historical investigation cannot prove that this or that event is an act of God, but it may be able to uncover the specific context of the events in which faith discerns God's actions.

Historical study of the Bible also reminds us that the narrative of the Bible refers to realities outside the text. The central narrative is not to be construed as a mere construct of the imagination of the community of faith. If the Gospels refer to the living God acting and suffering in Christ for our salvation, if the story they tell is not simply pious fiction, then historical study can never be *irrelevant* for Christian faith. The faith of the church does not stand or fall with the accuracy of every detail of the gospel story, as Calvin noted,[18] but faith does stand or fall with the truthfulness of the gospel portrayal of the central events of the ministry, death, and resurrection of Christ.

---

17. See Karl Barth, "The Strange New World within the Bible," in *The Word of God and the Word of Man,* 28-50.

18. See John Calvin, *Commentary on a Harmony of the Evangelists,* vol. 2 (Grand Rapids: Eerdmans, 1956), 89. Cited by William C. Placher, "Contemporary Confession and Biblical Authority," in *To Confess the Faith Today,* ed. Jack L. Stotts and Jane Dempsey Douglass (Louisville: Westminster/John Knox, 1990), 71.

It matters to faith whether Jesus really befriended sinners, blessed the poor, and gave his life willingly for others.

Historical study of the Bible serves still another theologically important function. It not only helps us to recognize the historical concreteness of revelation but also continually reminds us that the biblical writers were limited, fallible human beings. To deny their finitude is to rob them of their humanity. Contrary to the impression left by some doctrines of Scripture, the Spirit of God does not have to make puppets or parrots of the biblical witnesses in order to work through them. The grace of God does not destroy human freedom but renews and empowers it for partnership with God.

If we are embarrassed by the humanity of the biblical writers, we are also probably embarrassed by the humanity of Jesus the Jew from Nazareth and by our own humanity. Just as we are Docetists if we deny the full humanity of Jesus, so we are Docetists in our doctrine and interpretation of Scripture if we claim that the biblical witnesses were mere automatons under the control of the Spirit of God. If we affirm the full humanity of Jesus, we will also respect the humanity of the biblical witnesses.

To engage in historical study of the Bible is, of course, to accept risk. Some things that we previously held to be factual will be called in question. The difference between the thought world of the Bible and our own will widen. This is the risk of the historical study of the Bible, and it disturbs us. But the risk cannot be evaded because it is implied in the event of God's decisive presence and action in a finite human life. "The Word became flesh" (John 1:14), which means that the Word of God entered into the ambiguity and relativity of historical reality. The Incarnation involved risk and vulnerability, and no doctrine of biblical authority is acceptable that denies or minimizes that risk.[19]

Our emphasis on the importance of historical interpretation of Scripture is far from an endorsement of a positivist understanding of the historical task. Scripture records a history in which *God* is the primary actor. Historical interpretation that in principle excludes the activity of God is reductive and necessarily truncates the witness of Scripture. Moreover, to interpret the Bible historically is not simply to recall and record past events but to anticipate the fulfillment of promises contained in these events. The narratives of Scripture are told and retold by Israel and the church because the history of God's liberation that they recount is not yet finished. It is still open. The liberation begun in Jesus Christ points to a final liberation in which the whole creation will be set free (Rom. 8:21).

---

19. Cf. Walter Kreck, *Grundfragen der Dogmatik* (München: Chr. Kaiser, 1970).

No event can be fully understood apart from the future that it engenders. As a general principle of the interpretation of history, this thesis may be debatable, but such a principle is surely necessary in the interpretation of Scripture for those who believe in the resurrection of the crucified Jesus and his living lordship. To read the Bible historically in the deepest sense is to read it with an eye to the extension of its story of God's liberating activity in Christ into our own time and beyond. We must ask of Scripture not only what past it calls us to remember, but also what promises it wants us to claim here and now, and what future it wants us to pray and work for.

This means that we should not be surprised that the full meaning of the new freedom in Christ was not perfectly comprehended and actualized in the early church. This is evident, for example, in some of Paul's statements about the place of women in the church (1 Cor. 14:34). Still, the ferment and transforming power of the story of Christ the liberator are undoubtedly if imperfectly at work in the attitude of the New Testament church toward women. Episodes in the Gospels depict Jesus' new openness to and friendship with women. Paul himself composed a magna carta of freedom: "There is neither Jew nor Greek, there is neither slave nor free, there is neither male nor female: for you are all one in Christ Jesus" (Gal. 3:28) — a passage Krister Stendahl rightly describes as a "breakthrough," a radical new beginning of freedom incompletely realized in the early church, yet full of promise for the future under the guidance of God's Spirit.[20]

To read Scripture historically is to read it both critically and with sensitivity to the direction in which it moves, rather than with nostalgia for biblical times. There is a dynamic history of the transmission of tradition within Scripture itself. In the dynamic interpretative process within Scripture, there are "layers and layers of fresh reading" in new circumstances, and old teachings are sometimes seen to be problematic.[21] As Brian Blount argues, we interpret Scripture in the spirit of the scriptural writers themselves when we search not for the "last word" but for the "living word."[22] Our interpretation of Scripture must therefore include both a "hermeneutics of trust" (the human words of Scripture convey *God's* Word) and a "hermeneutics of suspi-

---

20. Stendahl, *The Bible and the Role of Women: A Case Study in Hermeneutics* (Philadelphia: Fortress-Facet, 1966).

21. See Walter Brueggemann, "Biblical Authority: A Personal Reflection," in Walter Brueggemann, William C. Placher, and Brian K. Blount, *Struggling with Scripture* (Louisville: Westminster/John Knox, 2002), 15. Brueggemann notes, for example, the abrogation of the Mosaic law of Deuteronomy 23:1-8 by Isaiah 56:3-8.

22. See Brian K. Blount, "The Last Word on Biblical Authority," in *Struggling with Scripture*, 51-69.

cion" (God's Word in Scripture is conveyed in *human* words). This is not a contradiction. If Scripture is viewed primarily as a witness to God's liberating love in Christ, as an earthen vessel that contains a great treasure (2 Cor. 4:7), then the passing on of its liberating and transforming message must be a creative and critical process rather than a mechanical repetition. As liberation theologians have emphasized in recent years, the Bible is faithfully interpreted when it is read as a source of freedom in Christ to overcome every bondage, including the use of the Bible itself as a weapon of oppression.[23]

2. *Scripture must be interpreted theocentrically; however, the identity of God is radically redescribed in the overarching narrative of Scripture as the triune God, i.e., the God of Israel who comes to us in Jesus Christ by the power of the Holy Spirit.* The central actor in the biblical drama is God. Scripture witnesses to the reality of God, to the purposes of God, to the kingdom of God. The content of the biblical story is God's faithfulness in acts of judgment and mercy in the covenant with the people of Israel and in the history of Jesus. The biblical narrative has many aspects, but the central theme is the work of the faithful God who takes up the cause of justice, freedom, and peace on behalf of the creation oppressed by sin and misery. Even in judgment the work of grace and promise is heard: "While we were yet sinners Christ died for us" (Rom. 5:8). In the resurrection of the crucified Jesus all of God's promises are decisively ratified. "All the promises of God find their Yes in him" (2 Cor. 1:20).

Who is the God of the scriptural witness? The answer is surely that God is the living and acting God, who is no abstract idea or figment of the pious imagination, but the one and only creator, reconciler, and redeemer. Yet the God of Scripture who does mighty deeds, creates the heavens and the earth, and delivers Israel from bondage, is also the God who suffers. If God is triumphantly present in the exodus of Israel from bondage, God is also present with Israel as it makes its bitter pilgrimage through the wilderness and suffers humiliation in exile.

Who is more majestic and powerful than the God of Scripture, the one who does wondrous things (Ps. 86:10) and whose glory the heavens declare (Ps. 19:1)? What power is comparable to that of God (Isa. 40:18, 25)? Who gives life to the dead and calls into existence the things that do not exist (Rom. 4:17)? Yet the power of the God depicted by Scripture is strange power. It is not the power of force but the power of Spirit (Zech. 4:6), and it is made known above all in the weakness of the cross of Jesus (1 Cor. 1:18ff.).

23. Cf. Mary Ann Tolbert: "One must defeat the Bible as patriarchal authority by using the Bible as liberator." Quoted by Letty M. Russell, *Feminist Interpretation of the Bible* (Philadelphia: Westminster, 1985), 140.

Again, whose freedom exceeds that of the God of Scripture, who is un-limited by any outside power? Yet the freedom of this God is far greater than the idea of freedom as complete independence from others. The free, self-determined God is free *for* others. God is free to take the form of a servant without ceasing to be God (Phil. 2:5ff.), free to become poor to make others rich, to suffer death to give others life (2 Cor. 8:9; John 3:16).

Thus a theocentric reading of the biblical story of liberation does more than provoke us to a new self-understanding or provide us with a new com-munal identity.[24] To be sure, it does these things. But primarily the witness of Scripture to God's activity newly identifies God. Scripture revolutionizes our understanding of our own identity, power, and freedom as creatures made in the image of God because it first overturns our understanding of the true identity, power, and freedom of God.

A theocentric reading of Scripture will necessarily be Christocentric, for all of the strands of the witness of Scripture to the identity and purpose of God converge in Jesus Christ. He is Emmanuel, God with us. As the author of the book of Hebrews writes, "Long ago God spoke to our ancestors in many and various ways by the prophets, but in these last days he has spoken to us by a Son" (Heb. 1:1-2). Luther's familiar statements that "Scripture is the cradle in which the Christ child lies" and that "Christ is King and Lord of Scripture" express well the Christian conviction that Jesus Christ is the center of Scrip-ture, that his ministry, death, and resurrection are the key to the interpreta-tion of Scripture. Barth makes the same point: "The Bible says all sorts of things, certainly; but in all this multiplicity and variety, it says in truth only one thing — just this: the name of Jesus Christ, concealed under the name Is-rael in the Old Testament, revealed under His own name in the New Testa-ment, which therefore can be understood only as it has understood itself, as a commentary on the Old Testament. . . . The Bible remains dark to us if we do not hear in it this sovereign name, and if, therefore, we think we perceive God and humanity in some other relation than the one determined once for all by this name."[25]

Yet while a Christian theocentric reading of Scripture is necessarily Christocentric, it is not Christomonistic. The God who is self-revealed in Je-sus Christ is none other than the creator of the heavens and the earth and the life-giving Spirit of God who opens the eyes and hearts of the readers of Scripture to receive its transforming message. *Christians read Scripture as wit-*

---

24. See David Kelsey, *The Uses of Scripture in Recent Theology* (Philadelphia: Fortress, 1975).

25. Barth, *Church Dogmatics*, 1/2: 720.

ness to the activity of the triune God. The God of the biblical witness is God the gracious source of all life ("Father") whose eternal Word became human to mediate abundant life to a world in captivity to sin and death ("Son"), and whose Spirit of freedom and new life in communion is moving the people of God and all creation to the consummation when God will be all in all ("Spirit"). In response to the activity of the triune God, men and women are called to repentance and faith. They are summoned and empowered to become partners in God's liberating and reconciling activity in the world. They are called to the living hope that the whole creation will be freed from all enslaving powers and will enjoy "the glorious liberty of the children of God" (Rom. 8:21).

If a consistently trinitarian interpretation of Scripture prompts a continuous revolution in our understanding of God, it also challenges the many ways we try to make God useful for our own cultural and political projects. The biblical story of God's liberating activity is both an authorization and a continual criticism of our various liberation movements. When the church automatically reacts to liberation theology and liberation movements with alarm, it merely shows that it no longer understands the message of Scripture. At the same time, all liberation movements are exposed to powerful temptations; they are tempted to identify God with their particular group and agenda and to equate liberation with the acquisition of power over others. The God of the biblical story, whose way of liberation is self-giving love, is always surprisingly different from what we imagine or wish divinity to be.

3. *Scripture must be interpreted ecclesially, i.e., in the context of the life and witness of the church; however, an ecclesial reading of Scripture differs not only from an individualistic reading but also from the control of Scripture by church doctrine or hierarchy.*

Every interpretation of Scripture reflects certain questions, needs, and interests of the interpreter. These questions, needs, and interests comprise a kind of horizon or boundary of our interpretive activity. Initially, our horizon may be defined by our own personal quest for salvation. We may first approach Scripture with our awareness of our own captivity, anxiety, guilt, frustration, alienation, loneliness, and despair, and our yearning for freedom and new life. In no way is this personal horizon of understanding Scripture as liberating word to be ignored or denigrated. There is an indelibly personal dimension to Christian faith and to the reading and interpretation of Scripture. The Word of God must be personally received and appropriated. Unfortunately, the horizon of the interpretation of the Bible for some Christians never extends beyond the significance of its message for their own life.

Interpreting Scripture ecclesially means reading, hearing, and interpreting Scripture within the horizon of the faith and practices of the whole community of believers. Participation in the witness, worship, and practices of the church prepares us for a proper reading of the scriptural witness. The Bible is not a collection of religious texts to be appropriated by individuals in whatever way they please; the Bible is the "Scripture" of the church.[26] The witness of Scripture establishes and orders the Christian community's faith and life. Thus, to interpret Scripture ecclesially means to listen to its witness in and with the whole community of faith, remembering that this community has acknowledged these writings to be canonical (that is, they comprise the rule or norm for identifying the Word of God) and confidently expecting that the Word of God will again address us through the biblical witness by the power of the Holy Spirit. To interpret Scripture ecclesially is to interpret it in the context of the memory and hope of the Christian community.

Reading and interpreting Scripture as the unique and normative witness to God's self-revelation given above all in Jesus Christ are skills learned by participation in the life of the Christian community. The skills of interpreting Scripture from its center and of rightly grasping the purpose of Scripture are cultivated as one takes part in the church's worship, prayer, proclamation, sacraments, confession of faith, practice of love and forgiveness, and service in the world.

The church is a community of interpretation, and it has certain rules of sound understanding of its sacred texts. These rules are not arbitrary. They are rooted in Scripture itself, which directs us to the life-giving Word (John 20:31; 2 Cor. 3:6). An ecclesial reading of Scripture will be informed, first of all, by the *rule of faith,* that is, the confessional consensus of the church about the central message of Scripture. Beginnings of a rule of faith are already present in the earliest confessions of the New Testament church (e.g., 1 Cor. 12:3; Mark 8:29). By the second century, Irenaeus is able to summarize the trinitarian and Christocentric rule of faith that is accepted by the church "scattered throughout the whole world."[27]

In addition to the rule of faith, an ecclesial reading of Scripture will be guided by what Augustine calls the *rule of love,* the purpose of Scripture to engender and increase our love of God and neighbor. We are called to love because God first loved us (1 John 4:19). This has clear implications for the interpretation of Scripture: "Whoever thinks that he understands the divine

---

26. See Phyllis A. Bird, *The Bible as the Church's Book* (Philadelphia: Westminster, 1982); Darrell Jodock, *The Church's Bible: Its Contemporary Authority* (Philadelphia: Fortress, 1990).

27. Irenaeus, *Against Heresies,* 1.10.1.

Scriptures or any part of them so that it does not build the double love of God and of our neighbor does not understand it at all."[28]

To the rule of faith and the rule of love, we should also add the *rule of hope*. God is "the God of hope" (Rom. 15:13), and "whatever was written in former days was written for our instruction, so that by steadfastness and by the encouragement of the scriptures we might have hope" (Rom. 15:4). By the rule of hope I mean that every sound interpretation of Scripture will freely acknowledge that we live by God's promise, that there is much that we do not understand, that "now we see in a mirror, dimly" (1 Cor. 13:12), that God is not yet finished with us or the world, that we and the whole creation groan for the fulfillment of God's redemptive purposes.

A mature reading and interpretation of Scripture thus presupposes a participation in the worship and life of the community of faith and its "rules" of interpretation. Interpreters of Scripture must be willing to be open to the wisdom of the church's fathers and mothers, sisters and brothers, past and present, near and far. Their witness serves as an important guide for our interpretation of Scripture in our own time and often deepens and corrects our incomplete and provincial understandings of its message of sin and salvation, captivity and liberation.

The classical creeds and confessions of the church have a special role in the task of scriptural interpretation in the life of the church. This is particularly true of the Apostles' and Nicene Creeds. They are a central part of the confessional tradition of most Christian churches and are widely used in worship and Christian education. The many confessions and catechisms of the churches (such as the Lutheran *Book of Concord*, the Presbyterian *Book of Confessions*, the Anglican *Thirty-Nine Articles*, the Methodist *Twenty-Five Articles of Religion*, and the *Catechism of the Catholic Church*) intend to offer what might be called exemplary interpretations of Scripture. Stated somewhat differently, creeds and confessions provide communally tested and approved rules for interpreting Scripture.[29] They not only instruct us about what is of central importance in Scripture but also show how the message of Scripture has been received by the church in particular places and moments in its history. Viewed in this way, the creeds, confessions, and catechisms of the church are not judicial instruments designed to punish offenders but hermeneutical documents to assist the church in a right understanding of Scripture. Their intent is to direct the church to the central and living truth of the scriptural witness as the church seeks to bear witness to the gospel today.

---

28. Augustine, *On Christian Doctrine* (New York: Liberal Arts Press, 1958), 30.

29. See George Lindbeck, *The Nature of Doctrine*, especially Chapters Four and Five.

Creeds and confessions do not supplant Scripture. They remain subordinate to its witness and can be corrected by it. An ecclesial reading of Scripture, while instructed by the church's confessions, remains open to new readings under the guidance of the Holy Spirit. In a Reformed understanding of confessions, they possess a real but relative and provisional authority in the life of the church. They too are normed by the scriptural witness. The principle "always in need of reform" *(semper reformanda)* by the Word of God must apply also to the church's confessional statements if the scriptural witness is to remain normative in the proclamation and life of the church.

4. *Scripture must be interpreted contextually; however, the context of our interpretation must not be confined to our personal history or to that of our immediate locality.* As participants in the worldwide Christian community, we must listen to interpretations of Scripture that come from localities other than our own, especially when these interpretations give voice to the poor and to the groaning of the whole creation for the justice, freedom, and peace of God's coming reign.

Interpreting Scripture contextually means more than being nurtured by the witness, life, and confessions of the local congregation or denomination of which we are members. If our reception and understanding of the witness of Scripture is not to be confined within the boundaries of our personal experience or locked within our particular church tradition and its established ways of reading Scripture, it is imperative that we listen carefully to interpretations of Scripture by Christians in contexts different from our own. We must remain open to the freedom of the Spirit who sheds new light on Scripture. The Spirit of God moves in surprising ways. Unfamiliar voices can challenge and enrich scriptural interpretation. If the Spirit is not to be quenched (1 Thess. 5:19), we must be open to new and disturbing readings of Scripture. No single interpretation of Scripture exhausts its message. All are in need of deepening and correction.

In particular, our interpretation of Scripture needs to be tested and deepened by understandings of its message that arise out of communities that know affliction and are struggling for life in the midst of poverty and injustice. Because of their long history of suffering, Jews approach Scripture with a sensitivity to the reality of evil and suffering in the world that is all too easily neglected by many Christians in Western societies. Many African Americans, Hispanics, and women read Scripture through Third World eyes, and this presents a deep challenge to First World readers, who all too often expect Scripture to endorse their comfortable, middle-class way of life. Training in a rich contextual reading of Scripture thus demands an ongoing ecumenical conversation and the Spirit-given courage "to hear the voices of people long silenced."[30] If we listen carefully to these voices, we will hear echoes of the cry for justice central in the message of the prophets (Isa. 1:16-17; Jer. 5:1; Amos 5:23-24; Mic. 6:8).

Recent liberation and other contextual theologies have underscored the fact that social and cultural factors are inevitably at work in the interpretation of the scriptural witness to revelation.[31] They also emphasize far more than does the classical theological tradition that both the Bible and church teaching have often been used in ways that have contributed to oppression rather than to liberation. For this reason, they insist that a privileged hearing should be given to the interpretation of the Bible by the marginalized and the poor of the world. Whatever criticisms may be made of contextual theologies, it should be noted that their intent is to seek not a revelation apart from the Bible, but a new reading of the Bible. Similarly, far from wanting to abandon the church as the environment in which Christian faith is nurtured, their aim is to rediscover the reality of the church among the poor and those who struggle for justice.

The claim that the experience of suffering and solidarity with oppressed people is the necessary context for responsible interpretation of Scripture is sometimes expressed in the phrase "the hermeneutical privilege of the poor." Properly understood, this phrase does not imply the moral or religious superiority of the poor. The poor, like the rich, are radically dependent on the grace of God for life itself, for new life, and for full life. What "the hermeneutical privilege of the poor" means is that the experience of suffering and poverty provides an opportunity for understanding the message of the Bible that frequently remains hidden to those who insulate themselves from the suffering of others and from their own suffering. The identification of God in the scriptural narrative of God's new and surprising work in Christ culminates in God's voluntary journey into solidarity with sinners, the poor, and the victims of injustice, and God's free acceptance of the way of suffering love for the redemption of all who are in bondage. "You know the grace of our Lord Jesus Christ, that though he was rich, yet for your sake he became poor, so that by his poverty you might become rich" (2 Cor. 8:9).

If we speak of the continuing and surprising activity of the Spirit to deepen and correct our understanding of the message of Scripture through the voices of the people of God in different times and places and even through the voices of those beyond the boundaries of the Christian commu-

30. "A Brief Statement of Faith," in *The Book of Confessions* (PCUSA), 10.4, line 70.
31. See *Lift Every Voice: Constructing Christian Theologies from the Underside*, ed. Susan Brooks Thistlethwaite and Mary Potter Engel (San Francisco: Harper & Row, 1990).

nity, have we not endangered the normativity of the scriptural witness, risked the loss of Christian identity, and undermined commitment to Christ? On the contrary, the point is to acknowledge that Jesus Christ is alive, that we have not yet exhausted the riches of the gospel, that the Spirit brings forth new light from the Word of God, and that we are called to faithful discipleship here and now.

From this perspective, the necessary context for interpreting Scripture is practical engagement in the living of Christian faith, love, and hope in a still unredeemed world. The non-coercive authority of the biblical witness finds its awaited hearing in gratitude for God's grace, in a new solidarity with the poor, in a commitment to justice, freedom, and peace shared with Christians everywhere and with all people of good will, and in a new sensitivity to the groaning of the whole creation for the coming of God's reign.

CHAPTER 4

The Triune God

C hristian theology begins, continues, and ends with the inexhaustible mystery of God. It speaks of God, however, not in vague and general terms, but on the basis of the particular actions of God attested in Scripture. The central task of a Christian theology, therefore, is to clarify the understanding of God that is proper to the Christian faith, to describe its own peculiar "logic" of God. To the questions Who is God? What is God like? How does God relate to us? a Christian doctrine of God responds in the light of the scriptural witness to God's history with the people of Israel and God's new covenant with all humanity in Jesus Christ. Since, as John Calvin insisted, our knowledge of God and our knowledge of ourselves are always inextricably intertwined,[1] the route that we take and the conclusions that we reach in the doctrine of God will profoundly influence everything else we say about Christian faith and life.

The Problem of God in Modern Theology

Talk of God has become a problem for many people today. While criticisms of traditional doctrines of God arise from various sources and take very different forms, they often focus on the human experience of domination by some coercive power, and on the human quest for freedom and fulfillment.

Perhaps foremost among these criticisms, especially among people influenced by the principles of the Enlightenment, is the charge that belief in God and affirmation of human freedom are incompatible. Critics of religious

1. Calvin, *Institutes of the Christian Religion*, 1.1.1.

belief argue that it is sustained only by uncritical and authoritarian habits of mind. According to Feuerbach, humanity impoverishes itself in religion, since God is simply the projection of our own hidden potential. In a similar vein, Freud called belief in God an infantile illusion that our needs will be met by an omnipotent parent.

Traditional theologies and church teachings are also called in question by those who speak for victims of injustice and oppression. Official doctrines of God, they contend, serve to justify and sanction existing conditions of misery and exploitation. In classical Marxist theory, religion is described as the opiate of the people.

Again, profound questions about the presence of God in history are raised for many people today by events of overwhelming evil. The long and torturous history of black slavery in North America compels some thinkers to ask whether God is a white racist;[2] the holocaust of six million Jews during World War II gives credence to the conviction that God is dead; the possibility of a world-encompassing nuclear holocaust seems to render all inherited claims about the sovereignty and goodness of God glib and even blasphemous; the spread of religious violence on a global scale links the name of God with appalling acts of terror.[3]

The problem of God is also a continuing topic of philosophical discussion in our time. An important critique is advanced by process philosophers and theologians, who argue that traditional doctrines of God are hopelessly inadequate because they view God as absolute and unaffected by the events of history. They charge that the tradition portrays the relationship of God and the world as unilateral and coercive rather than reciprocal and persuasive. The traditional view is considered utterly incompatible with the modern experience of reality as dynamic, processive, and relational; it is also said to be insensitive to the enormity of suffering in the world.

Feminist theology offers some of the most devastating criticisms of traditional doctrines of God. Representatives of this perspective charge that traditional thinking and imagery of God are bound up with patriarchal attitudes and structures that endorse and perpetuate relationships of domination. By patriarchy is meant "the male pyramid of graded subordinations and exploitations"[4] in which men lord over women, white people over people of color, and humanity over nature. Unchallenged, patriarchy erodes the credibility of

---

2. See William Jones, *Is God a White Racist?* (Garden City, N.Y.: Doubleday, 1973).

3. See Mark Juergensmeyer, *Terror in the Mind of God: The Global Rise of Religious Violence* (Berkeley: University of California Press, 2000).

4. Elisabeth Schüssler Fiorenza, *Bread Not Stone: The Challenge of Feminist Biblical Interpretation* (Boston: Beacon Press, 1984), xiv.

Christian faith. As Shug, a black woman in one of Alice Walker's novels, puts it, "When I found out I thought God was white and a man, I lost interest."[5] Sallie McFague summarizes the feminist critique of patriarchy and its legitimating theology by contending that at the heart of our most pressing issues today is the misuse of power. Whether we think of the exploitation of the natural environment, or of political, economic, racial, cultural, and gender oppressions, or of the development of weapons of incalculable destruction, the fundamental problem is "the question of power; who wields it and what sort it is. . . . Is power always domination?"[6]

The above list of charges against traditional doctrines of God is not meant to be exhaustive. It is intended simply to remind us of what are perhaps the most fundamental questions of theology: Who is the God worshiped and proclaimed by the Christian community? Is this God the enemy or the friend of human maturity and freedom? Is the sovereignty of God exercised in brute power or in costly love? Is God the source of reconciliation and peace or of violence and war?

In seeking to address these questions, we must first decide what route we shall follow. Shall we begin by developing a doctrine of God general enough to fit every religious conviction? Shall we argue, on the basis of common religious experience and allegedly universal principles, that God — whatever else this word might designate — is surely the one perfect, omnipotent, wise, good, and eternal being? If we were to follow this approach, we would postpone to some later point our thinking and speaking of God on the basis of the biblical witness, and particularly of its witness to God's revelation in Jesus Christ. Although this approach to the doctrine of God has a long and distinguished history in Christian theology, I think we should follow a different path.

While it is true that everyone begins an inquiry about the reality and identity of God with some prior ideas or unexpressed assumptions, a Christian theology should not uncritically adopt these often general and inchoate notions about God and should certainly not attempt to make them normative. Christian faith and theology do not speak of God in a general and indefinite way; they speak of God concretely and specifically. Christians affirm their faith in God as the sovereign Lord of all creation who has done a new and gracious work in Jesus Christ and who continues to be active in the world through the power of the Spirit. On the basis of this particular history

5. Walker, *The Color Purple* (New York: Washington Square Press, 1982), 177.

6. McFague, *Models of God: Theology for an Ecological, Nuclear Age* (Philadelphia: Fortress Press, 1987), 15-16.

of revelation and redemption, the Christian community confesses God to be the source, the mediator, and the power of new life. God is the majestic creator of the heavens and the earth, the servant redeemer of a world gone astray, and the transforming Spirit who empowers new beginnings of human life and anticipatory realizations of a new heaven and a new earth. To use the familiar terms of the biblical and classical theological tradition, God is "the Father, the Son, and the Holy Spirit." In brief, Christians confess the triune identity of God.

The Christian *confession* of God as triune is a summary description of the witness of Scripture to God's unfathomable love incarnate in Jesus Christ and experienced and celebrated in the community of faith. The *doctrine* of the Trinity is the always-inadequate attempt to interpret this witness in the most suitable images and concepts available to the church in a particular era. Rightly understood, the doctrine of the Trinity is not an arcane, speculative doctrine; rather, it is the understanding of God that is appropriate to and congruent with the gospel message. In applying the terms "appropriate" and "congruent" to this understanding of God, I am saying, negatively, that the doctrine of the Trinity is not a revealed doctrine. It did not descend miraculously from heaven, nor was it written by God on tablets of stone. It is the product of the meditation and reflection of the church on the gospel message over many centuries. In other words, the starting point or root of trinitarian faith is the good news of the love of God in Christ that continues to work in the world by the Holy Spirit. The doctrine of the Trinity is the church's effort to give coherent expression to this mystery of God's free grace announced in the gospel and experienced in Christian faith.

But isn't it simply preposterous to focus on the doctrine of the Trinity in constructing a Christian doctrine of God today? Isn't a trinitarian understanding of God a prime example of the *problem* of thinking and speaking of God rather than in any sense a credible response to that problem? While trinitarian language is still found in liturgy, prayers, and theological textbooks, is not this language for many Christians as well as non-Christians surrounded today by an impenetrable cloud? Is not this doctrine a paradigm of sterile theological speculation? Is it not both lacking in any practical significance and riddled with mathematical nonsense that demands a sacrifice of our reason and a demeaning submission to arbitrary church authority? Can this doctrine serve any other purpose than to obscure and obstruct the important causes to which enlightened people should dedicate themselves? And on top of all this, does not the language of "Father, Son, and Holy Spirit" simply prove that the Christian doctrine of the triune God is inescapably and irreformably sexist?

These questions show that the problem of God in modern theology confronts us in its most urgent and intractable form precisely in what we have called the distinctively Christian understanding of God: the doctrine of the Trinity. Is it possible to retrieve and re-present the Christian doctrine of the Trinity in a contemporary idiom and in all its revolutionary significance?

The Biblical Roots of the Doctrine of the Trinity

The biblical basis of the doctrine of the Trinity is not to be found simply in a few "proof texts" (such as Matt. 28:19). Its basis is the pervasive trinitarian pattern of the scriptural witness to God, foreshadowed in the Old Testament according to the Christian reading of it, and found more explicitly in the witness of the New Testament to the presence of the one and only God in the saving work of Jesus Christ and the renewing activity of the Holy Spirit.

Scripture affirms from beginning to end that there is but one God. Both Old and New Testaments share this faith in the sole sovereignty of "the Lord your God" (Deut. 6:4, Mark 12:29-30). The trinitarian faith of the church upholds rather than contradicts this unambiguous scriptural testimony. The first commandment is honored with equal zeal in the faith of Israel and in the faith of the Christian church: "You shall have no other gods before me" (Exod. 20:2).

The witness of the New Testament, however, is that the reality of the one God cannot be separated from God's love for the world in Jesus Christ and his renewing Spirit. The earliest Christian confession and experience thus implies a trinitarian understanding of God. In the New Testament account of the coming of God to rescue and renew the creation, there are three inseparable reference points. The love of God comes originally from the one called "Father," is humanly enacted for the world in the sacrificial love of the one called "Son," and becomes a present and vital reality in Christian life by the one called "Spirit." In Jürgen Moltmann's summary of the New Testament witness, the story of the gospel is "the great love story of the Father, the Son, and the Holy Spirit, a divine love story in which we are all involved together with heaven and earth."[7]

Thus Christians call God triune because this way of speaking accords with the biblical witness and with the experience of the church rooted in this witness. Christians confess that there is one God (Eph. 4:6), who is none

7. Elisabeth Moltmann-Wendel and Jürgen Moltmann, *Humanity in God* (New York: Pilgrim Press, 1983), 88.

other than the Lord God of Israel and of all creation, even as they confess that "Jesus is Lord" (1 Cor. 12:3) and do so in the power of the Holy Spirit who is also acknowledged as the Lord (2 Cor. 3:17). The God known in Jesus Christ by the Holy Spirit is God over us, God for us, and God in us — the loving God, the gracious Lord Jesus Christ, and the communion-creating Spirit of God (2 Cor. 13:13). These are not three Gods but three distinct personal expressions of the one, eternally rich God who is love (1 John 4:8). The biblical narrative of God's reconciliation of the world through Jesus Christ and of God's bringing the work of salvation to completion by the power of the Holy Spirit implies a trinitarian understanding of God (2 Cor. 5:18-20; Rom. 5:1-5; Eph. 1:3-14). So, too, does the universal Christian experience of salvation, which as Catherine LaCugna notes, is "the experience of being saved by God through Christ in the power of the Holy Spirit."[8]

Some theologians have contributed to a fuller understanding of the roots of trinitarian doctrine by attending to the early Christian practice of prayer and worship as well as to the early Christian confessions. Reflecting on such passages as Romans 8:9-30 and Galatians 4:4-7, Sarah Coakley describes early Christian prayer, as depicted by the apostle Paul, as an experience of incorporation into the love of God through Christ that is "ineluctably tri-faceted." Paul strains to express this experience by language that moves back and forth between "God," "Christ," and "Spirit." By the "Spirit" we are incorporated into "Christ" and receive adoption as children of "God." According to Coakley, we have evidence here not of a fully developed trinitarian doctrine, but of a "prayer-based trinitarian logic."[9]

If talk of the triune God is not to be wild speculation, it will always find its basis and its limit both in the biblical narrative of the love of God that comes to the world through Jesus Christ in the power of the Holy Spirit and in actual Christian experience of this love (Rom. 5:5). In Christian prayer and practice we are united with Christ by the Spirit and are drawn into the life of the triune God. This means that responsible trinitarian thinking must always begin with the so-called *economic Trinity* (i.e., the one yet threefold agency of Father, Son, and Spirit in the "economy" of salvation). All reference to the life of the so-called *immanent Trinity* (i.e., the eternal distinctions of persons within the being of God) rests on this basis. According to the gospel story,

---

8. Catherine Mowry LaCugna, *God for Us: The Trinity and the Christian Life* (San Francisco: Harper, 1991), 3.

9. Sarah Coakley, "Why Three? Some Further Reflections on the Origins of the Doctrine of the Trinity," in *The Making and Remaking of Christian Doctrine: Essays in Honour of Maurice Wiles*, ed. Sarah Coakley and David A. Pailin (Oxford: Clarendon Press, 1993), 29-56. See also Mark McIntosh, *Mysteries of Faith* (Cambridge, Mass.: Cowley Publications, 2000), 24-48.

God is active as "Father," "Son," and "Holy Spirit" as the source, the medium, and the effective promise of liberating and reconciling love. To this beginning point in God's relationship to us through Christ in the Spirit trinitarian theology must return again and again. When Christians speak of God as eternally triune, they simply affirm that the love of God that is extended to the world in Jesus Christ by the Holy Spirit is proper to God's own eternal life in relationship.

When the doctrine of the Trinity is turned into a purely speculative ontology of divinity, it is rightly criticized as arbitrary. We should not pretend that the revelation in Christ has given us exhaustive knowledge of the mystery of God. But Christians do not believe they are engaging in arbitrary speculation when they confess that what has been revealed of God in Jesus Christ and the Holy Spirit is altogether reliable and corresponds to God's innermost life. If God is expressed to us in three distinct personal ways, then there is a basis of this structure of divine love in God's own immanent, eternal being. God's own life cannot contradict what God is in relation to the world. In God's own life there is an activity of mutual self-giving, a community of sharing, a "society of love" (Augustine) that is the basis of God's history of love for the world narrated in Scripture. Hence proper trinitarian theology does not first speculatively posit a Trinity in eternity and afterward search for evidence of the Trinity in revelation and Christian experience. Rather, it begins concretely from the history of revelation and salvation attested by Scripture and experienced by Christians from the beginning of the church. Only on this basis do faith and theology declare that trinitarian communion belongs to God's own eternal being, as well as to God's relation to the world. The logic of trinitarian theology moves from the differentiated love of Father, Son, and Holy Spirit in the economy of salvation (the economic Trinity) to the ultimate ground of this threefold love in the depths of the divine being (the immanent Trinity).[10]

Classical Trinitarian Doctrine

Over the course of several centuries, the church formulated an explicit doctrine of the Trinity. Two milestones in the development of this doctrine were the Councils of Nicea (325 A.D.) and Constantinople (381 A.D.). The crux of the classical Niceno-Constantinopolitan teaching is that God is "one in essence, distinguished in three persons." While this technical language of fourth-century metaphysics (*mia ousia, treis hypostaseis*) is strange to us, the

---

10. See Karl Barth, *Church Dogmatics*, 1/1 (2d ed., 1975): 384-489.

intent is to describe the reality of the living God in conformity with the gospel story. The negative meaning of this affirmation of the unity and threefold self-differentiation of God is evident in its opposition to the distortions of trinitarian faith called subordinationism, modalism, and tritheism.

According to subordinationism, the names "Father, Son, and Spirit" describe different ranks or orders of deity. There is one great God — the eternal Father — and two exalted creatures or inferior divinities. Subordinationism is in the final analysis a strategy to protect God from contact with matter, suffering, mutability, and death. Such a strategy, however, conflicts with the gospel message of God's saving work through Jesus Christ (2 Cor. 5:18-19). How can Christ be the Savior, and how can the Spirit be the power of divine transformation here and now if they are not "very God of very God" but only exalted creatures or second-rank divinities?

According to modalism, the names "Father, Son, and Spirit" refer to mere masks of God that do not necessarily manifest God's inmost being. This would mean that the events of Jesus' ministry among the poor, of his crucifixion and resurrection, and of the outpouring of the Spirit were mere appearances and possibly unreliable indicators of the true nature of God. But how can believers be sure of what God is really like if all they know of God are these external masks that keep God's real identity deeply hidden?

According to tritheism, the names "Father, Son, and Spirit" refer to three separate and independent deities who collectively constitute the object of Christian faith. This view flatly contradicts the command of the Old Testament and of Jesus to love God, the one and only Lord, with all one's heart, soul, mind, and strength (Mark 12:30). How can the object of Christian trust, loyalty, and worship be three different Gods?

With its carefully conceived but now mostly puzzling description of God as "one in essence, distinguished in three persons," classical trinitarian doctrine rejects all versions of subordinationism, modalism, and tritheism. In support of the affirmation of the unity of God's being on the one hand and the equality and distinctions of the divine persons on the other, Christian theologians have proposed rules to govern thinking and speaking of the triune God. To protect the unity of God's being, the governing rule is, "All of the acts of the triune God in the world are indivisible." Hence the Father does not act alone in the work of creation, or the Son alone in the work of redemption, or the Spirit alone in the work of sanctification. Every act of God is the act of the one triune God. Balancing this rule is the rule of "appropriations" that guards the distinctions of the persons of the Trinity. While creation, redemption, and sanctification are all acts of the triune God, scriptural usage authorizes the appropriation of the act of creation primarily (though not exclusively) to the Father, the act of redemption primarily (though not exclusively) to the Son, and the act of sanctification primarily (though not exclusively) to the Spirit.

But what is the real point of all this technical trinitarian conceptuality with its complex accompanying rules? What is the positive and profoundly evangelical aim of classical trinitarian doctrine? The doctrine of the Trinity redescribes God in the light of the event of Jesus Christ and the outpouring of God's transforming Spirit. It wants to say that God is sovereign, costly love that liberates and renews life. It wants to say that God's love for the world in Christ now at work by the power of the Spirit is nothing accidental or capricious or temporary. It wants to say that there is no sinister or even demonic side of God altogether different from what we know in the story of Jesus who befriended the poor and forgave sinners. God *is* self-expending, other-affirming, community-building love. The exchange of love that constitutes the eternal life of God is expressed outwardly in the history of costly love that liberates and reconciles. Only *this* God who "loves in freedom" (Barth), both eternally and in relation to the world, can be worshiped and served as the ultimate power in full confidence and total trust.

To speak thus of God as triune is to set all of our prior understandings of what is divine in question. God is not a solitary monad but free, self-communicating love. God is not the supreme will-to-power over others but the supreme will-to-communion in which power and life are shared. To speak of God as the ultimate power whose being is in giving, receiving, and sharing love, who gives life to others and wills to live in communion, is to turn upside down our understandings of both divine and human power. The reign of the triune God is the rule of sovereign love rather than the rule of force. A revolution in our understanding of the true power of God and of fruitful human power is thus implied when God is described as triune. God is *not* absolute power, *not* infinite egocentrism, *not* majestic solitariness. The power of the triune God is not coercive but creative, sacrificial, and empowering love; and the glory of the triune God consists not in dominating others but in sharing life with others. In this sense, confession of the triune God is the only understanding of God that is appropriate to and consistent with the New Testament declaration that God is love (1 John 4:8).

In so interpreting classical trinitarian doctrine, our aim is to get beneath its "surface grammar," to penetrate to its deepest intention, its "depth grammar," rather than remaining stuck in the ancient conceptuality with all of its strange terminology. We do not truly respect doctrines if we simply repeat them as trained parrots might. Indeed, such mindless repetition often results in the subversion of the real intent of church teachings. Thus the important question for us is, What was then, and what is now, at stake in affirming that God is triune, that God is communicated to us in Jesus Christ by the Holy Spirit? The answer to this question is that trinitarian doctrine describes God in terms of shared life and love rather than in terms of domineering power. God loves in freedom, lives in communion, and wills creatures to live in a new community of mutual love and service. God is self-sharing, other-regarding, community-forming love. This is the "depth grammar" of the doctrine of the Trinity that lies beneath all the "surface grammar" and all of the particular, and always inadequate, names and images that we employ when we speak of the God of the gospel.

Distortions in the Doctrine of God

When attention to the doctrine of the Trinity declines, distortions of the Christian understanding of God appear. The demise of vital trinitarian faith is followed by a variety of unitarianisms.[11]

1. One distortion takes the form of the *unitarianism of the Creator,* or the first person of the Trinity. Here God is viewed as the first principle of the universe, the origin of all things, and not infrequently the "Father Creator" of a particular ethnic or national group. American civil religion is by and large a unitarianism of the Creator. God is acknowledged as the source of life, of certain inalienable rights, and of the providential guidance of American destiny. There is little awareness of sin in this understanding of our relationship to God and consequently little sense of the need for forgiveness, repentance, or radical transformation of life. American civil religion is, of course, not the only form of unitarianism of the Creator. It also finds expression in other national and tribal religions and in the vague theism espoused by many educated people whose doctrine of God is cut to the specifications of religion within the limits of Enlightenment reason.

2. Another distortion assumes the form of the *unitarianism of the Redeemer,* or the second person of the Trinity. Jesus is the exclusive concern of this kind of piety. Whether seen as a heroic personality or as the central figure of a religious cult, the unitarian Jesus has little connection with the Jesus proclaimed in the Gospels. When allegiance to "Jesus my Savior" is separated from the biblical affirmation of the lordship of God over all nature and history, salvation is defined in terms of the welfare of me and my little group.

11. Cf. H. Richard Niebuhr, "Theological Unitarianisms," *Theology Today* 40 (July 1983): 150-57.

Nothing else is of real concern. If all that counts is that you "Honk if you love Jesus," what does it matter if our environment is poisoned or if people are treated brutally because of their race, religion, or sex? The unitarianism of the second person is unable to discern any necessary connection between its cozy and sentimental Jesusolatry and passionate concern for the coming of justice for all people and for the renewal of the ravaged earth.

3. A third distortion in the Christian understanding of God appears as the *unitarianism of the Spirit,* or the third person of the Trinity. Here the experiences and gifts of the Spirit are everything. Little effort is made to test the spirits to see whether they are the Spirit of God's Christ, the Spirit who builds up the community and commissions it for service of God and others. Some "charismatic" groups skate dangerously close to a unitarianism of the Spirit. In saying this, I do not mean to denigrate the movements of spiritual renewal in the church today or undervalue their importance. The increased emphasis in recent years on the experience of the Spirit and the new attention to the doctrine of the Spirit in theology are no doubt legitimate protests against a Christianity that so often gives the appearance of lifeless antiquarianism or bureaucratized religiosity incapable of arousing and redirecting our feelings, affections, and dispositions. But the solution to this problem is not mere revelry in intense religious experiences. The point that I want to make here is simply that in the Christian church the experience of the Spirit is either the experience of the Spirit of the triune God or it is a divisive and even destructive experience. The Spirit who empowers reconciliation and liberation is the Spirit of Christ and of the one he called "Abba, Father."

Restatement of the Meaning of the Doctrine of the Trinity

I have contended that the doctrine of the Trinity expresses the distinctively Christian understanding of God. Whenever this understanding of God declines, the church is in danger of losing its identity. Rather than becoming mired in the surface grammar of trinitarian faith, I have tried to uncover its depth grammar.

From the earliest centuries of the church, the triune being of God has been recognized as a mystery that we cannot fully comprehend. Augustine, the person who perhaps spent more effort wrestling with the mystery of the Trinity than any theologian in the history of the church, said, "If you comprehend something, it is not God." Through the centuries discerning theologians have stressed the limitations of our knowledge of God and the inadequacy of all our language about God — including the trinitarian symbols. Today we are even more aware of how imperfect and historically burdened all language about God is. The search for new and more inclusive images of God that complement and correct the almost exclusively male images of the tradition is an important development in recent theology. This search will doubtless help us to retrieve much suppressed imagery of God in the biblical tradition. As the church's hymns and prayers increasingly employ a wide range of images of God, the spiritual life and theological sensitivity of both men and women in the church will be enriched.

At present the church has not arrived at any consensus on how to expand the exclusive masculine imagery of God in the tradition. Some urge doing away with all gender-specific imagery of God by restricting our theological language to impersonal metaphors; others propose speaking of the Spirit as feminine; and still others argue that it is both appropriate and necessary to use masculine and feminine images of each member of the Trinity.[12]

The argument against the first-mentioned option is the fact that in the Bible God is described most frequently in personal imagery. Of course, the biblical repertoire also includes impersonal metaphors of God such as rock, fire, and water, and our understanding and worship of God would be poorer without these images. Nevertheless, much would be lost if the church departed from the biblical practice of addressing God primarily as personal, as some*one* rather than some*thing*. The argument against the second option is that it offers only a partial remedy that may simply cover over or even exacerbate the problem. If female imagery were restricted to the Spirit, it would seem that language of the Trinity would still be controlled by male imagery.

In favor of the last mentioned option is the fact that the Bible depicts God not only as a father who cares for and protects his chosen people (1 Chron. 22:10; Ps. 103:13; Matt. 6:6-9) but also as a mother who gives birth to, feeds, and comforts her children (Isa. 49:15; 66:12-13). Jesus describes himself as desiring to gather the people of God together like a mother hen who gathers her brood under her wings (Matt. 23:37). As for the Spirit, Jesus teaches that to enter the reign of God one must be born by the Spirit, thereby portraying the Spirit's work as like a woman's labor in childbirth (John 3:5-6). This is only a sampling of the breadth of biblical imagery of God — all the more remarkable considering the patriarchal setting of the biblical witness. In view of this rich imagery, the language of Father, Son, and Holy Spirit, while constituting an enduring biblical baseline for the church, must not be absolutized in its theology and liturgy. The search for other imagery to speak

---

12. Cf. Elizabeth A. Johnson, *She Who Is: The Mystery of God in Feminist Theological Discourse* (New York: Crossroad, 1992), 47-57.

of the triune God should be affirmed.[13] At the same time, new images of God should be considered complements to, rather than replacements for, the traditional images. It must also be remembered that all of our images of God, old and new, masculine and feminine, personal and impersonal, receive a new and deeper meaning from the gospel story beyond the meanings that they have in the contexts in which they are ordinarily used. When we speak of God as father or mother, the meaning of these designations is determined finally not by our cultural or familial history but by the history of God's steadfast love for the world that stands at the center of the biblical witness.

As theologians and local congregations explore new images of God, it is utterly crucial, as many feminist theologians agree, that we not lose the trinitarian depth grammar.[14] I have defined this depth grammar of trinitarian faith as the grammar of wondrous divine love that freely gives of itself to others and creates community, mutuality, and shared life. God creates and relates to the world this way because this is the way God is eternally God. I want to expand this thesis by offering three additional interpretative statements about the doctrine of the Trinity.[15]

1. *To confess that God is triune is to affirm that the eternal life of God is personal life in relationship.* The Bible speaks of God as "the living God" (Matt. 16:16). God is not like the dead idols who can neither speak nor act. God speaks and acts creatively, redemptively, transformatively. The God of the biblical witness is not impersonal but personal reality that enters into liv-

---

13. See Brian Wren, *What Language Shall I Borrow? God-Talk in Worship: A Male Response to Feminist Theology* (New York: Crossroad, 1989). The strongly trinitarian Brief Statement of Faith (PCUSA) describes God as "like a mother who will not forsake her nursing child, like a father who runs to welcome the prodigal home" (10.49-50).

14. See Patricia Wilson-Kastner, *Faith, Feminism and the Christ* (Philadelphia: Fortress Press, 1983), 121-37; Catherine Mowry LaCugna, "The Baptismal Formula, Feminist Objections, and Trinitarian Theology," *Journal of Ecumenical Studies* 26 (Spring 1989): 235-50. LaCugna contends that "the trinitarian God is eminently God for us, whereas the unitarian God is eminently for himself alone" (243).

15. See Jan Milic Lochman, "The Trinity and Human Life," *Theology* 78 (April 1975): 173-83. The recent literature on the doctrine of the Trinity is vast. Among the more notable: Jürgen Moltmann, *The Trinity and the Kingdom* (San Francisco: Harper & Row, 1981); Catherine Mowry LaCugna, *God for Us;* Elizabeth A. Johnson, *She Who Is;* T. F. Torrance, *The Trinitarian Faith* (Edinburgh: T&T Clark, 1993); *Trinitarian Theology Today,* ed. Christoph Schwöbel (Edinburgh: T&T Clark, 1995); Robert W. Jenson, *Systematic Theology,* vol. 1: *The Triune God* (New York: Oxford University Press, 1997); David S. Cunningham, *These Three Are One: The Practice of Trinitarian Theology* (Malden, Mass.: Blackwell, 1998); *The Trinity,* ed. Stephen T. Davis, Daniel Kendall, and Gerald O'Collins (New York: Oxford University Press, 1999); Kathryn Tanner, *Jesus, Humanity and the Trinity: A Brief Systematic Theology* (Minneapolis: Fortress, 2001); Roger E. Olson and Christopher A. Hall, *The Trinity* (Grand Rapids: Eerdmans, 2002).

ing relationship with creatures. Moreover, according to trinitarian faith, God does not first come to life, begin to love, and attain to personhood by relating to the world. In all eternity God lives and loves as Father, Son, and Holy Spirit. In God's own eternal being there is movement, life, personal relationship, and the giving and receiving of love.

God is one, but the unity of God is a living unity. It is a unity of pleni-tude that includes difference and relationship. The Trinity is essentially a *koinonia* of persons in love. Some twentieth-century theologians, preemi-nently Karl Barth and Karl Rahner, are reluctant to speak of three "persons" in God because of modern philosophical conceptions of personhood. Their recommendation is to speak instead of "three modes of being" in God or "three distinct ways of subsisting."[16] However, instead of relinquishing the concept of person in reference to Father, Son, and Holy Spirit, trinitarian the-ology does far better to challenge regnant understandings of the meaning of personhood. The trinitarian "persons" are not to be understood as separate and autonomous selves. Instead, they have their personal identity in relation-ship. A trinitarian understanding of personal life questions modern views of personhood that equate personal existence with the self-consciousness and autonomy of the individual. In such understandings there is no reference to relationship with others as constitutive of personal life. The trinitarian per-sons are precisely not self-enclosed subjects who define themselves in separa-tion from and opposition to others. Rather, in God "persons" are relational realities and are defined by intersubjectivity, shared consciousness, faithful relationships, and the mutual giving and receiving of love.[17]

If in the New Testament witness the one God is described as the faithful Father, the servant Son, and the enlivening Spirit, then according to the doc-trine of the Trinity, these distinct ways of God's being present in the world and acting for our salvation are rooted in the eternal being of God. In the fe-cundity and dynamism of the eternal triune life there is differentiation and otherness rather than sheer mathematical oneness. Otherness is the presup-position of personal relationship; it is the sine qua non of the event of love. In contrast to sinful human attitudes and practices that rest on fear or hatred of the other and seek to remove or conquer the other, the triune God generates and includes otherness in the inner dynamism of the divine life. That God's own being is a being in personal differentiation and relationship is expressed

16. See Barth, *Church Dogmatics*, 1/1 (2d ed., 1975): 348ff.; Rahner, *The Trinity* (London: Herder, 1970), 103-15. Cf. Paul Tillich, *Systematic Theology*, 3: 286-94.
17. See John J. O'Donnell, *The Mystery of the Triune God* (London: Sheed & Ward, 1988), 100-111.

outwardly in the creation of a world filled with an extravagance of different creatures. So much of the spirit of conquest that manifests itself in our relationships with the natural world and with people of other nations, cultures, races, and gender stems from a fear of the other that ultimately betrays a monarchical rather than a trinitarian conception of God.[18]

2. *To confess that God is triune is to affirm that God exists in communion far deeper than the relationships and partnerships we know in our human experience.* The divine life is social and is thus the source and power of inclusive community among creatures, but it exceeds our capacity to describe. Since human beings are created in the image of God (Gen. 1:27), theologians have looked for "vestiges" or analogies of the triune being of God in the creation and especially in human life. In particular, two types of analogy have often been used in trinitarian theology. One is the so-called psychological analogy that is based on a view of personhood as constituted by differentiated but inseparable activities of the self. To be a person is to be a self-conscious subject possessing the intertwined faculties of memory, understanding, and will. The other type of trinitarian analogy is the so-called social analogy that takes the human experience of life-in-relationship as the best clue to an understanding of the triune life of God (a favorite triad being lover, beloved, and their mutual love). Traditional Western trinitarian theology has given primary emphasis to the psychological analogy,[19] while a number of contemporary theologians favor the social analogy and contend that the Eastern theological tradition offers considerable support for the use of this analogy.[20]

Both the psychological and social analogies have their strengths and weaknesses. Certainly neither can claim to comprehend fully the mystery of God. When the psychological analogy is stretched too far, there is the danger

18. Susan Thistlethwaite rightly observes that "the resistance to diversity . . . can be noted in the lack of consideration given the Trinity in modern theology" (*Sex, Race and God: Christian Feminism in Black and White* [New York: Crossroad, 1989], 122).

19. The classic statement of Western trinitarianism is Augustine's *On the Trinity*. For criticism of the primacy of the psychological analogy in Augustine's trinitarianism, see Colin Gunton, "Augustine, the Trinity, and the Theological Crisis of the West," *Scottish Journal of Theology* 43 (1990): 33-58. For a defense of Augustine, see Michael Rene Barnes, "The use of Augustine in Contemporary Trinitarian Theology," *Theological Studies* 56 (1995): 51-79.

20. The most influential Eastern trinitarian theologians are the Cappadocians, especially Gregory of Nyssa. Among his works is the essay "An Answer to Ablabius, That We Should Not Think of Saying There are Three Gods." See Cornelius Plantinga, Jr., "Gregory of Nyssa and the Social Analogy of the Trinity," *The Thomist* 50 (1986): 325-52. For the counterargument that Gregory of Nyssa is not a "social trinitarian," see Sarah Coakley, "'Persons' in the 'Social' Doctrine of the Trinity: A Critique of Current Analytic Discussion," in *The Trinity*, ed. Stephen T. Davis, Daniel Kendall, and Gerald O'Collins, 123-44.

of reducing God to a solitary individual and of neglecting the reality of personal relationship in God (the heresy of modalism). When the social analogy is pressed beyond proper limits, there is the danger of thinking of God as three separate individuals who decide to work in concert with each other (the heresy of tritheism). Fortunately, we do not have to choose between these analogies. The church has never declared one of them right and the other wrong, although it has rejected the dangers to which either may lead if pushed to an extreme. There is no reason why the two analogies should not serve to complement and correct each other. Every trinitarian theology does well to remember the lovely saying of Gregory of Nazianzus: "I cannot think of the one without being quickly encircled by the splendor of the three; nor can I discern the three without being immediately led back to the one."[21]

In the judgment of many contemporary theologians (mine included), much can be learned from fresh reflection on the social analogy.[22] Trinitarian faith attests the "sociality" of God. The God of the Bible establishes and maintains life in communion. God is no supreme monad existing in eternal solitude; God is the covenantal God. God's will for life in relationship with and among the creatures is an expression of God's faithfulness to God's own eternal life, which is essentially communal. According to classical trinitarian theology, the three persons of the Trinity have their distinctive identity only in deep and inseparable relationship with each other. Since John of Dasmascus, a revered Eastern Orthodox theologian, this ineffable communion of the triune life has been expressed by the Greek word *perichoresis*, "mutual indwelling" or "being-in-one-another." The three of the Trinity "indwell" and pervade each other; they "encircle" each other, being united in an exquisite divine dance; or to use still another metaphor, they "make room" for each other, are incomparably hospitable to each other.[23]

That God's life can be described in the light of the gospel with the beautiful metaphors of trinitarian hospitality and the dance of trinitarian love has far-reaching implications. It points to experiences of friendship, caring family relationships, and the inclusive community of free and equal persons as hints or intimations of the eternal life of God and of the reign of God that Jesus

---

21. Gregory of Nazianzus, *On Holy Baptism*, oration XL.41. Quoted by Calvin, *Institutes*, 1.13.17.

22. Cf. Jürgen Moltmann, *The Trinity and the Kingdom*; David Brown, *The Divine Trinity* (London: Duckworth, 1985); Cornelius Plantinga, Jr., "Social Trinity and Tritheism," in *Trinity, Incarnation and Atonement: Philosophical and Theological Essays*, ed. Plantinga and Ronald Feenstra (Notre Dame: University of Notre Dame Press, 1989); John Zizioulas, *Being as Communion* (Crestwood, N.Y.: St. Vladimir's Seminary Press, 1985).

23. For the metaphor of trinitarian hospitality I am indebted to Cornelius Plantinga, Jr.

proclaimed.[24] That God is a trinity of love means that concern for new community in which there is a just sharing of the resources of the earth and in which relationships of domination are replaced by relationships of honor and respect among equals has its basis in the divine way of life. In the words of Leonardo Boff, "the Trinity understood in human terms as a communion of Persons lays the foundations for a society of brothers and sisters, of equals, in which dialogue and consensus are the basic constituents of living together in both the world and the church."[25]

The Christian understanding of human life and Christian social ethics are thus grounded in trinitarian theology. This does not mean that the doctrine of the Trinity provides us with an elaborate blueprint for theological anthropology or a detailed program for the renovation of human society.[26] We must not forget that God is God, and we are creatures. It would be a mistake either to project our own ideas of ideal community onto God or to demand that our human communities perfectly reflect our vision of the triune life. Nevertheless, if God's being is in communion, then human life too is intended by God to be life in communion. The Christian hope for peace with justice and freedom in community among peoples of diverse cultures, races, and gender corresponds to the trinitarian logic of God. Confession of the triune God, properly understood, radically calls in question all totalitarianisms that deny the freedom and rights of all people, and resists all idolatrous individualisms that subvert the common welfare. The doctrine of the Trinity seeks to describe God's "being in love," God's "ecstatic," outreaching, ingathering love as the source of all genuine community, beyond all sexism, racism, and classism.[27] Trinitarian theology, when it rightly understands its own depth grammar, offers a profoundly personal and relational view both of God and of life created and redeemed by God.

Anne Carr points out the congruence of a theology of triune communion and the ideals and virtues that are of greatest concern to feminist theology. In her view, "the mystery of God as Trinity, as final and perfect sociality, embodies those qualities of mutuality, reciprocity, cooperation, unity, peace in genuine diversity that are feminist ideals and goals derived from the inclusivity of the gospel message."[28]

---

24. See Elizabeth A. Johnson, *She Who Is*, 220-23.

25. Leonardo Boff, *Trinity and Society* (Maryknoll, N.Y.: Orbis Books, 1988), 118-20.

26. For a strong warning against this use of trinitarian doctrine, see Kathryn Tanner, *Jesus, Humanity and the Trinity*, 81-83.

27. See Anthony Kelly, *The Trinity of Love: A Theology of the Christian God* (Wilmington, Del.: Michael Glazier, 1989), 147-49, 157-59.

28. Anne Carr, *Transforming Grace: Christian Tradition and Women's Experience* (San Francisco: Harper & Row, 1988), 156-57.

3. *To confess that God is triune is to affirm that the life of God is essentially self-giving love whose strength embraces vulnerability.* The triune God is the living God, and the life of God is a singular act of love. God's eternal act of self-giving love is communicated to the world in "the grace of the Lord Jesus Christ, the love of God, and the communion of the Holy Spirit" (2 Cor. 13:13). However scandalous the idea, the gospel narrative identifies God as the power of compassionate love that is stronger than sin and death.[29] To have compassion means to suffer with another. According to the biblical witness, God suffers with and for creatures out of love for them. Above all in Jesus Christ, God goes the way of suffering, alienation, and death for the salvation of the world. It is this compassionate journey of God into the far country of human brokenness and misery that prompts a revolution in the understanding of God that is articulated — although never fully adequately — in the doctrine of the Trinity. God loves in freedom not only in relation to us but in God's own eternal being. God can enter into vulnerable interaction with the world, even to the depths of temporality, deprivation, suffering, and death, because as Father, Son, and Holy Spirit God is essentially an inexhaustible history of mutual self-surrendering love.[30] This boundless love of the triune God is decisively revealed in the cross of Christ and is the eternal source and energy of human friendship, compassion, sacrificial love, and inclusive community.

A trinitarian understanding of God thus coheres with the witness of the Old and New Testaments, with the suffering love of the God declared by the prophets (see Hos. 11:8-9), and with all aspects of the gospel story: the compassion of Jesus for the sick, his solidarity with the poor, his parables of the Good Samaritan and the Prodigal Child, and above all his sacrificial passion and glorious resurrection. Moreover, a trinitarian faith redefines the meaning of salvation. If the triune God is self-giving love that liberates life and creates new and inclusive community, then there is no salvation for the creature apart from sharing in God's agapic way of life in solidarity and hope for the whole creation (cf. Rom. 8:18-39). Thus a trinitarian understanding of God and of salvation gives new depth and direction to our awakening but still fragile sense of the interdependence of life and our still half-hearted commitment to struggles for justice and freedom for all people.

If the life of the triune God is the mutual self-giving love of Father, Son, and Spirit, and if the triune God is active in history out of love for the cre-

---

29. See Eberhard Jüngel, *God as the Mystery of the World* (Grand Rapids: Eerdmans, 1983), 299-396.

30. See Hans Urs von Balthasar, *Credo: Meditations on the Apostles' Creed* (New York: Crossroad, 1990).

ation, it follows that we must not, as has often happened in the theological tradition, think of the Trinity only in retrospect, looking backward from God's dealings with the world to the Trinity before creation. We must think of the Trinity first of all as the life of God with and for us here and now, which we receive by faith, and in which we participate by worship and service as we hear and obey God's Word and Spirit.[31] Then, too, we must think of the Trinity prospectively, looking ahead to the glorious completion of the purpose for which God created and reconciled the world. The history of the triune God encompasses past, present, and future. It includes suffering and death but also new life and resurrection, and it moves forward to the consummation symbolized as the reign or commonwealth of God.[32] The glory of the triune God will be complete only when the creation is set free from all bondage and God is praised as "all in all" (1 Cor. 15:28). Trinitarian faith is thus expressed not only with our lips but also in our everyday life and practices, and it finds its completion not primarily in doctrinal definitions but in doxology, praise, and adoration.[33]

The Attributes of God

Our reflections on the triune reality of God point to the need for a thorough rethinking of the doctrine of the attributes of God, which have all too often been presented and debated without any reference to the life, death, and resurrection of Jesus Christ, or to the doctrine of the Trinity, which is simply a summary redescription of the God of the gospel.

The Christian theological tradition has frequently been ambiguous and confused in speaking of the attributes of God. It has tried to synthesize the confession that God is compassionate, suffering, victorious love revealed decisively in Jesus Christ with a number of speculative ideas about what constitutes true divinity, such as immutability, impassibility, and apathy. According to Augustine, for example, God does not truly grieve over the suffering of the world; according to Anselm, God does not experience compassion; according to Calvin, when Scripture speaks of God's compassion, it employs a figure of speech that is an accommodation to our finite understanding. Even the gospel witness to the suffering of Christ on the cross was not able to dislodge the

---

31. This is a central emphasis of Catherine Mowry LaCugna's *God for Us.*

32. See Jürgen Moltmann, *The Church in the Power of the Spirit* (New York: Harper & Row, 1977), 56-65.

33. See Moltmann, *The Trinity and the Kingdom,* 151-54.

ancient philosophical presuppositions of divine immutability and impassibility from theological reflection. Numerous theologians, including Calvin, attempted to reconcile God's presence in Christ with the conviction that God does not suffer. Looking for support in classical two-natures Christology, they affirmed that while the human nature of Jesus suffered, the divine nature remained impassible.[34]

Protestant and Catholic scholastic theology tended to treat the attributes of God in two virtually separate sets: one set containing the so-called absolute or incommunicable attributes (simplicity, infinity, immutability, impassibility, eternity, aseity, etc.) and the other containing the so-called relative or communicable attributes (holiness, love, mercy, justice, patience, wisdom, etc.). The first set was reached by the *via negativa,* or negative knowledge of God, that states what God is not by excluding from God all that is thought to be imperfect in the existence of creatures (God is *not* finite, i.e., infinite; God is *not* mutable, i.e. immutable). The second set was reached by the *via causalitatis,* or way of causality, that names God as the cause of all things and all their created virtues, and by the *via eminentiae,* or knowledge of God that begins with the virtues of creatures and then infers their perfect or eminent realization in God.[35]

The scholastic way of developing the doctrine of the attributes of God creates many problems from a biblical perspective and leads to serious consequences in both theology and ethics. Failure to rethink and reform our ideas of God's impassibility, immutability, and omnipotence in the light of the gospel sets the Christian doctrine of God at odds with the proclamation of Christ crucified. It may also support, however unintentionally, ways of thinking and patterns of behavior that are insensitive to the suffering of others, resistant to needed change, and prone to divorce power from compassion and responsibility.

No wonder Pascal expressed a preference for the "God of Abraham, Isaac, and Jacob . . . God of Jesus Christ, not the God of the philosophers and scholars." How can Christians talk about the impassibility of the God who "so loved the world that he gave his only begotten Son" for its salvation (John 3:16)? How can Christians talk about the immutability of God if the God of whom they speak is the living God of the biblical witness who acts and suffers, who blesses and judges, who listens to prayer and responds to the cries of

---

34. Calvin, *Institutes,* 2.14.2. See the discussion in Paul S. Fiddes, *The Creative Suffering of God* (New York: Oxford University Press, 1988), 25ff.

35. For the Reformed scholastic treatment of the divine attributes, see Heinrich Heppe, *Reformed Dogmatics* (London: George Allen & Unwin, 1950), 57-104.

those in distress? How can Christians who proclaim the message of God's weakness in the cross of Christ that confounds the powerful of this world allow the divine omnipotence to be identified with tyrannical power? Yet this is what so much of the Christian theological tradition and especially the old dogmatic textbooks, with their commitment to inherited metaphysical presuppositions, seemed unable to avoid.

In sharp contrast to the scholastic tradition, a number of modern theologians have labored at the reconstruction of the doctrine of the attributes of God.[36] Instead of discussing the attributes of God independently of the doctrine of the Trinity, they maintain that trinitarian doctrine and the revelation in Christ that are its basis is the proper context for everything Christians say of God. Karl Barth, the most influential trinitarian theologian of the modern era, finds the key to a Christian doctrine of the divine attributes, or as he calls them, the divine "perfections," in a trinitarian understanding of God centered in the person and work of Jesus Christ. The triune God is for Barth the one whose loving is free and whose freedom is loving. Hence Barth contends that the perfections of God are properly understood not in isolation but in dialectical pairs. Each perfection of divine love is to be set in the light of God's freedom, and each perfection of divine freedom is to be set in the light of God's love. According to Barth, grace *and* holiness, mercy *and* righteousness, patience *and* wisdom are the perfections of the divine love; and unity *and* omnipresence, constancy *and* omnipotence, eternity *and* glory are the perfections of the divine freedom. Barth's exposition of the perfections of God is basically an effort to reorient this doctrine to the scriptural witness to the living, triune God whose work of reconciliation is centered in Jesus Christ and brought to completion by the Holy Spirit. As Barth writes, "It is impossible to have knowledge of a divine perfection without having knowledge of God himself — knowledge of the triune God who loves in freedom."[37]

A full discussion of the divine attributes cannot be undertaken here. But enough can be said to indicate the direction in which a doctrine of the attributes of the triune God, guided by Scripture and attuned to the gospel of Jesus Christ, should move. My brief discussion will show my agreement with Barth that the attributes of God are best interpreted in pairs that point to the being and act of God as the one who loves in freedom.

36. See, for example, Karl Barth, *Church Dogmatics*, 2/1; Jürgen Moltmann, *The Crucified God* (New York: Harper, 1974); Daniel L. Migliore, *The Power of God* (Philadelphia: Westminster, 1983); Wolfhart Pannenberg, *Systematic Theology*, vol. 1 (Grand Rapids: Eerdmans, 1991); Elizabeth A. Johnson, *She Who Is;* Colin E. Gunton, *Act and Being: Towards a Theology of the Divine Attributes* (Grand Rapids: Eerdmans, 2003).

37. *Church Dogmatics*, 2/1: 323.

The *grace* and *holiness* of the triune God are inseparable. The grace of God is expressed in God's gift of life to the creation at the beginning and in the still greater gift of new life to fallen humanity in God's work of salvation in Jesus Christ and in the outpouring of the Holy Spirit to renew the people of God. Instructed by the biblical witness, we know that the grace of the triune God is not cheap but costly, holy grace, and we likewise know that the holiness of the triune God is not simply purity or faultlessness that places us under judgment but a gracious holiness. An encounter with the holy God is an encounter with the God who seeks to redeem and sanctify us and who calls us to new life, mission, and service (Exod. 3:1-10; Isa. 6:1-8).

The triune God has both *constancy* of purpose and is engaged in ever *new and changing* actions to fulfill that purpose. Is God properly described as immutable, as theologians have often taught? Far more accurate than the term "immutable" is the affirmation that the triune God is *constant, steadfast, and faithful* in character and purpose even as God does *new and unexpected* things consistent with the divine character to fulfill the divine purpose. This is surely what Scripture means when it affirms that the Lord God does not change (Mal. 3:6) and that Jesus Christ is "the same yesterday, today, and forever" (Heb. 13:8). An absolutely immutable, utterly changeless God would not be the living, triune God of Scripture but a dead God. Precisely because the grace of God revealed through Jesus Christ in the power of the Holy Spirit is constant and reliable yet new every morning, Christians affirm that God's *faithful, changeless love* is manifested in *changing, surprising ways*.

The love of the triune God is *vulnerable* yet *unconquerable*. This is a more appropriate way to speak of the God of the biblical witness than to call God "impassible." The intent of the doctrine of divine impassibility was to deny crudely anthropomorphic views of God. The life of God is not driven or controlled by the sorts of passions that rule and destroy human life in its alienation from God and from others. But the term "impassible" seems utterly bankrupt when used to describe the passionate lament of the God of the prophets (Hos. 11:8-9) or the agony of the Son of God in his passion and death (Mark 15:34), or the sighing of the Spirit on our behalf that is too deep for words (Rom. 8:26). While the superabundant love of God is free of all internal deficiencies and external constraints, God's love for the world is passionate and vulnerable. God's compassion for the poor and the suffering is real and profound. If Jesus Christ is the fullness of God's love, we know that the love of God does not spurn vulnerability and risk. There is no love without openness to rejection, suffering, and loss. To believe in the triune God who does not remain aloof from the world is to believe in a God who is *free to be compassionate toward us, free to become vulnerable for our sake, without ceasing to be God.* God's suffering with and for us is a *free act* of God whose aim is to bring salvation to those who are lost. The suffering of the triune God is not a sign of helplessness but a promise of the final victory of compassionate love (Rom. 8:35-39).

The *power* and *love* of the triune God are inseparable. To be sure, God is properly called omnipotent, but how shall we speak of the omnipotence of the triune God? Certainly not in the manner of debating whether God can square a circle or create a stone too heavy for God to lift. Nor is the omnipotent, all-determining power of God appropriately defined by saying it is like the power of a human emperor or monarch, only raised to the highest degree. The omnipotence of the triune God is altogether different from the human exercise of power to control and dominate others. The power of the triune God is *omnipotent love.* Christ crucified is the power of God unto salvation (1 Cor. 1:23-24). The love of God made known supremely in the cross of Christ has all the power necessary to accomplish the divine purpose of creating and redeeming the world and bringing it to its appointed goal. Because God's omnipotent love is God's own, it does not work by domination or coercion but is sovereign and effective without displacing or bludgeoning God's creatures.

The omniscience of the triune God is an infinitely deep *wisdom* that is exercised with gracious *patience.* As an attribute of the triune God, omniscience is not merely "knowing everything." It is not simply the complete possession of all possible information — an attribute that might be ascribed to a master computer in a science-fiction novel. The omniscience of the God of the biblical witness is far profounder than this. It is God's *wisdom* that Scripture extols, and the wisdom of God works in ways that are *hidden* and even outrageously *foolish* to the wise of this world (1 Cor. 1:23-24). In God's wisdom creatures are given space and time to develop their own existence and to respond freely to the love of God. God's wisdom is exercised both in righteous judgment and in patient love.

If we say that God is omnipresent, this cannot mean only that God is present always, everywhere, and in all things. Such an understanding of the omnipresence of God would be indistinguishable from pantheism. The truth of God's omnipresence is that God is *present everywhere* but *everywhere freely present.* God is present when and where and how God pleases. God is present to all creatures and in all events, but not in the same way. The Spirit of God is like the wind that "blows where it chooses, and you hear the sound of it, but you do not know where it comes from or where it goes" (John 3:8).

The unity of the triune God is no mere mathematical oneness or the unity of solitariness. The *unity* of the triune God is in *communion.* Communion means living unity that includes *differentiation and relationship*. In the unity — or better, loving communion — of the triune God there is difference without division, self-giving without self-loss, and eternal life in ceaseless harmony and peace.

The *eternity* of the triune God is *glorious*. God's eternity is altogether different from timelessness. The eternity of God is not antithetical to time. If it were, God would be imprisoned in eternity and could not companion with us in time. It would be nonsense to say, as Scripture does, that "when the time was fully come, God sent his son, born of a woman . . ." (Gal. 4:4). The true meaning of the eternity of the triune God is that God is *everlasting*. God's everlasting life is open to relationship with and participation in the temporal world. The good news of the gospel is that God has time for us. In coming to us in Jesus Christ and in giving us new life in the communion of the Holy Spirit the *beauty and glory* of the *eternal* God are multiplied.

The fatal flaw in many traditional expositions of divine attributes is that they ascribed predicates to God in ways that were not determined by the scriptural witness and the church's trinitarian interpretation of that witness. Barth rightly calls for a reconstruction of Christian thinking about the attributes of God in these words: "Who God is and what it is to be divine is something we have to learn where God has revealed [God]self. . . . We may believe that God can and must only be absolute in contrast to all that is relative, exalted in contrast to all that is lowly, active in contrast to all suffering, inviolable in contrast to all temptation, transcendent in contrast to all immanence, and therefore divine in contrast to everything human, in short that [God] can and must be only the 'Wholly Other.' But such beliefs are shown to be quite untenable, and corrupt and pagan, by the fact that God does in fact be and do this in Jesus Christ."[38]

The Electing Grace of God

If the Christian understanding of God follows a trinitarian logic, we will have to rethink not only the doctrine of divine attributes but also the doctrine of election or predestination.

Few doctrines in the history of Christian theology have been as misunderstood and distorted, and few have caused as much controversy and distress, as the doctrine of the eternal decrees of God, or double predestination. Although taught in some form by many classical theologians — Augustine,

---

38. Barth, *Church Dogmatics*, 4/1: 186.

Aquinas, Luther, Calvin — this doctrine has often been a distinctive mark of the Reformed theological tradition. The Westminster Confession, for example, states that by God's secret decrees and for the manifestation of God's glory, from all eternity "some men and angels are predestined unto everlasting life, and others foreordained to everlasting death."[39] Thus stated, the doctrine of election seems to make God an arbitrary tyrant and an enemy of human freedom. The result of this teaching appears to be virtually indistinguishable from fatalism. Far from good news, the doctrine that from eternity God has decreed some to salvation and others to damnation is "dreadful," as Calvin himself described it.[40]

According to the biblical witness, the electing grace of God is astonishing, but not dreadful. In the Bible election means that the God who freely chose Israel as covenant partner and who freely established a new covenant in Jesus Christ with Jew and Gentile alike is the God of free grace. Just as in the Old Testament Israel is chosen to be God's people not because of their power or virtue but solely by God's freely given love (Deut. 7:7-8), so in the New Testament the favor of God is surprisingly directed to sinners, the poor, and the outcast. The mystery of God's will is that in Jesus Christ, God chooses to be freely gracious to both Jew and Gentile (Rom. 11:25-36). Even the faith by which this grace is received is considered a free gift of God (Eph. 2:8). Thus the biblical theme of election is doxological; it praises the free grace of God as the only basis of creation, reconciliation, and redemption: "God chose us in Christ before the foundation of the world to be holy and blameless before him in love" (Eph. 1:4).

The development of the doctrine of election in Christian theology went awry when it was made to serve purposes that it was never intended to serve. The doxological intention of the doctrine has been obscured by a variety of motives: the desire to explain why some hearers accept while others reject the gospel message (Augustine); the determination to follow rigorously what appeared to be the logical implications of God's omnipotence and providential governance of the world (Aquinas); the insistence that the righteousness of God is evident in the damnation of the reprobate just as God's mercy is displayed in the salvation of the elect (Westminster Confession).

Within a trinitarian context, however, the doctrine of election has one central purpose: it declares that all of the works of God — creation, reconciliation, and redemption — have their beginning and goal in the free grace of God made known supremely in Jesus Christ. It affirms that the triune God

---

39. "The Westminster Confession," in *The Book of Confessions* (PCUSA), 6.016.
40. Calvin, *Institutes,* 3.23.7.

who lives eternally in communion graciously wills to include others in that communion. A trinitarian doctrine of election would therefore include the following affirmations:

1. *The subject of election is the triune God.* The electing God is not an arbitrary deity who exercises naked power and whose eternal decrees unalterably fix human destiny in advance. Just as God's attributes are predicates of the triune God decisively revealed in Jesus Christ rather than free-floating ideas about what divinity must be like, so God's election of human beings to be covenant partners corresponds to God's eternal triune love in freedom. It is the decision of the triune God to be God for the world, the divine determination to be God in relationship not only in God's own being but also in relationship to creatures. Election means that God chooses to share with others God's life in communion. God's decision to be God for us and with us, to come to us in the superabundant grace (Rom. 5:20) of Jesus Christ and the renewing power of the Holy Spirit, is no divine whim or afterthought. It represents God's primary intention from all eternity. It is the very foundation and starting point of all the works of God. Because election is God's eternal and irrevocable decision to be God for the world, the doctrine of election is appropriately included in the doctrine of God.

2. *Our knowledge of election has no other basis than the unfathomable love of God for the world in Jesus Christ that we share in the communion of the Holy Spirit.* What is the content of the knowledge of election when it is riveted to this basis? Having been chosen in Christ "before the foundation of the world," we know that we have no claim on God, that our salvation depends solely on God's grace, and that we can live in the confidence that nothing can separate us from the love of God in Christ Jesus (Rom. 8:39). Moreover, because the subject of election is the triune God who loves in freedom, and because in Christ we are called to freedom (Gal. 5:13) and given the Spirit of freedom (2 Cor. 3:17), we know that God's election, far from negating human freedom, intends our free service of God and our glad participation in the new life of communion with God and others. In addition, because God desires that everyone be saved (1 Tim. 2:4) and commissions the church to proclaim the gospel to all peoples (Matt. 28:19), we know that we must not set any a priori limits to the electing grace of God.

3. *The goal of election is the creation of a people of God and not simply the salvation of solitary individuals or the privileging of particular nations or ethnic groups.* The doctrine of election is not intended to cater to excessive self-concern or to fuel arrogant national, racial, or ethnic aspirations. Rather, God's electing grace aims to open human beings to the blessings and responsibilities of life in the new community of God's own making. Election is the

expression of God's will to create a community that serves and glorifies God. In the Old Testament, the people of Israel are the object of election (Lev. 26:12); in the New Testament, the object of election is Jesus Christ and all who are united with him. God purposes a new humanity in Christ in which individuals and entire peoples are free from preoccupation with themselves and free for thankful service to God and solidarity with others. Thus the doctrine of election must have a place not only in the doctrine of God but also in the doctrine of the Christian life and the vocation of the Christian community.

4. *The electing grace of God is accompanied by the righteous judgment of God, but these are not related like two parallel lines as has been suggested in many traditional doctrines of double predestination.* In the biblical witness election and rejection are not timeless divine decisions and are not independent tracks of the divine purpose. Rather, God's judgment operates in the service of God's gracious will. If this is the case, we must not separate God's grace and justice, and certainly must not posit an eternal decree of rejection alongside God's electing grace. God's Word to the world in Jesus Christ is not ambiguous: in him all of the promises of God are Yes and Amen (2 Cor. 1:20). But neither are we allowed to reduce the message that Jesus Christ has lived and died and been raised for all into an abstract guarantee of universal salvation. Grace is not cheap, and faith can never be separated from obedience. This is the clear teaching of Romans 9–11, the locus classicus of the biblical understanding of the relationship of grace and judgment, election and rejection. In this passage, the apostle Paul does not teach that some human beings (Jews) are eternally rejected while others (Christians) are eternally elected by God. Nor does he contend that glad and faithful human response to God's free grace is a matter of indifference since in the end all will be saved. Rather, his point is that God's mercy is a free gift (Rom. 9:18) and that God judges human sin and unfaithfulness. At the same time, God's judgment, while always serious, is not necessarily final, for God wills to have mercy on all (Rom. 11:32). If any are excluded from the community of grace at the end, it is because they have persisted in opposition to God's grace, not because they were excluded before the foundation of the world (cf. Matt. 25:34, 41).

Although Calvin's position has been interpreted in various ways, his decision to locate the doctrine of election in the context of the discussion of the life of faith rather than in an abstract consideration of the decrees of God (as happened in later Calvinism) shows that he intended to look to Christ as the "mirror" of election.[41] He rightly warned against viewing the doctrine of election in an arrogant, fearful, or merely curious manner, presenting it in-

41. Calvin, *Institutes*, 3.24.5.

stead as a doctrine that gives assurance and confidence to believers as they serve God and others. Moving boldly beyond Calvin, Barth developed a still more radically Christocentric doctrine of election, according to which Jesus Christ is both the Elected *and* the Rejected, and all others are strictly to understand their election *and* rejection as real only in him. This is why Barth can say of the doctrine of election that it is "the sum of the gospel" and that it is the best of all words that can be said or heard: that in Christ, God elects humanity as covenant partner, that apart from any need or constraint the freely gracious God chooses to be God for humanity.[42]

When the doctrine of election is rethought in a trinitarian context, the meaning and goal of election are clarified. The content of this doctrine is not the "dreadful" news that the purpose of God from all eternity is to save a certain number of elect and condemn a certain number of reprobate. The mystery of election is the mystery of God's will from the foundation of the world to share with others God's own life in communion to the praise of God's glorious grace.

The doctrines of the Trinity, the divine attributes, and the electing grace of God aim to identify God not in general terms but with Christian specificity. As suggested at the outset of this chapter, our knowledge of God and our knowledge of ourselves go hand in hand. Every view of what it means to be truly human implies a certain understanding of who God is, and every understanding of what is divine issues in a particular view of what it means to be human. If the doctrine of the Trinity is the distinctively Christian understanding of God, and if this understanding is to give direction and form to the Christian way of being in the world, the question that has to be put to the church today is obvious: Is the God of Christian devotion and practice the God who is the basis of personal life in relationship, the foundation of richly diverse human community, and the hope of the transformation of the world by the power of compassionate love? In short, do the personal and corporate lives of Christians give evidence of commitment to the triune God, the sovereignly gracious God who has come to the world in Jesus Christ and continues the work of renewal and transformation by the power of the Holy Spirit?

42. Barth, *Church Dogmatics*, 2/2: 3-194.

CHAPTER 5

The Good Creation

T he Bible proclaims good news in its very first verse: "In the beginning God created the heavens and the earth" (Gen. 1:1). The creation of the world is the first of the majestic and gracious acts of the triune God. It is God's calling "into existence the things that do not exist" (Rom. 4:17). While the good news of God's free grace has its center in the liberating and reconciling work of Jesus Christ and will have its final and victorious realization when God "makes all things new" (Rev. 21:5), the sovereign goodness of God is already at work in the act of creation. The triune God who eternally dwells in loving communion also welcomes into existence a world of creatures different from God. The creation of the world, its reconciliation in Jesus Christ, and its promised renewal and consummation are all acts of the one triune God, and they all exhibit the astonishing generosity and beneficence of this God.

Christian Faith and the Ecological Crisis

In the first article of the Apostles' Creed, Christians affirm their faith in God the creator, "Maker of heaven and earth." Like all articles of the creed, this article is rich with meaning and invites inquiry. A right understanding of the confession of faith in God the creator is perhaps more important today than ever before. The reason for this is the fact that in our time every exposition of the doctrine of God as creator and of the world as God's good creation is profoundly challenged by the ecological crisis. Evidence mounts almost daily that the crisis is of daunting proportions. The earth and the network of life that it sustains are in peril. In the view of some experts, the damage to the environment is already severe and in some cases perhaps irreversible. Nuclear accidents at Three Mile Island and Chernobyl; the frequent reports of oil spills and leaking chemical dump sites; the ominous warming of the earth and increased acidity of rain; the harm done to the ozone layer; the reckless pollution of air, streams, and fields; the decimation of the great rain forests of the earth; the loss of thousands of species of life; the development and use of chemical, biological, and nuclear weapons — these are but some of the items in the now-familiar litany of the degradation of the earth and the growing threat to all its inhabitants.

The gravity and scope of the ecological crisis give unprecedented urgency to the task of rethinking the Christian doctrine of creation. Any neglect, marginalization, or distortion of this doctrine in our time would only contribute to impending disaster. Development of a strong and comprehensive theology of the first article of the Apostles' Creed must be a major part of every Christian theology today.

Critics of the Christian tradition, however, see matters very differently. They charge that Christianity is a primary source of the ecological crisis; it is a major part of the problem rather than a possible part of the solution. According to these critics, the seed of the rapacious attitudes toward the natural environment characteristic of the modern era is to be found precisely in the Christian tradition and its scriptures. An accusing finger is pointed especially at the teachings that human beings alone are created in the image of God (Gen. 1:26a) and that they are commanded by God to exercise "dominion" over all the other creatures (Gen. 1:26b). Such teachings have given Western civilization religious justification for treating the natural environment in a ruthless manner; our wanton destruction of nature is sanctioned in the name of fulfilling the divine command. Thus historian Lynn White, Jr., who wrote what is considered the classic indictment of the Christian tradition's attitude toward nature, concludes that Christianity bears a "huge burden of guilt" for our present ecological crisis.[1]

While it is now widely agreed that White's charges are based on a simplistic and one-sided reading of biblical teaching and classical Christian doctrine, the challenge to Christian theology cannot be brushed aside. It would be a mistake to react in a purely defensive way to the criticism of the Christian theological tradition as unfriendly to the natural environment. As numerous studies have shown, negative and domineering attitudes toward the body and the physical world are present in many strands of Christian theology and even in the Bible itself.[2] Feminist theologians have underscored the link be-

---

1. White, "The Historical Roots of Our Ecologic Crisis," *Science* 155 (1967): 1203-7.
2. See H. Paul Santmire, *The Travail of Nature: The Ambiguous Ecological Promise of Christian Theology* (Philadelphia: Fortress, 1985).

tween the hierarchy of male over female and that of humanity over nature.[3] Such attitudes have offered little theological resistance to the spirit of conquest that has characterized the relationship of humanity to the natural environment in Western history. Torn out of its biblical context, the divine command to humanity to have dominion over the earth has been twisted into an ideology of mastery. There is, therefore, ample reason for Christians to repent of their complicity in the abuse of the environment and for Christian theology to engage in serious self-criticism.

An important first step in this process is to identify some of the deep-seated attitudes and practices that underlie the ecological crisis, and to consider the searching questions they pose for Christian theology and the church.

1. *Anthropocentrism.* Anthropocentrism is a view of the world as existing primarily to serve the needs and desires of humankind. "Man is the measure of all things," said the ancient Greek philosopher Protagoras. This doctrine has become a kind of motto of the modern attitude toward nature with devastating ecological consequences. Has Christian theology contributed to this view? The answer is, sadly, yes, in part. Many standard discussions of the doctrine of creation gave primary, if not exclusive, attention to the creation of human beings. That there were other beings created by God was certainly acknowledged, but they were often treated more like stage props than like important participants in the drama of creation and salvation.[4] Ludwig Feuerbach put it even more bluntly: "Nature, the world, has no value, no interest for Christians. The Christian thinks only of himself and the salvation of his soul."[5] Among the ways the anthropocentric perspective is evident in the theological tradition is its widely held utilitarian view of animals. Thomas Aquinas — a theologian second to none in affirming that the goodness of God is displayed in the diversity of creatures — nevertheless declared that "the life of animals and plants is preserved not for themselves but for man." Quoting Augustine from *The City of God*, Thomas says of the animals, "By a most just ordinance of the Creator, both their life and their death are subject to our use."[6] If Christian theology today is not unthinkingly to perpetuate such expressions of anthropocentrism in the tradition, must it not retrieve and draw out the implications of the radical theocentrism that is at the core of the biblical witness?

3. See Rosemary Radford Ruether, *Sexism and God-Talk: Toward a Feminist Theology* (Boston: Beacon Press, 1983).

4. Alan Lewis, *Theatre of the Gospel* (Edinburgh: Handsel Press, 1984).

5. Ludwig Feuerbach, *The Essence of Christianity* (New York: Harper & Row, 1957), 287.

6. *Summa Theologica*, 2-2, q. 64, a. 1. See Andrew Linzey, *Animal Theology* (London: SCM Press, 1994).

2. *Power as Domination.* At the heart of the ecological crisis is the misuse of power. Modern science and technology have acquired enormous power over the forces of nature and are able to use this power for good or ill. The desire to know the world and to put that knowledge to constructive use belong to the vocation of humanity. A radical rejection of modern science and technology in the name of some idealized pre-modern condition would be foolish and unhelpful. Yet it is true that the modern scientific project has frequently succumbed to the intoxication of power. The goal of science has too often been seen as the subjection of nature to human will rather than collaborating with nature for the common welfare of humankind and other creatures. According to Francis Bacon, knowledge is power, and the task of science is to force nature to give up its secrets. In Bacon's view, nature is related to humanity as slave to master. Bacon's language of master and slave shows that the view of power as domination has been a formative factor in Western science and technology. Has Christian theology contributed to this understanding of human power in relation to the environment? Yes, in part. When God is viewed as overwhelming power and humanity is seen as the image of God summoned to exercise divinely given "dominion" over the earth, theology becomes a potent contributor to the modern conquest of nature. But is the God of Christian faith rightly understood by this view of divine power, and is humanity rightly understood as the master of nature rather than its guardian and protector?

3. *Denial of Interconnectedness.* Anthropocentrism and the conception of power as domination feed and are fed by theoretical and practical denials of the interconnectedness and interdependence of all forms of life. An ecological consciousness is a consciousness of the delicate web of life and a respect for the existence and value of other creatures. When nonhuman forms of life are thoughtlessly destroyed in the name of human progress, the failure to respect and honor other beings is clear. Respect for other, nonhuman forms of life does not require that we attribute personhood to them. Rather, the question is whether other forms of life have a value in and of themselves, not entirely dependent on human purposes. The witness of Christian theology on this question has frankly been fragmentary and ambiguous. Some critics of the Christian tradition go much further: they charge that the Christian tradition sees no intrinsic moral and religious significance in the world of nature, that its value is only the value it has for human beings. Is the denial of the connectedness of life and the reduction of the value of other forms of life to their usefulness to humanity really compatible with a responsible Christian doctrine of creation?

4. *Assumption of Limitless Resources.* The assumption that natural re-

sources — clean air, pure water, fertile fields — are unlimited, or at least always renewable, underlies much of the exploitation of the earth for human purposes. We will never, so it is supposed, run out of the resources that are necessary to all life because they are supplied in inexhaustible abundance by the earth. Even if our natural environment should run out of these necessary resources, modern science and technology will always be there to provide alternative sources. This is part of the logic that has led to our ecological crisis. We continue, for example, to produce and drive large gas-guzzling vehicles and build ever-bigger homes that require ever-greater amounts of energy to heat in winter and cool in summer. We act as though resources are infinite. In so doing we manifest a callous disdain for future generations and for the poor of the earth who have never had just access to the world's limited resources. Has the Christian doctrine of creation been presented in a way that counters the ideas that natural resources are unlimited, that they are there solely for the purpose of humanity, that they may be squandered by some while others have little or no access to them, that the present generation may live in a manner that disregards the future of its children and its children's children?

5. *Unchecked Consumerism.* The market economy is driven by the desire to consume and possess, and this is a major factor in the ecological crisis. Not giving but consuming is the operative ethic. Not "I think, therefore I am," but "I consume, therefore I am" is the logic of late modernity. For this consumer mentality, the goal is to maximize one's possession and use of the world's goods. Not only things but even persons and relationships are turned into commodities. Jacques Derrida raises the question whether it is even possible to give a gift in a world determined by the principle of commodity exchange. What is called a gift is really a contract to receive something in return.[7]

Unchecked consumption in some societies is paralleled by widespread deprivation in others. While the inhabitants of some countries recklessly consume non-renewable resources of the earth, millions of others lack even the most basic necessities. Does uncontrolled consumerism have any basis in biblical teaching or in Christian theology and ethics, or does it contrast sharply with the divine economy of creation and salvation, an economy of extravagant gift-giving that results not in scarcity but in abundance for all?[8]

Even from this brief and partial listing of attitudes underlying the ecological crisis, it should be clear that this crisis is, at bottom, not primarily a

---

7. See Jacques Derrida, *Given Time: 1. Counterfeit Money* (Chicago: University of Chicago Press, 1992).

8. See M. Douglas Meeks, *God the Economist: The Doctrine of God and Political Economy* (Minneapolis: Fortress Press, 1989).

technical but a theological and spiritual crisis. Recovery of faith in God the creator and respect for the whole of God's creation is a matter of great urgency. In its early centuries, the church had to struggle against Manicheanism, a religion that denied the goodness and integrity of the material world. In particular, Manicheanism considered the human body contemptible and valued only the realm of pure spirit. Today, it is not only embodied human life but the earth itself and all the creatures that dwell on it that are at risk. The integrity of God's good creation is under assault, and the church must help to meet this challenge theologically and spiritually as well as in concrete practice.

Rereading the Scriptural Witness on Creation

A doctrine of creation sensitive to the ecological crisis will have to engage in a rethinking of the tradition rather than merely repeating it. This will require, in the first place, a rereading of Scripture. As already indicated, the witness of Scripture has sometimes been read in ways that have offered support rather than resistance to the destruction of the environment. In contrast to such readings, we can point to elements of the biblical witness that are strongly supportive of an ecological doctrine of creation.

Scripture presents nonhuman creatures as the inseparable companions of humanity in creation, reconciliation, and redemption. According to the first creation narrative in Genesis, God declares each group of creatures "good" and all of them together "very good" (Gen. 1:12, 18, 21, 25, 31). That God values and takes delight in all creatures is highlighted in the biblical assertion that not just humans but all creatures are able in some way to give glory to God their creator. "The heavens are telling the glory of God, and the firmament proclaims his handiwork" (Ps. 19:1). While the stars, the trees, and the animals do not speak or sing of the glory of God in the same way that humans do, in their own way they too lift up their praises to God, and for all we know, they do this with a spontaneity and consistency far greater than our own. The book of Job describes strange and wondrous creatures (Job 39–41) that seem to have no purpose other than to show the fecundity of God's grace. If God takes delight in all the creatures, and if they are all called in their own distinctive way to praise and glorify God, nonhuman creatures cannot be mere ancillary figures in a Christian doctrine of creation.

The earth belongs not to humans but to God (Ps. 24:1). Jesus delights in the lilies of the field (Matt. 6:28-29) and declares that God provides for the birds of the air (Matt. 6: 26). When the creation narrative states that human beings are created in the image of God and are given the command to have "dominion" over the earth, this must be understood in the context of the distinctive identification of God — not only in this passage but throughout the Bible — as the God not of arbitrary power but of free grace and covenantal love. Human beings are given the responsibility of caring for the whole of creation as God cares for it. It is a "dominion" of care and protection rather than of domination and abuse. As God's covenant with humanity makes clear, there are laws governing the cultivation of the earth and the use of the animals. Provision is made for the animals and the earth to have regular rest and to enjoy a Jubilee year in which all slaves are to be freed and the land is to be left fallow (Lev. 25:8-12).

While it is undeniable that there are passages of the Bible where God is described as exercising fierce suzerainty over the nations and nature, calling for acts of vengeance and even slaughter of the innocents in the conquest of Canaan by Israel (e.g., 1 Sam. 15:3), Christian faith does not find in such passages the central clue to the power and purpose of God. Certainly the reign of God proclaimed by Jesus and enacted in his life and death turns upside down every view of sovereignty as mastery over others: "You know that among the Gentiles those whom they recognize as their rulers lord it over them, and their great ones are tyrants over them. But it is not so among you; but whoever wishes to become great among you must be your servant, and whoever wishes to be first among you must be slave of all" (Mark 10:42-44). Seen in the light of what Christians hold to be the central biblical message, the command of God to humanity to have dominion calls for respect, love, and care for the good creation. It is a summons to wise guardianship rather than selfish indulgence, to leadership within the commonwealth of creatures rather than a license for exploitation. We might paraphrase the divine command to humanity as follows: "Let your faithful ordering of the world image the way in which the gracious God exercises dominion." According to the witness of Scripture at its deepest level, therefore, there is no absolute right of humanity over nature; on the contrary, human beings are entrusted with its care and protection.[9]

The Bible not only presents the nonhuman world as part of God's good creation; it also views the whole creation as mysteriously entangled in the drama of sin and redemption and included in the hope of God's coming kingdom. Humanity and the other creatures are bound together in suffering and hope. If all creatures experience the consequences of the divine judgment on human sin (Gen. 3), all are recipients of the divine promise (Gen. 9). Un-

---

9. "A Brief Statement of Faith" speaks of Earth as "entrusted to our care" by God the creator. (*The Book of Confessions*, PCUSA, 10.3, line 38).

der the present conditions of life, humanity and nature are caught in a web of mutual alienation and abuse. The separation of human beings from God insinuates itself into all other relationships, including that between humanity and nature. On the one side, there is brutal human exploitation and destruction of the natural environment; on the other side, there is tragic human suffering at the hands of destructive forces of nature, as such phenomena as cancers, earthquakes, hurricanes, and drought remind us. So the apostle Paul speaks of the natural world as groaning like a woman in childbirth, even as humanity also groans for its final liberation from suffering and death (Rom. 8:22-23). According to the biblical witness, we human beings exist in a solidarity of life and death with the whole groaning and expectant creation.

This inseparability of humanity and nature in the biblical view extends to their final destiny. The Bible includes the natural world in the promise and hope of redemption. Evidence of this is the divine covenant with Noah, symbolized in the rainbow after the flood, which explicitly includes all creatures. "God said, 'This is the sign of the covenant that I make between me and you and every living creature that is with you, for all future generations; I have set my bow in the clouds, and it shall be a sign of the covenant between me and the earth'" (Gen. 9:12-13). There are numerous visions of future redemption in the Bible, and they are staggeringly inclusive. They speak of a transformed, resurrected body (1 Cor. 15), of a new heaven and a new earth (Rev. 21), of the wolf dwelling in peace with the lamb and children playing with scorpions (Isa. 11), of a time of universal shalom when all creatures will live together in harmonious and joyful community.

If with the biblical witnesses we see ourselves as fellow creatures in company with all the inhabitants of the world of nature, if we understand ourselves as trustees rather than as masters of the earth, if we see nature as entangled with us in the drama of sin and redemption, and if we include nature in our hope for justice, freedom, and peace throughout God's creation, we will no longer want to rationalize our abuse of nature by alleging a God-given right to rule over the rest of creation as we please.

Reading Scripture with an eye to its sensitivity to the ecology of creation is an important task for which biblical scholarship has major responsibility. But this is only one of the requirements of a doctrine of creation for our time. It is the task of systematic theology to rethink all the major themes of the doctrine of creation.

Rethinking the Themes of the Doctrine of Creation

A Christian doctrine of creation, developed in the light of the revelation of God attested in Scripture, centered in Jesus Christ, and attentive to the ecological crisis of our time, will contain the following closely related themes.

1. To speak of the world as God's creation is first of all to make an affirmation about God. By calling God the "creator" and everything that constitutes the world "creatures," Christian faith affirms the *radical otherness, transcendence, and lordship of God.* There is, in other words, an ontological difference between God and the world, creator and creation. According to classical Christian doctrine, God creates *ex nihilo,* "out of nothing." "Nothing" is not a primordial stuff out of which the world was created. Creation "out of nothing" means that God alone is the source of all that exists. The creation of the world is an act of sovereign freedom. God is not like the craftsman of Plato's *Timaeus,* who imposes form and order on pre-existing matter. Nor is creation an emanation of the divine reality and thus partially divine. For Christian faith God is not a part of the world, and the world is not partly or secretly God. God is creator of all things — "the heavens and the earth" — and that means, as Langdon Gilkey puts it, "the nebulae, the amoebae, the dinosaurs, the early Picts and Scots, the Chinese, the Kremlin, You, I, our two dogs, and the cat."[10] God is the mysterious other on which all that exists radically and totally depends.

But to confess that God is creator is to say more. It is to say that *the free, transcendent God is generous and welcoming.* God was not compelled to create the world; creation is an act of free grace. Creation is a gift, a benefit. When we confess God as the creator, we are saying something about the character of God. We are confessing that God is good, that God gives life to others, that God lets others exist alongside and in fellowship with God, that God makes room for others. No outside necessity compelled God to create. Nor did God create because of some inner deficiency in the divine life that had to be satisfied. If creation is a necessity in either of these meanings, it is not grace.

While it is improper to speak of creation as "necessary," God nevertheless creates in total consistency with God's nature. The act of creation is a "fitting" act of God. It fittingly expresses the true character of God, who is love. Creation is not an arbitrary act, something God just decided to do on a whim, as it were. On the contrary, God is true and faithful to God's own nature in the act of creation. To speak of God as the creator is to speak of a beneficent, gen-

---

10. Gilkey, *Message and Existence: An Introduction to Theology* (New York: Seabury Press, 1979), 87.

erous God, whose outpouring love and purpose to share life-in-communion are freely, consistently, and fittingly displayed in the act of creation. The grace of God did not first become active in the calling of Abraham or in the sending of Jesus. In the act of creation, God already manifests the self-communicating, other-affirming, communion-forming love that defines God's eternal triune reality and that is decisively disclosed in the ministry and sacrificial death of Jesus Christ. God is love, and this eternal love of the triune God constitutes, in Jonathan Edwards's words, a "disposition to abundant communication."[11] Already in God's own trinitarian life of shared love, God aims at the coming into being of created community.[12] God is eternally disposed to create, to give and share life with others. The welcome to others that is rooted in the triune life of God spills over, so to speak, in the act of creation.

God's work of creation is aptly described not only as grace but also, in a sense, as "costly grace." It is an act of divine *kenosis*. Although the metaphor of divine kenosis is usually restricted to the "emptying" or self-humbling of the Son of God for our salvation (Phil. 2:5-6), there is a sense in which the act of creation is already a kind of divine kenosis — a self-humiliation or self-limitation — that others may have life, may have a relatively independent existence alongside God. As Emil Brunner writes, "The kenosis, which reaches its [highest] expression in the cross of Christ, began with the creation of the world."[13]

2. The doctrine of creation is at once an affirmation about God and an affirmation about the world and ourselves. So a second theme of this doctrine is that *the world as a whole and all beings individually are radically dependent on God*. Such radical dependence is far more than a sense of partial dependence on God in some regions of our experience or at some especially difficult moments of our life. In confessing that God is creator and that we are creatures, we acknowledge that we are finite, contingent, radically dependent beings. We express our awareness that we might not have been, that our very existence and every moment of our experience is a gift received from a source beyond ourselves.

The realization of this radical contingency, of our awareness of being primarily recipients of life, is what some philosophers and theologians have called the "shock of nonbeing." You and I are not necessary. We are creatures

11. Jonathan Edwards, *The End for Which God Created the World,* chap. 1, sec. 3.

12. Eberhard Jüngel, *God as the Mystery of the World* (Grand Rapids: Eerdmans, 1983), 384.

13. Brunner, *The Christian Doctrine of Creation and Redemption* (Philadelphia: Westminster, 1952), 20. See also John Polkinghorne, *Science and Creation: The Search for Understanding* (Boston: New Science Library, 1988), 62-63.

who exist at the pleasure of our creator. As contingent beings, our existence is precarious. We are frequently reminded of our frailty by sickness and failure, by the loss of loved ones and our awareness that we too must die, and even by the positive experiences of joy, happiness, and contentment — all of which come and go so quickly. Experiencing a moment of intense beauty that we would like to possess forever, feeling impotent in the face of injustice, witnessing the birth of a child, or being present at the funeral of a child — all this and so much more is taken up into our confession of our creatureliness. Our hold on life is fragile. We are finite. The resources of our community and nation are finite. The resources of the world are finite. Like the grass that withers and dies (Isa. 40:6), all creatures and the earth itself live on the edge of nonbeing. We did not bring ourselves into existence, and we cannot guarantee our continued existence. Friedrich Schleiermacher described the universal feeling of "absolute dependence" on God, and Rudolf Otto spoke of our "creature feeling." This is not simply a feeling about an event in the distant past called the creation of the world. It is a sense of being dependent here and now, always and everywhere, on the creative power of God. "Know that the Lord is God! It is God that has made us and not we ourselves" (Ps. 100:3).

This sense of being radically dependent on God for our very existence is closely related to the Christian awareness of salvation in Christ by grace alone. We are created and justified by grace alone. As creatures and as forgiven sinners, we are recipients of grace. In neither case is it a status that we have achieved through our own doing. Luther summarizes this faith awareness in his remark that "we are all beggars"; Calvin expresses the same conviction in the words "we are not our own . . . we belong to God."[14] It is, then, no coincidence that the apostle Paul brings together faith in God who raises the dead (our dependence on God for future life), who justifies sinners (our dependence on God for present life), and who brings into existence things which were not (our dependence on God for the creation and preservation of life) (cf. Rom. 4:17; 5:1). We are utterly dependent on God for the gift of life, for new life, and for the final fulfillment of life. This is what we confess when we call God our creator.

Radical dependence on God as a theme of the doctrine of creation must be properly interpreted, especially today when it is charged that Christian theology has often inculcated a spirit of passivity and servile dependence. The God on whom we are radically dependent is the God who wills us to be free and calls us to responsibility. Reliance on the God of the gospel is radical liberation from all servile dependencies. Thus, far from being a theological put-

14. Calvin, *Institutes of the Christian Religion,* 3.7.1.

down, the doctrine of creation is the basis of human dignity and freedom. But the freedom that God wills is a freedom for life in communion with and loving service of others. God our creator, the triune God, is the graciously liberating God who wills community in freedom.

3. A third theme of the doctrine of creation is that *in all its contingency, finitude, and limitation, creation is good* (if imperfect). If God is good, then for all its limitations, transience, and fragility, the gift of life God gives is good. This is emphasized in the Genesis creation narrative where the refrain is repeated: "And God saw that it was good" (Gen. 1:10, 18, 21, 25, 31).

The biblical affirmation that creation is good is easily turned into an ideology that obscures the brokenness of life and the reality of evil. This happens when this article of faith is separated from other faith affirmations about the actual fallenness of the world God has created — about sin, the work of reconciliation, and the hope in God's final victory over all those forces in the world that deform and distort God's good creation. When spoken casually and carelessly, the claim that God's creation is good can become an outrageous and even blasphemous assertion that every present state of affairs is good or that everything that happens is good. Hence what Christian theology does and does not say in affirming the goodness of creation must be briefly noted.

a. To say that creation is good is to reject every metaphysical dualism, to deny that some aspect or sphere of what God has created is inherently evil. Dualism in some form or other has insinuated itself into the theology and life of the church from its beginnings to the present. Consider some of the forms it has taken and continues to take: the spiritual is good, the physical is evil; the intellectual is good, the sexual is evil; the masculine is good, the feminine is evil; white is good, black is evil; human beings are good, the natural environment is evil. Over against all such dualisms, Christian faith declares that all that God has created is good. To regard any part of the creation as inherently evil — the Manichean heresy — is both slanderous and destructive.

b. Saying that creation is good is very different from saying that the world around us is useful to satisfy whatever purposes we have in mind. It is to say that God values all creatures whether or not we consider them useful. The affirmation that creation is good is the ground of respect and admiration for all beings. Not only humans but the animals — including the strange and frightening animals (cf. Job 39–41) — are God's creatures and deserve our respect. The inanimate as well as the animate world is God's creation and has its place within God's purposes and as such is to be honored. Human beings have no God-given right to exploit or deface or destroy the creation. The arrogant assumption of so much of our modern technocratic way of life — namely, that

103

What does that look like?

God loves only human beings (and usually only a fraction of them) — is an anthropocentric distortion of the Christian doctrine of creation.

c. To say that the world as created by God is good is not to say that it is "perfect" in some pollyannaish sense. The Bible is not especially interested in a past golden age when there was no need to struggle, no experience of suffering, and no death whatever. If all creatures are finite, limited, and vulnerable, and if challenge, risk, and growth are part of creaturely existence as intended by God, then there is no reason to suppose that *all forms* of suffering are inherently evil. There is, as Karl Barth puts it, a "shadow side" of the good creation.

d. To say that creation is good is not to deny that the world, as we know and experience it, is "fallen" and in need of redemption. There is much in the world that should *not* be. While creaturely existence entails finitude and limitations, the powers of disease, destruction, and oppression are not part of the creator's intention. God is not the cause but the opponent of evil forces in their individual and corporate expressions. I will say more about the mystery of evil in God's good creation in subsequent chapters; in this context, it is sufficient to note that when faith speaks of the goodness of creation, it refers not simply to the value of the reality brought into being at the beginning but also to the additional value this reality is given by virtue of God's continuing and costly love for it. The value of the life of creatures is determined not simply by the dignity the creator originally gave them but also by what divine love can do with them and intends for them. Thus Christian affirmation of the "good creation" encompasses the entire history of God's relation to the world from its beginning to its final consummation.

4. A fourth theme of the doctrine of creation is *the coexistence and interdependence of all created beings.* Luther is surely right in saying that one meaning of speaking of God as creator of heaven and earth is that "God has created me." And yet clearly God has created more than me, so Luther correctly goes on to say, "God has created me and all that exists."[15] In other words, creaturehood means radical coexistence, mutual interdependence, rather than solitary or monarchic existence. The creation of human beings with each other and with other creatures is an unmistakable theme of the Genesis creation stories. For all their differences, both narratives of creation in Genesis portray human beings as standing in organic relation to each other and to the world of nature.[16] God sets humanity in a garden and declares that "it is not good that the *adam* (human creature) should be alone" (Gen. 2:18).

15. Luther, "The Small Catechism," 2.2, in *The Book of Concord,* ed. Theodore G. Tappert (Philadelphia: Fortress, 1959), 345.

16. See George S. Hendry, "On Being a Creature," *Theology Today* 33 (April 1981): 64.

Karl Barth speaks of coexistence as the "basic form" of humanity, by which he means that we are human only in relation to God and to each other. Barth also contends that our essential relationality, or existence-in-coexistence, extends beyond the circle of human life. Human beings exist with the animals, with the soil, sun, and water and all the forms of life that they produce.[17] God is creator of a world whose inhabitants are profoundly interdependent. The world was created by God not as an assemblage of solitary units but for life together, and its structure of existence-in-community reflects God's own eternal life in triune communion. Relationality is a mark of the universe created by God. This is an extremely important theme, emphasized again in the next section of this chapter and developed further in Chapter Seven, on the doctrine of humanity in the image of God.

5. A fifth theme of the doctrine of creation is that *God the creator is purposive, and the world that God has created is dynamic and purposeful.* God continues to act as creator and preserver. To limit the work of God the creator to a single moment of the past would be, as Calvin said, "cold and barren."[18] The creative activity of God continues and has a goal. To be sure, this purposive activity of the creator and the purposefulness of the world cannot be directly "read off" what we perceive and experience. It is an affirmation of faith, not an empirical observation. There are clearly elements both of order and disorder, rationality and indeterminacy, cosmos and chaos in the world known to modern science. While the world described by scientific investigation is open to a faith interpretation, the evidence does not require that it be interpreted in this way. Some scientists conclude that the universe, destined to eventual hot or cold death, is meaningless.[19]

Yet if we take as our central clue God's way with the people of Israel and the decisive confirmation of that way in Jesus Christ, we are led to confess that creation has a purpose. God creates not by accident, nor by caprice, but by and for the Word of God. According to Scripture, Jesus Christ is the Word who was with God in the beginning and through whom all things were created (John 1:1-3; Heb. 11:3). He is the goal toward which the whole creation moves, and it is this divine goal that makes of the world a cosmos rather than chaos. In Christ "all things hold together" (Col. 1:17). The purpose for which God created the world is decisively disclosed in the life, death, and resurrection of Jesus Christ. With God the Father and the Holy Spirit, the Word of God is present and active in the creation, redemption, and consummation of the world.

17. See Barth, *Church Dogmatics*, 3/1: 168-228.
18. Calvin, *Institutes*, 1.16.1.
19. See Stephen Weinberg, *The First Three Minutes* (New York: Basic Books, 1977), 144.

In a trinitarian theology, creation is open, not closed. The Spirit of God, like the eternal Word, is at work in the world from its beginning, moving over the primeval waters (Gen. 1:2), giving life and breath to creatures (Ps. 104:30). The creative and re-creative Spirit of God continues to act everywhere, extending justice, building and restoring community, renewing all things. The Spirit acts freely, like the wind (John 3:8). Believers, however, recognize the Spirit mainly as the transforming power who comes from the Father and the Son and who liberates people for participation in the divine re-creative activity. Led by the Spirit, we are called to be God's partners — God's co-workers (cf. 1 Cor. 3:9) — in conducting creation to its appointed goal: the reign of God.

The promised goal of redeemed creation is described in the New Testament as a time of freedom, peace, and festivity. This messianic time of peace and festivity is prefigured in the sabbath rest that completes God's creative activity. Just as the first story of creation in Genesis moves toward its goal in the sabbath rest and enjoyment of the creator, so the history of the new creation finds its goal in the celebration and festivity of perfectly realized and fully enjoyed fellowship with God and other creatures in the new heaven and new earth. According to Jürgen Moltmann, "Israel has given the nations two archetypal images of liberation: the exodus and the sabbath."[20] The goal of the liberation of creation is both "external" freedom from bondage and "internal" freedom for the peace and joy of life in communion with God and other creatures.

When the creation of the world by God is set in the context of the whole activity of the triune God, we are able to describe creation not as something past and finished but as still open to the future. And the future for which creation is open is not only the coming of Christ to renew the creation but the participation of the creation in the end-time glory of God. Moltmann makes this point with a helpful revision of a medieval theological axiom. According to the scholastic theologians, "Grace does not destroy, but presupposes and perfects nature"; Moltmann's emendation reads: "Grace neither destroys nor perfects, but prepares nature for eternal glory."[21]

---

20. Moltmann, *God in Creation: A New Theology of Creation and the Spirit of God* (San Francisco: Harper & Row, 1985), 287.

21. Moltmann, *God in Creation*, 8.

Trinity, Creation, and Ecology

The recent literature on Christian theology and ecology is extensive and growing rapidly.[22] Several approaches to the topic stand out.[23] First, there is an apologetic approach that is concerned primarily to defend the Christian theological tradition against the charge that it is largely responsible for the attitudes toward nature that have brought about the ecological crisis. This approach has helped to counter some of the ill-founded charges against Christian theology, but it fails to stress the need for renewal and reformation of the tradition. Second, there is the approach of the process school of theology, which argues that a thorough conceptual reconstruction of the tradition is necessary if Christian faith and theology are to address the ecological crisis today in a credible and effective manner. Drawing upon the works of process thinkers like Teilhard de Chardin and Alfred North Whitehead, process theology has been a pioneer in reconceptualizing Christian theology in ways that, among other things, address ecological concerns. Some feminist theologians, combining feminist and ecological emphases within a process theological perspective, speak of their program as ecofeminism.[24] Third, there is a reformist, trinitarian approach. Unlike the approach of the apologists, it acknowledges the presence of anthropocentric strands in Scripture and the theological tradition and the need for theological reinterpretation and reformation, not mere defense of the tradition. Unlike the approach of process theology, however, the trinitarian approach finds the primary basis for theological revision and renewal in the central witness of Scripture and in a trinitarian "ontology of communion" rooted in Scripture. The reflections that follow relate most closely to the trinitarian approach in thinking about the relevance of Christian faith to ecological concerns.

During the past few decades many of the churches, including Roman Catholic, Eastern Orthodox, and Protestant denominations, have issued

22. For helpful introductions see Moltmann, *God in Creation;* James A. Nash, *Loving Nature: Ecological Integrity and Christian Responsibility* (Nashville: Abingdon, 1991); *Christianity and Ecology: Seeking the Well-Being of Earth and Humans,* ed. Dieter T. Hessel and Rosemary Radford Ruether (Cambridge: Harvard University Press, 2000); *All Creation Is Groaning: An Interdisciplinary Vision for Life in a Sacred Universe,* ed. Carol J. Dempsey and Russell A. Butkus (Collegeville, Minn.: Liturgical Press, 1999); and Larry Rasmussen, *Earth Community, Earth Ethics* (Maryknoll, N.Y.: Orbis Books, 1996).

23. My analysis is indebted to H. Paul Santmire, "In God's Ecology: A Revisionist Theology of Nature," *Christian Century,* Dec. 13, 2000, 1300-1305.

24. John B. Cobb, Jr., *Is It Too Late? A Theology of Ecology,* rev. ed. (Denton, Tex.: Environmental Ethics Books, 1995); Rosemary Radford Ruether, *Gaia and God: An Ecofeminist Theology of Earth Healing* (San Francisco: HarperSanFrancisco, 1992).

statements on the gravity of the ecological crisis and the need for a strong Christian theological witness in relation to it. A number of these statements — including the documents of the Canberra Assembly of the World Council of Churches (1990), which linked concerns of justice and peace with the "integrity of creation" under the theme, "Come, Holy Spirit, Renew the Whole Creation" — have been explicitly trinitarian. There is good reason for this emphasis. Joseph Sittler, one of the pioneers in the renewal of ecological concern in twentieth-century theology, argued that the doctrine of the Trinity has been neglected in much Western theology, with a resultant narrowing of the understanding of the salvific work of God. According to Sittler, when grace is limited to the forgiveness of sins, the grace of God that is already present in the gift of life is neglected. Sittler called for a recovery of the "Trinitarian amplitude" of the church's understanding of the grace of God and insisted on viewing the whole of the creation as the "field of grace."[25]

A trinitarian doctrine of creation is a vital resource for an ecologically responsible doctrine of creation for several reasons. The first reason is that *trinitarian theology holds together the affirmations of the transcendence of God over the creation and the immanence of God in the creation.* A Christian doctrine of creation must make both of these affirmations; it must affirm that the creation is the work of the transcendent, free God, and it must affirm that God the creator is not essentially alien to the creation or the creation to the creator. If either of these affirmations is neglected or lost, the result is either a monism in which God and the world are united without distinction, or a dualism in which God and the world are seen as essentially oppositional and alien to each other. A trinitarian doctrine of creation does not set God and the world in a "contrastive" relationship; the relationship of God and the world is not seen as essentially competitive.[26] Trinitarian doctrine holds together the transcendence and immanence of God in the act of creation by affirming that "God is the creator through the Son in the Spirit." This "trinitarian amplitude" of the gracious activity of God is a necessary presupposition of a strong ecological theology. The grace of the one triune God is present not only in history but also in nature, not only in the gift of forgiveness but also in the gift of creation and the gift of consummation.

A number of theologians have made this point by calling for a "cosmic Christology." Jürgen Moltmann approaches the matter from the doctrine of the Spirit. Creation is not only "creation by the Word," it is also "creation in the

25. Joseph Sittler, *Essays on Nature and Grace* (Philadelphia: Fortress, 1972), 2, 82.
26. See Kathryn Tanner, *Jesus, Humanity and the Trinity: A Brief Systematic Theology* (Minneapolis: Fortress, 2001), 2-5.

Spirit."[27] Moltmann thinks he has the support of Calvin for this emphasis. According to Calvin, "It is the Spirit who, everywhere diffused, sustains all things, causes them to grow, and quickens them in heaven and in earth."[28] Moltmann contends that a trinitarian understanding of "creation in the Spirit" is precisely what is needed for an ecological theology that takes in the cosmic breadth of God's activity and purposes. The Spirit is not to be reduced to the human spirit, nor is the work of the Spirit to be banished in favor of a mechanistic view of the world. The Spirit is the Spirit of the living, triune God. God not only transcends the creation, is not only incarnate in Jesus Christ, but is also present and at work throughout the creation. When Irenaeus spoke of the Word and Spirit of God as the "two hands of God," he expressed in symbolic form the trinitarian understanding of God that holds together what has often fallen apart in the history of the Christian doctrine of creation.

A second way in which a trinitarian understanding of God provides a resource for an ecological doctrine of creation is *the possibility it offers of viewing the coherence and rich diversity of the created order as rooted in and consistent with the life of the triune God.* Creation is cosmos and not utter chaos. As modern cosmology teaches, even the elements of chaos in our universe contribute to its unity and coherence. At the same time, the world contains extraordinary diversity. How to hold together the unity and manifoldness of reality has been a perennial problem of philosophy and theology. The relationship of unity and difference is not only a theoretical but a very practical issue that we cannot escape when we ask about the meaning of community, the goal of politics, or the rationale for ecological ethics. As Paul Santmire contends, the question is, where is the unity of the world to be found? The anthropocentric answer finds this unity in humanity; everything supposedly holds together in the human project. This view has not proven to be an ecologically friendly perspective. The theistic answer is to seek the unity of creation in a transcendent reality. But if this transcendent reality is construed as simply a necessary construct of human imagination, once again, though now indirectly and in idealist terms, the unity of all things is found in humanity. A trinitarian theology of creation finds the source of unity and difference and their harmony in the triune creator. As triune, God abides in loving communion that affirms difference and makes room for the other. The harmony of unity and difference in the triune creator is reflected in the creation of a cosmos richly differentiated. It is the triune God, creator, redeemer,

27. Moltmann, *God in Creation*, 9ff., and *The Way of Christ* (San Francisco: Harper-Collins, 1990), 274-305.

28. Calvin, *Institutes*, 1.13.14.

and consummator, present in the world by Word and Spirit, who provides the basis and the vision of an "ecological world-community."[29]

A third way in which trinitarian doctrine provides an essential resource for an ecological doctrine of creation is that it *underscores the goodness of creation, its groaning, and its longing to be renewed and perfected.* An adequate doctrine of creation must include all of these affirmations. Creation is a gift. Yet creation is wounded, and it remains incomplete. The doctrine of creation is not simply about the beginning of the universe. Creation has a history. It has its beginning in the love of God, continues by the grace of God, and will be brought to completion by the life-giving Spirit of God. The only adequate horizon for understanding creation as a dynamic, unfinished reality is the history of the triune God's relationship with it, a history that bears the sign of the cross as well as the promise of the resurrection. All of creation, and not humanity only, stands within this trinitarian history of God with the world. All of nature, and not humanity only, has its own integrity and value in the purposes of God. As Paul Santmire writes, "God has a universal, evolutionary history with all things." This history is "actualized by the agency of God's creative word and within the energizing matrix of God's life-giving Spirit." Santmire rightly emphasizes that humanity has its own special calling within the triune God's relationship with the world, and this should not be neglected. But all of God's creatures "have their divinely allotted and protected places and vocations," even if we are unable to say what these may be.[30]

Models of Creation

The primary candidates for understanding the relationship between God and the world are usually given the names theism, pantheism, and panentheism. Theism is the belief that God is the transcendent creator of the world, pantheism is the belief that the world is a mode of God's being, and panentheism is the belief that the world and God are mutually dependent. Since none of these positions as stated is entirely adequate to a trinitarian doctrine of God and creation, we need a different inventory of models and metaphors for understanding this relationship. While the creation of the world is a unique act, there is no reason why we should not expect *analogies* to this event in our own experience. We must remember, of course, that all analogies, metaphors, and models are imperfect when they are employed with reference to the di-

29. Moltmann, *God in Creation*, 12.
30. Santmire, "In God's Ecology," 1303-1305.

vine life and activity. They never exhaust what we are seeking to understand. As Sallie McFague reminds us, our language about God is inescapably metaphorical, and a metaphor says both that "it is, and it is not."[31]

George Hendry identifies several models or analogies used in Christian theology to speak of the divine act of creation. Each would claim some biblical support, and each has roots in common human experience.[32]

1. One obvious analogy is *generation*. We speak of procreation with reference to the human act of giving life to another. There are some hints of this analogy in the Bible. God is described as being like a "father" or "mother" to Israel. Yet while the procreation metaphor is present in the Bible, it is remarkably subdued by comparison with other religions of the ancient Near East. When the prophets of Israel, and later Jesus, speak of God as "father" or "mother," the metaphor points to God's creative love and parental care, not to an act of sexual procreation.

2. Another analogy of creation is *fabrication* or *formation*. The idea of fabrication is evident in the depiction of God as a builder (Ps. 127:1), and the idea of formation is evident in the depiction of God as a potter who forms clay into vessels (Jer. 18; Rom. 9:21) and when God is said to have formed human beings from the dust of the ground (Gen. 2:7). These analogies of fabrication and formation underscore the intentionality and purposefulness of God the creator, but they have two distinct disadvantages: they both presuppose a given material that is worked upon (thus obscuring the radicalness of God's creation of the world "out of nothing"), and they both assign a subpersonal status to what God brings into being.

3. A third analogy is that of *emanation*, which means literally a "flowing out," in the sense of water flowing from a spring, or light and heat radiating from the sun or a fire. According to this analogy, creation is an overflowing of God's fullness; it has its origin in the richness and abundance of deity. Earlier in this chapter I made some use of this imagery. However, the metaphor of emanation can suggest an impersonal and even involuntary process. Hendry points out that while the analogy of emanation is employed in classical theology with reference to the intratrinitarian relations — "light from light" in the Nicene Creed, for example — it did not gain wide acceptance as an analogy for God's creation of the world.

4. An analogy widely discussed today but not mentioned by Hendry is the *mind/body* relationship. In an effort to provide an alternative to oppres-

---

31. McFague, *Metaphorical Theology* (Philadelphia: Fortress, 1982), 13.

32. See George S. Hendry, *Theology of Nature* (Philadelphia: Westminster, 1980), 147-62; Ian Barbour, *Religion in an Age of Science*, vol. 1 (San Francisco: Harper & Row, 1990), 176ff.

sive hierarchical models, some theologians have proposed that the world be understood as the body of God. They argue that this analogy best expresses the intimacy and reciprocity of the relationship between God and the world.[33] The problem with this analogy, of course, is that it is incapable of articulating the gracious, nonnecessary, asymmetrical relationship of God to the world described in the Bible.

5. Finally, there is the analogy of what Hendry calls *artistic expression,* or what might also be called *play.* We often speak of the creation as a "work" of God. That way of speaking has its place, but it may connote something routine and mostly unpleasant, which is unfortunately the way work is often experienced in human life. It may be more helpful, therefore, to think of the creation of the world as the "play" of God, as a kind of free artistic expression whose origin must be sought ultimately in God's good pleasure.

According to the Bible, the creation is brought into being by the Word and Spirit of God. God speaks, and the world is given existence (Gen. 1). The Spirit of God moves over the primordial chaos (Gen. 1:2) and gives life to all creatures (Ps. 104:30). This divine creative activity occurs freely and spontaneously and thus displays features of play and artistic expression.

What are some of these features? First, true play is always free and uncoerced activity. All artistic expression — whether in music, drama, dance, painting, or sculpture — is creative, free, expressive, playful. While such playful activity has its own rules, they are not experienced as arbitrary but as defining a particular field of freedom. Second, there is free self-limitation in all artistic activity. Artists must respect the integrity of the medium with which they work, and for this reason some voluntary self-limitation is required. Third, when artists express themselves, they bring forth something really different from themselves, yet with their own image stamped upon it. And these artistic creations often acquire a life of their own. A classic piece of music or a classic literary text "speaks for itself." The characters of a novel or a drama acquire a personality and profile of their own and cannot be made to say or do just anything without the appearance of authorial violence or artificiality. Artistic creations are born in freedom, and they acquire a certain independence from their creators. Finally, while the artist needs certain materials, the result of artistic activity is of a different order from the materials used. A Mozart concerto or a Rembrandt painting is not simply a reassemblage of given materials but a "new creation."

The model of creation as artistic expression seems particularly appro-

---

33. See Sallie McFague, *The Body of God: An Ecological Theology* (Minneapolis: Fortress, 1993), 131-57.

not

priate for a trinitarian theology. The idea of God as an uninvolved and distant creator (a typical characterization in the Western philosophical tradition) is totally inadequate from a biblical perspective. On the other hand, the newly revived panentheistic description of the world as God's body, while emphasizing the intimacy of the relationship between God and the world, fails to depict appropriately either the freedom of God in relation to the world or the real otherness and freedom of the world. The model of artistic expression is attractive because it combines the elements of creative freedom and intimacy of relation between artist and artistic creation. Just as the love of God is freely expressed and shared in intratrinitarian communion, so in the act of creation God brings forth in love a world of free creatures that bear the mark of divine creativity.

Our failure to explore the metaphor of artistic activity or play in the doctrine of creation may be due in part to an unfortunate cleavage between theology and the arts in the modern period. And in part, as Moltmann suggests, it may be due to theology's regrettable disregard of the significance of the sabbath day of rest in the first creation narrative in Genesis. God's creativity comes to its conclusion in this story in the rest, celebration, and festivity of the sabbath, not in the making of humanity. As the completion and crown of creation, the sabbath is a reminder of the playful dimension of the divine creativity and a foretaste of the joy, freedom, and peace for which the world was created.[34]

Check it out?

The Doctrine of Creation and Modern Science

The preceding exposition should have made it clear that the Christian doctrine of creation is not a quasiscientific theory about how the world came into being. It is a deeply religious affirmation, shaped by the experience of the grace of God in Jesus Christ. It gives expression to our faith awareness that we are contingent, finite beings whose very existence is a gift from God. The stories of Genesis 1 and 2 are not scientific descriptions competing with modern cosmological theories but rather poetic, doxological declarations of faith in God, who has created and reconciled the world and each one of us.

The relation between faith in God the creator and modern science is an expanding field of inquiry.[35] Ian Barbour has provided the standard typology

---

34. Moltmann, *God in Creation*, 5-7, 276-96, 310-12.

35. The literature is extensive and growing rapidly. See A. R. Peacocke, *Creation and the World of Science* (Oxford: Clarendon Press, 1979); John Polkinghorne, *Science and Creation*;

of relating religion and science: conflict (one perspective simply rejects the claims of the other); independence (each field keeps to itself); dialogue (there is recognition that conversation is possible); and integration (attempts at some degree of harmonization or synthesis).[36] While the issues in the interaction between Christian theology and modern science are complex, several principles should be recognized.

First, we should note that *science and theology employ two very distinct languages,* are two different "language games" (Wittgenstein). On the one hand, there is the language of data, empirical evidence, causal connections, and probable theories; on the other hand, there is the language that describes the world as God's creation and employs rich symbols, images, and poetic cadences. To try to equate the scientific description of the origin of the world with the symbolic and metaphorical affirmations of the biblical narratives of creation is, as Karl Barth once put it, like trying to compare the sound of a vacuum cleaner with that of an organ. The language of science and the language of faith must be recognized in their distinctiveness; one should not be collapsed into the other. And the claim that only one of these languages is the voice of truth and alone provides access to reality is simply unfounded and arrogant.

But we must go on to say, secondly, that *while distinct, the two languages of science and theology are not totally different or mutually exclusive.*[37] They certainly need not be at war with each other as they have been for a good part of the modern era. Of course, if the Bible is asserted to be an inerrant textbook of natural science, that is the equivalent of a declaration of war on modern science by faith. And conversely, if evolutionary theory is claimed to be necessarily coupled with atheism, that is the equivalent of a declaration of war on faith by modern science. The warfare between science and theology in the modern period has had dramatic moments. When Galileo was forced to renounce his scientific judgment that the earth moves, his case became a symbol of enmity between science and faith. In the nineteenth and early twentieth centuries, the conflict has focused increasingly on the theory of evolution. The Wilberforce-Huxley debate, the Scopes trial, and recent controversies about "creation science" remind us of how widespread the confu-

---

Polkinghorne, *The Faith of a Physicist* (Princeton: Princeton University Press, 1994); Ian Barbour, *Issues in Science and Religion* (New York: Harper & Row, 1966); Barbour, *Religion in an Age of Science* (San Francisco: Harper & Row, 1990); Wentzel van Huyssteen, *Duet or Duel? Theology and Science in a Postmodern World* (London: SCM, 1998).

36. See Barbour, *Religion in an Age of Science*, 3-30.

37. Ian Barbour insists that "we cannot remain content with a plurality of unrelated languages if they are languages about the same world" (*Religion in an Age of Science*, 16).

sion has been and continues to be on both sides about the relationship of science and faith.

Despite the confusion, there is nothing inherently inconsistent in holding both to evolutionary theory and to faith in God the creator. However extensively we may have to revise our previous assumptions about the time span, stages, and processes of God's creative activity, this does not substantively affect the central claim of faith in God the creator. If some defenders of evolutionary theory think that faith in God is disproved by modern science, their conclusions are no more warranted by the theory itself than "creation science" is a required or even appropriate conclusion to be drawn from faith's affirmation of God as creator of the world. Both reductionism in science and imperialism in theology must be avoided. There are multiple levels in the world of our experience — physical, chemical, biological, personal, social, moral, religious — and each level is intelligible on its own terms as well as open to new understanding at a higher level.[38] This means that we can explore the congruence of scientific and theological understandings of the world without insisting on a proof or disproof of the one by the other.

Third, there is growing consensus among many theologians and scientists that *science and faith not only need not be at war with each other but each can and should influence and enrich the other.* Scientists increasingly recognize the dimension of personal participation and creative imagination in scientific inquiry.[39] They also emphasize that the scientific enterprise itself rests on assumptions and root metaphors that cannot be strictly proven. Stanley L. Jaki argues persuasively that assumptions that make modern science possible — that observed entities are objectively real, that they possess an inherent rationality, that they are contingent, and that the universe is a coherent whole — are entirely congruent with the Christian doctrine of creation.[40] One philosopher of science remarks that today it is not only the case that faith seeks understanding, but that scientific understanding is, at least in a broad sense of the term, in search of faith.[41]

Christian faith and theology have much to learn from modern biological research and scientific cosmology: that God has indeed created a dynamic and open rather than a static and closed universe; that God has created a highly differentiated rather than a monolithic universe; and that God has created a universe in which there is change, novelty, and indeterminacy as well as

38. On levels of cognitional activity, see Bernard Lonergan, *Insight: A Study of Human Understanding* (London: Longmans, Green, 1957), 271-78.

39. See Michael Polanyi, *Personal Knowledge* (Chicago: University of Chicago Press, 1958).

40. Jaki, *Cosmos and Creator* (Edinburgh: Scottish Academic Press, 1980).

41. Polkinghorne, *Science and Creation,* 32.

continuity, order, and coherence.[42] The pendulum may even have begun to swing too far in the opposite direction, that of expecting science to make clear what faith and theology only dimly intuit. This is at least the case in some popular writings that argue that quantum physics and the Big Bang cosmology offer a surer path to God than faith. Careless claims of this sort will not advance the conversation between modern science and theology.

What will assist progress is a new openness on both sides: of science to the dimension of mystery in its own work, and of faith and theology to a vision of God's purposeful activity that transcends the narrow framework of anthropocentrism. Theological anthropocentrism must be overcome by a new theocentrism — more specifically, by a revitalized trinitarian understanding of God — and by a doctrine of creation that is oriented to a future consummation embracing the whole creation of God, not fixated on the past. This does not mean a devaluation of human life but a revaluation of all creation. As Jürgen Moltmann writes, "The enduring meaning of human existence lies in its participation in [the] joyful paean of God's creation. This song of praise was sung *before* the appearance of human beings, is sung *outside* the sphere of human beings, and will be sung even *after* human beings have — perhaps — disappeared from this planet."[43]

Especially in view of the ecological crisis that we face today, it is imperative that we put the old warfare between Christian faith and modern science behind us. A *natural theology*, at least of the traditional sort, is not needed, or even helpful. But a *theology of nature* is of crucial importance.[44] It is also time to move beyond a policy of total separation or mutual indifference between scientists and their discoveries on the one hand and theologians and the vision of faith on the other. It is imperative that scientists and theologians enter into open dialogue with each other. Without one perspective seeking to absorb the other, each in its own way may point to the complex and fragile beauty of the interrelated world of God's creation.

---

42. See A. R. Peacocke, *Creation and the World of Science.*

43. Moltmann, *God in Creation,* 197.

44. See Hendry, *Theology of Nature,* 13-14; Barbour, *Religion in an Age of Science,* 183; and Polkinghorne, *The Faith of a Physicist,* 41-46.

CHAPTER 6

The Providence of God
and the Mystery of Evil

In Chapter One, I defined theology as faith seeking understanding and said that one aspect of this task is the quest for wholeness and coherence in our thinking about God, ourselves, and the world in the light of God's revelation in Jesus Christ. Our quest for coherence, however, must resist the temptation to build a system of ideas that pretends to know more than we do and thereby loses touch with both faith and lived reality. While we can have confidence in the truth of God revealed to us in Christ, our knowledge of God is not exhaustive. Just as the condition of faith is that of seeing only dimly (1 Cor. 13:12), so all theology is necessarily "broken thought," as Karl Barth described it. This fact comes home to us nowhere more forcefully than when we affirm the providence of God in the face of the reality of radical evil in the world. In relation to divine providence and the "problem of evil," the efforts of theology to clarify the claims of faith seem pitifully weak and unsatisfying. All grandiose theological systems that purport to have an answer to every question are exposed as illusory by the monstrous presence of evil and suffering in the world. Radical evil is the disturbing "interruption" (Arthur Cohen) of all theological thinking and speaking about God and especially about the providential rule of God.

Belief in Providence and the Reality of Evil

Christians confess the lordship and providential care of God over the world. God the creator does not abandon the creation, leaving it to run on its own, as deism teaches. The true God is no absentee landlord but remains ever faithful, upholding, blessing, and guiding the creation to its appointed goal.

God's continuing care for all creatures is attested in many passages of Scripture (e.g., Gen. 9:8-17; Ps. 104), perhaps the most familiar being the teaching of Jesus that God sends rain on both the just and the unjust (Matt. 5:45), feeds the birds of the air, clothes the lilies of the field (Matt. 6:26-30), and knows every hair on our head (Matt. 10:30).

A brief but pointed definition of providence is offered by the Heidelberg Catechism of 1563: providence is "the almighty and ever-present power of God whereby he still upholds, as it were by his own hand, heaven and earth together with all creatures, and rules in such a way that leaves and grass, rain and drought, fruitful and unfruitful years, food and drink, health and sickness, riches and poverty, and everything else, come to us not by chance but by his fatherly hand."[1]

This affirmation of God's providential activity is most severely tested by the reality and power of evil. As that which opposes the will of God and distorts the good creation, evil is neither illusion nor mere appearance nor a gradually disappearing force in the world. All theories that deny the reality of evil or minimize its power have been exposed as fantastic and worthless by the horrors of late modernity. An earlier era might have thought of evil as the result of cultural lag or inadequate education or insufficient social planning, and might have been convinced of the gradual and inevitable progress that the cosmos and humankind were making toward a paradise in which all suffering and evil would be eliminated. But at the beginning of the twenty-first century, in the wake of horrendously destructive wars, acts of genocide, and the grim possibility of biological warfare and nuclear annihilation, all such easy faith in progress has been discredited.

If evil cannot be explained away but confronts us with immense reality on the pages of our newspaper, in the cancer ward, and in "the brutal facts of modern historical life,"[2] theology cannot avoid the theodicy question: How can we continue to affirm the lordship of God in the face of such horrendous evil? Or, as the question is often formulated: If God is both omnipotent and good, why is there so much evil in the world? Must not the believer limit the power of God, disavow the goodness of God, or deny the reality of evil? The theodicy question presses itself on us with respect both to what is sometimes called natural evil — the suffering and evil that human beings experience at the hands of nature — and to what is described as moral evil — the suffering and evil that sinful human beings inflict on each other and on the world they

---

1. "The Heidelberg Catechism," A. 27, in *The Book of Confessions* (PSUSA), 4.027.
2. Arthur A. Cohen, *The Tremendum: A Theological Interpretation of the Holocaust* (New York: Crossroad, 1981), 81.

inhabit. In both spheres of experience, we soon find that our effort to relate our faith in God to the brutal facts of life leads into a labyrinth of tormenting questions.

1. "Natural evil" refers to injury and suffering caused by diseases, accidents, earthquakes, fires, and floods. We may think of a young mother mortally stricken by cancer, of an infant born with AIDS, of a young child who is killed by a runaway automobile, of thousands buried in a mud slide caused by a volcanic eruption, of hundreds killed in a plane crash in dense fog. Every pastor who makes hospital visitations and counsels with the bereaved knows that the pain and misery caused by such events are profound and sometimes devastating.

In seeking to cope with experiences of natural evil, we may be tempted to view vulnerability, finitude, and mortality as evil in themselves. But this would be a mistake. As we noted in the previous chapter, some limits and vulnerabilities belong to the goodness of life as created by God. Human beings are part of the natural order established by God and, like other creatures, are subject to its laws. Being a finite creature includes the possibility of pain, illness, grief, failure, incapacity, and the certainty of aging and eventual death. Creaturely life is transient; it has a beginning and an end (Ps. 90:10). God has created a world of both birth and death, both rationality and contingency, both order and freedom, both risk and vulnerability. In such a world, challenge, struggle, and *some* forms of suffering belong to the very structure of life. To wish the world were immune from *every* form of struggle and *every* form of suffering would be to wish not to have been created at all.[3] To insist that believers should be immune from the limits and risks of all creaturely existence would be petty and self-indulgent. Thus while finitude and mortality constitute the "shadow side" of life as created by God, they cannot be called inherently evil.

But even if we are careful to distinguish between finitude and evil, we are nevertheless confronted by an abysmal form of suffering in the natural order that appears to be absurd, excessive, and entirely out of proportion to any good that might arise from it. While the death of a person "in good old age and full of years" (Gen. 25:8) brings sorrow but usually does not threaten our faith, the death of a single child or young adult by leukemia or some other disease is more than sufficient to prompt the theodicy question.

Furthermore, the impulse to question God's providential guidance within the natural order is not confined to individual experiences of tragedy.

---

3. See Douglas John Hall, *God and Human Suffering* (Minneapolis: Augsburg, 1986), 49-71.

It forces itself on us in the interpretation of cosmic process as well as personal experience. Are not violent death and wasted life constitutive elements of the entire natural order? John Macquarrie comments on the "waste" present in the evolutionary process: "The process of evolution on the earth's surface looks more like a groping procedure of trial and error, with fantastic waste, than like the carrying through of a preconceived plan."[4]

The abysmal side of nature has led some to deny God or to equate God with destruction and evil. In Tennessee Williams's play *Suddenly Last Summer*, Sebastian, who is searching for God, is driven to delirium by seeing the large birds over the Encantadas Islands swoop down to devour all but a few of the newly hatched sea turtles as they struggle to reach the sea. Having witnessed this carnage, Sebastian tells his mother: "'Well, now I have seen Him!' and he meant God."[5] The shocking cruelty, terrible wastefulness, and apparent arbitrariness of the manifold occurrences of evil in nature can lead to doubt and even despair about the providential care and goodness of God.

2. The mystery of evil is equally impenetrable when we turn from the natural to the historical sphere of its operation. Whereas for the eighteenth century the symbol of the theodicy question was the Lisbon earthquake, for the twenty-first century it is the memory of such places as Auschwitz that interrupts all traditional theological reflection. The Holocaust of European Jewry during World War II by Nazi Germany has become the primary symbol of radical evil in an unredeemed world.

We are indebted to Jewish writers who have taken the lead in reflecting theologically about this thought-paralyzing experience. The massacre of six million Jews constitutes a scale of evil in history that numbs the mind and soul. With machine guns and gas ovens, Nazis destroyed millions of innocent people in the death camps for no other reason than their Jewish ancestry. The only motive behind this consummate act of genocide was sheer hatred. This gives the event an utterly diabolical character. The fact that it was perpetrated by a society that represented the very pinnacle of modern Western culture only underscores its horror. Nazis could not even claim that their demonic work was helpful to the German war effort, since there is abundant evidence that the opposite was the case. Jewish men, women, and children were senselessly and brutally annihilated not because of their unfaithfulness to the God of the covenant but precisely because of their membership in the covenant people.

4. Macquarrie, *Principles of Christian Theology*, 2d ed. (New York: Scribner's, 1977), 257.
5. Williams, quoted in Gordon D. Kaufman, *Systematic Theology: A Historicist Perspective* (New York: Scribner's, 1968), 310-11.

A moment of the horror of the Holocaust is captured in a single episode from Auschwitz, told by Elie Wiesel in his book *Night*. On one occasion, a young boy was hanged before all the prisoners for a minor infraction of the camp rules. As his body dangled from the rope, Wiesel was asked by someone, "Where is God now?" and a voice within him replied, "Where is He? Here He is — He is hanging here on this gallows. . . ."[6] The power of Wiesel's story comes from its focus on the profound crisis of faith in the experience of terrible affliction. Every experience of innocent suffering has an inescapable theological dimension. As Simone Weil shows in a valuable essay, affliction has many dimensions. It includes not only physical pain but also social rejection and self-hatred. Above all, however, "Affliction makes God appear to be absent for a time."[7] The experience of the absence — or death — of God is closely coupled with the experience of radical evil.

The event of the Holocaust is particular and unique, yet the witness to what happened there is joined by the witness of innocent sufferers everywhere: the black slaves in the United States, the victims of South African apartheid, the prisoners in the Stalin concentration camps, the hundreds of thousands incinerated at Hiroshima and Nagasaki, the countless number of lives lost in the Cambodian killing fields, the victims of "ethnic cleansing" in the Balkans, the millions of Rwandans slaughtered in tribal conflicts, the victims of "collateral damage" in various military ventures. The list is endless. Arthur Cohen writes, "When Jews insist that the *tremendum* of the death camps is unique, they speak correctly, but no less the other butchered people of the earth, butchered no less in their being and hence no less irrationally and absolutely."[8]

What the *tremendum,* by whatever name it is known, discloses is that evil is real and powerful, that it must be resisted, and that those who suffer under its weight sooner or later ask the psalmist's question, "How long, O Lord?" (Ps. 13:1), or the even more terrible question of Jesus, "My God, my God, why have you forsaken me?" (Mark 15:34).

Providence and Evil in the Theological Tradition

The classical doctrine of providence was not constructed by theologians insensitive to the reality of evil in the world. When they spoke of providence as

6. Wiesel, *Night* (New York: Bantam Books, 1982), 62.
7. Weil, *Waiting for God* (New York: Harper & Row, 1976), 120.
8. Cohen, *The Tremendum,* 36.

God's work of preserving the world in existence, ruling over all events, and directing the world to its final end, they did not ignore the power of the negation of God's will present in individuals, societies, and nations. This is evident in the impressive doctrines of providence developed by Augustine and Calvin.[9]

According to Augustine, God's providence is at work both in the lives of individuals and in history even though it is largely hidden. In his *Confessions*, Augustine recounts how God secretly but surely guided his life through many twists and turns toward faith in Christ and entrance into the church. The divine purpose was worked out not coercively, or from the outside as it were, but precisely in and through Augustine's own free decisions and actions. Later in the *City of God* he tries to help his readers see the providential hand of God at work amidst the disintegration of the Roman Empire. Tyranny, injustice, social breakdown, war, and other evil events are not caused by God but have their origin in the creatures' misuse of their freedom. Nevertheless, God permits these events to occur and uses them to accomplish the divine purpose. God exercises sovereignty over evil by bringing good out of what by itself is only negative and destructive.[10]

Calvin's doctrine of providence affirms God's governance over all events even more emphatically. Among Calvin's central aims is to oppose the idea that any event occurs by fortune, chance, or caprice. "All events are governed by God's secret plan," says Calvin; "nothing happens except what is knowingly and willingly decreed by God."[11] Holding that it is insufficient to affirm a "bare foreknowledge" of God, Calvin declares that God governs the course of nature and history down to the smallest details. God "directs everything by his incomprehensible wisdom and disposes it to his own end."[12]

Despite his emphasis on God's sovereign control, Calvin does not equate providence with fatalism; on the contrary, he teaches that while we are to look to God as the "first cause" of all things, we are also to give attention to the "secondary causes" in their proper place.[13] God has given human beings reason to foresee dangers and to exercise prudence. If danger is evident, we are not to plunge headlong into it; if remedies for suffering are available, we are not to neglect them. Like other classical theologians of divine providence, Calvin walks a tightrope between ascribing everything to God at the expense

9. See Langdon Gilkey, *Reaping the Whirlwind: A Christian Interpretation of History* (New York: Seabury Press, 1976), 159-87.

10. See Augustine, *City of God*, 13.4: "By the ineffable mercy of God even the penalty of man's offense is turned into an instrument of virtue."

11. *Institutes of the Christian Religion*, 1.16.3.

12. *Institutes*, 1.16.4.

13. *Institutes*, 1.17.6.

of the freedom and responsibility of creatures, and compromising the omnipotence of God by allowing some autonomy to creaturely activity.

For both Augustine and Calvin, divine providence is less a speculative doctrine than a practical truth. We can be confident that God reigns and that evil is firmly under God's control. This is a teaching with important benefits for the life of faith. In the first place, it teaches us the humility to receive adversity from God's hand even though we cannot understand the reason. Second, we are taught by the doctrine of providence to give thanks for the times when we prosper. And finally, trust in God's providence sets us free from all undue anxiety and care. Calvin sums up these points by saying that "gratitude of mind for the favorable outcome of things, patience in adversity, and also incredible freedom from worry about the future all necessarily follow upon this knowledge [of providence]."[14]

Within the framework of traditional doctrines of providence, there are at least three prominent answers to the theodicy question.

1. One familiar theodicy argument underscores the *incomprehensibility of God*. We do not know why there is so much evil in the world, or why it is distributed so unevenly, but we are nevertheless to trust God and have patience. This is a response to evil with considerable biblical support. Out of the whirlwind, God replies to Job's questions with a series of counterquestions that are intended to remind Job of his finitude and inability to grasp the ways of God with the world (see Job 38–41). "The story of Job," Calvin writes, "in its description of God's wisdom, power, and purity, always expresses a powerful argument that overwhelms men with the realization of their own stupidity, impotence, and corruption."[15]

We must surely agree that our knowledge of God's ways is limited and that sometimes silence is a far more appropriate response to the enormity of suffering than feeble attempts to answer the question why. A problem with this response, however, is that it may tend to suppress all questions and to encourage the unchallenged acceptance of *all* suffering. When used in this way, the theme of divine incomprehensibility does not have unanimous biblical warrant. Indeed, the book of Job itself is the most striking biblical example of permission to remonstrate with God and to call into question the divine governance. Although the picture of the pious, patient Job of the prologue and epilogue of the book is deeply imprinted in Christian consciousness, the rebellious and questioning Job of the poetic section is far less familiar. At the end of the book, it should be remembered, it is Job rather than his orthodox

14. *Institutes*, 1.17.7.
15. *Institutes*, 1.1.3.

critics who is commended by God for having spoken what is right (42:7). There is both theological and pastoral significance in the permission to question the justice of God in the face of outrageous suffering and evil.[16]

2. Another traditional theodicy argument interprets the experience of adversity as evidence of *divine punishment* (of the wicked) or *chastisement* (of the people of God). According to this view, God so governs the world that both the good and the wicked receive what they deserve, if not in this life, then in the life to come.[17] Calvin contends that "the scriptures teach us that pestilence, war, and other calamities of this kind are chastisements of God, which he inflicts on our sins."[18]

While there are some strands of the Bible that lend support to this conviction (for example, the Deuteronomic tradition, and the defenders of God in the book of Job), Jesus explicitly calls it in question. He teaches that the blind man was not born blind on account of his own or his parents' sins (John 9:1-3), and he claims that it was not because of their special wickedness that people in Siloam were killed when a tower fell upon them (Luke 13:4). The theodicy of divine punishment, which so easily blames the victim and often ignores the perpetrators, becomes especially repulsive and destructive when it is implied that God is punishing people who have incurable diseases or are murdered by the millions in the holocausts of history. Human deeds do have consequences, and sometimes a person's reckless or sinful behavior brings suffering in its train. But the theodicy of punishment sees the relationship between sin and suffering too simplistically. Not all suffering can be causally related to sin, and certainly not to the sin of the sufferer. To add guilt to the burden of suffering carried by the victims of natural evil or of human injustice is unconscionable.

3. Still another argument of traditional theodicy centers on the *divine pedagogy* that makes use of earthly sufferings to turn us to God and *to cultivate our hope for eternal life*. This argument teaches that Christians are to view all suffering as an opportunity for spiritual growth. They are to learn to have contempt for the present life and to meditate on the future life. God sends poverty, bereavement, diseases, and other perils to wean us away from this earth, to cause us to fix our eyes on heaven rather than on the goods of the present life.[19] The apostle Paul might be cited in support of this view: "I con-

---

16. See Kathleen D. Billman and Daniel L. Migliore, *Rachel's Cry: Prayer of Lament and Rebirth of Hope* (Cleveland: Pilgrim, 1999).

17. *Institutes*, 1.5.10.

18. Calvin, quoted in Dorothee Sölle, *Suffering* (Philadelphia: Fortress, 1975), 24.

19. *Institutes*, 3.9.1.

sider that the sufferings of this present time are not worth comparing with the glory that is to be revealed to us" (Rom. 8:18).

It should be noted, however, that the apostle is thinking primarily of sufferings that are willingly assumed by the Christian for the sake of Christ and the gospel. His statement ought not to be used to obscure the distinction between suffering that is willingly accepted for the sake of God's reign and suffering that arises from conditions that can and should be changed. While few Christians would want to contest the main point of the apostle — that hope in the final victory of God over evil can give meaning to innocent suffering — there is surely reason to question any interpretation of his teaching that would lead to ethical quietism or a depreciation of this life. Like Jesus, we can learn from our suffering (Heb. 5:8), but this is not to be converted into the general truth that suffering is good. The cries of victims must not be suppressed in this way, and any theodicy that suggests otherwise is dealing in mystifications.

The traditional theodicies summarized above have undoubtedly offered comfort and support to countless believers in particular situations. An element of truth is present in each of them. But they are all marked by a lack of sustained attention to the gospel story in their thinking about divine lordship and in their response to the reality of evil. At the beginning of the twenty-first century, all theodicy must be tested both by "the brutal facts of modern historical life" and by the biblical witness to the love of God in Jesus the crucified. This situation compels faith to rethink all inherited understandings of God, and in particular the ideas of divine omnipotence and omnicausality that are often presupposed in traditional doctrines of providence.

Rethinking Providence and Evil

Modern theologians have attempted to rethink the doctrine of providence in a way that respects both divine power and creaturely freedom. Divine activity and human activity are not mutually exclusive. God regularly works in and through creaturely agency to accomplish the divine purpose (Rom. 8:28).

Even a theologian as deeply respectful of his own classical Reformed theological tradition as Karl Barth could nevertheless say that its doctrine of providence was tragically flawed by a conception of divine omnicausality. Barth grants that the activity of God is "as sovereign as Calvinist teaching describes it,"[20] but he insists that the divine sovereignty must always be under-

20. Karl Barth, *Church Dogmatics*, 3/3: 131.

stood in the light of God's revelation in Christ. In practice, Barth contends, belief in providence in orthodox Reformed theology was indistinguishable from Stoic resignation, an acceptance of whatever happens as ordained by God. The consequence of such a teaching within modern culture was an inevitable "revolt against a capricious sovereign rule."[21] Failing to apply to the doctrine of providence the proper norm of Christian knowledge of God — namely, the revelation in Christ — the tradition became the herald of a "sinister deity." Hence Barth called for a "radical rethinking of the whole matter."[22] The Christian doctrine of providence is not a mere logical deduction from abstract claims about the omnipotence and goodness of God. It must be worked out in the light of a genuinely Christian (i.e., Christocentric and trinitarian) understanding of God as the one who loves in freedom, who wills to live in communion, and who from all eternity elects Jesus Christ and in him the people of God and all of creation.

Barth himself took important steps in this direction in his own doctrine of providence. Employing the categories of traditional theology, he describes divine providence as including God's preservation (conservatio), accompaniment (concursus), and governance (gubernatio) of all creatures. But he redefines each of these aspects of divine providence in the light of God's ways with the world in Jesus Christ. The God of creation and providence is none other than the God who covenants with Israel and with all creation, and whose faithfulness, judgment, and grace are supremely manifest in the person and work of Jesus Christ.

Accordingly, God *preserves* the whole creation and maintains it in existence. This act of preservation is not an arbitrary exercise of almightiness but an expression of God's faithfulness to the purpose for which the world was created. From all eternity the whole creation is chosen in and oriented to Jesus Christ as God's covenant partner. God's act of preserving the creation is thus an act of serving, an act of free grace to the creature, empowering and sustaining it for participation in the covenant of grace. God is not the impersonal or mechanical "first cause" of all that happens but the one whom Jesus revealed as the heavenly Father.

Moreover, God *accompanies* creatures in the exercise of their own vitality and freedom. That God accompanies the creatures means that God recognizes and respects the free activity of creatures and does not play the part of a tyrant. The creature is not a mere puppet or tool in the hands of the creator. God's activity and creaturely activity belong to two different orders; "God is

21. Barth, *Church Dogmatics*, 3/3: 116.
22. Barth, *Church Dogmatics*, 3/3: 118.

so present in the activity of the creature, and present with such sovereignty and almighty power, that God's actions take place in and with and over the activity of the creature."[23] In so accompanying the creature, God always respects the creature's finite autonomy in a way that corresponds to the singular union of divine and human activity in Jesus Christ.

Finally, God *governs* or rules over all things by guiding creation to its goal. This rule of God, often deeply hidden, is exercised by God's Word and Spirit and not by unilateral and coercive power. "God rules," Barth insists, "in and over a world of freedom."[24] God is present everywhere, always, and in all things, but God is not the sole actor. The God who wills to have communion with creatures gives them freedom to return love for love. In providence no less than in creation and redemption, God is the gracious Lord. All this clearly shows that Barth wanted to break free from a doctrine of providence based on a "logic of control" or domination (Farley).

While offering new direction for a Christian doctrine of providence that refuses to adopt a priori definitions of deity and omnipotence and concentrates instead on the grace of God as revealed in Jesus Christ, Barth's treatment of the reality of evil and of our part in the struggle against it leaves many questions unresolved. Evil for Barth is the alien power of "nothingness" *(das Nichtige)* that arises mysteriously from what God does *not* will in the act of creation. As Barth explains, "nothingness" is not nothing. While neither willed by God nor an equal of God, it has its own formidable and threatening power. It is that which contradicts the will of God manifested in Jesus Christ. God alone is able to conquer the power of nothingness: "The power of nothingness should be rated as low as possible in relation to God and as high as possible in relation to ourselves."[25]

A number of Barth's critics view his doctrine of nothingness as a lapse into metaphysical speculation.[26] They charge that Barth sometimes seems to treat the reality of evil and its conquest by God as a transcendental conflict that takes place over our heads, leaving unclear in what ways human beings are to be understood as active subjects in the struggle rather than mere onlookers. If evil is viewed as an alien sphere of power within the creation that God alone can overcome, will we not be disinclined to unmask proximate sources of human suffering and oppression and to take up the struggle against them?

23. Barth, *Church Dogmatics*, 3/3: 132.
24. Barth, *Church Dogmatics*, 3/3: 93.
25. Barth, *Church Dogmatics*, 3/3: 295.
26. See, for example, G. C. Berkouwer, *The Triumph of Grace in the Theology of Karl Barth* (Grand Rapids: Eerdmans, 1956).

We would be mistaken, however, to understand Barth's view of God's struggle against the power of nothingness as an invitation to passivity. For Barth it is precisely confidence in the superiority of God's grace that empowers believers to fight against evil and suffering in the world against seemingly impossible odds. Barth himself was very active in the church struggle during the Nazi period in Germany, and his theology has been an inspiration to many who have struggled against evil structures such as apartheid in South Africa.[27] Moreover, history itself testifies in favor of Barth's insistence that only God is able to conquer the power of radical evil. When individual human beings, groups, or nations, sure of their innocence and convinced of the utter wickedness of their enemies, claim for themselves the right and the power to rid the world of evil, they often become themselves agents of evil.

Nevertheless, the criticisms of Barth have some validity. Though he pioneered the modern reconstruction of the doctrine of providence, he did not sufficiently clarify the relationship between the activity of God and human activity in the struggle against evil. Nor did he sufficiently explore the relationship between patience and protest in a Christian doctrine of providence and in a Christian response to the reality of suffering and evil. These remain among the open questions in contemporary theological discussion.

Recent Theodicies

Numerous theologians after Barth have shared his criticism of the traditional doctrines of providence and evil but have proposed widely differing approaches to the task of rethinking these themes. Any review of recent theodicies and their corresponding understandings of providence would have to include the following.

1. *Protest theodicy.* This is the name given by John Roth to his own position, which has its basis and inspiration in the witness and reflection of the Holocaust survivor and author Elie Wiesel.[28] Jewish theologians Richard Rubenstein and Arthur Cohen may also be considered representatives of a protest theodicy. Assuming with the Bible a very strong view of the sovereignty of God, the tendency of this theodicy is to question the total goodness of God. There is simply too much tragedy, injustice, and murder in history.

27. For the argument that Barth must be understood as responsive to his social and political context not only in his occasional writings but also in the *Church Dogmatics*, see Timothy J. Gorringe, *Karl Barth Against Hegemony* (New York: Oxford University Press, 1999).

28. See Roth, "A Theodicy of Protest," in *Encountering Evil: Live Options in Theodicy*, ed. Stephen T. Davis (Atlanta: John Knox, 1981), 7-22.

We must be honest to our experience and to God and thus quarrel with the all-too-familiar refrain that God is love. Like Jacob who wrestles all night with a divine adversary and who is renamed Israel or "He who strives with God" (Gen. 32:22-32); like the psalmist who asks, "How long, O Lord?" (Pss. 13, 35, 74, 82, 89, 90, 94); like Job, who fiercely defends his innocence, and like Jesus who cries to God from the cross (Mark 15:34), we are compelled to protest against the silence and inaction of God, to remind God of the promises of the covenant even though God seems to have forgotten them. The reality that faith confronts forces it to "put God on trial," to be "for God by being against God."[29]

This is a theodicy with no easy answers but with the honesty to raise what earlier believers would have considered blasphemous questions and with a determination to be faithful to God even when it appears that God has ceased to be faithful. One might well demur from the theological conclusions that protest theodicy derives from the persistence of evil in nature and history while at the same time acknowledging the legitimacy of the protest as part of a faithful response to God.

2. *Process theodicy.* John Cobb, David Griffin, and Marjorie Suchocki are well-known representatives of process theodicy.[30] They approach the problem of evil from the perspective of process metaphysics. Refusing to compromise on the divine goodness, process thought argues that the solution lies instead in a radical restriction of divine power.

For the process theologians, God's power is essentially limited, and it is persuasive rather than coercive. Persuasion is the only way one power can influence another without violating the freedom of the other. God creates not ex nihilo but more like the Platonic Demiurge, who persuades recalcitrant matter as best God can. The world is a plurality of beings, all of which have some freedom and power of their own. God does not have, and never had, a monopoly on power. Thus there are some things God is simply unable to do — such as prevent the Holocaust, or stop a runaway car from killing a child in its path, or eliminate the possibility of cancerous growths in human beings.

In this view, God is responsible for evil in an indirect sense, because God has persuaded the world to bring forth forms of life that have the potential not only for great good but also, because the creature is free, for great evil. While indirectly responsible, however, God is not blameworthy. God always

29. Roth, "A Theodicy of Protest," 11, 19.

30. Cobb, *God and the World* (Philadelphia: Westminster, 1969), 87-102; Griffin, "Creation out of Chaos and the Problem of Evil," in *Encountering Evil*, 101-19; Suchocki, *The End of Evil: Process Eschatology in Historical Perspective* (Albany: State University of New York Press, 1988).

intends the good and always shares the suffering of the creatures in a world in which beauty and tragedy are interwoven.

Process theodicy is arguably the most comprehensive and consistent of modern theodicies, but at the same time it may also be the one most distant from the biblical witness. This is perhaps best seen in the fact that process theodicy, with its teaching that the sovereignty of God's love is metaphysically limited, can make little sense either of the doctrine of creation out of nothing or of the biblical hope in a definitive eschatological victory over suffering and evil.

3. *Person-making theodicy.* This is one of the most influential of modern theodicies, and John Hick is perhaps its ablest representative.[31] He distinguishes between the Augustinian and the Irenaean types of theodicy. In the former, evil is represented as the consequence of sin; in the latter, the possibility and experience of evil are conditions of the possibility of growth toward free and mature humanity in the image of God. The freedom and potential for growth with which human life is endowed can be abused, but without the real choice between good and evil, and without the possibility of learning through hard experience, the formation of character is simply impossible. According to Hick, God desires not puppets but persons who freely render their worship and adoration. Hence human beings are created incomplete and must freely participate in the process by which they come to be what God intends them to be.

Unlike process thinkers, Hick refuses to qualify the power of God working through love. He postulates the existence of worlds beyond this world in which persons continue their movement toward the fullness of life in love that God intends for all creatures. Some critics see this feature of Hick's theodicy as evidence of its speculative bent. Others note the functional similarity of the idea of the soul's progress beyond death with the Roman Catholic doctrine of purgatory.

While person-making theodicy does not entirely lack a social-ethical dimension, its weakness in this area is conspicuous. Far more attention is given to the possibility of growth through acceptance of suffering than to resistance to suffering that can and should be removed. To be sure, the idea of learning from and growing in suffering is deeply ingrained in the Bible; Jesus "learned obedience through what he suffered" (Heb. 5:8). Moreover, countless Christians as well as members of other religious communities have borne powerful witness to the working of grace even in the darkest of experiences. Still, it must not be overlooked that there are events of suffering and evil that in their immensity threaten to consume their victims. These events do not

31. See Hick, *Evil and the God of Love* (New York: Harper & Row, 1966); and "An Irenaean Theodicy," in *Encountering Evil*, 39-52.

seem reconcilable with the claim that every form of suffering is an opportunity for spiritual development. Marilyn McCord Adams calls such events "horrendous evils" and argues that they shake the foundations of Hick's soul-making theodicy.[32] Despite its strengths, Hick's theodicy proves to be less than satisfactory when it is tested by the experience of the *tremendum*.

4. *Liberation theodicy.* Liberation theology in its many forms must come to terms with the theodicy question, because the continuing reality of the suffering of the poor and the oppressed appears to stand in contradiction to the claim of this theology that God is at work in the world liberating the poor.

James Cone has addressed this problem. He refuses to diminish either the divine power or the divine goodness in order to arrive at an intellectually satisfying resolution of the dilemma. He acknowledges the plurality of responses to the mystery of evil in the Bible. He finds the deepest response in the theme of redemptive suffering (the Servant Songs of Isaiah) that comes to its fullest expression in the history of Jesus Christ. Cone interprets the biblical tradition, however, as a call to courageous human participation in God's *struggle against* suffering rather than a pious *acquiescence in* suffering. The African American religious tradition does not focus on the question of the origin of evil or on the submission of the victims of injustice to their masters. It is a faith tradition that sees in the cross God's struggle against evil and in the resurrection God's promise of the final victory of God over evil. God grants "power to the powerless to fight here and now for the freedom they know to be theirs in Jesus' cross and resurrection."[33]

When placed alongside much traditional theodicy, with its tendency to passivity in the face of evil, the important truth of liberation theodicy is readily apparent, but its dangers are evident as well. The struggle for justice must not be severed from the practice of forgiveness and the hope of reconciliation. Yet if there is a one-sidedness in the emphasis of liberation theodicy, the tradition has been no less one-sided.

The Triune God and Human Suffering

If we honestly acknowledge the persistence and power of evil in the world, can we still speak responsibly of divine providence? For Christians this question can be answered affirmatively if the lordship of God is consistently

32. See Marilyn McCord Adams, *Horrendous Evils and the Goodness of God* (Ithaca: Cornell University Press, 1999).

33. Cone, *God of the Oppressed* (New York: Seabury Press, 1974), 183.

redescribed in terms of the gospel narrative whose center is the ministry, crucifixion, and resurrection of Jesus Christ. A Christian approach to the lordship of God in relation to the reality of suffering must therefore be explicitly Christocentric and trinitarian.

A trinitarian understanding of God, rooted in the revelation of God in Christ, gives expression to the rich and differentiated expressions of God's relationship with the world as Father, Son, and Holy Spirit. God relates to creatures in ways appropriate to their own nature — to rocks and stones in one way, to plants in another way, to animals in another way, and to human creatures in still another way. God is present with the creatures both as co-agent and as co-sufferer.

As noted in an earlier chapter, subordinationism and modalism both cringe at the notion that God experiences struggle, suffering, and death. Trinitarian faith, however, recognizes that God's eternal being-in-love reaches out to the world. Far from being aloof, apathetic, and immutable, God freely becomes vulnerable out of faithful love for the world. The destructiveness of evil in creation can be overcome not by divine fiat but only by a costly history of divine love in which the suffering of the world is really experienced and overcome by God.

In an often-quoted passage, Dietrich Bonhoeffer wrote, "The Bible directs us to God's powerlessness and suffering; only the suffering God can help."[34] When turned into a slogan that is thoughtlessly repeated, the profound meaning of this statement is obscured. Only a suffering God can help us, but the suffering God is the triune God whose holy, self-giving, victorious love is at work from the creation of the world to its completion.

Perhaps more than any other modern theologian, Jürgen Moltmann has emphasized the deep connection between the event of the cross and a trinitarian understanding of God. What transpires in this event can be grasped theologically only in trinitarian terms. According to Moltmann, in his passion and death the Son of God experiences suffering and death out of love for the world. But the Father who sent him on his salvific mission also experiences the grief of loss of the beloved Son. And from this event of shared suffering love comes the Spirit of new life and world transformation. All of the suffering of the world is encompassed in the affliction of the Son, the grief of the Father, and the comfort of the Spirit, who inspires courage and hope to pray and work for the renewal of all things.[35] Some of Moltmann's critics

---

34. Bonhoeffer, *Letters and Papers from Prison* (New York: Macmillan, 1972), 361.

35. See Moltmann, *The Crucified God* (New York: Harper, 1974), esp. 235-49. Cf. Hans Urs von Balthasar, *Theo-Drama*, vol. 4: *The Action* (San Francisco: Ignatius, 1994), 319-28.

charge that he comes close to eternalizing suffering in God and thus risks turning theodicy into ideology. But Moltmann's intention is clearly to couple emphasis on the suffering of the triune God with hope in the eschatological victory of divine love over all evil and the participation of creation in God's eternal joy.

The crucial point is that a trinitarian understanding of divine providence and the reality of evil is marked not by a pagan notion of God as sheer almightiness but by the power of love at work in the ministry, cross, and resurrection of Jesus. Such a theology is centered not in a triumphalist "logic of control" but in the "logic of trinitarian love," the self-giving love of the creator, redeemer, and consummator of the world. The power of the triune God is not raw omnipotence but the power of suffering, liberating, reconciling love. An emphasis on God as Trinity gives providence a different face. The God who creates and preserves the world is not a despotic ruler but "our Father in heaven"; not a distant God but a God who becomes one of us and accompanies us as the incarnate, crucified, risen Lord; not an ineffective God but one who rules all things by Word and Spirit rather than by the power of coercion.

1. *The love of God the creator and provider is at work not only where life is sustained and enhanced but also where all that jeopardizes life and its fulfillment is resisted and set under judgment.*

According to the biblical witness, the God who created the heavens and the earth is the primary combatant in the struggle against all that threatens life. This is evident in the story of the exodus, the giving of the law, and the sending of the prophets to declare God's judgment on injustice and violence.

In the Gospels, Jesus' message of the coming reign of God and his ministry of liberation are presented as necessarily involving from the very outset conflict with forces that threaten to enslave and destroy human life. Jesus does the work of the one who sent him, healing the sick, blessing the poor, having table fellowship with social outcasts, and calling all people to repent and turn from the way of death to the way of life. Thus his journey to the cross is not a resignation to blind fate but a loving consent to the righteous will of the Father that evil be resisted to the bitter end. Far from being a basis for a Christian masochism, the passion story is, in J. B. Metz's words, a "dangerous memory" of God's passionate protest against the evil powers that resist the will of God and hold human life in bondage.[36]

Traditional theology has one-sidedly linked faith in providence with pa-

---

36. Metz, *Faith in History and Society: Towards a Practical Fundamental Theology* (New York: Seabury Press, 1980), 65-67, 88ff.

tience. It has often counseled the poor to accept their lot as ordained by God.[37] It has sometimes failed to help the sick and those who minister to them distinguish between mere resignation and faithful resistance to disease. The providence of the triune God does not foster fatalism. The divine *conservatio* works not only through our patience but also through our impatience and our courageous resistance to evil. For the Christian, evil is not to be resisted with evil, but it *is* to be resisted (cf. Rom. 12:21).

2. *The love of God the redeemer is at work both in the heights and in the depths of creaturely experience, both when the creature is strong and active and when it is weak and passive.* To confess that "in everything God works for good" (Rom. 8:28) is to affirm that God is ever faithful. Whether healthy or sick, whether sufferers or those who enter into solidarity with sufferers, we are not alone.

According to a Christian doctrine of providence, God does more than work for the preservation of life and against all that threatens it; God also intimately accompanies creatures in their activity and in their suffering. The God of free grace does not will to act alone and does not will that creatures should suffer alone. Although often overlooked by traditional theology, the divine *concursus* includes the fellow suffering of God.

The Bible portrays God as mourning with the people of Israel in their affliction. According to the psalmist, God is even present in the depths of Sheol (Ps. 139:8), an affirmation echoed in the statement of the Apostles' Creed that Christ descended into hell for us. In the Gospels Jesus is described as being moved with compassion for the crowds because they were harassed and helpless (Matt. 9:36). He healed the sick, had table fellowship with sinners, and associated freely with women and other marginalized people of his time. It is thus fully congruent with the biblical witness to say that God is present as co-sufferer with all the wretched of the earth, whether in cancer wards or in concentration camps. As revealed in the covenantal history with Israel and supremely in the history of Jesus Christ, God accompanies us not only in activity but also in agony and death.

God's accompanying of creatures in their suffering is sheer grace, unexpected companionship in the depths of affliction. The presence of another in the experience of suffering is a gift; the presence of the compassionate God in the experience of suffering is a gift precious beyond words. In God's companionship with sufferers, they are affirmed in their dignity and value in spite of the assault on their being by disease or their victimization by others.

People who suffer are under attack not only by physical pain and social

---

37. See Calvin, *Institutes*, 1.16.6.

oppression but also by a sense of worthlessness and abandonment. To speak of God's solidarity with victims is thus no mere rhetorical consolation but a life-renewing affirmation. The message that Jesus the Son of God has companionship with sinners and social outcasts, has compassion on the sick and the poor, and is finally crucified between two criminals outside the city gates has saving power because it overcomes the hopelessness and self-hatred that suffering at the hands of nature or our fellow creatures instills. Thus in the face of the fierce reality of evil, God's solidarity with victims is both judgment and grace — judgment on all insensitivity and inhumanity, and grace to all who are afflicted. God's companionship with those who suffer is a touchstone of a Christian doctrine of providence as well as an apt description of the call to Christian discipleship.

3. *The love of God the sanctifier is at work everywhere, preparing for the coming reign of God, planting seeds of hope, renewing and transforming all things.* Wherever a new freedom breaks the chains of bondage in an individual life or in the experience of an entire people, wherever new community in love and freedom takes shape, wherever hope is inspired against all odds, the Spirit of God who changes all things is present and active. The appearance of new life in the midst of death, wherever it may occur, is a sign that God's Spirit is still at work, transforming the groaning creation and moving it toward the completion of God's purpose in Christ.

God does indeed rule and overrule the events of each human life and all of history. But the way in which God rules and overrules a world of freedom and bondage, sin and suffering is by the power of Word and Spirit, the power of sacrificial love that is stronger than death. This is the way of the divine *gubernatio* in the light of the ministry, cross, and resurrection of Christ.

To be in Christ and to walk by the Spirit is to participate in the energy of God's liberating, sacrificial love and to be given new courage and hope by it. Only this holy love of God — extended to us in Jesus Christ and made effective in us by the Spirit of God (1 Cor. 13) — can transform a broken world and bring it healing and renewal. Only such love can persist in the struggle against disease and devastation and resist the bitterness they so often engender. Only such love can forgive sins — and without God's forgiveness of our sins and our forgiveness of the sins of others against us, no hope of real transformation of life is possible. Only the divine love that aims at new life and new community where all are free and all are affirmed can sustain the struggle for healing, justice, and peace without being captured by the spirit of hatred and revenge. Only a love that moves through the suffering of the cross to the promise of new life confirmed in the resurrection of Christ can be the basis of hope that does not despair in the face of personal and corporate disappointment and death. The Spirit of God is at work wherever there are such signs and beginnings of new life, new community, and new hope in the midst of death, separation, and hopelessness.

Providence, Prayer, Practice

At the conclusion of this chapter we must circle back to the point made at the beginning: all our reflections on providence and evil remain broken and incomplete. They prove incapable of yielding a definitive theoretical "solution" to the "problem of evil." Their aim must be far more modest. As Paul Helm writes, "Belief in providence enables Christians to put their pain in a different setting."[38] What I have proposed is no more than a prolegomenon to an understanding of the providence of God and the reality of evil in the "setting" of the Christocentric and trinitarian faith of the church.

Events of horrendous evil have the capacity to shake faith to the foundations. They may be experienced as events of God's absence, indifference, or hostility. In our personal, communal, or national life, violent forces may suddenly smash the images of God long taken for granted. Confidence in divine providence is especially difficult today in the face of global terrorism and global wars on terrorism. In a world where the cycle of violence and counterviolence threatens to spin out of control, can God have a providential plan for me, for my family, for my nation, for the world? The anguish of this question cannot be removed by well-crafted theoretical theodicies.

There are times when silence, companionship in suffering, and acts of compassion speak much more effectively than words. To those who ask where God was on September 11, 2001, when thousands lost their lives in the attack on the World Trade Center, some point to the acts of courage and self-sacrifice on the part of rescuers and co-workers as signals of a presence and activity of the Spirit of God in the midst of the maelstrom.[39] To the question of how we speak of God in relation to such an event, Rowan Williams calls attention to the ironic contrast between the overtly "religious" language used by the suicide bombers to justify their horrific violence and the simple, "secular" words of love and care for family members that characterized the final communication of some who were trapped in the towers and knew they were about to die.[40]

---

38. Paul Helm, *The Providence of God* (Downers Grove, Ill.: InterVarsity Press, 1994).
39. See James Martin, *Searching for God at Ground Zero* (New York: Sheed & Ward, 2002).
40. See Rowan Williams, *Writing in the Dust: After September 11* (Grand Rapids: Eerdmans, 2002), 3-12.

In the midst of horrendous evils, several things may become clearer than before.[41] First, no image of God, no doctrine of providence, can be compelling that is not rooted in and tested by the gospel of the crucified Lord. A doctrine of providence that teaches that no harm will come to me or to my nation because we consider ourselves God's chosen ones distorts the biblical message. If the theology of the cross is our interpretive key for events like September 11, we will beware of understandings of divine providence that rest on belief in our invulnerability, or our merit, or that serve mostly to confirm our personal or national innocence. W. Stacy Johnson wisely comments, "Trusting in God's promises is not the same thing as clinging to a particular vision of their fulfillment, as though we expected particular outcomes as an entitlement."[42]

Second, prayer has a necessary place in Christian life and theological work, most especially in response to the continuing power of radical evil. In honest prayer and honest theology we acknowledge that evil is within us as well as outside us, that our own resources to struggle against its power are not only severely limited but also marked by considerable ambiguity, that when we undertake to conquer evil with evil we only multiply it, and that our deepest hope can only be in God and not in ourselves. Occasions of horrendous evil may tempt us to lash out in unthinking fury, to make someone pay for the misery, to feel justified in any action we might take against those we deem guilty. Therefore Christ instructed his disciples to pray, "Your kingdom come, your will be done . . . forgive us our sins . . . deliver us from evil."

Third, while the search of faith for understanding never reaches full comprehension in this life, the call to discipleship in faith, hope, and love is clear. Christians know that they are summoned to watch, pray, and struggle for God's new world of justice and peace in the company of all who are afflicted and cry for deliverance. The biblical witness is far less interested in speculation on the origin of evil than in resistance to it in the confidence of the superiority and ultimate victory of God's love in Jesus Christ. A Christian response to the reality of evil will always be first of all practical. Solidarity with victims and costly ministry to the wounded and the dying are primary forms of Christian witness in the midst of shattering events. Here as elsewhere the primary task of theology is to interpret the tradition of faith from its center in Jesus Christ so as to allow it to become once again a transforming power in human life. New Testament faith in the power of God's love in Jesus

41. See my fuller response to September 11, written shortly after the event, "September 11 and the Theology of the Cross," in *The Princeton Seminary Bulletin* 23, no. 1 (February 2002): 54-58.

42. W. Stacy Johnson, "Probing the 'Meaning" of September 11, 2002," in *The Princeton Seminary Bulletin* 23, no. 1 (February 2002): 43.

Christ leads neither to arrogance nor to indifference. The apostle Paul's affirmations that "in everything God works for good" (Rom. 8:28) and that "nothing can separate us from the love of God in Christ Jesus" (Rom. 8:38-39) are best translated not into abstract theories but into concrete practices of Christian discipleship in solidarity with a groaning creation.

In the face of horrendous evils, questions like "Why did this happen?" and "Where was God?" assail believers. The questions cannot be quickly answered and should not be piously suppressed. They may have to be endured for a long time. But other questions must eventually be asked, too: Does God suffer as well as heal? Who is the God to whom we pray?[43]

---

43. See Gerhard Sauter, "'A City upon a Hill'? Die Religioese Dimension des amerikanischen Selbstverstandnisses und seine gegenwartige Krise," in *Der 11. September 2001: Fragen, Folgen, Hintergruende, hrsg. Sabine Seilke* (Frankfurt: Peter Lang, 2002), 80.

CHAPTER 7

Humanity as Creature, Sinner, and New Being in Christ

We human beings are a mystery to ourselves. We are rational and irrational, civilized and savage, capable of deep friendship and murderous hostility, free and in bondage, the pinnacle of creation and its greatest danger. We are Rembrandt and Hitler, Mozart and Stalin, Antigone and Lady Macbeth, Ruth and Jezebel. "What a work of art," says Shakespeare of humanity. "We are very dangerous," says Arthur Miller in *After the Fall*. "We meet . . . not in some garden of wax fruit and painted leaves that lies East of Eden, but after, after the Fall, after many, many deaths." The Bible and Christian theology give expression to this mystery of the dignity and the danger of human beings in three related affirmations: we are created in the image of God; we are sinners who deny and distort our created being; and we are forgiven sinners, enabled by God's grace to begin life anew in faith, to serve as Christ's disciples in love, and to move in hope toward the promised fulfillment of life in the coming reign of God. Recalling Calvin's dictum, we recognize that knowledge of God and knowledge of ourselves are intertwined. We cannot know God truly without being awakened to new self-recognition, and we cannot know our true humanity without a new awareness of the majestic grace of God.

Interpretations of "Image of God"

According to the first creation narrative in Genesis, God said, "Let us make humankind in our image, according to our likeness; and let them have dominion over the fish of the sea, and over the birds of the air, and over the cattle, and over all the earth, and over every creeping thing that creeps upon the

earth. So God created humankind in his image; in the image of God he created them; male and female he created them" (Gen. 1:26⊦27). The evocative
phrase "the image of God" has been interpreted in a number of different ways
in the history of Christian theology.

According to some interpreters, human beings in their upright stature
have a *physical resemblance* to God. Some passages of the Bible are strikingly
anthropomorphic in their depiction of God (such as Gen. 3:8ff.). However,
with its more characteristic emphasis on the transcendence and hiddenness of
God, the Old Testament lends little support to the notion of a physical resemblance between God and humanity and indeed explicitly forbids the making of
all images of God (Exod. 20:4). Similarly, while the New Testament community speaks of beholding the glory of God in the face of Christ (2 Cor. 4:6; John
1:14), it is not Jesus' physical correspondence to God that is meant but the correspondence of his intention and action to that of God. John Calvin, while not
flatly rejecting the interpretation of the image of God as physical resemblance,
was obviously concerned about excessive anthropomorphism.[1]

Perhaps the dominant Western interpretation of the image of God has
been that it resides in the *rational nature of human beings.* In the view of
many classical theologians, including Thomas Aquinas, the exercise of human reason is a participation in and reflection of the divine *logos* or reason by
which the world was created.[2] This high valuation of human reason has an element of truth in it, but it has fostered an intellectualization of Christian anthropology. If the essence of being human is seen primarily in the process of
abstract reasoning by which the physical dimension of life is transcended, a
corresponding depreciation of the emotional and physical dimensions of human existence results.

A related but different interpretation focuses on the reference of the
Genesis text to humanity's being given *dominion over the earth.* Humanity re-
sembles God in its exercise of power and dominion over the other creatures.
This interpretation of the image of God is often associated with a worldview
in which all relationships are construed in hierarchical patterns: God rules
over the world, the soul controls the body, men are the masters of women,
and humanity dominates the other creatures. As we saw in our discussion of
the doctrine of creation, this interpretation of the image of God in the modern era has often been used to legitimize the reckless exploitation of nature.
Patriarchy, racism, and colonialism are other forms of this spirit of mastery
over others. Against these views, I have contended that, rightly understood,

1. Calvin, *Institutes of the Christian Religion,* 1.15.3.
2. Thomas Aquinas, *Summa Theologica,* Pt. 1, q. 93, a. 4.

the dominion entrusted to humanity, like God's own exercise of dominion, involves respect, protection, and care for others rather than mastery and manipulation.

Still other interpreters have emphasized *human freedom* as the meaning of the image of God. Many modern philosophers and theologians have described the human being as essentially free, self-determining, and self-transcending.[3] Humans are both self-creators and creators of a world of culture that they superimpose upon the order of nature. In this free creative activity humans reflect the free creativity of God and thus become the image of God in the world. There is surely much to be said for this interpretation. But its serious limitations become evident in the frequency with which modern culture identifies the idea of freedom with the "disengaged subject," with mere independence from others, or even with sheer self-gratification.[4]

In agreement with numerous contemporary theologians, I would contend that the symbol "image of God" describes *human life in relationship* with God and with the other creatures. In the first story of creation in Genesis, the statement "God created humankind in his own image" is followed by "male and female he created them" (Gen. 1:27). To be human is to live freely and gladly in relationships of mutual respect and love. The existence of human creatures in relationship — the paradigmatic form of which is the coexistence of male and female — reflects the life of God who eternally lives not in solitary existence but in communion. Thus the image of God is not to be construed primarily as a set of human faculties, possessions, or endowments. It expresses self-transcending life in relationship with others — with the "wholly other" we call God, and with all those different "others" who need our help and whose help we also need in order to be the human creatures God intends us to be.[5]

The image of God is not like an image permanently stamped on a coin; it is more like an image reflected in a mirror. That is, human beings are created for life in relationships that mirror or correspond to God's own life in relationship. In light of the history of Jesus Christ, Christian faith and theology are led to interpret the *imago Dei* as an *imago Christi* and an *imago trinitatis*. Just as the incarnate Lord lived in utmost solidarity with and for sinners and the poor, and just as the eternal life of God is in communion, a triune "society

3. See Reinhold Niebuhr, *The Nature and Destiny of Man* (New York: Charles Scribner's Sons, 1955).

4. See Charles Taylor, *Sources of the Self: The Making of the Modern Identity* (Cambridge: Harvard University Press, 1989).

5. See Douglas John Hall, *Imaging God: Dominion as Stewardship* (Grand Rapids: Eerdmans, 1986).

of love" that is open to the world, so humanity in its coexistence with others is intended to be a creaturely reflection of the living, triune God made known to us in Jesus Christ and at work among us by the Holy Spirit.[6]

From the last few statements, it should be clear that the understanding of the image of God in Christian theology cannot be restricted to an exegesis of the first chapter of Genesis. The witness of this biblical text acquires new depths of meaning in the light of the gospel story. For Christian faith, Jesus Christ is the fullest expression of what God intends humanity to be. *This* human being is the "image of God" (2 Cor. 4:4; Col. 1:15) and our human destiny in him is to be conformed to the image of God. Hence the form of human life that we meet in Jesus the Christ will surely be the decisive factor in any Christian statement of what it means to be genuinely human.[7] That is not to say, of course, that a Christian understanding of human life can disregard other experiences and understandings of human existence. A theological anthropology cannot ignore the findings of cultural anthropology, psychology, sociology, and other disciplines. I mean simply that for Christian faith and theology, the life, death, and resurrection of Jesus will constitute the decisive norm of both true divinity *and* true humanity.

Created Humanity

I shall now attempt to describe the essential dimensions of human being in relationship with God and others under the headings of created humanity, fallen humanity, and new humanity in Christ.[8] In each case, I am viewing the phenomena of human life from the perspective of Christian faith. I begin with three theses regarding human life created by the triune God.

1. *Human beings, created in God's image, are freely addressed by God and free to respond to God.* Although modern anthropologies, both philosophical and scientific, have cut themselves loose from traditional Christian doctrine, they have nevertheless had to wrestle with the question of the distinctiveness of humanity. Understandings of human life have often oscillated between

6. See Stanley J. Grenz, *The Social God and the Relational Self: A Trinitarian Theology of the Imago Dei* (Louisville: Westminster/John Knox, 2001).

7. "In a sense the whole contribution of Christianity to a comprehension of the human consists of a single datum: Jesus Christ." Jose Comblin, *Retrieving the Human: A Christian Anthropology* (Maryknoll, N.Y.: Orbis Books, 1990), 223. For Karl Barth's attempt to develop a rigorously Christocentric anthropology, see *Church Dogmatics*, 3/2.

8. Cf. Peter C. Hodgson, *New Birth of Freedom: A Theology of Bondage and Liberation* (Philadelphia: Fortress, 1976).

angelism on the one hand and naturalism on the other. By *angelism* I mean the tendency to view human beings as disembodied minds, and by *naturalism* I mean the tendency to consider human beings as creatures whose behavior is entirely predictable and requires no reference to such intangibles as free will, the soul, or relationship to God.

In the modern era, philosophical and cultural anthropologists have sought to identify and describe the uniqueness of being human without falling into either angelism or naturalism. Thus they have spoken of the "self-transcendence" of humanity or its "world-openness" or its peculiar linguistic, cultural, and religious capacities and activities. To a far greater extent than other animals, human beings exist "exocentrically," that is, they are drawn outside themselves by the objects of their experience and especially by their relations with other human beings. According to Wolfhart Pannenberg, "the concept of human self-transcendence — like the concept of openness to the world which is to a great extent its equivalent — summarizes a broad consensus among contemporary anthropologists in their effort to define the special character of the human."[9]

The self-transcending freedom or openness to the world that is characteristic of human beings is of course finite and conditioned, not absolute. Human existence is embodied existence. We are psycho-physical unities, not disembodied spirits. We do not simply *have* bodies; we also *are* our bodies. We express ourselves and communicate with others through our embodied actions. Human flourishing cannot be separated from the satisfaction of bodily needs.

Moreover, human life is socially and historically embedded. We belong to particular societies, cultures, and historical epochs, and these help to define our human identity. What is most important to recognize, however, is that our particular embodiment and our historical embeddedness are not mere negative boundaries of human life; they are the condition of our finite but real freedom. No doubt genetics, history, and culture shape us in very definite ways: we did not choose to be born male or female, black or white, Russian or American. Nevertheless, we can choose to make something of these contingencies by turning them into occasions for the enrichment of life. While never absolute or unlimited, human freedom does involve the possibility of reshaping and redirecting the given of our experience.

From a Christian perspective, what I have been describing are symptoms or signs of human life as created by God. Our embodied existence is no

---

9. Wolfhart Pannenberg, *Anthropology in Theological Perspective* (Philadelphia: Westminster, 1985), 63.

obstacle to fellowship with God. On the contrary, in its affirmation of the goodness of embodied life as created by God, in its teaching that the Word became flesh in Jesus Christ, and in its hope in the resurrection of the body, Christian faith shows itself to be "the most avowedly materialist of all the great religions."[10]

According to Christian faith, our "exocentricity" and our finite but real freedom arise from the fact that, as embodied, historically conditioned beings, we are created for fellowship with God. The God who lives in relationship calls us to life in relationship. We are human as we are addressed by God. Our creator freely gives us life, calls us, covenants with us, and wants our response. God addresses human beings in their psychophysical totality and in their particular historical situations. God wants the free response of the whole person.

While the entire biblical witness portrays human beings as creatures to whom God speaks and from whom a response is awaited, this dialogical nature of human life in relation to God is made most explicit in the gospel narrative. Jesus is fully responsive to the will of God and the needs of others. His whole being and ministry are defined by total trust in and free obedience to the one he calls Abba and to the Spirit who commissions and empowers him for ministry. In the light of the humanity of Jesus, it becomes clear that being truly human means living in faithful response to the grace of God. God calls human beings out of isolation and into life in relationship. What God wants from human beings is not a mere echo or a mechanical reflex but a free and glad response. Human beings become free agents and historical subjects through being addressed by the living God who calls them to life in partnership and service. To be human is to respond in free obedience to God's gracious address.

2. *Being created in the image of God means that humans find their true identity in coexistence with each other and with all other creatures.* Once again, the findings of modern philosophy, anthropology, and psychology can offer help to theological anthropology. They emphasize that human existence is communal, not individualistic. We become and stay human in the tension between personal identity and communal participation. We exercise our freedom not in complete isolation but in continuous interaction with others.

Human life depends upon ecological systems and structures of interrelationship. Stated briefly, we live in dialogue.[11] Long before we are conscious

---

10. William Temple, *Nature, Man and God* (London: Macmillan, 1956), 478. See also chap. 2 of Comblin, *Retrieving the Human.*

11. The classic modern statement of dialogical personalism is Martin Buber, *I and Thou* (Edinburgh: T&T Clark, 1958).

of that fact, we exist in response to and interaction with others. We have to learn to trust others even before we take a single step on our own. What is true for individual development is also true for life in the political order. When Aristotle defined human beings as "political" animals, he meant that human beings must live and develop their capacities in the intricate relationships and interdependencies of the *polis,* or city. Being truly human and living in community are inseparable. This wisdom is beautifully captured in an African proverb: "I am human only because you are human."[12]

When we read with care the biblical accounts of creation, we are struck by the importance of interrelatedness in the depiction of the creation as a whole and of human beings in particular. In the first creation story (Gen. 1), humanity is part of a cosmic order established by God; in the second creation story (Gen. 2), humanity is created out of earth and placed in a garden inhabited by many other creatures.

Most strikingly, according to the biblical witness, human beings are created in the image of God not as solitary beings but in the duality of male and female (Gen. 1:27). As created by God, we are essentially relational, social beings, and this essential sociality and co-humanity is signified by our coexistence as men and women. We are created for life in community with others, to exist in relationships of mutual fidelity and mutual freedom in fellowship. This is the theological context of a Christian understanding of human sexuality. Human sexuality signifies and is appropriately expressed in mutually committed, reciprocally joyful, and lasting relationship with another.[13]

No theologian of the twentieth century has been more influential in the development of a theology of human relationality than Karl Barth. For Barth human existence is coexistence, and this fact is paradigmatically embodied in the coexistence of man and woman. Barth contends that if we ignore this particular expression of our co-humanity, if we obscure the significance of our existence in the mutual and reciprocal relationship of man and woman, we are likely to be tempted in every sphere of life by an inhuman vision of *homo solitarius.*

Barth makes three fundamental assertions in his elaboration of this theme: that human beings are *either* male *or* female and are called by God to affirm their particular sexual identity; that human beings are male *and* female and are called to find their human identity in mutual coordination with their sexual counterparts who are both similar and yet also irreducibly differ-

---

12. Allan Boesak, *Black and Reformed* (Maryknoll, N.Y.: Orbis Books, 1984), 51.

13. Barth uses the memorable phrase "Coitus without co-existence is demonic" (*Church Dogmatics,* 3/4: 133).

ent; and that human beings as male and female coexist in a definite and irreversible *order*.[14]

Each of Barth's assertions prompts questions. One might agree wholeheartedly with the contention that every human being should rejoice in his or her sexuality rather than deny or be ashamed of it, yet insist that Barth's first assertion must be immediately qualified — and more consistently than Barth himself does — by warnings against all stereotypical descriptions of the differences between male and female. Portrayals of men as intellectual and women as emotional, of men as objective and women as subjective, or as popular culture puts it, of men as being "from Mars" and women "from Venus," are sheer mythology and have no place in a serious theological anthropology.

Barth's second assertion must also be carefully qualified to avoid the implication that unmarried persons are any less called to a life in relationship with others than are those who marry, or that abiding friendships and committed partnerships of persons of the same sex may not also reflect in their own way the divine intention that human life is to be lived with and for others. As Paul Lehmann has contended, while Scripture unquestionably sees the relationship of man and woman as the *paradigmatic* and foundational instance of life in reciprocal love and fidelity, of commitment to life together with full respect for otherness and difference, this is not to be understood as a *limiting* or exclusive instance. A reading of Scripture governed by the centrality of God's steadfast covenantal love and the call to new life in community with God and others will not be constrictive in scope but open to a multiplicity of signs or parables of life in depth of fellowship made possible by God's grace.[15]

But the most problematic of Barth's assertions is the third, which posits an irreversible order in the relationship between man and woman. Barth acknowledges that every word used to describe this order is "dangerous" because of the possibility of stereotype and ideology.[16] Nevertheless, he speaks of the man in this relationship as "A," as "leader," as "superordinate," as "above," and the woman as "B," as "follower," as "subordinate," as "below." Despite the many qualifications he makes, Barth's depiction of this irreversible order of the relationship of man and woman has been widely and rightly rejected.[17] It is not only unacceptable to contemporary sensibilities but profoundly incompatible

14. Barth, *Church Dogmatics*, 3/4: 149-81.

15. See Paul L. Lehmann, *The Decalogue and a Human Future: The Meaning of the Commandments for Making and Keeping Human Life Human* (Grand Rapids: Eerdmans, 1995), 174.

16. Barth, *Church Dogmatics*, 3/4: 169.

17. See Paul Jewett, *Man as Male and Female* (Grand Rapids: Eerdmans, 1975); Jürgen Moltmann, *God in Creation* (San Francisco: Harper & Row, 1985); Rosemary Radford Ruether, *Sexism and God-Talk: Toward a Feminist Theology* (Boston: Beacon Press, 1983).

with Barth's own basic methodological principle of rethinking all Christian doctrine in the light of Jesus Christ and the new community of mutual love and mutual service that has its basis in him.

Contrary to Barth, it should be noted that in the first creation story there is no mention of hierarchy, of superiority or inferiority, or an above and a below, of a first or a second in the relationship between man and woman. We are simply told that male and female together constitute the image of God. The implication is that human beings are to live in "partnership," as Letty Russell puts it, speaking, listening, living, and working with each other.[18] The appropriate order of the relationship of man and woman in the light of the God of the gospel is not rigid hierarchy but mutual love and mutual service (Gal. 3:28; Eph. 5:21). To employ a trinitarian analogy, the relationship of man and woman is "perichoretic," a life of mutual indwelling and reciprocal love.[19] Neither in the perichoretic unity of the persons of the Trinity nor in the relationship of man and woman is there any place for a non-reciprocal "above" and "below," or a fixed and one-sided "superordination" and "subordination."

The Old Testament teaching that life in community is the clue to our human identity is confirmed and deepened by the gospel narrative. Jesus is depicted as the human-being-for-others, as someone who lives in the utmost solidarity with other men and women, especially with those who are defined by social and religious conventions as being outside community with God and God's chosen people. So to exist, says Christian faith, is to be the image of God whose being is in communion. As the eternal triune love makes room for others, so human beings in the image of God are called to discover true personhood in relationship with others.

3. *Being created in the image of God is not a state or condition but a movement with a goal: human beings are restless for a fulfillment of life not yet realized.* Human life is dynamic. It is propelled forward. Men and women are seeking, inquiring, expectant beings. In a familiar prayer, Augustine speaks of human life as in ceaseless movement: "You have made us *toward* yourself, and our hearts are restless until they rest in you."[20] This restlessness of the heart, the always unsatisfied drive in the human creature toward an ever-elusive goal, can be described phenomenologically, in the language of Wolfhart Pannenberg, as "world openness" or "openness to the future."

Whereas animals other than humans have drives or instincts that are

18. Russell, *The Future of Partnership* (Philadelphia: Westminster, 1979).
19. Cf. Alexander McKelway, "Perichoretic Possibilities in Barth's Doctrine of Male and Female," *Princeton Seminary Bulletin* 7 (1986): 231-43.
20. Augustine, *Confessions*, 1.1.1.

triggered by definite needs or particular objects, in the case of human beings there is a restlessness that is virtually boundless. Humans have a surplus of drives. They search not only for physical and emotional satisfaction but for a meaning in life that is very difficult to define or pin down. Human restlessness finds no goal in this world that is satisfying for very long. Moreover, the nonhuman animals are rather strictly confined to their environment; by contrast, human beings more readily transcend given environments, both natural and cultural. They create worlds of meaning that they continually transform, yet without ever finding full satisfaction. Humanity is created with a radical openness to the future, to the not-yet, to a fullness of life beyond every personal, social, or cultural achievement.[21] Humans are radically temporal beings, never content merely to preserve the past or to endorse the present without reservation. Being human means being open to a future that we cannot definitively envisage and certainly cannot fully actualize. There is at work in all creation, but especially in human life, a "call forward" to new freedom.[22]

This dynamism of human life is a symptom of what theology speaks of as human freedom for the coming reign of God. There are only hints of this dynamism of creaturely freedom in the Genesis creation narratives. Barth suggests that the tree of life in the Garden of Eden mentioned in the second creation narrative (Gen. 2:9; cf. Rev. 2:7) is to be understood as a kind of sacrament of the gracious promise of God.[23] Human life is oriented to and kept open by God's promise of abundant and abiding life that cannot be seized and possessed but can only be received as a gift again and again. In addition, according to the first creation narrative, God gives humans a commission or vocation that will shape their future. That vocation is to have dominion over the earth (Gen. 1:26, 28), a phrase which, I have contended, is rightly interpreted as a charge to guardianship and responsible stewardship. To be a steward is to be a partner with God in caring for the world God has created.

The witness of the prophets expands the Genesis narratives by describing human life in relation to the future as a choice — either to obey the commands of God that require justice, mercy, and humility, or to court judgment and destruction. According to the messianic tradition of the Old Testament, human life is to be lived in ceaseless expectation of the time when God will make all things new. The gospel of Jesus Christ further deepens this understanding of human life as oriented to the promises of God. By proclaiming

21. See Wolfhart Pannenberg, *What Is Man? Contemporary Anthropology in Theological Perspective* (Philadelphia: Fortress, 1970).

22. See John B. Cobb, Jr., *God and the World* (Philadelphia: Westminster, 1969), 42-66.

23. See *Church Dogmatics*, 3/1: 281-84.

the coming of God's reign, by prophetic acts that boldly inaugurate its arrival, and above all by his crucifixion and resurrection, Jesus definitively reveals that human life is not complete in itself but is oriented to God's future and the promise of fulfilled and abundant life. Human beings have a destiny; they are created and redeemed to glorify and enjoy God forever.[24]

The dimensions of created freedom that I have outlined — relationship to and responsibility before God, life in relationship with others, and openness to God's promise — are tightly bound to each other. Our created freedom is awakened by God's address to us, expanded by our coexistence with others very different from us, and directed toward a future fulfillment in the coming reign of God.

As is readily apparent, my interpretation of the "image of God" as human life in relationship is funded by a Christocentric and trinitarian understanding of God. If Jesus Christ in his unconditioned being-for-God and being-for-others is "the image of God," revealing who God is and what is our true identity as God's creatures, then an understanding of the life of God as life in communion calls for an understanding of human life as deeply relational in nature. To say that God is triune is to say also that human life is fulfilled only in relationship with God and others. As Stanley Grenz argues, "the retrieval of the doctrine of the Trinity has paved the way for a fully theological anthropology."[25] The triune God is not a solitary monad but lives in communion. God's triune life is the source and power of all life in relationship. Created in the image of God, we are called to be persons in communion with God and others.[26] We are called to participate in, and in some small way reflect, God's own life of relationship and communion.

Fallen Humanity

If Christian doctrine were to say of human beings only that they are created in the image of God, it would become sheer idealism. A Christian anthropology is, however, starkly realistic. As Reinhold Niebuhr puts it, "The Christian

---

24. When allowances are made for its time-bound language, the answer to the first question of the Westminster Shorter Catechism remains valid: "Man's chief end is to glorify God and to enjoy him forever." *The Book of Confessions* (PCUSA), 7.001.

25. Stanley J. Grenz, *The Social God and the Relational Self,* 16. "Christian theological anthropology is trinitarian theological anthropology" (23).

26. See Colin E. Gunton, "Trinity, Ontology and Anthropology: Towards a Renewal of the Doctrine of the *Imago Dei,*" in Christoph Schwöbel and Colin E. Gunton, eds., *Persons: Divine and Human* (Edinburgh: T&T Clark, 1991), 47-61.

view of human nature is involved in the paradox of claiming a higher stature for [human beings] and of taking a more serious view of [their] evil than any other anthropology."[27] While affirming the good possibilities of human existence as created by God, theological anthropology takes with utter seriousness the profound disruption, disorder, alienation, brutality, and oppression that characterize the actual human condition.[28] This condition is described in the assertion that we are "fallen," sinful creatures. Our alienation not only from God but also from our fellow creatures and ourselves is vividly portrayed in the Yahwist account of creation and fall (Gen. 2–3). Driven to disobedience by their desire to be gods or "like God," Adam and Eve are expelled from the Garden of Eden. This rupture of relationship with God is reflected in the poisoning of human relationships. The first human act outside the Garden is Cain's murder of Abel. The image of God in which humans were created is obscured and distorted by sin.

Our next task, then, is to describe in greater detail this condition of sin as a disruption of the created dimensions of human existence. If we are created for relationship with God who is wholly different from us and for relationship with other creatures who are relatively different from us, sin is a denial of our essential relatedness to those who are genuinely "other." We deny our dependence on the Other who is God and reject our need for our fellow creatures, most particularly those who seem so totally strange and "other" to us — the victim, the poor, the "leftover person."[29] Seen in this perspective, sin is "the depth of human intolerance for difference,"[30] intolerance for difference among creatures and, most basically, intolerance for difference between creatures and God. As in the case of the discussion of humanity as created, so in the description of fallen humanity, the embodiment of the image of God in Jesus Christ is our primary norm.

1. If being human in the image of God means life in free response to God who freely and graciously addresses us, then sin can be described as the denial of our relatedness to God and our need for God's grace. From this van-

---

27. Niebuhr, *The Nature and Destiny of Man*, 18.

28. For notable recent examinations of the doctrine of sin, see Cornelius Plantinga, Jr., *Not the Way It's Supposed to Be: A Breviary of Sin* (Grand Rapids: Eerdmans, 1995); Ted Peters, *Radical Evil in Soul and Society* (Grand Rapids: Eerdmans, 1994); Alistair McFadyen, *Bound to Sin: Abuse, Holocaust, and the Christian Doctrine of Sin* (New York: Cambridge University Press, 2000); Serene Jones, *Feminist Theory and Christian Theology: Cartographies of Grace* (Minneapolis: Fortress, 2000).

29. See Comblin, *Retrieving the Human*, 55.

30. Susan Thistlethwaite, *Sex, Race, and God: Christian Feminism in Black and White* (New York: Crossroad, 1989), 59.

tage point, sin is fundamentally *opposition to grace*. It is saying No to the invitation to receive God's gift of life with our praise and thanksgiving, saying No to a life of glad service to God, No to a life of friendship with our fellow creatures. Sin is the great refusal to live thankfully and gladly by the grace of God that makes personal life in community with diverse others possible. Sin is "grace denied."[31]

Thus we misunderstand the depth of sin if we see it merely as a violation of a moral code, a deviation from conventional behavior, doing something commonly considered "bad." Instead, sin is primarily the disruption of our relationship with God. As the psalmist writes, "Against you, you alone, have I sinned" (Ps. 51:4). This disruption of our relationship with God that is the essence of sin appears in many different forms. Two warrant special mention. Sin may take the form of rejecting God's grace and absolutizing ourselves. Declaring our freedom to be infinite, we proclaim ourselves God. This is the sin of the prideful, titanic, egocentric self. Often referred to simply as the sin of pride, it amounts to *active, self-centered idolatry*. It is the refusal to recognize the limits of the self and its dependence on God for life and the flourishing of life. Finitude and limitation are not evil in themselves, but they are often the occasion of anxiety and insecurity. Instead of living by a grace whose source is beyond ourselves, in our insecurity we seek to be our own God.

But the disruption of our relationship with God may take a very different form. Rejecting God's grace, we may despise ourselves and allow other creatures to take the place of God in our lives. This is the sin of self-rejection and self-hatred, and it easily leads to *passive, other-centered idolatry*. Sin as pride gets more than its share of attention in sermons and theological textbooks, but sin as self-hatred, self-negation, and self-loss is often ignored. Yet while less sensational, this form of sin is no less a turning from the gracious God who calls us to freedom, maturity, and responsibility in community. In our acquiescence to self-denigration we deliver ourselves over to shabby little idols and thus make of ourselves pitiful caricatures of what God intends for human life.

In recent years, feminist and other liberation theologians have rightly exposed the gross one-sidedness of traditional theology in its preoccupation with sin as pride.[32] They have insisted that, as human denial of grace, sin is

---

31. See Jones, *Feminist Theory and Christian Theology*, chapter 5.

32. Judith Plaskow, *Sex, Sin and Grace: Women's Experience and the Theologies of Reinhold Niebuhr and Paul Tillich* (Lanham, Md.: University Press of America, 1980). See Alistair McFadyen's helpful commentary on feminist theologies of sin in *Bound to Sin*, 131-66.

not only insurrectionary and sensational but is also banal, mediocre, and totally uninventive. An adequate doctrine of sin will recognize that sin against
the grace of God is not only titanic, Luciferian rebellion but also the timid,
obsequious refusal to dare to be fully human by God's grace. Judas's act of be-
trayal is sin in its aggressive form; the fear, denial, and flight of the other disciples in the hour of Jesus' trial is sin in its passive form.

2. If being human in the image of God means responding to God's call
to accept our freedom as a gift and to live freely with and for others, then sin
in dealings with fellow creatures takes the dual form of *domination* and *servility,* self-exaltation and self-destruction. As in the description of sin in relation
to God, so in the interpretation of sin in the relationship of human beings to
each other, we must note the duality of forms. The description of sin as domination and mastery over others is familiar to many people. They may quickly
identify as sinful the technocratic spirit that uses people and the world of nature merely to serve its own ends, the spirit of racial or national superiority
that is prepared to go to any lengths to get rid of the obnoxious presence of
those considered inferior or dangerous, the spirit of boundless will to power
that culminates in holocausts, genocidal war, and the destruction of entire
species of creatures.

Yet sin in relation to others manifests itself not only in this will to power
but also in the less obvious slide into powerlessness, into unquestioning passivity, self-dissipation, diffuseness, triviality, lethargy, and fear of initiative.
"Sin," writes Rosemary Radford Ruether, "has to be seen both in the capacity
to set up prideful, antagonistic relations to others and in the passivity of men
and women who acquiesce to the group ego."[33] We must be very careful here
not to engage in the practice of "blaming the victim." The point is not, for example, to heap guilt upon battered women who feel helpless and hopeless in
an abusive relationship, or to say that the poor are poor because they are lazy,
as we hear so often from right-wing politicians. The point is that distorted interpretations of sin not only overlook the apathy and inaction of the affluent
in the face of injustice; they also help to lock victims into their victimization
by undermining their will to break free.

Feminist psychiatrists and theologians have rightly objected to traditional doctrines of sin that focus exclusively on the experience of "making it,"
rising to positions of power, or being assertive and aggressive. Such a description of sin is often curiously off-target for many women in all cultures but
most especially for the desperately poor and exploited peoples, women and
men, of the Third World. The proper theological response to this distortion

---

33. Ruether, *Sexism and God-Talk,* 164.

in the tradition is not the simplistic device of distributing the two forms of sin — domination and servility, self-exaltation and self-abnegation — to the male and female populations respectively. That would be a new kind of ideology that would cover up rather than expose the insidious workings of sin in concrete human experience. What is essential to see is that sin has many faces, that it is, as Mary Potter Engel observes, a kind of hydra, a monster that grows two new heads for every one that is severed.[34]

As recent studies show, gender difference is not the only factor that needs to be taken into account in thinking about the many faces of sin. Race and class are also important factors. Thus what sin means in relation to the "survival" issues of most African American women is different from what it means in relation to the "fulfillment" issues of white middle-class women.[35]

Attention to differences of race, gender, and class deepens our understandings of sin and reminds us of its multifarious expressions. If many men in patriarchal societies need to repent of the sin of overbearing self-assertiveness, many women and poor people of every race and gender need to be liberated from paralyzing self-blame and destructive dependencies and encouraged to speak and act as persons created in the image of God. Mere passivity is the breeding ground of totalitarianism and inhumanity no less than outrageous pride. Both men and women of all races and classes are to some extent vulnerable to both forms of sin. Neither the inordinate love of self nor the secret hatred of self is the exclusive property of any sex, race, or class of people. Still, given the one-sided emphases of traditional theologies of sin, the major effort in any rethinking of the doctrine of sin today must be to dismantle those interpretations that serve as a religious ideology inculcating passivity in the face of injustice. The human freedom and maturity intended by God are destroyed both where one lords it over another and where one fails to resist being lorded over.

3. If being human in the image of God means being open to the coming of God's reign, then sin is *the denial of human destiny as appointed by God*. Once again, to grasp rightly the assault on human openness to God's future, we must attend to two contrary forms in which it may appear, analogous to pride and sloth, and domination and servility.

There is, on the one hand, the sin of indifference, apathy, and *resigna-*

34. Engel, "Evil, Sin, and Violation of the Vulnerable," in *Lift Every Voice: Constructing Christian Theologies from the Underside,* ed. Susan Brooks Thistlethwaite and Mary Potter Engel (San Francisco: Harper & Row, 1990), 163.

35. See Jacquelyn Grant, *White Women's Christ and Black Women's Jesus: Feminist Christology and Womanist Response* (Atlanta: Scholars Press, 1989), 195-201; Thistlethwaite, *Sex, Race, and God,* 77-91.

tion. The kind of resignation I have in mind is an unqualified acquiescence to the hellish forces of human history. It is total doubt and cynicism about the possibility of anything really changing, or rather of any real change for the better. What's the use of talking, let alone trying to do something about the injustice, war, and oppression that we or others may be experiencing, or that our community or society may be at least partially responsible for imposing on others? Don't we simply have to get used to the fact that life is messy and unfair, that war and poverty are perennial and inevitable realities in the world? And so we become resigned to fate. Tomorrow, we say, will be the same as today. As a result of this spirit of resignation, the little opportunities for greater justice, the small steps in the direction of peace and reconciliation, are mostly ignored or cynically dismissed. This attitude is false testimony because it denies our destiny as created in God's image and as heirs of God's promise in Jesus Christ.[36]

But on the other hand, no less a contradiction of our human openness to God's future is the sin of *presumption,* the violent effort to bring in God's kingdom with or without God. In this spirit of presumption and violence, there is limitless confidence in ourselves and our goodness, and a secret or open despair about the effectiveness of the gracious God who works through suffering love and whose power appears so weak and unpromising in comparison with guns and tanks. We will rid the world of evil, and by whatever means necessary to accomplish the task.

Christians today, no less than people of other faiths, are caught between pervasive apathy and acts of violence, apathy borne of hopelessness about the enormity of the evils that confront us and recourse to violence and coercion that seriously compromises or even destroys the goals of a better future. Either way, we can close off the future to which we are directed by God our creator and redeemer.

The Meaning of Original Sin and of Death as Enemy

The vexing question of the *origin of sin* has been a preoccupation of much traditional theological anthropology. Several of the proposed answers to this question are clearly in contradiction to the primary biblical emphasis on sin as rooted in the misuse or corruption of human freedom. The origin of sin is not to be traced back to bodily existence or human sexuality or some other

36. Cf. Karl Barth's description of the three primary forms of human sin: pride, sloth, and falsehood (*Church Dogmatics,* 4/1-3).

natural condition of life, as has been the tendency in some strands of Christian theology. Nor is the origin of sin to be found in ignorance or lack of education, as much Protestant liberal theology of the nineteenth century believed. Nor is the origin of sin to be located in a simplistic fashion in unjust social conditions, as is assumed by many social reform movements. Conditions of injustice are more properly seen as corporate expressions of human sinfulness rather than as its ultimate cause.

The biblical stories of the Garden of Eden and the fall of humanity (Gen. 2–3) are imaginative portrayals of the goodness of creation and the universality of sin rather than historical accounts of sin's origin. In the theological tradition there has been much fantasizing about the splendor of human existence in the golden age before the fall, but such thinking is not encouraged by the biblical witness. The Bible is far more interested in affirming the reality of sin, the need for repentance, and the divine promise of redemption than in longing for the recovery of a lost paradise. As Paul's discussion of Adam and Christ in Romans 5:12ff. shows, the Bible is eschatologically rather than protologically oriented in its thinking about sin and redemption.

The doctrine of "original sin," then, is not a theory of the origin of sin but the claim that the whole of humanity finds itself in a condition or state of captivity to sin. The theological tradition distinguishes between actual sins (particular transgressions of God's will) and original sin (the radical and universal sinful human condition). Original sin is radical (affecting every aspect of human life) and universal (affecting all human beings). Humanity under the condition of sin finds itself caught in a web of despoilment, corruption, pollution, and disintegration. These are hard words for those schooled in the tradition of the Enlightenment — perhaps especially for Americans. Commenting on the perilous sense of innocence that often afflicts American politics, Garry Wills offers this description of original sin: "We are hostages to each other in a deadly interrelatedness. There is no 'clean slate' of nature unscribbled on by all one's forebears."[37]

In the wake of the catastrophic evils of the twentieth century, all optimistic understandings of the origins and remedies of sin have been exposed as superficial. As much twentieth-century theological anthropology has emphasized — especially the still-powerful writings of Reinhold Niebuhr[38] — the doctrine of original or radical sin expresses a deep truth about the human condition even if it cannot be adequately stated without recourse to

---

37. Garry Wills, *Reagan's America: Innocents at Home* (Garden City, N.Y.: Doubleday, 1987), 384, quoted by Cornelius Plantinga, Jr., *Not the Way It's Supposed to Be*, 198.
38. See especially Niebuhr's *The Nature and Destiny of Man*.

paradoxical statements. Among the most important of these paradoxes are the following:

a. Sin is a *universal condition,* but it is also a *self-chosen act* for which we are responsible. Augustine speaks of an inherited sinfulness, Luther of the "bondage of the will," Calvin of the "vitiated and corrupted will," Edwards of the universal "evil disposition" of humanity.[39] Some of their arguments and metaphors may have overreached. Yet none of these theologians intended to deny human responsibility or the fact that sin is self-chosen. There is a tensive relationship here between universality and personal responsibility, and especially in the heat of argument it can be lost. When this happens, sin is reduced to fate and is no longer something for which all human beings are accountable. Niebuhr expressed the paradox in his oft-quoted epigram: "Sin is inevitable but not necessary."[40]

b. Sin insinuates itself into all human action, including not only what is widely condemned as *evil* but also what is commonly praised as *good.* This is not to say that distinctions between good and evil are unimportant; instead, it is to emphasize that sin may be most seductively and demonically at work under the guise of doing good. Again it is Reinhold Niebuhr more than any other modern theologian who has emphasized this point. A character in one of Elie Wiesel's novels comments on the entanglement of sin and innocence in human life: "Deep down . . . man is not only executioner, not only victim, not only spectator; he is all three at once."[41]

c. Sin is a corruption of the *individual* person, but it is also active and powerful in public and *corporate* structures of life. In modern society there is an increasing tendency to privatize sin and to restrict it to the behavior of individuals. Against this tendency stands the biblical witness with its emphasis on an encompassing reign of evil and the solidarity of all humanity in the old "Adam" of sin and alienation. Niebuhr exposes the tendency to privatize sin in modern society in his book *Moral Man and Immoral Society.*[42]

While these paradoxes do not provide a rational explanation of the origin of sin, they more adequately characterize the reality of sin than do theo-

39. Augustine, *On Original Sin;* Luther, *The Bondage of the Will;* Calvin, *Institutes,* 2.2; Edwards, *Original Sin.*

40. Niebuhr, *The Nature and Destiny of Man,* 263. Also Jones: "While we are not inherently sinful, no privileged area in our lives escapes it" (*Feminist Theory and Christian Theology,* 117).

41. Elie Wiesel, *The Town Beyond the Wall,* 174, quoted by Marilyn McCord Adams, *Horrendous Evils and the Goodness of God* (Ithaca: Cornell University Press, 1999), 200.

42. *Moral Man and Immoral Society: A Study in Ethics and Politics* (New York: Charles Scribner's Sons, 1932).

ries that attempt such an explanation. Sin is basically the refusal to live in right relationship with God and others, the denial of God's grace and the refusal to live in just and peaceful community that participates in and reflects God's own life in communion.

No less difficult than the question of the origin of sin is the question of the relationship between *sin and death*.[43] Following Paul's statement that "the wages of sin is death" (Rom. 6:23), the dominant view in Christian theology has been that Adam and Eve were created immortal and that death entered the world as a punishment for human sin. According to this view, death is strictly the "last enemy" to be destroyed finally by God (1 Cor. 15:26).

In the modern period this view has been challenged for several reasons. The first is the indisputable fact that mortality marked all life on earth long before the appearance of human beings. The second is the fact that human finitude implies limitation in time. Hence to speak of immortality as intrinsic to our created humanity obscures human finitude and threatens to blur the distinction between creator and creature. Christians indeed hope for everlasting life beyond death but this is a hope based not on what belongs inherently to human nature but solely on God's free grace and faithfulness. The third reason for challenging the adequacy of the traditional view is the fact that in a significant number of scriptural passages human mortality is not seen as inherently evil. In the Old Testament, longevity of life is considered a blessing, and it is possible to die "old and full of years" (Gen. 25:8; Job 42:17). A final reason for questioning the traditional understanding of the relationship of sin and death is the prominence of the idea of "natural death" in contemporary discussions about end-of-life ethical issues.

While the traditional view of death as the "wages of sin" contains an important truth, it is a truth that needs to be set in the wider framework of the whole history of God's relationship with humanity. The simplest formulation of a more comprehensive understanding of death is that both life and death must be seen in relation to the one God who is creator, redeemer, and giver of new life. As I stated earlier, a Christian anthropology and a trinitarian understanding of God are closely related.[44]

To speak of death in relation to God the creator is to speak of it as the

43. For distinct and in some cases opposing positions, see Karl Barth, *Church Dogmatics*, 3/2: 587-640; Eberhard Jüngel, *Death, the Riddle and the Mystery* (Philadelphia: Westminster, 1975); Karl Rahner, *On the Theology of Death* (New York: Herder & Herder, 1961); Wolfhart Pannenberg, *Systematic Theology* (Grand Rapids: Eerdmans, 1991), 2: 265-75.

44. For a discussion of human mortality in a trinitarian perspective, see David H. Kelsey, "Two Theologies of Death: Anthropological Gleanings," in *Modern Theology* 13, no. 3 (July 1997): 347-70.

limit and boundary of our finite existence. God created us as the embodied, temporally limited beings that we are. We have a beginning and an end in time. Our finite existence in space and time is the condition of the possibility of human freedom and of moral and spiritual growth. We pray to God to teach us to number our days (Ps. 90:12) because the days we have for the acquisition of wisdom and for spending ourselves in the love and service of God and others are not unlimited. If our time were infinite, no particular time would ever be decisive, urgent, precious. Even if no one in fact experiences death only in this way — as the created limit of our finite earthly existence — this does not alter the reality of our being finite creatures whose end in time might be something very different from what we as sinners experience it to be.

What in fact we experience death to be is an enemy, violence, negation, and utter loss. It is in relation to this actual experience of death under the condition of sin that Scripture speaks of death as the "wages of sin," and celebrates the reconciling work of God through Christ who has gained victory over sin and death for us. Under the condition of sin, death is not experienced as "natural" but as the sign of divine judgment. It is experienced as something that separates us from God and from all that we love and value. What death might be as the "natural" end of life is deeply concealed from us.[45] As it actually meets us, death is indeed, as Paul calls it, "the last enemy" (1 Cor. 15:26). The death we actually die is inextricably coupled with guilt and sorrow. We fear death because it ruthlessly exposes our flawed, incomplete, self-centered life. In the face of death we know that we cannot justify ourselves, and death thus becomes the great sign of judgment.

We die a burdened death because of the willful denial of relationship with God and others that marks our life. The connection between death and sin becomes apparent if we understand death as the fall into utter relationlessness. As the loss of all relationship, death is the "wages," that is, the definitive sign and inexorable consequence of life lived egocentrically, lived in willed separation from others rather than in self-giving love and communion.[46] For this reason, those who speak of death as enemy and curse are far closer to the truth of our actual experience of death than are those who domesticate or beautify it by such names as natural, or even friend or brother.

But the good news is that God has not left us alone in our sinful estrangement from God, from others, and from the truth of our own created being. The gift of God in Jesus Christ is the forgiveness of sins, companion-

---

45. Barth, *Church Dogmatics*, 3/2: 598.
46. On death as relationlessness, see Jüngel, *Death, the Riddle and the Mystery.*

ship in suffering and death, and liberation for new life in self-giving love. Trusting in the grace of God, and on this basis alone, we may approach our death as a conquered enemy. The grace of God in Jesus Christ removes the "sting" of death (1 Cor. 15:56). Because of Christ, "Whether we live or whether we die, we are the Lord's" (Rom. 14:8). Barth can therefore speak of those who look to the grace of God in Jesus Christ in life and in death as being "liberated for natural death," by which he means not "natural death" in the secular sense of mere biological cessation, but death shorn of its "sting" and now seen as the point of transition from "one hand of God to the other."[47]

A Christian theology of death will not stop here. It must go on to speak not only of "liberation for natural death," but also of God's ultimate victory over all death. Death is not the last word either in regard to human finitude or to human sin.[48] Everlasting life is the final goal of our created and reconciled existence. Since death is not yet completely defeated either in our persons or in the wider groaning creation, Christian faith and theology await a new heaven and a new earth where death will be no more. A trinitarian theology understands death not only in relation to God as creator and reconciler, but also in relation to God as the renewing, life-giving Holy Spirit. In the New Testament, it is especially Paul who reminds Christian believers that the new life experienced now in Christ by the power of the Spirit is only a foretaste of life eternal. The resurrection of the body is not yet an accomplished fact. We hope for the life of the world to come. In solidarity with the whole groaning creation, we await the consummation of God's redemptive activity.

From the preceding comments it should be clear that in Christian perspective, death has more than one face. It is the "natural" limit of all creatures, although its being a "natural" part of our existence as created by God is deeply hidden from us. Death is certainly also the inescapable reminder of God's judgment on sin that has been freely borne by Christ for us all. Death is also the moment of reception into the gracious hands of God. Death wears not only one of these faces but all three, because our life and death occur in the presence of the one God who is creator, reconciler, and redeemer; the source of life, the judge and renewer of life, and the giver of life everlasting.

---

47. The phrase is that of the distinguished theologian Heiko Oberman in the face of his dying. I owe this reference to Gerhard Sauter, "Dying with Dignity" (unpublished paper, Center of Theological Inquiry, December 18, 2002).

48. On the distinction between finitude and mortality, see Wolfhart Pannenberg, *Systematic Theology*, 3: 560.

New Humanity in Christ

Christian freedom is the beginning of a new freedom *from* the bondage of sin and *for* partnership with God and others. This fresh start has its basis in the forgiving grace of God present in the new humanity of Jesus with whom we are united by the power of the Holy Spirit. He is the perfect realization of being human in undistorted relationship with God. He is also the human being for others, living in utmost solidarity with all people, and especially with sinners, strangers, the poor, the disadvantaged, and the oppressed. He is, furthermore, the great pioneer (Heb. 12:2) of a new humanity that lives in radical openness to God's promised reign of justice, freedom, and peace. In his total trust in God, Jesus acts as our great priest, mediating God's grace and forgiveness to us; in his startling solidarity with all people, and especially with the poor and outcast, Jesus acts as our king, bringing us into the new realm of justice and companionship with the "others" from whom we have long been alienated; and in his bold proclamation and enactment of God's in-breaking reign, Jesus is the prophet who leads the way toward the future of perfect freedom in communion with God and our fellow creatures for which all creation yearns. To be Christian is to participate by faith, love, and hope in the new humanity present in Jesus. In the following chapters on Christology and the Holy Spirit and the Christian life, I will develop these themes at much greater length. In the present context, my aim is to depict briefly the new humanity in Christ as it compares and contrasts with the analyses of created humanity and fallen humanity offered in the previous two sections.

1. If being in the image of God means living by the grace of God, and if such a relationship with God is denied by the sins of self-glorification and self-abnegation, *faith is the simple trust and confidence in the benevolence of God extended to us by Jesus Christ in the power of the Holy Spirit.*[49]

As a free act of entrusting oneself to God, faith is the end of all idolatry, whether the idolatry of self or the idolatry of others in place of self. It is the glad response to the first commandment to love God with all our heart and mind and soul. Faith is the opposite of the will to absolute power that wants to lord it over others, but it is no less opposed to the indifferent slide into powerlessness that is coupled with self-hatred and debilitating doubt about one's ability or right to live and act with confidence and joy. As a free response to a trustworthy and gracious God who exercises power by making room for

---

49. Cf. Calvin's classic definition of faith as "a firm and certain knowledge of God's benevolence toward us, founded upon the truth of the freely given promise in Christ, both revealed to our minds and sealed upon our hearts through the Holy Spirit" (*Institutes*, 3.2.7).

others, faith differs both from centering the world around oneself and from rejecting oneself. The triune God of Christian faith does not envy human freedom. To the contrary, the gracious God empowers our freedom, sets us on our feet, and calls us to maturity and responsibility. When freedom is based on God's grace, people are liberated both from the drive to absolutize their freedom and from the desire to escape from the responsibility of freedom by merely going along with the seductive currents of history and culture around them.

2. If being in the image of God means life in mutual, helpful relations with others, and if this created structure of human life is distorted both by despising others and by hating ourselves, both by a lust for power and by a spirit of servility, then *love is the new way to be human with and for others supremely embodied in Jesus Christ and empowered in us by the Holy Spirit.*

Christian love is strong and freely self-giving. While it will express itself sacrificially, it will be different from destructive selflessness, passivity, or mere acquiescence to whatever pressures are at work in a situation. Like faith, Christian love is an act of freedom. It is the free practice of self-limitation and regard for the other. It is the willingness to assist others, especially those others called enemies, and the readiness to take the first step in promoting justice, mutuality, and friendship.

According to the biblical witness, love is not first of all a duty to be discharged; it is the joyful practice of a new freedom for others that we have received. Christian love is always preceded by God's surprising love for us. "We love because [God] first loved us" (1 John 4:19). We become and stay human when we acknowledge our solidarity with brothers and sisters everywhere, because this is the way we were created to live — not in self-important isolation from others but in deep and often costly solidarity with others. To be in Christ is to enter into an inclusive family where all are brothers and sisters and there are no more damaging hierarchical orderings of Jews and Greeks, masters and slaves, males and females (Gal. 3:28).[50] People whose freedom is rooted in God's grace and who are therefore surprisingly free to be with and for others — especially others called strangers and undesirables — will always be disturbing presences in a world that knows all too well both the coercive power of "masters" and the unresisting servility of "slaves" but scarcely can imagine the meaning of the "freedom of the glory of the children of God" (Rom. 8:21).

---

50. See the interpretation of this text in J. Louis Martyn, *Galatians* (New York: Doubleday, 1997), 373-83; cf. Elisabeth Schüssler Fiorenza, *In Memory of Her* (New York: Crossroad, 1983), 212.

3. If being in the image of God means a hunger for the coming of God's kingdom, and if this hunger is denied or distorted by the sins of despair and presumption, then *hope is the new freedom toward God's future in which we live in the expectation of the fulfillment of the gracious promise of God in Jesus Christ by the power of the Holy Spirit.*

The Spirit of Christ makes us restless for God's great consummation of the work of creation and redemption. No less than faith and love, hope is an exercise of human freedom. It is using our creative imagination to envision a more just society. It is discerning the real possibilities for friendship and peace, and working as best we can to realize them. It is committing ourselves, in the words of John Paul II, to a "culture of life" rather than a "culture of death." Christian hope is not utopian in the sense that we try to bring in God's kingdom ourselves. It is living and acting in a way that expresses confidence in God as Lord not only of the past and the present but also of the future. To live in Christian hope is to live in the expectation that by God's grace things can change, disease and death do not have the last word about human destiny, peace is possible, reconciliation between enemies can occur, and we are called to pray and work toward these ends. To live in hope means to persevere in the struggle for justice, reconciliation, and peace in the world even though good projects and noble causes will often meet with resistance and defeat. While never arrogant, Christian hope is confident in the ultimate victory of God.

Faith, love, and hope are ways of living into the image of God realized for us and promised to us in Christ. They are the gifts and practices of a new human relationship with God, a new way of being human in solidarity with others, a new expectation of God's coming reign, grounded and nurtured in "the grace of the Lord Jesus Christ, the love of God, and the communion of the Holy Spirit" (2 Cor. 13:13).

CHAPTER 8

The Person and Work of Jesus Christ

While Christian theology has many topics to explore, the decisive basis and criterion of all that it says is the person and work of Jesus Christ. This explains why in preceding chapters when I spoke of the triune God, creation, providence, humanity, sin, and evil, I looked to the revelation of God in Christ as the decisive clue. Likewise, when in subsequent chapters I take up the doctrines of the Holy Spirit, Christian life, the church, and Christian hope, it will again be my intent to anchor my thinking in the biblical witness to the purpose and activity of God made known preeminently in Christ. Theological reflection on any topic is *Christian* to the extent that it recognizes the centrality of Jesus Christ and the salvation he brings. For good reason the second article of the Apostles' Creed (which begins, "And [I believe] in Jesus Christ, [God's] only Son, our Lord . . .") is by far the longest. Neither the first article on God the creator nor the third article on the Holy Spirit and the church has any distinctively Christian content apart from its relationship to the second article. For Christian faith "the Father Almighty, Maker of Heaven and Earth" is identified as the Father of our Lord Jesus Christ, and "the Holy Spirit" is primarily defined as the Spirit that prepares the way for the coming of Christ, empowers his ministry, and brings his work to its consummation. Christology is not the whole of Christian doctrine, but it is the point from which all else is illumined.

Problems in Christology

Who is Jesus? How does he help us? Stated as simply as possible, these are the questions that have traditionally been discussed in theology under the head-

ings of Christology (the doctrine of the person of Jesus Christ) and soteriology (the doctrine of his saving work). In every age, the church has confessed that Jesus is Lord and that he brings salvation. Many Christians today,
however, are uncertain how these affirmations about Jesus are to be understood. Among the hard questions that every serious Christology must face in
our time are the following.

1. One question is how we are to make sense of the ancient Christological creeds. The unfamiliar concepts and the technical debates in the early
history of Christology pose serious challenges to any effort to understand and
communicate their meaning. The Nicene Creed speaks of the Son of God as
being "of one substance" with God the Father, and the Formula of Chalcedon
declares that Jesus Christ is "fully divine and fully human," two "natures"
united in one "person," "without confusion or change, division or separation." For many scholars as well as laypeople these classical Christological for-
mulas are cast in a language that is obscure, abstract, and far removed from
the experience of faith. In addition, critics say that the Christology of the old
creeds comes close to losing sight of the concrete historical reality of Jesus of
Nazareth in a maze of metaphysical speculation. Even theologians who disagree with these critics will acknowledge that the classical Christological
creeds must be interpreted and not merely repeated.

2. Another challenge to Christology comes from the rise of historical
consciousness and the application of the historical-critical method to the
Gospels. During the nineteenth century, historical-critical exegesis confidently expected to discover the "real Jesus" behind the allegedly encrusted
dogmas of the church and the biased faith confessions of the New Testament
community. Albert Schweitzer, who wrote the history of this movement, declared it a tremendous act of courage that nevertheless had to be judged a failure. Schweitzer concluded that Jesus could not be made attractive and accessible to the modern age as so many biblical historians attempted to do. When
these investigators peered down into the well of history, they managed to see
only their own faces reflected in the water below. According to Schweitzer, Jesus was an eschatological prophet whose message of the imminent coming of
the reign of God is utterly strange to the modern world.[1]

In recent decades, more sophisticated and chastened "quests for the historical Jesus" have been launched. While agreeing that a biography of Jesus is
impossible, given the nature of the Gospels as documents of faith and proclamation, many New Testament scholars now hold that an attitude of complete
skepticism regarding historical knowledge of Jesus is both unjustified and

1. Schweitzer, *The Quest of the Historical Jesus* (New York: Macmillan, 1961).

perilous. Such skepticism easily slips into docetism or into an uncritical identification of Jesus with the life and teaching of the church. One of the emphases of recent New Testament scholarship is that since Jesus was a Jew, albeit a "marginal Jew," his message and ministry must be understood within the setting of first-century Judaism.[2] Many New Testament scholars also agree that the center of Jesus' proclamation is the coming reign of God and that he enacts this reign in an anticipatory way by his unconditional love of God and his astonishing freedom to bless the poor, heal the sick, and extend forgiveness and table fellowship to sinners.

3. A third problem of modern Christology, closely related to the second, is the awareness of the remarkable variety of pictures of Jesus in the New Testament. The New Testament witnesses are united in their faith in Christ. Yet their portrayals of him as Savior and Lord are remarkably distinctive. Paul's Christology focuses on the cross and resurrection of Christ. Against all triumphalist views, Paul emphasizes that Jesus the risen Lord is none other than the one who was crucified. The cross of Christ is the very power and wisdom of God (1 Cor. 1:24). Mark tells the story of Jesus as a journey from Galilee to Jerusalem, a movement from a ministry of powerful deeds to death on the cross in ignominy and abandonment. According to Mark, the mighty deeds of Jesus can be properly understood only in the light of the redemptive purpose of God in the cross and resurrection. Matthew depicts Jesus as the authoritative messianic teacher whose exposition of the law brings to light a new and higher righteousness and whose life and death fulfill the promises of the Old Testament. Luke narrates the story of Jesus as the foundation of the continuing mission and expansion of the church, which is recounted in the book of Acts. For Luke, Jesus is Savior of the world, not only the one who fulfills God's promises to Israel. The Lucan Jesus is especially concerned with the outcast, the poor, women, and other marginalized people. John's Gospel focuses on the unique relationship between the "Son" and the "Father." John proclaims that Jesus brings light and life from God. For John, Jesus teaches and works according to the will of the Father, reveals the Father's love, and finally returns triumphantly to the Father who sent him, all for our salvation.

In addition to the several distinctive portrayals of Jesus already in the New Testament, there are, of course, countless interpretations of Jesus in the theology and art of the church and in secular art and literature. This remarkable treasury of Christologies has both positive and negative aspects. Its posi-

---

2. See John P. Meier, *A Marginal Jew: Rethinking the Historical Jesus,* 3 vols. (New York: Doubleday, 2001); Leander E. Keck, *Who Is Jesus? History in Perfect Tense* (Columbia: University of South Carolina Press, 2000).

tive side is that the rich array of understandings of Jesus Christ opens up to us aspects of his person and work that we might miss if we were limited to only one portrayal. A treasury of Christologies gives us a greater appreciation of the fullness of salvation in Christ, and awakens us to our freedom and responsibility to interpret the meaning of Christ for our own time and place.

But there is another, more problematic side to the proliferation of pictures of Christ. As Hans Küng has noted, there are so many different Christs — the Christs of piety and secularity, of ancient dogma and modern ideology, of dominant culture and counterculture, of political reaction and social revolution, of classical and popular literature, of moving religious art and mere kitsch — that the question of which Christ is the true Christ becomes unavoidable and urgent.[3] If it is true that diversity in Christology is not something to be feared, since it has its basis in the New Testament witness itself, nevertheless, enriching diversity must be distinguished from an anything-goes relativism. The latter would mean the loss of Christian identity and the inability to distinguish authentic faith in Christ from ideological distortions.

4. A fourth problem of Christology today is what often goes under the name of the scandal of particularity. In one form or another this problem has always confronted Christian faith and theology. The apostle Paul speaks of the message of Christ crucified as scandalous and foolish to most of its hearers (1 Cor. 1:23). In addition to the fundamental scandal of the cross, however, other scandals of particularity confront the church and Christology today. Some feminist theologians, for example, contend that patriarchal theology has in effect replaced the true scandal of the gospel with the scandal of the ontological necessity of Jesus' maleness.[4] Black and Third World theologians ask whether the church in the First World — mostly white and relatively affluent — obscures and subverts the scandal of Jesus' ministry to the poor and the oppressed.[5] Other theologians, concerned to foster new understanding and cooperation among the world religions, insist that we must renounce the false scandal of Christological imperialism and develop a "nonexclusive" and even a "nonnormative" Christology.[6] These are all serious concerns, and they must have their place in Christological reflection today.

3. Küng, On Being a Christian (New York: Doubleday, 1976), 126-44.

4. See Rosemary Radford Ruether, To Change the World: Christology and Cultural Criticism (New York: Crossroad, 1981), 45-56.

5. See Jon Sobrino, Jesus in Latin America (Maryknoll, N.Y.: Orbis Books, 1987).

6. See Paul F. Knitter, No Other Name? A Critical Survey of Christian Attitudes toward the World Religions (Maryknoll, N.Y.: Orbis Books, 1985).

The Person and Work of Jesus Christ

Principles of Christology

As a guide to our exploration of the doctrine of the person and work of
Christ that is mindful of the problems outlined above, we offer the following
working principles.

1. *Knowledge of Jesus Christ is not simply "academic" or historical knowledge; it is faith knowledge.* Faith in Christ is not just knowing *about* him but
trusting *in* him and being ready to follow him as the way, the truth, and the
life.[7] This is not, of course, to deny that there is a cognitive dimension of faith.
It is simply to say that the biblical witness and the proclamation of the church
do not intend simply to inform us about the fact that a man named Jesus once
lived a noble life, taught precious truths, and died a tragic death. When reference is made in the Bible and in church proclamation to Jesus, it is to declare
that his life, death, and resurrection are "for us," "for many," "for all" (Mark
10:45; Rom. 5:8; 8:32; 1 Cor. 15:22). What the Bible and the church want primarily to affirm about this person is that in him God brings forgiveness, liberation, reconciliation, and new life to the world. A soteriological dimension
is present in every layer of New Testament tradition and in all the classical
Christological affirmations of the church. The real "point" of Christology,
therefore, is neither to satisfy historical curiosity nor to engage in idle speculation; it is to affirm that in this Jesus, God is decisively present and graciously
active for the salvation of the world.[8] *Jesus is ethical teacher, not only*

KNOW ✱ 2. *Jesus cannot be properly understood if he is seen apart from the covenant of God with the people of Israel or if the scope of his saving work is limited
to certain individuals or to a select group rather than reaching out to the whole
creation.* The New Testament proclaims that Jesus is the fulfillment of the
covenant of God with his people and thus presupposes an understanding of
the history and hope of Israel.[9] Still more comprehensively, Jesus is seen as
the decisive embodiment of the eternal Logos of God who everywhere and
always impinges upon human life in the world both in grace and in judgment (John 1:1-14). This means Christology has a cosmic as well as a historical setting.[10] While it includes a concern for "my salvation," it must not be

enlightened teacher, we also follow his teaching, different. understanding of God. coming from law of Judaism but Jesus

7. Calvin asserts that the faith that embraces Christ is "more of the heart than of the
brain, and more of the disposition than of the understanding" (*Institutes of the Christian Religion*, 3.2.8).

8. See Schubert Ogden, *The Point of Christology* (New York: Harper & Row, 1982).

9. See Paul Van Buren, *Christ in Context* (San Francisco: Harper & Row, 1986).

10. The cosmic context of Christology has been given special attention in process theology. See W. Norman Pittenger, *The Word Incarnate* (New York: Harper, 1959); N. M. Wildiers,
"Cosmology and Christology," in *Process Theology*, ed. Ewert H. Cousins (New York: Newman

Jesus wants to do saving work, its about the individual but also about society — all of cosmos reduced to that concern. Nor should its cosmic dimensions be smothered by ecclesiocentric attitudes. In this sense, a "nonexclusive" Christology is demanded by the scriptural witness itself.

3. *The doctrines of the person and work of Christ are inseparable.* On the one hand, "to know Christ means to know his *benefits*," as Philip Melanchthon rightly insisted.[11] On the other hand, to know *Christ's* benefits, we must know who he is. While the traditional distinction of person and work is used in Christology for convenience, it can be seriously misleading. We cannot speak meaningfully of anyone's identity, and certainly not of Jesus' identity, apart from that person's life act.[12] Personal identity is constituted by a person's history, by his or her life story. The early church proclaimed who Jesus is in gospel narratives. It is by telling the story of Jesus, by narrating the whole gospel — his message, ministry, passion, and resurrection — that we are able to hold together the person and work of Jesus. That the New Testament does not split apart his person and work is evident in its interpretation of his name: "Call his name Jesus, for he will save his people from their sins" (Matt. 1:21).

4. *Every understanding and confession of Jesus Christ grows out of a particular situation and both reflects and speaks to particular needs and aspirations.* We must learn from understandings of Christ that are shaped by histories of suffering and hope very different from our own.[13] As already noted, the New Testament contains a plurality of Christologies, some focusing on the teaching of Jesus (such as the Q document and the Gospel of Matthew), some centering on the passion of Jesus (such as the Gospel of Mark and the letters of Paul), some emphasizing more the glory and triumph of the resurrected Lord (such as the Gospel of John). The one unsubstitutable Christ is inexhaustibly rich and gathers the whole range of human need and experience to himself. New situations call for new confessions of Christ, for he wills to be acknowledged as Lord and Savior in every time and place. Christians have both the

Press, 1971), 269-82. Denis Edwards, *Jesus and the Cosmos* (New York: Paulist Press, 1991), develops a cosmic Christology drawing on insights from Karl Rahner's theology.

11. Philip Melanchthon, *Loci Communes Theologici*, in *Melanchthon and Bucer*, ed. Wilhelm Pauck, Library of Christian Classics, vol. 19 (Philadelphia: Westminster, 1969), 21.

12. This is a prominent feature of Barth's Christology (see *Church Dogmatics*, 4/1-3) and of recent "narrative Christologies."

13. This is a major emphasis of liberation Christologies. See James H. Cone, *God of the Oppressed* (New York: Seabury Press, 1975), 108-37; Jon Sobrino, *Christology at the Crossroads* (Maryknoll, N.Y.: Orbis Books, 1978); Rosemary Radford Ruether, *Sexism and God-Talk: Toward a Feminist Theology* (Boston: Beacon Press, 1983), 116-38; Jacquelyn Grant, *White Women's Christ and Black Women's Jesus: Feminist Christology and Womanist Response* (Atlanta: Scholars Press, 1989), 195-222.

freedom and the obligation to confess Christ in appropriate and relevant ways in their own specific contexts, in continuity with the New Testament witness and in conversation with the particular experiences, needs, and hopes of people here and now.

5. *The living Jesus Christ is greater than all of our confessions and creeds, and he surpasses all of our theological reflection about him.* The risen Lord continually upsets our neat categories and classifications of him and the salvation he brings. "Who do you say that I am?" Jesus asks. "You are the Christ," Peter correctly replies. But in the next moment, when Jesus says that he must suffer and die to do the Father's will, Peter resists Jesus and shows that his previous understanding of him as the Christ is in need of correction (see Mark 8:27-35). No Christology can claim to exhaust the breadth and depth of the mystery of Christ. This is also true of the Christological creeds of the ecumenical church. They are milestones in the history of the church's confession of Christ, and they deserve our serious attention and respect. But they are not absolute. As Karl Rahner states — with the two-natures Christology of the Creed of Chalcedon (451 A.D.) in mind — the church's creeds are not the final word for our theological reflection, but points of departure.[14] We may have to quarrel with the language and conceptuality of the classical creeds even while, as members of the same community in which these creeds arose, we will certainly want to be instructed by them. Our faith is in God revealed in Christ and not in a particular theological system or Christological formulation. We are to trust and obey Christ in life and in death, but that is something very different from absolutizing a particular doctrine of Christ, whether ancient or modern.

Patristic Christology

In the centuries after the New Testament period, the church's confession that Jesus is Lord and Savior had to be restated in new contexts and defended against serious misunderstandings. This demanded intense theological work and the use of new conceptual forms. Since the Christological debates and decisions of the patristic church have greatly influenced all subsequent Christological reflection, we need to examine these developments.

The initial milestone in the development of Christology in the post-apostolic era was the *first ecumenical council of the church held in Nicea in 325 A.D.* This council was convened to counter the threat to Christian faith posed

---

14. Rahner, "Current Problems in Christology," in *Theological Investigations*, vol. 1 (Baltimore: Helicon Press, 1965), 149-200.

by Arianism. According to Arius and his followers, Jesus Christ, the divine Logos, was the preeminent creature rather than the eternal Son of God. True divinity, Arius argued, could not be subject to any limitations and certainly not to suffering and death. Hence Christ, while the unique revealer of God and our redeemer, could not be truly God with us. Although he was as much like God as a creature could be, he was not equal with God. He did not share in God's being. "There was when he was not," said Arius. While the intent of Arius was to honor and exalt God above every creature, he could speak of divine transcendence only in the sense of being the opposite of everything created. For Arius it was inconceivable to speak of God as coming among us as one of us. The God of Arius could not share divine life and love with creatures.

Nicene theology, defended especially by the great fourth-century theologian Athanasius, represents a completely different conception of God and a resounding affirmation of the full divinity of Christ. For Nicea, the qualities that constitute the divinity of the God of the gospel are not absoluteness, incommunicability, and invulnerability. On the contrary, the God of the gospel is defined by the act of self-giving love. This is the understanding of God that underlies the Nicene declaration that Jesus Christ is truly the Son of God, "God from God, light from light, true God from true God." In opposition to the Arian view, the Nicene Creed affirms that the Son of God incarnate in Jesus Christ is "begotten, not made" and is "of one substance" *(homoousios)* with God the Father. The Nicene Creed, reaffirmed and amplified at the Council of Constantinople in 381 A.D., is both the church's premier creedal formulation of trinitarian faith and the decisive creedal declaration of the full divinity of Jesus Christ.

Although the Council of Nicea settled the issue of the divinity of Christ, the church was now faced with the questions of how to affirm also the full humanity of Christ and how to understand the unity of his divinity and humanity. In the attempt to resolve these issues, two major schools of Christology emerged, centered in Alexandria and Antioch. If we keep in mind the differing emphases of these two schools, we will better understand the complex and often tangled history of Christological controversy from the Council of Nicea to the Council of Chalcedon in 451 A.D. and the councils immediately following it.[15]

The *Alexandrian school,* led by Athanasius and later by Cyril of Alexandria, represented what scholars call the "Word-flesh" type of Christology. The primary emphases of this school were on the divinity of Christ and the unity of his person. The one subject of the history of Jesus Christ is the second per-

---

15. For an overview of fourth- and fifth-century Christology, see J. N. D. Kelly, *Early Christian Doctrines* (New York: Harper & Brothers, 1958), 280-343.

son of the Trinity, the Word of God incarnate. According to the Alexandrians, the eternal Word of God "assumed" or "took on" flesh in the Incarnation (John 1:14; Phil. 2:7). Because of its emphasis on the unity of the person of Christ, the Alexandrian school was sharply opposed to the tendency to separate the divine and human natures of Christ that characterized the Antiochian school, and particularly the views of Nestorius. From the Alexandrian perspective, such separation denied the reality of restored communion with God accomplished on our behalf by the Word of God incarnate. In Athanasius's famous statement, "God became human that we might become divine."[16] Realization of this purpose required the real union of divine and human natures in the person of Jesus Christ. An extreme expression of Alexandrian Christology, later rejected by the church, was offered by Apollinarius. In the effort to explain how the divine and human natures were united in one person, he taught that the Word of God replaced the human mind of Jesus in the Incarnation.

The *Antiochian school,* represented most prominently by Theodore of Mopsuestia and Nestorius, emphasized the full humanity of Christ. In contrast to the Alexandrian "Word-flesh" Christology, the Antiochian school defended a "Word-human being" Christology. In other words, the Antiochians championed the full humanity of Jesus. Nestorius's refusal to speak of Mary the mother of Jesus as *theotokos,* "God-bearer," infuriated Cyril of Alexandria. Whereas the Alexandrian school spoke of the Word "assuming" flesh, the Antiochian school spoke of the Word "indwelling" a human being. The Antiochians insisted on the distinction between the divine and human natures of Christ in part because of their concern to protect the divinity from the corruptibility and suffering of creatures, and in part because of their conviction that only if Christ were truly human could his obedience and faithfulness undo sin and death in human nature and achieve our salvation. Just as the Alexandrians were never able to express the full reality of the humanity of Jesus Christ in a way that was satisfactory to the Antiochian school, the Antiochians were never able to express the unity of the person of Jesus Christ in a way that was satisfactory to the Alexandrian school. If the teaching of Apollinarius was an extreme expression of the Alexandrian tendency to emphasize the divinity of Christ and the unity of his person, the Nestorian separation of the two natures was the extreme expression of the Antiochian concern to guard the full humanity of Christ and the immutability and impassibility of the divine nature.

These complex Christological debates after Nicea led eventually to the *Council of Chalcedon in 451 A.D.,* the fourth ecumenical council of the church

---

16. Athanasius, *On the Incarnation,* 54.

and the second great milestone in the development of classical Christology. According to Chalcedon, Jesus Christ is "fully divine, fully human, two natures in one person, without confusion or change, separation or division."[17] Chalcedon places the distinction of what is divine and what is human in Christ at the level of "natures" *(physeis)* and the unity of the incarnate Word at the level of "person" *(hypostasis)*. Most historians of doctrine view Chalcedon as a careful balance of the emphases of the Alexandrian and Antiochian schools. This creed did not "solve" the Christological problem but drew the boundaries within which orthodox confession of Christ was to occur.[18] On the one hand, concerns of the Antiochian school were incorporated in the unambiguous affirmation of the full humanity of Jesus Christ and in the declarations of the unity of the two natures "without confusion and without change." These emphases repudiated the Apollinarian truncation of the humanity of Christ or any other Christology that might cast suspicion on Christ's full humanity. On the other hand, the repeated assertions of Chalcedon that Jesus Christ is one person and the declaration that the divine and human natures are united "without separation or division" vindicated the concerns of the Alexandrian school. The Definition of Chalcedon set the standard of all subsequent Christological confession in the majority of Christian churches, Eastern Orthodox, Roman Catholic, and Protestant.

Christological controversy did not end at Chalcedon. At the fifth ecumenical council (Constantinople, 553 A.D.), the "personal union" *(unio hypostatica)* of divine and human natures in Jesus Christ was made still more explicit. According to traditional interpretations of this doctrine, the human nature of Christ, considered in itself and apart from its union with the Word of God, is *anhypostasis,* that is, lacking concrete existence. This means that the humanity of Christ is not an independent subject existing prior to or apart from the Word of God. The positive side of this doctrine is that the humanity of Christ is affirmed as *enhypostasis,* that is, existing in perfect union with the person *(hypostasis)* of the Word of God. In other words, the humanity of Jesus Christ comes to personhood only in union with the Word of God. This doctrine of the humanity of Christ as *anhypostasis/enhypostasis* is clearly a strengthening of the Alexandrian interpretation of Chalcedon.

---

17. For the full text of the Formula of Chalcedon, see *Christology of the Later Fathers,* ed. Edward Rochie Hardy, Library of Christian Classics, vol. 3 (Philadelphia: Westminster, 1954), 372-74.

18. For the view that Chalcedon is basically Alexandrian, see John A. McGuckin, *St. Cyril of Alexandria: The Christological Controversy* (Leiden: Brill, 1994); for the view that Chalcedon tilts in the Antiochian direction, see Robert W. Jenson, *Systematic Theology,* vol. 1 (New York: Oxford University Press, 1997).

At the sixth ecumenical council (Constantinople, 681 A.D.) the Antiochian concern was more prominent. According to this council, the two distinct natures of the one incarnate Lord include two wills and two centers of action. While the two wills are distinguishable, the human will is perfectly subordinate to the divine. A decisive Gospel text for this doctrine of the two wills of Christ is his prayer in Gethsemane, "Not what I want, but what you want" (Mark 14:36).

In this brief survey of patristic Christology at least one other doctrinal development deserves mention. An important way of affirming the unity of the person of Jesus Christ in the patristic period took the form of the doctrine of the "communication of properties" *(communicatio idiomatum)*. According to this doctrine, because divine and human natures are perfectly united in the incarnate Lord, there is a "communication" or "exchange" of properties. Predicates appropriate to each nature can be affirmed of the one person. Hence it is possible to say, "The Son of God suffered"; that is, while suffering is an attribute that belongs to the human nature, because of the communication of properties, it can also be ascribed to the incarnate Son of God. Likewise, it is possible to say, "Jesus is the Lord"; that is, while lordship is an attribute that belongs to the divine nature, because of the communication of properties, it can also be ascribed to Jesus as the humanity of God incarnate.[19]

While the doctrine of the communication of properties may strike many people today as an exercise in abstract speculation, the intent of the doctrine is profoundly soteriological. This is best seen in the closely related teaching of the "wonderful exchange" *(admirabile commercium)*, a central theme of the early fathers and of many later theologians.[20] Calvin, for example, develops the theme in the following beautiful passage: "This is the wonderful exchange which, out of his measureless benevolence, [the Son of God] has made with us, that, becoming Son of man with us, he has made us sons of God with him; that, by his descent to earth, he has prepared an ascent to heaven for us; that, by taking on our mortality, he has conferred his immortality upon us; that, accepting our weakness, he has strengthened us by his power; that, receiving our poverty unto himself, he has transferred his wealth to us; that, taking the weight of our iniquity upon himself (which oppressed us), he has clothed us with his righteousness."[21]

19. See John of Damascus, *Exposition of the Orthodox Faith*, Book 3, chaps. 4-5.

20. See Hans Urs von Balthasar, *Theo-Drama: Theological Dramatic Theory*, vol. 4: *The Action* (San Francisco: Ignatius, 1994), 244-49.

21. John Calvin, *Institutes*, 4.17.2. For an example of the theme of exchange in Luther, see "The Freedom of a Christian," in *Luther's Works*, 31: 351.

Rethinking Classical Affirmations of the Person of Christ

In the church's confession of Jesus Christ, reference is made to the historical person Jesus of Nazareth, and some theological claim is made about him, often in the form of a special title. The earliest Christian confessions took the form "Jesus is the Christ" (Mark 8:29) and "Jesus is Lord" (1 Cor. 12:3). In these confessions, Jesus is recognized as genuinely human, and he is said to have a unique relation to God and to be the sole agent of our salvation. While the creeds of Nicea and Chalcedon set the direction and provided the standard of all subsequent Christology, affirmation of Jesus as Lord and Savior today requires more than the mere repetition of these creeds. In the following presentation, my intent is to reaffirm the Christological confession of the early church and to remain in broad agreement with the declarations of Nicea and Chalcedon. But we also need to recognize some deficiencies of the classical Christological tradition and to explore proposals for its reformulation.

1. Jesus is *fully human*. While the New Testament does not give us materials for a biography of Jesus, there can be no doubt that it refers to a concrete human being who is like us in all respects, with the exception of being "without sin" (Heb. 4:15), which is essentially alienation from and hostility to the grace of God. Like every human being, Jesus was "born of a woman" (Gal. 4:4). As a first-century Jew, he was deeply influenced by the culture and religious heritage of his people. He grew and matured physically, intellectually, and spiritually (Luke 2:40). An itinerant preacher of the coming kingdom of God, he had no home of his own. He experienced hunger and thirst. He became tired. His knowledge was not unlimited. From personal experience he knew the pain of grief when a loved one dies. He had real, rather than make-believe, temptations. He knew both acclaim and rejection. In the end he was betrayed, arrested, humiliated, tortured, and finally crucified.

If we acknowledge that confession of the full humanity of Jesus necessarily implies, among other things, his intellectual and physical limitations, his experience of the full range of human emotions including joy, anger, grief, and compassion, and his real suffering and death, we thereby refuse to go the way of the Docetists, who were embarrassed by all this. In their view, Jesus' humanity was only an "appearance": he did not really suffer or die. Some of the Docetists even contended that Jesus never left footprints and never blinked his eyes. Against all docetic views, the mainstream of Christian teaching has affirmed the full humanity of Jesus. Jesus was not a mere phantom. He was not a lifeless puppet kept in motion by strings controlled from above. Jesus prayed, spoke, acted, and suffered as a real human being. The basic objection to any crass or subtle qualification or reduction of Jesus' humanity is soteriological. In the memorable phrase of Gregory of Nazianzus, "That which he has not assumed, he has not healed."[22] If God in Christ is not present to us in the depths of our human finitude, misery, and godforsakenness, then whatever this person may have said or done, he cannot be the Savior of human beings, who know finitude, misery, and godforsakenness all too well. If God in Christ does not enter into solidarity with the hell of our human condition, we remain without deliverance and without hope. For the classical Christological tradition, the full humanity of Jesus is the precondition of the inclusiveness of his salvation.

However, if we said no more than this, our affirmation of the full humanity of Jesus would remain, like the creedal tradition, formally correct but insufficiently guided by the concrete gospel narrative. According to that narrative, Jesus was not simply a human being but a *singular, disturbing, even revolutionary* human being. In the power of the Spirit, Jesus proclaimed the coming reign of God and acted in God's name with an astonishing freedom. He spoke of God as *Abba,* "dear father," taught his hearers to love their enemies, and announced God's grace to sinners and the poor. He summarized his mission by quoting the prophet Isaiah: "the Spirit of the Lord is upon me, because he has anointed me to bring good news to the poor; he has sent me to proclaim release to the captives, and recovery of sight to the blind, to let the oppressed go free, to proclaim the year of the Lord's favor" (Luke 4:18-19; cf. Isa. 61:18-19).

Jesus' proclamation and ministry transgressed the supposed boundaries of God's grace and thus shocked the sensibilities of the guardians of religious tradition. He blessed the poor, healed the sick, cast out demons, befriended women, and had table fellowship with sinners. His words and actions seemed blasphemous to his critics. Furthermore, his announcement of the inbreaking reign of God made him vulnerable to the charge of being a political conspirator. The disturbing ministry of Jesus thus led to his crucifixion as a blasphemer and a possible threat to imperial rule.[23]

Jesus is indeed fully human, but his is a new humanity. The intimacy of his relation with God and his solidarity with sinners and the oppressed are new and offensive. He is the human being radically free for God's coming reign and therefore radically free for communion with and service to the neighbor. Like the father in the parable of the prodigal child, Jesus extends the welcoming love of God to those who are thought least deserving of it (Luke

---

22. Gregory of Nazianzus, Epistle 101, in *Christology of the Later Fathers*, ed. Edward R. Hardy, Library of Christian Classics, vol. 3 (Philadelphia: Westminster, 1954), 218.

23. Cf. "A Brief Statement of Faith," in *The Book of Confessions* (PCUSA), 10.2, lines 19-20: "Unjustly condemned for blasphemy and sedition, Jesus was crucified. . . ."

15:11ff.). Like the good Samaritan of another parable, Jesus comes to the aid of wounded humanity at great cost to himself. Thus when Christians call Jesus fully human, their claim is not simply that he is *a* human being but that he is the norm and promise of a new humanity in relation to God and to others.

That the humanity of Jesus is a new humanity grounded in God's grace is the point of the biblical and creedal affirmations that Jesus was "conceived by the Holy Spirit" and "born of the Virgin Mary." "Conceived by the Holy Spirit" emphasizes that God's grace is uniquely at work in and through this human life by the power of the Holy Spirit. "Born of the Virgin Mary" signifies that salvation comes not from humanity's own inherent possibilities but from God alone.[24] The aim of these affirmations, then, is neither to "prove" the divinity of Jesus, nor to praise virginity as an especially holy estate, nor simply to report a gynecological miracle.[25] Rather, they proclaim that Jesus' humanity is God's humanity, that Jesus and the salvation he brings are the sheer gift of God.

It is with this understanding of the full humanity of Jesus that we should take up the serious questions that have been raised for Christology by feminist theologians. Can a male be the savior of women, or does the particularity of Jesus' gender preclude him from being a universal savior? This question obviously grows out of the history of oppression that women have experienced and that has all too often been supported in the church by direct or indirect reference to the fact that the one who is said to be the norm of full humanity was male. If true humanity is by definition masculine, then women must always be less than fully human. A response to this concern must emphasize, as a number of feminist theologians do, that the New Testament sees the full humanity of Jesus not in his maleness but in his shocking love, his prophetic criticism, his inclusive freedom for God and for others.

No doubt the assumptions of patriarchal culture more or less pervade the biblical witness as a whole. Nevertheless, the message and ministry of Jesus, while not immune from this influence, also contain profound challenges to patriarchy. In his parables of the reign of God (which include not only the story of the forgiving father [Luke 15:11ff.] but also the story of the woman who searches for her lost coin [Luke 15:8ff.]), in the new imagery he uses of God and of his own ministry (Luke 13:34), in his friendship with women, and in his advocacy of the cause of the poor and the oppressed, Jesus' proclamation, life, and death were prophetic and scandalous. Hence, a Christology

---

24. For Karl Barth's interpretation of these affirmations, see *Church Dogmatics,* 1/2: 172-202.

25. See Jürgen Moltmann, *The Way of Jesus Christ: Christology in Messianic Dimensions* (San Francisco: HarperCollins, 1990), 82.

faithful to the biblical witness will always have a critical and subversive dimension. It will be iconoclastic in relation to self-serving understandings of God and the support that these understandings give to oppressive attitudes and relationships.

More specifically, it is a complete distortion of the humanity of Jesus as depicted in the gospel story to claim that maleness is an ontological necessity of the incarnation of the Word of God, or that because Jesus was male, women should not be ordained to the office of ministry.[26] If we follow the description of Jesus in the gospel story, we will surely agree that the theological significance of the humanity of Jesus resides not in his male gender but in his unconditional love of God and his shockingly inclusive love of others. This and this alone makes the life and death of Jesus a radiant expression of the eternally self-giving, other-affirming, community-forming love of the triune God.

2. Jesus is not only fully human but also *fully divine.* The classical creeds declare the divinity of Jesus Christ without reservation and do so in faithfulness to the New Testament witness: "God was in Christ reconciling the world to himself" (2 Cor. 5:19). If this affirmation means anything, it means that what Jesus does and suffers is at the same time the doing and suffering of God. The preaching of Jesus is more than the word of a prophet; in his preaching God decisively addresses us. Jesus does not simply announce the coming reign of God; the reign of God is embodied in his person and work. When Jesus forgives sinners, this is not just the pardon offered by a human being; it is also God's forgiveness expressed and enacted in this human being. Jesus' companionship with the poor and sick is not just a caring human being's companionship with suffering fellow creatures; it is God's solidarity with these people made concrete in what this human being does and suffers. Jesus' passion and death for us is not just the martyrdom of another innocent victim in an unjust world; it is also God's suffering, God's taking death into the being of God and overcoming it there for our salvation. The resurrection of Jesus from the dead is not the victory of a solitary human being over death; it is God's victory over sin and death for us all in the raising of this man Jesus.

God acts, suffers, and triumphs in and through Jesus. In Jesus Christ we do not have less than God's very own presence in our humanity. In this person the eternal God suffers and acts for our salvation. However strange their

---

26. Elisabeth Schüssler Fiorenza: "An understanding of the incarnation in terms of biological gender positivism does not square with the tradition according to which the *humanity* and not the *masculinity* of Jesus has saving significance" ("Lk. 13:10-17: Interpretation for Liberation and Transformation," *Theology Digest* 36 [Winter 1989]: 303-19); similarly, Jacquelyn Grant: "The significance of Christ is not his maleness but his humanity" (*White Women's Christ and Black Women's Jesus,* 220).

language, this is the point of the ancient creeds of Nicea and Chalcedon, which declare that Jesus Christ is "of one substance" with the Father and that he is "fully God" as well as "fully human." The concern here is again soteriological. No human being alone can save us. If Jesus Christ is not *God* with us, if the life and forgiveness that he offers are not God's own life and forgiveness, if his self-giving, sacrificial love poured out for our sake is not *God's* own love, then he cannot be Savior and Lord. Christian faith cannot compromise either on the full humanity or on the full deity of Jesus Christ.

But if this Jesus is God with us, then a radical conversion of our ordinary understandings of the words "God" and "Lord" is required. This is not made explicit by the creed of Chalcedon. As in the case of the confession of Christ's full humanity, Chalcedon speaks of his divinity in a rather formal and abstract manner that fails to bear the specific imprint of the gospel narrative. This narrative does not invite us to think first of what everyone supposes divinity to be and then to recognize in Jesus the presence of that supposed divinity. Instead, it describes the coming of God's Word, or God's Son, in the actions and sufferings of a servant who humbles himself and becomes obedient even to the death on a cross (Phil. 2:5ff.). Just as the gospel story surprisingly redefines the meaning of true humanity by describing Jesus' intimate relationship with God and his shocking fellowship with sinners and the poor, so this story unexpectedly redefines the meaning of true divinity and genuine lordship by depicting the actions and sufferings of a humble servant who gives his life unconditionally for the redemption and renewal of the world. Christian faith sees no less than God in the transforming, suffering, and victorious love at work in Jesus' ministry, cross, and resurrection. But precisely in this person, divinity and lordship are radically redefined in terms of a surprising love that welcomes sinners, makes itself vulnerable for the sake of others, and is shockingly partisan toward the weak, the poor, and the outcast.[27]

3. The affirmation that Jesus is fully human and fully divine points to the *mystery of the unity of his person.* According to classical Christological doctrine, the two natures of Christ are united in one person (or hypostasis) "without confusion or change" and without "division or separation." Critics have charged that this doctrine of one person in two natures leaves us with the impression of the artificial joining of two discrete material objects, like two boards that are glued together. Even theologians who are in basic agree-

---

27. In *White Women's Christ and Black Women's Jesus,* Jacquelyn Grant argues that black Christians do not have the white liberal's problems with confessing Jesus as God and Lord. For blacks Jesus is "the divine co-sufferer, who empowers [black people] in situations of oppression" (212).

ment with Chalcedon have called for a rethinking and restatement of its teaching in more dynamic terms.

One proposal is to rethink the doctrine of the two natures in terms of "two sets of relationships," the relationship of Jesus to the Father and the Spirit on the one hand, and the relationship of Jesus to other human beings on the other.[28] Another proposal is to speak not of a union of divine and human "natures" but of the unique history of Jesus Christ, in whom divine and human agency are united without confusion or separation. Assumed here is the idea of "double agency," at once divine and human, in the history of Jesus Christ. Is the idea of double agency, explored by some philosophers and theologians, a coherent idea, and if it is, can it be employed to interpret the doctrine of the union of divinity and humanity in Christ?[29] Or does the idea of double agency risk reintroducing the Nestorian fallacy of a merely external, voluntary union of two separate subjects?

In his book *God Was in Christ*, Donald Baillie argues that while the personal unity of the humanity and divinity of Christ is a "paradox" that we can never fully grasp, we can nevertheless know something of its reality by analogy from our own Christian experience. At the heart of Christian existence is the experience of divine grace that precedes and enables human freedom. In every age the Christian testimony has been that we are most truly human, most fully ourselves, most profoundly free when we live in response to God's grace. As the apostle Paul writes, "I worked . . . though it was not I, but the grace of God that is with me" (1 Cor. 15:10; see also Gal. 2:19-20). When God acts, human action is not displaced. Divine grace and human freedom are not mutually exclusive. The grace of God does not negate but permits and establishes truly free human action.[30]

While Baillie's argument is suggestive, important clarifications are needed. First, the union of the Word of God and humanity in Jesus Christ is an utterly *unique* union. It is not like the union of form and matter, or the union of soul and body, or the union of two friends. Nor is it rightly under-

28. See Schwöbel, "Christology and Trinitarian Thought," in *Trinitarian Theology Today*, ed. Christoph Schwöbel (Edinburgh: T&T Clark, 1995), 143.

29. Barth has a discussion of double agency in his doctrine of *concursus divinus* or "the divine accompanying" in *Church Dogmatics*, 3/3: 90-154, but rejects it as a model for interpreting the Christological mystery. For a discussion of the idea of "double agency" in Barth's theology, see George Hunsinger, *How to Read Karl Barth: The Shape of His Theology* (New York: Oxford University Press, 1991), 185-233.

30. Baillie, *God Was in Christ* (New York: Scribner's, 1948), 106-32. "Human nature, at the contact of God, does not disappear," writes John Meyendorff; "on the contrary, it becomes fully human" (*Christ in Eastern Christian Thought* [Washington: Corpus Books, 1969], 64).

stood as simply a notable instance of God's relationship to and presence in all creatures. Even the participation of Christians in Christ and of Christ in them, while real, is not the same as the event of incarnation in which the Word of God is united with human nature. The union of God and humanity in Jesus Christ is a singular act of God. Undoubtedly, Baillie's reference to the "paradox of grace" in Christian experience intends to guard the uniqueness and singularity of the Incarnation. However, this intention is somewhat obscured by the fact that Baillie's argument moves strictly from Christian experience to an understanding of the person of Christ, rather than moving also in the reverse direction. Our experience cannot explain the reality of God with us in Christ; his reality illumines ours. In his light we understand more clearly that human existence as intended by God is not life closed within itself, but life in depth of relationship with God and others. Analogies of the union of God and humanity in Christ taken from the sphere of personal relationships of friendship and love are not to be summarily dismissed. But it should always be remembered that they will be at best imperfect intimations of the mystery of the union of God and humanity in Christ.

Second, the union of the Word of God and humanity in Jesus Christ is an *asymmetrical* union. That is, the activity of God is primary and prevenient; the human response is secondary and subsequent. The union of the Word of God and humanity in Christ is not a relationship of equal partners, not a symmetrical relationship of cooperation between equals. The eternal Word of God is the initiating subject of the history of Jesus Christ. What the early Christological tradition tried to say with its now obscure notions of the anhypostatic and enhypostatic humanity of Christ might be more clearly expressed by speaking of the utter prevenience and generosity of divine agency that creates and makes room for free human response.

Third, the union of the Word of God and humanity in Christ is a *dynamic* union. Traditional Christological conceptuality has an inert, ahistorical quality about it. It does not easily allow for ideas of movement, history, interaction, encounter, and development. It is as though the union of God and humanity had no place for the genuine growth of Jesus as a human being or for a deepening of his relationship with God and others (Luke 2:40). The union of the divine and human in Christ, however, is not to be identified simply with the moment of his conception or birth. His actual ministry, passion, and death must also be considered in any account of the union of divinity and humanity in him. As Kathryn Tanner states: "Jesus does not overcome temptation until he is tempted, does not overcome fear of death until he feels it, at which time this temptation and fear are assumed by the Word. Jesus does not heal death until the Word assumes death when Jesus dies; Jesus does not conquer sin until he assumes or bears the sin of others by suffering death at their hands."[31] We should think of the union of divine and human "natures" in Jesus Christ not statically but dynamically.

Fourth, the union of the Word of God and humanity in Jesus Christ is a *kenotic* union. A Christology that goes beyond yet is faithful to Chalcedon may legitimately speak of a "kenotic unity" of God and humanity in Jesus Christ.[32] The idea of *kenosis* comes from the Christological hymn of Philippians 2:5ff. Kenosis (literally, "emptying") is the act of free self-limitation and free self-expenditure. In Jesus Christ, God and humanity are united in mutual self-giving love. It is a union in the Spirit in which there is reciprocal self-limitation and total openness of each to the other. The divinity and humanity of Jesus are neither confused (monophysitism) nor separated (Nestorianism). In the Word of God become human, the Word of God lives in loving unity with this human being, and this human being lives in loving unity with the Word of God. A unique unity of free divine grace and free human service takes place. Taking Philippians 2:5ff. as our guide, the unity of divinity and humanity in Jesus Christ is best described as a kenotic union rooted in the Spirit of mutual self-surrendering love.

The act of kenosis that characterizes the life of the incarnate Lord does not entail a negation or diminution of God's nature (as nineteenth-century kenotic Christologies mistakenly taught). As emphasized in our discussion of the doctrine of the Trinity, the very nature of God is self-giving, other-affirming, community-creating love. Life in mutuality and fellowship does not diminish but defines the reality of God. In the eternal life of God there is interaction and exchange between "Father" and "Son" in the uniting love of the "Spirit." The unity of the triune God is a communion of reciprocal, self-giving love.

The trinitarian communion of love is thus the eternal ground and prototype of the union of true God and true humanity in Jesus Christ.[33] The mystery of the person of Christ has its proper setting against the background of the trinitarian mystery in which personhood and communion are inseparable. Being a person means being in relationship. In the Incarnation, God freely and lovingly assumes this human life, and this human life freely and lovingly responds to God. In the history of Jesus Christ, God's freedom for and faithful-

---

31. Kathryn Tanner, *Jesus, Humanity and the Trinity* (Minneapolis: Fortress, 2001), 28.

32. See Lucien J. Richard, *A Kenotic Christology* (Lanham, Md.: University Press of America, 1982).

33. According to Walter Kasper, "In the last resort, the mediation of God and man in Jesus Christ can only be understood in the light of Trinitarian theology." *Jesus the Christ* (New York: Paulist Press, 1976), 249. See also Schwöbel, "Christology and Trinitarian Thought," 113-46.

ness to humanity and humanity's freedom for and faithfulness to God are perfectly united. In him the perfect love of God and a perfect human response are one. Seen from one perspective, God elects Jesus as God's "chosen," God's "beloved" (Matt. 12:18); seen from another perspective, Jesus is entirely devoted to God and freely subordinates his will to God's (Luke 22:42). In perfect mutual love, divinity and humanity are distinct yet personally united in Jesus Christ.

In summary, while faint analogies of the unity of divinity and humanity in the incarnate Lord may be found in the "paradox of grace" in Christian life, or even in common human experiences of intimate personal relationship in which two may think, will, and act as one, the identity of Jesus Christ as described by Scripture and creed is a mystery beyond comprehension. The relationship of God to Jesus and of Jesus to God has its basis and fullest analogy in the mystery of the eternal exchange of love in the life of the triune God.

Rethinking Classical Interpretations of the Work of Christ

While the ministry, death, and resurrection of Christ all belong to the liberating and reconciling work of Christ, the cross has been the center of attention in most doctrines of atonement in Western theology. The New Testament uses many different metaphors to express what happened in Christ's death for us. We find financial, legal, military, sacrificial, and other metaphors, all of which contain treasures of meaning. Despite the familiarity of these metaphors, they can still surprise us with fresh insight.[34] Some of the New Testament metaphors of the work of Christ have been expanded into elaborate theories of atonement. Even if no single understanding of the atoning work of Jesus Christ has received ecumenical approval, there have been several prominent theories of atonement in Christian theology.[35]

1. One of these is called the cosmic conflict or *Christ the Victor* theory. This theory — a favorite among many patristic theologians — develops the battle metaphor found in some New Testament passages (e.g., Col. 2:15). According to this view, the work of atonement is a dramatic struggle between God and the forces of evil in the world. The deity of Christ is deeply hidden in human form. The evil forces are thus fooled into thinking he is an easy prey. Gregory of Nyssa uses the colorful image of a fish unsuspectingly swallowing

---

34. See Colin E. Gunton, *The Actuality of Atonement: A Study of Metaphor, Rationality, and the Christian Tradition* (Grand Rapids: Eerdmans, 1989).

35. On what follows, see Gustav Aulén, *Christus Victor* (New York: Macmillan, 1951).

the bait on a fishhook. Under the veil of his humanity, Christ triumphs over the demons, the devil, and all the principalities and powers that hold human beings captive. By his cross and resurrection, Christ decisively defeats these powers and thus frees their captives.

While this theory helpfully emphasizes the reality and power of evil forces that hold humanity in bondage, and while it correctly stresses the costliness and assurance of God's victory, its limitations are readily evident. It is especially misleading if its imagery of bait on a fishhook is interpreted in a literalistic way that reduces the humanity of Jesus to a mere disguise to fool the evil powers, or if its language of a cosmic battle between God and the devil serves to undermine the awareness of human responsibility for its sinful condition. Thinking of the atoning work of Christ in this way would make believers mere spectators of a cosmic struggle that takes place over their heads. Some critics of the Christ the Victor theory have also asked whether it is overly triumphalist and leads to a denial of the continuing power of evil and sin in history and in our own lives.

Despite these limitations, the cosmic battle theory of the atonement enshrines at least two deep truths. One is that God achieves the liberation and reconciliation of the world not by employing coercion or brute force but by the foolish wisdom of the cross. God does not defeat evil by evil means but through the power of divine love. As Gregory of Nyssa puts it, "God's transcendent power is not so much displayed in the vastness of the heavens, or the luster of the stars, or the orderly arrangement of the universe or his perpetual oversight of it, as in his condescension to our weak nature."[36] Another truth embedded in the cosmic battle theory is that evil forces are not only destructive but self-destructive. As morally offensive as the idea that God uses deception in the work of salvation may be, what the crude images of this theory intend to convey is that God's hidden or "foolish" way of redeeming humanity is wiser and stronger than the apparently invincible forces of evil. It is worth noting that some feminist theologians have called for a retrieval of the insights of the classical battle theory of the atonement.[37]

2. Another influential theory of atonement is the Anselmian *satisfaction* theory. It is rooted in biblical passages that suggest vicarious suffering as the way by which humankind is redeemed (e.g., Isa. 53; Gal. 3:13). The theory finds classic expression in Anselm's *Cur Deus Homo?* ("Why Did God Become

36. Gregory of Nyssa, "Address on Religious Instruction," in *Christology of the Later Fathers*, ed. Edward Rochie Hardy, Library of Christian Classics, vol. 3 (Philadelphia: Wesminster, 1954), 301.

37. See Darby Kathleen Ray, *Deceiving the Devil: Atonement, Abuse, and Ransom* (Cleveland: Pilgrim, 1998).

Human?"). Anselm's reflections on this question arise out of the medieval thought world and presuppose then-current understandings of law, offense, reparations, and social obligations. God and humans are related like feudal lords and their serfs. Since disobedience dishonors the lord, *either* satisfaction must be given *or* punishment must follow. The satisfaction that is due to God on account of the offense of sin is infinite. While humanity *must* provide this satisfaction, only God *can* provide it. "None but God can make this satisfaction . . . none but a human being ought to do this."[38] For this reason God has become human in Christ. In his perfect obedience unto death, satisfaction is rendered, justice is done, God's honor is restored, and sinners are forgiven.

The humanity of Christ is given a more significant role in this theory of atonement than in the cosmic conflict theory. Moreover, the seriousness of sin and the costliness of redemption are expressed in a way that was intelligible to the church in the medieval period. But the satisfaction theory as traditionally presented also raises serious questions. Most important of all, it seems to set God in contradiction to Godself. It draws upon the juridical metaphors of the New Testament in a way that brings mercy and justice into collision. In other words, the Anselmian theory makes the act of forgiveness something of a problem for God. Grace is made conditional on satisfaction. But is conditional grace still grace? According to the New Testament, it is not God but humanity who needs to be reconciled. In the New Testament God is not so much the object as the subject of reconciliation in Christ.

Standing firmly in the tradition of the Anselmian satisfaction theory, John Calvin nevertheless wavered on the question whether the motive of the atonement was the need to satisfy God's righteous anger or whether God was moved by pure and freely given love for the world. While also deeply indebted to the Anselmian tradition, Karl Barth moves beyond both Anselm and Calvin by consistently interpreting the atoning work of Christ as motivated solely by the holy love of God.[39]

Another failing of the satisfaction theory, as traditionally stated, is that it does not adequately distinguish between a substitute and a representative. Dorothee Sölle has made this point rather convincingly. The world of substitution is the impersonal world of replaceable things. When a part of a machine wears out, a new part can be substituted. Representation, however, belongs in the world of persons and personal relationships. A representative

---

38. Anselm, *Cur Deus Homo?* Bk. 2, chap. 6.

39. See Bruce McCormack, *For Us and Our Salvation: Incarnation and Atonement in the Reformed Tradition,* Studies in Reformed Theology and History (Princeton Theological Seminary, 1993).

stands in for us, speaks and acts for us, without simply displacing us. In other words, a representative does not divest us of responsibility. Parents, for example, represent their children until their maturity, when they are able to speak and act for themselves. The atoning work of Christ is more faithfully and understandably interpreted as an act of personal representation rather than a work of mechanical substitution.[40]

3. A third prominent theory of atonement is often called the *moral influence* theory. It is also described as the "subjective" theory, in contrast to the "objective" emphases of the two theories already outlined. In the moral influence theory Christ reconciles humanity neither by some cosmic battle nor by some legal transaction — both of which would appear to be complete apart from any participation of those on behalf of whom the action is performed. Rather, Christ shows God's love to us in such a compelling way that we are constrained to respond in wonder and gratitude. The atoning work of Christ is complete only when it is appropriated in the act of faith and allowed to transform one's life.

Abelard, a contemporary of Anselm, is often named as the foremost representative of the moral influence theory of the atonement. The Abelardian theory is sometimes called exemplarist. However, it is not at all clear that Abelard reduces the work of Christ to that of mere example. Some passages in Abelard's writings indicate that for him the love of God in Christ is a divine benefit, a creative gift that generates the response of love in us. While it cannot be said that Abelard himself succeeded in clarifying the fact that the power of the love of God in Christ is greater than any mere example, his line of thought can certainly be extended to include this explanation. What Christ does is revelatory and exemplary, but "above and beyond its exemplary value, there is in it a surplus of mysterious causal efficacy that no merely human love possesses."[41]

The moral influence theory has its strength in emphasizing the unconditional nature and transforming power of God's love and in stressing the importance of our human response. While attending primarily to the "subjective" side of atonement, the theory might also be developed in a way that recognizes the objective web of illusions and self-deceptions that constitute our sinful condition as well as the objective power of the revelation of God's sacrificial love that shines into our sin-darkened world. Still, it is undoubt-

40. Sölle, *Christ Our Representative* (Philadelphia: Fortress, 1967).
41. Philip L. Quinn, "Abelard on Atonement: 'Nothing Unintelligible, Arbitrary, Illogical, or Immoral about It,'" in *Reasoned Faith*, ed. Eleonore Stump (Ithaca, N.Y.: Cornell University Press, 1993), 296.

edly true that many versions of the moral influence theory, especially in the modern era, have tended toward a sentimentalization of God's love, underestimated the power and tenacity of evil in the world, and depicted Jesus as merely a good example for people to follow. Still relevant is H. Richard Niebuhr's critique of a naive form of liberal theology in America: "A God without wrath brought people without sin into a kingdom without judgment through the ministrations of a Christ without a cross."[42]

These theories of atonement, and the New Testament metaphors on which they are based, are not mutually exclusive. Of course, at various times in the history of theology there have been those who have argued that one or another of them embodies total and exclusive truth. When such absolutization of one image or one theory occurs, there is a loss of the riches of the New Testament proclamation and the centuries-long meditation of the church on the meaning of the atoning work of Christ.

Moreover, each of the three theories can be reclaimed and reinterpreted for our own time, with its particular sense of bondage and cry for liberation. Through the ministry and cross of Christ, God does something decisive on behalf of oppressed humanity, liberating us from evil forces that enslave us, freeing us from our burden of guilt, restoring moral order in a disordered world, setting us free from the illusions and self-deceptions that bring destruction on our neighbors as well as ourselves, and awakening new faith, hope, and love in us. It is instructive that in the current hymnody of the church all three views of the atonement are represented, as can be seen, for example, in the three hymns "A Mighty Fortress Is Our God" (Christ the Victor), "O Sacred Head Now Wounded" (satisfaction), and "God of Grace and God of Glory" (moral influence).

John Calvin's doctrine of the three offices of Christ *(munus triplex)* offers help in keeping our understanding of the atonement open and inclusive. Calvin says that Christ acts as our prophet, priest, and king.[43] In this doctrine of the three offices, Calvin is able to include the teaching of Jesus, his sacrificial death, and his lordly rule. We might restate Calvin's teaching of the three offices of Christ as follows: Christ as prophet proclaims the coming reign of God and instructs us in the form of life appropriate to that reign (moral influence); Christ as priest renders to God the perfect sacrifice of love and obedience on our behalf (satisfaction); Christ as designated king rules the world despite the recalcitrance of evil and promises the ultimate victory of God's reign of righteousness and peace (Christ the Victor).

---

42. Niebuhr, *The Kingdom of God in America* (New York: Harper Torchbook, 1959), 193.
43. See Calvin, *Institutes,* 2.15.

In his elaborate doctrine of reconciliation, Karl Barth also makes use of the idea of three offices of Christ, imaginatively weaving them together with the classical doctrines of the two natures (divinity and humanity) of the one person of Christ and his two states (humiliation and exaltation). This yields the themes of "The Lord as Servant" (God in Jesus Christ acts humbly as our priest, redeeming us from our sin of pride), "The Servant as Lord" (humanity in Jesus Christ is exalted by grace to royal partnership with God, liberating us from our sin of sloth), and "The True Witness" (the union of God and humanity in Jesus Christ is radiant truth, carrying its own prophetic power and dispelling our sin of falsehood).[44] Calvin's and Barth's theologies of the person and work of Christ are richer for their inclusive approach to the wealth of metaphors in the New Testament witness and the mutually corrective motifs of classical theology.

Our reflections on several prominent views of atonement suggest that fruitful interpretations of the work of Christ should be guided in our time by the following principles:[45]

(1) We should respect the riches of the New Testament metaphors of atonement and the diversity of classical formulations rather than seeking to reduce everything to one common denominator.

(2) The atoning work of Christ encompasses the whole gospel story: his ministry, teaching, cross, and resurrection. None of these should be omitted or isolated from the others.

(3) The work of atonement is based on God's gracious initiative, but it also calls for a human response. An adequate doctrine of atonement will give both factors their appropriate attention.

(4) The grace of God includes judgment, and the judgment of God serves the purpose of grace. A doctrine of atonement should not present the grace and judgment of God as conflicting with each other.

(5) The atoning work of God in Christ has significance for individuals, society, and the entire cosmos.

Violence and the Cross

The Scriptures unanimously affirm that the death of Jesus was "for us," "for our sins," "for many," "for the world." "Christ died for our sins in accordance with the Scriptures" (1 Cor. 15:3). This scriptural affirmation is present, ex-

---

44. Barth, *Church Dogmatics*, 4/1-3.

45. Cf. Paul Tillich's summary of principles of the doctrine of atonement in *Systematic Theology*, 2: 173-76.

plicitly or implicitly, in the ancient ecumenical creeds. Jesus Christ "suffered under Pontius Pilate, was crucified, died, and was buried" (Apostles' Creed). All this was done "for us and for our salvation" (Nicene Creed). Is there a way of understanding this confession of "Christ crucified for us" that speaks with particular directness to our own time?

Perhaps the primary reason we have such difficulty in making sense of the death of Jesus as "for us" is that it is an event of violence. We are often experts not only in covering up the violence that pervades our lives and the workings of our world but also in skillfully disguising the violence that was present in Christ's death for us.[46] In many churches, worshipers have become accustomed to gilded and bejeweled crosses. Emperors have embraced the cross as a symbol of imperial majesty and glory. In hiding the violence of the event that stands at the center of the gospel drama, we turn the message of the costly love of God into a sentimental fairy tale, or a symbol of domination, or some other distortion of its true meaning. Alternatively, we acknowledge the violence of the cross but place the blame on some despicable group (often the Jews) or on God (as in theories of atonement that say the cross was necessary to appease the wrath of God).

No less than the world of antiquity, ours is a world of fearful and systemic violence. The Holocaust is the most vivid twentieth-century reminder of this fact. Hopes that the twenty-first century might represent a new beginning have been quickly shattered. The "cold war" of the second half of the twentieth century has been supplanted by the terrorism and the wars on terrorism of the first decade of the twenty-first century. A numbing fear of biological, chemical, and nuclear warfare has spread in the wake of appalling suicide bombings and various military responses to them. If there is any constraint on violence and lawlessness at the international level, its characteristic form is the construction of systems of mutually assured destruction. International relations, however, are not the only realm where the reality of violence is encountered. In the social and economic domains, unbridled competition and self-aggrandizement are glorified even if it means advancing one's fame and fortune at the expense of others. As statistics show, the domestic sphere is all too often not an arena of harmony and tranquility but a field of violence, where spouses are battered and parents abuse their children. Even the ecclesiastical domain is tarnished by episodes of abuse of power and exploitation of the most vulnerable.

---

46. I am indebted in the following paragraphs to the work of René Girard (*Violence and the Sacred*) and Gerhard Forde's reflections on Girard's work in *Christian Dogmatics*, vol. 2 (Philadelphia: Fortress, 1984), 79-99.

This is the real world where the drama of salvation unfolds. It is a world saturated with violence, a world of both hidden and overt savagery — the poor exploited, women beaten and raped, the innocent slaughtered, children abused, the earth plundered, prophets murdered. The message and ministry of Jesus clash profoundly with this world. He announces God's forgiveness of sinners, promises the future to the poor, welcomes outcasts and strangers, calls all to repentance and a new way of life characterized by love of God and others. His words and deeds arouse strong opposition from political and religious leaders alike. When Jesus proclaims and enacts the reign of God in a world built on violence, it is no arbitrary religious doctrine but profoundest truth that Jesus *must* suffer. That is, the boundless love of God must collide with a world where the desire to dominate incites the desire to retaliate and the use of violence is met by acts of counter-violence. As the risen Jesus explains to the disciples on the way to Emmaus, did not the Christ have to suffer all this and enter into his glory? (Luke 24:26). It was divine "necessity" — the necessity of God's gracious and non-coercive love — that the love of God be fully expressed in all its vulnerability in Jesus Christ. It was sinful human "necessity" — the necessity of a world order of our own making — that this one who mediated God's forgiveness and inaugurated the reign of God characterized by justice, freedom, and peace should become the victim of our violence because he threatened the whole world of violence that we inhabit and will to maintain.

We are not all equally blameworthy for the terrible webs of violence and death that envelop our personal lives, our society, and our world. But we are all caught up in these webs. We are all part of vicious circles of violence, whether as victims or victimizers or, most likely, some of both. A world imprisoned in these circles of violence is a veritable hell.

It belongs to the good news of the gospel that for our sake Christ "descended into hell." This sentence of the Apostles' Creed is so provocative and unsettling that it is sometimes simply omitted. Yet it is gospel. It gives vivid expression to the depth and unrestricted range of God's self-giving love in the crucified Christ. According to some interpreters, Christ's descent into hell refers to a missionary journey undertaken between the crucifixion and resurrection of Jesus Christ to preach the gospel to the inhabitants of the realm of the dead. Other interpreters, including John Calvin and Karl Barth, understand the descent into hell to refer to the terrible experience of loneliness and abandonment that Christ experienced for our sake on the cross, a terror far greater than his physical agonies alone. I agree with the second school of interpretation, but would go on to further describe the hell into which Christ descended for our sake as the world where violence and cruelty reign, where communion with God and others is under terrible and constant assault, and where the presence of God is deeply hidden.[47]

It is in a world captive to the way of violence that Jesus lived and died for us all. But God raised the crucified Jesus and made him the chief cornerstone of a new humanity that no longer espouses the way of violence, that no longer needs scapegoats, that no longer wills to live at the expense of victims, that no longer imagines or worships a bloodthirsty God, that is no longer interested in legitimations of violence, but that follows Jesus in the power of a new Spirit. We may briefly identify three aspects of Christ's death for us as it impinges on our world of violence.

1. *Christ died for us in order to expose our world of violence for what it is — a world that stands under God's judgment, a world that is in deadly bondage and that leads to universal destruction.* The life of Jesus and its culmination in the event of crucifixion is the revelation of the nonviolent love of God that sets us all, individually and corporately, under judgment. Nietzsche once said that because God is dead, everything is permitted. The claim that this message is good news is a lie. The fictitious freedom that is born of the will to replace and if possible murder God leads eventually to homicide, genocide, and biocide. "Christ died so that we might know that *not* everything is permitted."[48]

2. *Christ died for us in order to extend the healing love of God to all the violated and to mediate the forgiving love of God to all the violators.* The life and death of Christ are more than the revelation of God's judgment on our world of violence. They are supremely the gift of God's own costly love, mediating God's forgiveness and friendship in the midst of our violent world. In Jesus Christ God takes the sin, the hatred, and the violence of the world into God's own being and extinguishes them there. The language of violated and violators, victims and perpetrators, oppressed and oppressors can itself become a dehumanizing tool, and it should not be allowed to imprison our theological reflection. It does not speak the deepest truth about us, since we are all to some extent on both sides of these opposing terms. The crucified Christ embodies the love of God in our violent world, conquering the hatred that inspires violence and the spirit of revenge that prompts counter-violence. In the teaching, ministry, and crucifixion of Christ, God exposes the lie of the inevitability of the circle of violence and counter-violence. God refuses to oppose evil with evil. The cross is God's free and costly gift of love

47. On the descent into hell, see David Lauber, "Towards a Theology of Holy Saturday: Karl Barth and Hans Urs von Balthasar on the 'descensus ad inferna'" (Princeton Theological Seminary doctoral dissertation, 1999).

48. José Porfiro Miranda, *Being and the Messiah*, quoted in Leonardo Boff, *Passion of Christ, Passion of the World* (Maryknoll, N.Y.: Orbis Books, 1988), vii.

whose goal is the transformation of the world. Whenever the message of the cross of Christ is rightly preached and heard, whenever people of faith gather at the Lord's table to celebrate life in Jesus Christ and its promise of a new creation, whenever forgiveness is offered in the name of Christ and received in the power of the Spirit, the deadly circle of violence and counter-violence is broken, and the rule of violence begins to yield to a new world of compassion and solidarity.

3. *Christ died for us in order to open, in the midst of our violent world, a new future of reconciliation and peace for a new humanity and a new creation.* Seen in the light of the resurrection, the history of Jesus that comes to its climax in crucifixion is the indelible promise of the victory of the nonviolent love of God that wills peace and reconciliation throughout the creation. There is good news in the message of the cross that becomes radiantly clear in God's resurrection of the crucified: "God has not undergone the cross in order to eternalize it and deprive us of all hope. On the contrary, God has assumed it because God means to put an end to all the crosses of history."[49] The cross and resurrection of Jesus Christ inscribes deeply into human history the truth that God's compassion is greater than the murderous passions of our world, that God's glory can and does shine even in the deepest night of human savagery, that God's forgiving love is greater than our often paralyzing awareness of our guilt, that God's way of life is greater than our way of death.

Dimensions of the Resurrection of Christ

The resurrection of Christ stands at the center of the New Testament witness. It is attested in all four Gospels and has a prominent place in the other apostolic writings. "He is not here," says the angel to the women at the tomb. "He has been raised!" (Matt. 28:6). The earliest accounts of the resurrection of Christ are found in two basic forms: stories of the empty tomb (such as Mark 16:1-8), and stories of the appearances of the risen Lord (such as 1 Cor. 15:1-11 and Luke 24:13-35). There is little point in playing off one of these ancient resurrection traditions against the other. Whichever tradition is judged to be earlier, the fact remains that, as the apostle Paul declares, the Christian faith stands or falls with the truth of the resurrection of the crucified Jesus (1 Cor. 15:14).

Interpretations of the resurrection of Christ must avoid two extremes. On the one hand, the truth of the Easter message cannot be demonstrated by

---

49. Boff, *Passion of Christ, Passion of the World*, 144.

modern historical research. Faith in the resurrection of Christ is not reducible to the claim that the corpse of Jesus was resuscitated. Even if there were strong evidence that the tomb of Jesus was empty, this would not prove the claims of faith, as the New Testament witnesses already recognized (Matt. 28:11-15). This is not to say that faith and theology can simply avoid the many critical literary and historical questions that surround the Easter proclamation. But as Rowan Williams warns, it is possible to become so preoccupied with these sorts of questions that "the question of why the resurrection should be good news *now* almost disappears."[50]

On the other hand, the meaning of the resurrection of Christ must not be reduced to a change of mind and heart on the part of the early disciples. In this view the resurrection was not something that happened *to* Jesus, a new act of God by which the crucified Jesus was raised from the dead. Instead, the resurrection is something that happens *in* the disciples. According to Rudolf Bultmann, for example, the resurrection is a symbol of the rise of faith in the saving significance of the cross as proclaimed in the early Christian message: "The faith of Easter is just this — faith in the word of preaching."[51] What remains unclear in this interpretation is whether anything happened beyond the crucifixion that prompted the word of preaching and the response of faith. The danger exists here of reducing the resurrection of Christ to an internal and largely private occurrence that neither changes nor challenges the public world ruled by sin, violence, and death.

As attested in Scripture, the resurrection of Christ is an event that cannot be captured within the limits of a purely historical or a purely private perspective. "Resurrection" in the biblical sense of the word belongs to late Jewish and early Christian apocalyptic hope. It points to the event in which, despite the suffering and persecution of God's people, the final fulfillment of God's covenant promises has begun. God's raising of the crucified Jesus to new life is God's concrete confirmation of the promise that evil will finally be defeated and justice will reign throughout God's creation. Within this framework of apocalyptic eschatology, the message "Jesus is risen" requires a multidimensional interpretation.

There is, first, the crucial *theological* dimension. God is faithful. The God of Israel, who alone can open graves and bring the dead to life (Ezek. 37), raised the crucified Jesus. "The God of Abraham, the God of Isaac, and the

---

50. Rowan Williams, *Resurrection: Interpreting the Easter Gospel* (Cleveland: Pilgrim, 2002), 110.

51. Rudolf Bultmann, "The New Testament and Mythology," in *Kerygma and Myth: A Theological Debate* (New York: Harper & Row, 1961), 41.

God of Jacob, the God of our ancestors has glorified his servant Jesus" (Acts 3:13). What happened on Easter morning was neither a matter of course nor a remarkable feat of human imagination. Nor did Jesus raise himself from the dead. To speak of resurrection is to speak of God.[52] The resurrection of Jesus is an act of God, an act of the faithful and gracious God who makes an unexpected and glorious new beginning in the drama of salvation. Just as Jesus died for us, so also he was raised for us. A world of sin, violence, and death rendered its verdict on him. But God has rendered a contrary verdict, reversing and canceling the verdict of the world. The resurrection of Jesus is thus the "verdict of the Father" that confirms the Father's boundless love for the Son and for the world for which the Son gave his life.[53] In the resurrection of the crucified, God has spoken a mighty and irrevocable yes to Jesus and in him to all the world, altering the human situation once and for all.

Second, there is the *Christological* dimension of the resurrection. All of the resurrection narratives of the New Testament emphasize the identity of the risen Christ with the crucified one. The risen Christ is none other than the one who for our salvation assumed our flesh, lived among us as a humble servant, and was obedient even unto death on a cross (Phil. 2:5-11). It is this Jesus who was raised by God from the dead. As Scripture reports, the risen Christ "showed them his hands and his side" (John 20:20). By his resurrection from the dead, the servant Lord now appears in the radiance of his being. His way of *kenosis* (emptying) ends not in irredeemable tragedy but in *plerosis* (fullness), not in heroic death but in fullness of life. In his resurrection, the very same one whose glory remained mostly hidden prior to Easter (cf. Isa. 53:1-3) now shines radiantly. The light of the resurrected Christ dispels all darkness. His love cannot be held captive by a world ruled by sin and drenched in violence and death. Accordingly, the message that Christ is risen is met by fear, awe and amazement, rendering those who hear it speechless at first (Mark 16:8). As David Bentley Hart writes, the glory of the resurrected Christ "transgresses the orderly metaphysics" that rule our world.[54] It subverts our conceptions of what is necessary, upsets our worldviews of what is possible, shatters the "glamour of violence" that blinds us, and sets in its place the splendor of the truth of God's reconciliation and peace realized in Jesus Christ.[55] In the risen one, our humanity is seen in its exaltation. Easter is the

---

52. See Karl Barth, *The Resurrection of the Dead* (London: Hodder and Stoughton, 1933; reprinted Wipf and Stock, 2003).

53. *Church Dogmatics*, 4/1: 283-357.

54. David Bentley Hart, *The Beauty of the Infinite: The Aesthetics of Christian Truth* (Grand Rapids: Eerdmans, 2003), 389.

55. Hart, *The Beauty of the Infinite*, 349.

beginning of the freedom of the glory of the children of God (Rom. 8:21). As Irenaeus declares, the glory of God is humanity alive.[56]

Third, there is a *pneumatological* dimension of the resurrection. The gospel tells the story of God's Son, "who was descended from David according to the flesh and was declared to be Son of God with power according to the Spirit of holiness by resurrection from the dead" (Rom. 1:3-4). According to the Gospel of John, the risen Lord breathes the Spirit on his disciples (John 20:22). The resurrection of Christ is, in the apostle Paul's words, the "first fruits" (1 Cor. 15:20, 23) of the new creation, and believers participate in the new life in Christ by the power of the Spirit. The Spirit gives again the gift of life that Christ has given once for all. By the Spirit, the light that shone in the crucified and risen Christ continues to shine. By the Spirit, the love of the crucified and risen Christ reaches into human hearts and minds: "God's love has been poured into our hearts through the Holy Spirit that has been given to us" (Rom. 5:5). The Father freely gives the Son, the Son freely gives himself for us, and the Spirit is God freely giving again. "God simply continues to give, freely, inexhaustibly, regardless of rejection. God gives and forgives; he fore-gives and gives again."[57] The cross and resurrection of Christ thus manifest the trinitarian plenitude of God's self-giving love for the world: the Father's giving is boundless, the Son's giving is glorious, the Spirit's giving again is life-transforming. By the Spirit the living Christ brings new life to his disciples and gives them a mission. An integral part of the resurrection narratives is the apostolic commissioning to proclamation and service. By the authority of the risen Christ and in the power of the Spirit, the disciples are sent forth to teach the truth of Christ, to baptize in the name of the triune God (Matt. 28:19-20), and to serve others (John 21:15-17).

Fourth, the reception of the resurrected Christ has an *ecclesial* dimension. The apostolic proclamation of the resurrection of the crucified must be received by a personal act of faith. Yet it is never an isolated experience and perception. The splendor and power of the resurrected one creates a new community. Through the witness, life, and practices of that community — "the body of Christ" — the truth of Christ crucified and risen is proclaimed. As Rowan Williams points out, in the gnostic gospels of the early Christian era, the risen Christ "returns in discarnate shape to give his apostles detached instructions for their own escape." For the New Testament witnesses to the resurrection, however, "the church is where Jesus is met, where bodily historical graces and reconciliation are now shown."[58] The story of the walk to

---

56. Irenaeus, *Against Heresies*, 4.20.7.
57. Hart, *The Beauty of the Infinite*, 351.
58. Williams, *Resurrection*, 93-95.

Emmaus is especially instructive in this regard. As they walk together on Easter morning, two disciples talk despondently about their shattered hopes. When a stranger joins them on the road, they do not recognize that it is Jesus. The risen Lord becomes known to them as he interprets the word of Scripture and breaks bread with them (Luke 24:13-35).

In underscoring the role of the church as the body of Christ in the apprehension and reception of the risen Christ, we do not say that the risen Christ is identical with, or only a pious construct of, the community of faith. That would be another way of emptying the reality of his resurrection into the response of his witnesses. The risen Christ comes *to* his disciples; he is not secretly identical with them or merely a product of their imagination. The community of faith is where the living Christ is often encountered, acknowledged, confessed, and obeyed, but it is not the ultimate source and power of the risen Lord. "The church," says Williams, "still meets Jesus as the other, a stranger; it never absorbs him into itself so that he ceases to be its lover and its judge."[59]

Fifth, there is a *political* dimension of the resurrection of Christ. N. T. Wright makes the arresting claim that the message "Christ is risen" was and is "political dynamite."[60] Like the declaration that the risen Jesus is Lord (1 Cor. 12:3; John 20:28) — a declaration inseparable from the Easter message — the proclamation that Christ is risen constitutes a challenge to all principalities and powers of the world. If Christ is the risen Lord of the world, Caesar is not.[61] If by the resurrection God has declared this Jesus to be the "Son of God" and in doing so has affirmed his lordship, then not only the tyranny of sin and death but also the tyrannical claims and violent regimes of emperors and empires ("the institutionalization of sin and death," as N. T. Wright describes them) are put in question and radically subverted.[62] "Because of the resurrection," Hart writes, "it is impossible to be reconciled to coercive or natural violence, to ascribe its origins to fate or cosmic order . . . all violence, all death, stands under judgment as that which God has and will overcome."[63]

Jon Sobrino also emphasizes the political dimension of the resurrection of Christ. He understands the resurrection message as proclaiming the triumph of God over all injustice and violence, the event that gives all victims of history a new and lasting hope. According to Sobrino, the cross of Christ and the suffering of all "crucified people" of history "provide the most apt setting for the un-

---

59. Williams, *Resurrection*, 95.

60. N. T. Wright, *The Resurrection of the Son of God* (Minneapolis: Fortress, 2003), 730.

61. N. T. Wright, *The Resurrection of the Son of God*, 225.

62. N. T. Wright, *The Resurrection of the Son of God*, 729.

63. Hart, *The Beauty of the Infinite*, 394.

derstanding of the resurrection of Jesus."[64] Sobrino notes that in the earliest resurrection accounts, it is in Galilee — symbol of the place of the poor and the despised — that the risen Jesus will be found. Disciples of the risen Jesus will find him as they take up their ministry in the "Galilees" of history. All this has a very practical meaning for Sobrino. Following the crucified and risen Jesus necessarily entails struggle and conflict. The God of life who raised Jesus from the dead opposes all idols of death, and so too must his disciples. While not a call to arms, the Easter message is a call to permanent resistance to all injustice and violence. The cross and the resurrection of Jesus are inseparable. They express both God's solidarity with victims and the efficacy of God's boundless love. So understood, the cross ceases to be a manifestation of love without power, and the resurrection ceases to be a manifestation of power without love.[65]

Finally, there is the *cosmic* dimension of the resurrection of Christ. We might also speak of this as the eschatological dimension of Christ's resurrection. As Jürgen Moltmann states, the resurrection of Christ is the beginning of God's new world. It is "the first preliminary radiance of the imminent dawn of God's new creation."[66] The resurrection of Christ is the sign, the promise, and the beginning of the coming new world of God. Moltmann's particular emphasis in his theology of the resurrection is its cosmic scope. He contends that, at least in the Western church, the resurrection of Christ has been seen too narrowly as offering hope for the future of humanity. While the Easter message certainly includes this hope, the new world that it envisions and opens is not limited to human destiny. In addition to the hope for persons and communities, the resurrection of Christ also means hope for the whole cosmos groaning for release from bondage to death (Rom. 8:18-25). Christ died not only in solidarity with sinners, and not only in solidarity with all human beings who suffer violence. He also died in solidarity with all living creatures captive to the reign of death. Hence, properly understood, the resurrection of Christ is the "first fruits" of the coming universal reign of God, the event that inaugurates the coming of God's gift of new life for the whole creation. To believe in the resurrection of Christ is to believe that God will not only triumph over the violent death that reigns in human history but also will triumph over the tragic death to which all life is presently subject.[67] In this comprehensive sense, proclamation of the resurrection of Christ crucified is "gospel," good news indeed.

64. Jon Sobrino, *Christ the Liberator* (Maryknoll, N.Y.: Orbis Books, 2001), 14.

65. Sobrino, *Christ the Liberator*, 87-88.

66. Jürgen Moltmann, *The Way of Jesus Christ: Christology in Messianic Dimensions* (San Francisco: HarperCollins, 1990), 220.

67. Moltmann, *The Way of Jesus Christ*, 253.

CHAPTER 9

Confessing Jesus Christ in Context

Confession of Jesus Christ takes place in particular historical and cultural contexts. Our response to the questions of who we say Jesus Christ is and how he helps us will be shaped in important ways by the particular contexts in which these questions arise. In this chapter my aim is to explore in greater detail some recent efforts to take seriously the social and cultural contexts of Christology.

Why devote a chapter of an introduction to theology to the topic of contextual theology in general and contextual Christology in particular? First, it is a reminder that all theology is contextual, that historical and cultural context is a factor in all Christian life, witness, and theology. Traditional European and North Atlantic theologies are no less contextual than African American theology or feminist theology. Second, it is a recognition that there is no risk-free way of engaging in the task of Christology. If there is risk in a Christology that is self-consciously contextual, the same is true of every attempt to say who Christ is and what sort of salvation he brings. Third, the whole church has something to gain from the newer contextual Christologies (or as they are sometimes called, local Christologies) and much to lose by ignoring or dismissing them. This chapter should therefore be read not as an optional appendix to the previous chapter but as an important extension of its reflections on the person and work of Christ.

The Particularity and Universality of the Gospel

There are both external and internal factors prompting the development of contextual Christologies.[1] Some of the external factors are easily identified. Many Christians in Asia, Africa, and Latin America are convinced that their theological reflection must attend to their own distinctive non-Western cultures and forms of thought. They chafe at the Western cultural imperialism that has often accompanied the spread of Christianity into their lands. They wonder why faith in Jesus Christ can be expressed with the help of Western philosophical conceptualities but not with the aid of Asian or African forms of thought. In North America and Europe, many black and Asian Christians and women of all races contend that traditional theologies have ignored their particular histories and struggles.

Equally important, however, are the internal factors that make the development of contextual Christologies both possible and necessary. The Christian gospel centers in God's work of reconciliation in Jesus Christ. According to the scriptural witness and the church's ecumenical creeds, God comes to us not in abstract principles or ideas but in a concrete history. Christianity is a historical and incarnational faith focused on the activity of God in the calling of the people of Israel and above all in the coming of God in the person and work of Jesus of Nazareth. Yet for all its particularity, this activity of God among the people of Israel and supremely in Jesus Christ is proclaimed as having universal significance. Christ lived, was crucified, and was raised from the dead "for all." God's way to universality is through the particular. This has profound implications for the church's witness to Jesus Christ throughout the world. Just as God's decisive self-communication is through incarnation in a particular human life, so the transmission of the gospel message by the church makes use of concrete and diverse languages, experiences, philosophical conceptualities, and cultural practices.

The missiologist Andrew Walls speaks of the "translation principle" that is present in the transmission of the gospel. God's act of self-communication through incarnation is an act of divine translation par excellence, and it provides the theological basis of the necessary work of translation in the proclamation and mission of the church. Jesus Christ, the Word of God incarnate, lived in a particular locality, belonged to a particular ethnic group, and spoke a particular language. Witness to and appropriation of God's act of self-communication in its scandalous particularity prompts a

---

1. See Stephen B. Bevans, *Models of Contextual Theology* (Maryknoll, N.Y.: Orbis Books, 1992), 5-10.

continuing translation process as the Christian message is transmitted in new places and times. According to Walls, "Incarnation is translation. When God in Christ became man, divinity was translated into humanity. . . . The first divine act of translation thus gives rise to a constant succession of new translations. Christian diversity is the necessary product of the incarnation."[2]

The practice of the early church offers abundant evidence of the translation principle in the spreading of the gospel. We have not one but four Gospels, each of which proclaims Christ in a distinctive way that is shaped by its particular context. Paul declares that he has become "all things to all people" that he might "by all means" save some (1 Cor. 9:22). This does not mean, of course, tailoring the gospel so that it no longer offends anyone. It does mean, however, that the labor of interpretation is necessary if the gospel is to be proclaimed clearly to different people in different cultural settings. The true scandal of the gospel must be distinguished from false scandals created by the assumption that only one language and one culture can be vehicles of the gospel message.

Recognition of the inseparable bond between the particularity and universality of the gospel helps to explain both the necessity and the challenge of contextual theology. On the one hand, if we seek to emphasize the universality of the gospel by generalizing its message and stripping it of all historical contingency, we lose sight of the gospel's own particularity and its power to receive and transform human life in all its historical particularity and diversity. On the other hand, if we emphasize one particular expression of the gospel to the exclusion of all others, we lose sight of its universal power. Robert Schreiter states the problem in this way: "In the midst of the tremendous vitality that today's Christians are showing, one set of problems emerges over and over again: how to be faithful both to the contemporary experience of the gospel and to the tradition of Christian life that has been received."[3]

In the previous chapter an attempt was made to interpret and summarize the church's common affirmations about the person and work of Jesus Christ. No doubt this restatement also bears the marks of the particular historical context in which the present book is written and the particular ecclesial tradition of its author. The point of the present chapter is to recognize that there is necessarily a catholic (universal) and a local (particular) dimension to the confession of the person and work of Christ. Christology will

---

2. Andrew Walls, *The Missionary Movement in Christian History: Studies in the Transmission of Faith* (Maryknoll, N.Y.: Orbis, 1996), 27-28.

3. Robert J. Schreiter, *Constructing Local Theologies* (Maryknoll, N.Y.: Orbis Books, 1986), xi.

increasingly have to attend to both of these dimensions. This will require a willingness to listen to interpretations of Christ and his saving work that arise out of different locations and histories from that of the dominant Western theological tradition. Mutual criticism and correction will certainly be a part of the dialogue between the "catholic" theological tradition and the more recent, self-consciously "contextual" theologies. But so too will mutual enrichment. Emerging contextual Christologies have the potential to show that the gospel of Jesus Christ addresses human life in all its historical and cultural diversity and that nothing genuinely human is alien to the gospel.

Latin American Christology

Some of the most creative work in Christology in recent years comes from Latin American liberation theology. Among its leaders are Gustavo Gutiérrez, Jon Sobrino, Leonardo Boff, José Míguez Bonino, and Juan Luis Segundo.[4] While Latin American Christology is far from monolithic and has shown the capacity for self-correction and fresh lines of thought, there are several common emphases that can be identified and that will no doubt continue to influence the work of Christology in the entire ecumenical church.

According to Latin American theologians, Christology cannot be done in a vacuum. It *must attend to the concrete setting, the particular historical situation in which the biblical message is read and heard.* Dehumanizing poverty is an overwhelming reality in Latin America. For centuries the history of Latin American people has been marked by colonial exploitation followed by debilitating dependence on First World nations. The quest for liberation from this dependency — economically, culturally, and spiritually — is the context of Latin American Christology. The setting of reflection about Christ for Latin American liberation theologians is "the world of the poor": "The setting does not invent the content, but away from this setting it will be difficult to find [Christ] and to read adequately the texts about him."[5]

---

4. Gustavo Gutiérrez, *A Theology of Liberation*, 15th anniversary ed. (Maryknoll, N.Y.: Orbis Books, 1988); Jon Sobrino, *Christology at the Crossroads: A Latin American Approach* (Maryknoll, N.Y.: Orbis Books, 1978); idem, *Jesus the Liberator* (Maryknoll, N.Y.: Orbis Books, 1993); idem, *Christ the Liberator* (Maryknoll, N.Y.: Orbis Books, 2001); Leonardo Boff, *Jesus Christ Liberator* (Maryknoll, N.Y.: Orbis Books, 1978); Juan Luis Segundo, *Jesus of Nazareth, Yesterday and Today*, vol. 2, *The Historical Jesus of the Synoptics* (Maryknoll, N.Y.: Orbis Books, 1985); Jose Miguez Bonino, *Faces of Jesus: Latin American Christologies* (Maryknoll, N.Y.: Orbis Books, 1984).

5. Sobrino, *Jesus the Liberator*, 28.

Latin American theologians interpret Scripture in the light of their situation and their situation in the light of Scripture. Within this hermeneutical circle they affirm that *God in Christ enters into solidarity with the poor.* Latin American liberation theologians insist on beginning in Christology "from below" (that is, starting with the concrete historical ministry of Jesus) rather than "from above" (that is, starting with the doctrines of the Trinity and the incarnation of the eternal Logos). According to Sobrino, "If the *end* of Christology is to profess that Jesus is the Christ, its *starting point* is the affirmation that this Christ is the Jesus of history."[6] Only by beginning with the biblical witness to the ministry and crucifixion of Jesus of Nazareth will we properly understand the classical Christological dogmas of the church.

When we begin "from below," with the "historical Jesus" and his ministry in first-century Palestine, we find ourselves face to face with one who proclaimed the near advent of God's kingdom of justice and freedom, who blessed the poor, forgave sinners, had table fellowship with the outcast, befriended women, collided with the self-righteous custodians of the law, and evoked the suspicion and anger of the Roman authorities with his message and ministry. If we focus on the concrete ministry, suffering, and death of Jesus, we cannot avoid the conclusion that the God revealed and made present by Jesus enters into solidarity with the poor.

Critics of this emphasis charge that it distorts the universal offer of salvation in the biblical proclamation. For Latin American liberation theologians, however, the theme of God's solidarity with the poor is an expression of inclusivity, not exclusivity. Since it is the poor who are being unjustly excluded, it must be the poor who are included first of all in the divine economy of salvation.[7]

For Latin American theologians, *the sin that keeps people in bondage and the salvation that frees them have both personal and political dimensions.* The characteristic emphasis of this theology is, to be sure, on the social and political aspects of the gospel. This is a response to the entrenched and damaging privatization of Christian faith and life. While such privatization may fit well with the dualisms that permeate modern Western culture, in the eyes of Latin American theologians it is a distortion of the biblical message. There are corporate structures of sin and injustice. Jesus did not confront only sinful indi-

---

6. Sobrino, *Christology at the Crossroads,* xxi.

7. See Julio Lois, "Christology in the Theology of Liberation," in *Mysterium Liberationis: Fundamental Concepts of Liberation Theology,* ed. Ignacio Ellacuria and Jon Sobrino (Maryknoll, N.Y.: Orbis Books, 1993), 168-93.

viduals but a sinful structure of life. Similarly, he saw salvation as more than the rescue of isolated souls to fellowship with God. Rather, he proclaimed and inaugurated the kingdom of God, the rule of the gracious and righteous God that encompasses the whole of life.

Although Latin American Christology characteristically underscores the corporate, political dimension of sin, it does not ignore the importance of the personal dimension of sin and salvation. It speaks of the need of a theology of "integral liberation" and of a "spirituality of liberation." Sentimental views of the poor and neglect of the need of all people for repentance and conversion have nothing to do with integral liberation.[8]

Latin American liberation theologians are aware that the political significance of the ministry of Jesus cannot be sought in simplistic parallels between the action of Jesus and what Christians should do today in their particular situations. The attempt, for example, to find a link between Jesus and the Jewish revolutionaries called Zealots in order to justify revolutionary action by Christians today is misguided. The proper analogy is between Jesus' struggle against the forces of injustice as part of his ministry in the name of the coming reign of God and the struggle of Christians today for justice in the hope of a time of reconciliation and peace for all people by God's grace.

In Latin American Christology, *the cross and resurrection of Christ are given a distinctive interpretation.* Jesus was killed as a consequence of his scandalous message and ministry, not because it was demanded by God, as taught by some theories of atonement. The cross was not necessary to change God's attitude toward human beings. Rather, it is the culmination of a life totally dedicated to God and God's reign. "Jesus' life as a whole, not one of its elements, is what is pleasing to God."[9] "What does Jesus' cross really say? It says that God has irrevocably drawn near to this world, that he is a God 'with us' and a God 'for us.'"[10]

From the perspective of Latin American liberation theology, the danger of ideology in Christian teaching is most pronounced in the interpretation of the cross. The cross is not an event demonstrating that God wants everyone to suffer as much as possible. In many places — not least in Latin America — the message of the cross has repeatedly been used to undercut resistance to injustice and to help keep the oppressed in their place. However, what this

---

8. See Gustavo Gutiérrez, *We Drink from Our Own Wells: The Spiritual Journey of a People* (Maryknoll, N.Y.: Orbis Books, 1984).

9. Sobrino, *Jesus the Liberator,* 229.

10. Sobrino, *Jesus the Liberator,* 231.

misuse of the proclamation of the cross obscures is the world of difference between suffering that is imposed on others and suffering that is willingly assumed for the sake of assisting others to gain release from their bondage. Far from being an ideological defense of suffering caused by exploitation and abuse, the cross is a sign of the suffering of God in the passion of Christ and stands as a protest against unjust suffering as well as a promise of God's companionship with the oppressed.

Likewise, the resurrection of Christ is wrongly construed as only drawing attention to life beyond death rather than also calling for real transformation of this world. "What is specific about Jesus' resurrection is . . . not what God does with a dead body but what God does with a victim. . . . God is the God who liberates victims."[11] The resurrection is the divine promise of the comprehensive transformation of life and the universal triumph of God's righteousness.

For Latin American liberation theologians, *knowledge of Christ is inseparably linked to following Christ.* Faith affirmations and Christian praxis are inseparable. We will never rightly understand Christ or his proclamation, ministry, death, and resurrection until we find ourselves where he placed himself — in the company of those who are afflicted and unjustly treated and who cry out for the justice and freedom that they have lost or never known. Sobrino argues that "the only way to get to know Jesus is to follow after him in one's own life; to try to identify oneself with his own historical concerns; and to try to fashion his kingdom in our midst. In other words, only through Christian praxis is it possible for us to draw close to Jesus. Following Jesus is the precondition for knowing Jesus."[12]

Sobrino's axiom of Christology is open to the criticism that it is one-sided. We must surely also say that knowing Jesus rightly is the precondition of following him. Otherwise we might be following not Jesus but an image of Jesus of our own making. Nevertheless, Sobrino's emphasis, appropriately qualified, is a much-needed reminder to the church in his situation as well as to the church universal that the pursuit of Christology apart from the dangerous practice of following Christ is bound to miss the point.

What changes will Latin American liberation theology undergo in the future? From many different quarters there has been a barrage of criticisms of liberation theology. The major criticisms concern the movement's utopian tendencies, the overdependence on Marxist analysis, the suspicion of a "low" Christology, and of course for the Vatican, the challenge to episcopal author-

---

11. Sobrino, *Christ the Liberator*, 84.
12. Sobrino, *Christology at the Crossroads*, xiii.

ity that finds expression in the local groups or "base communities" in which liberation theology has flourished. In the wake of these criticisms, a careful reader should acknowledge both the abiding insights of Latin American liberation theology as well as some of its flaws.[13] One of its flaws, at least in its early phase, was to be less than attentive to matters of race and gender and thus to all the voices long silenced. Rebecca Chopp observes, "As Latin American liberation theology pushes further to examine its own diversity, its own mosaic of culture and practices, its future will have to extend more and more to include the voices, and not merely the faces, of women, of blacks, of Amerindians, and others who have not yet spoken even within Latin American liberation theology."[14]

African American Christology

Without question, African American or black theology is the pioneering contextual theology of North America, and its influence has now extended worldwide. Black theology first appeared in the period of the civil rights struggle in the United States in the 1960s, but its roots go back centuries in the history and experience of African American Christians. A dynamic movement, black theology has gone through several phases, from intense activism to academic establishment to reconnection with the experience and mission of the black church.[15] As is true of other contextual theologies, there are many voices within black theology and they have different and sometimes mutually corrective emphases. As will be noted, black theology has shown the capacity for vigorous self-criticism.

Black theology is rooted in the history and experience of African American people. It affirms the value and inspiration of black history and culture as the story of a courageous people who, undergirded by faith in God, have struggled against oppression and survived despite long and brutal mistreatment. First as an enslaved people and then as repeated targets of racist attitudes and practices in both the wider society and the established churches, African American Christians have made a distinctive witness to the God of the gospel. Black theology emerges from this history and social context, yet it

13. See Nancy E. Bedford, "Whatever Happened to Liberation Theology?" *The Christian Century* 116 (Oct. 20, 1999): 996-1000.

14. Rebecca S. Chopp, "Latin American Liberation Theology," in *The Modern Theologians,* ed. David F. Ford (Malden, Mass.: Blackwell, 1997), 409-25.

15. See M. Shawn Copeland, "Black, Hispanic/Latino, and Native American Theologies," in *The Modern Theologians,* 357-67.

is not wholly derived from or determined by this context. While emphasizing that what people think about God, Jesus Christ, and the meaning of Christian discipleship is shaped by their particular history and status in a given society,[16] black theology insists that the faith of African American Christians cannot be explained by any kind of reductionism. It is not simply a product of its context. The Christian gospel speaks with power both *out of* and *to* the experience of African American people.

According to black theologians, *the encounter with Scripture through the lens of the experience and faith of the black community results in a rediscovery of the good news of God's liberation of the oppressed*. For black theology this rediscovery is comparable in importance to the rediscovery by Luther of the gospel of justification by grace through faith alone over against the teaching that salvation rests on our good works, and the rediscovery by Barth of the radical otherness of God in contrast to the domesticated divinity of Protestant liberalism.[17] The African American experience is used as a "window into the world" of Scripture and its liberating message, and the insights that are achieved are offered to all.[18]

Reading the Bible through the eyes of a people who continue to struggle for freedom, and centering their interpretation on the person and work of Jesus Christ, a number of black theologians declare that *Christ is "black."* This affirmation must be properly understood: Christ is called "black" because of his solidarity with the poor and the outcast in his ministry and in his death by crucifixion alongside two criminals. James Cone writes, "Christ is black . . . not because of some cultural or psychological need of black people, but because and only because Christ really enters into our world where the poor, the despised, and the black are, disclosing that he is with them, enduring their humiliation and pain and transforming oppressed slaves into liberated servants."[19]

Black Christology unambiguously acknowledges Jesus as Savior, fully divine and fully human.[20] It charges, however, that the real meaning of these orthodox affirmations has often been obscured or even subverted by a racist mindset. In other words, although Christ was confessed by the estab-

---

16. See James H. Cone, *God of the Oppressed* (New York: Seabury, 1975).

17. See James Cone, *For My People: Black Theology and the Black Church* (Maryknoll, N.Y.: Orbis Books, 1984), 41.

18. Brian K. Blount, *Then the Whisper Put on Flesh: New Testament Ethics in an African American Context* (Nashville: Abingdon, 2001), 22.

19. Cone, *God of the Oppressed*, 136.

20. See James H. Evans, Jr., *We Have Been Believers: An African-American Systematic Theology* (Minneapolis: Fortress, 1992), 96.

lished churches to be both divine and human, the true humanity of God incarnate did not seem to include the suffering humanity of black people. Evidence of this is the support given by many white churches in nineteenth-century America to the institution of slavery. Cone asks, "What are we to make of a tradition that investigated the meaning of Christ's relation to God and the divine and human natures in his person, but failed to relate these christological issues to the liberation of the slave and the poor in the society?"[21]

Black Christology concentrates on the meaning of the ministry, cross, and resurrection of Christ for the poor and despised of the earth. As Cone contends, the identity of Jesus must be seen in who he was, who he is, and who he will be. Jesus is "who he was . . . the one who lived with the poor and died on the cross"; Jesus is "who he is," present now with the poor, helping them to "struggle for the maintenance of humanity in a situation of oppression"; Jesus is "who he will be," the coming Lord who empowers the oppressed to "'keep on keeping on' even when their fight seems fruitless."[22] For black theology, the history of salvation attested in Scripture is marked by the scandal of particularity, from the exodus of the people of Israel from bondage in Egypt to the ministry of Jesus among the despised today.

While black theology emphasizes God's partiality toward the poor, it does not deny the universal scope of grace. Understandable anger is evident, especially in the early writings of black theologians. Nevertheless, most black theologians reject an "inordinate focus" on the particularity of blackness that would jeopardize the universalism of the gospel and turn the Christian message into a racial ideology.[23]

Black theology is not just a church theology but also a "political theology." *It seeks to unmask evil forces, including but not limited to the pervasive racism that marks the attitudes, structures, and practices of the North American church and North American society.* The language of struggle and conflict that permeates black theology is upsetting to many of its readers because it seems to them to call for violent retaliation. But in fact black theology has never endorsed a spirit of revenge or called for preemptive acts of violence. As Cone shows, black theology has been stamped by the life and witness of two North American black leaders — Martin Luther King, Jr., and Malcolm X. King's consistent message was one of non-violent resistance, while

---

21. Cone, *God of the Oppressed*, 114.

22. Cone, *God of the Oppressed*, 108-37.

23. Cf. James H. Cone, *A Black Theology of Liberation* (Philadelphia: J. B. Lippincott, 1970) and Cone, *For My People*, 225, n. 6.

Malcolm X confronted racism in a tough and uncompromising voice, endorsing the right of blacks to defend themselves against violence. Yet like King, Malcolm X also envisioned, at least in the final period of his life, a universal harmony of people of all races. Cone sees the life and witness of these two leaders as ultimately converging strands of the faith and hope of the black community.[24]

If the first generation of black theologians was primarily interested in exposing the endemic racism of American society and the church in America, and in spelling out the political implications of the biblical message of liberation, the following generations have moved on to explore black history and culture as a resource for Christian faith and theology today. Dwight N. Hopkins uses slave religion as a primary source for the construction of a black theology focused on three doctrines: "God, in constructive black theology, is the Spirit of total liberation for us. Jesus is the fulfillment of the Spirit of total liberation revealed to be with us. And human purpose is the Spirit of total liberation in us."[25]

Like other liberation theologies, black theology insists that *confessing Christ is inseparable from following Christ.* This is not an expression of anti-intellectualism, although it could be employed to that end. It is instead a rejection of the damaging separations of theology and ethics, theory and practice, mind and body, person and society, and church and world that are sins against the integrity of the gospel and the indivisibility of human life.

Black theology has shown a remarkable capacity for expansion and transformation. It *does not consider either its own work or the life of the black community to be immune from criticism.* A radical encounter with the gospel seen through the window of the black experience stands in judgment not only on the dominant society but also on oppressive practices and attitudes in the black community. As in all communities, there are realities of life in the black community "still in desperate need of liberation and transformation, not only from without (where the problems are more obvious), but also from within (where the problems may be even more destructive)."[26] Womanist theologians in particular have raised serious questions about the absence of women and women's concerns in the project of black theology. These criti-

---

24. James H. Cone, *Martin, Malcolm, and America: A Dream or a Nightmare?* (Maryknoll, N.Y.: Orbis Books, 1992); Peter J. Paris, "The Theology and Ethics of Martin Luther King Jr.: Contributions to Christian Thought and Practice," in *Reformed Theology for the Third Christian Millennium,* ed. B. A. Gerrish (Louisville: Westminster/John Knox, 2003).

25. Dwight N. Hopkins, *Down, Up, and Over: Slave Religion and Black Theology* (Minneapolis: Fortress, 2000), 158.

26. Blount, *Then the Whisper Put on Flesh,* 188.

cisms have led in recent years to frequent dialogue and important collaboration between black theologians and womanist theologians.[27]

M. Shawn Copeland raises other concerns that must be addressed by black theology in the future. Among them is the need for increased "engagement with critical black biblical scholarship" and sustained wrestling with the doctrinal history of the church. Copeland asks, "How is black theology to tease out more adequately the soteriological implications of the Nicene/Chalcedonian formulation?"[28]

Within the African American church, dedication to Christ and his way has been cultivated and sustained primarily not by academic theologies, however important they may be, but by a *distinctive tradition of vibrant worship, inspiring preaching, and moving songs of sorrow and joy* that recount conditions of suffering, remember Jesus the Savior, celebrate his presence, and express hope in his coming reign. One of the most powerful ways the confession of Christ has found expression in the African American church is through a unique and rich musical heritage.[29] This heritage is one of the many precious gifts of the African American church to the church universal.

The flowering of African American theology in recent decades has helped to awaken the African American church and indeed the church universal *to the history and vitality of the church in Africa.* Christology today cannot ignore the distinctive understandings and images of Jesus in African worship and theology. Attentive both to the biblical witness and to the history and piety of their people, some African theologians privilege images of Jesus such as the great "Healer" of every affliction, the primal "Ancestor" who has gone before us and who shares our humanity, and the mighty "Chief" or "Victor" over all forces of evil and destruction. These distinctive African "faces of Jesus" invite Christians everywhere to discover fresh dimensions of the grace of God in Jesus Christ.[30]

---

27. See Dwight N. Hopkins and Linda E. Thomas, "Womanist Theology and Black Theology: Conversational Envisioning of an Unfinished Dream," in *Dream Unfinished* (Maryknoll, N.Y.: Orbis Books, 2001), 72-86.

28. Copeland, "Black, Hispanic/Latino, and Native American Theologies," 361-62.

29. "These musical forms [African American spirituals] are the richest available historical resource for a black Christology." Evans, *We Have Been Believers*, 81. See James H. Cone, *The Spirituals and the Blues* (New York: Seabury, 1972); cf. Blount, *Then the Whisper Put on Flesh*, 90.

30. See *Faces of Jesus in Africa*, ed. Robert Schreiter (Maryknoll, N.Y.: Orbis Books, 1991); and Kwame Bediako, "The Doctrine of Christ and the Significance of Vernacular Terminology," in *International Bulletin of Missionary Research* 22 (1998): 110-11.

Feminist, Womanist, and Mujerista Christologies

Feminist theology is probably the most influential of recent theological movements. The central concerns of feminism can be simply stated even if their ramifications are complex and extensive. According to one feminist theologian, "a feminist . . . simply means someone (male or female) who recognizes that women are fully human, acknowledges the imbalance and injustice that for centuries has, in church and society, characterized the situation of women, and is committed to righting that wrong."[31] Covering a wide spectrum of thinkers, Protestant and Roman Catholic, conservative, progressive, and radical, feminist theology is not a monolithic system of theology or an undifferentiated theological school. Nevertheless, it displays many common emphases.[32]

Like other contextual theologies, feminist theology arises out of a particular history and context. Its context is *the particular experience of women in church and society* where they have been systematically relegated to an inferior status and excluded from many spheres of activity and leadership. This culturally inscribed and theologically supported system of male domination and female subordination — called patriarchy by feminist theology — perpetuates engrained sexist attitudes and patterns of injustice and contributes to secret or overt abuse and violence.

The purpose of feminist theology is *to expose and struggle against the systemic injustice of patriarchy.* It tries to accomplish this task by reclaiming the importance of women's experience, by exposing the distorted views of women present in Scripture, church history, and Christian theology, by demonstrating the long hidden or suppressed contributions of women to the community of faith, and by restating Christian doctrine and reforming church liturgy and practices in ways that are faithful to Christ and the gospel and hence profoundly inclusive of women and men.

Feminist Christology argues that many traditional Christologies have buttressed rather than challenged the attitudes and structures of patriarchy. As noted in the previous chapter, feminist theologians repudiate the explicit or unspoken assumption that the maleness of Jesus is an ontological necessity of his work as Savior. To the contrary, they contend that "Jesus the Christ's ability to be savior does not reside in his maleness but in his loving, liberating history in the midst of the power of evil and oppression."[33] According to

---

31. Anne Carr, "Feminist Views of Christology," *Chicago Studies* 35 (Aug. 1996), 128.

32. For a recent survey, see Lisa Isherwood, *Introducing Feminist Christologies* (London: Sheffield Academic Press, 2002).

33. Elizabeth A. Johnson, *She Who Is: The Mystery of God in Feminist Theological Discourse* (New York: Crossroad, 1992), 167.

Rosemary Ruether, Jesus stands within the dynamic prophetic tradition of Scripture and announces a new humanity in which the poor and the outcast are welcomed and the equality of women and men is affirmed. As proclaimer of the liberating Word of God and as representative of liberated humanity, Jesus is not an exemplar of patriarchy but instead discloses the "kenosis of patriarchy."[34]

Wary of making Jesus a hero figure, other feminist theologians concentrate on a revision of conventional interpretations of the earliest Christian community. They emphasize Jesus' vision of the inclusive reign of God and the discipleship of equals that began around him. In the earliest Christian community, relationships were inclusive and non-hierarchical, and women played a highly significant role. Indeed, as the empty tomb traditions suggest, women were probably the earliest Christian proclaimers of the resurrection.[35]

A number of feminist theologians have contended that in the earliest Christian community Jesus was understood as the incarnation of the wisdom (sophia) of God. They underscore the importance of the figure of divine wisdom in the Old Testament where wisdom is portrayed as female and as being in the beginning with God (such as Prov. 8). Speaking of Jesus as the wisdom of God offers the possibility of expanding the range of images to interpret his identity and saving work in continuity with the classical Christological creeds of the church.[36]

Perhaps the two most troublesome areas of traditional Christian doctrine and practice for feminist theology are the metaphors and images used in the classical doctrine of the Trinity and the established interpretations of the atoning death of Christ. While some feminist critics of the traditional trinitarian language of Father, Son, and Holy Spirit charge that it makes the Christian understanding of God inherently sexist, other feminists identify the real problems as a *univocal or literalistic view of our language about God and the exclusive use of only one set of images of God.* Elizabeth Johnson argues that a major part of the language problem in the church stems from a loss of the sense of the mystery and incomprehensibility of God that is so prominent in the ancient apophatic tradition of theology. According to Johnson, we must recognize that all of our language about God is inadequate even as we are called to bear our witness to God known through Jesus Christ in the power of

34. Rosemary Radford Ruether, *Sexism and God-Talk: Toward a Feminist Theology* (Boston: Beacon Press, 1983), 137.

35. See Elisabeth Schüssler Fiorenza, *Jesus: Miriam's Child, Sophia's Prophet: Critical Issues in Feminist Christology* (London: SCM, 1995).

36. Johnson, *She Who Is*, 164-67.

his Spirit. We are not required to limit our language about God to the exact words that Scripture uses, provided that our words faithfully characterize the living God mediated through the scriptural witness, the witness of the church, and the present experience of the people of God.[37]

Regarding the death of Christ, *many feminist theologians take issue with traditional doctrines of the atonement.* They reject interpretations of the death of Jesus that separate it from his ministry, that depict the reason for his death as the punishment that he must bear for us so that we might receive forgiveness from God the Father (thus eliciting the charge of divine child abuse), and that tend to glorify suffering, victimization, and surrogacy with all their damaging effects in the lives of women.[38]

These topics are vigorously debated within feminist theology itself. Some feminist theologians contend that interpretations of classical atonement doctrine as fostering child abuse and purchasing forgiveness at the cost of brutality are misreadings of the biblical and theological tradition.[39] Moreover, some feminist theologians argue that acts of self-giving and self-dispossession for the sake of others, when voluntary, are not inherently oppressive. On the contrary, such acts can be seen as an acceptance of human vulnerability and a manifestation of risk-taking love that counters the mentality of absolutized selfhood and the spirit of domination of others regnant in patriarchal culture. Sarah Coakley contends that the repression of all forms of vulnerability is a danger to Christian feminism. Accompanying the dismissal of all vulnerability is the "concomitant failure to confront issues of fragility, suffering or 'self-emptying' except in terms of victimology. And that is ultimately the failure to embrace a feminist reconceptualizing of the power of the cross and resurrection."[40]

Just as there is lively debate among black theologians over the priority of particular and universal emphases in the interpretation of the Christian message, so there is *lively debate among feminist, womanist, and mujerista theologians.* Black women theologians (womanist theologians), and Hispanic women theologians (*mujerista* theologians), while closely related to feminist

---

37. Johnson, *She Who Is,* 7.

38. See Delores S. Williams, *Sisters in the Wilderness: The Challenge of Womanist God-Talk* (Maryknoll, N.Y.: Orbis Books, 1993).

39. Leanne Van Dyk, "Do Theories of the Atonement Foster Abuse?" in *Dialog* 35, no. 1 (Winter 1996): 21-25; JoAnne Marie Terrell, *Power in the Blood: The Cross in the African American Experience* (Maryknoll, N.Y.: Orbis Books, 1998).

40. Sarah Coakley, "Kenosis and Subversion: On the Repression of 'Vulnerability' in Christian Feminist Writing," in *Powers and Submissions: Spirituality, Philosophy and Gender* (Oxford: Blackwell, 2002), 33. See also Johnson, *She Who Is,* 246-72.

theology, offer critical voices within it. They emphasize the oppressive power of racism and classism in addition to sexism in society and the church. Womanist theologians thus criticize the failure of theologians, white or black, to engage the evil of sexism, as well as the failure of white feminist theologians to engage the evils of racism and classism not only among men but also among white and often affluent women.[41] *Mujerista* theologians, who are well aware of the machismo mentality and its demeaning and abusive attitudes and behavior, voice similar criticisms in the Hispanic theological community.[42] Writings of womanist and *mujerista* theologians have opened the possibility of a deeper sense of solidarity and a commitment to cooperation among women of all colors and classes.

Hispanic Christology

The context of Hispanic theology is the *history of struggle and the experience of discrimination against Hispanic or Latino/a people in North America*. Hispanic theology is closely related to Latin American liberation theology and shares many of its themes: the importance of social location; starting with the historical Jesus; God's partiality toward the poor; the inseparability of faith and practice. But it also has its own distinctive emphases and themes. This summary will make special use of the Christological writings of the Mexican-American Roman Catholic theologian Virgilio Elizondo and the Christology of the Protestant Cuban-American theologian Justo Gonzalez.

Virgilio Elizondo writes as a faithful Roman Catholic who cherishes the unity of the faith, affirms the church's Christological doctrines, and also celebrates the particularities of the faith and practices of Hispanic Christians. His central concept in Christology and ecclesiology is *mestizaje* or cultural and racial mixture.

In his reflections on the "Galilean journey" of Jesus, Elizondo attempts to retrieve the significance of Jesus' Galilean locus for Hispanic Christians and for the ecumenical church.[43] Elizondo finds several layers of meaning in the fact that Jesus was a Galilean. To be a Galilean Jew classified one as an out-

---

41. See Jacquelyn Grant, *White Women's Christ and Black Women's Jesus: Feminist Christology and Womanist Response* (Atlanta: Scholars Press, 1989); Stephanie Y. Mitchem, *Introducing Feminist Theology* (Maryknoll, N.Y.: Orbis Books, 2002).

42. See Ada Maria Isasi-Diaz, *En la Lucha/In the Struggle: A Hispanic Women's Liberation Theology* (Minneapolis: Fortress, 1993).

43. Virgilio Elizondo, *Galilean Journey: The Mexican-American Promise* (Maryknoll, N.Y.: Orbis Books, 2000).

sider in many respects — geographically, socially, culturally, linguistically, and religiously. Galilee was a region where people of mixed origins lived; an economically marginalized region separated from the center of power in Jerusalem; a region known not only for its distinctive dialect but also associated with ignorance of the religious law and laxity in observing Jewish religious customs and ceremonies. According to Elizondo, that Jesus the Son of God was a Galilean has great significance both for our understanding of the Incarnation and for the goal of God's work of salvation in him. Among the claims Elizondo makes in his reading of the "Galilean journey" of Jesus are the following.

The Galilean identity of Jesus concretizes the scandalous meaning of the Incarnation. "The human scandal of God's way does not begin with the cross, but with the historico-cultural incarnation of his Son in Galilee."[44] In Jesus, "God becomes not just a human being, but the marginated, shamed, and rejected of the world."[45] Like other contextual or liberation theologians, Elizondo focuses on the "historical Jesus" but not in the same manner as the academic guild and its various quests of the historical Jesus. Elizondo is concerned with the concrete person and work of Jesus in his particular historical setting as described by the Gospels.

The Galilean identity of Jesus underscores *the conflictual character of Jesus' message of the kingdom of God and his ministry among the marginalized that came to a climax on the cross.* "It was not just the death on the cross that was salvific, but the entire way that climaxed on the cross. It is in the conflictual tensions of the way from Galilee to Jerusalem that the full impact of the salvific way of Jesus emerges."[46] Although Jesus entered into conflict with those who opposed the kingdom he proclaimed and embodied, he refused to return the violence of his enemies with violence. According to Elizondo, Jesus is "the aggressive prophet of nonviolent love."[47]

Elizondo sees *an analogy between the Galilean identity of Jesus and the "mixed" identity of Mexican-Americans.* This is perhaps the most provocative element in Elizondo's Christology, and it has aroused questions and objections from other Hispanic theologians. For Elizondo, Jesus' origin and formation in Galilee marked by social and cultural *mestizaje* points to the presence of divine grace in and through humanity defined by *mestizaje:* "Mestizaje is

---

44. Elizondo, *Galilean Journey,* 53.

45. Virgilio Elizondo, "Mestizaje as a Locus of Theological Reflection," in *Mestizo Christianity: Theology from the Latino Perspective,* ed. Arturo J. Banukelas (Maryknoll, N.Y.: Orbis Books, 1995), 19.

46. Elizondo, *Galilean Journey,* 69.

47. Elizondo, "Mestizaje," 20.

the beginning of a new Christian universalism."[48] While reference to Jesus as *mestizaje* prompts criticisms similar to those leveled at the claim of some African American theologians that Jesus is black, Elizondo's aim is to speak not in racially exclusive terms but of "a new universalism that bypasses human segregative barriers."[49] Mexican-Americans may find new hope and dignity in hearing the good news of God's presence and activity in Jesus the Galilean, who like them was a despised and marginalized *mestizo*.[50]

For Elizondo, *the mission of Mexican-American Christians becomes clear in the light of the identity and saving work of the Galilean Jesus.* The *mestizaje* people are a chosen people, chosen not for privilege but for a mission. They are to be an inclusive people, the agents of a new creation. While called to confront the idolatrous systems of evil that favor the few and deprive the many, this does not mean a call to arms or to violence. Rather, "It is in our fiestas that our legitimate identity and destiny are experienced."[51] The fiestas are celebrations of "the beginning of the ultimate eschatological identity [of the people of God] where there will be differences but not division."[52]

Although Elizondo clearly assumes the truth of the Christological creeds of the church, he does not explain how they are related to his interpretation of the person and ministry of the Galilean Jesus. This is, however, an important concern in the work of the Protestant Cuban American theologian Justo Gonzalez. Like Elizondo, Gonzalez calls for a liberative reading of Scripture. He claims that all Hispanic theologies agree that responsible scriptural interpretation "must throw light on our current situation, help us to understand it, and support us in the struggle for justice and liberation."[53] Unlike Elizondo, however, Gonzalez tries to show how classical Christological doctrine and Hispanic context may helpfully inform each other. According to Gonzalez, the affirmations of the Councils of Nicea and Chalcedon speak with surprising relevance to the Hispanic church today.[54]

---

48. Elizondo, *Galilean Journey*, 124.

49. Elizondo, *Galilean Journey*, 124.

50. See Miguel H. Diaz, *On Being Human: U.S. Hispanic and Rahnerian Perspectives* (Maryknoll, N.Y.: Orbis Books, 2001). I am indebted to Ruben Rosario-Rodriguez, Ph.D. candidate at Princeton Theological Seminary, for helping me understand the contributions and challenges of Hispanic theology.

51. Elizondo, "Mestizaje," 25.

52. Elizondo, "Mestizaje," 25.

53. Justo L. Gonzalez, "Scripture, Tradition, Experience, and Imagination: A Reflection," in *The Ties That Bind: African American and Hispanic American/Latino/a Theologies in Dialogue*, ed. Anthony B. Pinn and Benjamin Valentin (New York: Continuum, 2001), 64.

54. See Justo Gonzalez, *Mañana: Christian Theology from a Hispanic Perspective* (Nashville: Abingdon, 1990).

Gonzalez offers the creed of Nicea as one example. In confessing the eternal divinity of Jesus Christ, Nicea at the same time protested against the "Constantinization" of God. By "Constantinization" Gonzalez means the accommodation of the God of the gospel to the understandings of divinity familiar to the Hellenistic world. Although Arius was biblically learned, he was unable to break free of his philosophical and religious milieu and think of the suffering Jesus as one with the majestic and transcendent God. The temptation to abandon the living God of Scripture and settle into a "theology of the status quo" with its assumptions about what constitutes true power and glory was acute for Arius and continues to be so now. To affirm that the one who proclaimed good news to the poor and who was crucified between two thieves is the very Son of God and "of one substance" with the Father constitutes a scandal to all who think of God, then and now, as a super-emperor. In other words, Nicea revolutionizes our understanding of the nature of divinity and the nature of true power.

According to Gonzalez, the creed of Chalcedon, with its affirmation of the true divinity and true humanity of Christ, also fights all forms of "Constantinization" and its damaging effect on the very souls of the oppressed. People in bondage are often tempted to accept theological rationales for their condition. Such rationales were available in the early centuries of the church in the form of Docetism. For the Docetists, Jesus only appeared to be human. He was in fact a purely heavenly being, untouched by the realities of human suffering and death. By affirming the full humanity of Jesus Christ, Chalcedon flatly rejected Docetism and, in so doing, repudiated a heresy that is still a temptation to Christians today. Addressing Hispanic Christians in particular, Gonzalez notes how individuals who feel powerless may succumb to the message of many television preachers who dodge the issue of the transformation of life here and now and instead encourage the poor to forget about their present misery and think only of the life to come. Such a message is a modern version of Docetism.[55]

Chalcedon rejected not only Docetism but also adoptionism, Apollinarianism, and Nestorianism. Gonzalez argues that each of these ancient heresies tempts Hispanic Christians today, although the names under which they appear may be very different. Modern adoptionism, for example, denies the embodiment or the grace of God in Jesus Christ in favor of the idea that Jesus wins the favor of God by his works. This is the Christological counterpart to the American myth that everyone can make it to the top if he or she tries hard enough. Unless the oppressed are taught that Jesus Christ is God with and for

55. Gonzalez, *Mañana*, 143.

us, not "the local boy who makes good," they will think of themselves as unworthy failures. The adopted Jesus is not good news for those on the bottom of the social scale.[56]

Thus, the creeds of Nicea and Chalcedon, as Gonzalez rereads them in the Hispanic context, are far from outdated. Their affirmation that the true God has become truly human in Jesus Christ for our salvation is as important for the Hispanic church today as it has been for the church in other times and places. But to grasp this point requires that these creeds be interpreted in a way that addresses the context of Hispanic Americans. Gonzalez agrees with critics of Chalcedon who say that the creed does not define the true divinity and true humanity of Jesus Christ as attested in Scripture with sufficient concreteness: "It is precisely in his being for others that Jesus manifests his full divinity, and it is also in his being for others that he manifests his full humanity."[57] When properly interpreted, however, the ancient Christological creeds are indispensable guides for a contextualized proclamation of the gospel of God's unmerited grace in Jesus Christ.

Asian American Christology

Among the most recent contextual theologies in the United States is Asian American theology. While still in its beginning stages, this theology will no doubt continue to grow as the number of Asian American Christians steadily increases. Asian Americans come from many different countries with very diverse cultural and linguistic backgrounds. While there are many common concerns, there is no single Asian American theology. My summary is based largely on the Korean American theological literature.[58]

The context of Asian American theology is the experience of Asian immigrants and their families in the United States. This context is characterized by a *complex intersection of two widely different cultures.* Just as in black theology there is a meeting of the continents of Africa and North America, and just as in Hispanic theology there is a confluence of the cultures of North and South America, so in Asian American theology there is an encounter of Western and Eastern cultures.

A number of Asian American theologians *draw upon Eastern philosoph-*

56. Gonzalez, *Mañana,* 145.
57. Gonzalez, *Mañana,* 152.
58. I am indebted to Kevin Park for his study of Korean-American theology in his dissertation, "Emerging Korean North American Theology: Toward a Contextual Theology of the Cross" (Princeton Theological Seminary, 2002).

ical, religious, and literary traditions and cast their theological work in a style or form that they consider more suitable to Asian peoples than typical Western categories and styles of thinking. Some are directly or indirectly influenced by Asian concepts like Yin and Yang. They favor an inclusive, complementary, "both-and" form of thinking in distinction from what they see as the exclusive, oppositional, "either-or" way of thinking common in the West. Other Asian American theologians make use of seminal Asian concepts like *tao* and *han* in their theological work or draw upon images and scenes of life from Eastern cultures. Graphic examples of the use of Asian images are found in the work of the Japanese American theologian Kosuke Koyama, who served as a missionary in Thailand for several years. Koyama speaks not of "systematic" or "dogmatic" theology but of "water buffalo theology," a theology that is intelligible to poor farmers of southeast Asia who cultivate the fields with the help of water buffalo rather than tractors.[59] C. S. Song, a prominent Chinese American theologian, understands theology as essentially storytelling. He tells the stories of Asian peoples, especially the poor and the oppressed, and interprets these stories in the light of the story of Jesus.[60]

A key concept in the work of several Asian American theologians is "marginality." According to J. Y. Lee, "The incarnation . . . was divine marginalization. . . . Christ became the margin of marginality by giving up everything he had."[61] Acknowledging the limitations of all analogies when speaking of God and the work of salvation, J. Y. Lee nevertheless compares the marginalization experienced by Asian Americans in the United States to the self-marginalization of God in Jesus Christ. Just as God experienced rejection and humiliation in emigrating from a heavenly place to this world, so the Asian American emigrants experience rejection and humiliation when they give up everything and come to America: "Where they once held professional-level positions in their native land, here they started as janitors, launderers, cooks, and other marginal workers."[62]

Sang Hyun Lee develops the theme of marginality in a somewhat different way. For him marginality, or living on the boundary of two worlds, has both negative and positive aspects for Asian Americans. Negatively, it is the experience of being pushed to the margins of the dominant society, largely because of racial prejudice. In this negative sense, being marginal is not a matter of choice but an involuntary situation. Positively, marginality offers

59. Kosuke Koyama, *Water Buffalo Theology* (Maryknoll, N.Y.: Orbis Books, 1974).

60. C. S. Song, *The Believing Heart: An Invitation to Story Theology* (Minneapolis: Fortress, 1999).

61. J. Y. Lee, *Marginality: Key to Multicultural Theology* (Minneapolis: Fortress, 1995), 83.

62. Lee, *Marginality*, 83.

the opportunity for creative action at the intersection of cultural differences and the chance to exercise a prophetic voice for justice over against structures of injustice and exclusion.[63]

That *Jesus was a Galilean and therefore knew the condition of marginality firsthand* is a theme of Asian American Christology as it is of Hispanic Christology. While Elizondo emphasizes the *mestizo* or mixed racial and cultural dimension of the Galilean situation, Sang H. Lee emphasizes more the cultural, political, and religious marginalization of Galilee in relation to the power center of Jerusalem. The point for both is that the meaning of the Incarnation and the saving work of Christ cannot be divorced from his life and activity in a context of marginalization. The appeal to the Galilean context of the message and ministry of Jesus is an effort to ground a theology of marginalization not only in the doctrinal theme of incarnation but also in the historical concreteness of the New Testament witness to the person and work of Jesus.

One striking example of the use of the insights of Asian culture in the development of Asian American theology is the concept of *han. Han* is a Korean word for the anger, resentment, and bitterness of those who have been unjustly treated. Andrew Sung Park proposes that the concept of *han* illuminates the meaning of sin and the saving work of Christ. Sin is almost always discussed in terms of the perpetrator, seldom in terms of its effect on the victim. "The traditional doctrine of sin has been one-sided, seeing the world from the perspective of the sinner only, failing to take account of the victims of sin and injustice."[64] The victim, like the perpetrator, is in a kind of bondage, not a bondage of guilt requiring forgiveness, but a bondage of anger and resentment requiring liberation. The saving work of Christ must therefore be seen not only as God's forgiveness of sinners but also as God's liberation of victims from the burdens of anger, resignation, or hatred toward those who have wronged them that, if left to fester, will destroy all joy in life and obstruct the possibilities of transformation and renewal.

Like other contextual theologians, *Asian American theologians are generally critical of standard Western interpretations of the death of Jesus such as the satisfaction theology of the atonement.* They emphasize instead the solidarity of Jesus even unto death with the poor, the abused, and the suffering. In his writings, Kosuke Koyama emphasizes the radical critique of domineering

63. See Sang Hyun Lee, "Pilgrimage and Home in the Wilderness of Marginality," *Princeton Seminary Bulletin* 16, no. 1 (1995); and Kevin Park, "Emerging Korean North American Theology," 72-119.

64. Andrew Sung Park, *The Wounded Heart of God: The Asian Concept of Han and the Christian Doctrine of Sin* (Nashville: Abingdon, 1993), 10.

power that is declared in the passion and death of Jesus. In both religion and politics, there is ample evidence of the idolatry of imperial "centrism," that is, those who are at the center of power, wealth, and influence and who want to control and exploit those at the periphery. Christians believe that Jesus is the center of all things, yet he realizes his centrality by moving in compassion to the periphery. "Over against . . . destructive centrism in the world of religion and politics, the crucified Christ affirms his centrality by giving it up for the sake of the periphery. This is his way to shalom."[65] For C. S. Song, the most important clues to who the real Jesus is and what salvation he brings will be found among "people who are poor, outcast, and socially and politically oppressed. What Jesus has said and done is not comprehensible apart from men, women, and children who suffer in body and spirit."[66]

Asian American women also wrestle with the meaning of Jesus as Lord in the context of histories of subordination and oppression. Does following Jesus Christ reinforce the pattern of passive dependency of women? Does choosing Christ mean choosing a male whom they are to love despite his neglect and abandonment? According to Chung Hyun Kyung, the answer of many Asian Christian women to these questions is a resounding "No." Jesus "affirms, respects, and is actively present with them in their long and hard journey for liberation and wholeness. Asian women are discovering with much passion and compassion that Jesus takes sides with the silenced Asian women in his solidarity with all oppressed people."[67]

Many of these proposals of Asian American theologians, like those of other contextual theologies included in this chapter, are arresting. They demand both careful hearing and responsible assessment. Peter C. Phan suggests two important criteria of such assessment: first, appropriateness, or "the relative coherence of this message with the life and teaching of Jesus as mediated through the Bible and Christian tradition"; and second, adequacy, or "the power to speak the Christian word in the contemporary idiom in order to understand and transform the condition of the addressee."[68]

---

65. Kosuke Koyama, "The Crucified Jesus Challenges Human Power," in *Asian Faces of Jesus*, ed. R. S. Sugirtharajah (Maryknoll, N.Y.: Orbis Books, 1993), 155.

66. C. S. Song, *Jesus: The Crucified People* (New York: Crossroad, 1990), 12.

67. Chung Hyun Kyung, "Who Is Jesus for Asian Women?" in *Asian Faces of Jesus*, 226.

68. Peter C. Phan, *Christianity with an Asian Face: Asian American Theology in the Making* (Maryknoll, N.Y.: Orbis Books, 2003), 118.

The Local and the Global in Christology

At first glance, the great variety of local and contextual theologies and their particular views of Christ and the salvation he brings may seem both bewildering and threatening. One may be tempted to dismiss the polymorphic witness to Christ in local theologies as simply confusing, divisive, and heterodox, and seek refuge in the familiar language and categories employed by the classical Christological creeds and their interpretation in the established theological traditions. But this would be a mistake. We are not faced with an either/or choice but with the need for dialogue. The particular witness of contextual or local Christologies and the common Christological confession of the whole church need each other if effective translation of the gospel is to occur in our pluralistic world.

The worldwide church needs to hear the witness of the local churches and their experience of the living Christ. In terms of sheer numbers, the "center" of Christianity has shifted from Europe and North America to Africa and South America. With the likely growth of Christianity in China, its voices will doubtless make a new and distinctive contribution to Christian witness and theology in the twenty-first century.

In recent decades, the many voices of world Christianity have begun to be heard. Vatican II was the first ecumenical council of the Roman Catholic Church in which there was strong representation from the Third World. Any future ecumenical council of the church, hoping to speak to and on behalf of Christians everywhere, will necessarily have representation from an unprecedented diversity of race, language, culture, theology, and liturgical practice. Without local theologies, the voice of the church as a worldwide community becomes overly abstract and theoretical. Local theologies offer particular and concrete witnesses to Christ and the salvation he brings that need to be heard and absorbed by the church universal. These voices sometimes raise disturbing questions, but the questions are not artificial or merely academic. They arise from lived experience, and they prompt reflection and call for response and perhaps reformation.

But if the church catholic needs to hear the voices of local theologies, the converse is also true: the local churches need to hear the common witness of the worldwide church as expressed in classical creeds, confessions, and liturgies. If the temptation of ecumenical confessions of the faith is to remain imprisoned in abstractions, the temptation of local witness and confession is to fall victim to provincialism and one-sidedness. While fresh expression of the meaning of Christ in concrete contexts is vitally important, such expressions must not be separated from the larger, overarching story of God's work of salvation attested in Scripture and summarized in the ecumenical creeds of the church. The summary of the overarching story of Scripture known in the early church as the "rule of faith" played an essential role in the life and mission of the church as it expanded into new regions and cultures. One-sidedness in theology is not always avoidable; indeed it is doubtful that any theology worth its salt has not engaged in one-sided emphases. But one-sidedness in theology, whether conservative or liberal, is a failing when it becomes hardened, closes its ears and heart to the voices of others, and renders itself irreformable.

If the contextual and ecumenical concerns of Christology are to be held together, if they are to correct and enrich each other, then at least two principles suggest themselves:

First, *every effort at ecumenical theology must be genuinely open to the voices of contextual theologies.* It must want to "hear the voices of people long silenced."[69] The era of a trickle-down theory of divine truth emanating always from some center, whether Rome, London, Geneva, New York, or wherever, is over. Ecumenical theology must test itself by its capacity to hear and integrate all that the Word and Spirit of the living Christ is saying through the local churches. Listening to the voices of Christians in cultures and situations different from that of mainline North American churches should not be undertaken as a grudging concession. Rather, listening to these different voices is an opportunity, in the words of Andrew Walls, for a fresh "discovery of Christ." The reality of Jesus Christ has meanings and dimensions "never guessed before," and in the ecumenical exchange of insights and gifts we may be offered surprising glimpses of "the glory of the completed, redeemed humanity."[70]

Second, *local theologies must be genuinely concerned to speak not only in and to their own context but from that context to the worldwide community of Christian believers.* As Robert Schreiter notes, "A local community's theology should impel it to move outward from itself. It must make some contribution to the way in which the whole of the Christian church understands itself, either by affirming what is already known in the tradition or by extending it to new circumstances."[71] It would be a short-circuiting of the task of local theology if it remained insular and in-house rather than contributing the insights it has won to all the people of God. The purpose of every local theology is that

---

69. "A Brief Statement of Faith," in *The Book of Confessions* (PCUSA), 10.4, line 70.

70. Walls, *The Missionary Movement*, xviii. See also Margaret O'Gara, *The Ecumenical Gift Exchange* (Collegeville, Minn.: Liturgical Press, 1998).

71. Schreiter, *Constructing Local Theologies*, 120.

the witness of the whole church may be deepened, enriched, and perhaps corrected. The apostle Paul spoke of the diversity of gifts that are given so that all might benefit. No member of the body of Christ can say to other members, "I have no need of you" (1 Cor. 12:21). Responsible local theology must be ecumenical in intent even as truly ecumenical theology must be open to the insights and the calls to action that come from local theologies.

This is not an easy agenda for theology. But ease is not what the church should expect in its mission or what theology should expect in its task. The Formula of Chalcedon, Karl Rahner says, is a crucial point of departure and not the end of Christological reflection. Theology is in constant movement and self-correction. Or in the words of Karl Barth, the dogmas of the Christian faith are points where the confession of the church has come to a "provisional halt."[72] The task of theology is to continue the journey of faith seeking understanding by "beginning again and again at the beginning." The beginning is the living Lord Jesus Christ whose story is told in Scripture, enlivened by the Spirit, summarized in the church's rule of faith, and retold by faithful Christians in different cultural idioms and in different times and places.

---

72. Karl Barth, *The Göttingen Dogmatics*, vol. 1 (Grand Rapids: Eerdmans, 1991), 39.

CHAPTER 10

The Holy Spirit and the Christian Life

C hristians affirm that God is the creator who has graciously called the world into existence and made human beings in the image of God. They also confess that God was decisively present in the person and work of Jesus Christ to reconcile the world and to liberate humanity from its bondage to sin, death, and all other evil powers that threaten to ruin God's good creation. If the creed of the church ended abruptly with these first two articles of faith in God the creator and reconciler, it might seem to be speaking of events now historically remote and of truths that have little to do with our life here and now. In Martin Luther's words, "Of what help is it to you that God is God, if he is not God to you?"[1] John Calvin makes the same point: "As long as Christ remains outside of us, and we are separated from him, all that he has suffered and done for the salvation of the human race remains useless and of no value for us."[2]

The third article of the creed affirms that God is not only *over* us and *for* us but also at work *in* us. It speaks of the Holy Spirit and the new humanity in Christ. How do men and women participate in the great drama of creation, reconciliation, and transformation? What power enables humanity to have a share in the life and activity of the triune God? What new attitudes, practices, and relationships are to characterize those who have encountered God's grace in Jesus? To what goal does our history and the history of the whole creation move? A reply to these questions must begin, as the third article of the creed begins, with an affirmation of faith in the Holy Spirit.

---

1. Martin Luther, "A Meditation on Christ's Passion," in *Luther's Works*, 42: 3-14.
2. Calvin, *Institutes of the Christian Religion*, 3.1.1.

Neglect and Recovery of the Doctrine of the Holy Spirit

The doctrine of the Holy Spirit has seldom received the attention given to other doctrines of the faith such as Christology and ecclesiology. Some theologians have even spoken of the early creedal definitions of the doctrine of the Holy Spirit as almost "slipshod."[3] Symptomatic of the church's neglect and suspicion of the Spirit are many instances of official church opposition to movements that have stressed the presence and power of the Spirit. The Montanists of the second century, the Waldensians of the twelfth century, the radical reformers of the sixteenth century, and the Christian base communities of our own time have all come under suspicion because of their emphasis on the working of God's Spirit. The institutional church has always looked on the experience of and appeal to the Spirit as potentially subversive and in need of control.

Routine neglect and suspicion of the work of the Holy Spirit has damaging effects on both Christian life and Christian theology. It can lead to distortions in the understanding of God, the doctrine of Scripture, the significance of the natural order, the value of human culture, the interpretation of Christ and his work, the nature of the church, the freedom of the Christian, and the hope for the final fulfillment of life. When the work of the Holy Spirit is forgotten or suppressed, the power of God is apt to be understood as distant, hierarchical, and coercive; Christocentric faith deteriorates into Christomonism; the authority of Scripture becomes heteronomous; the church is seen as a rigid power structure in which some members rule over others; and the sacraments degenerate into almost magical rites under the control of a clerical elite.

In recent years, however, there has been a resurgence of interest in the Holy Spirit and Christian spirituality both in theology and in the life of the church.[4] A number of factors have contributed to this development.

1. Viewed in broad cultural perspective, the new interest in the Holy Spirit is a protest against depersonalization and bureaucratization in both modern society and the church. It is a protest against the domination of form over vitality, structure over purpose, external authority over free consent. When questions are settled simply by quoting passages from the Bible or citing the doctrines of the church, this is rightly judged by many people as but

---

3. See George S. Hendry, *The Holy Spirit in Christian Theology* (Philadelphia: Westminster, 1956), 13.

4. This is reflected in the theme chosen for the seventh assembly of the World Council of Churches in Canberra, Australia, in 1990: "Come, Holy Spirit — Renew the Whole Creation."

another instance of the ethos of control and coercion. To know God as Spirit is to experience God as a liberating rather than a coercive power.

2. Equally important, the new interest in the Holy Spirit is evidence of a widespread hunger for a deeper faith, for a new relationship with God, for the experience of genuine love and lasting friendship, and for the spiritual resources to deal with the personal and corporate crises of our time. Many people in modern technological society feel lonely and ignored. They often experience utter helplessness in the face of the impersonal forces that affect their lives. Cultural institutions that once provided meaning, support, and companionship are disintegrating. Help in dealing with these personal and cultural crises can scarcely be found in secular philosophies that exalt self-reliance and the spirit of individualism. The hunger for new life, new community, new joy finds expression in the renewed interest in the Spirit and in the search for a new spirituality.

3. Recent interest in the Holy Spirit may also be connected with the sense of historical distance and cold objectivity that seems endemic to modern consciousness. Even a so-called Christocentric theology is not immune to the acids of historical distance and objectivistic ways of thinking. What is the significance of the objective reality of salvation in Christ if there is no personal appropriation of this reality and no actual participation in its transforming power?[5]

4. Renewed interest in the Holy Spirit may also be related to the experience of emptiness and "burnout" of many pastors, church leaders, and countless other people who have taken part in the various social and political movements of reform in recent years. The spiritual life has sometimes been neglected or even denigrated by social activists as an unnecessary vestige of the past. But it has now become apparent that perseverance in struggles for justice, peace, and freedom cannot be sustained apart from a vital spirituality.

5. The new interest in the Holy Spirit is also clearly associated with developments in the ecumenical church. Among the more important of these are the remarkable worldwide expansion of the Pentecostal churches that have historically placed great emphasis on the Spirit, the growing influence of the Eastern Orthodox Churches which have argued for centuries that the Western church's spiritual life and its theology of the Spirit are defective, and the emergence of the Christian base communities in Latin America and in

---

5. Yves Congar states as the most important conclusion of his extensive writings on the Holy Spirit that there can be "no Christology without pneumatology and no pneumatology without Christology." *The Word and the Spirit* (San Francisco: Harper & Row, 1986), 1.

other parts of the world where the Bible is read under the guidance of the Spirit and in an atmosphere of discovery and celebration.[6]

6. Most important of the factors promoting recent interest in the Holy Spirit is a better appreciation of the prominence of the work of the Spirit in both the Old and New Testaments. The literature on the topic of the Spirit by biblical scholars and systematic theologians has grown rapidly. Commenting on the tendency to read Scripture in a fragmentary or even atomized manner, one theologian notes what is undoubtedly a common failing: not allowing "the whole story of the Spirit, as we receive it in the Old Testament, in the Gospels, the Book of Acts and again in the Epistles of Paul, to make a conjoint impact on [us] in the way we all have so often done with the whole story of Jesus."[7]

After a long period of concentration on Christology in Western theology, is it now time for attention to shift in the direction of pneumatology? This question has been raised in our time even by Karl Barth, the great advocate of Christocentric theology in the twentieth century. Barth would be the first to remind us, however, that a recovery of the importance of the Spirit must not come at the expense of the centrality of the church's witness to Jesus Christ.[8]

be able to explain statements in italics

A Sketch of a Theology of the Holy Spirit *226-235*

Whatever the various factors at work in the recent resurgence of interest in the person and work of the Holy Spirit, the principal elements of this doctrine are in need of rethinking today.[9]

1. *A Christian theology of the Holy Spirit will take its bearings from the biblical witness to the work of the Spirit of God in the history of Israel, in the ministry of Jesus, and in the life of the early church.*

In the Old Testament, the Spirit is the creative breath of God giving life to all creatures (Ps. 104:29-30; Job 33:4). The Spirit gives gifts of intelligence,

6. See Jose Comblin, *The Holy Spirit and Liberation* (Maryknoll, N.Y.: Orbis Books, 1989).

7. John McIntyre, *The Shape of Pneumatology: Studies in the Doctrine of the Holy Spirit* (Edinburgh: T&T Clark, 1997), 16.

8. See Barth, "Concluding Unscientific Postscript on Schleiermacher," in *The Theology of Schleiermacher* (Grand Rapids: Eerdmans, 1982).

9. Important recent titles on the doctrine of the Holy Spirit include Yves Congar, *I Believe in the Holy Spirit*, 3 vols. (New York: Seabury Press, 1983); Jose Comblin, *The Holy Spirit and Liberation;* Alasdair I. C. Heron, *The Holy Spirit* (Philadelphia: Westminster, 1983); Jürgen Moltmann, *The Spirit of Life: A Universal Affirmation* (Minneapolis: Fortress, 1992); Michael Welker, *God the Spirit* (Minneapolis: Fortress, 1994); John McIntyre, *The Shape of Pneumatology;* Clark H. Pinnock, *Flame of Love: A Theology of the Holy Spirit* (Downers Grove, Ill.: InterVarsity, 1996).

skill, and artisanship to further the purposes of God among God's people (Exod. 31:1-11). The Spirit offers assurance of forgiveness of sins (Ps. 51:10-12), gives courage to the downtrodden (Hag. 2:4-5), brings new life out of death (Ezek. 37), restores hope (Joel 2:28-29), and promotes justice in the land (Isa. 11:1ff.). A special feature of the Old Testament understanding of the Spirit is that the Spirit of God is given to God's chosen servants, commissioning and empowering them to restore justice in the land when the weak and the poor are oppressed (Isa. 42:1-4a; 61:1-4). In these and many other ways, the Spirit of God is presented by the Old Testament as God's creative, sustaining, saving, and renewing power who rescues not only individuals but the entire people of God from forces of disintegration and self-destruction.[10]

In the New Testament, too, the Spirit of God is a prominent actor. The Synoptic Gospels describe the life and ministry of Jesus as empowered by the Spirit from beginning to end (Luke 4:18ff.). The special prominence of the work of the Holy Spirit for the evangelist Luke is indicated by the fact that he begins his Gospel with the story of the birth of Jesus to Mary by the power of the Spirit and starts his sequel to the Gospel (the Acts of the Apostles) with the account of the coming of the Spirit to the disciples at Pentecost. The early church clearly understood itself as living in the time of the long-promised outpouring of the Spirit (Joel 2:28-32; Acts 2:17-21). Paul thinks of the Spirit in the closest possible relation to the risen Christ and interprets the work of the Spirit as the "firstfruits" of the harvest of God's coming reign (Rom. 8:23). For the evangelist John, the Spirit is sent to bear witness to Christ and to lead the disciples into the fullness of truth in him (John 14:26).

2. *A Christian theology of the Holy Spirit will give special attention to the work of the Holy Spirit in binding believers to Christ and creating new life and new community in him.* While the work of the Spirit has been underdeveloped in much of the theological tradition, the New Testament contains a rich and multidimensional description of the Spirit's work. Six aspects of this work can be identified:

a. The work of the Spirit is *re-presentative.* It is by the power of the Spirit that Christ is made present to believers. By re-presenting Christ — by bringing Christ into the present — the Spirit spans the gap between the then and there and the here and now. By the work of the Spirit, the Christ attested in Scripture and proclaimed in the church does not remain a mere object outside of us or a distant event of the past from which we are separated by a "broad, ugly ditch" of space and time (G. E. Lessing). Christ is not merely a memory of someone long gone or someone who may arrive in the future; he

10. See especially Michael Welker, *God the Spirit.*

is present here and now to us — in the power of the Spirit. As Calvin writes, it is through the "energy of the Spirit" that we come to "enjoy Christ and all his benefits."[11]

b. A second aspect of the work of the Spirit is the creation of new life. According to John's theology, the Spirit is the agent of our second birth. Just as we are born from our natural mother's womb in our first birth, so we must be born anew by the power of the Spirit. The Nicene Creed follows 1 Corinthians 15:45 in naming the Spirit the "life giver." While this designation refers primarily to the new life in Christ, it probably also has in mind the activity of the Spirit at the creation of the world (Gen. 1:2). The Spirit is the power of transformation from the old to the new, from enslavement to the powers of sin and death to a new life in communion with God and others.

As recipients of new life from the Spirit, Christians are enabled both to speak of God's mercy and righteousness and to act as co-workers with God in the renewal of creation. The disciples' new power of communication across different languages given by the Spirit is dramatically depicted in Acts 2. And the Spirit's empowerment to witness and serve is underscored in Paul's description of the gifts of the Spirit. Given new life and gifted by the Spirit, all members of the community of faith become contributors to the common welfare, partners in the creative and redemptive work of God.

c. Another aspect of the work of the Holy Spirit is *liberative.* "Where the Spirit of the Lord is, there is freedom" (2 Cor. 3:17). The freedom that the Spirit gives is not sheer vitality or lawless freedom. It is not "consumer freedom" or the freedom to do whatever one pleases. Instead, the Spirit frees us to take on the "mind" of Christ (Phil. 2:5), to live according to the "law" of Christ (Gal. 6:2). It is the freedom to love God and others, the freedom for life in right relationship. The Spirit frees believers for a pattern of life that reflects the pattern of God's self-giving love in Jesus Christ. Because injustice destroys right relationship with God and others, the Spirit of God energizes resistance to injustice (cf. Isa. 42:1ff., 61:1ff.). The New Testament associates the coming of the Spirit with the liberation of life from every bondage and with a new freedom for the service of God. Inasmuch as the work of Christ is essentially one of liberation ("For freedom Christ has set us free," Gal. 5:1), the activity of the Spirit is a continuation of the work begun by Christ. The liberating work of the Spirit that brings freedom for new and abundant life in communion with God and others is present not only in human life but throughout the creation that groans and longs to participate in "the freedom of the glory of the children of God" (Rom. 8:21).

11. Calvin, *Institutes,* 3.1.1.

d. Still another aspect of the work of the Holy Spirit is the *communal.* The Spirit is the power who unites us to Christ and to each other. This has also been called the incorporative work of the Spirit: "Through the agency of the Spirit, believers are caught up, as it were, in the life of the Godhead, incorporated through the activity of the Spirit into the Son, given there the firm and assured status of children of God by adoption, enabled to join the Son's ceaseless prayer of Abba to the Father."[12] This uniting or incorporating power of the Spirit is not the power of mere togetherness of the like-minded or the kinship of people of the same family, race, economic class, or nation. It is the power of new community that unites strangers and even former enemies. It creates community where formerly there were insuperable barriers. "There is no longer Jew or Greek, there is no longer slave or free, there is no longer male and female; for all of you are one in Christ Jesus" (Gal. 3:28). United in Christ by the power of the Spirit we are one community; we are members of one body and mutually dependent on one another. By drawing us into new solidarity with Christ and each other, the Spirit remakes us as persons-in-community who no longer live as isolated, self-centered individuals.

e. Of great importance is the *promise* associated with the work of the Holy Spirit and the strong hope this sustains in the lives of believers. The Spirit at work in the Christian community is said to be the "firstfruits" (Rom. 8:23) or, in another metaphor, the "first installment" or "guarantee" (2 Cor. 1:22; 5:5) of the future that God is bringing. As the power of God's promised future, the Spirit awakens hope, yearning, and restlessness for the completion of God's redemptive work and the establishment of justice and peace throughout the creation. The Spirit sighs in us and in all the creation for God's coming kingdom. The Spirit keeps hope alive and incites fresh visions of God's new world. Where there is no vision or hope, no discontent or protest against present injustice and evil, there is assuredly no presence of the Spirit in the biblical understanding of this term.

f. A further brief comment should be made about *the gifts or charismata of the Spirit.* According to the biblical witness, there are many diverse gifts of the Spirit, and each should be respected. In celebrating the diversity of spiritual gifts, we recognize our mutual dependence and encourage mutual support. As the apostle Paul teaches in 1 Corinthians 12–14, however, the most important gifts are not the sensational ones, such as speaking in tongues, but the gifts of faith, hope, and above all love. While Paul does not want to outlaw

---

12. *We Believe in the Holy Spirit: A Report by the Doctrine Commission of the General Synod of the Church of England* (London: Church House Publishing, 1991), 10.

speaking in tongues within the Christian community, it is clear that neither he nor any other New Testament witness considers this phenomenon crucial for Christian spirituality. The primary criterion of life in the Spirit is an unconditional love of God and a correlative love of others, especially those who are commonly considered strangers and even enemies. Such love is motivated by God's love for sinners and the poor in Christ.

We should not denigrate any of the various gifts that the Spirit gives to members of the church, but we should test their authenticity by the criterion of whether they serve the common good rather than promoting division and contention in the community. A true gift of the Spirit builds up the community and contributes to the common good rather than serving only the self-aggrandizement of a few.

3. *A Christian theology of the Holy Spirit will speak of a correspondence between the work of the Holy Spirit in the economy of salvation and the activity of the Spirit in the eternal life of the triune God.*

If the Holy Spirit does all the things recounted in Scripture and confirmed in Christian experience — unites us with Christ, pours the love of God into our hearts, gives us new life, helps us to pray, liberates us for love of God and neighbor, makes of us one people called to serve and glorify God, gives gifts of service to all members of the community, assures us of the promises of God and awakens in us the hope for the consummation of God's redemptive purposes — if the Holy Spirit does all these things, then the Spirit is indeed the "Spirit of God" (Rom. 8:14), the "Spirit of Christ" (Rom. 8:9), the "Spirit of Truth" (John 14:17), the "Spirit of life" (Rom. 8:2). As such, the Holy Spirit is to be worshiped and glorified together with the Father and the Son. According to classical trinitarian logic, sound theological reflection begins with the work of Jesus Christ and the Holy Spirit for our salvation attested in Scripture and experienced in Christian life and prayer and only on that basis moves to affirmations about God's eternal being.[13]

Christian faith and theology speak of the Holy Spirit as the Spirit of the triune God. What the Spirit does in us and in the world has its basis in the eternal life of God. For trinitarian faith, God is the living God whose eternal being is dynamic communion in love. God's being is the act of mutual sharing of life and love among Father, Son, and Holy Spirit. As emphasized in Chapter Four, the three persons of the Trinity are not to be understood as separate selves living in isolation from each other. Rather, their personhood is constituted by their relationships with each other. They are so deeply and inseparably united that they "indwell" each other in what Jonathan Edwards,

13. See Basil, *On the Holy Spirit* (Crestwood, N.Y.: St. Vladimir's Seminary Press, 1980).

following one strand of Augustine's trinitarian imagery, boldly calls "the society of the three persons in the Godhead."[14]

The Spirit is the uniting and consummating love of the Trinity, the energy of the life of communion, the gift of mutual love and friendship. The life of the triune God is not a closed circle but in the power of the Spirit is open to the world. Thinking and speaking of the uniting, bridging, and culminating activity of Spirit in the eternal triune life is not something that we dream up, not a mere projection of our wishes and fantasies. It is based on the revelation and experience of the Spirit as the gift of the love of God poured into our hearts, as the power of new community in Christ, as the comforter who unites us to God through Christ, as the promise of the completion of God's purposes. Because God in relation to us is faithful to God's own being, there is a correspondence between the uniting, gift-giving, and consummating work of the Holy Spirit in the economy of salvation and the activity of the Spirit as the bond of unity, love, joy, and peace in the eternal triune life.

The relation of the Holy Spirit to the Father and the Son has been the topic of a long-standing controversy in the trinitarian theologies of the Eastern and Western churches. These churches share much in common in their understandings of the Spirit. Both declare that the Spirit is the Lord and lifegiver, fully equal to the Father and the Son. Both declare that all of the divine attributes that belong to the Father and the Son belong also to the Spirit. Both declare that the Spirit, together with the Father and the Son, is to be worshiped and glorified. Both speak of the Spirit as "person," no less than the other members of the Trinity.

Despite these major agreements, a divergence in doctrine occurred between East and West over the question of the "procession" of the Spirit. As background for understanding this question, we must explain the distinction made in classical trinitarian theology between the "missions" and the "processions" of the Son and the Spirit. The term "missions" refers to the sending and activity of the Son and the Spirit in the creation, reconciliation, and redemption of the world. Eastern and Western theologies are agreed that every work of God involves the presence and cooperation of all three persons of the Trinity. Corresponding to the missions of the triune God in relation to the world *(ad extra)* are the eternal "processions" of the Son and the Spirit within the Trinity *(ad intra)*. From all eternity there is in the triune life a "begetting" of the Son and a "proceeding" of the Spirit.

In the Niceno-Constantinopolitan Creed of 381 A.D. the Spirit is said to

---

14. *The Works of Jonathan Edwards,* vol. 18: The "Miscellanies," 501-832, ed. Ava Chamberlain (New Haven: Yale University Press, 2000), 110.

proceed "from the Father." Beginning in the sixth century, the Western church added to the creed the phrase *filioque*, "and from the Son." As a result, in the revised creed in the West, the Holy Spirit is said to proceed "from the Father and from the Son." The church in the East has rejected this addition as an illegitimate, unilateral action on the part of the Western church and has continued to affirm that the Spirit proceeds only from the Father (cf. John 15:26).

Is anything important at stake in this disagreement? According to Western theology, the *filioque* doctrine declares that Christ and the Spirit are inseparable. If the work of the Spirit were completely independent from that of Christ, the church would be unable to make responsible judgments about various experiences and movements claiming to be authorized by the Spirit of God. The church would also be vulnerable to all sorts of natural theologies that do not look to Christ as the decisive revelation of God.[15] Furthermore, according to Western theology, the unity of the Trinity is guarded by the *filioque* because the Spirit is the common bond between Father and Son.

According to Eastern theologians, however, the *filioque* has the effect of subordinating the Spirit to Christ. It thus promotes a Spirit-deficient Christology and a Spirit-deficient ecclesiology in which power is divorced from spiritual presence. Furthermore, Eastern theologians contend that by obscuring the uniqueness of the Father as the sole source of the Son and the Spirit, the *filioque* threatens the unity of the Trinity. Again according to Eastern theology, the *filioque* obscures the activity of the Spirit in all creation and history rather than only where the Word incarnate is explicitly proclaimed and confessed.

Some progress toward a resolution of this ancient controversy has been made in recent ecumenical studies and conversations. Further progress depends on whether the two sides can reach agreement on several points. (1) The Western church was clearly at fault in unilaterally emending the creed. Even if there were strong theological reasons for the change, the issue should have been debated and resolved by the whole church. (2) Neither the Western nor the Eastern model of the procession of the Spirit fully captures all forms of the relationships of the persons of the Trinity depicted in the New Testament witness. (3) The debate about the "procession" of the Spirit has one-sidedly focused on the question of the *origin* of the Spirit from the Father (or Father and Son). Interest in relationships of origin should be complemented by attention to the *goal* of trinitarian movement. The Spirit's activity in the ministry of Jesus and in the life of the church points to the coming reign and eschatological glory of the triune God.[16]

15. For a vigorous defense of the *filioque*, see Karl Barth, *Church Dogmatics*, 1/1: 448-89.
16. See Jürgen Moltmann, *The Trinity and the Kingdom* (San Francisco: Harper & Row,

In the New Testament, Jesus and the Spirit are not competitors, nor is one subordinate to the other. They are interdependent.[17] Jesus is both the receiver and the giver of the Spirit. On the one hand, Jesus is the gift of the Spirit. He is, according to the infancy narratives, conceived by the Spirit (Matt. 1:20; Luke 1:35). At his baptism the Spirit descends and remains on him (John 1:32). Jesus is the one anointed by the Spirit for the ministry of good news to the poor and liberation to those in bondage (Luke 4:18ff.), the one who heals the sick and casts out demonic forces in the power of the Spirit (Matt. 12:28), the one who is himself raised from the dead by the Spirit (Rom. 1:4). In these accounts, the Spirit of God is the actor and Jesus the recipient or mediator of the Spirit's action. On the other hand, the Spirit is the gift of the risen Christ (John 20:22), the one promised and sent by Christ as promised (John 15:26; Luke 24:49). The Spirit is the power that teaches us what is the mind of Christ (1 Cor. 2:16), pours the love of God into our hearts (Rom. 5:5), empowers our new life in Christ (Rom. 8:11), and motivates and equips us for discipleship and service (Rom. 8:14). In these accounts, the Spirit is the recipient or the mediator of the action of Christ. The intimacy of the relation of Christ and the Spirit in the New Testament is such that on the one hand, as Calvin says, Christ is "useless" without the Spirit, and on the other hand, the test of authenticity of the presence of the Spirit is whether there is witness to and confession of Jesus as Lord (1 Cor. 12:3).

Finally, there is considerable discussion today about the appropriateness of using female imagery of the Spirit. We should not make much of the fact that the word for Spirit is feminine in Hebrew *(ruach)*, although it is neuter in Greek *(pneuma)*, and masculine in Latin *(spiritus)*. More pertinent are New Testament descriptions of the nurturing and empowering activities of the Spirit and the fact that in the conversation with Nicodemus in the Gospel of John, Jesus speaks of the work of the Spirit as like a mother who gives birth (John 3:3-6).[18]

Some theologians propose that the Holy Spirit is the feminine counterpart to the incarnate Son of God. They suggest that the Word and Spirit of God can be described respectively as the Son and Daughter of God, working together to make us all adopted children of God. Following Irenaeus's image of Word and Spirit as the "two hands" of God, Jose Comblin suggests that just as the Word of God is incarnate in a single human being, so the Spirit of God is intimately present in one inclusive community, bringing to birth and nurtur-

---

1984); David Coffey, "The Holy Spirit as the Mutual Love of the Father and the Son," *Theological Studies* 51 (1990): 193-229.

17. See Hendrikus Berkhof, *The Doctrine of the Holy Spirit* (Grand Rapids: Eerdmans, 1965).

18. See Virginia Ramey Mollenkott, *The Divine Feminine: The Biblical Imagery of God as Female* (New York: Crossroad, 1984).

ing God's new humanity. According to Comblin, a theology of the maternity of the Spirit might counterbalance the excessive masculinity of the church's traditional ways of imaging God and its understanding of divine power.[19]

But while speaking of the Spirit of God in feminine imagery is suggested by some biblical passages and should be welcomed in both theology and liturgy, the name "Spirit" should primarily serve to remind us that God is beyond gender and that we must avoid the danger of making idols of any images and metaphors of God. A number of feminist theologians warn of possible gender stereotyping that may accompany talk of the Spirit as female. The triune God is neither an exclusive male fraternity nor a divine company composed of two males and one female. That the triune God is also called Spirit teaches us to think and speak of God as uniquely personal, allowing gender-specific imagery yet also far transcending all such imagery. That God is Spirit should remind us of the limits of all of our language about God.[20] The triune God lives in perfect communion and mutual self-giving love. Beyond saying that, we do well to emulate the pious wonder and reverent modesty in our thinking and speaking of the triune God that has characterized the classical theological tradition at its best.

4. *While taking its bearings from the biblical witness and being centered on the Spirit's activity of binding believers to Christ, incorporating them into the church as the body of Christ, and equipping the church for mission, a Christian theology of the Holy Spirit will affirm that the Spirit is present and active also outside the church.*

A Christian theology of the work of the Holy Spirit must not be confined to the life and witness of the church. There is a cosmic dimension of the work of the Spirit. If the Spirit is like the wind that "blows where it wills" (John 3:8), we must expect and be open to the working of the Spirit beyond the walls of the church. The Spirit of God is present and at work in the world of nature, in the restlessness of the human heart, in the work for justice and harmony in human relations, in the search for truth in the sciences, in the skills of creative artists, and in the histories of the world religions.

The cosmic work of the Spirit is a complex topic. It is sometimes discussed under the themes of "common grace" and "general revelation." Augustine and Calvin, both Christian humanists, offer helpful guidance on the topic. According to Augustine, "Every good and true Christian should understand that wherever he may find truth, it is his Lord's."[21] Calvin is of the same

---

19. Comblin, *The Holy Spirit and Liberation*, 39.

20. See Krister Stendahl, *Energy for Life: Reflections on the Theme "Come, Holy Spirit — Renew the Whole Creation"* (Geneva: WCC Publications, 1990), 6-8.

21. Augustine, *On Christian Doctrine* (New York: Liberal Arts Press, 1958), 54.

opinion: "If we regard the Spirit of God as the sole fountain of truth, we shall neither reject the truth itself, nor despise it wherever it shall appear, unless we wish to dishonor the Spirit of God."[22] Among contemporary theologians, Jürgen Moltmann has emphasized the importance for theology and the church of recognizing the cosmic work of the Spirit. The Spirit of God is the Spirit of life, everywhere at work empowering all that supports and enhances life and peace in God's creation, and struggling against all forces of disintegration, destruction, and death.[23]

A theology of the Spirit of God that takes into account its cosmic dimension has two important implications. The first is the recognition of the freedom of the Spirit and the acknowledgment that the church, as witness to and servant of the universal reign of God, is not itself the completed realization of God's reign. The second implication is the responsibility of the church to discern the work of the Spirit of God and to distinguish God's Spirit from other spirits at work in the world. In this regard the ministry of Christ and the proclamation of Christ crucified and risen are of fundamental significance. Calvin puts the matter well: All understanding of the work of the Spirit is an "unstable and transitory thing in God's sight, when a solid foundation of truth does not underlie it."[24] Apart from the light of Christ, a discussion of God the Spirit would be like wandering in a labyrinth.[25]

The Christian Life: Justification

Christian life is based on the grace of God in Jesus Christ to whom we are united by the power of the Holy Spirit. On its objective side, new life in Christ is rooted in God's transforming work of justification, sanctification, and vocation. On its subjective side, Christian life is the free personal appropriation of God's grace in faith, love, and hope.[26]

Christian life in the power of the Spirit is a dynamic process of transformation into the likeness of Christ that is set in motion by the gracious initiative of God. It begins with justification, continues in sanctification, and

22. Calvin, *Institutes*, 2.2.15.

23. Jürgen Moltmann, *The Spirit of Life*.

24. Calvin, *Institutes*, 2.2.16.

25. Calvin, *The Gospel According to St. John*, trans. T. H. L. Parker (Grand Rapids: Eerdmans, 1959), 213.

26. I am here following the broad outline of Barth's treatment of the Christian life in terms of justification, sanctification, and vocation in his *Church Dogmatics*, 4/1-3. Cf. Tillich, *Systematic Theology*, 2: 176-80.

moves to its goal in vocation. Life in Christ is patterned after the life, death, and resurrection of Jesus Christ and is thus a continuous dying to an old way of life and a rising to a new way of life. It is both mortification and vivification, both a receiving of and responding to God's grace, both gift and task, both being freed and exercising new freedom, both being loved and loving others. To be a Christian is "to grow up in every way" in Christ (Eph. 4:15), to be on the way to the fullness of our new humanity in him.

As the first moment of this process, *justification is God's gracious forgiveness of sins that is received by faith alone* (Rom. 3:23-28). Accomplished and manifested in Jesus Christ, it is God's free, unconditional, and unmerited acceptance of us in spite of our sin and alienation from God, from others, and from ourselves. "Justification" is a term from the judicial sphere and means "acquitting" or "making right." That we are justified means that our broken relationship with God has been restored by an act of free grace and forgiveness. God's act of justification is by grace alone *(sola gratia),* in Christ alone *(solus Christus),* received by faith alone *(sola fide).*

The doctrine of justification is sometimes expressed in the abbreviated form: we are justified by faith. However, a major distortion of the doctrine occurs if it is taken to mean that faith is the human act by which we merit justification. God's act of justification is a free gift and is in no way dependent upon us, although it calls for our response. Thus a more adequate brief statement of the doctrine is that we are justified by grace through faith. We cannot merit justification even by our act of faith. Faith is simply the appropriate response of trust and acceptance of God's unconditional acceptance of us.

The act of faith is not rightly understood when it is viewed as mere assent to propositions presented to us by the church or the Bible. Christian faith is the act of personal trust in God made known in Christ, not bare assent to propositions about God or Christ. The Reformers distinguished between two ways of believing. One way is to believe certain things *about* God — for example, that God exists, or that Christ performed miracles. Luther called this historical or factual knowledge rather than faith in the proper sense. The other way is to believe *in* God. When I put my faith in God, "I not only believe that what is said about God is true, but I put my trust in him, surrender myself to him."[27]

The doctrine of justification is, in Luther's words, "the centerpiece of our teaching."[28] This is echoed by Calvin, who calls the doctrine of justifica-

---

27. Martin Luther, "A Brief Explanation of the Ten Commandments, the Creed, and the Lord's Prayer," in *Works of Martin Luther* (Philadelphia: Muhlenberg Press, 1943), 2: 368.

28. Luther, *Stufenpsalmen* of 1532-33, quoted by Bernhard Lohse, *Martin Luther's Theology: Its Historical and Systematic Development* (Minneapolis: Fortress, 1999), 258, n. 2.

tion "the main hinge on which religion turns."[29] Luther reports that the breakthrough in his understanding of the gospel occurred when he came to realize that the "righteousness of God" of which Paul speaks in Romans 1:17 is not a punitive but a gracious righteousness. Before his discovery, Luther had understood God's righteousness to mean the righteousness that is revealed in God's punishment of sinners. "I hated the righteous God who punishes sinners," Luther writes. But when he grasped that the gospel reveals the righteousness with which the merciful God justifies by grace through faith, Luther felt as though the gates of paradise had been opened to him. "A totally other face of the entire Scripture showed itself to me."[30]

In classical Lutheran theology, the doctrine of justification has been described as "the article by which the church stands or falls."[31] It would be a mistake, however, to suggest that for the Reformers all Christian doctrine can be reduced to the doctrine of justification. The fullness of the event of Jesus Christ does not find its complete expression in this or any other single doctrine.[32]

The differences in the interpretations of the doctrine of justification by the sixteenth-century Reformers and the teaching of the Roman Catholic Church as expressed in the Council of Trent were real. At the same time, the dispute was complicated by sharp polemics and mutual misunderstandings. Roman Catholic theologians believed that the Reformers' doctrine of justification taught only a purely legal change of status in the believer's relation to God and thereby disregarded the importance of a transformed Christian life and the call to obedience and service. The Reformers charged that the Roman Catholic teaching made good works a prerequisite for attaining the justifying grace of God. They taught that new life and good works are the *fruits* rather than the *precondition* of God's act of justification by grace alone to be received by faith alone.[33]

In 1999, after years of study and discussion, official representatives of the Roman Catholic and Lutheran Churches signed a Joint Declaration on

29. Calvin, *Institutes*, 3.11.1.

30. *Luther's Works*, 34: 336-37.

31. See Carl E. Braaten, *Justification: The Article by Which the Church Stands or Falls* (Minneapolis: Fortress, 1990); Eberhard Jüngel, *Justification: The Heart of the Christian Faith* (Edinburgh: T&T Clark, 2001).

32. "The *articulus stantis et cadentis ecclesiae* is not the doctrine of justification as such, but its basis and culmination: the confession of Jesus Christ in whom are hid all the treasures of wisdom and knowledge (Col. 2:3); the knowledge of his being and activity for us and to us and in us." Barth, *Church Dogmatics*, 4/1: 527.

33. See especially Martin Luther, "Two Types of Righteousness," in *Luther's Works*, 31: 297-306.

the Doctrine of Justification. This declaration does not resolve all issues. Nevertheless, it is significant that these churches were able to make this common confession: "By grace alone, in faith in Christ's saving work and not because of any merit on our part, we are accepted by God and receive the Holy Spirit, who renews our hearts while equipping and calling us to good works."[34]

While this official declaration is cause for celebration, it does not fully accomplish the theological task of interpreting the doctrine of justification for our own time. Far from being an outmoded teaching, the doctrine of justification, when properly understood, continues to have enormous relevance today. There are many ways by which we try to justify ourselves, render our lives acceptable and meaningful to others, to ourselves, and perhaps also to God. We do this not necessarily by "good works" but often by plain hard work or by acts that we think will win the approval of others. Who is entirely immune from this desire for approval and is not anxious about being rejected? In modern society, we are all to some degree continuously on trial, not unlike the accused in Franz Kafka's story *The Trial*, who is tormented by the fear of being condemned by an anonymous judge. The quest for acceptance and the drive to succeed border on idolatry in our competitive society. Both as individuals and as a people, we are terrified by the prospect of failing to win the recognition and love that we crave.

The desperate search for acceptance is no doubt at work in the epidemic of drug addiction in American society. While the motivations for using drugs are complex, the sense of hopelessness, worthlessness, and the absence of significant affirmation by others are no doubt important factors. The turn to drugs exposes the heartlessness of our social structures and relationships as well as the universal human vulnerability to the self-imposed bondages that are called addictions.

Although not often noted, our consumerist way of life is also an addiction. Modern societies create artificial needs through advertising and seduce us into seeking identity and meaning in accumulating material possessions. Whether in bondage to the spirit of possession or success, we are driven by the desire to "make it," to feel valued, accepted, and loved. In view of all this, anyone who thinks that the doctrine of justification has little relevance for people in our sophisticated society captive to many kinds of addictions — whether of money, work, leisure, fame, sex, or the more frequently mentioned forms of substance abuse — is simply out of touch with reality.

One of the most impressive twentieth-century restatements of the doc-

---

34. *Joint Declaration on the Doctrine of Justification: The Lutheran World Federation and the Roman Catholic Church* (Grand Rapids: Eerdmans, 2000), 3.15.

trine of justification by grace through faith was offered by Paul Tillich in a sermon entitled "You Are Accepted." "Just accept the fact that you are accepted," said Tillich, "accepted by a power that is greater than you."[35]

But perhaps an even more powerful expression of the doctrine of justification comes out of the struggle of blacks for justice and freedom in North America and South Africa. An important element of the message of such eloquent preachers as Martin Luther King, Jr., and Jesse Jackson could be summarized in the affirmation that "we are somebodies." Interpreted in the light of its gospel roots, this affirmation means that we are of worth despite the negative evaluation of the society in which we live or even our own negative self-evaluation. We are of worth not because our employers or teachers say so, not even because the president of the United States or the American constitution says so; we are "somebodies" because God our creator and our redeemer says so. It is because we are creatures made in the divine image, because we are children of God, persons for whom Jesus Christ suffered, died, and was raised again, persons in whom the Spirit of God is at work — because of all this, we are somebodies. That is the basis of our dignity, our worth, our human rights, and our human responsibilities.

A similar discovery is made by a character in Alice Walker's novel *The Color Purple*. When Celie expresses surprise that her friend Shug thinks that God loves her even if she doesn't do things like go to church, sing in the choir, and feed the preacher, Shug replies, "But if God love me, Celie, I don't have to do all that. Unless I want to."[36] Far from being irrelevant, such rediscoveries of the biblical message of justification by grace have revolutionary potency. We can be certain that the Caesars of history tremble when people discover that their worth is not determined by what they achieve or by what state and society bestow or withhold from them. Their identity and value are given to them by God, who loves, affirms, and accepts them as they are — whoever they may be. Because God in Jesus Christ has said Yes to them, they are not "nobodies" but "somebodies."

The Christian Life: Sanctification

If justification by grace through faith is the foundation of the Christian life, *sanctification is the process of growth in Christian love.* The word "sanctification" means "to make holy," but for some people that definition may be more a hindrance than a help. We should not understand holiness here in the sense of

35. Tillich, *The Shaking of the Foundations* (New York: Scribner's, 1948), 162.
36. Walker, *The Color Purple* (New York: Washington Square Press, 1982), 176.

moral flawlessness or religious otherworldliness. It certainly has little to do with the smug attitudes of a so-called Moral Majority. Becoming holy or sanctified in the New Testament sense means being conformed to the image of Christ by the working of the Holy Spirit in our lives. The essential mark of this Christlikeness is that free, self-giving, other-regarding love that the New Testament calls *agape*. Released from the compulsive power of self-centeredness, we are enabled to love God and our neighbors with a joyful heart.

Justification and sanctification are inseparable because by faith we are united with Christ. To participate in Christ by faith is to receive a "double grace," as Calvin puts it. We are justified or forgiven in Christ and thus reconciled to God, and we are sanctified by Christ's Spirit so that we may cultivate a new life in conformity with Christ.[37] The two aspects of this double grace are distinguishable but not separable, just as the cross and resurrection of Christ are distinguishable but inseparable moments of his work of reconciliation on our behalf. Barth describes the indissoluble relationship between justification and sanctification with characteristic precision: Justification is the basis and presupposition of sanctification; sanctification is the aim and consequence of justification.[38]

It is a mistake to think of sanctification as primarily what *we* do in contrast to justification as solely *God's* work. John Wesley, well-known for his insistence on the importance of the sanctified life, was one with the continental Reformers and the classical theological tradition in insisting "that we are sanctified as well as justified by faith. . . . Exactly as we are justified by faith, so are we sanctified by faith."[39] Just as faith is properly understood as a response to the divine justification of human life on account of Christ, so love of God and our fellow creatures is properly understood as a response to the divine sanctification of human life in Christ. Sanctification is first of all the gift of God, and only then also a human calling.

The term "growth" must be used with care in reference to the Christian life. Any suggestion of an undisturbed process of development or a neatly ordered sequence of stages should be avoided. There is, to be sure, real movement in Christian life, but it is neither quantifiable nor predictable. On the topic of sanctification, Luther and Wesley seem to be at irreconcilable odds, with Luther emphasizing justification almost to the neglect of sanctification and Wesley emphasizing sanctification even to the point of a doctrine of

37. Calvin, *Institutes*, 3.11.1.

38. Barth, *Church Dogmatics*, 4/2: 508.

39. "The Scripture Way of Salvation," in *John Wesley's Sermons: An Anthology*, ed. Albert C. Outler and Richard P. Heitzenrater (Nashville: Abingdon, 1987), 376.

Christian perfection. But to properly understand their different emphases, their different historical circumstances must be kept in mind. In his battle against all forms of self-justification, Luther, rooted in Pauline theology, insists that we are simultaneously justified and sinful *(simul iustus et peccator)*. Luther's emphasis does not preclude real deepening of Christian faith and genuine growth in Christian life, but it stresses the radicalness of human sinfulness and our continuing dependence on God's forgiveness. Wesley, for his part, ministering in the midst of the moral breakdown that accompanied the Industrial Revolution, urges Christians to become "perfect" in the love of God and neighbor and teaches that at least some Christians have arrived at this goal even in this life. Basing his teaching on the call of Jesus to "be perfect as your heavenly Father is perfect" (Matt. 5:28), Wesley does not deny that sin continues as a powerful force in the life of believers but calls for greater trust in the transforming work of the Holy Spirit.[40]

If we respect the freedom of God's grace and the limitless disguises that sin assumes, we will avoid oversimplification in our portrayals of the process of growth in Christian life. Yet we will also insist that, in the environment of the Spirit of God who is at work in the Christian community, real growth in Christian faith, love, and hope does occur. Several criteria or marks of growth in Christian life may be briefly mentioned.[41]

1. The first is *maturing as hearers of the Word of God*. Christian life is shaped and normed by the Word of God, whose unique and primary witness is the Scripture of the Old and New Testaments. This Word proclaims God's grace and judgment and calls its hearers to repentance, conversion, and new life. Maturing as hearers of the Word means approaching Scripture not as a magical answer book but as the church's primary witness to the sovereign, holy love of God supremely revealed in Jesus Christ. The Spirit of God uses the witness of Scripture to form and reform Christian life and to build and strengthen Christian character.

Mature hearing of the scriptural witness involves opening oneself to all its formative influences: its narratives, poetry, parables, songs of praise, directives, promises, laments, and warnings. Mature hearing also involves listening to this witness not as an isolated individual but in community. And it means allowing ourselves to be opened to new and surprising readings of Scripture by Christian communities in very different contexts from our own. The inter-

---

40. See Jürgen Moltmann's comparison of Luther and Wesley on justification and sanctification in *The Spirit of Life: A Universal Affirmation*, 161-71.

41. See John Calvin, *Institutes*, 3.1-10; Karl Barth, *Unterricht in der christlichen Religion* (Zürich: TVZ, 2003), 3: 306-33; Paul Tillich, *Systematic Theology*, 3: 231-37.

pretations of Scripture by the poor and the afflicted especially will correct and deepen interpretations with which we are more familiar. When this kind of persistent and open attention to Scripture occurs, we can be sure that the Spirit of God is at work.

What we are calling mature hearing of the Word of God will involve our readiness to assume responsibility for the fresh interpretation and living out of the witness of Scripture in the present situation. Above all, mature hearing of the Word of God issues in a continuing transformation of life by the concrete practice of love of God and love of neighbor.

2. A second mark of Christian growth is *maturing in prayer*. Prayer is a concrete expression of our love of God. It is personal communication with God, calling upon God as a strong and caring father or mother (cf. Matt. 6:9; Rom. 8:15; Isa. 66:13). For the Christian, God is not some*thing* but some*one* — and primarily someone who is spoken *to*, rather than only spoken *about*. Moreover, this someone addressed in prayer is not feared as a tyrant but genuinely loved as the sovereign and free God who exercises dominion with astonishing goodness and mercy. Prayer is thus our acceptance of the invitation to call upon God in confidence. Maturing in prayer does not mean mastering certain techniques or becoming virtuosos of the spiritual life. It means, on the contrary, being open and honest to God, praising God but also crying to God in our need, and even sometimes crying out against God.[42]

Prayer is the fundamental exercise of the new human freedom in partnership with the Spirit of God. Calvin calls prayer "the chief exercise of faith."[43] While it includes adoration and thanksgiving, prayer is essentially bold petition. As instructed by Jesus, we are to pray *first* for the hallowing of God's name, for the coming of God's reign, for the doing of God's will, *and then also* for daily bread, for forgiveness, for deliverance from temptation (Matt. 6:9-13). Maturing in prayer means being ready to learn, in the presence of the God of costly grace, the difference between what we want and what we need. It means learning that every fruitful human action is rooted in prayer for God's reign, for God's forgiveness, and for God's empowering grace.[44]

3. A third mark of Christian growth is *maturing in freedom*.[45] Freedom

---

42. See Patrick D. Miller, *They Cried to the Lord: The Form and Theology of Biblical Prayer* (Minneapolis: Fortress, 1994).

43. Calvin, *Institutes*, 3.20.

44. See Jan Milic Lochman, *The Lord's Prayer* (Grand Rapids: Eerdmans, 1990); Karl Barth, *Prayer*, 50th Anniversary Edition, with essays by I. John Hesselink, Daniel L. Migliore, and Donald K. McKim (Louisville: Westminster/John Knox, 2002).

45. The two classical Reformation texts are Calvin, "Christian Freedom" in *Institutes*, 3.19; and Luther, "The Freedom of the Christian," in *Luther's Works*, 31: 333-77.

flourishes where the Spirit of God is at work (2 Cor. 3:17). God's Spirit does not work like a steamroller: it does not crush us, but sets us free and empowers us for new life.

To live in the power of the Spirit of Christ is to grow in a new freedom. Calvin describes this freedom as having three parts: freedom from the law as a means of self-justification; freedom for joyous obedience of God's will summed up in the commandment to love God with all our heart and our neighbors as ourselves; and freedom in indifferent matters *(adiaphora)*.[46] Christian freedom has a negative side. It is a freedom from bondage to sinful ways of life in which we seek to be our own god and disregard the welfare of others. Christians are called to freedom from bondage to ideologies of race, nation, domination, and wealth. They are also set free from religious legalisms that strain at a gnat and swallow a camel (Matt. 23:24). When Paul speaks of a "law of Christ" (Gal. 6:2), he does not mean a law that produces new anxiety about our standing before God. He means life in conformity with Christ's self-giving love that guides the exercise of our new freedom.

If Christian freedom can be described negatively as freedom from the terror of having to win God's favor and from our multiple idolatries, it can be described positively as freedom for the service of God and others. Embracing God's mercy and forgiveness, we are freed to forgive others.[47] Augustine aptly characterizes Christian freedom in the statement "Love God, and do what you will."[48] The point of this remark is that if we love God above all else, we will freely do what God wills. Freedom in Christ is utterly different from the self-indulgence that characterizes consumer culture. It is a heightened readiness to be servants in God's work of reconciliation in Christ. Struggle against hostility, injustice, and other evils at work within us and around us is the inseparable companion of Christian freedom.

Christian growth thus means increasing freedom *from* all that undercuts the love of God and neighbor, and increasing freedom *for* new opportunities of Christlike service. Such service is costly, and in this sense suffering is a component of the process of sanctification. This has nothing to do with the idea of suffering for suffering's sake; it has everything to do with the freedom to face suffering for the sake of the coming reign of God's justice and peace.

---

46. Calvin, *Institutes*, 3.19.2-7.

47. See L. Gregory Jones, *Embodying Forgiveness: A Theological Analysis* (Grand Rapids: Eerdmans, 1995).

48. Augustine, *Homilies on 1 John*, 7.8, in *Augustine: Later Works*, ed. John Burnaby (Philadelphia: Westminster, 1955), 316.

As Moltmann notes, in a superficial, apathetic, and dehumanized society, willingness to risk suffering can be a sign of spiritual health.[49]

4. A fourth mark of Christian growth is *maturing in solidarity*. By "solidarity" I mean regard for and love of all our fellow creatures. This means in the first place love of our fellow human beings, and especially the poor and the neglected.[50] Growth in Christian life is a process of entering into solidarity with ever-wider circles of community that are created and nourished by the Spirit. This new spirit of solidarity presupposes a *metanoia*, a repentance or renewal of the mind, whereby we cease to be attentive only to ourselves and become increasingly conscious of and sensitive to the needs of others. Sensitivity to and struggle against injustices in society and church are part of maturing in solidarity with others.

Hearing the Word of God and partaking of the sacraments are concrete and regular practices of the community of faith that help to engender this new way of thinking, feeling, and living in the new solidarity in Christ with the whole groaning creation. If they do not serve this purpose, they are empty religious rites.

Christian life in many congregations is stifled by the fact that membership is all too homogeneous. Too many congregations are like birds of a feather that have flocked together. Christian growth involves openness to and a search for heterogeneous and inclusive community. Church membership and mission should not be mere reflections of the socioeconomic, cultural, racial, and gender divisions of secular society. Increasing solidarity with strangers, people commonly considered undesirables, and even those labeled enemies is a criterion of growth in Christian life. But maturing in solidarity for the Christian also entails solidarity with the whole realm of nonhuman creatures. Regnant anthropocentrism in our everyday attitudes, our lifestyles, and our economic and political decisions is an obstacle to growth in Christian life. Growth in solidarity always comes at a cost. It is costly both in the sense of requiring us to give up self-centered ways of thinking and living and in the sense of arousing opposition and perhaps even persecution from those who see the movement toward solidarity as a deadly threat rather than a blessing. Classical theological descriptions of the Christian life, following Scripture, have rightly always emphasized the inescapability of cross-bearing in the life of the disciples of the crucified Lord.[51]

49. Moltmann, *The Crucified God* (New York: Harper & Row, 1974), 115.

50. Solidarity with the poor is the central theme of Latin American liberation spirituality. See Gustavo Gutiérrez, *A Theology of Liberation* (Maryknoll, N.Y.: Orbis Books, 1973), and *We Drink from Our Own Wells* (Maryknoll, N.Y.: Orbis Books, 1984).

51. Cf. Calvin, *Institutes*, 3.8.

5. Another mark of growth in Christian life is *maturing in thankfulness and joy.* The Heidelberg Catechism sums up the Christian life in the single, lovely term "thanksgiving." In the same confessional tradition, the "Brief Statement of Faith" includes these lines: "In gratitude to God, empowered by the Spirit, we strive to serve Christ in our daily tasks, and to live holy and joyful lives."[52] Of course, the joy and thanksgiving that are marks of Christian life are very different from superficial optimism or artificial cheeriness. Christian thanksgiving and joy are also different from the self-righteous attitude of the person who thanks God that he or she is so much better than thieves, rogues, adulterers, and tax collectors (Luke 18:11). We are speaking instead of the thankfulness and joy of those who know they are utterly dependent on the mercy of God and who express their gratitude in heartfelt praise, open friendship, and joyful service. Such thanksgiving and joy grow out of confidence in God, who by the Spirit has already begun the renewal of life in Christ and whose grace will ultimately triumph over all evil, sin, and death.

Grace generates thanksgiving; *charis* brings forth *eucharist.* For this reason, the eucharistic meal — anticipation of the joyful messianic banquet — will always be at the center of Christian worship alongside the proclamation of the Word of God. There is much to protest and much to struggle against in the church and in society, in one's own life and in the life of the body politic. As Calvin and other theologians of the Christian life have emphasized, cross-bearing is a signature of growth in grace. Still, in the midst of struggle and cross-bearing, we grow as we continue to give thanks. We show ourselves to be maturing Christians as our capacity for thanksgiving, praise, and joy go hand in hand with our readiness for costly discipleship.

6. A final mark of growth in Christian life is *maturing in hope.* Christian life is a pilgrimage. It is life on the way to the fulfillment of God's purposes for us and for the world. Christians seek "a homeland," a "better country," the "city" that God is preparing (Heb. 11:13-16). Mature hope does not give up on this world, for it is God's world. Nor does mature hope rest on our ability to build the reign of God on earth, for only God can do that. Mature Christian hope prays and works for the coming of God's reign and the doing of God's will, but it also knows how to wait on God.

Calvin offers a beautiful summary of the conviction that animates mature Christian life in its many aspects: "We are not our own; we are God's."[53]

---

52. *The Book of Confessions* (PCUSA), 10.72-74.
53. Calvin, *Institutes*, 3.7.1.

The Christian Life: Vocation

Christian life is life in movement toward a goal. God not only justifies and sanctifies human life in the power of the Spirit but also gives it a particular vocation and a great hope. When this aspect of God's work of liberation and reconciliation is neglected, a certain narrowness and even narcissism creeps into the life of faith and the work of theology.

The themes of election and vocation are deeply embedded in the biblical witness. God calls Abraham, chooses the people of Israel, summons the prophets, sends Jesus of Nazareth, and commissions the followers of Jesus for service in the world. Indeed, Scripture speaks of the election of the people of God in Jesus Christ before the foundation of the world (Eph. 1:4). But in spite of the pervasive presence of the themes of election and vocation in the Bible, they are virtually forgotten or unintelligible doctrines for many Christians today.

God freely elects creatures to be partners in the mending of creation. Election is a call not to privilege, but to service. Israel is chosen by God to be a blessing to all the nations of the earth (Gen. 12:2-3). The servant of God is to be a light to the nations (Isa. 42:6; 49:6). Jesus Christ is the chosen Son of God, who obediently does the work of God and calls others to take part in this work (John 4:34; 15:16). Human beings are called to be co-workers with God in the mission of liberation and reconciliation. They receive new dignity and purpose when they are given this task. Every gift of the Spirit of God includes a responsibility. As Dietrich Bonhoeffer puts it, the grace of God is freely given, but it is not cheap. We have been called and commissioned to costly service.[54]

The vocation of a Christian is not to be confused with having a job by which one earns one's livelihood. Whatever one's job or profession, as a Christian one is called to be a partner in God's mission in the world. Christian life involves inward growth and renewal, but it does not turn in on itself as does so much contemporary literature on the importance of self. Christian life is in movement outward to others and forward to the future of the completion of God's redemptive activity. The Christian vocation is the ministry of liberative reconciliation, the call to invite all into a new community where justice is cherished and where freedom and love flourish, a community that is grounded in Christ, empowered by the Spirit, and destined for participation in the eternal communion of the triune God. Universal participation in the love of the triune God made known in Christ and effectively at work in the activity of the Holy Spirit is the goal of Christian mission.

54. Bonhoeffer, *The Cost of Discipleship* (London: SCM Press, 1959), 45.

Christians live by the promise of God and thus in creative hope. There is work to be done, a message to be proclaimed, forgiveness to be offered and practiced, service to be rendered, hostility to be overcome, injustice to be rectified. Guided by the Word and Spirit of God, Christians take up these tasks in confidence and hope in the final fulfillment of God's promise of a new humanity in a new heaven and a new earth. Christian life is more than acceptance of the forgiveness of sins and more than personal transformation, even if it can never be without these. Christian life is also the vocation to participate in the preparation of all creation for the coming reign of God marked by God's justice, freedom, and peace. It is the highest of callings and is empowered by "the grace of the Lord Jesus Christ, the love of God, and the communion of the Holy Spirit" (2 Cor. 13:14).

CHAPTER 11

The New Community

The Nicene Creed contains the familiar words, "I believe in . . . one, holy, catholic, and apostolic church." For many Christians, the doctrine of the church, or ecclesiology, is perhaps the least interesting and the most irritating topic of Christian theology. "Jesus yes, church no" nicely summarizes the anger and frustration that discussion of the church frequently arouses. Faith in God the creator, trust in Christ and his reconciling work, and experience of the transforming power of the Holy Spirit may be recognized as vital aspects of Christian faith and theology. As a rule, their importance is not doubted even when questions are raised about their proper interpretation. This is not the case, however, with the doctrine of the church. Ecclesiology is a subject many associate with the politics of organization and management but hardly with realities indispensable to Christian faith and life. Such an attitude contrasts sharply with the understanding of the church in the Bible and in classical Christian confessions. Augustine went so far as to declare, "I would not believe the gospel unless the authority of the catholic church moved me."[1] Calvin would have had some reservations about this provocative declaration but he often wrote with deep affection for the church as the "mother" of believers.[2]

My thesis in this chapter will be that the church is not incidental to God's purposes. God enters into covenant with creatures and seeks their partnership. If there is communion in the eternal life of God and God wills us to share in that communion, then questions regarding the nature of the church and its mission in the world today, far from being matters of secondary im-

---

1. Augustine, "Against the 'Foundation Letter' of the Manichees," in *The Works of St. Augustine,* ed. J. E. Rotelle (New York: New City Press, 1990), 1.19.

2. Calvin, *Institutes of the Christian Religion,* 4.1.4.

portance to the understanding of Christian faith, are quite central. The end for which the world was created and redeemed is deep and lasting communion between God and creation, a commonwealth of justice, reconciliation, and freedom based on the grace of God. While flawed and always in need of reform and renewal, the church is nonetheless the real beginning of God's new and inclusive community of liberated creatures reconciled to God and to each other and called to God's service in the world.

The Problem of the Church

While there are many problems that people have with the church today, several are widespread and deep-seated.

1. A great deal of misunderstanding and even hostility to the church results from the *individualism* that saturates American culture. Some of our most powerful cultural myths and images center on the self-made and independent individual, who achieves success in life without assistance from others. Independence rather than interdependence is our cultural bias, and this has an impact on the prevailing understandings of Christian faith and life. A sense of the importance of community is, of course, not entirely absent from modern Western society. Characteristically, however, the groups to which the self-sufficient individual or private person belongs are "voluntary societies," groups one chooses to join and in which one remains a member for as long as they meet one's needs and serve one's purposes. In much white North American Christianity, this translates into a self-centered piety in which the church is quite secondary and entirely optional. Being a Christian is an individual matter and is not essentially bound to life with others. This individualism hides the profound hunger for companionship and community that runs beneath the surface of life in America.[3]

2. Not only is religious belief and practice individualized in modern culture, it also assumes a *privatized* form. That is, the world of work and public affairs is separated from the world of domesticity, leisure, personal nurture, and religion. The process of privatization severs the message and mission of the church from the larger questions and struggles of life. If any purpose of the church is recognized, it is to serve the needs of private individuals and small homogeneous groups.

3. Still another obstacle to a proper understanding of the church is its ac-

---

3. See Robert N. Bellah et al., *Habits of the Heart: Individualism and Commitment in American Life* (Berkeley and Los Angeles: University of California Press, 1985).

commodation to *bureaucratic organization*. Bureaucracy is a system of administration marked by anonymity, adherence to fixed rules, hierarchy of authority, and the proliferation of officials. The ultimate in modern bureaucracy is the reduction of personal relationships to communication with a machine. The church is subject, like all organizations, to bureaucratic pressures. Forgetful of its distinctive being and calling, the church seeks success and respectability by mimicking the organizational structures and managerial techniques of profitable corporations. When the church succumbs to these pressures, it loses its true identity and its distinctive mission in the world.

4. Another major source of the problems that many people have with the church is to be found in the conspicuous and disturbing discrepancy between the expressed faith of the church and its *actual practice*. As Nietzsche wrote, "They would have to sing better songs to make me believe in their Redeemer: his disciples would have to look more redeemed!"[4] There is a chasm between what is proclaimed and what is practiced. As a result, the language about the community called *church* sounds shamelessly triumphalist and unreal. "The church is one" (Does it only appear to be broken into countless racial, national, and class factions?); "the church is holy" (Does it only seem to be a community of very fallible and sinful people?); "the church is catholic" (Is it merely an illusion that the church is often provincial and hypocritically self-interested?); "the church is apostolic" (Does it only appear to have frequently set itself above the apostles?).

As Joseph Haroutunian points out, statements like these embarrass and upset us because we know that the church is different from what we say it is.[5] To the extent that Israel and the early church were a people up against the wall — poor, weak, and in peril — their language about the reality of the people of God had a dignity. It was intended to comfort and support God's little, marginal, often persecuted people. But when the same language is used to describe the church as we know it, the language goes false on us. We know that the language is only cosmetic, and we become embarrassed or angry. Because of their sensitivity to this predicament, a favorite motto of ecumenical church leaders in this century has been "Let the church be the church!" (John Mackay). Let the church live and act like the body of Christ, the temple of the Spirit, and the servant people of God. This is a summons to the church to stop preening itself with all sorts of metaphysical compliments without any corresponding social reality and praxis.

---

4. Nietzsche, *Thus Spake Zarathustra*, quoted in Hans Küng, *The Church* (New York: Sheed & Ward, 1967), 150.

5. Haroutunian, "The Realization of the Church," *Theology Today* 17 (1960): 137-43.

Missing in the individualized, privatized, bureaucratic, and cosmetic forms of Christianity today is any real understanding of the interconnectedness of life that is expressed in all the basic doctrines and symbols of classical Christian faith. Christians confess their faith in the triune God whose reality is constituted by the welcoming love of Father, Son, and Holy Spirit. Christians believe in God the creator, redeemer, and sanctifier, who wills not to be alone but to have a covenant partner; whose costly grace in Jesus Christ inaugurates a new freedom for relationship with God and with others; and whose transforming Spirit establishes new community-in-freedom that anticipates the redemption of all creation. The Christian understanding of God as trinitarian communion and of salvation as the free participation of creatures in God's "society of love" highlights the importance of the church for Christian faith and theology.

Thus the call for the reform and renewal of the church today does not derive from a "craze for modernity" but from a fresh apprehension of the gospel that gave the church life.[6] When we honestly admit the problems of the church — which have their roots in our forgetfulness of the profoundly social meanings of all the articles of the faith as well as in our failure to hold together faith and practice — we may begin to catch sight of the mystery of the church. The mystery is that through the free grace of God in Jesus Christ at work in the world by the power of the Holy Spirit, God is breaking down all walls of separation and making "one new humanity" (Eph. 2:15). The mystery of the church is that it is called to bear witness to and participate in the trinitarian love of God, the God who gives existence to others, shares life and power, and lives in the mutual giving and receiving of love. The church is called to be the beginning of new human life in relationship, solidarity, and friendship beyond all privatism, classism, racism, and sexism.

New Testament Images of the Church

In the New Testament the church (*ecclesia,* "assembly" or "congregation") refers to the new community of believers gathered to praise and serve God in the power of the Holy Spirit in response to the gospel of the ministry, death, and resurrection of Jesus Christ. The word "church" can designate either local assemblies of Christians or the universal Christian community.

If we probe further the concept of *ecclesia,* we find that the New Testament describes it as a new communal reality constituted by the grace and call

6. See Küng, *The Church,* xi.

of God. It is a distinctive form of human life in relationship with God and others. Centered on the reconciling love of God in Christ and empowered by the Spirit for service, the *ecclesia* is human life in process of re-formation and renewal. Its existence and proclamation bear witness to the coming reign of God. Among the distinguishing marks of human life in the *ecclesia* is the breaking down of the walls separating people from God and each other. Life in the *ecclesia* is to be marked by praise of God, service to others, generosity, interdependence, forgiveness, and friendship. In the *ecclesia* power and responsibility are to be shared, and there is always to be a special concern for the poor, the weak, and the despised.[7]

In the New Testament the church and its distinctive form of life are related to but never identified with the coming reign of God. The church is a sign and provisional manifestation of the reign of God. The triumphalist identification of the church with the reign of God has been the source of much arrogance and destructiveness in church history. The church anticipates and serves the coming reign of God but does not fully realize it.

The New Testament describes the church in many different images and metaphors. In his book *Images of the Church in the New Testament,* Paul Minear lists some ninety-six different images or analogies of the church found in the New Testament.[8] Clearly, there is a surplus of biblical images in regard to the church as there is also in regard to God and the person and work of Jesus Christ. Among the many images of the church are "the body of Christ" (1 Cor. 12:27), "the salt of the earth" (Matt. 5:13), "a letter of Christ" (2 Cor. 3:2-3), "fishers for people" (Mark 1:17), "branches of the vine" (John 15:5), "the field of God," "the building of God" (1 Cor. 3:9), "God's temple" (1 Cor. 3:16), a building on a rock (Matt. 16:18), "the bride of Christ" (Eph. 5:23-32), "God's own people" (1 Pet. 2:9), a "new Jerusalem" (Rev. 21:2), "the household of God" (Eph. 2:19), "strangers and foreigners" (Heb. 11:13), and "the poor" (Luke 6:20).

From this rich inventory of New Testament imagery of the church, four major clusters may be identified:[9]

1. One set of images centers in the description of the church as the *people of God,* and especially the exodus people of God. The theme of the covenant between God and God's elect people is deeply embedded in both the Old

7. For a penetrating analysis of the sociality of the life of faith, see Edward Farley, *Ecclesial Man: A Social Phenomenology of Faith and Reality* (Philadelphia: Fortress, 1975).

8. Minear, *Images of the Church in the New Testament* (Philadelphia: Westminster, 1960).

9. Cf. Peter C. Hodgson, *Revisioning the Church: Ecclesial Freedom in the New Paradigm* (Philadelphia: Fortress, 1988). I am indebted to Hodgson's study at a number of points in this chapter.

and the New Testaments. "I . . . will be your God, and you shall be my people" (Lev. 26:12). "You are . . . God's own people, in order that you may proclaim the mighty acts of him who called you out of darkness into his marvelous light" (1 Pet. 2:9). According to this cluster of images, the church is not primarily a building or an organization but a people, a community, and specifically the people of God who have been called by God. Related to this image of the church as the people of God are images such as chosen race, holy nation, new Israel, sons and daughters of Abraham, remnant, and the elect. A basic function of this constellation of images is to connect the Christian community to the historic Israelite community of God based on the covenant promises and to describe this people as an exodus, pilgrim community, a people called out for a special task and set on the way toward a new homeland. One of the great achievements of the Second Vatican Council was to give renewed prominence in its "Dogmatic Constitution on the Church" *(Lumen Gentium)* to this image of the church as the people of God[10]

2. A second set of images related to the first describes the people of God as a *servant people.* This is a very prominent motif of the Old Testament. Repeatedly, Yahweh calls for the liberation of the people of Israel "that they may serve me" (Exod. 8:1; 9:1; 10:3). The theme of a servant people is no less important in the New Testament. Just as the Lord of this community is a servant Lord, so the community called by God is to be a community of servants. "The Son of Man came not to be served but to serve and to give his life a ransom for many" (Mark 10:45). Christians are likewise to be servants — "servants for Jesus' sake" (2 Cor. 4:5). Called to serve God and others, the church is not to exercise power in a self-centered way or to lord it over others, but to be ready for costly service (Matt. 20:25-26). There are many images that cluster around this service image. The people of God are co-workers, helpers, ambassadors, and witnesses. All of these images suggest that this particular community has its reason for being not in itself but in its task, which is to serve God and the world created by God. The church's service of God finds expression in its worship, prayer, and praise; the church's service to the world takes the form of witness in word and deed to God's grace and God's call for justice. These two aspects of the service of the church are integrally related, as in Jesus' twofold commandment to love God with our whole heart and to love our neighbors as ourselves.

3. A third set of images focuses on the metaphor of the church as the *body of Christ.* This description of the church occurs in the Pauline letters

10. See *The Documents of Vatican II,* ed. Walter M. Abbott, S.J. (New York: Guild Press, 1966), 15-96.

(above all, 1 Cor. 12:12-31). The community participates in one Lord, one Spirit, one baptism, and thus becomes "one body." We have been united with Christ in baptism (Rom. 6:5) and our true identity is no longer found in ourselves but is hidden with Christ in God (Col. 3:3). Organic union with Christ is also a theme of the Gospel of John, in which Jesus speaks of himself as the vine and his disciples as the branches (John 15:5). These organic images of the church as the body of Christ and as the branches of the vine of Christ have been enormously influential in the history and theology of the church. The images convey the common dependence of all members of the body on the one head, who is Christ (Col. 1:15-20; Eph. 5:23). They also express the mutual dependence of all members of the community on one another. Believers are all one in Christ Jesus (Gal. 3:28) and the variety of gifts they have been given are for the enrichment and edification of the whole community.

4. A final set of images portrays the church as the *community of the Spirit,* the community of the end-time, filled by the gifts of the Spirit. In the renewing experience of the Spirit of God, the New Testament church sees important evidence of the fulfillment of the promises of the prophets (Acts 2:17ff.). Racial, gender, and class divisions are broken down (Gal. 3:28); strangers are welcomed; the sharing of power replaces domination. Empowered and guided by the Spirit who has been given as the "pledge" (2 Cor. 1:23) and "firstfruits" (Rom. 8:23) of God's glorious new age, the community of the Spirit is a new creation, the sign of God's new humanity. This cluster of eschatological symbols of the church points to the radical new beginning of life realized in the coming of Christ and his Spirit and the promise of a comprehensive renewal and transformation of all creation. The church serves and suffers but also celebrates and hopes, because it already experiences a foretaste of new life and joy in the *koinonia,* the fellowship of the Holy Spirit. As a sign of the coming reign of God, the church is an "alternative community" in which a new Spirit of freedom reigns and in which the most wretched are included and even enemies are welcome.[11]

Critique of Current Models of the Church

Instructed by these New Testament images of the church, it is possible to review critically some models of the church both past and present. Whereas fa-

11. See David J. Bosch, *The Church as Alternative Community* (Potschefstroom: Instituut vir Reformatoriese Studie, 1982).

miliar images and symbols of the church are derived from Scripture and are often used in worship and ordinary faith discourse, the term "model" refers to a theoretical construct that is employed to deepen our understanding of a complex reality. Avery Dulles identifies several models of the church: institution, mystical communion, sacrament, herald, and servant.[12] In the following paragraphs I will make use of his categories but develop them in my own way. It is important to bear in mind that each model can easily lead to distortions of the true nature and purpose of the church.[13]

1. Among the most influential models of the church is that of an *institution of salvation*. This view defines the church primarily in terms of divinely authorized structures, officers, procedures, and traditions. As institution, the church has a definite form and organization. The chain of power and authority is precisely determined. Some organizational features — structures of leadership, patterns of worship, authoritative writings — are, of course, already evident in the church of the New Testament period. Within a century or two, the structures of canon, bishop, and doctrine had developed to provide stability and coherence to the community. However, according to Dulles, a predominantly institutional view of the church was characteristic neither of the patristic period nor of the Middle Ages. It achieved dominance only in the nineteenth century.

Institutional structure is, of course, an essential component of the life of the church as fully human. The church is an "earthen vessel" (2 Cor. 4:7) of a great treasure. Some kind of structure and order is a necessity in any historical community. It is sheer romanticism to suggest otherwise. But the institutionalist view of the church, when made primary and especially when allied with state power, has done far more harm than good. It has not resisted the temptation to see the purpose of the church as institutional survival and increase of power rather than faithful witness and costly service. One might describe the characteristics of the church according to the institutional model as being rather like those of an imperial state. Typically, order in this church is hierarchical rather than representative or interactional. Power always flows from the top to the bottom. Furthermore, power is centralized in the hands of the few who are supposedly ordained by God to rule over the silent and powerless masses of believers. Above all, the prevailing mentality is one of maintenance of the institution and, if possible, extension of its power.

While all this is portrayed in traditional Protestant polemics as the typi-

---

12. Dulles, *Models of the Church* (New York: Doubleday Image Books, 1974).

13. For a recent critique of distortions in the understanding of the church today, see Leander E. Keck, *The Church Confident* (Nashville: Abingdon, 1993).

cally Roman Catholic version of the church, the truth is that the tendency of the institutional structures of the church to grow and harden into institutional*ism* has proved to be very real in both Roman Catholic and Protestant ecclesial life. When this happens, hierarchy triumphs over community, and the mentality of survival supplants the spirit of service. In the Reformed churches, there has been much emphasis on the priesthood of all believers, on the offices of ordained ministry as functional rather than metaphysical, and on the stirring motto, *ecclesia reformata semper reformanda* — "The church reformed, always in need of being reformed." Such principles fight against the tendency toward institutional sclerosis, but they have often been honored more in word than in practice. Whereas Roman Catholic institutionalism identifies the church with the hierarchy, Protestant institutionalism identifies the church with its own patterns of organization, tests of orthodoxy, and books of order.

The strongest criticism of the over-institutionalized church comes today neither from liberal Roman Catholic nor classical Protestant sources but from Latin American liberation theology. We do not rightly understand this theology unless we recognize that one of its important concerns is critique and reformation of a hierarchical, over-centralized, and anxious institutional church. In the judgment of liberation theologians, the institutional church all too often exercises power in a manner resembling that of totalitarian governments and exploitative corporations. Leonardo Boff even compares the institutional church to a business enterprise with an elite in charge of the capital (the sacraments) and with the masses reduced to mere consumers.[14] Because the church is not immune to the temptation to seize and abuse power, the structures of the church must be continuously challenged and converted by the gospel and its summons to risk-taking service.

2. Another model of the church portrays it as *an elite community of the Spirit.* According to this view, the church is not so much a formal organization as it is a closely knit group whose members share a common experience of God's revivifying Spirit. Whereas the church in its traditional form is large, hierarchically organized, impersonal, and often insensitive to the needs of individuals, the typical spiritual community is small, personal, and loosely organized. It tries to develop a strong sense of belonging and mutual support among its members. In sociological terms, if the church as institution represents the "church" type of Christian social life, the church as intimate community of the Spirit represents the "sect" type.[15]

---

14. See Boff, *The Church: Charism and Power* (New York: Crossroad, 1985), 43.

15. For the distinction between "church" and "sect," see Ernst Troeltsch, *The Social Teachings of the Christian Churches*, 2 vols. (New York: Macmillan, 1956).

When the church is understood primarily as the intimate community of the Spirit, its reason for being is the cultivation of spiritual experiences and the promotion of interpersonal relationships. The church as intimate community takes different forms. In Catholicism an ecclesiology of mystical communion, developed partly in reaction to deadening institutional and hierarchical structures, has encouraged a more personalist understanding of the church and has recognized the importance of the gifts of the Spirit to all the people of God. Protestantism has produced a variety of understandings of the church as spiritual community. One appears in the charismatic movement, which emphasizes the gifts of the Spirit and special experiences of spiritual healing and renewal. Individuals who have had these experiences often form close, mutually supportive groups.

The model of the church as intimate community undoubtedly addresses real human needs. Many people in modern society are desperately lonely and battle-scarred. They seek a safe refuge and a community where they can feel at home. Some are physically and spiritually broken by their efforts to survive in a depersonalized and indifferent social order, and they cry out for spiritual healing and new meaning for their lives. With its emphasis on prayer, meditation, spiritual exercises, and exchange of personal experiences, the church as intimate community cultivates a more personal and egalitarian experience of life in community than does the institutional model of the church. Whatever its limitations, such ministry to individuals in need is an essential element of the mission of the church. Much of Jesus' ministry, it may be noted, was devoted to the healing of the sick in body as well as in spirit (Mark 1:32-34).

But there are serious weaknesses in this model as well. These become especially evident when the understanding of Christian community is uncritically borrowed from movements in contemporary culture and ecclesial life becomes indistinguishable from encounter sessions, sensitivity groups, and other kinds of therapeutic gatherings. It is not always clear what distinguishes such communities as specifically Christian. An ecstatic experience of the holy or an experience of intimacy and bonding with another does not necessarily constitute an experience of Christian faith. Moreover, therapy-oriented communities tend to concentrate on the individual's growth at the expense of the larger social responsibilities of the community. Currently popular New Age spirituality provides evidence of this fact. A church that copies such patterns of spirituality and intimate community becomes simply a haven from an insensitive and bureaucratic society and its depersonalizing effects. It becomes, in other words, an escape from, rather than a renewing critique of, the larger society that is in need of transformation. While the church is indeed the community of the Spirit in which all have gifts and in which power is shared, the New Testament views this new Spirit-guided community as called to serve God's purpose of both personal and world transformation.

3. Another current model of the church is that of *sacrament of salvation.* Increasingly prominent in Roman Catholic theology since Vatican II, the model of the church as sacrament of salvation emphasizes that in its worship, witness, and service, the church is the sign of the continuing presence of the grace of God in Jesus Christ. As interpreted by some theologians, the model draws attention primarily to the church's own sacramental life, and particularly to participation in the eucharist. In the community nourished and renewed by eucharistic action, the redemptive work of Christ is extended to all humanity. One of the strengths of the sacramental model is its combination of the objective and subjective aspects of the life of the church, which tend to be separated in the models of the church as institution or intimate group.

But the model of the church as sacrament also has its weaknesses. It can lean toward ecclesiocentrism, often in the form of preoccupation with liturgical correctness. The presence of Christ and the Spirit may be sought exclusively in the rites of the church. This may be accompanied by a corresponding loss of the church's social witness and service. While some Latin American liberation theologians have adopted the model of the church as sacrament, they use the phrase to refer to the church's calling to embody God's redemptive activity in history through the practice of solidarity with the poor. As a sacramental community, the church should signify, in its internal structures and its social praxis, the liberation of life that it announces by Word and sacrament.[16]

4. A fourth prominent model of the church is that of *herald of good news.* This is the understanding of the church that has been primary in the Protestant traditions. It is based on the conviction that the church's mission is above all to proclaim the Word of God and to call the nations to repentance and new life. Men and women are to be summoned to put their faith in Jesus as Savior and Lord. All matters of institutional structure and satisfaction of personal needs are to be subordinated to the task of proclamation and evangelization.

An evaluation of the model of the church as herald must begin with the acknowledgment that the proclamation of the gospel is indeed a primary task of the community of faith. However, this task has often been construed in rather narrow terms. When the model of the church as herald dominates or even excludes other models, it is easy for the church to take a patronizing and

---

16. Cf. Gustavo Gutiérrez, *A Theology of Liberation* (Maryknoll, N.Y.: Orbis Books, 1988), 143ff.

self-righteous attitude toward people and cultures to whom the Word is to be proclaimed. Then the church only speaks and never listens. If the church as herald is not to be an instrument of domination, it must be willing to learn as well as to teach. Moreover, a holistic understanding of the church's proclamation is often missing from this model. Preoccupation with the delivery of the message may override the concern to meet concrete human needs for food, shelter, medical care, education, and meaningful employment.

5. A fifth current model of the church portrays it as *servant* of the servant Lord. This may also be called the diaconal model. According to this view, the church is not primarily an institution whose purpose is survival and expansion, nor an intimate community designed to foster the personal growth of individuals who feel neglected and depersonalized by modern society, nor merely the herald of a message. The church is a servant community called to minister in God's name on behalf of fullness of life for all of God's creatures.

According to this model, the church serves God by serving the world in its struggle for emancipation, justice, and peace. Dietrich Bonhoeffer defined the church as the community that exists for others. "The church," he wrote, "must share in the secular problems of ordinary human life, not dominating but helping and serving."[17] This model of the church for others, a church that is servant rather than master of the world, has been influential in many modern ecclesiologies. It plays an important role both in the emphasis on the church's mission of reconciliation in the midst of conflict and in the call to the church to participate in the struggle for the liberation of the oppressed.

Taking as its primary theme God's work of reconciliation in Jesus Christ, the Confession of 1967 of the Presbyterian Church (U.S.A.) describes the service of the church as a participation in God's ministry of reconciliation. This ministry includes both the church's proclamation of the gospel and the church's efforts to foster reconciliation in societies torn by racism, international conflict, indifference to poverty, and sexual exploitation.

Liberation theologies have a rather different take on the meaning of the church as servant. Suspicious of premature calls to reconciliation that often bypass the reality of oppression and the need to struggle against it,[18] they understand the proper service of the church as participating in God's liberating activity in the world, exposing conditions of bondage, calling for the conversion of people and corporate structures, prompting prophetic action on be-

17. Bonhoeffer, *Letters and Papers from Prison* (New York: Macmillan, 1967), 204.
18. The *Kairos Document*, for example, written during the struggle against apartheid in South Africa, criticizes both a "state theology" that endorses apartheid and a "church theology" that avoids real struggle against injustice with talk of reconciliation.

half of justice and freedom, and sustaining believers in their solidarity with the poor and their struggle against the powers of evil and injustice.

The concrete form of ecclesial life that helped to give birth to liberation theology is the "Christian base community."[19] These base communities or "house churches," prominent in Latin America but a growing phenomenon throughout the Third World, are often in the thick of movements for social change. Made up of small groups of people in particular localities who gather to pray, interpret the Bible together, and relate their faith to their common, everyday problems, the Christian base communities understand themselves as experiments in a new way of being the church. Often led by laity, the base communities are far more communitarian than hierarchical in structure. Power is shared rather than centralized. In the light of the gospel, the people analyze such problems as water or electricity shortages, inadequate sewers, widespread unemployment, low wages, lack of schools, police harassment, and state persecution. They consider strategies for change and offer support to each other in their various tasks.[20] Yet the Christian base communities cannot be reduced to mere political action groups. While it is true that they are decidedly oriented to the practice of faith in the world, they find strength to persist in their mission in a distinctive spirituality of prayer, Bible reading, and eucharistic fellowship.

The servant model of the church has much to contribute. At its best, it helps to overcome the split between the spiritual and the mundane, between concern for evangelization and struggle for justice, a split all too frequent in other models of the church. Like Bonhoeffer, Karl Barth insisted that the church exists for the world. Because God first and supremely exists for the world, the church, according to Barth, is to exist not for itself but for others.[21] The missionary character of the church is not incidental but instead essential to its very being as the people of God.

Yet, as with other models of the church, there are also dangers of distortion in the servant model. One distortion would be the virtual equation of the church with an agency for social improvement. Another would be an inadequate understanding of service. Many feminist theologians hold that the idea of service has been systematically misused and that as a result, it may no longer be the most appropriate way to characterize the new life in

19. See *The Challenge of Basic Christian Communities*, ed. John Eagleson and Sergio Torres (Maryknoll, N.Y.: Orbis Books, 1982).

20. See Carl Mesters, *Defenseless Little Flower* (Maryknoll, N.Y.: Orbis Books, 1989).

21. Says Barth, "As the people created by Jesus Christ and obedient to him, it is not subsequently or incidentally but originally, essentially, and *per definitionem* summoned and impelled to exist for God and therefore for the world and men" (*Church Dogmatics*, 4/3.2: 762).

Christ.[22] They argue that for women in particular, service has meant always being submissive and allowing others to dominate one's life rather than entering into the new freedom and friendship in Christ (John 15:15) that empowers caring and healing ministries. While service of God and others is central to Christian identity, its meaning must be carefully distinguished from servitude and self-negation.

Overactivity and incessant busyness are other ways in which the servant model of the church may be misinterpreted. The church may forget what the basis and goal of its service is, with the result that ecclesiology is reduced to social function. When the church understands itself only in terms of its practical service to the world, it subordinates proclamation of the gospel and nurture of the spiritual life to zeal for political action. Closely related to this is the ever-present danger of an uncritical identification of the reign of God with a particular program of social and political change. Ironically, a church that has lost the capacity for self-criticism and is no longer aware of the need for reform within its own life can hardly be expected to be an agent of reform in the wider society. When the servant model of the church is construed simply as social activism, the true nature and purpose of the church are endangered. The church no longer takes seriously the many forms of bondage from which human beings need to be liberated — the sins of pride, greed, apathy, presumption, and self-indulgence, no less than such structural forms of sin as economic exploitation, racism, sexism, domestic abuse, and state-sponsored violence. It makes little sense to set these various liberation concerns against each other.

An important conclusion of this review of prominent models of the church is that perhaps the greatest obstacle to a proper understanding of the church is the tendency to absolutize one historical form or one particular image or model of the church. The gospel of the crucified and risen Jesus Christ is always greater than our theologies, including our theologies of the church. When the church keeps its eyes on Christ and remains open to the Holy Spirit, it is in touch with the one necessary power of continuous reform and renewal of ecclesial life. The dangers of ecclesiocentrism and triumphalistic attitudes are ever present. No single image or model of the church is capable of saying all that must be said about its nature and mission. For this reason, in the following sections I venture two crucial affirmations about the church that need to be kept in dialectical tension with each other. By word, sacrament, prayer, and life together, the church participates, in a provisional and incomplete way, in the triune love of God; by its manifold ministries of witness and compas-

---

22. See, e.g., Susan Nelson Dunfee, *Beyond Servanthood: Christianity and the Liberation of Women* (Lanham, Md.: University Press of America, 1989).

sion and its service of justice, reconciliation, and peace in the world, the church participates, always imperfectly, in the mission of the triune God.

The Church and the Call to Communion

Consistent with the trinitarian emphases throughout this book, I am convinced that ecclesiology needs to be developed in closer relationship with trinitarian doctrine.[23] A trinitarian ecclesiology will take its basic clue from the fact that the most fundamental Christian affirmation about God revealed in Jesus Christ through the continuing activity of the Holy Spirit is that God is the triune God who loves in freedom. The God whose eternal life is the act of shared love enters into covenant with the people of Israel and through Jesus Christ opens this covenant to all people. The triune God reaches out to the world in holy, free, extravagant love that embraces sinners. According to trinitarian doctrine, God's own life is in communion, and the end for which God created and reconciled the world is deep and abiding communion between God and creatures.

While it is true that understanding the church as a communion or *koinonia* in Christ by the Spirit has a long history in Christian theology, there has been a remarkable revival of interest in this theme in recent Roman Catholic, Eastern Orthodox, and Protestant theology.[24] The ecclesiology of communion has been the topic of a study by the World Council of Churches,[25] and appears frequently in recent Vatican documents on the church. Communion ecclesiology goes hand in hand with the recovery of trinitarian theology during the past half century. If the life of God is understood as the eternal communion of Father, Son, and Spirit; if the divine life is envisioned as a dynamic movement of giving and receiving of love that is appropriately described as a mutual "indwelling" *(perichoresis);* if the creation and redemption of the world by the triune God are understood as free gifts that open to creatures new life in communion with God and each other; if being in Christ is a participa-

---

23. According to Colin E. Gunton, "the manifest inadequacy of the theology of the church derives from the fact that it has never seriously and consistently been rooted in a conception of the being of God as triune" ("The Church on Earth: The Roots of Community," in *On Being the Church: Essays on the Christian Community,* ed. Colin E. Gunton and Daniel W. Hardy [Edinburgh: T&T Clark, 1990], 48).

24. See Robert W. Jenson, *Systematic Theology,* vol. 2: *The Works of God* (New York: Oxford University Press, 1999), 167-269; Dennis M. Doyle, *Communion Ecclesiology* (Maryknoll, N.Y.: Orbis Books, 2000).

25. *On the Way to Fuller Koinonia: Official Report of the Fifth World Conference on Faith and Order,* Faith and Order Paper no. 166, ed. Thomas F. Best and Gunther Gassmann (Geneva: World Council of Churches, 1994).

tion in the life of God through Christ in the Spirit, then it is entirely fitting to describe the nature of the church as essentially the beginning of new life in communion. Human life comes to completion by participation in and reflection of the triune love of God. As it participates in the love of God through Christ in the Spirit, the church becomes a sign and a provisional realization of the destiny of humanity and indeed of the entire creation. While by no means identical with the coming reign of God, the church's proclamation and practice are to be a witness to and an anticipatory participation in God's reign.

According to the Apostles' Creed, the church is "the communion of saints" *(communio sanctorum)*. The Latin word *sanctorum* can mean both "communion of the holy ones" and "communion in the holy things." As Barth explains, the church as the communion of saints embraces both meanings. The church is "the communion of the *sancti,* i.e., of those who are sanctified by the Holy Spirit, of all Christians of every age and place." But the church is also a "communion in the *sancta,*" i.e., "the holy relationships in which [Christians] stand as *sancti;* the holy gifts of which they are partakers; the holy tasks which they are called upon to perform; the holy position which they adopt; the holy function which they have to execute."[26] As together Christians worship and praise God, pray for forgiveness and forgive each other, intercede for those in need, hear the Word proclaimed, baptize, celebrate the Lord's Supper, and go forth to serve in the name of Christ, they participate in the gift of new life that is God's very own. "The cup of blessing that we bless, is it not a communion in the blood of Christ? The bread that we break, is it not a communion in the body of Christ?" (1 Cor. 10:16).

One of the advantages of describing the church as life in communion is that it helps to connect ecclesiology to other central Christian doctrines. The Trinity is divine life in communion; humanity is created and redeemed by God for just, loving, and peaceful communion that participates in and reflects the divine life; the church is a concrete sign and provisional realization of new community with God and with others through Christ in the Spirit. The koinonia of the church centers in the sharing of the gospel and the celebration of the sacraments. As I shall emphasize in the following section, this koinonia is not closed but open to the world in mission and service. The church is called to be a sign of God's grace to sinners and of God's call of all people and all creation to new life in Christ. From this perspective, there is an unambiguous answer to the question, What does it mean to be "saved"? To be saved is to participate in God's gift of forgiveness and new life through Jesus Christ whose fruit is reconciliation, communion, and peace with God and

---

26. *Church Dogmatics,* 4/2: 642-43.

others. By faith in God that works through love (Gal. 5:6) we take part in this new life here and now in a preliminary and incomplete way, and in hope we await the fulfillment of life in communion with the triune God.

If the confession of the church as the "communion of saints" is not to be misunderstood, it must be clear that the "saints" are forgiven sinners. Until the consummation of God's redemptive activity, there is daily need of repentance and prayer for forgiveness within the communion of saints. A church that considers itself identical with God's reign, or that no longer passionately hopes for the fulfillment of God's work of reconciliation and communion, denies the reality of the church as the provisional representation of God's coming reign.

The ecclesiology of communion underscores the utter centrality for the church of the practices of prayer, proclamation, praise, celebration of the sacraments, study of Scripture, mutual forgiveness, bearing one another's burdens, and service of needy neighbors. These are practices that give concrete expression to communion with God in Christ by the power of the Holy Spirit. Christian communion is life together in Christ, a way of knowing by participation and not by mere cognition. Communion with God and each other is a reality that cannot be fully grasped or definitively formulated in a set of propositions. Life in communion is affectional, moral, and aesthetic as well as cognitive. It is life together in faith, hope, and love, the gifts of the triune God. One of the key scriptural texts of the ecclesiology of communion is the prayer of Jesus for his disciples "that they may all be one. As you, Father, are in me and I am in you, may they also be in us" (John 17:21). Other important texts include Paul's description of the Lord's Supper as a sharing or communion in the body and blood of Christ (1 Cor. 10:16), of the apostle's sharing in the sufferings of Christ (Phil. 3:10), and of the church's participation in the communion of the Holy Spirit (2 Cor. 13:13; Phil. 2:1).

Called to communion with the triune God and with one another, the church is radically different from both a collectivism that disregards the particularity of persons and an aggregate of individuals who know only a world of lonely, isolated selves. Just as the persons of the Trinity are not self-contained individuals but have their identity in mutual, free, self-giving relationships, just as the life of the triune persons is life with, for, and in each other, so the church is called to life in communion in which persons flourish in mutually supportive relationships with others. In such communion the church becomes *imago Trinitatis,* an analogy of, and partial participation in, the triune life of God.[27]

---

27. See John Zizioulas, *Being as Communion: Studies in Personhood and the Church* (Crestwood, N.Y.: St. Vladimir's Seminary Press, 1985).

It can be argued that an ecclesiology of communion is especially relevant in an age of fragmentation. Strong centrifugal forces of pluralism are at work in our postmodern world. Postmodernity is characterized by fragmentation of the world and the self, of truth and justice. In this context, recovery of the reality of the church as the provisional representation of new life in communion offers hope. An ecclesiology of communion, however, is based on far more than the desire to say something helpful in the postmodern era of fragmentation. What is at stake in an ecclesiology of communion is the right understanding of the very nature of God and the end for which God has created and redeemed the world. What is involved is the very meaning of salvation. Through Christ and in the Spirit, God opens to the world the new life marked by forgiveness of sins, reconciliation of enemies, and communion in the love of God.

The Church and the Call to Mission

Understanding the church as called to communion is one essential aspect of a trinitarian doctrine of the church. But it is not the only essential aspect. Of equal importance is the understanding of the church as called to mission. The church does not exist for itself alone any more than God has chosen to exist for God alone. Because the triune God is a missionary God, the church is called to be a missionary church rooted in the trinitarian missions.[28] The church is the community called into being, built up, and sent into the world to serve in the name and power of the triune God.[29] The mission of the church is to participate in the reconciling love of the triune God who reaches out to a fallen world through Jesus Christ in the power of the Holy Spirit.

Understanding the mission of the church in the context of the trinitarian missions differs in important ways from other understandings of the church's mission. Sometimes the mission of the church is described as the effort to save people from eternal damnation; sometimes to expand the power

---

28. On the theme of *missio Dei*, see Barth, "Die Theologie und die Mission in der Gegenwart," *Zwischen den Zeiten* (1932), 189-215; *Ad Gentes* (Vatican II); Lesslie Newbigin, *The Open Secret: Sketches for a Missionary Theology* (Grand Rapids: Eerdmans, 1978); David J. Bosch, *Transforming Mission: Paradigm Shifts in Theology of Mission* (Maryknoll, N.Y.: Orbis Books, 1991); Darrell Guder, "From Mission and Theology to Missional Theology," *The Princeton Seminary Bulletin* 24, no. 1 (2003): 36-54; Daniel L. Migliore, "The Missionary God and the Missionary Church," *The Princeton Seminary Bulletin* 19, no. 1 (1998): 14-25. The following discussion follows closely some sections of my essay.

29. This is the structure of Karl Barth's doctrine of the church in *Church Dogmatics*, 4/1-3.

and influence of the church; sometimes to share the blessings of Western culture with people of other cultures; sometimes to transform the world into the reign of God. All such rationales for mission are inadequate. The church's mission has a trinitarian basis: the triune God who lives eternally in mutual self-giving love wills to include all creatures in that communion of love. By God's Word and Spirit, the welcoming love of God is extended to the world. The mission of the church has its basis and model in this movement of God to the world, this *missio Dei* or divine missionary activity. The reconciling mission of the incarnate Word and the transforming mission of the Spirit identify the God of Christian faith as a missionary God.

The missionary activity of the church should be understood as a participation in the mission of Jesus Christ. As we noted in chapter 8, the saving work of Christ has been described, especially in the theologies of Calvin and Barth, in terms of his threefold office as priest, prophet, and king. As priest, Jesus Christ is the mediator, the one who in his ministry, cross, and resurrection brings God's forgiveness and new life to the world and renders to God the obedience that is God's due. As prophet, Jesus Christ instructs and guides believers in the will of God and exposes the idolatry, injustice, and violence that rule in all domains of human life. As king, Jesus Christ protects and defends the people of God and claims their obedience and service.

The doctrine of the threefold office of Christ also brings clarity and direction to the understanding of the church and its mission. Of course, to speak of the church's mission in terms of the threefold office of Christ cannot possibly mean that the church replaces Christ as the primary missionary, or that the church perfects an essentially defective mission of Christ. On the contrary, the living Christ continues his missionary work in the world, and the church is called to participate in his work and to be guided by it. Hence the church's mission will always include the priestly activity of proclaiming forgiveness and reconciliation in the name of Christ; it will always include the prophetic activity of teaching God's will made known in Christ and denouncing injustice and oppression as opposing God's will; and it will always include the royal activity of being a protector and advocate of the weak and lowly and using what resources and influence it has not for its own sake but for the sake of God's coming reign of justice and peace that has dawned in power in the royal life, death, and resurrection of Christ.[30] If it is Christ-centered, the missionary activity of the church will follow the way of the cross and will show a

---

30. See Philip W. Butin, *Reformed Ecclesiology: Trinitarian Grace According to Calvin*, Studies in Reformed Theology and History 2, no. 1 (Princeton, N.J.: Princeton Theological Seminary, 1994).

partiality to outsiders, strangers, and all those considered alien, unworthy, or disturbingly different.[31]

As a participation in the missions of the triune God, the missionary activity of the church is not only Christ-centered; it is also accompanied and empowered by the mission of the Spirit of God. The mission of the Spirit, at work in the world from its beginning, is brought to consummate focus in Christ.[32] If the Spirit of God is present in the giving, renewing, and restoring of life throughout the creation, the defining mark of the Spirit's work is the creation and nurture of a people of God united in Christ. In one respect, the mission of the Spirit follows on the mission of Christ. The Spirit is sent by Christ from the Father to bring the work of redemption to its completion. In another respect, however, the mission of the Spirit precedes the mission of Christ, in that the mission of Christ gathers up all that the Spirit has been preparing beforehand. The mission of the Spirit is life-giving and life-enhancing. It creates and sustains personal life in new and inclusive community. Where the Spirit of the Lord is, freedom is there (2 Cor. 3:17). The Spirit brings freedom from all the forces and fears that destroy human life, and freedom for the fullness of life in the just and peaceful community that God intends.

The coming of the Spirit at Pentecost, recorded in Acts 2, provides an illuminating paradigm of the missionary work of the Holy Spirit. The Spirit is the power of God to step over boundaries, to overcome separation and alienation. At Pentecost the coming of the Spirit brings about unprecedented communication and new communion among people previously incapable of understanding each other. The Spirit breaks down the barriers that separate people. Communication among people of diverse languages and cultures becomes a reality. The Pentecost experience is an experience of new unity and mutual understanding in Christ in the midst of great diversity.[33] To be baptized into Christ by the power of the Holy Spirit is to become a member of a community in which real differences remain but the differences are embraced and relativized by a deeper unity: "There is no longer Jew or Greek, there is no longer slave or free, there is no longer male and female; for all of you are one in Christ Jesus" (Gal. 3:28).

The missionary activity of the church in the power of the Spirit will thus be marked by four features. First, it will be missionary activity that fosters just and inclusive community. In this new community those once considered

---

31. See Patrick R. Keifert, *Welcoming the Stranger: A Public Theology of Worship and Evangelism* (Minneapolis: Fortress, 1992).

32. See Stephen B. Bevans, "God Inside Out: Toward a Missionary Theology of the Holy Spirit," in *International Bulletin of Missionary Research* 22 (1998): 102-5.

33. See Michael Welker, *God the Spirit* (Minneapolis: Fortress, 1994).

strangers will be embraced as sisters and brothers in Christ. Difference and otherness will not be considered mortal threats but a summons to find our new identity in Christ that transforms our relationship to each other.[34] Second, it will be missionary activity that expects and welcomes the ministerial gifts of all its members to be used for the well being and peace of the whole. The Spirit of God, far from being miserly or partisan, lavishes gifts on all. Third, the church's missionary activity will be motivated by thanksgiving and joy rather than by fear or a sense of burdensome obligation. Just as the church's participation in the missionary activity of Christ is characterized by joy (Luke 10:17), so the church's participation in the life and mission of the Spirit is marked by joy and peace (Rom. 15:13). As the church engages in mission, it looks confidently to God's Word and Spirit and prays, "Come, Lord Jesus!" "Come, Holy Spirit!" Finally, the missionary activity of the church will recognize, welcome, and support the presence of the Spirit in all fields of human endeavor — in the sciences as well as the arts, in politics as well as religion — where life and peace are enhanced and death and destruction are combated.

From what has been said of the church as called to communion and mission, it should be clear that it is a cardinal mistake to look for analogies and clues for understanding the church and its missionary activity in the principles, structures, and strategies of growth typical of corporations, clubs, academies, and other forms of organization familiar to us. The life and mission of the church have their basis in the free grace of God and not in our clever strategies and programs. The church does not "have" the living Christ at its disposal or "possess" the Spirit as something under its control. Rather, the church is called to participate in the missions of Christ and the Spirit. As John V. Taylor writes, "Our theology would improve if we thought more of the church being given to the Spirit than of the Spirit being given to the church."[35] If we seek an analogy of the new community in Christ empowered and guided by his Spirit, our reference must be to the triune life of God. In the triune life there is an eternal giving and sharing of life and love. Personhood is profoundly relational and difference enriches rather than subverts equality. The church of Jesus Christ in the power of the Spirit is called to be a community of love and service in which all participate in an exchange of gifts given by the "gifting God."[36] In Christ, by the power of the Spirit, all re-

34. See Miroslav Volf, *Exclusion and Embrace: A Theological Exploration of Identity, Otherness, and Reconciliation* (Nashville: Abingdon, 1996).

35. See John V. Taylor, *The Go-Between God: The Holy Spirit and the Christian Mission* (London: SCM Press, 1972), 133.

36. See Stephen H. Webb, *The Gifting God: A Trinitarian Ethics of Excess* (New York: Oxford University Press, 1996).

ceive a new identity and enter into reconciled and reconciling community. In this way the church anticipates, however partially and brokenly, the coming reign of the triune God.[37]

Classical Marks of the Church

Since the church is not identical with the reign of God but is only its witness and provisional representation, it should not be surprising that the life of the people of God is filled with dynamic tensions. In the two previous sections we have identified two inseparable aspects of the reality of the church: the church as communion and the church as mission. But there are many other tensions in ecclesial life. When the tensive elements in the life of the church are no longer held together in such a way that they correct and enrich each other, they begin to struggle against each other and threaten to destroy the identity and unity of the church.

It is destructive to drive a wedge between the church as a charismatic community and the church as an institution with order and structure. Spiritual vitality without some form and structure is chaotic, just as institutional form without spiritual vitality is empty and deadening. Order in the church should be understood functionally, not ontologically; provisionally, not permanently; interactionally, not hierarchically. The order of the church must always be subject to reform by God's Word and Spirit.

It is destructive to compel people to choose between the worshiping church and the socially involved church. Praise and prayer must not be set against service and action in the name of Christ, or vice versa. What kind of prayer is it that fails to open people to the service of God in the world? And what kind of Christian action is it that is not rooted in prayer for the hallowing of God's name, for the forgiveness of our sins, and in all the other petitions of the Lord's Prayer?

It is destructive to separate the church of the Word and the church of the sacraments. A good Reformed church, according to the stereotype, is a church of the Word and not a sacramental church; and a good Catholic church, the stereotype continues, is a sacramental church and not a church of the Word. This is a deeply injurious dichotomy. What is the Word that is not accompanied by its concrete enactment in the sacraments? What is a sacrament that is unaccompanied by the strong and clear Word of God?

---

37. See Miroslav Volf, *After Our Likeness: The Church as the Image of the Trinity* (Grand Rapids: Eerdmans, 1998).

It is destructive to permit a split to develop between an inclusive church and a partisan church. We must not so interpret the inclusiveness of the church that we are afraid ever to take sides on crucial issues of justice and peace. Otherwise reconciliation becomes a cheap word for avoiding all conflict and lacking the courage to take a stand. On the other hand, the partisanship of the church must always have a catholic or inclusive intention. If it is true that the universality of the church is achieved only through particularity, it is also true that the church's commitment to particular people and their needs must always aim at universality.

The dynamic tensions of ecclesial existence must be kept in mind in any helpful reinterpretation of the classical "marks" of the church. According to the Nicene Creed, the church is "one, holy, catholic, and apostolic." These are often cited in the theological tradition as the marks or essential characteristics of the true church.[38]

1. What is meant by the *unity* of the church? The unity of the church is not to be found primarily in structures, offices, doctrines, or programs. It is a distinctive unity rooted in "one Spirit . . . one Lord, one faith, one baptism, one God and Father of all" (Eph. 4:4-6). It is a unity of fellowship with God through Christ in the Spirit. The unity of the church is a fragmentary and provisional participation in the costly love of the triune God. Unity in the love of this God must not be equated with lifeless uniformity or deadening sameness. The unity of the church is a unity formed in Christ in whom our isolated self dies and in whom we find new identity in mutual relationship with others.

The love of God, and the unity of the church that is grounded in it, is a lavish celebration of the communion of the different. As creator of heaven and earth, God gives existence to a vast diversity of beings. As reconciler, God unites in new fellowship those who were once estranged from God and from each other. As sanctifier, God the Holy Spirit brings together a community made up of people of many nations, cultures, and ethnic groups and empowers them with many gifts for mutual service in the church and in the world. The New Testament speaks of the unity of the church as an expression of the unity of the triune God. It is a unity of participation in and reflection of the communion of Father and Son in the Spirit (John 17:21), a unity of those previously estranged who, having been reconciled by the cross of Christ, now have access in one Spirit to the Father (Eph. 2:18). The unity generated by the triune God is thus no stifling, suffocating unity, an impoverished numerical oneness. It is a differentiated and rich unity that is confessed by faith, shared

---

38. In the following reflections I am especially indebted to the work of Jürgen Moltmann, *The Church in the Power of the Spirit* (New York: Harper & Row, 1977).

in love, and awaited in hope. The unity of the church is experienced now only in part. The one church is *in via,* on the way toward the fulfillment of the promises of God in Christ. It is the pilgrim church, celebrating now the coming of a new unity of humanity around the Lord's table, but at the same time looking forward to the great eschatological banquet in which all the people of the earth, from east, west, north, and south, will sit together in peace and joy in the presence of their Lord (Luke 13:29).

2. What is meant by the *holiness* of the church? Holiness does not mean becoming "holier than thou," developing an attitude of moral superiority that leads to separation from those deemed inferior. As emphasized earlier, the church is a community of forgiven sinners. The holiness of the church is not grounded in itself but in Christ, whose life, death, and resurrection justifies believers by grace and sets them on the path of sanctification. The church is holy by participation in the holy love of God. God's love is holy not because it holds itself aloof from sinners and strangers but precisely because it embraces them without reservation. This is God's holiness and justice revealed in Jesus Christ: that God justifies, accepts, and loves sinners despite their unworthiness.

By analogy, the true holiness of the church is seen not in impeccable conformity to conventional moral rules but in the courageous criticism of injustice, acts of solidarity with the poor and the outcast, and the sharing of friendship and power with the weak and despised. As is true of all the marks of the church, the confession that the church is holy is an utterance of faith and hope. It receives its warrant from the promise of God and not from an empirical description of its life. Yet this confession is not solely about the future. There are or should be signals of a new form of human life taking shape in the community called the church. Men and women of Christian character and discipline should be formed within this community who are able to resist the style of life characteristic of a self-centered consumer society, who lead the way in opting for a simpler way of life, and who show openness to the needs of others, especially the poor.

3. What is meant by the *catholicity* of the church? The classical definition of catholicity is "what is believed everywhere, always, and by all" (Vincent of Lerins). The church is catholic or universal in a number of senses. It is present in all parts of the world and in all periods of history. It has many parishes, but it is not provincial. These are readily accepted meanings of the church's catholicity. The problem is that catholicity too often is understood as a sort of abstract universality hovering above the particularities of culture and history. A related mistake is the association of catholicity with a noncommittal attitude, a neutrality that strives to please all and offend none.

The church today needs to interpret the meaning of *catholic* as inclusive of all kinds of people. In order to be catholic in this sense, it is, paradoxically, necessary for the church to be partisan. If the Gentiles are being excluded from hearing the good news of freedom in Christ, then it becomes necessary to be partisan for the Gentiles, as was the apostle Paul, precisely to affirm the catholicity of the church and the universality of the lordship of Christ. If particular racial groups and certain economic classes are being turned away from the church, either directly or indirectly, because they do not find their concerns and needs taken seriously, then it is necessary to become partisan for these people, as black theology, feminist theology, and other forms of liberation theology do. When the church makes an option for the poor, it demonstrates rather than denies its catholicity. The other side of this coin, however, is that every partisan act of the church must be intentionally universal, or it becomes not the partisanship of God but a divisive and destructive party spirit.

4. What is meant by the *apostolicity* of the church? According to some churches, an essential mark of the church is the legitimate ordination to church office by bishops who stand in historical succession with the apostles. While this might be seen as a sign of continuity with the apostles, the church's apostolic character cannot be guaranteed by a chain of succession in some external and mechanical sense. Nor is the apostolic character of the church to be restricted to the ordained clergy. Every baptized person is summoned to be a witness to the good news of God's in-breaking kingdom in Jesus Christ and in this sense to take part in the apostolate of the church. The church is apostolic insofar as it conforms in faith and life to the gospel of Jesus Christ attested by the prophets and the apostles. This apostolic succession of faithfulness to the gospel should manifest itself both in what the church proclaims and in how the church lives and bears its witness. It should determine the way in which the church seeks to communicate the gospel and carry out every aspect of its mission in the world. Specifically, true apostolic witness to the gospel eschews force, intimidation, and deception as strategies to win adherents, whether in the form of a blatant appeal for state power to secure the church's position and influence or the more covert forms of threat and coercion or narrow appeals to self-interest employed in certain kinds of evangelism, both on and off television. As the apostle Paul pointed to his scars and persecutions in order to demonstrate his apostolate (2 Cor. 11:23ff.), so the apostolic church will show its faithfulness to the gospel by carrying out its mission in the weakness and poverty that the grace of God uses to God's glory and humanity's salvation.

While the Nicene marks of the church are affirmed by virtually all

Christian traditions, the Protestant Reformers also defined the true church in a different way. They asked, What is the basis of the unity, holiness, catholicity, and apostolicity of the church? Their answer to this question was: the pure preaching and hearing of the Word of God and the right administration of the sacraments. According to Luther, "if the church is without the Word, it ceases to be the church."[39] Calvin and Luther agree on this point: "Whenever we see the Word of God purely preached and heard, and the sacraments administered according to Christ's institution, there, it is not to be doubted, a church of God exists."[40] The Reformers' view was necessary and appropriate to counter the schismatic tendencies in their own reform movement as well as to respond to the charge of the established church that the Reformation movement rejected the Nicene understanding of the church. In fact, the two sets of marks of the church are complementary. Without the Reformation set, the Nicene marks could be interpreted triumphantly or moralistically; without the Nicene set, the Reformation marks could be interpreted schismatically.

At the beginning of the twenty-first century, with the gulf widening between the rich and poor of the world, it is important to ask whether these two classical sets of marks of the church are exhaustive, at least as they have been traditionally interpreted. Since the New Testament period, it has been a principle of ecclesiology that the church is where Christ is. But where is Christ? The answers to this question in the history of doctrine are familiar: Christ is where the bishop is; Christ is in the eucharistic celebration; Christ is where the gospel is preached and heard; Christ is where the gifts of the Spirit are manifest. While there is some truth in all these responses, none of them explicitly includes the response given in Matthew 25:31ff.: Christ is present among the poor, the hungry, the sick, and the imprisoned. Those who minister to the wretched of the earth minister to Christ. The true church is not only the church of the ear (where the gospel is rightly preached and heard), and not only the church of the eye (where the sacraments are enacted for the faithful to see and experience); it is also the church of the outstretched, helping hand. Have the church and theology neglected the clear answer of Matthew 25:31ff. to the questions of where Christ is and how we shall recognize the true church? Christ is among the poor, and the church is the people of God free enough to enter into solidarity with the poor. If this is not the only answer that should be given to the question of where Christ is, it is one that the church must never ignore.

39. Luther, "Concerning the Ministry," in *Luther's Works*, 40: 37.
40. Calvin, *Institutes*, 4.1.9.

CHAPTER 12

Proclamation, Sacraments, and Ministry

P roclamation, sacraments, and ministry are closely related doctrines. Especially the latter two continue to divide Christian churches. Indeed, they are the principal topics on which the efforts toward ecumenical consensus and the reunion of the churches repeatedly stall. Agreement would be easily secured if it were enough to say that, like every human community, the church has regular practices that clarify its identity and support its mission, and needs to order its life and choose leaders to guide it. But such agreement, while valid in sociological terms, would fall short of the theological understanding that faith seeks. Since proclamation of the Word and celebration of the sacraments are vital to Christian faith and life, and since ministerial office and church polity should cohere with the central message and mission of the church, theology must not abdicate its responsibility for careful reflection on these themes.

Proclamation of the Word

Theology and preaching are distinct yet mutually related activities. On the one hand, the responsibility of preaching is a major stimulus to theological reflection; on the other hand, a central task of theology is to evoke, assist, and at times criticize preaching. Theology serves preaching by testing its faithfulness to the gospel, by reminding it of the fullness of God's revelation in Jesus Christ, by urging that preaching be more compelling, more concrete, more self-critical, less trivial, less intimidated by dominant cultural assumptions.[1]

1. See Fred B. Craddock, *Preaching* (Nashville: Abingdon, 1985); Gerhard O. Forde, *Theology Is for Proclamation* (Minneapolis: Fortress, 1990).

Proclamation of the Word and celebration of the sacraments belong together. They presuppose and complement each other because in their different ways they both attest and mediate the free grace of God in Jesus Christ. Proclamation may be defined as faithful witness to the Word of God addressed to specific people in a particular time and place. The following theses amplify this definition:

1. Proclamation of the Word of God is *human testimony to the gospel of Jesus Christ, whose effectiveness depends ultimately not on the preacher but on God.* The preacher does not become superhuman when he or she mounts the steps of the pulpit. If the words of a preacher truly convey the Word of God, that is not due to the preacher's brilliance or eloquence but to the sovereign and free grace of God the Holy Spirit. The Spirit of God does not scorn the service of creatures, but makes effective use of it. Honest acknowledgment of human limitations and prayerful confidence in God's grace are thus essential presuppositions of the proclamation of the Word of God. An arrogant or self-serving spirit is especially reprehensible in a preacher. As Karl Barth states, "as ministers we ought to speak of God. We are human, however, and so cannot speak of God. We ought therefore to recognize our obligation and our inability, and by that very recognition give God the glory."[2]

2. Proclamation of the Word of God is *based on the witness of the scriptural text.* As used in Christian theology, the phrase "Word of God" has three meanings: (1) the incarnate or living Word of God, who is Jesus Christ; (2) the written Word of God, or Scripture; and (3) the proclaimed Word of God, or the preaching of the gospel in the present. These three forms of the Word are inseparably bound to each other in a definite order. When present proclamation is faithfully based on the original witness of Scripture to the living Word of God incarnate in Jesus Christ, it becomes God's Word to people here and now by the power of the Spirit.

The claim that preaching should be *based* on the witness of Scripture is certainly intended to reject a view of preaching as arbitrary invention. But it also differs from the idea that preaching is the mere repetition of biblical words or ideas. Proclamation is re-presentation; it is proclaiming the same message the apostles proclaimed, but proclaiming it in different words in a different time and place. Authentic proclamation requires reflection and imagination. Restatement of the gospel is necessary if the preacher is to be faithful to the apostolic gospel. Proclamation is new witness in the here and now to the promise and claim of God addressed to the world in the covenant history with Israel and supremely in Jesus Christ.

2. Barth, *Word of God and Word of Man* (New York: Harper, 1957), 186.

Encountering the Word of God through Scripture is never a matter of course. Just as God is surprisingly revealed in the hiddenness of the cross of Christ, so the Word of God is conveyed through the historical contingencies of Scripture. The witness of Scripture must be studied, pondered, questioned, and argued with.[3] Preacher and congregation return again and again to Scripture, now disturbed and infuriated by it, now comforted and strengthened by it, in the expectation that the Spirit will once again address us through the witness of prophets and apostles with a life-giving word.

3. Proclamation of the Word of God is an act of *witness to the truth*. Being a witness is among the most solemn of human acts, requiring utmost attention and commitment. As Paul Ricoeur notes, its most familiar location in common human experience is the courtroom, where the truth is at issue and justice is at stake.

Several features of the act of witness stand out. First, the witness is sworn to tell the truth. Second, faithful witnesses draw attention not to themselves but to someone or some event distinct from themselves. Third, the need of witnesses arises from the fact that what they tell us is quite different from a general truth that can be known in advance or that is universally accessible. Witnesses attest particular events. Fourth, the act of witness is self-involving. It requires personal participation, commitment, and courage. Fifth, because the truth is often resisted, the commitment of the witness in its most solemn form may become a commitment unto death. The link between witness and risk-taking is preserved in the New Testament word *martus,* "martyr." While not in itself proof that a witness speaks the truth, commitment and risk-taking distinguish what a witness does from detached observation or passive transmission of information.[4]

4. Proclamation of the Word of God employs the medium of *language.* Christian witness is certainly not limited to the linguistic realm. There is a witness of deeds as well as a witness of words. Still, proclamation of the living Word of God takes the primary form of verbal communication.

Human beings have been endowed with the capacity to communicate and to understand through language. For good or ill, language shapes human life. Individuals and communities may be condemned to bondage or introduced to a new freedom by the particular stories that they tell and retell and by the metaphors and parables that they employ to understand the world,

---

3. For a remarkable example of wrestling with the scriptural witness, see Phyllis Trible, *Texts of Terror* (Philadelphia: Fortress, 1984).

4. Cf. Paul Ricoeur, "The Hermeneutics of Testimony," in *Essays on Biblical Interpretation,* ed. Lewis S. Mudge (Philadelphia: Fortress, 1980), 119-54.

themselves, and the ultimate reality called God. We think and speak of God, if at all, in carelessly or carefully chosen words and images.

The importance of language in human life is recognized and honored by the seriousness with which the church takes up the task of proclaiming the gospel. While the writers of Scripture knew that there are experiences, insights, and sighs of faith too deep for words (Rom. 8:26), they also declared that "faith comes from what is heard, and what is heard comes by the preaching of Christ" (Rom. 10:17).

Christian proclamation necessarily uses language in arresting, disturbing, uncommon ways. This is why metaphor, image, and story are so prominent in Christian talk of God. In the proclamation of the gospel, language is stretched to its limits in the attempt to point to the reality of God, the gracious creator, redeemer, and sanctifier. How could the language of proclamation not be jolting, even shocking, when at the heart of the Christian message is the story of Christ crucified and raised for the salvation of the world? If God's grace is surprisingly present in the midst of our everyday life, how could the language of proclamation, like the literary forms of the Bible, not abound in fresh imagery, startling metaphor, and arresting parable?[5]

While no particular words or forms of speech are inherently adequate to speak of God, some are more fitting than others to point to the identity and action of God attested in Scripture. If, as we have emphasized, the revelation of the living God takes its decisive form not in a set of eternal truths but in the life-act of a person, the proclamation of the church will give a certain priority to the biblical narratives, and especially the Gospels, that speak of God as a living, acting, personal, and gracious reality.

5. While the content of the proclamation of the Word of God is rich and deep, it is also fundamentally simple. It is the *gospel*, the "glad tidings" of God's astonishing faithfulness to humanity and the entire creation in all their sin and brokenness. The task of proclamation is to present this "gospel of God" (Rom. 1:1), this announcement of God's gift of forgiveness and new life in Jesus Christ, in all its inner consistency, intelligibility, and clarity, in all its inexhaustible fullness, irresistible appeal, and liberating power. The content of Christian proclamation is not "whatever Scripture says" but "what Scripture is all about" — that is, the central biblical message.

Although the gospel is fundamentally simple, it is not simplistic; while affirmative, it is never trivial or cheap. The gift that it announces is accompanied by a call for disciplined life of love and service and by a warning of

---

5. See Thomas G. Long, *Preaching and the Literary Forms of the Bible* (Philadelphia: Fortress, 1989).

judgment. Lutheran and Reformed theologies make this point in distinctive ways.

A notable emphasis of Lutheran theology is that if Christian proclamation is to avoid trivializing the grace of God announced in the biblical witness, it must clearly distinguish between law and gospel and know the importance and place of each. Summarizing the teaching of the Lutheran Confessions on this point, Edmund Schlink writes, "The law terrifies; the Gospel comforts and cheers the terrified person. The law beats a man down; the Gospel raises him up and strengthens him. The law accuses and condemns; the Gospel pardons and bestows. The law punishes and kills; the Gospel makes free and alive."[6]

While the concern to distinguish Christian proclamation from the announcement of "cheap grace" (Bonhoeffer) and to fight every reduction of the gospel to moralism is crucial, the Reformed theological perspective holds that it is equally important to avoid a dualistic understanding of the Word of God. If law and gospel should not be confused, neither should they be divorced. God's Word to the world in Jesus Christ is a strong and unambiguous Yes (2 Cor. 1:20), but it is a Yes that contains both promise and direction. At the center of Christian preaching is not an abstract law/gospel dialectic but the message of the free grace of God in Jesus Christ crucified and resurrected for our salvation. This message both liberates and empowers us for the love of God and others. In the light of the gospel, the law functions not only as judgment but also as guide to the new life in Christ. Only if preaching focuses on the whole Christ of the biblical witness will it avoid both the moralistic preaching rightly criticized by Lutheran theologians and the preaching of a gospel that lacks direction for the new life in Christ rightly criticized by Reformed theologians.[7]

6. The proclamation of the Word of God always takes place in particular situations. If Christian witness always has a text, it also always has a particular *context*. It does not deal in general truths about God, the world, and humanity. If that were the case, the content of proclamation would not be the living Word of God but timeless truth that leaves everything as it is. As witness to

6. Schlink, *Theology of the Lutheran Confessions* (Philadelphia: Fortress, 1961), 104. See also Carl E. Braaten, *Justification: The Article by Which the Church Stands or Falls* (Minneapolis: Fortress, 1990), 143-53.

7. In the Reformed tradition, the proper purpose of the law is to give direction to love and to provide order for the life in community that God intends. See John Calvin on the three uses of the law, and particularly on its chief "third use" to guide believers in the new life in Christ (*Institutes of the Christian Religion*, 3.7.6-14). See also Karl Barth, "Gospel and Law," in *Community, State, and Church*, ed. Will Herberg (Garden City, N.Y.: Doubleday Anchor, 1960), 71-100.

the living Word of God, Christian proclamation speaks to particular people in a specific time and place. It addresses a particular situation here and now with a specific message. It calls men and women to concrete decision and concrete action. Christian proclamation is not vague, neutral, safe discourse about God, but concrete witness to the gospel that aims at a concrete response. The Christ attested in Christian proclamation is, to be sure, "the same yesterday, today, and forever" (Heb. 13:8), and loyalty to this person is essential in all Christian witness. But as the living Lord, Jesus Christ addresses us as the gift and claim of God in ever-new and context-specific ways, and his voice must be heard and obeyed anew. When the contextuality of proclamation is lost, so also is the presence of the Spirit, who alone gives life to the written or spoken word (2 Cor. 3:6).[8]

7. To the question of *how* the Word of God is to be preached, the answer of the Westminster Larger Catechism, while clearly reflecting the language and piety of the seventeenth century, still commands respect: "They that are called to labor in the ministry of the Word are to preach sound doctrine, diligently, in season, and out of season; plainly, not in the enticing word of man's wisdom, but in demonstration of the Spirit and of power; faithfully, making known the whole counsel of God; wisely, applying themselves to the necessities and capacities of the hearers; zealously, with fervent love to God and the souls of his people; sincerely, aiming at his glory, and their conversion, edification, and salvation."[9]

What Are Sacraments?

While proclamation of the Word of God is an indispensable means of grace, it does not exhaust the many different ways in which the extravagant love of God is communicated to us. In addition to proclamation, there are sacraments. Sacraments are "visible words,"[10] embodiments of grace, enacted testimonies to the love of God in Jesus Christ.

8. On the importance of contextuality in preaching, see Justo L. Gonzalez and Catherine G. Gonzalez, *Liberation Preaching: The Pulpit and the Oppressed* (Nashville: Abingdon, 1980); also Nora Tisdale, *Preaching as Local Theology and Folk Art* (Minneapolis: Fortress, 1997).

9. The Westminster Larger Catechism, Q. 159, in *The Book of Confessions* (PCUSA), 7.269. I am indebted to Dawn DeVries for drawing my attention to this passage in a lecture on the preaching of the Word as a means of grace in the Reformed tradition.

10. See Robert W. Jenson, *Visible Words: The Interpretation and Practice of Christian Sacraments* (Philadelphia: Fortress, 1978).

An often-repeated definition of sacraments was formulated by Augustine, who called them "visible signs of an invisible grace." The definition offered by the Westminster Shorter Catechism is more specific: A sacrament is "a holy ordinance instituted by Christ wherein by visible signs Christ and the benefits of the new covenant are represented, sealed, and applied to believers."[11] Sacraments are palpable enactments of the gospel by means of which the Spirit of God confirms to us the forgiving, renewing, and promising love of God in Jesus Christ and enlivens us in faith, hope, and love. The presence of Christ in the proclamation of the Word and the presence of Christ in the practice of the sacraments are not two different Christs but the same Christ present in different ways.

The Bible does not provide a definition of a sacrament, nor does it specify their number. In the New Testament, the Greek word *musterion* — literally "mystery," later translated in the Latin as *sacramentum*, or "sacrament" — refers to the presence and purpose of God made known in Jesus Christ, not specifically to baptism, the Lord's Supper, or other rites (Eph. 1:9-10). In the early Middle Ages, the number of sacraments varied widely. Since the thirteenth century, their number has been set at seven in the Roman Catholic and Eastern churches: baptism, confirmation, eucharist, penance, ordination, marriage, and anointing of the sick.

The Reformation churches reduced the number of sacraments to two or three, with baptism and the Lord's Supper always recognized as the most important. It was argued that sacraments were to be limited to those practices clearly instituted by Christ and the apostles. Even more important than the Reformers' reduction in the number of sacraments, however, was their insistence on two basic points: first, the inseparability of Word and sacrament; and second, the importance in both Word and sacrament of the working of the Spirit and of the response of faith. These emphases countered every quasi-magical view of the nature and efficacy of the sacraments.[12]

From the earliest times, two tendencies in interpreting the sacraments have been evident. One emphasizes the *objective reality* of God's grace in and through the sacraments. Those who hold to this view see the sacraments as divinely appointed rites that, when properly administered, convey grace and salvation if there are no impediments. The sacraments are said to be effica-

---

11. Westminster Shorter Catechism, in *The Book of Confessions* (PCUSA), 7.092.

12. As Martin Luther put it, "it is not the water that produces these effects, but the Word of God connected with the water, and our faith which relies on the Word of God connected with the water. For without the Word of God the water is merely water and no Baptism" ("The Small Catechism," 4.10, in *The Book of Concord*, ed. Theodore G. Tappert [Philadelphia: Fortress, 1959], 349).

cious in themselves *(ex opere operato).* This tendency is found, for example, in Ignatius, who speaks of the Lord's Supper as the "medicine of immortality"; in Augustine, who held against the Donatists that the effectiveness of the sacrament does not depend upon the purity or worthiness of the celebrant; and in the traditional Roman Catholic doctrine of transubstantiation, according to which the substance of the bread and wine is changed into the substance of the body and blood of Christ when the eucharist is properly administered by a duly ordained priest.

The second tendency in the interpretation of the sacraments emphasizes the importance of *our faith response.* According to this view, the sacraments are dramatic signs of the grace of God and are effective not in themselves but only as they are received by faith. The sacraments are not so much something done *to* us as something that *we* do — we repent, we confess our faith, we vow to be faithful. According to this view, the purpose of the sacraments is to give people the opportunity to bear public witness to their faith. The sacraments are public acts of commitment and public expressions of loyalty to Christ.

These two tendencies struggle with each other in the church and in theology up to the present. The danger of the more objective view by itself is that it minimizes the importance of the response of faith and seems to disregard the freedom of the Spirit. Viewed purely objectively, the grace of God mediated by sacramental action is depersonalized and reified. The danger of the more subjective view by itself is that it obscures the unconditional and objective reality of God's grace. These two tendencies are not to be correlated respectively with the Roman Catholic and Reformation traditions. Elements of both tendencies are present to some degree in both traditions.

Both Catholic and Protestant theologians today increasingly emphasize the personal character of God's self-communication in Word and sacrament. There is an effort to get beyond the impasses of traditional sacramental controversies. One way of doing this is to redefine the meaning of sacrament in such a way that Christ becomes the paradigm of what is sacramental, and the theology of the sacraments becomes more adequately trinitarian. Thus Karl Barth, Karl Rahner, and Edward Schillebeeckx contend that Jesus Christ is the primary sacrament. It is in Christ that the decisive presence and activity of God in and through a finite reality occurs. This Christocentric redefinition of sacrament underscores the free, personal presence of God's grace in concrete, worldly form while also insisting that grace, as personal presence, makes room for and calls for free personal response.

If Christ is the primary sacrament, then those rites of the church that are called sacraments will correspond to their archetype. The sacraments are celebrated in Christ and re-present Christ. God comes to human beings personally by the power of the Holy Spirit in the concrete, worldly media of spoken word and enacted sacrament. The gospel of God's costly love is both spoken to us and enacted in our midst. Both Word and sacrament re-present in different ways the gift and demand of God's unconditional grace in Jesus Christ by the power of the Holy Spirit.

Since Vatican II it is possible to speak of a growing convergence among Roman Catholic and Protestant theologians in the understanding of the sacraments. This convergence is marked by several features: (1) an emphasis on the inseparability of Word and sacraments; (2) a trinitarian and Christocentric interpretation of both the proclamation of the Word and the celebration of the sacraments; (3) an effort to interpret the sacraments in a way that illuminates the "sacramental" character of the whole of creation; and (4) a concern to make as explicit as possible the connection between the sacraments, Christian life, and Christian ethics.

The Meaning of Baptism

Christian baptism is the sacrament of *initiation* into life in Christ. It marks the beginning of the journey of faith and discipleship that lasts throughout one's life. In baptism a person is immersed in water, or water is poured or sprinkled upon him or her, in the triune name of God.

1. Authorization of baptism is often found in the command of Jesus: "Go therefore and make disciples of all nations, baptizing them in the name of the Father and of the Son and of the Holy Spirit, and teaching them to obey everything that I have commanded you. And remember, I am with you always, to the end of the age" (Matt. 28:19-20).

Important as this passage has been in the history of baptismal practice, baptism is based not only on the *command* of Jesus but on the *act* of Jesus in freely submitting himself to baptism. Jesus commences his vocation, his obedient response to the call of God, by being baptized by John. In this act, Jesus enters into solidarity with lost humanity. He begins the life of costly love and service that eventually leads to his passion, death, and resurrection. Jesus' baptism thus signifies his solidarity with the sinners and outcasts of this world and his complete obedience to his Father's will. As described by the evangelists, this self-identification of Jesus with sinful humanity is met by God's identification of him as the beloved Son and by the descent of the Spirit of God on him (Mark 1:9-11).

Jesus uses the image of baptism in relating the life of his disciples to his own mission of self-expending love: "Are you able to drink the cup that I drink, or be baptized with the baptism that I am baptized with?" (Mark 10:38). The event of baptism thus marks the beginning of the Christian's participation in the life, death, and resurrection of Christ. It signals one's death to an old way of life and one's birth to the new life in Christ. Christians are given a Christian name, and their whole life becomes a journey of faith in which they enter ever more fully into their baptismal identity. They become participants in the life and love of the triune God in whose name they are baptized.

2. The New Testament unfolds the meaning of baptism in many rich images. Each of them is important and complements the others.[13]

a. Baptism is described as a *dying and rising* with Christ. The descent into the water signifies the Christian's identification with the passion and death of Christ, whereby the power that sin has in the old way of life is broken, and the Christian's ascent from the water signifies a participation in the new life based on the power of the resurrection of Christ (Rom. 6:3-4).

b. Baptism is also pictured as the *washing* of a sin-stained life. Just as water washes away the dirt of the body, so God's forgiveness washes away the sins of those who are truly repentant (1 Cor. 6:11). Those who are pardoned and cleansed by Christ receive in baptism a fresh start in life and a new ethical orientation.

c. Baptism is further portrayed as a *rebirth* by the Holy Spirit and a receiving of the gift of the Spirit (John 3:5; Acts 2:38). While the Holy Spirit is at work everywhere in creation, giving and renewing life, the New Testament closely associates the gift of new life in the Spirit with baptism.

d. *Incorporation* is another image of baptism in the New Testament. By this act we are united with Christ, with each other, and with the people of God in every time and place. Welcomed into the covenant community by baptism, we are no longer solitary individuals, but instead members of a new family and citizens of a new society (Eph. 2:19). This new society is one in which there is neither Jew nor Greek, neither slave nor free, neither male nor female (Gal. 3:28).

e. Baptism is also a *sign of God's coming reign*. It is the beginning of the Christian's movement in faith toward that reign. By baptism Christians receive the Spirit as the "firstfruits" (Rom. 8:23) of the harvest to come and are set in solidarity with the whole groaning creation, which eagerly awaits the fulfillment of God's purposes and the coming of God's justice and peace.

3. If baptism is the commencement of Christian life, signifying a dying

---

13. For the following, see *Baptism, Eucharist and Ministry* (Geneva: World Council of Churches, 1982).

and rising with Christ, a cleansing from sin, a receiving of the life-giving Spirit, a welcoming into God's new society of love, and the start of a faith journey toward God's coming renewal of all things, what sense does it make to baptize infants?

Both Luther and Calvin defended infant baptism, although they rejected aspects of the theology of baptism taught by the Roman Catholic Church.[14] However, strong objections to infant baptism have been raised for centuries by those in the Baptist traditions. More recently, they have been raised within Reformed theology by Karl Barth.[15] Barth's objections to infant baptism can be summarized as follows:

a. Infant baptism has no explicit basis in Scripture. While the possibility that infant baptism was practiced in the apostolic age cannot be excluded, all evidence seems to point to the conclusion that it became a practice of the church only in the post-apostolic period.

b. Barth argues further that infant baptism has led to the disastrous assumption that people become Christians virtually by birth. Grace is thus cheapened, and the gospel is spread by subtle and sometimes overt coercion. In Barth's judgment, infant baptism has contributed to the serious sickness and impotence of the church in the modern era.

c. Barth's central theological argument is that infant baptism obscures the meaning of baptism as an entrance into free and responsible Christian discipleship. In baptism there is first an action of God (baptism with the Spirit) and then a corresponding human action (baptism with water): there is a divine gift and a human response. Baptism attests God's grace and marks the beginning of the new life in Christ. Since baptism is a free and glad human answer to God's gracious activity in Jesus Christ, and since this answer must be fully responsible, Barth thinks that infant baptism obscures and distorts the meaning of baptism.

What can be said in response to Barth's objections? In reply to his first point, reference has often been made to the covenantal promises of God given to believers and to their children (Acts 2:39), as well as to the fact that entire households were sometimes baptized in the apostolic period (Acts 16:33). Still, the historical evidence is slim, and it must be conceded that the case for infant baptism cannot be made on the grounds that it was undeniably practiced in the New Testament church.

14. For Luther, see Jonathan D. Trigg, *Baptism in the Theology of Martin Luther* (Leiden: Brill, 1994); for Calvin, Francois Wendel, *Calvin: Origins and Development of His Religious Thought* (Durham: Labyrinth, 1963), 318-29; also B. A. Gerrish, *Grace and Gratitude: The Eucharistic Theology of John Calvin* (Minneapolis: Fortress, 1993), 109-23.

15. See Barth, *Church Dogmatics,* 4/4 (Fragment).

Nor can we deny Barth's second charge that infant baptism has been subjected to much abuse in the history of the church. A similar criticism, however, could be leveled against virtually every theological doctrine and liturgical practice of the church. The distortion of a doctrine or the abuse of a practice calls for correction and reform but not necessarily elimination.

The real issue, then, is the theological *permissibility* of infant baptism under certain conditions. Should churches baptize only adults or *may* they baptize infants as well as adults, and under what conditions?

Common to both infant and adult baptism practices is the affirmation that we are recipients of the gift of God's love and are claimed for God's service. Just as in the Lord's Supper we are fed by the bread of life and the cup of salvation, so baptism declares that we are first of all recipients of an action, that something is done *for* us. Whether baptized as children or adults, our baptism signifies primarily what God has graciously done for us, and it is upon this that faith rests.

It can be argued that the two forms of baptism — infant and adult — together express the full meaning of baptism better than each would alone. In other words, their meanings are complementary rather than mutually exclusive. Adult baptism gives greater play to the conscious and free response of a person to God's forgiving love in Jesus Christ. It stresses explicit public confession and personal commitment to the way of Christ. But if practiced exclusively, adult baptism may tend toward a view of faith as preceding rather than responding to God's initiative. It may also foster a false individualism to the extent that it neglects the importance of the community in the process of one's growth in faith and Christian discipleship in both childhood and adulthood. The fact that in traditions that baptize adults exclusively there is often a dedication and commitment service for infants and their parents points to the need for some public recognition of the responsibility of the church for nurturing children in the life of faith.

Infant baptism, on the other hand, declares the sovereign grace and initiative of God. It demonstrates that even when they are helpless, human beings are loved and affirmed by God. It proclaims, as Karl Rahner says, that God loves this child.[16] It expresses God's loving reception of the child into a covenant community that takes responsibility for helping this child to mature in faith. It makes clear that baptism is a beginning of the process of growing into Christ, and that this process of growth cannot take place without a supportive community of faith.

Since the chief objection to infant baptism is that it undercuts the ne-

---

16. Rahner, *Meditations on the Sacraments* (New York: Seabury, 1977), 1.

cessity of free and conscious acceptance of the life of discipleship, it is imperative that the practice of infant baptism be dissociated from every semblance of the dispensation of cheap grace. Some kind of "commissioning" service must link together infant baptism and the free, personal response of the person baptized. Baptism and faith *are* inseparably related. The question is simply one of time. Must the response of faith on the part of the baptized be simultaneous with or immediately follow the event of baptism? After all, as Barth would surely agree, God is patient. God's grace is not coercive but gives humanity time. Of course, the patience of God must not be used as an argument for casually postponing a response. It is appropriate, however, to refer to God's patience in giving children who have been baptized time to come of age, stand on their own feet, and respond freely and gladly to the call to discipleship already at work in their lives. In the meantime, there *is* a faith that is already responding to the enacted grace of God in the baptism of the infant. It is the faith of the parents and the community in whose midst the child is baptized. While their faith cannot simply substitute for that of the child, it can help prepare the way for the child's eventual free response to her or his baptism. Parents and congregation vow to provide a Christian environment for their children until the day when they are ready to speak for themselves.

Does the Holy Spirit work in infants? Geoffrey Bromiley is surely right to say that it would be shocking to answer this question in the negative. The Holy Spirit can and does work in the lives of infants and children through the ministrations of their parents, guardians, teachers, and friends. Why not also through the proper practice of infant baptism?[17] The working of God's Spirit is not restricted by gender, race, or class. Neither is it restricted by age.

I conclude, therefore, that while the practice of infant baptism is not absolutely necessary in the life of the church, it *may* be permissible. And whether it is permissible depends on whether it is being practiced as a routine social rite, or as a form of cheap, magical grace, or instead with the clear understanding that it proclaims the unconditional grace of God in Jesus Christ and calls both parents and community to responsibility for the care, nurture, and guidance of the baptized child in the life of faith, hope, and love.

Infant baptism, responsibly practiced, is a sign of *God's gracious initiative* in creation and redemption. It is a powerful expression of the fact that God loves us even before we begin to respond to God in trust and love. It proclaims the love of God as sheer gift.

Further, infant baptism is a sign of *human solidarity* in the presence of

---

17. Cf. Bromiley, *Children of Promise: The Case for Baptizing Infants* (Grand Rapids: Eerdmans, 1970).

God. At no stage of human life are we isolated from each other or from God. The grace of God draws us deeply into relationship; it is formative of new community. Because the grace of God aims at the transformation not only of individuals but also of our life together as families and communities, the practice of infant baptism is theologically legitimate and meaningful.

Finally, infant baptism is a sign of *covenantal responsibility* as a community of faith and most especially as parents of the child brought to baptism. If people are indifferent to or negligent of their responsibility as parents to bring up their children in a home and a congregational environment that guides them toward their own free, personal decision about Christian faith and discipleship, it is unlikely that their sense of social responsibility will be very strong in regard to people beyond the family circle or local church. Especially in our age of broken homes, one-parent families, and many abused and abandoned children, infant baptism could be a strong and unambiguous declaration of the fact that God loves these and all children. When infant baptism is taken with appropriate seriousness, parents and other members of the congregation of Jesus Christ are called to responsibility for the care and nurture of children in the life of faith.

4. A special problem for the theology of baptism today is whether it is permissible to substitute other words for the traditional trinitarian formula in the service of baptism to avoid gender-specific language of God. This question does not have an easy answer. On the one hand, the classical trinitarian images are part of the service of baptism recognized by the ecumenical church and cannot be removed by unilateral action of a congregation or denomination without serious repercussions in ecumenical relationships. Moreover, if we were to speak of the triune God *only* with reference to God's relation to us — for example, as creator, redeemer, and sanctifier — such terms, while fundamental in Christian language of God, would not properly identify the relationships of the triune persons in God's own being. Exclusively functional trinitarian language veers in the direction of modalism.

On the other hand, exclusive masculine imagery of God courts idolatry and must be challenged. We should eschew liturgical fundamentalism that refuses *any* modifications, expansions, or alternatives to the traditional trinitarian formula. Baptism "in the name of Father, Son, and Holy Spirit" is not a magical incantation. It is a witness to the love of the triune God who lives in communion and who welcomes all into the new human community founded on grace alone.

Brian Wren is doubtless correct in pleading for more serious theological work, more creative imagination, and more responsible expansion of our language of the triune God in hymn, prayer, and liturgy. Guided by God's Word and Spirit, the church should be open to fresh trinitarian imagery that will complement — not replace — the traditional trinitarian images.[18] Among the proposals meriting careful consideration is to expand the baptismal formula so as to interpret the traditional images in gender-free words. This might, for example, take the form: "I baptize you in the name of the Father, and of the Son, and of the Holy Spirit; the Source of Life, the Word of Life, and the Gift of Life."[19]

The Meaning of the Lord's Supper

Celebration of the Lord's Supper goes back to the beginnings of the church. It is a central part of the Gospel tradition. According to the apostle Paul, who repeated a tradition he received, "The Lord Jesus on the night when he was betrayed took bread, and when he had given thanks, he broke it, and said, 'This is my body that is for you. Do this in remembrance of me.' In the same way he took the cup also, after supper, saying, 'This cup is the new covenant in my blood. Do this, as often as you drink it, in remembrance of me.' For as often as you eat this bread and drink the cup, you proclaim the Lord's death until he comes" (1 Cor. 11:23ff.).

1. If baptism is the sacrament of the foundation of Christian life in God's grace, the Lord's Supper is the sacrament of the *sustaining* of Christian life by that same grace. If baptism is the sacrament of the beginning of Christian life, the Lord's Supper is the sacrament of *growth* and nourishment in Christian life. If baptism marks the gift of God's love in Jesus Christ that welcomes us into his body by the power of the Spirit, the Lord's Supper marks the triune God's ever new *sharing* of life and love that draws us more deeply into communion with God and each other and strengthens us for service in the world.

The Lord's Supper gathers together the past, present, and future of God's creative and redemptive work. In the great prayer of thanksgiving that is an integral part of the eucharistic service, we are reminded of all of God's lavish gifts in the creation and preservation of the world, and most of all of

18. See Wren's arresting suggestions in *What Language Shall I Borrow?* (New York: Crossroad, 1989).

19. See David S. Cunningham, *These Three Are One: The Practice of Trinitarian Theology* (Malden, Mass.: Blackwell, 1998), who proposes "Source, Wellspring, Living Water"; also see Gail Ramshaw, "In the Name: Towards Alternative Baptismal Idioms," *The Ecumenical Review* 54 (2002): 343-52.

Christ's life, death, and resurrection for our salvation. But for the community of faith, Christ is no mere memory: he makes himself present here and now in the power of the Spirit through the breaking and eating of the bread and the pouring and drinking of the wine, and those who partake of this meal are made one body, one people in him. Furthermore, in this sacrament Christians are summoned to hope in Christ's coming again. They look eagerly for the consummation of the liberating and reconciling activity of God in which they are now participants and co-workers. Thus in the celebration of the Lord's Supper, the whole range of Christian life in time is expressed — memory of the crucified Lord, provisional experience of his presence here and now through the Spirit, and hope for the swift coming of God's reign of justice, freedom, and peace in fullness.

2. Since there has been extensive and often acrimonious dispute among the churches about the nature of Christ's presence in the Lord's Supper, any discussion of this topic should be prefaced by the reminder, repeated often in this book, that every theological formulation is provisional rather than absolute and that "the reality of fellowship in the church always precedes theological understanding."[20] Of the numerous interpretations of the presence of Christ in the Lord's Supper, four have been especially influential.

a. The first is the traditional Roman Catholic doctrine of *transubstantiation*. According to this view, the "substance" of the elements of bread and wine is transformed by the power of God into the substance of the body and blood of Jesus Christ. The "accidents," or outward form, of the elements — those qualities that can be seen, tasted, and felt — remain the same. This view presupposes Aristotelian and Thomistic philosophical concepts and distinctions that are no longer familiar to most people. It can be argued, however, that the real intent of this doctrine is actually to avoid magical views, even if its popular versions tend to come very close to this.

In more recent Catholic theology, new interpretations of the doctrine of transubstantiation have been proposed. According to one suggestion, there is a transignification (a change of meaning) of bread and wine, while according to another there is a transfinalization of the elements (a change of end or purpose). The point of these interpretations is that what something is cannot be separated from its context and use. Changes in context and use entail changes in meaning and identity, as when a piece of paper becomes in another context a letter bearing a message. This way of thinking about the change that occurs in the bread and wine bypasses the older Aristotelian conceptuality and the problems it has created. Although it has not been recognized in official Cath-

---

20. Wolfhart Pannenberg, *The Church* (Philadelphia: Westminster, 1983), 148.

olic teaching, it has the potential of overcoming some of the disagreement among the churches about the "changing of the elements."[21]

b. Another view of the presence of Christ in the sacrament is the Lutheran doctrine of "sacramental unity."[22] This is sometimes called *consubstantiation*, although Luther himself did not use this term. While Luther rejected the Catholic doctrine of transubstantiation as a binding theory, his own doctrine of the presence of Christ in the Lord's Supper is emphatically objective and realistic. Christ is present "in, with, and under" the elements of bread and wine, as fire permeates and envelops a glowing ember. The Lutheran doctrine stresses that Christ is present not just "spiritually" but bodily. And he is present even to those who eat unworthily and to their judgment. The idea of a merely "spiritual" presence of Christ was anathema to Luther. "No God like that for me!" he declared.[23]

c. A third view is found in the central strand of the *Calvinist or Reformed* tradition. This interpretation agrees with Catholics and Lutherans in affirming the real presence of Christ, but its special emphases are that Christ is present by the uniting power of the Holy Spirit and is received by faith. Calvin's interpretation of the real presence is subtle. On the one hand, he resists interpretations of the Lord's Supper that would mechanically affix Christ to the elements; on the other hand, he rejects views that would deny that Christ is really and efficaciously present in the Supper. For Calvin, in our faithful eating of the bread and drinking of the wine Christ joins us to himself by the grace and power of his Spirit. Christ is present in the whole eucharistic action rather than in the elements viewed in isolation from the use God makes of them. When Calvin says that Christ is present not corporeally but "spiritually," he means that Christ is present to faith by the power of the Holy Spirit. He does not mean that Christ is present only figuratively or as a mere idea or memory. For Calvin there is a Spirit-actualized correspondence between the eating and drinking of the bread and wine and the receiving of the real presence of Christ for the upbuilding of Christian life. "The sacraments," Calvin says, "profit not a whit without the power of the Holy Spirit."[24]

Brian Gerrish summarizes Calvin's understanding of the Lord's Supper

21. See Edward Schillebeeckx, "Transubstantiation, Transfinalization, Transignification," *Worship* 40 (1966): 366; Alasdair I. C. Heron, *Table and Tradition: Toward an Ecumenical Understanding of the Eucharist* (Philadelphia: Westminster, 1983), 164.

22. See Bernhard Lohse, *Martin Luther's Theology: Its Historical and Systematic Development* (Minneapolis: Fortress, 1999), 309.

23. Martin Luther, "Confession Concerning Christ's Supper," in *Luther's Works,* 37: 218.

24. Calvin, *Institutes,* 4.14.9.

in the following six propositions: (1) "The Lord's Supper is a gift." (2) "The gift is Jesus Christ himself." (3) "The gift is given with the signs." (4) "The gift is given by the Holy Spirit." (5) "The gift is given to all who communicate." (6) "The gift is to be received by faith."[25]

Calvin's admission that he did not have a definitive explanation of the real presence of Christ in the eucharist is worth noting: "Now if anyone should ask me how this takes place, I shall not be ashamed to confess that it is a secret too lofty for either my mind to comprehend or my words to declare. And, to speak more plainly, I rather experience than understand it. . . . In his sacred supper [Christ] bids me take, eat, and drink his body and blood under the symbols of bread and wine. I do not doubt that he himself truly presents them, and that I receive them."[26]

d. Still another interpretation is known as the *memorialist* doctrine. The celebration of the Lord's Supper is essentially a memorial or reminder of what Christ did for human salvation in his passion, death, and resurrection. The language of lively or vivid "memory" replaces the language of "real presence" in this interpretation of the Lord's Supper. What are traditionally called "sacraments" are, from the memorialist perspective, more appropriately named "ordinances." Christ has instituted these ordinances and has commanded his followers to express their loyalty to him by continuing to practice them. The ordinances of baptism and the Lord's Supper are, therefore, essentially acts of commitment and obedience. They are means by which Christians tell the story of Christ and his saving work and their own participation in and identification with him. Christians recall the drama of salvation and declare their commitment, loyalty, and obedience to Christ by these symbolic acts of baptism and Lord's Supper.[27]

3. Two major tendencies in the interpretation of the Lord's Supper continue to stand in some tension with each other. The one tendency sees this sacrament primarily as a sacrifice; the other tendency sees it primarily as a meal. According to current Roman Catholic teaching, the eucharist is a sacrifice of praise and thanksgiving to the Father for the work of creation and redemption, a re-presentation of the sacrifice of Christ on the cross, and a uniting of Christians with the self-offering of Christ.[28] For most Protestants, the Lord's Supper is primarily a meal in which the self-gift of God in Christ

25. Gerrish, *Grace and Gratitude*, 135-39.

26. Calvin, *Institutes*, 4.17.32.

27. For a fuller statement of this understanding of baptism and the Lord's Supper, see Stanley J. Grenz, *Theology for the Community of God* (Nashville: Broadman and Holman, 1994), 665-704.

28. *Catechism of the Catholic Church* (San Francisco: Ignatius Press, 1994).

is remembered, celebrated, and proclaimed until Christ comes in glory. It involves sacrifice strictly in the sense of the church's offering of the sacrifice of praise and thanksgiving to God in response to the once-for-all sacrificial love of God in Jesus Christ.[29] As recent ecumenical dialogues have shown, these different emphases, once misunderstandings have been set aside, do not have to be seen as mutually exclusive, and lines of convergence become evident.[30]

The sacrament called the Lord's Supper has many other names — holy communion, eucharist, divine liturgy, the breaking of the bread. But by whatever name it is called, it is a deeply trinitarian celebration. In the whole action of the Lord's Supper, thanksgiving is given to God through Christ in the Spirit. It is a *meal of thanksgiving* to God for the gifts of creation and redemption; a *meal of communion* with the crucified and living Christ who is God's gift to the world; and a *meal of joy and hope* in the power of the Spirit who gives us new life and *provides a foretaste of the great messianic banquet* of the end time, when God's liberating and reconciling activity will be completed. If the trinitarian and eschatological nature of this meal were more fully acknowledged, new possibilities of rapprochement between Roman Catholic, Eastern Orthodox, and Protestant theologies of the Lord's Supper would follow.[31] In particular, recovery of the importance of the *epiclesis,* the invocation or prayer for the coming of the Holy Spirit in the eucharistic service, would correct the tendency to focus solely on what happens to the bread and wine and on one particular moment of the service when the bread and wine are consecrated. It would underscore the church's utter dependence on the Spirit of God for the gift bestowed in the whole action of this meal.[32]

29. See Calvin, *Institutes,* 4.18.13-16. See also D. M. Baillie, *The Theology of the Sacraments* (New York: Scribner's, 1957), 115.

30. See *Baptism, Eucharist and Ministry.* In 1993 Lutheran and Reformed churches established full communion even while recognizing continuing differences in the interpretation of the Lord's Supper. Employing the principle of "mutual affirmation and admonition," these churches agreed that their respective interpretations were diverse witnesses to the one gospel: "The theological diversity within our common confession provides both the complementarity needed for a full and adequate witness to the gospel (mutual affirmation) and the corrective reminder that every theological approach is a partial and incomplete witness to the gospel (mutual admonition)." *A Common Calling: The Witness of Our Reformation Churches in North America Today,* ed. Keith F. Nickle and Timothy F. Lull (Minneapolis: Augsburg, 1993), 66.

31. See Michael Welker, *What Happens in Holy Communion?* (Grand Rapids: Eerdmans, 2000).

32. Lukas Vischer asserts that "the prayer for the presence of the Spirit shows that the church must always appear before God with empty hands" ("The Epiclesis: Sign of Unity and Renewal," *Studia Liturgica* 6 [1969]: 35). According to an agreement reached by a Roman Catho-

The Lord's Supper discloses what human life by God's grace is intended to be — a life together in mutual sharing and love. Just as the meaning of Christian baptism is inseparable from Jesus' own baptism as the commencement and epitome of his own singular life of love, obedience, and service, so the meaning of the Lord's Supper is inseparable from Jesus' practice of table fellowship with sinners and the poor throughout his ministry (Mark 2:15; Luke 15:1-2). This has unmistakable ethical implications. A proper understanding of the Lord's Supper must include not only the present reality of communion with Christ but also the promise of the coming joy of the messianic reign of justice, freedom, and peace. The Lord's Supper is a concrete sign and seal of God's promise of a new, liberated, and reconciled humanity in a new heaven and a new earth. To eat and drink at this table is to be united with Christ by the Spirit and to be challenged to extend the self-giving, other-affirming, community-forming love of the triune God to all people. All are invited to this table, but most especially the poor, the sick, and the outcast (cf. Luke 14:15-24). Understood in this way, the Lord's Supper has profound significance for Christian ethics and for the mission of the church in the world today.

Baptism, the Lord's Supper, and Ethics

I have spoken of baptism as the sacrament of solidarity and of the Lord's Supper as the sacrament of sharing. This way of describing the two great sacraments of the Christian community has the advantage of bringing out the essential connection between sacramental action and Christian ethics. Baptism and the Lord's Supper are not practiced merely out of reverence for ancient tradition or because of their aesthetic value. In these symbolic actions Christians receive their identity and their vocation. Together with the proclamation of the Word, the sacraments are means of grace by which God calls, strengthens, and commissions the church for its mission in the world.

Baptism is the sacrament of *God's solidarity with the world* in all its sinfulness and estrangement. In Jesus Christ, God entered into unconditional solidarity with sinful and lost humanity. Christ was baptized for lost humanity, and Christian baptism is the first step of participation in the life, death,

---

lic and Lutheran dialogue commission, "It is through the Holy Spirit that Christ is at work in the Eucharist. All that the Lord gives us and all that enables us to make it our own is given to us through the Holy Spirit. In the liturgy this becomes particularly clear in the invocation of the Holy Spirit (epiclesis)" (*Das Herrenmahl* [Paderborn: Verlag Bonifacius, 1980], p. 20). See also *Baptism, Eucharist and Ministry*, 10ff.

and resurrection of Christ. In baptism Christians are given a new identity. They are defined as children and partners of the triune God, who from all eternity wills to live in solidarity with others.

Baptism is the sacrament of *human solidarity in Christ with each other,* and especially with all those who are different, strange, and even frightening to us. There can be no baptism into Christ without a deepening of the sense of solidarity with fellow creatures and with all their needs and yearnings. In Christ there is neither Jew nor Gentile, neither slave nor free, neither male nor female (Gal. 3:28). Apparently an early baptismal confession, this New Testament text declares the unprecedented solidarity of life in Christ. Baptism creates a solidarity that defies and shatters the divisions and barriers that sinful human beings have created. Racism, sexism, and other ideologies of separation are doubly reprehensible when they exist within or are supported by the Christian church, since they are a denial of the solidarity that is God's intention for human life made in the image and reconciled by the activity of the triune God.

Baptism is also the sacrament of *human solidarity with the whole groaning creation.* It is a sign of God's coming reign and of the promised transformation of all things. Nature is present in the act of baptism most conspicuously in the use of water. If God uses water in baptism to signify the cleansing and renewal of humanity in Christ, can the church disregard the implications of this for its stewardship of the natural world? Can Christians who begin a life of new solidarity in baptism remain indifferent to the despoilment of the earth's water, soil, and air by reckless policies of pollution? Ought not baptismal theology, among its many rich meanings and dimensions, also remind us at the beginning of the twenty-first century that God is the creator and Lord of the whole cosmos and has appointed human salvation to be inextricably bound together with the call to stewardship and protection of the natural order?

As baptism signifies multidimensional solidarity, so the Lord's Supper signifies multidimensional sharing. The Lord's Supper is, in the first place, the sacrament of the *sharing of the divine life with humanity.* The triune God, who is eternally rich in love and fellowship, freely and graciously shares that life of love with humanity in Jesus Christ. Sharing life with others, whatever the cost, is God's own way of being. That is the identity of God disclosed in the life and death of Jesus Christ and articulated in the doctrine of the Trinity.

The Lord's Supper is therefore also the sacrament of *human participation in the divine life by sharing life with each other.* As a public, open, joyful, hopeful meal, the Lord's Supper is a foretaste of a new humanity. Christians cannot eat and drink at this table — where all are welcome and none goes hungry or thirsty — and continue to condone any form of discrimination or any social or economic policy that results in hunger or other forms of deprivation. The Lord's Supper is the practice of "eucharistic hospitality," in which strangers are welcomed into the household of God.[33] Christians cannot share this bread and wine while refusing to share their daily bread and wine with the millions of hungry people around the world.[34] There is an intrinsic connection between responsible participation in the Lord's Supper and commitment to a fairer distribution of the goods of the earth to all its people.

The Lord's Supper, whose natural elements are grain and the fruit of the vine, is also a symbolic recognition of *the shared life and common destiny of humanity and nature.* The natural order shares in God's work of giving life to human beings and of granting them new life. And conversely, human beings share in the care and cultivation of the earth and receive with thanksgiving its good gifts. The Lord's Supper is a beautiful portrayal of the interconnection and interdependence of personal, communal, and cosmic salvation.

Ludwig Feuerbach, the great humanist philosopher of the nineteenth century, contended that all Christian doctrines were simply secret ways of speaking about human potential in a natural environment. He concluded his book *The Essence of Christianity* with an interpretation of the sacraments. His final words on the topic: "Therefore let bread be sacred for us, let wine be sacred; and also let water be sacred! Amen."[35] A Christian interpretation of baptism and the Lord's Supper will not succumb to Feuerbachian reductionism. We must surely say far more than Feuerbach, but we must not say less. Water that symbolizes our new life in solidarity with Christ and with others must be kept clean and pure. Bread and wine that symbolize Christ's sharing of life and love with us must also be shared by us with all who are hungry and thirsty.

The Meaning of an Ordained Ministry

If all Christians are called to participate in God's ministry of liberation and reconciliation through Jesus Christ, and if all have been given the gift of the

---

33. See L. Gregory Jones, "Eucharistic Hospitality," *The Reformed Journal,* March 1989, 12-17. Jürgen Moltmann makes the same point: "The Lord's Supper takes place on the basis of an invitation which is as open as the outstretched arms of Christ on the cross." *The Church in the Power of the Spirit* (New York: Harper & Row, 1977), 246.

34. Cf. Monika K. Hellwig, *The Eucharist and the Hunger of the World* (New York: Paulist Press, 1976); Anne Primavesi and Jennifer Henderson, *Our God Has No Favourites: A Liberation Theology of the Eucharist* (Turnbridge Wells, England: Burns & Oates, 1989).

35. Feuerbach, *The Essence of Christianity* (New York: Harper Torchbooks, 1957), 278.

Holy Spirit, what is the meaning and necessity of an "ordained ministry"? Does not the office of ordained ministry contradict the vocation of all Christians to service of God and neighbor? Does it not foster elitism and hierarchy in the church? A response to these questions may be given in the form of several important distinctions.

1. As used in Christian theology, the word "ministry" has both *a general and a particular meaning.* In my discussion of Christian vocation in Chapter Ten, I emphasized that all Christians are called to the worship and service of the triune God. All are given the vocation of love of God and love of neighbor, all are called to follow Jesus Christ and to be his faithful witnesses in word and deed, all are given gifts by the Spirit to make their unique contribution to the life of the community and its mission to the world. In this *general* sense of ministry, often expressed in the Reformation tradition as "the priesthood of all believers," all Christians are called to ministry and are empowered for this task by the Holy Spirit.

But there is also a *particular* meaning of the term "Christian ministry." Among the diverse gifts of the Spirit to the church is the calling and ordination of certain people to the ministry of Word and sacrament. Ministry in this sense is an office that is ordained by God to provide for regular and responsible preaching of the gospel, celebration of the sacraments, and leadership in the life and service of the church. So crucial are these activities to the life and well-being of the community of faith that they are not left to chance occurrence or haphazard preparation. In every time and place, the church needs leaders who are qualified to preach, teach, administer the sacraments, and offer guidance in Christian faith and life.

2. The call to the ministry of Word and sacrament has both *an inward and an outward aspect.* People are called to this ministry by the Holy Spirit, who bestows special gifts and motivates their recipients to dedicate their lives to the gospel ministry. The apostle Paul refers to this inward call of God when he says, "Woe to me if I do not proclaim the gospel" (1 Cor. 9:16).

But the call to ordained ministry also has an outward aspect. It is mediated by the community of faith. Since the office of ministry is conducted on behalf of the entire community, it is essential that the will of the Spirit be expressed not only to the individual called but also through the community's acknowledgment of that calling. Hence schools are established to prepare leaders for the church, candidates for the ministry undertake a regimen of study and prayer and submit themselves to examination, and formal calls to ministry are issued by congregations on behalf of the whole people of God.

People called both inwardly and outwardly by the Spirit of God for leadership responsibilities are set apart by a service of ordination. In this service the ordinand promises to be faithful to Christ and to the whole people of God. Other ordained leaders lay hands on the ordinand as a sign of commission to ministry, and the church prays for the Spirit to empower the ordinand's ministry.

3. Ordination is properly understood *missiologically rather than ontologically.* That is, ordination is not a mysterious change of ontological status elevating the person ordained over other Christians. It is being commissioned and authorized to a particular task in the power of the Spirit. There is no basis in Scripture for thinking of ordination to the ministry of Word and sacrament as a "higher" or "fuller" ministry in comparison with other ministries of Christians. The clergy do not constitute a separate class of Christians. A hierarchical division between clergy and laity is a wound in the life of the church.

This is not to say, however, that ministry can be reduced to mere function. The person of the minister cannot be simply divorced from the task of ministry. Ministry presupposes not only thorough educational preparation but also deep commitment to God and a sincere desire to serve Christ. Ordained ministry is a distinctive calling and not just a role one plays or a job one does.

Yet ministers of the gospel of Jesus Christ convey a great "treasure in clay jars" (2 Cor. 4:7). Like other believers, ordained ministers are fallible human beings. The people they serve may sometimes expect their pastors to be perfect saints. They may wish for infallible advisors, brilliant preachers, courageous leaders, people who are always in charge of things, with an answer for every question and a faith that contains no uncertainty or doubt. But the terrible and happy truth, as Karl Rahner puts it, is that ministers are often weak as well as occasionally strong: they too live in fear and trembling; they too cry, "Lord, I believe, help me in my unbelief" and "Lord, be merciful to me, a sinner." Nevertheless, they preach the gospel that transforms the world. Ministers must therefore continuously remind their people and themselves not to take offense at their humanity. Their plea, Rahner contends, must be: Do not be offended by our failures. Take our frailty and weakness as a promise that God's grace is victorious even through the ministry of ordinary people. From our inadequacy, "learn that God has no horror of human beings."[36]

One implication of the fact that God calls ordinary human beings to ordained ministry and is not embarrassed by their humanity is surely that a policy of obligatory celibacy for all ordained ministers or priests must be judged as theologically flawed as well as practically unwise. A vow of celibacy

---

36. Karl Rahner, *Meditations on the Sacraments,* 61-62.

is certainly to be honored when it is taken freely, with careful deliberation, and in service of Christ. But the idea that it is a requirement for all ordained ministers has no foundation in Scripture, has not been the practice of the Eastern church, and was not the uniform practice of the Western church during its first thousand years. Numerous theologians, priests, and countless laity in the Roman Catholic Church are raising criticism of the policy of obligatory celibacy with increasing frequency.

In summary, theology must avoid both a *sacralizing of ministry* that separates ordained leaders from the rest of the people of God and a *demeaning of ministry* that trivializes the importance of this office in the life of the church. If it is a caricature of ministry to consider those in this office superior to and holier than other Christians, it is equally scandalous when ordained ministers ignore the disciplines of spirit and body requisite to faithful ministry of the gospel in an anxious effort to be trendy or just part of the crowd. The proper perspective on ministerial identity comes not from our idealized views of ministry, nor from secular models of what it means to be a successful leader (like the manager of a corporation or a media celebrity) but from the biblical witness to Christ and his exercise of ministry.

4. Every ministry of Christ must be characterized by *service rather than domination*. Jesus said that he came to serve rather than to be served (Mark 10:45), and he commanded his disciples to exercise authority differently from those who lord it over others (Mark 10:42-44). Whatever church order is adopted — episcopal, presbyterian, congregational, or some other — the meaning and exercise of power must be determined by the gospel of Jesus Christ and not by secular understandings and uses of power, such as the power to dominate and control others. If a church has moderators, superintendents, bishops, or even a pope, all must understand themselves as servants of the servant Lord and should discharge their responsibilities accordingly.

The purpose of every ministry is to build up the whole people of God in faith, hope, and love for more effective service in the world. All church order and church offices must therefore be tested continuously by the criterion of basic coherence with the ministry of Christ and by the practical test of whether a particular way in which the church's life is ordered in fact helps the whole church to take part in this ministry.

While ministry is not authoritarian, it does involve the exercise of authority. Servants of Christ are not like leaves blown about by the wind. Christian service is not servile subjection to power structures outside the church or within it. Especially within the Reformed tradition, service of the Word of God includes the freedom and responsibility to speak against the community when it obscures or departs from the gospel and to challenge whatever powers there be when they subvert justice and resist the coming of God's reign. The authority of the ordained minister is based not on his or her person but solely on the gospel of Jesus Christ. It is an authority that is always exercised in partnership with the whole people of God. Ministerial authority is inherently collegial rather than monarchical in nature.

While various ministries of leadership have been recognized in the church since its beginning, no particular church order can claim exclusive New Testament authorization. A threefold pattern of ministry is acknowledged by many churches: bishops or synods to oversee the work of several churches in a particular area; presbyters to lead in the proclamation of the Word and the celebration of the sacraments in a local congregation; and deacons to lead in service of the needy.

However widely adopted this threefold pattern may be, the question of church order remains one of the most contentious issues in ecumenical discussions. Does church order — whether episcopal, synodal, or congregational — belong to the well-being *(bene esse)* of the church, or to the very essence *(esse)* of the church? Must all churches recognize and adopt one form of church order as divinely given if they are to enjoy full communion with each other? Inseparable from these questions is, of course, the issue of papal primacy. Is the papal office to be understood primarily as the ultimate seat of jurisdiction in the church, or is it to be understood primarily as a sign of the visible unity of the church? In his much discussed 1995 encyclical *Ut Unum Sint* ("That they may all be one"), Pope John Paul II invited other churches to "a patient and fraternal dialogue" about the proper exercise of the papal office in the new ecumenical situation.[37]

Order is certainly important in the life of the church. Polity does matter. The question is whether or not the principles of church order are consistent with the gospel of Jesus Christ and whether they support rather than suffocate the freedom and the gifts of the Spirit to all the people of God. Guided by these criteria, every church order should value open, conciliar decision-making, should aim to build consensus in the church in a spiritual rather than a dictatorial and coercive manner, and should be open to reform under the guidance of the Spirit and in response to new situations.[38]

5. Ordination to ministry of Word and sacrament is *inclusive rather than*

---

37. Pope John Paul II, Encyclical Letter *Ut Unum Sint* (Vatican City: Liberia Editrice Vaticana, 1995). See the discussion of this encyclical in *Church Unity and the Papal Office: An Ecumenical Dialogue on John Paul II's Encyclical "Ut Unum Sint,"* ed. Carl E. Braaten and Robert W. Jenson (Grand Rapids: Eerdmans, 2001).

38. On church order as based on the distinctive character of Christ's lordship, see Karl Barth, *Church Dogmatics,* 4/2: 676-726.

exclusive. No groups of people should be excluded from the exercise of this office on the basis of such criteria as gender, race, or sexual orientation. A doctrine of ministerial inclusivity is based not on a theory of natural human rights but on the free grace of God, who summons people of all races, classes, nations, and genders to all ministries of the church.[39]

In our time, the most important development in Christian ministry is the recognition by many churches that the Spirit of God extends the call to ministry of Word and sacrament to women as well as men. This will no doubt be a point of tension among the churches for years to come. Arguments advanced against the ordination of women include the contention that Jesus chose only male apostles, that only a male can properly represent the person and work of Christ to the people of God, and that ordination of women would be a major departure from a centuries-old tradition of the Roman Catholic Church.

From a Reformed perspective, these arguments are entirely unconvincing. There is ample evidence that women played an important leadership role in the life of the New Testament church. Furthermore, the argument that only a male can represent the person and work of Christ seems finally to rest on the assumption that God is masculine, and disregards the fact that the one who presides in prayer, proclamation, and eucharistic celebration represents not only God to the people but also the people to God, at least half of whom — and in many congregations the majority of whom — are women. As for the argument from tradition, the response must be that the actual work of the Spirit of God in the ministries of many ordained women in the church today is a confirmation of the power of the gospel and a reminder that the church is always in need of being reformed *(semper reformanda).* Not only for many Christians in the Reformation churches but for increasing numbers of Roman Catholic Christians as well, the continued exclusion of women from the ministry of Word and sacrament by some churches is a great scandal to the gospel, a denial of the freedom of the Spirit to work in new and surprising ways among the people of God, and an increasing impoverishment of the church and its mission today.

---

39. According to "A Brief Statement of Faith," the Spirit "calls women and men to all ministries of the church." *Book of Confessions* (PCUSA), 10.4, line 64.

CHAPTER 13

The Finality of Jesus Christ
and Religious Pluralism

S erious reflection on the relationship between Christian faith and other religions is one of the most important tasks facing the church and theology
in the twenty-first century. With the relentless advance of globalization in
economy, politics, culture, and communication, and with the increasing
awareness of the religious factor in national and international tensions and
conflicts, the need for Christian theology to engage in the development of a
theology of the religions is both real and urgent. By a Christian theology of
religions I mean something different from the descriptive study of the history,
beliefs, and practices of the various religions of humanity. That is also an important endeavor. But a Christian theology of religions has the distinctive
theological task of asking about the place of the plurality of world religions
within the purposes of God made known in Jesus Christ. A crucial aspect of
this task is to clarify how it is possible to maintain the conviction that Jesus
Christ is Lord and Savior of the world and at the same time to honor the integrity and value of other religions.

The Ambiguity of Religion

A discussion of the lordship of Jesus Christ in the context of modern religious
pluralism appropriately begins with a recognition of the ambiguity of religion. Religion is ambiguous in at least three senses.

There is ambiguity regarding the *definition* of religion. Among the
many ways of defining religion are worship of and beliefs about God or gods,
recognition of an ultimate reality, or the sense of awe and reverence in rela-

tion to that which is considered sacred.[1] There is also ambiguity in the *inter-pretation* of religion. Some interpreters contend that the various religions share a common essence and that they differ only at the level of the symbols and rituals in which the encounter with the holy is expressed; others reject the assumption of a common essence and argue that every religion must be understood in its distinctiveness and particularity. Most important, the ambiguity of all religions is evident in their *actual history and practice,* in their proven capacity to promote good and evil, truth and superstition.

The critique of religion has ancient roots and has found voice both inside and outside the church. Plato rejected the myths of the gods of Mount Olympus as a corrupting influence on their worshipers. Aristotle's understanding of God as the unmoved mover whose perfection inspires desire and love in all creatures was far removed from the popular religious ideas of his time.

Exercising judgment on idolatrous beliefs and practices is a prominent feature of the biblical witness. Indeed, a good case can be made that the biblical tradition is the most ancient and powerful source of religious criticism. The prophets of ancient Israel condemned all forms of idolatry and harshly judged the attention given by prevailing religious practices to external rituals instead of attending to the important matters of justice and mercy (Mic. 6:1-8). Jesus stood within this prophetic tradition. In his teaching and ministry he rebuked those who used prayer and other religious practices and beliefs to hide the love of self under the pretense of love of God. Jesus condemned religious piety and practice that subverted the love of God and neighbor and served as a means of self-justification and the neglect of the weak and the poor.

The critique of religion had a prominent place in Enlightenment philosophy. The zenith of this critique is found in the writings of David Hume and Immanuel Kant. Hume's *Dialogues on Natural Religion* and Kant's *Religion within the Limits of Reason Alone* radically question the ability of human reason to verify the claims of faith. For Kant the essence of religion is essentially universal moral duty. The doctrines of particular faith communities have little practical moral significance. Of the doctrine of the Trinity Kant states that even if one were able to understand it, "nothing whatever would be accomplished for human betterment."[2]

---

1. For a list of nine different definitions of religion, see Charles Taliaferro, *Contemporary Philosophy of Religion* (Oxford: Blackwell, 1998), 21-24, 30.

2. Immanuel Kant, *Religion within the Limits of Reason Alone* (New York: Harper & Brothers, 1960), 133.

The philosophical critique of religion in the nineteenth and twentieth centuries is especially associated with the great "masters of suspicion," Karl Marx, Friedrich Nietzsche, and Sigmund Freud. Each argued that there was a hidden dynamic beneath the surface of religious practice. Drawing on Feuerbach's projection theory of religion, Marx called religion "the opium of the people." In his view, religion is the self-administered narcotic of distressed human beings that serves to relieve the pain of exploitation and oppression. In brief, religion tries to assuage the misery of life in this world by offering the consolation of life in another world. As a result, religion hinders efforts to transform present conditions of life and fosters conformity to present unjust conditions. Hence, according to Marx, the critique of religion is the necessary foundation of the critique of all social, political, and economic structures.

Nietzsche attacked Christianity as a religion of resentment in which weakness and mediocrity are made virtues while strength and genius are despised. In a famous parable, Nietzsche has a madman announce the death of God, and in *Thus Spoke Zarathustra*, Nietzsche proclaims the advent of the superior human being who will transcend the conventional religious beliefs and moral values of the past. Freud, the father of modern psychoanalysis, dismissed religion as an infantile illusion, the continuation into adulthood of a child's dependence on its parents out of a sense of weakness and an inability to cope with the challenges of life. Religion is the camouflaged longing of finite, mortal human beings to be protected by an omnipotent power.

Among the theological critics of the Christian religion in the nineteenth and twentieth centuries, Søren Kierkegaard and Karl Barth stand out. Kierkegaard attacked the conventional Christianity of the established church in Denmark for its loss of existential seriousness and its domestication of the scandal of the gospel. Barth mounted an equally blistering assault on the reigning theology of Protestant liberalism of the nineteenth and early twentieth centuries. In his Romans commentary, Barth excoriated the idols of church and society, called the god of bourgeois religiosity a "no-god," and declared that religion is unbelief, the place where human life is most clearly exposed as discordant and diseased. He later added that the gospel, far from confirming the self-aggrandizing claims of the church and the arrogant self-righteousness of the pious, meant the "end" of the church and the "abolition" of religion.[3] Barth's powerful critique of religion in the name of the God who is "wholly other" remains one of his most controversial contributions to church and theology.

Barth's criticism of religion is frequently viewed as entirely negative. It

---

3. Karl Barth, *Church Dogmatics*, 2/1: 280-361.

is said to lead inevitably to a fatal theological endorsement of secularism or to an uncritical endorsement of Christianity as the only true religion. This is not accurate. Barth did not think that the gospel simply deconstructs religion and puts secularism in its place. Nor was Christianity protected from his radical critique of religion. For Barth the revelation of God in Jesus Christ brings judgment on all religion, beginning with the Christian religion. Moreover, in speaking of the gospel as the "abolition" of religion, Barth used the German word *Aufhebung,* which means both "abolition" and "elevation." In other words, the revelation of God brings not only judgment on all religion but also the power to transform human beings and their religious life.

Although Barth's evaluation of religion was no doubt one-sided, it would be a mistake, in pendulum-like fashion, to swing to the opposite extreme. The religions of the world are indeed complex and ambiguous realities. It serves little purpose to demonize or to glorify them. In a religiously pluralistic world, a Christian theology of the religions should neither imperially dismiss other religions nor uncritically endorse all religions as basically the same. A theology of the religions today should be guided by two principles.

First, *a theology of the religions will recognize that there are real and not merely surface differences among the world religions and will avoid abstract definitions of an essence common to all religion.* The distinctive truths and values of the religions are obscured by the common essence approach. When a theology of religion stays at an abstract level, it circumvents the concrete reality of the world religions.[4] Modern scholars of religion are increasingly emphasizing the importance of the study of the particular religions and have reservations about speaking of religion in the singular or in terms of a common or universal essence. The aim of the modern discipline of the history of religions is to understand religion not in general or in the abstract but as it confronts us in all its historical particularities.

While this emphasis on particularity in the study of religion should be greeted by theology as a significant advance, it is an advance that is not without its own hazards. For it can lead to a purely descriptive presentation of the beliefs and practices of the religions with little concern about questions of truth and value. Indifference to or suppression of these questions leads only to a superficial tolerance, "a falsely understood liberalism in which one trivializes the question of truth or no longer even dares to ask it."[5] When one simply brackets the questions of truth and value in the study of the religions,

4. Jacques Dupuis, *Toward a Christian Theology of Religious Pluralism* (Maryknoll, N.Y.: Orbis Books, 1997), 8.

5. Hans Küng, *Christianity and the World Religions* (New York: Doubleday, 1986), xviii.

the result is a kind of "consumer pluralism" (Rowan Williams) extended now to the domain of the religions.

This leads directly to the second principle that should inform a theology of the religions. *A theology of the religions will be undertaken from a particular faith perspective and will necessarily involve critical judgment.* A theology of the religions must avoid the paths of distant neutrality or even sheer relativism. While all religions of humanity command our respect, they are not beyond critical examination. Religious belief and practice are far from being consistently innocent and commendable. As millennia of religious history and recent events have reminded us, religion can be directed to destructive and lethal ends.

As a reminder of the ambiguity of religion, a Christian theology of the religions might well begin its reflections with a frank acknowledgment of the evils that have been done in the name of Christianity and other world religions. We should not ignore or dismiss a multitude of ugly facts. Brutal medieval crusades were conducted in the name of Christ the Lord; many churches and their leaders provided theological justification for the enslavement of millions of Africans and the elimination of native Americans in North America; the Spanish conquistadors slaughtered countless native South Americans under the sign of the cross; on theological grounds women have been systematically subordinated to men and excluded from positions of leadership in church and society; six million Jews were destroyed in the Shoah by genocidal policies designed and carried out by at least nominally Christian people taught for centuries to harbor contempt for Jews; violent conflicts between Roman Catholics and Protestants in Northern Ireland have continued to the present; bloody battles erupt periodically between Hindus and Muslims over Kashmir; at different times Muslims and Christians or Muslims and Jews have engaged in prolonged warfare; in recent years the practice of terrorism on an international scale as well as military responses to it have not lacked in religious slogans and justifications. The list could easily be extended, but it is already long enough to make the point of how preposterous it would be to view religion and the religions through rose-colored glasses. More than preposterous, it is perilous to fail to recognize how any religion can be and has been used in the service of evil ends.[6] All religions are ambiguous historical phenomena.

Recognition of the ambiguity and the sometimes appalling misuse of religion, including Christianity, must therefore go hand in hand with recognition of what is good and truthful in the different religious traditions.

6. See Charles Kimball, *When Religion Becomes Evil* (San Francisco: Harper, 2002).

Barth's theological critique of religion, while one-sided, must not be ignored. As the Confession of 1967 states, "The reconciling word of the gospel is God's judgment upon all forms of religion, including the Christian."[7] That is certainly not all that a Christian theology of the religions will want to say, but it cannot say less.

Types of Christian Theologies of the Religions

The unconditional nature of Christian commitment to Jesus Christ as universal Savior and Lord is sometimes expressed by the phrase "the finality of Christ." Can Christians continue to affirm the "finality" of Christ in a world where the plurality of cultures and religions increasingly points to the need for a spirit of openness and dialogue?

In many surveys of views of the relationship of Christianity to the other religions, three types are identified: exclusivism, inclusivism, and pluralism.[8] Exclusivism asserts that Jesus Christ alone is the way, the truth, and the life, and there is no salvation other than through faith in him. Other religions may possess some knowledge of the truth of God, but they are not ways of salvation. Inclusivism teaches that Jesus Christ is the definitive revelation of God, that the salvation accomplished in him embraces all people, and that it is somehow made available to all. Pluralism holds that all religions mediate knowledge of the mystery of God, and all are equally valid ways of salvation. Each of these positions has a distinctive understanding of the sense in which the revelation of God in Jesus Christ is "final."

While the simplicity of this now standard typology of theologies of religion is attractive, it has serious limitations. One weakness is that it can lead to a pigeonholing mentality that ignores the important overlap of positions and obscures significant differences among theologians placed in any of the three categories. A second weakness is that since the category of inclusivism is more complex and less sharply defined than exclusivism and pluralism, many critics see it as a hopeless effort to construct a mediating position. Critics on the right complain that its universalist leanings make it a compromise with pluralism, while critics on the left charge that its Christocentric commitments show that it is simply a variant of exclusivism. Inclusivism thus becomes an ill-defined category, and the debate about the relationship of Christian faith

7. *The Book of Confessions* (PCUSA), 9.42.
8. See Alan Race, *Christians and Religious Pluralism* (Maryknoll, N.Y.: Orbis Books, 1982).

and other faiths tends to polarize between exclusivism and pluralism. Theologically, the problem with the exclusivist/pluralist polarity, as Christoph Schwöbel rightly notes, is that neither position takes seriously the concern of Christian faith for both the particularity and the universality of God's grace.[9]

Paul Knitter has recently proposed another typology of theologies of the religions that attempts to give a greater sense of the range and complexity of the different positions. He identifies four types: complete or partial replacement of the other religions (evangelical); fulfillment of the other religions (Vatican II Roman Catholic); mutuality of the religions (liberal Protestant and liberal Roman Catholic); and acceptance of the particularity and incommensurability of the religions (postliberal).[10] Knitter's recognition of the need for a more adequate typology underscores the fact that reflection on a theology of the religions is still at a relatively early stage, where even the questions being asked are not always clearly sorted out. Is Jesus Christ the only Savior? is not the same question as, Is salvation possible for adherents of religions other than Christianity? and neither of these questions is the same as asking, Is dialogue among the religions necessary, and if so, what are its goals? The following list of types of theologies of religions is indebted to Knitter's recent typology but also expands upon and diverges from it.

1. The first type declares that Jesus Christ alone is Savior and Lord of all and that salvation is possible only through explicit faith in him. Since Jesus Christ is the only Savior of the world, "the way, the truth, and the life" (John 14:6), and since the other religions do not know or proclaim the grace of God in Jesus Christ, neither revelation nor salvation is to be found in religions other than Christianity. In type 1, dialogue with other faiths, under the assumption that Christians may have something important to learn from these encounters, is downplayed if not rejected. In brief, the Christian religion is true and all other religions false.[11] Knitter calls this position the "total replacement" type.

The most serious objection to this position is that it fails to distinguish between Jesus Christ and our ideas and understandings of Jesus Christ. To

---

9. Schwöbel, "Particularity, Universality, and the Religions: Toward a Christian Theology of the Religions," in *Christian Uniqueness Reconsidered,* ed. Gavin D'Costa (Maryknoll, N.Y.: Orbis, 1990), 30-46. In his essay "The Finality of Christ," Rowan Williams also tries to escape from "the textbook options prescribed for interfaith dialogue — exclusivism, inclusivism, and pluralism." *On Christian Theology* (Oxford: Blackwell, 2000), 95.

10. Paul Knitter, *Introducing Theologies of Religion* (Maryknoll, N.Y.: Orbis Books, 2002).

11. See Harold Lindsell, "Missionary Imperative: A Conservative Evangelical Exposition," in *Protestant Crosscurrents in Mission: The Ecumenical-Conservative Encounter,* ed. Norman A. Horner (Nashville: Abingdon, 1968), 57.

confess Christ as Lord is not to say that we are in possession of all that Christ is and means. Openness to the truth of Christ that has not yet dawned upon us is a basic aspect of authentic Christian commitment.

2. A second type also holds fast to the confession that Jesus Christ alone is Savior and Lord and that salvation is possible only through explicit faith in him. But type 2 differs from type 1 in recognizing the presence of some knowledge of God in other religions and in cautiously approving of dialogue between Christians and members of other communities of faith, provided that Christian truth claims are not set aside or watered down. Knitter speaks of this type as "partial replacement."

In elaborating a type 2 position, Carl Braaten, an evangelical Lutheran theologian, argues that two distinctions are essential in a theology of the religions: the distinction between revelation and salvation, and the distinction between law and gospel. "God reveals himself in many ways," Braaten contends, "but there is salvation in the name of Jesus Christ alone."[12] Other religions know something of the law of God, but this is not a saving knowledge because it is not knowledge of the God of the gospel. God speaks through nature, conscience, the moral law, and the world religions, but in these ways God does not speak the gospel of God's grace and forgiveness in Jesus Christ. Summarizing what is to be found in other religions, Braaten says, "Revelation, yes, salvation, no."[13]

3. A third type teaches that Jesus Christ, the Savior and Lord of the world, is the "fullness" of God's truth and grace. All religions find their fulfillment in Christ. This view is represented by the "Document on the Relationship of the Church to Non-Christian Religions" *(Nostra Aetate)* adopted by the Vatican II Council.[14] According to the teaching of Vatican II, the non-Christian religions contain intrinsic values and possess authentic rays of truth about God. They can thus be seen as preparations for the reception of the fullness of the truth of the Christian gospel *(praeparatio evangelica)*. In effect, type 3 adapts the famous formula of Thomas Aquinas — "Grace does not destroy nature but fulfills it" — to the relationship of Christ and other religions. The grace of God in Jesus Christ does not destroy or replace the truths found in the other religions; it fulfills them. Knitter appropriately labels this position the "fulfillment" type.

12. Carl E. Braaten, "Hearing the Other: The Promise and Problem of Pluralism," in *Currents in Theology and Mission* 24 (1997): 395.

13. Braaten, "Hearing the Other," 396; see also Braaten, *No Other Gospel! Christianity among the World Religions* (Minneapolis: Fortress, 1992).

14. *The Documents of Vatican II,* ed. William M. Abbott (New York: Guild Press, 1966), 660-71.

As the official teaching of the Roman Catholic Church since Vatican II, understanding the grace of God in Jesus as the fulfillment of the religions represents a relatively new development in Catholic doctrine. For centuries prior to Vatican II, the central teaching of the Roman Catholic Church regarding those outside the church was summarized in the statement "Outside the church there is no salvation" *(extra ecclesiam nulla salus)*. However, at Vatican II the Church declared that it "rejects nothing which is true and holy" in the other religions and acknowledges in them "a ray of that Truth which enlightens all men."[15]

The Vatican II Declaration on the Church and the Religions offers brief descriptions of the rays of truth reflected in other religions. In Hinduism believers "contemplate the divine mystery and express it through an unspent fruitfulness of myths and searching philosophical inquiry." "Buddhism in its multiple forms acknowledges the radical insufficiency of this shifting world. It teaches a path by which men, in a devout and confident spirit, can either reach a state of absolute freedom or attain supreme enlightenment by their own efforts or by higher assistance." "Upon the Moslems, too, the Church looks with esteem. They adore one God, living and enduring, merciful and all-powerful, Maker of heaven and earth."[16]

Because God wishes all to be saved (1 Tim. 2:4), and because rays of truth and some measure of divine grace are present in non-Christian religions, Vatican II exhorts Christians to engage in "dialogue and collaboration with the followers of other religions." As part of their witness, it encourages Christians to "acknowledge, preserve, and promote the spiritual and moral goods" found in believers of other faiths, as well as the values in their society and culture. In particular, the Declaration urges Christians and Muslims "to forget the past," "to strive sincerely for mutual understanding," and "to make common cause" in fostering social justice, moral values, peace, and freedom.[17]

Whether Vatican II teaches that salvation is possible through the other religions, or whether its statements can at least bear that interpretation, is a matter of continuing dispute.[18] Whereas types 1 and 2 emphatically deny that salvation is possible through other religions, type 3 either leaves the door slightly ajar or remains silent.

4. Type 4 agrees with the previous three types in affirming that Jesus

15. *Documents of Vatican II*, 662.

16. *Documents of Vatican II*, 662-63.

17. *Documents of Vatican II*, 663.

18. See David Wright, "The Watershed of Vatican II: Catholic Approaches to Religious Pluralism," in *One God, One Lord: Christianity in a World of Religious Pluralism*, ed. Andrew D. Clarke and Bruce W. Winter (Grand Rapids: Baker Book House, 1992), 207-26.

Christ alone is Savior and Lord of all, but it differs from them in holding that the saving grace of God decisively known in Jesus Christ is in some manner present to all people whether they have heard the Christian gospel or not. Salvation is therefore possible in and through the other religions. This is the position often described as the "inclusivist" type. While it can take a number of different forms, it is most frequently associated with the theology of Karl Rahner. Perhaps the greatest Roman Catholic theologian of the twentieth century, Rahner developed a theology of the religions that affirms the saving grace of Christ *within* the religions rather than seeing Christ as standing necessarily *against* the religions.

How is it possible to teach that God's redeeming grace is present in the other religions and that a saving faith can take root in them while at the same time holding that there is salvation only through Jesus Christ? How can Rahner affirm the saving grace of Christ within the religions while declaring that there is a "pressing obligation to engage in missionary activity"?[19] Rahner's reasoning runs as follows. If, as Scripture teaches, God wills all persons to be saved (1 Tim. 2:4), and if God seeks to accomplish what God wills, the grace of God supremely manifest in Jesus Christ must be freely at work in all human life. By God's grace, there is in the depths of the existence of every human being the "permanently present possibility of a salvific relationship of freedom to God."[20] Moreover, since human beings are by nature social beings whose fundamental decisions are mediated through the particular forms of their social and historical life, the non-Christian religions must have some kind of positive role in the mediation of divine grace. Rahner concludes that non-Christians who are faithful to the light that is mediated to them within their religious communities may be called "anonymous Christians."[21] Since for Rahner being *knowingly* Christian is the intrinsic goal of the "anonymous Christian," he sees no contradiction between his theory of the anonymous Christian and his insistence on the "pressing obligation" of missionary activity.

Although Rahner's theology was a major influence at Vatican II, his position goes beyond the official declarations on the religions by that council in at least two ways. First, Rahner not only holds that non-Christians can know some truths about God but also that they can come to a saving relationship

19. Karl Rahner, "On the Importance of the Non-Christian Religions for Salvation," in *Theological Investigations,* vol. 18 (New York: Crossroad, 1983), 289.
20. Rahner, "On the Importance of the Non-Christian Religions," 291.
21. Karl Rahner, "Anonymous Christians," in *Theological Investigations,* vol. 6 (Baltimore: Helicon, 1969), 390-98. See also Rahner, *Foundations of Christian Faith* (New York: Seabury Press, 1978), 311-21.

with God if they respond faithfully to the knowledge that is made known to them. As noted above, the Vatican II documents are either ambiguous or silent about this possibility. Second, Rahner goes beyond Vatican II in contending not only that non-Christians may be "anonymous Christians" but also that other religions can be historical channels of a saving knowledge of God. While acknowledging that the non-Christian religions are "incomplete, rudimentary, and partially debased," Rahner argues that they can nevertheless be used by God as "ways of salvation by which human beings approach God and his Christ."[22]

Critics of Rahner charge that his talk of "anonymous Christians" lacks support in both Scripture and tradition. Furthermore, Rahner's theory is criticized as a subtle form of theological imperialism. Some have asked why a Buddhist may not turn Rahner's doctrine of anonymous Christianity upside down and speak of Christians as "anonymous Buddhists." Others have asked whether the moralistic tone of this position, which is accepting of all people who observe the law of God, are sincere, and show good will, does not contradict the gospel proclamation of God's acceptance of sinners and lawbreakers by grace alone.[23]

5. A fifth type primarily emphasizes the differences of the religions while being at the same time open to the possibility of salvation for those who have not heard of Jesus Christ or who in this life reject what they have heard. George Lindbeck, a leading representative of this type, underscores the radical particularity and otherness of the religions.[24] He describes religions as unique and irreducible languages and forms of life. Lindbeck thinks that a theology of the religions like Rahner's neglects the real differences among the religions, trying unsuccessfully to build metaphysical bridges between the religions by using ideas like implicit faith, pre-linguistic experiences of grace, "anonymous Christian," and "anonymous Christianity."

For Lindbeck explicit confession and worship of Jesus Christ as Savior and Lord of all distinguishes Christian faith from the other religions. At the same time, Lindbeck contends that the principle of attending to the particularity of a religious tradition must be upheld not only in dealing with Christian faith but with other faiths as well. All religions must be understood in their distinctiveness, which means careful attention must be given to their own self-descriptions. While Lindbeck's emphasis makes dialogue among the

---

22. Rahner, "On the Importance of the Non-Christian Religions," 295.

23. See Lesslie Newbigin, *The Open Secret: Sketches for a Missionary Theology* (Grand Rapids: Eerdmans, 1978), 196.

24. George A. Lindbeck, *The Nature of Doctrine: Religion and Theology in a Postliberal Age* (Philadelphia: Westminster, 1984).

religions a more difficult enterprise than it is often imagined to be, he does not view meaningful dialogue as impossible. This is true especially if dialogue takes the form of what may be called "ad hoc" encounters on specific issues and concrete possibilities of cooperation rather than the grandiose effort to achieve comprehensive doctrinal agreements. Lindbeck thinks that in these ad hoc encounters Christians can become better Christians, and conversely, "one of the ways in which Christians can serve their neighbors may be through helping adherents of other religions to purify and enrich their heritages, to make them better speakers of the languages they have."[25] On the matter of the salvation of non-Christians, Lindbeck sees no reason why Christians may not hold that non-Christians encounter and receive the grace of Christ either in their last moments of life or in the life hereafter.

Lindbeck's stress on the radical otherness of the religions combined with affirmation of the unrestricted possibility of salvation has certain resemblances to the emphases of Karl Barth. Reference to Barth in relation to the type 5 form of a Christian theology of religions is one of the points where my typology differs from Knitter's. Both Barth and Lindbeck emphasize the universality as well as the particularity of the Christian gospel. Because Knitter limits himself to a few passages in Barth's early writings, he concludes that Barth is a representative of a severe form of exclusivism. In fact, Barth's position is far more complex and combines an unprecedented emphasis on the particularity of the gospel of Jesus Christ with a striking call to Christians to hope and pray for the salvation of all. While Barth did not explicitly extend his emphasis on the particularity of Christian faith to the other religions, it is arguable that this is a step fully consistent with his theology.

In Barth's view the confession that Jesus Christ is *the* light of life and *the* incarnate Word of God does not mean there are no "true words" and "other lights" outside the Bible and the Christian church. The church has the responsibility to listen carefully to these words and attend to these lights outside the boundaries of the church, to test them, and to remain open to them as unexpected ways by which the living Word of God addresses the church.[26] Granted, Barth does not explicitly include the beliefs and practices of other religions among the other words and lights that the church encounters in the world. Nevertheless, the general structure of his overall argument is at least open to this interpretation.

While Lindbeck and Barth are united in focusing on the particularity of the grace of God in Jesus Christ and in avoiding every attempt to build meta-

25. Lindbeck, *The Nature of Doctrine,* 61-62.
26. Barth, *Church Dogmatics,* 4/3.1: 114-35.

physical bridges between the Christian faith and other religions, their emphases are somewhat different. Barth resists an undialectical identification of
God's revelation in Jesus Christ with the language of Scripture and church
and acknowledges the freedom of God to speak in unexpected ways. Thus in
his doctrine of "other words" and "other lights," he argues that the capacity of
Jesus Christ to address us "is not restricted to his working on and in prophets
and apostles and what is thus made possible and actual in his community. His
capacity transcends the limits of this sphere."[27] Jesus Christ speaks for himself
in other witnesses than Bible and church and in doing so challenges and enriches our knowledge of him. Jesus Christ is himself "rich and strong enough
to display and offer himself to our poverty with perennial fullness."[28] Barth
also has distinctive reasons for remaining open to the possibility of universal
salvation. He bases this possibility on the unequivocal Yes of God to humanity in Jesus Christ from the foundation of the world rather than on any speculation about what non-Christians might decide at death or after death.

6. Type 6 places far greater emphasis on the indispensability of dialogue
among the religions than any of the preceding types. Knitter calls this the
"mutuality" type of theology of the religions. According to this type, Christians and people of other faiths must take their own faith commitments with
utmost seriousness but must also enter into genuinely open dialogue with
other faith communities. In these dialogues there will be real giving and receiving on both sides. Paul Tillich, Hans Küng, John Cobb, and Jürgen
Moltmann are among the prominent representatives of this appeal for open,
give-and-take dialogue among the religions. Each would affirm the universal
saving significance of Christ, but each would also claim that our knowledge
of Christ and salvation in him is augmented, corrected, and to some extent
completed in the encounter with other religions.

According to Tillich, all are enriched in interreligious dialogue, as believers on both sides of the conversation discover latent or forgotten dimensions in their own tradition.[29] Hans Küng contends that all religions are
"ways of salvation" even if all religions also contain a mixture of truth and
falsehood. Just as Christian faith in dialogue may serve as a "critical catalyst"
for the other religions by helping to elicit what is deepest and best in them, so
also Christian faith will be challenged and clarified in the dialogue because it
will have to discover what is the depth and fullness of God's revelation in

---

27. Barth, *Church Dogmatics*, 4/3.1: 118.
28. Barth, *Church Dogmatics*, 4/3.1: 99.
29. See Paul Tillich, *Christianity and the Encounter of the World Religions* (New York: Columbia University Press, 1963).

Christ.[30] John Cobb speaks of Christ as the creative dynamic at work in all the religions: "The more deeply we trust Christ, the more openly receptive we will be to wisdom from any source, and the more responsibly critical we will be both of our own received habits of mind and of the limitations and distortions of others."[31]

Critics of this emphasis on the indispensability of dialogue charge that it is inclined to lose the centrality of *Jesus* Christ, the sharp edges of the Christian gospel, and the urgency of its being proclaimed throughout the world. Küng denies these charges, saying that his aim in promoting dialogue is to encourage Christian self-criticism in the light of the other religions and to engage in Christian criticism of the other religions in the light of the gospel.[32]

Likewise, Moltmann rejects the charge that the way of dialogue leads to an abandonment of the gospel. According to Moltmann, dialogue with other faiths can be a concrete expression of Christian life formed by the gospel. If Christians believe in a God who is self-giving love and who aims at reconciliation and peace in the creation, they cannot wish to be closed and invulnerable in their relationships with others. They trust "in a God who can suffer and who in the power of his love desires to suffer in order to redeem. Therefore, in their dialogue with people of a different faith, Christians cannot testify through their behavior to an unalterable, apathetic and aggressive God. By giving love and showing interest in others, they also become receptive to the other and vulnerable through what is alien to them. They can bear the otherness of the other without becoming insecure and hardening their hearts. The right thing is not to carry on the dialogue according to superficial rules of communication, but to enter into it out of the depths of the understanding of God."[33] In Moltmann's view, the scandalous message of the "crucified God" will always be the basis and norm of a Christian encounter with the other religions, while the "finality" of Christ will be seen not as something we already fully possess but as a promised reality that has already come and yet whose coming we still await.

7. The seventh type is different from the preceding types in contending that a theology of religions must move away from Christocentrism to a radical theocentrism. It is not Jesus Christ but God or "Ultimate Reality" that must be made central. John Hick, the preeminent representative of a pluralist

---

30. See Hans Küng, *On Being a Christian* (New York: Doubleday, 1976), 86-116.

31. John Cobb, "The Religions," in *Christian Theology*, ed. Peter C. Hodgson and Robert H. King (Minneapolis: Fortress, 1985), 373.

32. See Küng, *Christianity and the World Religions*, xvii.

33. Jürgen Moltmann, *The Church in the Power of the Spirit* (New York: Harper & Row, 1977), 160-61.

theology of the religions, calls for a "Copernican revolution" in theology, "a shift from the dogma that Christianity or Christ is at the center to the realization that it is God who is at the center, and that all the religions of humanity, including our own, serve and revolve around that God."[34]

Hick's pluralist approach to the theology of the religions focuses not on the particularity of the religions but on what they are thought to hold in common. According to Hick, the religious traditions are like pilgrims climbing to the top of the same mountain but from different sides. Pluralism in this sense seeks to relativize the historical particularities of the individual religions and tries to identify the "theocentric" or "ultimate reality-centered" core in all of them. For Hick and like-minded pluralists, respect and tolerance should replace all efforts at proselytism and conversion.

While Christians accept Christ as Savior, all religions have their own saviors and all offer salvation. Hick interprets Christian affirmations about Christ, such as the uniqueness or "finality" of Christ as Savior and Lord, not as ontological truth claims but as the poetic or exuberant language of love for the one through whom Christians have come to know God.[35] Hick's position raises the truth question in an acute form and leads to thin generalities that fail to represent well any particular religious tradition. For Christians, it is not a "supreme being" or "ultimate reality" as such who is worshiped as God but the one who covenanted with the people of Israel and who in sovereign grace became a humble servant in Jesus Christ for the salvation of the world.

Paul Knitter shares some of Hick's commitments to the pluralist path in speaking of Christianity and the other religions. However, Knitter sees important differences between himself and Hick. For one thing, Knitter wants to hold on to the uniqueness of Jesus in a stronger sense than Hick. For Knitter Christian affirmations about Jesus are not only expressions of strong affections but also "performative" declarations that call others "to recognize and accept the power that is available to them in Jesus."[36] Again, Knitter emphasizes that all talk of God is confessional, that we all speak from some particular perspective, and that it is therefore unavoidable that Christians will relate to other religions with unabashedly Christian convictions. All bring to religious dialogue certain "nonnegotiables." Finally, unlike Hick, Knitter gives considerable attention to the task of Christian mission and emphasizes the inseparability of a theology of the religions that takes seriously the religiously

34. John Hick, *God and the Universe of Faiths* (New York: St. Martin's Press, 1973), 131.

35. John Hick, "Jesus and the World Religions," in *The Myth of God Incarnate*, ed. John Hick (London: SCM, 1977).

36. Paul F. Knitter, *Jesus and the Other Names: Christian Mission and Global Responsibility* (Maryknoll, N.Y.: Orbis Books, 1996), 70.

"other" and a theology of liberation that is concerned about the suffering and oppressed "other."

Toward a Trinitarian Theology of the Religions

There is a serious omission in the usual way the debate about Christian faith and other faiths is framed — with its customary either/or choice between "exclusivism" and "pluralism." I refer to the lack of attention to the doctrine of the Trinity as the church's own hermeneutical framework for interpreting the biblical drama of salvation. An increasing number of theologians agree that "the significance of the doctrine of the Trinity for Christian theology of world religions remains vastly underdeveloped."[37] More specifically, the work of the Holy Spirit is neglected, or when it is included, it is not always related to the work of Christ. In two recent seminal studies, Jacques Dupuis, a Roman Catholic, and Mark Heim, a Protestant, contribute to the development of a trinitarian theology of world religions.[38]

Dupuis and Heim are both committed to the uniqueness of God's work of salvation in Jesus Christ. They also share the conviction that the other religions have a positive place within the providence of God. Both argue that all religious traditions must be considered in their particularity and concreteness, and consistent with this emphasis, both believe that a trinitarian understanding of God must be the centerpiece of a Christian theology of the religions.

Dupuis builds on the achievements of Vatican II, which recognized elements of truth and grace in the other religious traditions to an unprecedented degree. As we noted earlier, a major question in Roman Catholic theology of the religions after Vatican II has been whether salvation might be mediated to non-Christians through their respective religious traditions. Dupuis proposes to pursue the question further by asking: What place do the other religions have in God's overall plan of salvation? Dupuis's exploration focuses on a trinitarian doctrine of the Spirit. He contends that the Holy Spirit is active not only in the lives of individuals of other religious traditions but also in these religious traditions themselves. The Spirit of God is universally present and active, both anticipating the event of Jesus Christ and subsequently extending his salvific work beyond the church. According to Dupuis, "the Spirit spreads

---

37. Braaten, *No Other Gospel!* 7.

38. Dupuis, *Toward a Christian Theology of Religious Pluralism*; S. Mark Heim, *The Depth of the Riches: A Trinitarian Theology of Religious Ends* (Grand Rapids: Eerdmans, 2001).

throughout the world, vivifying all things."[39] This cosmic work of the Spirit is to sow the seeds of the Word in all cultures and traditions.

While emphasizing the universal work of the Spirit, Dupuis rejects any doctrine of God's saving grace that is centered on the Spirit separated from Christ. The universality of the work of the Spirit is understood as the Spirit's preceding, accompanying, and following the work of Christ. For Christian faith "the action of the Spirit and that of Jesus Christ, though distinct, are nevertheless complementary and inseparable."[40] From ancient times trinitarian doctrine has recognized this twofold activity of God by Word and Spirit. As the only Son of God, the work of Christ has saving significance for all of humanity, but according to Dupuis, the Christ-event does not "exhaust" God's saving power.[41] Dupuis therefore rejects both an abstract "pneumatocentrism" and an abstract "Christocentrism," the former separating the work of the Spirit from Christ and the latter separating the work of Christ from the Spirit. We are not to think of two independent or parallel economies of salvation. The work of Christ and the Spirit are two inseparable and complementary aspects of the one economy of salvation of the one triune God. Dupuis favors the imagery of Irenaeus: Christ and the Spirit are the "two hands" of the triune God.[42]

According to Dupuis, the trinitarian reality of God is the basis of both the actuality and the theological legitimacy of religious pluralism. In God's providence, and through the various religious traditions, all human beings tend to the ultimate goal of communion with the triune God.[43] Christ is the culminating point of the economy of salvation, but the work of the Spirit is important both in leading the world to Christ and in guiding believers into the riches of Christ.[44] While the grace of God in Jesus Christ is rightly called "constitutive" for the salvation of all, other religious traditions and their practices "can mediate secretly the grace offered by God in Jesus Christ and express the human response to God's gratuitous gift in him."[45]

Like Dupuis, Heim sees the Trinity as the key to a Christian theology of the religions. He contends that a trinitarian inclusivism is the best alternative

---

39. Dupuis, *Toward a Christian Theology of Religious Pluralism*, 243. Cf. Rahner: "Christ is present and operative in non-Christian believers and hence in non-Christian religions in and through his Spirit" (*Foundations of Christian Faith*, 316).

40. Dupuis, *Toward a Christian Theology of Religious Pluralism*, 197.

41. Dupuis, *Toward a Christian Theology of Religious Pluralism*, 83, 298.

42. Dupuis, *Toward a Christian Theology of Religious Pluralism*, 195, 300.

43. Dupuis, *Toward a Christian Theology of Religious Pluralism*, 313.

44. Dupuis, *Toward a Christian Theology of Religious Pluralism*, 300.

45. Dupuis, *Toward a Christian Theology of Religious Pluralism*, 303.

to exclusivism on the one hand and a relativistic pluralism on the other; "The Trinity is Christianity's pluralistic theology," Heim writes.[46] In Heim's reading of the Christian theological tradition, the doctrine of the Trinity has always been, at least implicitly, the larger framework for thinking about other religions, whether in terms of a general revelation through creation (focus on the Father), or a universal presence and activity of God (focus on the Spirit), or a hidden activity of the eternal Word incarnate in Jesus (focus on the Son). Heim argues that a trinitarian theology should recognize the validity of all three of these approaches.[47] A trinitarian theology of the religions upholds the Christian claim of the universal and constitutive significance of Jesus Christ for salvation. It also affirms the possibility and necessity of attending to the particularity of the religious traditions and of being able to discern the work of God in them.

According to Heim, the triune God is unfathomably rich and includes difference within the divine unity. Because of "the depth of the riches" of the triune God, religions other than Christianity may offer ways to realize a particular dimension of the life of the triune God even if they do not offer the fullness of salvation that consists in participation in the trinitarian life of communion. Heim sums up his position: "Each religion's end involves relation to a particular aspect of the triune divine life."[48] Seeing the religions in a trinitarian light, Heim can conclude that religions belong to the providential will of God. The religions offer an eternal pluralism of religious ends that befit "the depth of the riches" of the divine life, and at the same time they constitute penultimate paths to salvation in the distinctively Christian sense of communion with the triune God.

Dupuis's and Heim's proposals for a trinitarian approach to a theology of religions are still in process of development. They will satisfy neither the exclusivists nor the relativizing pluralists. But they offer a fresh route to explore in this still nascent area of theological study. They both seek to avoid a Christomonism that floats free of the doctrine of the Trinity just as they both try to avoid a vague and amorphous theocentrism. They attempt to hold fast to the concrete person and work of Jesus Christ and the particular Christian understandings of God and salvation while at the same time seeking to relate to other faith traditions with sensitivity and openness. The move toward a trinitarian theology of the religions is consistent with the emphasis placed in this book on the trinitarian understanding of God revealed in Jesus Christ by

---

46. Heim, *The Depth of the Riches*, 33.
47. Heim, *The Depth of the Riches*, 136.
48. Heim, *The Depth of the Riches*, 268.

the Holy Spirit and the understanding of salvation as the fulfillment of life in communion with God and other creatures.

Salvation in Other Religions?

The question of whether or not salvation is possible through other religions is answered with an unambiguous no by exclusivists (types 1 and 2) and an unconditional yes by pluralists like John Hick (type 7). Less clear, or perhaps more complex and nuanced answers to this question are given by inclusivists (types 3-6). Some clarifications are needed when the question of salvation in other religions is raised.

1. One needed clarification is the *meaning of the term "salvation."* In Scripture and classical Christian theology, salvation is the fulfillment of life in relationship with God and others. It includes rescue from the bondage of sin and evil, forgiveness and healing, renewal of life and reconciliation with God, with neighbors and enemies, one's self, and the natural world. Salvation is more than a return to pristine creation, more even than the reconciliation with God and our fellow creatures that is present in the life of faith, hope, and love here and now. Salvation means final fulfillment of life in perfect and everlasting communion with God and our fellow creatures.

Heim argues that the debate about salvation in other religions will not shed much light unless it is recognized that there are many different understandings of the final end of human life. Both those who deny and those who affirm salvation through other religions overlook this fact. In Heim's view, it is a mistake to assume that all religions aspire to the same end, that they all share a common understanding of salvation. He therefore speaks of "salvations" in the plural, or even more carefully, of distinct "religious ends." There are, in other words, different understandings of human destiny, different interpretations of the end for which the various religions instruct and prepare their adherents.

According to Heim, only Christianity offers salvation in the specific sense of depth of communion with God and the other creatures of God. Other religions have quite different views of the end or fulfillment of life. The ends envisioned by the different religions include moksha (Advaita Hinduism), total submission to the will of Allah (Islam), and self-emptiness (Buddhism), as well as salvation (Christianity). The distinctiveness of the Christian understanding of salvation is a corollary of the Christian trinitarian understanding of God who wills to communicate God's self to us in Christ and the Spirit. Because trinitarian faith understands the life of God as life in communion, salvation means the fulfillment of reconciliation accomplished in Christ and the everlasting communion of believers with God and others. This understanding of "salvation" is not offered by other religions. Nevertheless, Christians should recognize that it is possible for persons of other faiths to attain valuable religious ends other than the Christian end through their own religious traditions.

Heim thinks his view offers many advantages. For one, it encourages "greater clarity among Christians about the distinctive nature of salvation."[49] For another, it makes room for "the providential role for the religions in the divine plan other than or in addition to serving as channels for salvation as Christians understand it."[50] In other words, the distinctiveness of the good news of the gospel is not diminished if we acknowledge religious ends other than salvation. The distinctiveness of the gospel of salvation is highlighted rather than obscured by the recognition of a plurality of religious ends that have their own integrity and value.[51]

Heim's provocative proposal has not gone unchallenged. Dupuis charges that Heim's thesis seems to call in question God's universal will to save (1 Tim. 2:4). If we say that God wills to save some but not others, does this not divide the being and will of God? Does not God's will to save endure even when it is ignored or rejected? Would not a division within the will of God go against the grain of the biblical witness and eventually result in an unraveling of the doctrine of the Trinity? At stake for Dupuis is not only affirmation of the unified will of the triune God but also "the unity of the human race both in its origin in God from creation and its destiny in him through salvation."[52] Are not the theology of universal human dignity and universal human rights based on the assumption of a common human origin and a common human destiny?

2. A second clarification needed in discussions of the question of whether or not salvation is possible through other religions concerns the *scope of salvation.* Often the question of salvation is cast in terms of the individual and his or her ultimate happiness, as though the individual's fulfillment could be isolated from the wider scope of God's purposes for all humanity and the entire creation. When we begin with the question, "Will I be saved?" we are led next to ask, "Who else will be saved besides me?" Lesslie Newbigin rejects this starting point as a flawed way of dealing with the ques-

49. Heim, *The Depth of the Riches,* 293.

50. Mark Heim, *Salvations: Truth and Difference in Religion* (Maryknoll, N.Y.: Orbis Books, 1995), 160; Heim, *The Depth of the Riches,* 291-92.

51. Heim, *The Depth of the Riches,* 293.

52. Dupuis, *Toward a Christian Theology of Religious Pluralism,* 312.

tion of salvation. The fundamental question is not "Will I be saved?" but "How shall God be glorified? How shall God's amazing grace be known and celebrated and adored?"[53] In other words, the drama of God's work of salvation in the world includes, but is not limited to, single individuals or single nations. Asking where and how God is being glorified and what part we are to play in God's great drama of salvation are more appropriate ways of relating to people of other faiths than asking first of all who will be saved.

3. A third important clarification needed in the discussion is the distinction between the question of whether or not salvation is possible through other religions and the question of *universal salvation*. The issue of universal salvation has a long history in Christian theology. The earliest debates occurred over Origen's theory of *apokatastasis panton* (literally, "restoration of all things"). Apokatastasis is the teaching that all creatures will eventually be saved. Although the church eventually condemned Origen's teaching, some of his defenders say that he likely considered the topic of universal restoration not as a fixed dogma but as a question for exploration. In other words, he considered it a possibility to be hoped for rather than a certainty of Christian faith.

As commonly understood today, universalism is the view that God will and indeed must save all. The argument for universalism is generally advanced along two fronts. One is that God will and must save all because God is love. God cannot finally reject the creatures of God's own hand. Love seeks the good of the beloved regardless of the cost or the time involved.

The second line of argument for universalism is that given God's infinity and human finitude, it is inconceivable that God will not eventually find a way to redeem even the most wayward or resistant of creatures. Human beings have the freedom to say no to God, and God respects that freedom. But God is God and has the will and the time to prepare the way for an eventual affirmative response from all creatures, either in this life or the next.

The fact that biblical texts relevant to the theme are not easily harmonized helps to account for the long-standing disputes about universal salvation. There are biblical texts depicting a double end of the drama of salvation (e.g., Matt. 10:28; 18:8-9; 25:31-46; Luke 16:19-31), and there are biblical texts suggesting a restoration or consummation of all things (e.g., Rom. 5:18-19; 1 Cor. 15:22; Col. 1:20; Eph. 1:10). What answer one gives to the question of universal salvation depends in large part on which of these two strands of the biblical witness receives priority in one's overall interpretation of the scriptural message.

53. Lesslie Newbigin, *The Gospel in a Pluralist Society* (Grand Rapids: Eerdmans, 1989), 179.

What are the theological arguments for leaving *open* the possibility of salvation being mediated through other religions, with the understanding that such openness is not identical with a doctrine of universal*ism?*

1. Openness to God's grace in and through other religions has its basis in the *freedom of the triune God*. We cannot restrict the freedom of God to work when and where and how God pleases. An affirmation of divine freedom is not an endorsement of universalism. The arguments for the necessity of universal salvation will be unconvincing to those who affirm that the free grace of God cannot be turned into a metaphysical necessity. Salvation is and remains God's free gift. God is not obligated to save anyone or humanity as a whole. God's saving grace is not motivated by need or necessity but solely by God's good and free decision to be God for the world. A recent statement approved by the 214th General Assembly of the Presbyterian Church (USA) is carefully constructed to affirm both the uniqueness of the saving work of Jesus Christ and the freedom of God to accomplish God's purposes as God determines:

> Jesus Christ is the only Savior and Lord, and all people everywhere are called to place their faith, hope, and love in him. No one is saved by virtue of inherent goodness or admirable living, "for by grace you have been saved through faith, and this is not your own doing; it is the gift of God" (Eph. 2:8). No one is saved apart from God's gracious redemption in Jesus Christ. Yet we do not presume to limit the sovereign freedom of God our Savior, who desires everyone to be saved and to come to the knowledge of the truth (1 Tim. 2:3-4). Thus, we neither restrict the grace of God to those who profess explicit faith in Christ nor assume that all people are saved regardless of faith. Grace, love, and communion belong to God, and are not ours to determine.[54]

2. Openness to God's grace in and through other religions is rooted in *the boundless love of the triune God made known in the missions of God's Word and Spirit*. There is a "wideness" in God's mercy:[55] "When I am lifted up from the earth, I will draw all people to myself" (John 12:32). Just as we cannot place boundaries on the freedom of God, neither can we restrict the scope of God's mercy. But to allow that God's mercy through Word and Spirit encompasses the possibility of salvation in religions other than Christianity is not to say that these religions possess the power of salvation in themselves. Neither

---

54. "Hope in the Lord Jesus Christ," 2002 General Assembly, Presbyterian Church (USA).

55. Clark Pinnock, *A Wideness in God's Mercy: The Finality of Jesus Christ in a World of Religions* (Grand Rapids: Zondervan, 1992).

the Christian religion nor other religions have this power as a possession. The power resides in the grace of God embodied in Christ and made effective by the Holy Spirit. Wherever and whenever persons are reconciled with God and with their neighbors, this is an event of free grace that may make use of religious structures but is not inherent in them. We must not turn God's love and mercy into a commodity at our disposal.

3. Openness to God's grace in and through other religions is *congruent with Christian hope and prayer.* Doctrines like universal*ism* on the one hand, or "outside the church there is no salvation" on the other hand, say far more and far less than the Christian gospel authorizes us to say. They impose different kinds of necessity on God, and this must be resisted by Christian faith and theology. Although Karl Barth has sometimes been described as a universalist, he repeatedly rejected the designation. The reason Barth did so is that he refused to tie the hands of God or to make the promise of salvation into a guarantee. Barth's concern was to let God be God and to resist the temptation to imprison God in a conceptual system or a religious tradition. According to Barth, while Christians should not adopt a universalist theology, they have reason to hope and pray for the salvation of all. "The church will not then preach an apokatastasis, nor will it preach a powerless grace of Jesus Christ or a wickedness of men which is too powerful for it. But without any weakening of the contrast, and also without any arbitrary dualism, it will preach the overwhelming power of grace and the weakness of human wickedness in face of it."[56] Critics say that Barth is here attempting to walk a very narrow tightrope. This may be true, but maintaining a precarious balance may well be the difficult assignment required of sound theology in dealing with this topic.

Christians and Jews

The relationship between Christians and Jews is unique. This is not to say that Christians are to see themselves as friends of Jews but enemies of Muslims, Hindus, and Buddhists. Nor is it to say that Christians are to endorse uncritically every policy of the state of Israel, especially in relation to the Palestinian people, or baptize every alliance, particularly every military alliance, between the United States and Israel as arrangements ordained and blessed by God.[57]

56. Karl Barth, *Church Dogmatics*, 2/2: 447.

57. For a critique of the treatment of Palestinians by Israeli state power as an endangerment to the integrity of Judaism, see the works of the Jewish theologian Marc H. Ellis, the most recent being *Practicing Exile: The Religious Odyssey of an American Jew* (Minneapolis: Fortress, 2002).

It is simply to recognize that Christians and Jews share the history of God's covenant promises attested in Scripture and are part of the one people of God. The question of the relationship of Christianity and Judaism cannot be considered as simply one instance of the question of the relationship between Christianity and other religions. The church cannot be the church apart from the people of Israel; the church's very identity is bound up with the Jews as the elect people of God.

Different answers to the question of the relationship between Christians and Jews are already evident in the New Testament. But for most of its history the church has thought of itself as supplanting the people of Israel as God's elect. The church has often been seen as God's people of the new covenant that has superseded the election of Israel under the old covenant. In more severe versions of this doctrine of supersession, as it has come to be known, the church has preached and taught contempt for the Jews. According to this teaching, the Jews rejected their Messiah and the Savior of the world, were primarily responsible for his death, and have been rightly punished for their sin in their subsequent history. Examples of this teaching and its terrible consequences can readily be found in all periods of church history.

In the post-Holocaust era, many Christian churches have publicly repudiated the doctrine of contempt for the Jews and have expressed repentance for the church's attitude toward and treatment of the Jews in the past.[58] In addition to manifesting a penitent spirit, these official church pronouncements are encouraging evidence of a recovery of the recognition of the deep and inseparable relationship of Israel and the church in recent Christian theology.[59]

The classical New Testament text on the topic of Israel and the church is Romans 9–11. In this passage Paul argues that the people of Israel remain God's elect people. Far from Israel's being finally rejected by God, Gentile Christians are to understand themselves as "grafted" into the root of the tree of God's people. Paul's hope is that after his worldwide missionary activity among the Gentiles, the Jews too will acknowledge Jesus as Messiah and that

---

58. See encyclical of Pope John Paul II; 1994 ELCA Declaration to the Jewish Community repudiating the anti-Jewish views of Martin Luther and expressing repentance for Christian treatment of the Jews through the centuries; 1987 PCUSA Document on Theological Understanding of the Relationship Between Christians and Jews, expressing repentance for the church's complicity in anti-Jewish attitudes and actions and acknowledging that Jews are already in a covenantal relationship with God.

59. The literature is extensive. For brief discussions of the issues, see Jürgen Moltmann, *The Church in the Power of the Spirit* (New York: Harper & Row, 1977), 136-50; Robert W. Jenson, "Toward a Christian Theology of Israel," in *Jews and Christians: People of God*, ed. Carl E. Braaten and Robert W. Jenson (Grand Rapids: Eerdmans, 2003), 1-13.

in the end "all Israel" will be saved (11:26). As one New Testament scholar puts it, Paul sees his missionary work as a "colossal detour" in which God, far from ceasing to be faithful to Israel, intends to bring about the salvation of Jews and Gentiles.[60]

Ecclesiology and missiology today must take seriously Paul's passionate defense of the faithfulness of God to Israel and the corollary of the inseparable relationship between Israel and the church. There is one covenant of grace constituting one covenant people. Through the redemptive activity of Jesus Christ and the pouring out of God's Spirit on people of all nations and languages, the once-excluded Gentiles are now being included within the covenant people.

The indissoluble relationship of church and Israel is concretized above all in the fact that Jesus Christ was born a Jew. However scandalous the idea, "salvation is from the Jews" (John 4:22). Barth put the matter as sharply as possible: anti-Semitism is hostility to the gospel; enmity to Jews is enmity to Jesus Christ.[61]

In addition, the scriptures of Israel are also the scriptures of the church. Even if the church reads Israel's scriptures in the light of the apostolic witness to Jesus Christ, the church is bound to Israel's scriptures for the right understanding of its own identity and mission. Any church that devalues or cuts itself off from the Hebrew scriptures proves by that act that it has ceased to be the church.

Moreover, the triune God worshiped by Christians is none other than the Holy One of Israel. In worshiping the triune God, the church worships the God who established and keeps covenant with Israel. On the basis of God's work of salvation in Jesus Christ, and the outpouring of the gifts of the Spirit on people of all nations, the church does not claim to believe in another God than the Holy One of Israel but to have a fuller understanding of the one and only God.

The bond between church and Israel is also seen in their common but differentiated election and mission. The Jewish people understand their mission as being faithful to the Torah, whereby they are to become a light to all the nations. The mission of the church in the power of the Holy Spirit is to proclaim to all nations the God of Abraham, Isaac, and Jacob made known above all in Jesus Christ and his saving work.

---

60. Ernst Käsemann, "Paul and Early Catholicism," in *New Testament Questions of Today* (Philadelphia: Fortress, 1969), 241.

61. Barth, "Die Kirche und die politische Frage von heute," in *Theologische Fragen und Antworten* (Zürich: Zollikon, 1957), 85.

Finally, Israel and the church are bound together in hope. Israel still awaits the Messiah. For its part, the church awaits the new coming in glory of Jesus the crucified and risen Messiah. Thus "the mission of Christianity is to be seen as the way in which Israel pervades the world of the Gentile nations with a messianic hope for the coming God."[62] Israel's insistence that God's promises have not yet been perfectly fulfilled is a necessary reminder to the church that is repeatedly tempted to identify itself with God's coming reign. The witness of Israel is also an indispensable witness to a world in which God's name continues to be dishonored, and injustice and violence continue to mar God's creation.

Important differences between Christians and Jews on matters of faith and hope remain. Yet their continuing disagreements may be viewed as those of younger and older siblings in the same household of the gracious father (cf. Luke 15:11-32). They are called to respect the distinctive and irreplaceable witness God has given each to bear to the other and to the world. According to Barth, the appropriate witness of the church to Israel is the witness of authentic Christian life. Barth further contends that the modern ecumenical movement suffers more from the absence of Israel than from that of Rome or Moscow. We can go a step further than Barth and say that only as the church gains a proper understanding of its irrevocable bond with Israel will it be prepared for a deeper understanding of its relationship to other world religions. This is especially true of the church's relationship to Islam, which also finds its roots in the faith of Abraham.

Witness to Jesus Christ in a Religiously Pluralistic World

A Christian theology of the encounter between Christianity and the other religions will emphasize both the particularity and the universality of God's grace in Jesus Christ. Its task is to do this without falling into a narrow Christocentrism on the one hand or an abstract theocentrism on the other. A Christian theology of the religions will be deeply trinitarian.

Affirming the universality of God's grace requires an openness to the working of the Word and Spirit of God beyond the boundaries of the church. It also requires the abandonment of those understandings of the atoning work of Jesus Christ that see it as limited in its scope. God's fundamental word to the world in Jesus Christ is a resounding Yes. There is, of course, a di-

---

62. Jürgen Moltmann, *The Way of Jesus Christ: Christology in Messianic Dimensions* (San Francisco: HarperCollins, 1990), 2-3.

vine No, a divine judgment, contained within this Yes. Nevertheless, as the apostle Paul writes, all the promises of God find their Yes in Jesus Christ (2 Cor. 1:20). The free grace of God is inclusive. This is the testimony of Scripture. The life, ministry, death, and resurrection of the incarnate Word of God are characterized by a radical inclusiveness. He has table fellowship with tax collectors and sinners, befriends women, the poor, and the outcast, and finally gives his life for his enemies as well as his friends.

But affirmation of the freedom and universality of God's grace is not to be equated with an abstract universalism. To affirm God's free grace is to refuse to make God captive to some metaphysical necessity. Universal salvation is not a divine obligation. God is not a prisoner of any metaphysical scheme, including the scheme of eternal double decrees or the necessity of a universalist logic. While never arbitrary, God's grace is free; while freely given, God's grace is costly. Theology and the church have no authority either to declare that God must save all or that God can save only through the ministry and witness of the church. What the church is called to proclaim is the good news that there is no encumbrance on God's side to including all in the company of the redeemed. It is called to proclaim that all men and women are summoned to receive and rejoice in the free grace of God realized once for all in Jesus Christ.

To gather together the threads of this chapter, I offer three theses.

1. *Christians are called to relate to non-Christians in the confidence that the grace of God made known in Jesus Christ is at work by the power of God's Spirit even where it is not recognized as present.* Christians should approach non-Christians in a spirit of confidence and openness. We do not glorify Jesus Christ by slandering adherents of other religions. As Krister Stendahl writes, "We must learn to sing our song to Jesus Christ with abandon, without telling negative stories about others. For it is simply not true that our faith and our devotion would be weakened by our recognizing the insights and the beauty and the truths in other faiths."[63] The God who is supremely revealed in Jesus Christ is at work by the Spirit in all places and among all people. Trusting this is so, Christians will be willing to listen as well as to speak, recognizing that they have something to learn as well as something to teach, that they have something to receive as well as something to give. Our theologies, however excellent they may be, do not exhaust the reality of God, and our Christologies, however comprehensive and profound, do not exhaust the richness of Jesus Christ. There are riches of God's grace still to be discov-

---

63. Krister Stendahl, *Energy for Life: Reflections on the Theme, "Come, Holy Spirit — Renew the Whole Creation"* (Geneva: WCC Publications, 1990), 50.

ered. These riches are made known primarily in the ever-new proclamation of the Word, in the celebration of the sacraments, in the fellowship of believers, and in the service of the poor. But they are also made known, however secondarily, in the words and lights that Christians encounter in the witness and practice of the other religions.

2. *The encounter of Christians and non-Christians requires genuine dialogue, yet without relinquishing the responsibility to communicate the gospel as faithfully and as compellingly as possible.* Christians should speak and act in this encounter with others as committed and unashamed Christians, not pretending to be otherwise, and not seeking the presumed safety and detached objectivity of mere observers. A potential danger lurks in the call to openness in dialogue with persons of other faiths when it is undertaken by those who have largely forgotten or have become alienated from their own Christian theological heritage. As John Cobb cautions, "We may be so ready to learn from others, so ashamed of the imperialistic attitudes of our past, and so unsure of our inherited beliefs that encounter with new wisdom causes us to abandon our own inheritance."[64] That said, Christian theology in dialogue, like all Christian life, necessarily entails some risk. In dialogue, Christians make themselves vulnerable to new light, open themselves to the voice of the living Christ in unexpected places, ready for deepened perception, widened horizons, and new understandings of the depths and riches of God's love for the world in Jesus Christ.

Dialogue between Christianity and the other religions is right and necessary because a proper understanding of the biblical message demands it and the search for peace and reconciliation in the world requires it. The "finality" of Jesus Christ, therefore, should not be understood by Christian believers as meaning that they are in present possession of the full truth of Christ. Jesus Christ is far greater than any Christology. The confession of Christ must therefore be confidently expectant rather than overly defensive, prospective rather than only backward-looking. While Christians are confident that no future revelation of God will contradict what has been revealed in Jesus Christ, they readily acknowledge the incompleteness of their present knowledge of God. Now we know in part; we do not yet see God as we shall one day (1 Cor. 13:12).

3. *The interaction of Christians and non-Christians should be encouraged at the grassroots level and fostered in cooperative efforts on matters of common concern and commitment.* Even where there is an impasse on doctrinal agreement, cooperation in relation to such issues as peace among the nations, jus-

64. John Cobb, "The Religions," in *Christian Theology*, 373.

tice for all people, help for the hungry, respect for human rights, and the care of the environment is often possible. This experience of common endeavor, itself of intrinsic value, may also help Christian and non-Christian believers to understand better each other's religious faith and practice.

Thus while commitment to Jesus Christ as the definitive embodiment of God's character and purpose belongs to the nonnegotiable core of Christian faith, Christians humbly acknowledge that they are far from comprehending "the breadth and length and height and depth" of the love of God in Jesus Christ (Eph. 3:18-19). They acknowledge that God is free and cannot be imprisoned in any doctrinal systems, religious institutions, or rituals. They confess that God's Spirit is at work in the world everywhere and always. As people called to faith, love, and hope, Christians await the completion of God's purposes. In the meantime, they seek to be faithful to the light that shines in the face of Jesus Christ. They are confident that the brightness of his light increases rather than decreases as they witness to him in a pluralistic world. In this spirit, they venture to enter into sincere dialogue with people of other faiths and, wherever possible, seek to cooperate with all others in works of justice, compassion, and peace, in the expectation that in these encounters faithful followers of Christ have something to give and also something to receive.

CHAPTER 14

Christian Hope

C hristian faith is expectant faith. It eagerly awaits the completion of the creative and redemptive activity of God. In the language of Scripture and creed, Christians hope and pray for the coming of God's "kingdom" (Matt. 6:10), for "a new heaven and a new earth" (Rev. 21:1), for "the resurrection of the body and the life everlasting" (Apostles' Creed), for the "final triumph of God" over death and all the forces that resist God's will and disrupt the creation (Confession of 1967, PCUSA). Eschatology, or the doctrine of the last things, is reflection on the Christian hope for the completion of human life in perfect fellowship with God and others and for the consummation of God's purposes for all creation.

The fact that we are taking up the doctrine of hope in this final chapter should not be taken as evidence that it has less importance than doctrines discussed earlier. On the contrary, we might just as well have begun this introduction to theology with eschatology as concluded with it. Modifying Anselm's famous definition, we might have described Christian theology at the outset as "hope seeking understanding" *(spes quaerens intellectum).*[1]

Apart from hope in God, every Christian doctrine becomes distorted. A doctrine of revelation would be flawed if it did not acknowledge that we now see in a mirror dimly and not yet face to face (1 Cor. 12:12); a doctrine of the triune God would be deficient if it did not recognize that God is an inexhaustible mystery, that God's grace to us is an unfathomable gift, that we must cling to God's promise and "hope in the Lord" (Ps. 131:3) both now and in all eternity; a doctrine of creation would be incomplete if it failed to emphasize that the creation still groans for its liberation and completion (Rom.

---

1. See Jürgen Moltmann, *The Theology of Hope* (New York: Harper & Row, 1967), 33.

8:22); a doctrine of humanity would be dreary and pretentious if it were stripped of eschatology and lacked the conviction that our life is now hidden with Christ in God (Col. 3:3); a Christology would be seriously truncated if it failed to affirm that the Lord is not only the one "who is and who was" but also the one "who is to come" (Rev. 22:20); our doctrines of the church and its sacraments would be masquerades if they succumbed to ecclesiastical triumphalism, portrayed the church as owner and dispenser of God's gifts, and had little interest in the completion of God's reign of justice, freedom, and peace throughout the creation. Not only at the end but also from the very beginning, Christian faith and theology look to the coming glory of God and the fulfillment of the promise of God contained in the gospel of Jesus Christ.

The Crisis of Hope in an Age of Terrorism

The biblical witness is a book of hope. From Abraham and Sarah to the present day, the people of Israel have placed their hope in the promises of God who has entered into covenant with them. Trusting in God's faithfulness, they have hoped for the messianic reign of God, for deliverance from evil, and for God's blessing of justice and peace on all who keep God's commandments. The prophets envision a time of universal concord when the Lord shall be glorified in all the earth, when nations "shall beat their swords into plowshares, and their spears into pruning hooks" (Isa. 2:4), when justice and peace shall prevail throughout the creation.

The New Testament, too, is saturated with the spirit of expectation. Jesus proclaims in word and in deed that the reign of God is at hand (Mark 1:15). He teaches his disciples to pray, "Your kingdom come" (Matt. 6:10). In his ministry of forgiveness and healing, and above all in his resurrection from the dead, the New Testament church sees the beginning of God's victory over all the forces of sin and death in the world (1 Cor. 15:57). The early followers of the crucified and risen Lord eagerly await the final triumph of God when "death will be no more" (Rev. 21:4). They speak of God as the "God of hope" (Rom. 15:13), and their persistent prayer is "*Maranatha* — our Lord, come!" (1 Cor. 16:22), "Come, Lord Jesus" (Rev. 22:20).

However, as the church expanded, adapted to its cultural environment, and eventually became the official state religion under the Roman emperor Constantine, hope in the glorious coming of Christ and in the transformation of the world was increasingly marginalized. Ecclesiastical triumphalism replaced the passion for God's coming reign. While hope in personal survival beyond death remained, hope for the transformation of all creation waned.

331

To be sure, the embers of a greater hope continued to burn beneath the surface of established Christian doctrine and institutional church life. Hope erupted from time to time like a mighty volcano in various apocalyptic movements — the Montanists in the second century, the followers of Joachim of Fiore in the Middle Ages, the Munzerites during the sixteenth-century Reformation, the black Christian slaves in the American South.[2] But in mainstream, orthodox Christianity, the earth-shaking hope of the New Testament was largely forgotten. In its place, other kinds of hope have come to dominate both secular and religious consciousness in the modern era.[3]

1. Beginning with the Enlightenment and continuing to the early twentieth century, critics scorned the apocalyptic hope of the Bible as the product of ignorance and fear. For enlightened society, biblical eschatology was definitely out of style except as it was trimmed to the culturally acceptable form of the *liberal theory of progress.* Human history, like all of life, was a steadily upward-moving process. Education and modern science virtually guaranteed the progress of the human race.

To a considerable extent, Christian theology acquiesced in this reduction of hope to the limits of Enlightenment reason. The teachings of Jesus were seen as encouragements to humanity on its path of scientific and moral progress. Eschatology became, as Karl Barth said, a "harmless little chapter at the conclusion of Christian Dogmatics."[4]

With the rediscovery of the utter strangeness of New Testament eschatology by Johannes Weiss and Albert Schweitzer at the beginning of the twentieth century, the equation of Jesus' proclamation of the coming reign of God with the idea of progress was discredited. The rise of dialectical theology in Europe after World War I was in large part a retrieval of radical biblical eschatology. According to the early Barth, "If Christianity is not altogether thoroughgoing eschatology, there remains in it no relationship whatever with Christ."[5]

After two devastating world wars, the Holocaust, the development of nuclear weapons, the ominous signs of ecological disaster, and powerful movements of social unrest and revolution in many parts of the world, the idea of gradual but inevitable progress in history now seems pure fantasy. With the shattering of its dreams, the liberal humanism of Western society

2. See Gayraud S. Wilmore, *Last Things First* (Philadelphia: Westminster, 1982).

3. For the history of Christian eschatology in the modern period, see Gerhard Sauter, *What Dare We Hope? Reconsidering Eschatology* (Harrisburg: Trinity Press International, 1999).

4. Barth, *The Epistle to the Romans,* trans. Edwyn C. Hoskyns (London: Oxford University Press, 1933), 500.

5. Barth, *The Epistle to the Romans,* 314.

has experienced a crisis of hope. The postliberal and postmodern world is no longer confident that reason, science, and technology are unambiguously on the side of life against death or that they are able to guarantee a golden future for humanity.

2. The liberal theory of progress is not the only modern claimant to supersede the eschatological hope of the Bible. Among modern philosophies of the future, none has been more influential than *Marxist utopianism.* For a century and a half, it has offered humanity a secularized and militant version of biblical hope.

In his *Philosophy of Hope,* Ernst Bloch develops a neo-Marxist interpretation of all human experience and cultural activity as moved by a passionate hope for a future that transcends all alienation.[6] Bloch calls his philosophy of hope the legitimate heir of the revolutionary apocalyptic hope of the Bible. He has no interest in demythologizing the biblical hope in order to make it more acceptable to the bourgeois world. Instead, his aim is to release the social critique and prophetic vision conveyed in the dangerous memories and eschatological images of the Bible. The fantastic imagery of cosmic judgment and renewal is no embarrassment to Bloch as it has been so often to acculturated Christianity. In his view, such images are an appropriate language to speak of the incalculable conflict and suffering experienced in history and the radical transformation of life that is required to set things straight. For Bloch, of course, it is not God but the revolutionary proletariat who will execute the "final judgment" on capitalist oppressors and establish "the new heaven and the new earth" of socialism.

In a nuclear age, however, both official and revisionist Marxist hope, no less than the easy optimism of liberal humanism, are in crisis. After decades of Marxist police states and Stalinist concentration camps, the promise of a new humanity created through armed revolutionary struggle has become increasingly hollow. Marxist critics may still serve to awaken Christians to dimensions of the biblical hope that they are tempted to forget in affluent consumerist societies. But as dramatized by the fall of the Berlin Wall, the collapse of the Soviet Union, and the emergence of democratic states in Eastern Europe, the power of Marxist utopianism is on the decline. Many who previously held to this ideology have begun to look for a hope beyond this hope, for a fulfillment of life that Marxism has promised but has not been able to realize.

3. Today the question of what Christians dare to hope for is raised in a radically new situation. It is a situation marked by the memory of the Holocaust and other horrors of the twentieth century, the danger of chemical, bio-

---

6. Bloch, *The Philosophy of Hope,* 3 vols. (Cambridge: MIT, 1985).

logical, and nuclear warfare, the widening gap between the relatively rich and the desperately poor among and within nations, the worldwide epidemic of AIDS, and the mounting environmental crisis. For the present generation, the word "future" is not so much a fascinating as an anxiety-producing word.[7]

In recent years, fear of what the future has in store has been further deepened by acts of terrorism and counter-terrorism on an international scale. The destruction of the World Trade Center on September 11, 2001, has become an ominous symbol of a new age of "apocalyptic terror." The hopes and fears of the early twenty-first century are riveted on random, desperate acts of terrorism, often fueled by an apocalyptic interpretation of reality.[8]

An apocalyptic view of the world and the coming judgment of God is of course represented or presupposed in many biblical writings. One New Testament scholar even describes apocalyptic as "the mother of Christian theology" (Ernst Käsemann). The book of Revelation (*Apokalypsis* in Greek) in particular portrays the coming cosmic warfare between Christ and Antichrist, good and evil, in vivid apocalyptic symbols and images. Arising out of the persecution of the church at the end of the first century, the book of Revelation encourages Christians to resist the imperial Roman cult and its dehumanizing power. It offers assurance of God's coming judgment and triumph over all evil forces. For many reasons, the book of Revelation has long been a storm center of interpretation.[9] Yet while containing holy war imagery and disturbing cries for vengeance, its message is not a call to arms but a summons to non-violent resistance and readiness for martyrdom rooted in a theology of the cross and resurrection of Christ.[10]

Apocalyptic movements of the present, driven more by desperation than by hope, differ fundamentally from the hope of the New Testament. In its most virulent form, contemporary *neo-apocalypticism* weds a gruesome portrayal of final cosmic warfare with terrorist political action. It divides the world into the good and the evil, demonizes all who are considered enemies, is absolutely convinced of the righteousness of its own cause, and calls for holy warfare. Its adherents often see themselves as the agents of

---

7. See Sauter, *What Dare We Hope?* 164.

8. See Mark Juergensmeyer, *Terror in the Mind of God: The Global Rise of Religious Violence* (Berkeley: University of California Press, 2000); Robert Jay Lifton, *Destroying the World to Save It: Aum Shinrikyo, Apocalyptic Violence, and the New Global Terrorism* (New York: Henry Holt and Company, 1999).

9. Luther doubted that the book of Revelation preached Christ adequately; Calvin passed over Revelation in his otherwise complete set of commentaries on the New Testament.

10. See Adela Yarbro Collins, *Cosmology and Eschatology in Jewish and Christian Apocalypticism* (Leiden: Brill, 1996), 198-217.

God's judgment and justify their use of violence as not only condoned but commanded by God. This lethal combination can be found today in violent apocalyptic movements not only in Islam but in scattered Christian and Jewish sects as well.[11]

Apocalypticism in contemporary America takes many different forms. These range from fundamentalist sermons and books announcing the imminent end of the world to religious communities who have abandoned the world doomed to destruction and gather to await the second coming of Jesus, to violent political action groups intent on meting out God's end-time judgment. The most radical groups are convinced that murder and acts of mass destruction directed at the enemies of God have divine endorsement.[12]

Most Christian preachers and writers who interpret current events in terms of apocalyptic warfare do not directly encourage people to engage in acts of violence. They see present world events as fulfillments of biblical descriptions of the end time and as heading, by God's predetermination, toward the cataclysmic end of history. They assure true believers that they have a way of escape from the worldwide holocaust soon to come. For decades, the writings of Hal Lindsey (including *The Late Great Planet Earth*) have defined a popular form of fundamentalist Christian apocalypticism in North America. More recently, other writers have offered enormously successful fictional narratives of the "rapture" of the saints and the events that follow in end-time history (like the *Left Behind* series). The popularity of these works of Christian neo-apocalypticism, which seems to surge with every new outbreak of violence in the Middle East, raises many disturbing questions.

Given the threat of nuclear, chemical, and biological warfare, the conflicts among the nations over territory and natural resources, the spread of terrorism and wars on terrorism, and the sense of powerlessness and impending catastrophe that overwhelms many people today, it is not difficult to understand why these doomsday teachings are so influential. The failure of the theology of the mainline denominations in North America to offer alternative interpretations of the disturbing eschatological and apocalyptic themes of the Bible has helped to create a kind of theological vacuum in the popular imagination that is being filled by predictions and detailed descriptions of the imminent, violent end of the world.

11. On apocalyptic in contemporary Judaism, see Gershom Gorenberg, *The End of Days: Fundamentalism and the Struggle for the Temple Mount* (New York: Oxford University Press, 2000); for its presence in Islam, see David Cook, *Studies in Muslim Apocalyptic* (Princeton, N.J.: Darwin Press, 2002).

12. See Mark Juergensmeyer, *Terror in the Mind of God*; Charles Kimball, *When Religion Becomes Evil* (San Francisco: Harper, 2002).

What I have called neo-apocalypticism feeds on fear. It offers to allay this fear by describing the exact timetable of the awful events of the end as ordained by God and predicted by the Bible. With the reestablishment of the modern state of Israel as a base date, and drawing on a few obscure texts in Ezekiel, Daniel, 1 Thessalonians, and the book of Revelation, neo-apocalypticists identify the biblical battle of Armageddon with a coming thermonuclear holocaust. True believers will be "raptured" or caught up in the clouds to be with the Lord (1 Thess. 4:17). Rescued by Christ out of a world plunging toward destruction, they will not have to endure the terrible years of tribulation. The return of Jesus Christ and the rapture of faithful Christians from the terrible end times is, according to Lindsey, "the real hope for the Christian, the blessed hope of true believers." By God's plan, the responsibility for evangelizing the earth during those years will be assigned to 144,000 converted Jews. All this will happen, readers are warned, in their lifetime.

Despite its considerable popularity, contemporary apocalyptic literature is a serious departure from the hope based in the gospel of Jesus Christ.

a. The neo-apocalyptic way of reading Scripture is a distorted reading rather than a serious interpretation of the biblical message as a whole. The life, ministry, death, and resurrection of Christ become quite secondary to the arbitrary speculation about the final events of history. Texts are torn out of their historical context and made to fit into a schema of the interpreter's own devising.

b. The timetable for the end events is highly deterministic. The wheel of apocalyptic destiny moves on its own momentum and nothing can stop it. Missing is any call to Christians to help steer history in a direction different from the predicted universal conflagration. There is no encouragement to take some responsibility for the future of the creation. Knowing that they will be exempted from the terrors to come, believers can be mere observers of world events and calmly await their salvation.

c. The world is divided into true believers and infidels, "us" and "them." Reconciliation with the enemy, often identified with nations hostile to the United States, or with leaders and supporters of the United Nations, is impossible. The conscience of the true believers remains undisturbed. They are not called to repentance, not summoned to do justice and love mercy.

d. The real object of hope in this version of apocalyptic eschatology is the event called the rapture. After terrifying descriptions of cosmic holocaust, with seas of blood running six feet deep, believers are told, "Believe in Jesus Christ and you will be raptured. You will escape all of these horrors." Such a message is entirely lacking in a sense of solidarity with the whole creation and with all humanity groaning for emancipation from sin, suffering, and death.

e. Most conspicuous in this neo-apocalyptic depiction of the end time is the absence of a theology of the ministry, cross, and resurrection of Jesus Christ. Eschatology is torn away from the person and work of Christ. Armageddon replaces Golgotha. Faith, love, and hope are severed. The church will be safe in heaven when all hell breaks loose. Witnessing for God on the earth in the final days of cosmic war will be the task of converted Jews. One can imagine the justified sarcasm of death-camp survivors should they be asked to respond to this picture of the future: "The self-centered and complacent church never was around when helpless victims were machine-gunned, men and women gassed, the heads of children bashed in by rifle butts. So it will be no surprise when the church is absent once again in the conflicts of the days ahead. Then, as before, faithful Jews and Christians will be left alone to bear a terrible witness to God."

In contrast to the neo-apocalyptic reading of Scripture, the New Testament hope is centered not on a blessed rapture but on the coming of the crucified and resurrected Jesus and the accompanying call to faithful discipleship in the here and now. It is a hope focused on the redemptive power of God, whose judgment is real and severe but whose mercy endures forever.[13]

Principles for Interpreting Christian Hope

In view of the crisis in which human hope finds itself today, Christian theology must not default on its responsibility to "give an account" of the hope of Christians (1 Pet. 3:15). If not the liberal belief in progress, or Marxist utopianism, or the neo-apocalyptic hope of rapture amidst impending nuclear holocaust, what is the Christian hope? The answer to this question is not made easier by the often *confusing and contradictory interpretations* of Christian hope in twentieth-century biblical and theological scholarship. While the majority of biblical scholars and theologians of Christian hope would be united in their opposition to the views of naive liberalism, militant Marxism, and fundamentalist apocalypticism, their own interpretations of biblical hope are often set in opposition to each other. We can iden-

---

13. My critique of Lindsey, first presented in an unpublished lecture in 1979, was used by J. Christiaan Beker in *Paul's Apocalyptic Gospel* (Philadelphia: Fortress, 1984), 26-27. For a different critique of modern apocalypticism, see Gordon D. Kaufman, *Theology for a Nuclear Age* (Philadelphia: Westminster, 1985).

tify four pairs of opposing interpretations of eschatology in biblical and systematic theology.

a. One conflict is between futurist eschatology (Albert Schweitzer) and realized eschatology (C. H. Dodd). Is the kingdom of God proclaimed in the New Testament an already present reality, or is it still entirely in the future?

b. Another conflict is between individual eschatology (Bultmann) on the one hand and corporate eschatology (the early Moltmann, the liberation theologians) on the other. Does the kingdom of God have to do with new life for the individual, or does it concern social, economic, and political fulfillment?

c. Still another conflict takes the form of historical eschatology (modern Western theology) versus cosmic eschatology (Eastern theology, process theology). Is the kingdom of God the fulfillment of human life, or does it comprehend the whole of nature and cosmic process?

d. Finally, there is the conflict between eschatology that focuses primarily on God's activity (dialectical theology) and eschatology that concentrates primarily on human activity (Social Gospel theology, recent theologies of praxis). Is the kingdom of God solely God's work, or are human beings to take it upon themselves to build the kingdom by their own effort?

These conflicts result from one-sided interpretations of biblical eschatology. The reign of God for which Christians hope is *already* inaugurated in Jesus Christ but is *not yet* complete. It embraces personal *and* communal fulfillment. It encompasses history *and* cosmic process. It is a divine *gift* yet also *calls* humanity to partnership with God. In our context of many false hopes and widespread hopelessness, Christian hope must be expressed anew in all its fullness.

Christians hope in the final victory of the creative, self-expending, community-forming love of the triune God. Hence they hope in the triumph of the love of God over all hate, of the justice of God over all injustice, of God's freedom over all bondage, of community with God over all separation, of life with God over the power of death. Yet this hope becomes indistinguishable from cheap optimism if it fails to share the present agony of the world.

In the world as we know it, death seems to have the last word. Each human life, the whole of human history, and the entire cosmos drive inexorably toward death. The death that is at work in our own lives, in history, and in nature is far more than biological termination. It is the power of negativity and destruction that threatens the fulfillment of life created and redeemed by God. Disease, disability, alienation, injustice, oppression, war, and a host of other evils constantly remind us that "in life we are in death." Only those who take the reality of death and the grave with utter seriousness can begin to grasp the meaning of life as a sheer gift of God and the joyous hope of resurrection to new life by the grace of God.[14]

Christian hope amid the ravages of sin, evil, and death has many dimensions.[15] This must include, of course, hope for the *fulfillment of personal life*. Protestant theologians have not written much about this dimension of hope in recent decades. As their emphasis has shifted to the political dimensions of Christian hope, the question of the meaning of hope in relation to the death of individuals has been pushed to the side. Some Roman Catholic theologians (notably Karl Rahner) have developed a theology of death in which the death of each person becomes a final opportunity to freely relinquish oneself, to give oneself into the gracious hands of God in trusting self-surrender.[16] However one evaluates such a theology of death, the fact remains that theology cannot ignore the death of individuals or their hope for fullness of life. If human beings are created in the image of God, forgiven and loved by God in Christ, and through the work of the Spirit experience even now the beginnings of new life in relation to God and others, then hope of personal fulfillment is no mere relic of an antiquated piety: it is an integral part of Christian hope. The idea that personal human life is expendable and unimportant to God is alien to the biblical witness.

But Christian hope is not limited to the fulfillment of individual life. It insists that *personal and communal fulfillment are inseparable.* Christians thus work and hope for the transformation of life in community. As individuals we know that our lives are intimately intertwined with those of friends and neighbors near and far. When by grace we rise above our egocentricity, we realize that there can be no salvation for us as persons apart from the transformation of the many communities and institutions to which we belong: family, society, humanity as a whole. The expansion of Christian hope to include new life for societies and economies ruled by the power of death has been a major contribution of political and liberation theologies in our time. If our hope is in the triune God, it must necessarily be a hope not of the salvation of isolated individuals but of people in community.[17]

Christian hope also has a cosmic dimension. It *encompasses the entire*

14. For an example of Christian faith and hope in the face of death and loss, see the moving book of Nicholas Wolterstorff, *Lament for a Son* (Grand Rapids: Eerdmans, 1987).

15. See Jürgen Moltmann, *The Coming of God: Christian Eschatology* (Minneapolis: Fortress, 1996).

16. See Rahner, *On the Theology of Death* (New York: Herder & Herder, 1961).

17. See Jürgen Moltmann, *The Theology of Hope* (New York: Harper & Row, 1967); Moltmann, *The Trinity and the Kingdom* (San Francisco: Harper & Row, 1981); Gustavo Gutiérrez, *A Theology of Liberation* (Maryknoll, N.Y.: Orbis Books, 1988), 121-42.

creation. The fulfillment for which we yearn cannot be found apart from the renewal and transformation of the heaven and the earth to which we are bound in life and in death.[18] At the beginning of the twenty-first century, increasingly surrounded by an environmental wasteland, we are learning how important it is to us as individuals and as societies to be able to hope that by God's grace new blossoms may yet break forth in the desert and that life-giving waters may yet flow in the wilderness (Isa. 35:1-2, 5-7).

Christian hope in God's final triumph over sin, evil, and death is multidimensional; it is personal, corporate, and cosmic. The final victory belongs to God, not to death (1 Cor. 15). This conviction must guide any restatement of the meaning of the eschatological symbols of the Bible and the Christian creeds. As essential hermeneutical principles for interpreting Christian hope today, consider the following proposals:[19]

1. *The language of Christian hope is language stretched to the limits, language rich in symbol and image.* We should not pretend to have precise and detailed information about the future. The symbolic language of hope is to be taken seriously but not literalistically. When we speak of life beyond death, or of a resurrected body, or of a new heaven and a new earth, we speak in images, metaphors, and parables.[20] We must have the humility to recognize with Luther that "as little as children know in their mother's womb about their birth, so little do we know about life everlasting."[21]

2. *Christian hope is grounded in the resurrection of the crucified Jesus, sustained by the presence and promise of the life-giving Holy Spirit, and oriented to the glory of the triune God.* The God of Christian hope is the triune God, the creator, redeemer, and consummator. From the foundation of the world, the purpose of the triune God has been to share life with others, to create a com-

---

18. Process theologians and theologians engaged in the dialogue between science and theology have placed particular emphasis on this dimension of the Christian hope. See John B. Cobb, Jr., and David Ray Griffin, *Process Theology: An Introductory Exposition* (Philadelphia: Westminster, 1976), 111-27; John B. Cobb, Jr., *Is It Too Late? A Theology of Ecology* (Beverly Hills, Calif.: Bruce, 1972); John Polkinghorne, *The God of Hope and the End of the World* (New Haven: Yale University Press, 2002).

19. Cf. Karl Rahner, "The Hermeneutics of Eschatological Assertions," in *Theological Investigations,* vol. 4 (New York: Seabury Press, 1974), 323-46.

20. John Calvin recognized this in his sober and restrained writings on eschatology: "For though we very truly hear that the Kingdom of God will be filled with splendor, joy, happiness, and glory, yet when these things are spoken of, they remain utterly remote from our perception, and, as it were, wrapped in obscurities, until that day comes when he will reveal to us his glory, that we may behold it face to face" (*Institutes of the Christian Religion,* 3.25.10).

21. Luther, quoted by Hans Schwarz, in *Christian Dogmatics,* vol. 2, ed. Carl Braaten and Robert Jenson (Philadelphia: Fortress, 1984), 586.

munity of love in which all are united without loss of enriching differences. Through the work of Christ and by the power of the Spirit, we are invited to participate in the eternal life and glory of the triune God. As the power of self-giving, other-affirming, community-forming love, the triune God is the God whose glory is in the triumph of life over death, of justice over injustice, and of reconciliation and peace over hostility and war.

3. *Christian eschatological symbols must be interpreted non-dualistically and must be shown to encompass the quest for fulfillment and wholeness in all dimensions of life.* It is necessary to exercise a hermeneutics of suspicion and to dismantle all the harmful dualisms in the interpretation of Christian hope — between the spiritual and the physical, between personal and communal fulfillment, between hope for humanity and hope for the whole creation. The activity of God always finds its consummation in embodiment.[22]

4. *Christian eschatological symbols, rightly understood, relativize all historical and cultural achievements of humanity.* Christian hope differs from all utopianisms that eventually capitulate to the ideas that the end justifies the means and that the present must be sacrificed for the future. Authentic Christian hope will certainly stand in opposition to present injustice and to every effort to absolutize the status quo. However, in the struggle for justice, equality, and human rights, Christians will always insist on "more" — on a different, greater future than what is ever achievable by human effort and ingenuity, a hope beyond hope. Utopian hope finds in humanity itself the resources and capacities to remove all suffering, establish universal justice, and complete history. A Christian theology of hope, by contrast, knows that the fulfillment we seek is an incalculable gift of God. Consequently, Christian hope will generate criticism both of the status quo and of all absolutized programs of progress and strategies of revolution. Christian symbols of the end are symbols of total and permanent revolution.[23]

5. *Christian hope and its rich symbols are immensely evocative and give birth to creative human activity.* When properly interpreted, Christian hope in-

22. For a discussion of this thesis, see Jürgen Moltmann, *God in Creation* (San Francisco: Harper & Row, 1985), 244ff. The critique of dualism in Christian eschatology, as in other areas of Christian doctrine, has been a major emphasis of feminist theology. See Rosemary Radford Ruether, "Eschatology and Feminism," in *Lift Every Voice: Constructing Christian Theologies from the Underside,* ed. Susan Brooks Thistlethwaite and Mary Potter Engel (San Francisco: Harper & Row, 1990), 111-24.

23. During the Russian revolution of 1917, Karl Barth called attention to "the revolution of God" that sets in motion a spirit of "permanent revolution." See Paul L. Lehmann, "Karl Barth, Theologian of Permanent Revolution," *Union Seminary Quarterly Review* 28 (Fall 1972): 67-81.

cites the imagination to dream new dreams and motivates individuals and societies to fresh effort to find ways of helping to "make and keep human life human" in the world (Paul Lehmann). This may seem to contradict what I just said about the critical, relativizing function of Christian hope and eschatology. However, the point of differentiating between what only God can do and what human beings are called to do is not to minimize the importance of the latter but to free us from ultimately stultifying presumption. Christian symbols of the end do indeed speak of the coming reign of God as a gift. Yet to acknowledge the gift of grace is also to be commissioned to a task. We cannot bring in God's reign by our own efforts, but we can and should be encouraged by our hope in God to work for a world of greater justice, freedom, and peace. In brief, Christian hope enlivens rather than paralyzes human imagination and action in the direction of God's coming new heaven and new earth.[24]

Classical Symbols of Christian Hope

Eschatology has traditionally focused on four clusters of symbols of the end of history and the completion of human life. Every Christian understanding of these symbols will be guided by the history of Jesus Christ as the decisive expression of the triune God's sovereign love for the world. As I have emphasized throughout this survey of Christian doctrine, the love of God is freely shared in all eternity, is graciously extended to the world in creation and incarnation, and moves toward the consummation of all things when God will be fully glorified by a liberated and redeemed creation.

1. One cluster of Christian symbols of hope centers on the *parousia* of Christ. *Parousia* means "arrival" or "coming" and refers in the New Testament to the coming of the crucified and risen Jesus in glory. In expectation of this final coming, the church prays: "Come, Lord Jesus" (Rev. 22:20). "Without the symbol of the Second Coming, without apocalyptic," David Tracy writes, "Christianity can settle down into a religion that no longer has a profound sense of the not-yet, and thereby no longer a profound sense of God's very hiddenness in history."[25]

Hope in the parousia of Christ emphasizes, first of all, that Christian hope is hope in *someone,* not in *things* or *ideas,* however desirable and valuable they may be. Christians do not simply hope for life, joy, freedom, justice,

---

24. See Carl E. Braaten, *Eschatology and Ethics* (Minneapolis: Augsburg, 1974).

25. David Tracy, "Form and Fragment: The Recovery of the Hidden and Incomprehensible God," in *Reflections* 3 (Autumn 2000): 80.

and peace in the abstract. They do not hope simply for their individual survival or the survival of family members or their nation or the human race. Christians hope in the coming of Jesus Christ, in whom all that is good has its basis and meaning and without whom all would be empty and worthless. Christian hope is hope in Christ the coming Lord and *his* reign.

Second, hope in the parousia of Christ is not blind hope in a totally unknown future. The Christ whose arrival is awaited is the Christ who has already come. He has come in his ministry of forgiveness of sinners and healing of the sick, in his feeding of the hungry and blessing of the children, in his passion and resurrection, and in the outpouring of the Holy Spirit. He continues to come in Word and sacrament and in ever-surprising encounters of his presence among the hungry, the thirsty, the naked, and the imprisoned who cry out for help. Christians do not hope for the coming of a Lord who is now simply absent and altogether unknown. The one whose parousia is awaited is the very same one whose humble and hidden comings have awakened and continue to sustain our hope in his final coming in glory.

Third, all of our present experiences of the coming of the Lord are fragmentary and provisional. God's justice and peace are not yet realities throughout the creation. The world is not yet redeemed; God's work of salvation is still unfinished. Sin and suffering, alienation and death still mar the creation and are still all too present in the lives of believers. The final act of the drama of redemption has not been played out. So the church prays, "Your kingdom come" (Matt. 6:9), and "Come, Lord Jesus" (Rev. 22:20), and continues to eat the bread and drink the cup of the Lord's Supper "to proclaim the Lord's death until he comes" (1 Cor. 11:26).

In their hope for the final arrival of Jesus Christ and his consummated reign, Christians make no claim to know either the date or the manner of this coming. They have been told not to spend their time speculating about the timetable of the last events, but simply to keep alert (Mark 13:32-33). They are to live in the confidence that the very same crucified and risen Lord who is at the center of the church's memory and present experience of God's liberating and reconciling activity will also be at the center of the final act of the drama of redemption. Whatever the ultimate future of humanity and the cosmos may hold, God's action in the end will be fully congruent with what God has done in the history of the covenant decisively confirmed for the world in Jesus Christ. God with us in Jesus Christ is faithful and will not abandon the people of God or the whole creation. That is what the church confesses when it confesses hope in the second coming of Christ.

2. Another cluster of Christian symbols of hope centers on the "resurrection of the dead" (Nicene Creed) and the companion symbol of the "resurrec-

tion of the body" (Apostles' Creed). These symbols acquire their Christian meaning, of course, from the event of the resurrection of Christ. *Resurrection* is an apocalyptic image symbolizing the holistic and inclusive character of Christian hope. The inclusiveness of hope in resurrection has several aspects.

In the first place, the symbol of resurrection encompasses soul and body. The ancient doctrine of the immortality of the soul is, from a Christian perspective, mistaken on at least two counts.[26] The belief in the immortality of the soul posits an inherently indestructible element of human life which is separable from the mortal, corruptible body that it temporarily inhabits. Christian hope in the resurrection of the body, by contrast, does not rest on an immortality that is supposedly an inherent possession of the individual or humanity as a whole. Instead, Christians hope in the resurrection as a gift of God analogous to the sheer gift of creation at the beginning and to the undeserved and superabundant gift of forgiveness and reconciliation in Christ. Moreover, God wills to give new life to the whole person, not merely to a disembodied soul. Even if we cannot adequately conceive of a resurrection body (see 1 Cor. 15:35-44), the symbol stands as a bold and even defiant affirmation of God's total, inclusive, holistic redemption.

The second aspect of inclusive hope in the resurrection power of God is closely connected with the first. If God's promise includes the body, then it also embraces society, the body politic, and indeed the entire cosmos with which our bodies are so intimately bound up. In contrast to the individualism and anthropocentrism of the doctrine of the immortality of the soul, resurrection hope envisions not simply a future for me or my family or the human species but for the whole cosmos. Christians hope for a changed, transformed world, for a "new heaven and a new earth."

The third aspect of the inclusiveness of hope in resurrection is that it embraces those who have already died as well as those now living and those still unborn. Rightly understood, Christian hope is breathtakingly inclusive. It is not narrower but broader than secular hopes for a golden age of the future in which only those living at that time will participate.[27] There is no more emphatic expression of resistance to all the forces of disease, negativity, evil, and death in the world than the hope in God's resurrection of the dead. All the ways of God — the triune God — begin and end in deep and inclusive communion that spans all space and all time.

26. Cf. Oscar Cullmann, *Immortality of the Soul or Resurrection of the Dead?* (New York: Macmillan, 1958).

27. For a discussion of the resurrection power of God with reference to the victims of injustice, see Peter C. Hodgson, *God in History: Shapes of Freedom* (Nashville: Abingdon, 1989), 224ff.

3. The symbol of the *last judgment* is an awesome and, to many people, terrible element of Christian eschatology. They may think of the famous *Dies Irae* (day of wrath) that became a part of the Catholic mass for the dead. Or they may think of Michelangelo's somber painting of the last judgment on the wall of the Sistine Chapel, in which Christ the irate judge gestures rejection to the damned who are lying at his feet, their faces distorted with despair and their bodies mangled with pain. The martyrs of the faith who surround Christ seem to take satisfaction in the torment of the damned.

Christian hope in the last judgment must be sharply distinguished from all self-righteousness and resentment. The gospel of Jesus Christ and the motive of resentment and revenge are absolutely incompatible. The God who is decisively revealed in the cross of Christ does not exercise vindictive judgment.

In reaction to a doctrine of final judgment as divine revenge, however, liberal Protestantism too quickly dismissed the symbol of the last judgment altogether. The result was a sentimentalizing of Christian faith, hope, and love. God is indeed a "consuming fire" (Heb. 12:28-29), not a doting grandfather. But the fire of God is the fire of a loving judgment and a judging love that we know in the cross of Christ to be for our salvation rather than our destruction.

In distinction from both lurid portrayals of the last judgment in the tradition of the church on the one hand and superficial liberal dismissals of the reality of divine judgment on the other, a faithful and adequate interpretation of the symbol of the last judgment will have three primary emphases. First, we shall *all* be judged by God. Hence we must never assume, or act as if we assumed, that the sins of others will be exposed and condemned while only ours will be forgiven. We shall all have to pass through the fire of God's purifying love (cf. 1 Cor. 3:13, 15). Second, the very same Christ who was crucified and raised for us will also be our judge on the final day. We are not confronted now with a gracious, forgiving Lord but then with a vengeful, vindictive judge. Third, the criterion of judgment, now and then, is nothing other than the self-giving, other-including love of God decisively made known in Jesus Christ. We will not be judged by whether we have said, "Lord, Lord" (Matt. 7:21) or whether we have subscribed fully to certain orthodox doctrines. If we are guided by the scene of the final judgment in Matthew 25, the question we will have to answer will be something like this: In response to God's superabundant mercy to us, have we shown mercy, or only loved ourselves?[28] Orthodox belief and petty legalism are not the criteria by which human lives are finally measured. The criteria are simple trust in God's grace and joyful par-

28. See Hans Urs von Balthasar, *Credo: Meditations on the Apostles' Creed* (New York: Crossroad, 1990), 70-71.

ticipation in Christ's agapic way of life that manifests itself in often quite ordinary service of others, and especially of the poor, the sick, and the outcast.[29]

4. A final set of Christian symbols of hope centers on the promise of *eternal life in the reign of God* ("heaven") and the possibility of *eternal death* ("hell"). In considering these symbols, we are not to be preoccupied with such matters as "the furniture of heaven or the temperature of hell" (Reinhold Niebuhr). Moreover, we should note that the symbols of eternal life and eternal death are not given equal weight in the biblical witness. The coming of the reign of God is promised; the references to final destruction and hell constitute a warning that is not to be ignored.

The symbols of the consummated reign of God, or the new heaven and new earth, point to the fulfillment of reconciliation and to everlasting life in depth of fellowship with the triune God. Fulfillment of life does not mean we will become God. We are and will remain creatures. Nor will we lose our humanity and become angels. Rather, our human identity will be fulfilled in perfect communion with God and with others in God. Eternal life will be more than a return to pristine creation; it will also exceed the fragments of reconciliation we experience in the present by God's grace. Eternal life is unceasing joy in the completion of reconciled life: "the reconciliation of *all things* (Col. 1:15-20) — reconciliation between human beings and God, reconciliation among human beings themselves, internal reconciliation within human beings, and reconciliation of human beings and the nonhuman environment."[30] Eternal life is unbroken and unending communion with God, whose being is in communion. As Jonathan Edwards envisions it, heaven is "a world of love." "There in heaven this fountain of love, this eternal three in one, is set open without any obstacle to hinder access to it. There this glorious God is manifested and shines forth in full glory, in beams of love; there the fountain overflows in streams and rivers of love and delight, enough for all to drink at, and to swim in, yea, so as to overflow the world as it were with a deluge of love."[31]

When heaven is interpreted as the joy of fulfilled reconciliation and life in communion with the triune God, it is seen at once to be the consummation of both personal life and life in community. All of the biblical images of

29. These brief comments on the final judgment are developed further in my essay, "From There He Shall Come to Judge the Living and the Dead," *The Apostles' Creed*, ed. Roger Van Harn (Grand Rapids: Eerdmans, 2004).

30. Miroslav Volf, "Enter into Joy! Sin, Death, and the Life of the World to Come," in *The End of the World and the Ends of God: Science and Theology on Eschatology*, ed. John Polkinghorne and Michael Welker (Harrisburg: Trinity Press International, 2000), 275.

31. Jonathan Edwards, "Heaven Is a World of Love," in *The Works of Jonathan Edwards*, vol. 8, *Ethical Writings*, ed. Paul Ramsey (New Haven: Yale University Press, 1989), 370.

eternal life are profoundly communal — a new heaven and a new earth, a marriage banquet, a new Jerusalem coming down from heaven, a choir of countless people of every nation and language singing endless praise to God. Eternal life, then, is no infinite extension of the existence of isolated selves, no perpetuation of individualism into infinity. Eternal life means unending participation in God's eternal "blessed society" (Edwards). The social nature of humanity as created and redeemed by God finds its provisional representation in the church as the body of Christ, and will find its final fulfillment "in the sharing of life with all others who together share the life of God."[32] Life in communion is not the loss but the perfecting of personal identity in relationship with God and others: "Heaven, fellowship with the Trinity, is . . . the end for which all human beings were created."[33]

The everlasting life of God is inexhaustibly rich. The redeemed will never be sated or bored by it, never feel they have gotten to the bottom of it. The "rest" and "peace" of eternal life will not be an eternal sleep. There will be unending discovery and joy in communion. In the praise and service of the triune God there will be ever new surprises and adventures as God's gift of life and love "goes on unfolding boundlessly."[34] "The old creation," says John Polkinghorne, "is a world that contains sacraments. . . . The new creation will be wholly sacramental, for God will be 'all in all' (1 Cor. 15:28)."[35]

By contrast, hell is simply wanting to be oneself apart from God's grace and in isolation from others. Hell is that self-chosen condition in which, in opposition to God's agapic love and the call to a life of mutual friendship and service, individuals barricade themselves from others. It is the hellish weariness and boredom of a life focused entirely on itself. Hell is not an arbitrary divine punishment at the end of history. It is not the final retaliation of a vindictive deity. Hell is self-destructive resistance to the eternal love of God. It symbolizes the truth that the meaning and intention of life can be missed. Repentance is urgent. Our choices and actions are important. God ever seeks to lead us out of our hell of self-glorification and lovelessness, but neither in time nor in eternity is God's love coercive.[36]

32. Zachary Hayes, *Visions of a Future: A Study of Christian Eschatology* (Wilmington, Del.: Michael Glazier, 1989), 196.

33. Jerry L. Walls, *The Logic of Eternal Joy* (New York: Oxford University Press, 2002), 107.

34. Von Balthasar, *Credo,* 103. This is also a prominent theme of the eschatology of Jonathan Edwards.

35. John Polkinghorne, "Eschatology: Some Questions and Some Insights from Science," in *The End of the World and the Ends of God,* 40. Polkinghorne adds, "I do not believe in panentheism as a present reality, but I believe it will become an eschatological reality."

36. See Hans Küng, *Eternal Life: Life after Death as a Medical, Philosophical and Theological Problem* (New York: Doubleday Image Books, 1985), 129-42.

Will there be universal salvation? Will hell be empty? Will God's love prevail even over the most recalcitrant of creatures? This is "the most disputed question in Christian eschatology."[37] It is not a question that Christian faith and theology can answer with a presumptuous guarantee of yes or no. There are biblical passages that issue sharp warnings and suggest a double outcome of history (e.g., Matt. 24:36-42; 25:31-46), and passages that point toward the redemption of all things (e.g., 1 Cor. 15:22; Rom. 11:32). It is best, as Karl Barth has suggested, not to try to resolve this tension theoretically, but to hope and pray, on the basis of the superabounding love of God in Jesus Christ, for a redemption of the world far greater than we are prone to desire or even able to imagine.[38]

Eschatology and Ethics

The symbols of Christian hope — the coming of Christ in glory, the resurrection of the dead, the last judgment, the promise of eternal life, and the warning of eternal death — are both spiritually and ethically profound. By comparison, the hope of bourgeois Christianity is shallow and banal, and the apocalyptic terrorisms of political and religious groups on the right and the left are dehumanizing and destructive.

Unfortunately, the church has largely lost the link between Christian hope and Christian ethics, and it is a matter of urgency that this link be recovered in our time. Our hope is in God and not in our own resources, but precisely for that reason we are empowered to engage in ministries of consolation, resistance, and transformation. Rightly understood and practiced, Christian hope brings to our activities and struggles in this life the passionate expectation of all-encompassing renewal. Conversely, only in the life of discipleship is the true meaning of Christian hope grasped. This dialectical relationship of Christian hope and Christian ethics — that hope in God permeates the life of discipleship, and the life of discipleship drives us back again and again to hope in God — needs to be spelled out in greater detail.

1. *Hope empowers us to enter into solidarity with the groaning creation and to persist in the struggle for the renewal of all things.*

---

37. Jürgen Moltmann, *The Coming of God*, 237.

38. Barth, *The Humanity of God* (Richmond: John Knox Press, 1960), 61-62. Hans Urs von Balthasar takes the same position: "I would like to request that one be permitted to hope that God's redemptive work for his creation might succeed. Certainty cannot be attained, but hope can be justified." *Dare We Hope "That All Men Be Saved"?* (San Francisco: Ignatius Press, 1988), 187. Cf. Tillich, *Systematic Theology*, 3: 406-9.

Genuine Christian hope — hope in the final triumph of God, in the completion of God's redemptive work in Christ, in God's promise of resurrection — moves and empowers believers to enter into real solidarity with afflicted humanity and with the whole groaning creation. Based solely on the grace of Christ and the gift of the Holy Spirit, Christian hope liberates us for the praise and service of God in a needy world. Christian hope is not an abstract theory but a living practice. It is not an exercise in freewheeling speculation. As John Webster writes, "Christian eschatology is practical rather than speculative."[39]

Christian hope does not close our eyes to the suffering of the world. On the contrary, Christians believe that God cherishes the world, has created and redeemed it, and wills to have abiding communion with it. If we hope in fulfilled life beyond death, we cannot be indifferent to suffering life before death. As Jürgen Moltmann has put it, "those who hope in Christ can no longer put up with reality as it is, but begin to suffer under it, to contradict it. Peace with God means conflict with the world, for the goad of the promised future stabs inexorably into the flesh of every unfulfilled present."[40]

Surely one of the most pressing challenges to people inside and outside the church today is to enter into an ever-widening circle of solidarity with all who suffer.[41] We are tempted to be ethical individualists, or perhaps ethically sensitive family members, or people with a sense of solidarity with our particular class, gender, race, or nation. The Christian gospel of the self-expending, other-regarding, community-forming love of the triune God frees us to enter into solidarity with all creatures. We are thus freed by grace to become hopeful not only for a small circle of family and friends but for the whole human family, not only for the human family but for all of creation. Our hope as Christians embraces not only our present generation but generations past and those yet to come. Any society whose policies callously neglect the present needs of the poor or recklessly disregard the health and welfare of future generations is deeply anti-Christian.

In saying that Christian hope should stretch our imagination, widen our vision of salvation, and deepen our solidarity with other people and with the whole groaning creation, we are not arguing that the visions and symbols of Christian hope are to be espoused merely because they are useful to us. On

39. John Webster, *Word and Church: Essays in Christian Dogmatics* (Edinburgh: T&T Clark, 2001). Webster quotes Moltmann: a theology of hope is "a theology for combatants, not onlookers" (*The Coming of God*, 146).

40. Moltmann, *The Theology of Hope*, 21.

41. For a moving statement of this concern in strictly humanist terms, see Jonathan Schell, *The Fate of the Earth* (New York: Alfred A. Knopf, 1982).

the contrary, Christian hope is "well-founded hope."[42] Christians hold that the biblical visions of hope are not fantasies but give expression to the truth that God purposes to liberate and reconcile all creation and is faithful to that purpose. Only the truth can really free us for costly service (John 8:32). Human beings will not persist in struggling and hoping for that which they know to be merely make-believe.

At the beginning of the third millennium since the gospel of Jesus Christ was first proclaimed, the world still groans for freedom from many bondages. If we have cause to rejoice that the long cold war between East and West is over, many divisions of peoples and nations nevertheless remain. Nuclear, chemical, and biological weapons continue to proliferate. The gap between rich and poor peoples of the earth is widening. Racism and sexism persist in all parts of the globe. Our despoliation of the environment proceeds at a reckless pace. Terror and counter-terror threaten without warning to turn city buses, cafes, office buildings, churches, synagogues, and mosques into scenes of carnage.

Ethics has very much to do with how we deal with difference and otherness. In a world become a global village, a new solidarity among people of diverse races, gender, and cultures and a new sense of common destiny with all of God's creatures is needed more than ever. The Christian gospel frees us to include friends, strangers, and enemies — all the "others" — in our love, our prayer, and our hope. We are called to forgiveness, reconciliation, and unrestricted solidarity because the triune God loves in freedom, abides in communion, and wills to be glorified by the participation of all creation in God's own life of shared love.

This does not mean that Christians should see themselves as "builders of the kingdom of God on earth." Understanding the relationship of Christian hope and Christian ethics in this way is as distant from the scriptural witness as is the opposite view of a purely otherworldly hope that no longer has any interest in this world and the possibilities of its transformation. In contrast to both of these views, Christian hope encourages the search for and support of positive "indications," "intimations," or "parables" of the coming reign of God.[43] It looks for "anticipations of God's future in history" and motivates efforts to "prepare the way" for God's coming reign by speaking, praying, and working for justice for all and peace among the nations.[44]

42. See Hendrikus Berkhof, *Well-Founded Hope* (Richmond: John Knox Press, 1969).
43. See Barth, *Church Dogmatics*, 4/3.2: 937-38.
44. See Jürgen Moltmann, "The Liberation of the Future and Its Anticipations in History," in *God Will Be All in All: The Eschatology of Jürgen Moltmann*, ed. Richard Bauckham (Minneapolis: Fortress, 2001), 265-89.

2. As we wait, pray, and work for God's transformed world in which life will flourish and the forces of evil, death, and destruction will be overcome, we learn the meaning of hoping in God rather than in our own abilities and achievements.

If Christian hope cultivates a new spirit of solidarity, it is also true that the life of costly discipleship reminds us again and again that our hope is finally based on nothing else than the sovereign grace of God. All that creates, preserves, transforms, and fulfills life is by grace — that is a brief summary of Christian theology from prolegomena to eschatology.

Christians learn the meaning of hope in the grace of God only in the practices of discipleship. These practices include proclaiming and hearing the gospel, gathering around the Lord's table, and sharing with others the forgiveness, peace, reconciliation, liberation, and hope that are the gifts of God. They include gestures of friendship and peace, passing on to others the apostolic benediction of the grace of the Lord Jesus Christ, the love of God, and the communion of the Holy Spirit (2 Cor. 13:13). They include hospitality to strangers and the service of the needy. As the church waits and prays, it also acts. Christian hope, I have insisted, does not immobilize people, but makes them eager to get to work. It is not escapist hope, but creative hope. It seeks for provisional manifestations, anticipatory realizations of God's new world of justice and peace.

Yet while anticipatory signs of God's reign are to be found in every triumph over disease and suffering and in every victory for justice and peace, we are also reminded, personally and corporately, of the incompleteness of these victories. We cannot perfect the world. We are unable to heal every disease or right every wrong. We cannot raise the dead. As Edward Schillebeeckx writes, "There is human hurt for which no social or political cure exists."[45] We are a pilgrim people, and there is a "homeland," a "better country," than we presently inhabit and that our hearts seek (Heb. 11:14, 16). Therefore Christians are never to equate their efforts and achievements with what Karl Barth calls the "great hope," the "great righteousness," the "great peace," by which he means the reign of God that comes as a gift from God. Instead, Christians are to proclaim the gospel and work with imagination and energy for the realization of many "little hopes," for more justice, more peace, more compassion in our families, our communities, our churches, our nations, and our international relationships.[46] We are most loyal to the earth when our ultimate loy-

---

45. Schillebeeckx, *Jesus: An Experiment in Christology* (New York: Seabury Press, 1977), 624.

46. See Barth, *The Christian Life* (Grand Rapids: Eerdmans, 1981), 205-13, 260-71.

alty is to God alone. That is the ethical corollary of the first commandment to "have no other gods" than God (Exod. 20:1); it is also the point of the command of Jesus to "strive first for the kingdom of God and his righteousness and all these things will be given to you as well" (Matt. 6:33).

In reliance on the "God of hope" (Rom. 15:13), Christians dare to persevere in a life of service and costly discipleship when others have given up the task as hopeless. There is so much pain and suffering in the world, so much destruction and death, that we become weary and are tempted to despair. Yet hope in God sustains us. While avoiding every foolish confusion between God's coming reign and their always meager, inadequate, and flawed efforts to prepare its way, Christians are nevertheless called to struggle against apathy and resignation and to plant seeds of hope and new life that God will water and bring to fruition. The call to hope, even and especially in the darkest hour, is beautifully expressed in the statement attributed to Luther: "If I knew tomorrow that the world would end, I would still plant an apple tree today."[47]

Christian hope offers no guarantee of quick or easy success. It remembers that Christ was crucified. True hope is thus learned only as it is practiced in companionship with the crucified Christ and those whose suffering he shares.[48] Only in that location is it possible to discover that God's grace is sufficient. Only at Golgotha and in the many places of suffering in the world that remind us of the one who suffered there can we begin to repent and learn to love and to hope. In these places of darkness and pain, North American Christians might learn to ask elementary but necessary questions: Will we continue to squander our wealth on ever more sophisticated armaments instead of using it to help feed the poor and heal the sick? Will we persist in a way of life that makes it difficult or even impossible for others — the poor, the oppressed, future generations — to have enough food, sufficient supplies of energy, drinkable water, arable land? Must not Christians in more affluent countries understand their responsibility as Christian disciples today to resist the spirit of limitless consumption so widespread in North Atlantic societies? Would not the cultivation of a new Christian ascesis, a simpler way of life, be one practical expression of authentic Christian hope in our time?

This is the spirit of Christian hope: to share the gospel of God's gift of unbounded love; to struggle against the forces of violence and death; to take risks for justice, freedom, and peace for all people; to hasten and to wait (2 Pet. 3:12) for the consummation of God's purposes for the world; to resist

---

47. See Gerhard Sauter, "Our Reasons for Hope," in *The End of the World and the Ends of God,* 221.

48. See Nicholas Lash, *Theology on the Way to Emmaus* (London: SCM Press, 1986).

the temptation to fight injustice with injustice and violence with violence; to live in the confidence that nothing can ever separate us from the love of God in Christ Jesus our Lord (Rom. 8:38-39); and through it all, to discover ever new reasons to give thanks and glory to God. Because it fosters love of the enemy and help for the needy while refusing to acknowledge any human institution, movement, power, or possibility as ultimate, Christian hope time and again infuriates the Caesars of this world and confounds the ideologues of the right and the left. This strange hope in the triumph of the love of God made known in the crucified and resurrected Lord differs radically from our idolatrous hopes in the triumph of our culture or nation — or of our domesticated ideas of God and God's reign.

Christians hope in the steadfast love of God that raises the dead and brings a transformed heaven and earth filled with God's righteousness, freedom, and peace. They hope for the coming of God's glory, for the final "healing of the nations" (Rev. 22:2), for the realization of God's reign of justice and peace throughout the creation (Isa. 9:6-7), for the end of all crying and all death (Rev. 21:4), for everlasting life in God's joyful "world of love" (Edwards). They hope not only to see God but also to serve, glorify, and enjoy God forever. Christian hope is hope in a fulfillment of life beyond all that we deserve or can even imagine — hope in the consummation of life in the joyful communion of the triune God.

Thus Christian theology, like Christian faith, hope, and love, appropriately ends in doxology:

> For from God, and through God, and to God are all things.
> To God be the glory forever.
>
> (Rom. 11:36)

APPENDIX A

Natural Theology: A Dialogue

The initial division of many standard textbooks in theology goes under the name of "natural theology." While it assumes different forms, the purpose of natural theology is to establish a knowledge of God, or at least a readiness for knowledge of God, common to all people. To clarify the possibility and limits of natural theology, distinctions are sometimes made between common grace and extraordinary grace, and between general revelation and special revelation. According to natural theology, common grace and general revelation make possible a knowledge of God that is plain everywhere and always through "the things that have been made" (Rom. 1:20), and is apprehensible through human reason, conscience, and common experience. Extraordinary grace and special revelation, by contrast, refer to the unique action and self-disclosure of God in relation to the people of Israel and in the history of Jesus Christ as made known through the witness of Scripture. The expectation is that once natural theology has prepared the way, a theology based on special revelation can do its job of refining and deepening the understanding of God.

The project of natural theology has been the topic of vigorous and complex controversy for centuries both among philosophers and theologians. For our purposes, it is sufficient to identify briefly three positions taken in this controversy. (1) According to one tradition of natural theology, the existence of God can be demonstrated by reason. Shared by both Protestant and Catholic scholastic theologies, this view was made an official teaching of the Roman Catholic Church at Vatican I in 1870. (2) According to a more recent understanding of natural theology, while a strict proof of the existence of God is not possible, and while the revelation of God in Christ is normative, there is nevertheless an important religious dimension in all human experience and

354

genuine knowledge of God in all religions. Different versions of this position are held by such influential theologians as Paul Tillich, Karl Rahner, and Hans Küng. (3) According to a third view, all efforts to formulate a natural theology, old or new, are misguided; they invariably obscure the distinctiveness of God's revelation in Jesus Christ, which is the supreme norm of Christian theology and of Christian faith and life. Karl Barth, the best-known representative of this position, does not deny that there are other little lights and other good words than the great light and the decisive Word of God in Jesus Christ. But while insisting that Christians should be open to these other lights and words, Barth distinguishes this attitude from a program of natural theology.

This will do as a rough introduction to the problem. If we use our imagination, we can listen in on an agitated conversation about natural theology among the following four theologians.

Karl Barth. Barth's theology, presented in his *Church Dogmatics* (13 vols.), is rigorously Christocentric.

Paul Tillich. Tillich's magnum opus is his *Systematic Theology* (3 vols.), in which he develops a "method of correlation" between existential questions and theological answers.

Karl Rahner. Perhaps the most prolific and influential of twentieth-century Roman Catholic theologians, Rahner is the author of *Theological Investigations* (20 vols.). His method is based on transcendental philosophy and attempts to expose the dimension of mystery in all human experience.

Ecumenist. This figure represents some of the concerns of such contemporary theologians as the Roman Catholic Hans Küng *(Christianity and the World Religions)* and the Protestant John B. Cobb, Jr. *(Beyond Dialogue: Toward a Mutual Transformation of Christianity and Buddhism)*, whose goal is to foster mutual understanding and respect among the world religions.

An Unusual Meeting

BARTH: Paul Tillich, you old rascal! Imagine meeting you here. What have you been up to since we last met in Basel? I hope you have stopped all that method-of-correlation nonsense since you went to heaven. You did go to heaven, didn't you, Paul?

TILLICH: Karl, you haven't changed a bit. I see that you're still smoking that old pipe of yours as if it were your ultimate concern, and still wise-cracking your way through uncomfortable situations. Yes, I did make it to heaven, but no, I haven't stopped advocating my method of correlation. What I *have* tried to get stopped are those endless performances of *The Magic Flute* that you and Mozart keep organizing. I am not sleeping well with all the racket you make.

BARTH: Sorry about your insomnia, Paul, although as I recall you were quite a night owl on earth. But you know my weakness for Mozart's music; it is the passion of my life second only to the passion for good theology.

TILLICH: We're both passionate theologians, Karl. Do you remember the time I boxed your ears by saying that your Word of God theology was too wordy?

BARTH: Yes, and I gave you a good kick in the shins by replying that your abysmal God beyond God was an abomination. But enough of this friendly chatter. We have obviously been summoned here for some important reason, and if I'm not mistaken, we are about to be joined by our two Catholic friends, Karl Rahner and Ecumenist.

ECUMENIST: Greetings, gentlemen, and thank you all for coming. I tried to have John Calvin join us, too, but he is taking a required seminar on inclusive language and sends his regrets. Let me come directly to the point. The reason we have been brought together is that theology today seems to be afflicted by an epidemic of confusion about method. My hope is that after talking with each other a bit, we could issue an impressive consensus statement. It wouldn't take us very long, and it would be a great ecumenical event.

BARTH: Splendid idea, Ecumenist. And I have just the right strategy. Why don't I write the document while the rest of you take a little nap? Then when you wake up, you can all sign it, and we can get back to where we came from. Where did you say you came from, Paul?

RAHNER: Karl, I don't think your plan is quite what Ecumenist had in mind. You see, the chief theological confusion today is about what used to be called natural theology, about how our knowledge of mystery and transcendence which arises out of common human experience and is expressed in all the religions relates to our knowledge of God based on the particular revelation in Christ. What we would like to accomplish at this meeting is the preparation of a manifesto for a new way of viewing natural theology. We want to vindicate the value and necessity of an analysis of human existence — its possibilities, limitations, and hidden dimensions — that would be based simply on common reason and common human experience and would form an essential, if preliminary, ingredient in all theological work.

BARTH: What!? Someone please pinch me. Did I hear right? Do you honestly think I will be party to a consensus statement with you people on the reconstruction of natural theology? Haven't I made my position plain enough in a little essay titled "Nein!" and in thirteen fat volumes of the *Church Dogmatics*? And Ecumenist, shame on you! The odds at this meeting are scandalous. It's three against one.

RAHNER: Now wait a moment, Karl. We all know how absolutely opposed you are to what has been called natural theology in the past. But each of us — Paul, Ecumenist, and I — are just as opposed as you are to some of the things that have traditionally been called natural theology.

TILLICH: No doubt about it. For instance, none of us here is in the least interested in trying to rejuvenate the classical proofs of the existence of God. They are in my judgment failures as rational arguments, and theology is ill advised to try to use them today to convince people of God's existence. At the same time, however, I think these classical arguments are remarkable expressions of the *question* of God implied in human existence. "Natural theology," or as I would prefer to call it, "philosophical theology," does not give answers about God that compete with Christian revelation; it simply analyzes the existential question of God to which the Christian revelation is addressed.

RAHNER: I might add to what Paul has said that the proofs for the existence of God are really reflexive elaborations of a more basic and original knowledge. The point is that we all live surrounded by mystery. All of our knowing and doing presuppose an infinite horizon of mystery. At a primordial and preconceptual level, we human beings are oriented to the inexhaustible mystery we call God. What I call "foundational theology" — I do not use the term "natural theology" — is the attempt to clarify this primordial and universal human experience of the holy mystery called God.

ECUMENIST: All this makes good sense to me. I also refuse to practice natural theology in the traditional scholastic sense. I do not think that we can prove the existence of God by a purely rational thought sequence. On the other hand, I do not think we can limit knowledge of God to the biblical revelation. This would lead to disaster for theology and the church. I think we can and must carry on a discussion about God with everyone who is willing to listen and to speak about the matter — humanists, atheists, Marxists, and most certainly people of other religions. I think we can show that human life requires a fundamental trust in reality that is re-presented and thematized in the great religions of humanity. I don't think we are left with the unhappy alternative of *either* a purely authoritarian assertion of God *or* a purely rational proof in the sense of the old natural theology.

357

BARTH: Well, well, well. You all seem to be convinced that you are not engaged in anything so tasteless as natural theology. I do get the uneasy feeling, however, that I am standing before three wolves in sheep's clothing who are all loudly declaiming "We are not wolves." Brother Paul talks of the necessity of analyzing the questions implied in the modern human situation so that the Christian message may then be addressed to those questions. Father Karl wants to speak of a primordial experience of God that is presupposed by the special categorical knowledge of God contained in the Christian proclamation. And courageous Ecumenist — *et tu,* Ecumenist? — wants to show that all human life presupposes fundamental trust in reality, however inarticulate, and that the specifically Christian understanding of God both corrects and completes what we dimly may know of God apart from God's revelation in Jesus Christ. Do I understand you all correctly so far?

Tillich and Barth

TILLICH: Yes, I think you do. But if we are to get beyond this point in our discussion, I think it would be least confusing if the three of us, whom you have identified as crypto-natural theologians, had an opportunity to go one-on-one with you. And since I have the floor at the moment, I will begin by saying that you, Karl, are an ass.

BARTH: Paul, thank you for the delightful compliment. I take you to mean that I am like Balaam's ass — one who speaks for the Lord.

TILLICH: No, not Balaam's ass, Karl, just a plain old stubborn ass who refuses to concede the obvious. No matter how many fat volumes you write to the contrary, you simply cannot disregard the actual questions people have without ending up talking only to yourself. You cannot give people answers if they are not aware of the questions those answers are supposed to address. The only people your theology of revelation will ever speak to are those who respond to all the familiar words like Pavlov's dogs drooling every time they hear the right bells.

BARTH: You have a delightful menagerie in your imagery, Paul — asses, dogs, and who knows what else. Well, let me add another beast to your zoo — the ostrich — and ask you to get your head above the ground of being long enough to hear my position as *I* state it. I do indeed think that all Christian theology must have its center in God's self-revelation in Jesus Christ. We will, of course, have all kinds of questions when we start, continue, and end with this revelation. But we must not elevate our existential questions to systematic importance such that the revelation in Christ is allowed to speak only to these questions and only so far as it meets our prior criteria of meaningful communication. If we are attentive, open, and responsible as theologians, we will discover that revelation questions us, reformulates the questions that we may have thought were so important at the beginning. If we center on Christ, all of our questions will be included and addressed. If we insist on starting with our own urgent and often self-serving questions, we will probably end up with our own predictable and probably self-serving answers. That's not revelation.

TILLICH: What you have just described seems to me a closed circle. If you are in the circle, fine. But if you are outside the circle, the whole thing sounds like gibberish. We have to help people see that faith in God is not just the experience of a little religious clique but that all people are human insofar as they experience a "depth dimension" in life, insofar as they have some "ultimate concern." When we understand faith as ultimate concern, we break out of all closed circles.

BARTH: I am amused to be told that my theology creates a closed circle, since many of my sharpest critics charge that my understanding of the grace of God in Jesus Christ leads irresistibly toward universalism. Be that as it may, I see that you are still sawing away on that old theme of ultimate concern. You must know that I have always found your approach to faith much too general and abstract. With all these generalizations about ultimate concern, one is bound to miss the uniqueness and particularity of Christian faith in God made known in Jesus Christ as attested in Scripture.

TILLICH: But even in its uniqueness, Christian faith bears some resemblances to other faiths. There are common elements that can be discovered and that make comparison and contrast possible. In other words, there are at least some formal similarities among all world religions and quasireligions. They are all expressions of what I call ultimate concern, and they are all quests for human salvation — that is, for our human well-being as opposed to nonbeing.

BARTH: I do not deny that common features can always be seen among faiths, but this process usually results in a lot of bloodless generalities. If you want to know what Christian faith is, start with its hard particularities. Don't assume in advance that it is simply one instance of faith in general. I rather suspect, by the way, that the same procedure would also be helpful in trying to understand Islam or Hinduism. In any case, I contend that the method of concentrating on the particular event of revelation is basic for a right understanding of Christian faith. Do you recall the astonishing precision and specificity of Calvin's definition of faith: "a firm and confident knowledge of God's benevolence to us, founded on the gracious promise of Christ, illumined to our minds and sealed in our hearts by the Holy Spirit"?

TILLICH: But surely the particular knowledge of God in Christian faith presupposes some prior knowledge of God, just as surely as the New Testament proclamation of the in-breaking of God's kingdom in Jesus presupposes the Old Testament understanding of God. Do I need to remind you that Calvin did not *begin* his *Institutes* with the definition of faith you have just cited? He began with a recognition of a "seed of religion" present in every human heart. The particular presupposes the general. I can know something about baking a pie regardless of the particular pie to be baked. There are common elements: pie pan, crust, oven, and so on, and certain rules governing the process of pie-making in every case.

BARTH: Have you ever baked a pie in general? I would prefer eating an apple pie to one of your pies in general.

TILLICH: No, I haven't baked a pie in general, but I can understand something about baking pies without baking this or that particular pie.

BARTH: As you know, Paul, Christian theology has always insisted that God cannot be confined to any of our categories, and certainly not the category of pies. So let's drop the analogy. My point is simply that faith is created by and oriented to the incarnate love of God in a very particular person named Jesus of Nazareth. The particular nature of Christian faith is determined by the distinctive and unsubstitutable person who is the object of faith.

TILLICH: True enough, but why can't I make you see that we can still have some understanding of faith or ultimate concern as a possibility of human existence regardless of its concrete manifestation?

BARTH: I suspect it is because you want to talk about faith as a general human possibility, while I want to talk about revelation as a particular gift received by faith.

TILLICH: You are a victim of your own false dichotomy. Of course revelation is a gift, but a gift can be accepted or rejected. To talk about a gift rightly is to talk about the possibility of accepting or rejecting it. If faith is not an always-present human possibility, then it is something thrown at people like a stone. Some gift that is.

BARTH: There you go again, making a complete caricature of my position with your analogy of stone-throwing. I do not doubt the importance of receiving a gift, but it is sheer folly to confuse the gift with the reception. When children open their packages on Christmas morning, their attention is entirely upon the content of their gifts and not upon their remarkable capacity to receive. My concern is that we allow Christian faith to be openness to something genuinely new rather than accommodating it to our previous knowledge and experience.

TILLICH: How can we ever know anything if we do not already know something about it? There must be some basis for recognizing the new. Otherwise we couldn't even ask questions about it.

BARTH: I think that line of reasoning is suspicious. Maybe we could take a little clue from the history of science, where great discoveries have been made not when the old has been presupposed as a condition for recognizing the new but when the new has broken into all our previous assumptions and demanded a new understanding of everything we thought we were so certain of before. The coming of the genuinely new compels us to raise questions we hadn't dreamed of before. In this sense, maybe theology will win recognition as an exemplary science just to the extent that it faithfully acknowledges the utter *novum* of its object.

TILLICH: I call this breaking in of the new a *kairos*. And as you yourself have now admitted, the experience of a *kairos*, an opportune moment when the old foundations are shaken, occurs in some form or other not only in relation to Christian revelation and faith but in many spheres and dimensions of human life. Revelation indeed shakes the foundations of our knowledge and experience, but there can be no shaking if there are no foundations.

Ecumenist and Barth

ECUMENIST: I'm simply going to interrupt here. Since you two are in a rut, let me see if I can recast the issue.

BARTH: Ecumenist, my good friend and, after Pope John XXIII, my favorite Catholic theologian — do they ever greet you at the Vatican like that, Ecumenist? Before we lock horns, let me ask you a little question. Have you told Pope John Paul II that he is not infallible? Do it, Ecumenist, but do it gently. Make it easy for him; tell him Barth wasn't infallible either.

ECUMENIST: I'm glad to hear your confession of fallibility, Karl, especially since there are a lot of your followers — Barthians, we call them — who sure talk as if they were infallible.

BARTH: Ecumenist, how many times have you heard me say "I am not a Barthian"? Why just the other day, I jumped out in front of a very serious-looking Presbyterian theologian and said, "Boo! I'm not a Barthian. Why do you want to be one?" You should have seen how scared he was.

ECUMENIST: Well, let's see whether you are a Barthian or not. Do you still insist on that sharp distinction between religion and revelation? Do you still insist on seeing all human religion as the pinnacle of human arrogance and unbelief?

BARTH: The answer is yes to both questions. Revelation is God's self-manifestation and self-communication in Jesus Christ. In the light of Jesus Christ, all human religion — and I emphasize, Ecumenist, that includes also our Christian religiousness — stands under the judgment of God. We take our religion, our dogmas, our rituals, our institutions, our moralities with frightful seriousness. But invariably at work in all this is our arbitrary attempt to storm heaven, our secret urge to justify and sanctify ourselves, to strengthen our conviction that we are able to master life and to bring it to fulfillment by ourselves.

ECUMENIST: Yes, yes, we are well acquainted with your theological criticism of religion, and I will admit that the whole church is deeply indebted to you for it. You have helped to liberate the gospel from thoughtless entanglements with bourgeois Western culture and nationalistic ideologies. You have helped us — at least indirectly — to enter into conversation with humanists, atheists, and Marxists, because your insistence on theological criticism of religion recognized the element of truth in all the secular critiques. You dared to argue that the modern atheistic critique of religion is only an echo of God's far more potent criticism of it. Moreover, your criticism of the identification of Christian faith with Western culture has helped the younger churches of the world — in Asia, Africa, and South America — to claim their freedom and responsibility to interpret the Word of God in their own time and culture.

BARTH: Ecumenist, this is supposed to be a dialogue, not a testimonial. But I hear a qualification beginning to surface.

ECUMENIST: Indeed, there is. Your theological critique of religion played an important role in its time, but it was always one-sided, and its continuation today would simply be a tragedy. We find ourselves in a new situation that calls for a new kind of Christian apologetics. We need to argue for the reasonableness of faith in God, to show that our development as individuals, our confidence in the worthwhileness of life, and our sense of the importance of ethical activity all presuppose a fundamental trust in a reality beyond ourselves. Furthermore, your diatribe against religion is simply too indiscriminate and too vague to be adequate for the church in our time. We live in an age when close and frequent contact between the world religions is a fact that we can no longer ignore. Christian theology today simply cannot be done responsibly in splendid isolation from the other religions.

BARTH: Well, you know that I have nothing against fundamental trust, but surely it makes a big difference in what or whom you place this trust. If I was one-sided when I said "Nein!" to every open or covert support for the German Christians who wanted the church to place at least part of its fundamental trust in Hitler and the German Third Reich, then so be it. After the horrors of this century, anyone who talks about fundamental trust as something unambiguously good is simply naive. On the other point you mentioned, if you have read carefully what I have written on the subject of religion, you know that I have always insisted that our evaluations of the non-Christian religions must be characterized by charity and great modesty. Not because of some liberal doctrine of "tolerance" — which all too often hides an arrogant and patronizing attitude — but because of the freedom of the grace of God in Jesus Christ who has reconciled us all, in all of our religiousness.

ECUMENIST: Your reply is a good example of what I mean by the evasiveness and vagueness of your teaching on the religions. On the one hand, all religion stands under God's judgment; on the other hand, we are all, regardless of our religion, and whether we recognize it or not, already reconciled to God through the grace of Christ. This is a curiously ambiguous approach. You criticize Tillich for what you call his vague talk about faith as ultimate concern, but then you deal with the subject of religion as though Buddhism, Hinduism, Islam, and all the other religions could be lumped into a single laundry bag called religion. I see here a fatal lapse in your insistence on beginning with the particular and the concrete in our theological work. Why doesn't that hold for our understanding of the other religions as well?

BARTH: My point is simply that Christian theological reflection on world religions must always be from the standpoint of revelation in Christ, or it ceases to be Christian. There may indeed be important words and, yes, revelations that other religions have to convey to us, and we must be open to hear what they have to say that may deepen or correct our understanding of the Word of God in Jesus Christ. But as Christians we can recognize and honor the truth of these words only as they reflect some aspect of *the* Word of God. If you can speak of the religions more concretely, more discriminately than I did, by all means do so, but unless you give up your task as a Christian theologian, your study will be guided by the light of the revelation of God in Christ.

ECUMENIST: I have no quarrel with the insistence that our theological work as Christians must never dodge the normative question of truth. Nor do I contest for a moment that our conversations with people of other faiths will seek to lift up the specificity of God's self-revelation in Jesus Christ. As I have said over and again, we must always be asking what constitutes the specifically Christian, what is unique about Christian faith in relation to the other religions. But frankly, Karl, there is a chasm between us. I don't think the differences among the religions have much significance for you, and I suspect that means that religions other than Christianity have no constitutive significance for you. You never allow the religions to come into conversation with you on their own terms. Let me put it sharply. You refuse, a priori and systematically, to allow the religions not only to stand under the judgment of revelation but to be bearers of truth about God and hence also media of revelation and ways of salvation in their own right.

BARTH: Surely you don't think that I bind God's grace to the Christian church. God is freely and graciously at work everywhere in the world, including in the world of religions. But we Christians can only speak of what God is doing in the world in the light of the history of revelation and reconciliation in Jesus Christ. Otherwise, we are on the slippery slope of relativism.

ECUMENIST: I don't endorse relativism or syncretism any more than you do. I am only saying that we can learn from our encounter with the non-Christian religions as also ways of salvation, just as they will be better and richer for their encounter with an honest, open, humble, and faithful witness to Jesus Christ. I am saying that we should approach our non-Christian brothers and sisters not as though God were completely alien to them, not as though God's grace were entirely strange to them, not as though we were bringing the re-creative love of God into their lives for the very first time. Rather we should approach them as people among whom God has already been at work, both in judgment *and* in grace. This does not mean that we should abandon Christian mission; on the contrary, it means that our missionary task should be carried out in a new spirit of openness, self-criticism, and thankfulness for what is true, good, and beautiful in other religions, without compromising on our allegiance to what God has revealed in Jesus Christ.

BARTH: That's a long speech, Ecumenist. And there's much in it that I agree with. Have I not emphasized repeatedly that God has objectively reconciled the whole world in Jesus Christ? He is the way of salvation! And just for that reason the question of whether religions other than Christianity are *also* ways of salvation is a terribly misleading question, since it assumes that *Christianity* or the *Christian church* is the way of salvation. You are certainly correct in saying that we must not relate to non-Christians as though God were not already for them. Jesus Christ has died and been raised for them as well as for us. That ontological fact determines their lives no less than ours. All this talk about being "inside" or "outside" the church is very relative and never more than provisional. What we may offer, if anything, to those provisionally "outside" is the good news of their and our reconciliation in Christ.

ECUMENIST: Your position is a conundrum. On the one hand, you say that God's revelation places all religion under judgment. On the other hand, you have working for you a kind of Christocentric ontology of universal scope that declares that all people are already reconciled in Jesus Christ. If we took only the first affirmation seriously, what you call revelation in Jesus Christ would be utterly dehistoricized and would be no more closely related to historical Christianity than to any other historical phenomenon. If we took only the second affirmation seriously, we would seem to be committed to a kind of a priori universalism. What in the world *is* your theology of world religions?

BARTH: I am not sure that I have a "theology of world religions," if by that is meant some way of systematically relating Christian faith to all the other faiths of humanity by including them all under some general explanatory theory. Why can we not say *both* that every religion stands under judgment, is in need of new light and reformation, *and* that God is graciously at work long before we come on the scene to bear our witness to Jesus Christ or to enter into dialogue with people of other faiths? Let the call to mission and dialogue be motivated by joy and thanksgiving rather than by either arrogance or fear.

ECUMENIST: I honestly do not think you have shown us how to do this, Karl, and that is why I believe we are in need of a post-Barthian approach to the question of the relationship between revelation and the religions.

BARTH: Don't forget to tell them that I'm not a Barthian!

Rahner and Barth

RAHNER: I think it's time for our tête-à-tête, Karl. I hope the fact that we have the same first name is a sign of a much deeper bond between us. I have learned much from your theology.

BARTH: And I have admired your creative theological activity from afar. Your volumes of *Theological Investigations* must be almost as large now as the *Church Dogmatics*. Or have you already surpassed me? No matter, we both know now that they won't let you bring them into heaven. You have to leave them in the cloakroom.

RAHNER: Like Paul and Ecumenist, I have no zeal for the traditional natural theology. What I am concerned to show is that the holy and gracious mystery of God is present as the milieu in which we live and move and have our being. In all our striving after truth, we confront an unfathomable mystery that ever eludes us. We reach out to the future to shape it by our actions, and we are in the presence of the absolute future that we cannot control.

BARTH: I have not read your theology carefully, so pardon me if I say that it sounds to me faintly similar to what we Protestants have heard ad nauseam from the school of Schleiermacher and Bultmann. [To Ecumenist:] Why didn't you invite them?

RAHNER: I am well aware of your criticisms of anthropocentric theology, but I think that whole debate is trapped in hopeless dichotomies — nature or grace, philosophy or theology, experience or revelation. I speak of my anthropology as a Christocentric anthropology. I see human life as surrounded and moved by grace before we become conceptually clear about that grace through the decisive self-revelation of God in Jesus Christ.

BARTH: In other words, you are going to make a distinction between a universal, primordial, preconceptual knowledge of God and the particular, categorical knowledge of God mediated to us through historical revelation. I find this distinction troublesome. I think you are going to end up saying that the Christian gospel tells us what we knew deep down all along. That really worries me.

RAHNER: Perhaps you misunderstand me. I sometimes think that what I am after is not so far from your own claim that all human beings are embraced by the love of God in Jesus Christ even if they do not know it. My way of saying this is that indeed many people do not know it — conceptually, categorically, with "the top of their minds." Still, they may experience something of the holy mystery of God in everyday things and may surrender themselves to that mystery. This act of surrender is an act of faith, and I would call a person who freely surrenders herself to the holy mystery that encompasses all human life an "anonymous Christian." In other words, people may have an experience of judgment and grace even though they do not articulate this experience in terms of the knowledge of God mediated by the particular historical revelation in Christ.

BARTH: Then what you call explicit Christian faith is nothing more than the use of a definite set of religious symbols to express a universal religious experience. The churches with declining membership should really take to your idea of "anonymous Christians." It will do immediate marvels for church rolls and General Assembly reports. Just imagine one such report: 246 "confessing Christians" and, at last count, 7,259 "anonymous Christians."

RAHNER: That's a flippant response, and you know it, Karl. I could just as easily say that your theology provides an elixir for exhausted Christians and their flagging programs of evangelism: "No need to panic; everyone is already reconciled even if they don't yet know it." I am not downgrading the importance of historical revelation, the proclamation of the Word, and the celebration of the sacraments. I am saying that there is a condition of the possibility of our hearing and understanding the proclaimed Word. This possibility is itself a gift of grace. Perhaps an example of what I mean by the experience presupposed by the proclaimed Word would be helpful.

BARTH: I'm all ears.

RAHNER: Sleeping is a regular part of our everyday experience. We take it for granted. Yet it is, when we pause to think about it, an exceedingly mysterious phenomenon. Human creatures, who are so distinguished by their freedom and who engage most of their waking energy in the effort to master the world and provide security for themselves, let go of themselves in falling asleep, give up control of themselves, commit themselves to the mystery that enfolds them in sleep — a mystery that they do not understand and that they have not created. If we ponder the matter, we may see that falling asleep is an act of confidence in the reliability and goodness of a power greater than ourselves, an act of faith in and surrender to what is beyond our control. You see, we do know something about surrender and trust to a nameless mystery, and it is this primordial knowing that makes it possible for us to receive the gospel message in freedom. In faith we surrender ourselves freely into the hands of the gracious God, who is not an alien power altogether extrinsic to our being but, as you might put it, Karl, a friendly mystery at work in us.

BARTH: There is something peculiar going on here. Karl, if you are saying that in the light of the gospel, in the light of Christ's dying and rising for us and of our dying and promise of rising in him, we are liberated to see the whole range of human phenomena, including the familiar act of sleeping, in a completely new way, I agree entirely and wish you well in your further theological investigations. But I would not call this natural theology, old, new, or otherwise. I would say that what you are doing is discovering parables or analogies of the concrete grace of God in Jesus Christ in the wide field of nature, history, and human experience. Bravo, I would say to this agenda. It is precisely what I myself substituted for so-called natural theology. If we view the act of sleeping and many other events and phenomena through the spectacles of the gospel, we may arrive at your conclusions. But I'm afraid this is not what you are doing, or that it is not only what you are doing, or that neither of us is completely sure what you are doing. You seem to want to move both from revelation to experience and from experience to revelation. Can you have it both ways?

RAHNER: Why not? Are both ways not in some sense included in the reality of the Incarnation? And have you yourself not expounded at length on the two inseparable movements of the Incarnation: the movement of God from above to below and the movement of a free human being from below to above?

A Final Exchange

ECUMENIST: I'm not going to give Karl a chance to answer that question. Our time is up, and, gentlemen, we have failed to capitalize on an extraordinary ecumenical opportunity. We are obviously not going to be able to produce a consensus statement on natural theology as I had hoped. Theological students will have to continue to suffer in the present theological confusion.

TILLICH: Take heart, Ecumenist. We can each leave our own document stating our own position on the issue. I just happen to have a copy of mine in my pocket. The first sentence reads: "The purpose of every sermon is to expose the depth dimension of our life and to awaken infinite concern."

ECUMENIST: Well, I must confess that I, too, brought a document of my own along. It is entitled: "Peace on Earth and Peace among the Religions," and its central appeal to all Christians is this: in the emerging dialogue of the world religions, expect to enrich others with your faith, and expect to be enriched by theirs.

RAHNER: My definitive statement on the subject will require at least two volumes, but I do happen to have with me a draft of a new essay, "On Discerning the Presence of God in the Everyday."

BARTH: Yes, of course, I brought one, too. It begins: "Are there *parables* of the kingdom of God in nature, experience, culture, and religion? — Yes. Shall we pursue a new *natural theology*? — No." And there is only one footnote in the whole text. It reads: "Don't forget, I'm not a Barthian!"

The Resurrection: A Dialogue

N o issue has been more widely debated in modern theology than the relationship of Christian faith and history. This issue comes to a sharp focus in the various interpretations of the New Testament witness to the resurrection of Jesus of Nazareth. The affirmation that God raised the crucified
Jesus from the dead, far from being peripheral, stands at the very center of the
New Testament proclamation. Without the Easter witness, Christian faith
would either not exist at all or would be something very different — perhaps
a religious sect that recalled the tragic death of its great founder and teacher.
On this point there would be virtually universal agreement among Christian
theologians. According to Rudolf Bultmann, the New Testament documents
are so permeated with the Easter faith that all attempts to reconstruct the history behind the texts are exceedingly shaky. Karl Barth goes so far as to say
that while we might imagine a New Testament that had only the resurrection
narratives, we certainly could not imagine a New Testament without them.
Wolfhart Pannenberg and Jürgen Moltmann place the resurrection of Jesus at
the very center of their eschatological reinterpretations of Christian faith.

But while Christian theologians agree on the importance of the Easter
witness, they interpret it in very different ways. Interpretations of the resurrection are like windows through which we may gain a glimpse of the salient
features of a theology — most especially its particular understanding of the
relation of faith and historical inquiry, the authority of Scripture, the sense in
which God is said to act, and the hope Christians have for personal, political,
and cosmic renewal. We may be able to get a better sense of the possibilities

---

An earlier version of this dialogue appeared in *Theology Today* 33 (April 1976): 5-14.

and problems of different theologies of the resurrection if we are allowed to eavesdrop on an imaginary conversation among four theologians. The participants are:

Rudolf Bultmann. A noted New Testament scholar, Bultmann is best known for his program of the demythologization and existential interpretation of the New Testament. His many writings include *Theology of the New Testament* and a commentary on the Gospel of John.

Karl Barth. Introduced in Appendix A, Barth engaged in a long-term controversy with Bultmann concerning the relationship of faith and history and the proper interpretation of the New Testament. Barth contended that Bultmann dissolved Christian faith and theology into anthropology, and Bultmann charged that Barth was philosophically and hermeneutically naive.

Pannenbergian. This speaker may be considered a more or less faithful disciple of the contemporary theologian Wolfhart Pannenberg, who emphasizes the reasonableness of faith, the need for a new Christian apologetic to be developed in relation to modern science, and the inseparable link between Christian faith and the results of historical inquiry. Pannenberg's writings include *Revelation as History; Jesus — God and Man; Theology and the Philosophy of Science;* and *Anthropology in Theological Perspective.*

Moltmannian. This member of the dialogue has obviously been greatly influenced by eschatological theology, or the theology of hope, whose primary voice in recent decades has been that of Jürgen Moltmann. The position represented is also akin to many political and liberation theologies. Moltmann's writings include *Theology of Hope; The Crucified God;* and *The Trinity and the Kingdom.*

Resurrection and Historical Reason

BARTH: Have I ever told you my joke about modern theologians? Bonhoeffer is good beer; Tillich is beer; Bultmann is foam.

BULTMANN: Your attempt at humor is no more successful than your attempt to understand me. But I do share your view of Bonhoeffer. His theological sophistication was never more evident than when he called *your* theology a positivism of revelation. You throw doctrines indiscriminately at people: Virgin Birth, the Trinity, and all the rest. Then you say, in effect, "Like it or lump it."

MOLTMANNIAN: Well, now that you two have had a chance to greet each other, maybe we can get on with our conversation. Did you all see the big news in the Sunday *New York Times*? Front page story! "Archaeologists have uncovered the skeleton of a young man crucified and buried outside the walls of Jerusalem some two thousand years ago."

BULTMANN: Yes, and as might have been expected, the journalists and TV anchormen concluded their coverage with the comment: "And some people are raising the question whether this skeleton might be that of You Know Who." I must say that I feel rather fortunate that I demythologized my theology some years back.

PANNENBERGIAN: If that remark was supposed to be funny, I find your sense of humor rather tasteless. Your attitude toward history and its relation to faith is thoroughly cavalier. Just for openers, there is not a shred of evidence this skeleton might be that of Jesus of Nazareth. If anything, such an archaeological find gives support to the historicity of the gospel narratives. It shows that criminals were crucified by the Romans during the time of Jesus in precisely the manner described by the Gospels.

BULTMANN: Faith is not dependent on the results of historical inquiry, as you seem to be suggesting. Of course, faith presupposes the fact that Jesus of Nazareth really lived and died. But the Easter *kerygma* is independent of the claims and counterclaims about the historicity of the traditions of the New Testament.

Mostly Barth and Bultmann

BARTH: I suspect, Pannenbergian, that I am closer to you than to Bultmann on this issue. But let's not forget that the heart of Christian faith — that Jesus was raised from the dead by God — can neither be refuted nor supported by historical evidence of the sort you mentioned. The resurrection is an act of God, and this makes it historical in a unique sense.

PANNENBERGIAN: After that comment, I'm not so sure you *are* closer to my position than to Bultmann's. You seem to be tearing the resurrection out of history and locating it in some nebulous theological domain where God acts, a domain far removed from the nitty-gritty of actual human history. The resurrection of Jesus is a historical event. It is a public fact, if you like. If it isn't something that really took place in history, then the message of the church is a deception, and we are still in bondage to sin and death.

BARTH: I think you misunderstood what I said. My point is simply that the resurrection, while an event that really happened, is not historical in the same sense as, say, Caesar's crossing of the Rubicon, or even the crucifixion. The resurrection is a historical event in the sense that it really happened in space and time. But I should willingly concede that it is not a historical event in the sense that it can be shown to have occurred or not to have occurred by the modern historian with his critical method and assumptions. I do not subscribe to the weak-headed idea that the resurrection was merely a change of mind on the part of the disciples. The idea that nothing has happened except what modern historians by their critical procedures can establish to have happened is pure myth and deserves to be demythologized.

BULTMANN: I suppose these pontifical comments about weak-headed people and myth were spoken for my benefit, so let me try to make my position clear. I also think that the Easter faith is historical. But this does not mean that Christian faith asserts that the resurrection can be historically demonstrated, which it obviously cannot. Nor does it mean that, as Barth says, the resurrection is an event that happened in space and in time, even though historical science has no access to this event. In my judgment, this is a completely unintelligible claim. We cannot disregard what Ernst Troeltsch has taught us about the principle of analogy in modern historical reasoning without bringing Christian faith into a disastrous clash with the ethics of modern critical inquiry. It is an axiom of critical historical reason that we can understand the past only on the basis of some analogy with present knowledge and experience.

BARTH: Now who's pontificating? Your principle of analogy is going to compel you to reduce the event of the resurrection to a subjective experience of the disciples.

BULTMANN: To believe in the resurrection is not to commit oneself to unintelligible and nonsensical claims. To believe in the resurrection is to believe in the redemptive significance of the cross of Jesus for one's own life. The believer says, "When I am confronted with the message of Jesus crucified, I know that faith means radical dependence on the grace of God." To make that confession is to accept a completely new self-understanding. As a historian, I am interested in the archaeologist's discovery of a skeleton of a crucified Jew. As a Christian, I couldn't care less.

BARTH: Talk about unintelligibility! Your interpretation of the resurrection seems to me completely incoherent. What you appear to be saying is that the resurrection didn't really occur at all and that the rise of faith in the disciples and in us *is* the resurrection. You rob the Easter faith of an objective basis and put it in the category of a hallucination. Unlike you, when I say that the resurrection is an act of God, an event of revelation, I do not empty this act of its objectivity and concreteness. I do not reduce it to a mere cipher for a change of mind by the disciples.

Mostly Pannenbergian

PANNENBERGIAN: Hold on, you two. Don't you see that you are both equivocating? You both talk about the resurrection as historical in some very strange sense — an inaccessible event of revelation or new self-understanding. This is utterly out of touch with what the word "historical" ordinarily means. Thus you both end up divorcing faith from concrete history. You are both prisoners of the principle of analogy. To speak of history is to speak of the singular, the particular, the unique. The modern historian does not say: This could not have happened because it is not part of my experience. He says: What is the evidence? This is the question that in different ways both of you want to bypass.

MOLTMANNIAN: I agree with you, Pannenbergian, that the principle of analogy, as Bultmann apparently insists on using it, should not be allowed to go unquestioned. If we demand that something can be considered historically real only if it can be conformed to our present experience, history is closed a priori, and our understanding of it can never allow for the coming of the genuinely new and unexpected. I prefer to speak of the resurrection as an "event of promise," an event that makes history, that opens it up, that disturbs all our so-called established facts, and that makes us dissatisfied with the status quo of human alienation, suffering, and injustice. If this is the direction in which you are moving, Pannenbergian, then I am with you. But you seem so preoccupied with verifying the resurrection as an event of the past that I wonder if you will do justice to its future-orientation, its promissory character. I could subscribe to the idea of the "eschatological verification" of the resurrection, but I simply do not think we are now in a position to offer proof of the historicity of the resurrection witness.

PANNENBERGIAN: Then you are also engaging in a lot of woolly thinking. All of you want to claim that the Easter faith is historical, but from that point on you *all* engage in systematic ambiguity. This results in a de facto divorce of the resurrection from history. Barth says that the resurrection takes place in history, but the history it takes place in is not accessible to ordinary historical investigation. What is this suprahistory? Faith and theology are brought into total disrepute by this talk of suprahistory, *Heilsgeschichte,* and *Horse-*

geschichte. If historical evidence is not relevant to the affirmation or denial of the alleged event of Jesus' resurrection, then what we call the resurrection is no more historical than the dying and rising of the ancient Egyptian god Osiris.

MOLTMANNIAN: Your criticisms are appropriate if they are directed against Barth, but you can't seriously lay these charges against me. I am just as concerned as you are to engage in critical conversation with modern historical reason.

PANNENBERGIAN: Well, Moltmannian, even though I much prefer your description of the resurrection as an event of promise to Barth's talk of it as an event of revelation, I think your disregard of the factual evidence for the Easter faith finally puts you in the same position as Barth. I, too, have spoken of an "eschatological verification" of faith affirmations, but if this sort of language is not to remain mythological and meaningless — in short, a cop-out — we will have to engage in some hard-nosed analysis of historical reasoning. We will have to show that history is open, that the meaning of an event cannot be separated from the interpretative context in which it originally occurred, and that the full meaning of any event can finally be determined only at the end of history, when it can be seen in the context of universal history. The openness of history and of historical reason has to be shown convincingly to the modern world. Otherwise the proclamation of the resurrection will get a hearing only in the church, and Christianity will retreat more and more into a pocket of unintelligibility and irrelevance.

BULTMANN: You don't have a corner on the concern about the intelligibility of the Christian message. I have spent my entire scholarly career on the issue of faith and understanding.

PANNENBERGIAN: Sure you have, but you say in effect that the resurrection was not something that happened *to Jesus* but is something that happens *in us*. We understand ourselves anew as we discover the redemptive meaning of the cross of Jesus for us. Well, read the New Testament accounts. If they say anything at all, they say that the resurrection was something that happened first to Jesus and was subsequently made known or revealed to the disciples. So you see, I find myself disagreeing with all of you. You all disengage the resurrection from the domain of public history, the history that we live, the history that critical historians deal with. Whether you locate the resurrection in some suprahistorical sphere and call it "event of revelation" or "event of promise" or place it in some existential domain and call it a "new self-understanding" really makes little difference. There's more than a touch of Docetism in all of your positions.

BARTH: I do hope that this discussion isn't going to degenerate into a name-throwing contest, though I've got a pretty good arsenal if you want to try me out. Let's get one point straight: *I* did not say that the resurrection takes place in some suprahistorical sphere. Those are your words, Pannenbergian, and they do not represent my position. What I did say was that the resurrection of Jesus took place in space and time and in this sense is like every other event. In addition, I said that there could be no historical demonstration that this event occurred in space and time, at least short of the conclusive and universal revelation of Jesus' lordship at the parousia. The Easter faith of the disciples was not a conclusion reached by reasoning from facts on which everyone could agree. The resurrection really happened, but *that* it happened was revealed. Jesus himself appeared to the disciples. This act of his appearance is quite beyond modern historical inquiry and its procedures of proof.

PANNENBERGIAN: But that is what I emphatically reject. You are splitting apart revelation and reason, faith and history. Of course the historian cannot *demonstrate* that the resurrection occurred in the same way that the chemist can demonstrate that water is composed of two parts hydrogen and one part oxygen. You are assuming a positivistic notion of historical knowledge that has long been abandoned by most historians. The historian does not provide conclusive demonstrations in this positivistic sense. I have said that each historical event can be fully known only at the end of history, and this obviously precludes the positivistic model of what is involved in historical interpretation. Still, we are not excused from the task of offering the most reasonable interpretation of the evidence at hand. We make inferences on the basis of available evidence. We then make informed judgments that we are prepared to support with arguments. Historical judgments cannot be arbitrary and capricious; they must be reasonable and arguable. When we say "Jesus is risen," we are making a truth claim. We are advancing a claim to the historicity of this event. We are claiming that the judgment that this event took place in space and time is the most reasonable historical explanation of the evidence, and we must remain open to correction on the basis of additional evidence or more convincing interpretations of the evidence. The apostle Paul, at least, was not squeamish about citing eyewitnesses to the resurrection to support the claims of faith.

BULTMANN: You know, of course, that I think Paul undercut his message with that list of eyewitnesses to the risen Jesus in 1 Corinthians 15. As for the traditions of the empty tomb, they are clearly later legendary accretions.

PANNENBERGIAN: I am not arguing that we have to accept all the New Testament traditions uncritically. Of course, the tradition of Easter faith underwent a development and some legendary additions were made. But we will only understand the meaning of the claim "Jesus is risen" as we enter into the horizon of interpretation of the early Christian community instead of prematurely judging that *this* can't happen or *that* is simply impossible. We won't even know what in the world we are talking about when we use the word "resurrection" until we grasp what meaning it had in the context of Jewish and Christian apocalyptic. For apocalyptic all of history is oriented toward the eschatological future of God. The early disciples believed that the resurrection of Jesus signaled and anticipated the general resurrection and final judgment toward which universal history moves. Neither for New Testament believers nor for us can affirmation of the resurrection of Jesus be separated from one's understanding of the whole of reality. My main point is that we have to be reasonable, rather than irrational, in our effort to communicate the faith to the modern mentality. Unless we are able to offer reasons for our belief in the resurrection of Jesus, as the early church itself tried to do, we render Christian faith completely arbitrary and authoritarian. We evacuate the Easter message of all intelligibility and truth claim.

BULTMANN: Now listen, Pannenbergian, your position strikes me as fantastically naive and presumptuous. You take upon yourself the task of telling historians how to do their job. I am not sure you really appreciate the critical rigor of historical investigation. You speak of historians as if they could never pose a threat to the historicity of the biblical narratives. Critical historians interrogate their sources like a prosecuting attorney interrogates a witness in a courtroom. They say, "This is what we are told happened. But did it really happen that way, or at all?" And historians carry out this inquiry on the basis of presuppositions rooted in common human experience.

PANNENBERGIAN: "Common human experience" is a pretty vague notion.

BULTMANN: Is it? I don't accept as historical fact reports of a person walking on water, because this completely contravenes our present knowledge and experience of reality. Suppose someone who tried to assassinate the President of the United States were brought to trial and said to the court: "I didn't fire the gun at the President. It was an 'act of God.' The Holy Spirit pulled the trigger." What would you do, Pannenbergian? Would you say: "Let's look at the evidence. Check the FBI files and see what we have on this Holy Spirit character." My point is that we often argue from the analogy of common experience.

This is why I simply can't see how a resurrection from the dead could function as an historical explanation.

PANNENBERGIAN: That's because you have an incredibly narrow idea of what historians do. History is precisely the arena of the unique, the singular, the once-for-all. There are no a priori laws of history that can be used to answer historical questions or exclude certain possibilities without first looking at the evidence. The resurrection of Christ from the dead cannot be called unhistorical simply because it violates some general law like "resurrections from the dead don't happen."

BARTH: Well, I certainly agree with that. Bultmann has always seemed to me to take his radical skepticism much too seriously. But I must say, Pannenbergian, that what bothers me about your line of argument is that you seem to make faith dependent on the conclusions of historical-critical reason. Your approach seems to be: first knowledge, then faith. As you know, I simply reject this as the proper method of theological inquiry. *Fides quaerens intellectum,* "faith seeking understanding" — this is the right procedure for theology. Otherwise faith ceases to be faith and becomes the conclusion of a historical or metaphysical argument. We simply have to begin with the reality of the resurrection of Jesus. We do not establish the truth of the risen Lord; his truth establishes us as forgiven and liberated persons.

Mostly Moltmannian

MOLTMANNIAN: OK, Barth, we have heard this line from you before, and up to a certain point it makes sense. But I think that Pannenbergian has grasped something about the resurrection that is missing in your theology of revelation, and that is the proleptic, anticipatory, promissory nature of this event. If we are rightly oriented to the resurrection of Christ, we should not be facing the past but should be moving into the future of righteousness, peace, and new life promised by God in this event of the raising of the one who was crucified. The resurrection is the ground of Christian hope and the basis of the commission of the church. If we really believe in the resurrection of Jesus, this will manifest itself in our being a pilgrim people, an exodus community, a people called to take part in the struggle against injustice and for the liberation and transformation of all things from the chains of the law and of death.

PANNENBERGIAN: Since I interpret the resurrection as a proleptic event as you also seem to want to do, I am not sure what you find objectionable in my approach.

The Resurrection: A Dialogue

MOLTMANNIAN: I am afraid that your preoccupation with a new interpretation of history and historical reason means a loss of the sense of liberation for service that is inextricably connected with the apprehension of the resurrection in the New Testament church. If I may baptize a saying of Marx, the real task of theology is not to provide a new interpretation of the world but to take part in its transformation. The proclamation of the resurrection of the *crucified* Jesus does more than create anticipation; it sets us in contradiction to present injustice.

BULTMANN: Well, without trying to baptize Marx, let me say that I too want to talk about freedom from the past, openness to the future, and the transformation of life by the gospel of the crucifixion and resurrection of Jesus. This is precisely why I find the abstract way in which all of you speak of this message to be completely sterile and boring. You are so anxious about preserving its "objectivity." Barth wants to make sure that we remember to say that it happened in space and time. But he doesn't feel compelled to give any support to this statement. It just hangs in mid-air, and believing in the resurrection of Jesus comes to involve assenting to some unintelligible claim. This is dishonest. I don't think that Christian faith is this sort of sacrifice of moral and intellectual integrity. So, perhaps surprisingly, I have considerable admiration for Pannenbergian's refusal to allow faith to be equated with intellectual irresponsibility. The problem is that he ends up identifying faith with assent to objective historical statements. The New Testament has a different texture. It is a summons to you and to me to accept the crucified Jesus as God's redemptive act for us, a summons to us to say, Yes, God's presence in the world is realized in the paradoxical form of the crucified one — a summons therefore to live entirely in dependence upon God's forgiveness. This involves dying to my old anxious and grasping self and allowing God alone to be my future and my hope.

MOLTMANNIAN: *My* future and *my* hope! That's just the problem with your interpretation of the Easter message, Bultmann. You individualize and privatize the message. Sure, you talk about transformation and new life. But what you mean is transformation of *my* consciousness. You have split self and world apart. I don't think the early church did that. When they proclaimed the resurrection of Jesus from the dead, they understood this to be the beginning of *world* transformation. I appreciate your criticism of a false kind of objectivism and an anxious searching after proofs and demonstrations in theology. But your interpretation of transformation is much too narrow, too provincial, too individualistic. To believe in the resurrection of the crucified is not just to have a new *self*-understanding. It is to understand and relate to

God differently. It is to understand and act in the social and political *world* differently. It is to believe in the faithfulness of God in the face of personal and political structures of death. The confession that the crucified one has been raised always has been and continues to be the expression of a subversive faith with revolutionary implications for our social-political as well as personal spheres of life.

PANNENBERGIAN: Well, Moltmannian, I am certainly impressed by the way you have demolished Bultmann, and of course I agree with much of what you have said. I am interested in a public theology with all its attendant difficulties rather than a theology that simply caresses the convictions of an insulated community. But, Moltmannian, you're evading the real issue of this conversation. We're talking about the historicity of the resurrection of Jesus. Stop trying to play the role of junior social prophet and recognize that the real task of theology is to provide a responsible account of the claims of Christian faith.

BARTH: The real question is what theological responsibility means. When you say responsible, Pannenbergian, I think you mean engaging in apologetics, vindicating Christian truth claims before the bar of reason. However aggressive it may seem, apologetics is always theology that has lost its nerve. Real theological responsibility means being responsive to the one concrete and living center of the biblical witness, Jesus Christ, the crucified and risen Lord. Bultmann says that I have no support for the claim I make that the resurrection is an event in space and time. The New Testament texts are my support! Surely they present the resurrection as an event in space and time, as a real happening to which the disciples responded.

BULTMANN: But the texts need to be interpreted! Your simple appeal to the fact that the texts say so would land us in biblicism and fundamentalism.

BARTH: That was a low blow. You know full well that I am no fundamentalist. I fought that mentality for forty years. Of course the texts need to be interpreted. But if you think you can skirt around the claim that the resurrection was an objective event, an event that happened in space and time, you are not interpreting the texts: you are manipulating them to say what you want them to say.

BULTMANN: I see that the elderly Barth still possesses a volatile temper.

BARTH: You bet I do, particularly when there is as much at stake as there is here. We're arguing about the heart of the gospel. You say that the message of the resurrection challenges people to understand themselves anew in the light of the saving significance of the cross. And I say that this will not do. The New

Testament speaks of a second and victorious act of God beyond the cross of Jesus. You make the apostolic message a mere summons to realize what has become possible because of the cross. And I say that the apostolic message proclaims not the *possibility* of new life but the *realization* of new life in Jesus the risen Lord. The new world of God created in the resurrection of Christ is objectively true, even if only believers acknowledge it subjectively as true.

PANNENBERGIAN: The way you two knock your heads together amuses me. You have so many things in common: a positivistic notion of historical inquiry, a fear of engaging in apologetics vigorously and unashamedly, a suspicion of every attempt to provide reason and evidence for the claims of faith, and, naturally resulting from all this, a curious ambiguity about the sense in which the resurrection can be said to be a historical event. You know, when I read the New Testament accounts of the resurrection, I don't get the impression, as Bultmann does, that the biblical witnesses thought that the desire for evidence of the resurrection was illegitimate. When you disparage such evidence, you make faith in Jesus and his claims for himself completely arbitrary and authoritarian. The resurrection is God's vindication of Jesus' claims to authority. It is God's certification that Jesus was who he said he was. It is that event in history that proleptically realizes the goal of history.

MOLTMANNIAN: In my judgment, Pannenbergian, we must emphasize that the resurrection of Jesus is *God's* vindication, *God's* proof, *God's* promise. Otherwise we will be pursuing a theology of glory separated from a theology of the cross. In my view, it is really the identity of God that is the basic issue of the resurrection narratives. Who is the God made known in the raising of the crucified Jesus? The God present in the cross and resurrection of Jesus is the triune God. To speak of God as triune is to say that the event of cross and resurrection defines God as the Father who in love surrenders the Son, as the Son who in love is obedient to the Father's will, and as the Spirit of love who holds Father and Son in communion in their greatest distance from each other and who opens this communion to the world. On the cross God takes suffering and death into the divine life for the sake of the salvation of the world. In the resurrection the joy of God's final victory over evil is promised.

PANNENBERGIAN: You are surely aware that my theology of the resurrection is also eschatologically oriented and that I am as thoroughly trinitarian in my theology as you try to be in yours. So I still don't see what you find so objectionable in my theological work.

MOLTMANNIAN: I suspect that it has to do with the lack of attention to the significance of the cross in your theology and to the consistently conservative political implications that you draw from your interpretation of the biblical witness. As I understand the gospel message, to know this God of cross and resurrection is to take part in the suffering and joy of the history of divine love that wants to transform all things. We continue to live in the brokenness and incompleteness of history under the signature of the cross. The cries of the oppressed and the groaning of creation have not ceased. Authentic Easter faith manifests itself, therefore, not in impressive intellectual or historical proofs but in the spirit of sacrifice and service that comes from God's own history of suffering, liberating, and reconciling love for the world. I see you, Pannenbergian, as advancing a theology of the resurrection that is continually tempted to become a theology of glory. My theology of the resurrection tries to avoid this by consistently emphasizing that God raised the *crucified* Jesus from the dead and calls us to solidarity with the victims of history in the hope of the renewal of all things.

Summations

BARTH: Since that last speech is probably going to require an interpretation as long as my *Church Dogmatics,* we had better call it a day. But before we do, I want to challenge each of you to say on what text you would preach your next Easter sermon. I have always believed that theology is for the sake of better, more faithful preaching. So what I am asking is this: How would our interpretations of the resurrection work themselves out in our Easter sermons? For my part, I would like to preach on the text in which the angel announces to the disciples at the tomb, "He has risen. He is not here" (Mark 16:6). I think I would emphasize that an angel brought this message, that it was revelation, and that above all else it was good and joyful news.

BULTMANN: I have always been especially attached to the Gospel of John. I think I would preach on the word of the risen Lord to Thomas: "Have you believed because you have seen me? Blessed are those who have not seen and yet believe" (John 20:29). In light of our previous discussion, I think my emphasis in this sermon would be pretty self-evident. Easter faith is an existential response to the scandal of the cross; it is not a matter of being a privileged eyewitness of a spectacular event in history called the resurrection.

PANNENBERGIAN: I would want to preach a sermon emphasizing the centrality of the fact of the resurrection for our faith. A good text would be the Pauline claim: "If there is no resurrection of the dead, then Christ has not been raised; if Christ has not been raised, then our preaching is in vain and your faith is in vain" (1 Cor. 15:13-14). I would try to bring out both sides of Paul's argument: that the intelligibility of the resurrection of Christ depends on an understanding of reality as radically open to the new, and that the actuality of the resurrection is the basis of the Christian interpretation of reality and of the whole of Christian faith and life.

MOLTMANNIAN: My choice for an Easter text is perhaps a little unexpected, but that is surely appropriate for the subject matter. I would preach on the text from the Apocalypse: "Behold I make all things new" (Rev. 21:5). I would emphasize that only the church that risks itself in the service of the crucified and risen Christ, attending to the pain and suffering of the world, will hear that word of promise.

Political Theology: A Dialogue

The relationship between Christian faith and current struggles for justice, freedom, and peace has become one of the central issues in theology to-day. In recent decades, Christians have not only been involved but have of-fered theological justifications for their involvement in the civil rights move-ment, the black liberation struggle in the United States, the women's liberation movement, the struggle against apartheid in South Africa, the praxis of solidarity with the poor and the formation of Christian base com-munities in Latin America, the protest against totalitarian rule and oppres-sion in Poland, Haiti, and the Philippines, the worldwide opposition to the nuclear arms race, resistance to American military intervention in the 1960s in Vietnam and in the 1980s in Central America, participation in the sanctu-ary movement — the list could be extended almost indefinitely.

Some critics have condemned such activity as a damaging politicization of the church that has diverted it from its true mission. However, for most Christians it has become increasingly clear that the real issue is not *whether* there is an inseparable link between faith and political practice but *how* this link is to be understood. What follows is an imaginary exchange among sev-eral political theologians who seek to clarify their positions on this issue. The participants are:

Karl Barth. Since he has been introduced in the preceding two appendi-ces, it is sufficient to say here that he was a leader of the German Confessing Church in its resistance to Nazism, that his early participation in the socialist movement has become a focal point in some recent interpretations of his the-ology, and that he wrote a number of occasional essays on theology and polit-ical issues, some of which are collected in *Community, State and Church* and *Against the Stream.*

Reinhold Niebuhr. Far and away the most influential American ethicist and political theologian of the twentieth century, Niebuhr addressed national and international issues with prophetic insight and analytical power for four decades. Among his many writings are *Moral Man and Immoral Society, The Nature and Destiny of Man, The Irony of American History,* and *The Children of Light and the Children of Darkness.*

Liberationist. This is a composite figure who does not speak for any single Latin American liberation theologian but who obviously is influenced by such writers as Gustavo Gutiérrez *(A Theology of Liberation; We Drink from Our Own Wells)* and Leonardo Boff *(The Church: Charism and Power).*

Feminist. This speaker, too, is a composite figure and should not be identified without qualification with any particular contemporary feminist theologian. Among the most widely read feminist theologians today are Rosemary Ruether *(Sexism and God-Talk),* Phyllis Trible *(God and the Rhetoric of Sexuality),* Sallie McFague *(Models of God),* Elisabeth Schüssler Fiorenza *(In Memory of Her),* and Letty Russell *(The Future of Partnership).*

A Gathering of Political Theologians

BARTH: Since I don't believe in chance, an invisible hand must have been at work in arranging another of these unlikely conversations. The dear Lord must have a marvelous sense of humor.

LIBERATIONIST: I can assure you that the Vatican had nothing to do with it. As you know, they're a little nervous about all this free-wheeling debate among theologians. They think it usually leads to confusion among the faithful as to what the church teaches. While I do not share this view, I have my own reasons for not being very optimistic about what will come of our meeting.

NIEBUHR: That we have gotten together at all, even if only in someone's imagination, is one of those impossible possibilities about which I have written. The surprises and twists of history defy rational explanation. The fact is that we are here, political theologians all, with the opportunity of discovering, if not where we agree, at least where, why, and to what extent we disagree.

FEMINIST: I've been trying to figure out why the four of us were selected. True, we have all been involved in political struggles as theologians and have written more or less extensively on the relationship of Christian faith and political responsibility, but for goodness' sake, so have lots of other people — Joseph Ratzinger, Michael Novak, and Pat Robertson, to mention a few. What a conversation about political theology we might have had with any or all of them!

NIEBUHR: I am not sure it would have been a conversation; more likely it would have turned into a shouting match or even a riot. Maybe there's some value in four clearly left-of-center political theologians like us finding out how much ground we share, if any. We all have been tagged as liberals, radicals, or even "commies" at some time or other.

BARTH: Indeed, we have, Reinie. In fact, I think you were responsible for stuffing me in a bag like that once or twice. But never mind. Even if we can't hope for a Barmen-like Declaration to result from this meeting, that is no reason we cannot engage in an open and friendly conversation. Part of the problem of most theologians is their lack of a sense of humor; they take themselves and what they call the present situation with such frightful seriousness.

FEMINIST: That is a rather predictable and gratuitous remark, Karl. As some of us see the matter, the church and theology are not nearly serious enough about the oppression and exploitation of people around the world. It's all so cozy to be reminded to be friendly and to keep a sense of humor, but the fact is that millions of people are dying because of the apathy and complicity of the church. I honor your prophetic leadership of the church in the struggle against Nazism, but what you lost sight of in those infinite expanses of the *Church Dogmatics* is that there are forces at work in the world today that are as sinister and destructive as Nazism.

LIBERATIONIST: Olé! The question of the church's political commitment and responsibility is not a topic for friendly conversation in the safety and decorum of an academic seminar. It is a life-and-death issue for millions of people, at least in Latin America and other parts of the Third World. My guess, Feminist, is that what happened in the cases of our friends Karl and Reinie is that their work became increasingly detached from pastoral and political praxis. As their theology and ethics became ever more theoretical — however concrete or even pragmatic it claimed to be — they were tolerated, and perhaps to some extent co-opted, by the ruling powers. When Karl was the "red pastor" of Safenwil, or involved in the German Church Struggle, and when Reinie was a Detroit pastor forced to speak out against the exploitative policies of the auto magnates, or incensed by the ravages of the Great Depression, their theology had social critical power. In those days they spoke out of the social struggle and in solidarity with suffering people.

BARTH: I was involved in the religious socialist movement early on. But I was never really caught up in its ideology. What was important to me as a pastor was union organizing and helping the working people struggle for their rights. I do not believe I ever abandoned the commitment to justice and peace that animated my early ministry. I do think I later put that commitment on a firmer theological foundation and guarded better against confusion of the kingdom of God with any human politics — whether right, center, or left.

FEMINIST: But Karl, that's precisely my point, and I think Liberationist's, too. Your theology, which is usually impeccably orthodox, tries to walk a tightrope between a desire for pure Word-of-God theology and occasional pronouncements and actions in relation to particular social and political issues and movements. But that is simply not possible — or rather it is possible only at the expense of serious and sustained involvement of the church and theology in the most vital political struggles of our time. By the way, I hope you noticed that I said your theology was "usually" impeccably orthodox, since at least in the case of your teaching about the ordered relationship of man and woman in the image of God — according to which man always is the leader and woman always the follower — you are both dead wrong and, in the only sense that counts, terribly heretical. If you had remained a theologian of praxis instead of pontificating about what God says from your safe professorial chair in Basel, you might have learned from some of your female comrades in the struggle for justice that Galatians 3:28 rather than Ephesians 5 is the important clue for a genuinely Christian understanding of the relationship of man and woman.

BARTH: After that tongue-lashing, I am more persuaded than ever that the charge to women to keep silent in the church (1 Cor. 14:34), while by no means to be construed as a general rule, may well be a necessary command in exceptional cases. As far as I am concerned, the question is not whether faith and theology are to hover above history or whether concrete decisions are to be risked in the praxis of faith. My position is that the church never speaks or acts "on principle." It makes its evaluations and judgments spiritually and by individual cases. The real question for me is what norm or criterion finally guides our political decisions and praxis. I am far more respectful of the contextuality of Christian decision-making than you suggest, but I am even more passionately concerned that the political decisions of Christians be guided by the Word of God attested in Scripture.

Niebuhr and Barth

NIEBUHR: Well, Karl, even if you do insist on the concrete risk-taking of Christians, Feminist and Liberationist are right in pointing out the folly of trying to develop a political theology that is based on the Word of God alone and that does not interact with, and stand corrected by, the concrete experiences of individuals and societies. As you will recall, I warned you long ago about this business of turning theology into a kind of airplane that soars so high above the world of experience and history that it can no longer make discriminating judgments regarding the persons and events below, which appear so tiny and insignificant from that distance. I think responsible theology and ethics should refuse to ride in this high-altitude airplane. We are human beings, not God, and we must form our judgments and make our decisions as finite, fallible human beings.

BARTH: Where in the world do I deny that? Should I laugh or cry at your charge that I think we fly to heaven in some kind of eschatological airplane and play God? My point is simply that our political decisions as Christians, which must always be as concrete and well informed as possible, must always be disciplined and directed by exegetical attention to the Bible. "Exegesis, exegesis, exegesis!" I told my students in Bonn before being expelled from Germany by the Nazis. I still think that is sound advice for all theology and ethics. It is bad theology and bad Christian ethics to argue that the Christian view on any particular social or political issue is settled by appeal to some vague notion like the Judeo-Christian tradition, the perennial philosophy, the mind of Christ, or whatever.

NIEBUHR: Your obsession with biblical exegesis makes theology captive to biblical literalism. You want to establish biblical authority in all matters of Christian faith and practice with as little recourse as possible to sources of truth and right that come from common reason, universal conscience, or cultural history. That way of thinking drives us straight into theological obscurantism.

BARTH: So in your eyes I am a literalist and an obscurantist. I have learned not to be intimidated by these bogeyman slogans substituting for arguments. I happen to believe, as I thought you did too, that the Word of God is like a sword that cuts through our self-righteous confidence that God is always on our side. I am unalterably opposed to any identification of the biblical message with the going cultural values of Western society, whether these are focused on the infinite worth of the individual, as with the old liberal school, or on the glory of free enterprise, as with our present so-called neoconservatives. You're not one of them, are you, Reinie?

NIEBUHR: You know darn well I'm not. You are absolutely right about the substitution of self-righteous civil religion for prophetic biblical teaching and the easy replacement of the hard truths of classical Christian faith with the naive creeds of modern culture. I have no quarrel with you in your effort to extricate Christian faith from the idolatries of our day. What I do object to is your remedy, which is almost as bad as the disease. You destroy all commerce between Christian faith and the philosophical, ethical, and anthropological disciplines. You refuse to enter into a debate with modern culture to show that its analysis of the human situation is superficial and its expected redemptions are illusory. Your isolationist theology belies your claim that the political decisions of Christians should be as well informed as possible. Where do you enlist the help of social scientists and politicians in describing the dynamics of specific political issues? All you want to do is preach the gospel and wait for the Holy Spirit to validate it.

BARTH: In one sense, at least, that is just what I think we should do, but it is a preposterous reading of my theology and a complete distortion of my lifelong engagement in political issues to charge me with isolationism and otherworldly quietism. Have you ever heard of Barmen?

NIEBUHR: Yes, I have, and it illustrates the point I am making. Your brand of political theology is strictly for the church in the most extreme crises, where the issues of good and evil are obvious. In these circumstances, your theology can arouse Christians to heroic action. However, in situations of great complexity and ambiguity, where the devil is not so obvious, your eschatological extremism is impotent. That is why you never found yourself able to make a clear decision against the threat of communist totalitarianism as you had against Nazi totalitarianism. So when Hungary was invaded by the Soviet Union, we heard only silence from the Barth who once roared like a lion against Nazism.

BARTH: As you should know by now, that "silence" in relation to the invasion of Hungary was a careful and painful response to a particular and very complex situation that you and some other Western church leaders tried to oversimplify for your own propagandistic purposes. Anyone who knows anything about me and my theology knows my strong support of democratic government. But I did not then, and I do not now, see Russia as the evil empire and the United States as the incarnation of goodness and innocence. In relation to the conflict between these two superpowers that developed after World

War II, a different response from the church was and is needed in comparison with the one I helped to mobilize against Hitler. The church needs to search for and promote a third option rather than allow itself to become the religious echo of one or the other of these superpowers. It seems to me that in this case it is you who refused to recognize the importance of the particular situation in which Christians have to make their political decisions with a "nicely calculated more or less." Instead, you simply waved the flags of Western self-righteousness, which came to haunt you in the 1950s with the McCarthy witch hunt and in the 1960s with the terrible war in Vietnam. I think you have written something about the irony of history?

NIEBUHR: I see that we both have warrior's instincts and go for the jugular. I will not deny that your perception of the myth of American innocence and the pretensions of American power may have been sharper than mine in that period when I argued a little too one-sidedly for the legitimate exercise of limited power to counter the Soviet threat. While I regret not having criticized the American Vietnam war policy earlier than I did, that still does not alter my fundamental rejection of your feeble and obscure efforts to assist the church to make enlightened and discriminating judgments in the political sphere. You have only your spiritual intuition to offer, and of course in the case of Nazism it was brilliant. But the church needs something more than intuition robed in the garments of the Word of God.

BARTH: I have never rested my case on so-called intuition. I have argued that Christian political decision-making must follow the direction and line of God's own political action in Jesus Christ. We may discern parables or analogies of the kingdom of God in every protection of human rights, in preferential care for the poor and the oppressed, and in open societies that have fundamental freedoms of speech, assembly, and the like. While God's action in Jesus Christ does not supply blueprints for Christian political actions, it points in a definite and unswerving direction. Among the political options open to the Christian community in a particular situation, it will choose the one that most suggests an analogy or correspondence with the gospel of Jesus Christ. This is not "intuition," and it is not biblicism, at least not in the sense of thinking we can find the biblical "answers" to our particular political problems ready-made for us.

NIEBUHR: Your attempt to develop a political theology based solely on the Word of God by the device of reasoning analogically from the gospel story just doesn't work. It amounts to a tour de force. Your clever analogies are designed to protect the sole authority of the Word of God and to claim independence of the insights of cultural history, natural law, the moral conscience, political theory, or social analysis. But the whole process is simply an illusion. To begin with the obvious, your references to the Bible are bound to be selective. Other interpreters might come up with analogies very different from yours. For example, one might argue from the biblical description of God as Lord and King and of God's people as servants that a monarchy or even dictatorship is an appropriate way of ordering human life in accordance with God's action. Admit it, Karl, your preference for democracy and a system of law that protects human rights owes much more to general cultural history than you are willing to say.

BARTH: It is now very clear to me that you have a thoroughly mistaken notion of what I think biblical interpretation involves. Whatever may be the case with your American fundamentalists, for me the Bible is to be interpreted in the light of its central testimony to God's covenant history with Israel fulfilled in Jesus Christ. That covenant history discloses both the true identity of God and the true identity of humanity as God's covenant partner. All of the terms that we ascribe to God and all that we think we know about God's purposes must be reexamined, corrected, and transformed in the light of the covenantal activity of God. In terms of this history, God is not just any Lord, but a Lord who becomes a servant. God is not just any king, but a king who humbles himself and exalts humanity to royal partnership with God. If you can find in monarchy and even dictatorship an analogy to this history of this God, you are close to desperation.

NIEBUHR: It all seems to me to be a very devious and dubious way of trying to circumvent the fact that the Christian faith owes something to general culture. To ignore this fact, especially in our ethical analyses and political decisions, can only lead to self-deception and a ghetto mentality. Instead of engaging in exegetical gymnastics to display these kingdom-like analogies of yours that are supposed to guide our political action, political theology should take as its task a realistic analysis of a particular political situation informed by an interpretation of the classical Christian symbols of sin, the Christ, the cross, and so on. In the interaction of concrete political analysis and the interpretation of symbols like the cross, in which God's justice and love intersect, depth is given to our political theory and realism and hope to our political proposals. As a political ethicist, I take Christian symbols not literally but with utmost seriousness.

BARTH: Again, you misrepresent my approach. I do not advocate or practice ignorance of cultural history, philosophy, social and political analysis, or anthropological studies. I believe that there are many little lights of creation, culture, and history that we would be not only foolish but disobedient to ignore. These lights must be honored, but they are little lights that for the Christian never substitute for the one great light of God's revelation in Jesus Christ. In other words, that great light of Jesus Christ is the criterion by which we recognize and affirm the truth that is present in all the little lights of our experience, cultural history, and common sense.

NIEBUHR: What you have just said may be a significant step beyond the impression of a cleavage between faith and culture that many of your earlier writings left. Still, I am not satisfied with this latest version of your position. For you the little lights of creation, experience, and cultural history can be in the last analysis only reflections of the great light of revelation in Jesus Christ. I see the relationship as much more dialectical. Our knowledge of God's revelation in Jesus Christ is continually tested, corrected, or verified by common experience and general culture. It is, for example, unfortunate that the Confessing Church did not allow its opposition to Nazism to embrace the inviolability of Jews as human beings rather than limiting its concern to the church and the freedom of its proclamation. A Christian approach to political theory, social criticism, and the struggle for justice must recognize that the church is heir to both the prophetic biblical tradition and the Enlightenment tradition of political rights. These two traditions constitute a creative synthesis — Christian realism, I call it — the elements of which must be kept in mutually corrective and mutually enriching interaction.

Liberationist and Niebuhr

LIBERATIONIST: Reinie, I share a number of your misgivings about Barth's approach to the relationship of faith and politics. Despite his courageous leadership of the Confessing Church, I find it difficult to grasp the connection between his explicit biblicism and his professed contextualism. He is of course right when he says that we all move by some process of analogy between the proclamation of the kingdom of God in the Bible and the present situation. But there is a lot of residual idealism in his failure to begin with concrete situations and reflect critically on them in the light of revelation. I am, therefore, much closer to you than to him on the matter of the positive interaction of human experience and social analysis with what is called revelation or Word of God. Barth's analogies of the kingdom of God seem to me well intentioned but terribly vulnerable to all sorts of ideological manipulation.

NIEBUHR: But, if I am not mistaken, you also have a number of reservations about my work. Well, it so happens that I have some questions for you, too, so why not fire away?

LIBERATIONIST: All right. For starters, I question the social location of your theology no less than Barth's. You value what you call the wisdom of experience and general cultural history as a means of testing, correcting, or confirming the teachings of the Bible and the Christian tradition. But precisely whose experience and whose cultural history do you have in mind? As far as I can see, you don't even try to break out of the model of theology as primarily an apologetic enterprise designed to convince enlightened nonbelievers of Europe and North America of the limitations of their understandings of human life and the depth dimensions that they overlook because of their disdain of the profound symbols of the Judeo-Christian tradition. My theology of liberation, however, is aimed not at the sophisticated and usually well-to-do nonbeliever of the Western world but at the nonperson of so much of the Third World. It begins with the experience of the poor and their struggle for justice and freedom.

NIEBUHR: I am surprised that you would consider me insensitive to the concern of God for the poor. What I call Christian realism is to a large extent a retrieval of the prophetic tradition of the Old Testament — with its word of judgment on the abuse of the poor by the wealthy and powerful — as well as a reclaiming of the apostolic teaching: "God chose what is low and despised in the world, even things that are not, to bring to nothing things that are" (1 Cor. 1:28).

LIBERATIONIST: Advocacy of the cause of the poor is one thing, but solidarity with the struggle of the poor — with which liberation theology begins — is something else. It presupposes a clear and unqualified commitment to the cause of the poor, and out of this experience the biblical message is heard and understood in a new way. By comparison, your prophetic theology retains many of the features of complacent North American liberalism.

NIEBUHR: I happen to think that there are elements of the liberal tradition well worth preserving. What bothers me about your call to an unconditional commitment to and struggle with oppressed people is the danger of identifying particular political strategies and commitments with the kingdom of God or the absolute good. I would have thought that the lesson of history in the twentieth century is that a reign of terror is not far away when any people claim unequivocally that they are the privileged bearers of God's will. A reservation about this sort of presumption is a very important element in Christian realism.

LIBERATIONIST: I find your Christian realism a very slippery concept. It is presumably supposed to mean living by God's grace without illusions and denials of the finitude and sinfulness of all human activity. It is clearly targeted against all utopian thinking. But whether you like it or not, your Christian realism has become in many cases indistinguishable from a hard-nosed pragmatism that uniformly defends the existing state of affairs. It has the effect of blaming the victims of oppression if they take action to overcome their bondage and become subjects of their own history.

NIEBUHR: Don't put that reactionary label on me. You know I am far from denying the legitimacy of revolution in certain circumstances. What I am arguing is that God is more mysterious and hidden than either the self-righteous possessors of power or the unselfcritical leaders of revolutionary movements allow. They both illicitly claim to be the guardians or executors of God's will. The point of the eschatological biblical symbols, in my judgment, is that the final meaning of history cannot be realized by humanity's own effort. History cannot complete itself, but depends for its completion on a power beyond itself. The eschatological symbols thus mitigate our pride without destroying our hope.

LIBERATIONIST: I think you see the relationship between biblical eschatology and politics primarily in a negative way. I see the relationship more positively. Historical action presupposes confidence in the future. Biblical eschatology — especially Jesus' proclamation of the coming kingdom of God — ignites rather than suffocates hope and effort at historical transformation. I am therefore much more appreciative than you of the importance of utopian thinking. True utopian thinking involves both a denunciation of the existing order and an annunciation of what may yet be in contrast to what is. The effective denunciation and annunciation of utopian thinking can be achieved only in concrete praxis. You too quickly identify utopian thinking with the ideology that masks rather than discloses real possibilities of change.

NIEBUHR: I am well aware of the utopian mentality and how the failure of its schemes leads invariably to disillusionment and brutality. The basic error of this way of thinking is its pretentious conviction that always someone or some institution outside the self is solely responsible for all injustice and evil in the world. The profound truth of the symbol of original sin is thereby ignored. Marxism is the greatest of modern utopias, and its historical failures are such that I would have thought it would not be quite the temptation to you liberation theologians that it appears to be. Have you kept up with what happened in Eastern Europe and the Soviet Union?

LIBERATIONIST: We in Latin America have not and do not intend to adopt Marxism uncritically, any more than we intend to be mesmerized by the European and North American ideology of "democratic capitalism." We seek our own third way (here I applaud the insight and independence of Barth), and that way may indeed be a form — but *our own form* — of democratic socialism.

NIEBUHR: I am happy to hear that. You may know that I was once very active in the Christian socialist movement, but I gradually moved away from it, as its principles seemed helpless before the harsh realities and dark ambiguities of modern history. It was caught up, for example, in a naive pacifism that ignored the urgency of resistance to the demonic movement of Nazism. My own endorsement of democracy sums up my Christian realism: the creation of humanity in the image of God makes democracy possible; the sinfulness of humanity makes democracy necessary.

LIBERATIONIST: Even this wise saying can so easily become a mask that covers reality rather than a light that shines on it. It may hide a sophomoric confidence in the electoral process and in the system of checks and balances within "democratic" societies that ignores actual control of government by moneyed interests and that is totally ignorant of the experience of the poor within and outside those societies. The cry for transformation arises from the experience of suffering, and without attending to that experience even our best democratic theories and systems become masks of injustice. This is why for me the purely theoretical debate for or against democracy, or capitalism versus socialism, has an unreal quality. A paradigm shift is required if we are to avoid this unreality in our theology and our political commitments. We must enter into solidarity with the poor on the wager that it is this experience in which the coincidence of the transforming grace of God and the struggle for justice and freedom becomes evident.

NIEBUHR: You have not understood me rightly if you think I am interested only in minimal and undisturbing advances in justice and not in radical transformation. On the contrary, it is precisely when we recognize the impossible but relevant ideal of sacrificial love as disclosed in the cross of Christ that all of our relative achievements of justice are questioned. The call for relative justice and mutual love in all our social relations is the historical approximation to the impossible ideal of sacrificial love. But God's suffering love symbolized by the cross defines the limits of history and points to a completion of human life and history by resources that are not our own. For this reason I think that the Christian's engagement in political struggle is most responsible when it is de-absolutized, unburdened of all its pretensions. I am deeply concerned that the loss of emphasis in liberation theology on some of the central symbols of the faith — atonement, justification, Trinity — or that the transmutation of these symbols into a code language for uncritical participation in all liberation struggles may result in a politicization of the church and its theology no less disastrous than that of neoconservative political theology on the other end of the spectrum.

LIBERATIONIST: There is an old adage of scholastic theology, *abusus non tollit usum*, which I believe is relevant here. Of course, liberation theology and its social expression — the base Christian communities — are subject to distortion and can be made into fronts for the recruitment of members for a strictly secular liberation movement. But no fair-minded reading of my books, which deal at length with the need for a spirituality of liberation to sustain and continually convert the liberation commitment, could charge my theology with the sort of abuse of which you speak.

Feminist and Liberationist

FEMINIST: Liberationist, I think an understandable nervousness is evident in what we've heard from both Karl, with his appeal for a pure theology of the Word, and from Reinie, with his summons to tough-minded Christian realism. These are probably the two greatest theologians of Europe and North America in the twentieth century, but the relationship of their theological reflection to concrete praxis remains more or less ambiguous. In this regard they represent rather than transcend the approach of academic theology with which the method of liberation theology fundamentally disagrees. The church of the future will remember their work with gratitude but will not be able to follow in their steps.

BARTH [to Niebuhr]: See, Reinie, we're already passé.

LIBERATIONIST: I agree, Feminist, and that means that the church and theology must take up a new agenda focused on the experience of genuine solidarity with the suffering of the poor. Can we expect an alliance of at least some segments of the church in both the First and the Third World on this agenda?

FEMINIST: I hope so, but it won't be easy. Representatives of various liberation theologies will have to have a lot of patience and listen to each other carefully, and that will sometimes prove painful. For example, from my own feminist perspective, I have some pretty hard words to address to your project of liberation theology.

LIBERATIONIST: Well, if you give me the chance to tell you what's on my mind that I think you need to hear, I'm willing to listen for the moment.

FEMINIST: Your theology of liberation is sharply critical of the praxis of the church, but in my judgment, quite uncritical and even naive in regard to the traditional doctrine of the church. You fail to explore in any depth the connection between the doctrinal tradition, with which you seldom express disagreement, and the actual practice of the church that you challenge.

LIBERATIONIST: I'm startled to hear you say that. Don't I criticize the separation of the spiritual and the material, and every purely otherworldly interpretation of Christian hope, to mention only a few points?

FEMINIST: Yes, of course. But your method of doing theology does not seem to me to recognize sufficiently the necessity both of prophetically denouncing injustice in the present situation in the light of the biblical tradition, and of critically engaging the tradition in the light of our new experience of God's work in the world. I hear a great deal of the former in your work but rather little of the latter. We are both Catholics, and deeply committed to the church, so that's not the issue. The issue is whether loyalty to what the tradition is really about must not include, if it is to be honest and free, criticism of many aspects of the tradition.

LIBERATIONIST: Are you speaking in particular about patriarchal language about God and the question of the ordination of women?

FEMINIST: Those are merely symptoms of a much larger issue. I am asking whether you are prepared to approach the biblical texts and the history of Christian doctrine with a hermeneutics of suspicion, ready to expose and criticize those elements of the tradition that enter into complicity with attitudes and practices of injustice in society and in the church. I do not see how any responsible political theology or theology of liberation can avoid this task.

LIBERATIONIST: My own effort, I suppose, has been concentrated on the retrieval of the power and illumination of the Word of God in relation to the suffering of the poor and their struggle for liberation. That for me has been an all-consuming task. Anything else would be — well, a harmful distraction. Note, please, I do not say that what you are asking for is unimportant. Indeed, I am happy to see that some of my fellow liberation theologians are doing the sort of thing you want, but I have not found that to be my most pressing task.

FEMINIST: But surely, the way the church itself exercises its power, the kind of leadership and extent of participation that it fosters, the freedoms that it cultivates or denies in its own life, the honesty or dishonesty with which it treats its own history of complicity with oppression — these matters are hardly peripheral to the quest for integral liberation. The church cannot call for freedom in the institutions and relationships of society while it represents in its own life a rigid, hierarchical, closed society.

LIBERATIONIST: I certainly cannot quarrel with that, but why do I have the feeling that you have still not expressed your central concern, which has to do with the sexism of the whole tradition, as well as its present manifestations in the church and society?

FEMINIST: That is indeed my central, although not my only, concern in the struggle for integral liberation. And I am frankly distressed that it is all but absent from your own analysis of oppression and exploitation in your writings. Sexism is deeply embedded in the Christian tradition, including the biblical tradition. The very best theological minds of this century — Niebuhr, Barth, Rahner — have hardly been able to recognize it as a problem. We will never come to terms with this sexism — which is the oldest and most virulent form of oppression — until we expose and denounce it in our own tradition of faith. It is certainly part of political theology, as I understand it, to uncover the sexism in Barth's theology of man and woman in which woman is by divine ordination set in subordination to man; to uncover the inadequacy of Niebuhr's description of human sin as predominantly pride, thus showing his own masculine bias and his disconnection from the experience of women and minority peoples, whose temptations to self-hatred and resignation are far greater than to pride; and to expose the lack of attention to the special plight of Latin American women in your own liberation theology. Have you ever examined the consistently sexist character of your language about God?

LIBERATIONIST: I have been helped by the contribution of women like yourself to a deeper understanding of oppression and liberation. My experience is that women assume a significant leadership role in all aspects of the life, reflection, and service of the base communities, and I would certainly want to do all that I can to encourage this. If I have showed insensitivity to the plight of Latin American women in my earlier writings, I regret this. I do now see far better than before how traditional structures of the church and certain interpretations of traditional doctrines serve to strengthen and perpetuate the system of *machismo* in our societies. Sentimentalized portraits of the Blessed Virgin would be an obvious example. It is chilling to consider that our macho attitudes simply reflect in our own man/woman relationships something of the abuse and exploitation that our whole society experiences at the hands of imperialist powers.

FEMINIST: Nor should we overlook the fact that in the Christian tradition this exploitative attitude toward women goes hand in hand with a similar attitude toward nature. In patriarchal societies, nature is viewed simply as raw material to be used by human beings to satisfy not only their needs but their every desire. A liberation theology that does not expand its concern to the cosmic scale is inadequate for our age of nuclear weaponry and runaway industrial pollution. The whole earth is groaning for liberation.

LIBERATIONIST: All right, but now I must be permitted the opportunity to address you with my concerns. I am disturbed, first of all, that women, and especially North American women, seem rather inattentive to the danger of supplanting the question of economic oppression with the issues of linguistic sexism and environmental abuse. I agree that liberation must be integral and comprehensive, but my impression is that we have some way to go before we can be mutually confident that our various liberation agendas are not simply fighting each other. That would be truly tragic. It would simply fall into the long-established strategy of the powerful: divide and conquer.

FEMINIST: You are entirely right about this, and I must express my embarrassment when a North American woman indiscriminately attacks the masculine ego without any attempt to understand the special experiences of suffering of men in oppressed minorities or in poor countries, or when a middle-class North American woman fails to distinguish her own situation from that of her sisters in Latin America.

LIBERATIONIST: Not only in Latin America. There are rather strikingly different experiences of oppression represented in North America by white middle-class women and most black women. I believe you are now beginning to hear from these black women, who call themselves *womanist* rather than *feminist* theologians, and who insist that their primary struggle is for survival rather than self-fulfillment. My guess is that much of Latin American liberation theology will find itself closer to black womanist than to liberal feminist theology.

FEMINIST: I see womanist theology as a challenge to and a radicalization of the feminist movement, and I think that it will serve to deepen and strengthen it.

LIBERATIONIST: Then, too, you must forgive us if we smile when we are told that we neglect concern for the natural environment in our theology of liberation. The traditional cultures of the Third World have a deeply reverent attitude toward nature. It is precisely the colonialization and neocolonialization of our societies that has brought ecological havoc. So again, you see, I am still inclined to consider the economic factor as more important than either the sexual or the ecological or the racial, although with regard to the latter I have learned much from my black friends in North America and South Africa. I am prepared to listen further to others so long as they speak out of real experiences of suffering and are not just advancing theoretical constructs to entertain themselves and those who debate with them.

Prayer and Politics

BARTH: We must conclude our conversation for the time being. The earlier predictions of a lack of a clear consensus appear to have been accurate. Before we part, may I suggest that we strike a little blow against the popular opinion that we political theologians have no use for prayer. I for one want it to be carefully noted that my final reflections on Christian ethics in the *Church Dogmatics* are an extended meditation on the first two petitions of the Lord's Prayer: "Hallowed be Thy name. Thy kingdom come." Prayer and political responsibility are thoroughly intertwined in the Christian life.

NIEBUHR: Neither of us, Karl, could ever be accused of being soft on pietism when it is mixed with political irresponsibility. But I entirely agree with your point about the inseparability of political action and prayer for the kingdom. My political theology is summed up in the prayer I have used so often: "Lord, give me the courage to change what I can change, the serenity to accept what I cannot change, and the wisdom to know the difference."

LIBERATIONIST: I am not so sure that in the situation in which I do theology it is appropriate to balance so nicely the prayer for courage to work for change and the prayer for serenity to accept the unchangeable. Perhaps you will allow me to modify your prayer: "Lord, give us the courage to change what we can change even though we have been taught for so long that we must accept our hunger, poverty, and disease as things which you will. And give us the wisdom to distinguish courage from arrogance." With this modification, I can express agreement with the point that you and Karl have made. I have long contended that we need not only new theological concepts but a new spirituality that informs our thought and action. In the context of the liberation struggle, prayer is far from "useless." My friends, the poor are teaching the church to pray in a new way, which, if my reading of the Gospels is correct, is also a very old way.

FEMINIST: I will simply call to mind the Song of Mary: "My soul magnifies the Lord, and my spirit rejoices in God my savior. . . . God has put down the mighty from their thrones and exalted those of low degree" (Luke 1:46-47, 52).

A Glossary of Theological Terms

accommodation The idea that God adapts revelation so that it can be grasped by finite creatures. Calvin, with whom this idea is often associated, explains that anthropomorphic images and metaphors of God found in the Bible, such as describing God as having hands or being jealous, are the result of God's accommodation to our weakness. According to Calvin, the Incarnation is the primary instance of accommodation. In the humanity of Christ God "has accommodated himself to our little measure lest our minds be overwhelmed by the immensity of his glory."

adiaphora A Greek word meaning "indifferent things." *Adiaphora* are peripheral or non-essential matters that are not to be made binding on the Christian conscience. They include ceremonies, customs, practices, and viewpoints neither commanded nor forbidden by the Word of God. According to Calvin, knowledge of Christian freedom in relation to *adiaphora* is of great importance, "for if it is lacking, our consciences will have no repose and there will be no end to superstitions."

adoptionism The view that Jesus was a human being "adopted" by God and elevated to divine sonship at some point in his life. The time of his adoption has been variously set at his baptism, his birth, or his resurrection from the dead. Rejecting all adoptionist Christologies, the creeds of Nicea and Chalcedon follow John 1:1 and other New Testament texts in declaring that Jesus Christ is the eternal Son of God who became human for our salvation.

Alexandrian school Centered in Alexandria, Egypt, this school of patristic thought included Clement of Alexandria, Origen, Athanasius, and Cyril of Alexandria. In Christology, the Alexandrian school emphasized the full divinity of Christ and the personal unity of his divine and human natures. Athanasius championed the Nicene declaration of Christ's equality with God the Father against Arianism, and Cyril emphasized the unity of the incarnate Word over against the Antiochian (especially Nestorian) tendency to separate the divine and human natures of Christ. For the

Alexandrians, salvation depended on the reality of the union of God and humanity in Christ.

analogy Analogy means "likeness" or "similarity." Use of some form of analogy is indispensable in theology because creator and creatures are radically different. Theologians who speak of an "analogy of being" *(analogia entis)* insist on some similarity as well as difference between the being of God and the being of creatures. Real if limited knowledge of God is thus possible on the basis of knowledge of ourselves and other creatures. Other theologians, emphasizing the radical discontinuity between God and creatures, reject the analogy of being and employ instead an "analogy of faith" *(analogia fidei)*. Theology governed by the analogy of faith does not attempt to understand God in terms of created reality but interprets created reality in the light of God's self-revelation in Jesus Christ.

anhypostasis/enhypostasis Technical Greek terms used in post-Chalcedonian Christology to guard the unity of the person of Christ. That the human nature assumed by the Word in the Incarnation is *anhypostasis* means that it has no independent existence *(hypostasis,* in Latin, *persona)* apart from the Word. That the human nature is *enhypostasis* means that it receives its hypostasis or concrete existence when united with the Word.

Antiochian School Centered in Antioch, Syria, the Antiochian school of theology was the great competitor of the Alexandrian school for the leadership of the church in the fourth and fifth centuries. It included Diodore of Tarsus, Chrysostom, Theodore of Mopsuestia, and Nestorius. In their Christology the Antiochians emphasized the full humanity of Christ and the distinction between his divine and human natures. Their insistence on the distinction rested in part on their concern to protect divinity from the corruptibility and suffering of creatures, and in part on their conviction that only if Christ were truly human could sin and death be undone and salvation achieved in human nature.

apocalyptic Refers to a literary genre found in the Old Testament (e.g., Isa. 27; Daniel), in intertestamental writings (e.g., 1 and 2 Ezra), and in the New Testament (e.g., Mark 13, Revelation). These writings speak of a "revelation" *(apokalypsis)* of the hidden plan of God to bring about the destruction of evil and the ultimate victory of God's purposes throughout the creation. Filled with visions and symbols, apocalyptic writings arose out of situations of severe oppression and persecution. The New Testament scholar Ernst Käsemann called apocalyptic the "mother of Christian theology."

apokatastasis A Greek term meaning "universal restoration" (Acts 3:21) and interpreted by some patristic theologians, notably Origen, to refer to the final redemption of all creatures. While the view that universal salvation is a certainty of faith (universal*ism*) has been rejected by church teaching, a number of twentieth-century theologians, including Karl Barth and Hans Urs von Balthasar, hold that we are not forbidden to pray and to hope for universal salvation even if there is no necessity or guarantee that God's redemptive purposes will be consummated in this way.

apophatic theology   From the Greek *apophasis,* meaning "negation." Apophatic theology holds that God cannot be grasped by the categories of finite reason and hence can only be spoken of in the form of negations: God is not finite (infinite), not mortal (immortal), not changeable (immutable). The negative way of apophatic theology implies that mystical experience is the true way to knowledge of God. Pseudo-Dionysius (fifth-sixth century) is the most famous of apophatic theologians and his influence, especially in Eastern Orthodoxy, has been profound.

apostolic succession   As understood in many Protestant churches, apostolic succession refers to the church's faithful transmission of the gospel message that has its origin and norm in the witness of the apostles. In churches with episcopal polity, apostolic succession means the legitimate ordination to church office by bishops who stand in historical succession with the apostles.

appropriation   The practice, based on biblical usage, of ascribing or "appropriating" a particular attribute or act to one of the persons of the Trinity, even though all attributes and acts of the triune God are indivisible and cannot be assigned exclusively to one of the persons. Thus the act of creation is appropriated to the Father, the act of redemption to the Son, and the act of sanctification to the Spirit, even though, strictly speaking, all are acts of the one triune God. The doctrine of appropriations helps guard the truth of the distinctions within the Trinity just as the doctrine of perichoresis helps guard the truth of the unity of the Trinity.

ascension   Scripture (Luke 24:51; Acts 1:9-11) and the Nicene and Apostles' Creeds declare that after his resurrection Jesus "ascended into heaven." The doctrine of the ascension of the risen Jesus affirms that he rules from heaven as head of the church and Lord of the world and that he continues to be present and active in the world in the power of the Holy Spirit. An important aspect of this doctrine is that the presence of Jesus cannot be directly identified with the structures and practices of the church or the events and movements of history. The doctrine thus calls in question every ecclesiastical or secular triumphalism.

aseity   Based on the Latin *a se,* "from himself," the term "aseity" is used in classical theology to describe God's self-existence or underived being in contrast to the derived and dependent being of creatures. Anselm interpreted aseity as God's necessary being as opposed to the contingent being of creatures; Barth interpreted aseity as God's actuality in sovereign freedom and divine self-determination.

Asian American theology   The project of expressing Christian faith and theology in the context of the distinctive heritage and experience of first- and second-generation Asian American Christians. Some major themes of Asian American theologians are the experience of marginality, racial discrimination against Asian Americans in

North American society, and the challenge of bearing a unique and prophetic witness at the intersection of Western and Asian cultures.

atonement   Atonement or "at-one-ment" refers to the reconciling act of God in Jesus Christ, especially though not exclusively through his passion and death, that mends the broken relationship between God and humanity caused by sin. While the New Testament is unanimous in declaring that Christ lived and died "for us" ("Christ died for our sins," 1 Cor. 15:3), there are many images and metaphors of atonement in Scripture, and there is no single official church dogma defining the work of Christ as there is of his person. Nevertheless, several "theories of the atonement" have been especially influential: the ransom or "classical" theory of early Greek Fathers like Origen and Gregory of Nyssa; the satisfaction theory formulated by Anselm; and the exemplarist or "moral influence" theory associated with Abelard.

baptism   Baptism is the sacrament (some churches say "ordinance") of initiation into the Christian community. Commanded by Christ (Matt. 28:19) and practiced in all Christian churches, baptism takes the form of a public confession of faith and immersion in, pouring of, or sprinkling with water in the name of the triune God, Father, Son, and Holy Spirit. The rich symbolism of baptism includes washing away of sin, dying and rising to new life in Christ, being born to new life by the Spirit, and being welcomed as a child of God into the family of faith. Disagreement continues among the churches whether only those able to make a free and responsible confession of faith should be baptized (Baptist churches), or whether the children of believing parents may also be baptized (Roman Catholic, Eastern Orthodox, and many Protestant churches).

black theology   Black theology interprets the biblical witness and historic Christian doctrine within the context of the history and experience of African Americans. Biblical themes such as the exodus of the people of God from bondage, the critique of injustice by the prophets, and the ministry, crucifixion, and resurrection of Jesus illuminate and in turn are illuminated by the African American experience of bondage, systemic racism, and the struggle of African Americans for freedom and justice. Among the prominent emphases of black theology are God's solidarity in Christ with the poor and the oppressed, the value in God's sight of people of color, and the courageous and faithful witness of the African American churches in the midst of suffering. The witness of African American churches finds expression in a distinctive heritage of worship, preaching, music, and social action. James Cone is one of the pioneers and leading representatives of black theology.

canon   The Greek term literally means "rule" or "standard." By speaking of Scripture as "canon" and of its writings as "canonical," the church acknowledges that Scripture is the basic standard or criterion of Christian faith, life, and theology. In the Protestant churches, the canon of Scripture is composed of 39 books of the Old Testament and 27 books of the New. In the Roman Catholic Church several other writings found in the Greek Septuagint but not contained in the Hebrew Scriptures (e.g., The Wisdom of Solomon) are also included within the Old Testament canon.

Chalcedon Site of the fourth ecumenical council of the church (451 A.D.). The Formula of Chalcedon declares that Jesus Christ is truly God, truly human, existing in two natures united in one person "without division or separation, confusion or change." This decree, which set the standard of orthodox Christology in most churches East and West, incorporates the concern of the Alexandrian school for the unity of the person of Christ as well as the concern of the Antiochian school for his full humanity. Both monophysitism (the extreme Alexandrian tendency) and Nestorianism (the extreme Antiochian tendency) are rejected. The Oriental Orthodox churches, such as Armenian, Coptic, and Syrian, are non-Chalcedonian.

charismata A Greek word meaning "gifts" used by the apostle Paul in 1 Cor. 12:8-11 to speak of the unique endowments given by the Holy Spirit to Christians to equip them for their particular ministries in the community of faith. Paul emphasizes that all Christians receive gifts and that all gifts are to be used for the enrichment and nurture of the whole community.

communication of properties According to this doctrine, the union of divine and human natures in the one person of Christ includes a communication or interchange of properties *(communicatio idiomatum)*. The incarnate Word takes on the attributes of human nature and his human nature participates in the attributes of divinity. Hence we can say of the incarnate Word, "The Son of God suffered," and "Jesus is Lord of all creation." Rooted in the Christology of the Fathers, this doctrine has been interpreted rather cautiously in the Reformed tradition because of its concern to respect the distinctions between the natures, more boldly in the Lutheran tradition because of its concern to assert the union of the natures in the person of Christ. Luther's teaching of the ubiquity or omnipresence of the body and blood of Jesus Christ in the celebration of the eucharist rests on the doctrine of the communication of properties.

communion of the saints Affirmation of the "communion of the saints" is an article of the Apostles' Creed. It is based on the biblical teaching of the "communion" or "fellowship" (koinonia) of believers in Christ that is created and sustained by the Holy Spirit and that constitutes the church as the one body of Christ. The Latin term *communio sanctorum* can mean both a communion of the saints *(sancti)* of all times and places with each other, and a communion of the saints with the holy things *(sancta)* of God, including proclamation of the Word, celebration of baptism and the Lord's Supper, and participation in the church's worship and service in the world.

consubstantiation The interpretation of the eucharist according to which, after the consecration, the substances of the body and blood of Christ co-exist in union with rather than as replacements of the substances of the bread and wine. This explanation, which some late medieval theologians discussed as an alternative to transubstantiation, is also attributed to Luther. He held that the body and blood of Christ are really present "in, with, and under" the bread and wine of the eucharist and used the analogy of the co-presence of fire and iron in a red-hot iron.

covenant   A promissory relationship established by God with the world and particularly with the people of Israel. Based on God's grace and faithfulness and calling for obedience and service, covenant in the biblical sense must be distinguished from a legal "contract" agreed upon by equal partners. God's covenant with Israel is summarized in the promise, "I will be your God and you shall be my people" (Lev. 26:12; Jer. 7:23; 11:4; 30:22). Scripture describes various covenants of God with Noah, Abraham, Moses, and David. The prophet Jeremiah speaks of a "new covenant" that will be written not on tablets of stone but on human hearts (31:31ff.). Scripture proclaims the realization of this new covenant in Jesus Christ in whom all the promises of God are fulfilled.

creatio ex nihilo   A Latin phrase meaning "creation out of nothing." Affirming that all that exists is the result of the sovereign, free love of God, the doctrine of the creation of the world out of nothing is congruent with, although not explicitly taught in, the scriptural witness (cf. Rom. 4:17). The world is not part of God's being, nor does anything co-exist eternally with God (e.g., eternal unformed matter) out of which the world is created. "Creation out of nothing" stands in contrast to every form of dualism and pantheism in understanding the relationship between God and the world.

creationism   Also known as "creation science," creationism opposes the theory of evolution and the estimates of the age of the universe by modern cosmology. It holds that the world was created by God in a manner corresponding closely to the biblical accounts and is perhaps 10,000 years old rather than many billions of years old as modern cosmology teaches.

deism   The view that after creating the world God is no longer actively related to it. The God of deism neither providentially guides the world nor acts within it in any way. Some deist thinkers likened the relationship between God and the world to an omniscient clockmaker who constructs a perfect clock that is able to run on its own and needs no help from its maker. This view of the relationship between God and the world, held by a number of Enlightenment thinkers, was strongly influenced by the emergence of modern science and its accompanying optimism.

descent into hell   According to the Apostles' Creed, after Christ was crucified, died, and was buried, "he descended into hell." This doctrine has a complicated history. 1 Peter 3:18-20 is usually cited as one of its exegetical bases. In the theological tradition two streams of interpretation are identifiable. One understands the descent as a missionary journey of Christ into hell (or sheol/hades, the collective abode of the dead) to preach the gospel and to liberate those imprisoned there, although there is no consensus about who are the ones liberated (the Old Testament saints? the righteous pagans? all people?). The other stream of interpretation understands the descent into hell as Christ's experience of separation from God on the cross when he endured God's judgment on sin on our behalf (Calvin, Barth).

dialectical   Refers generally to a mode of thought that seeks to hold in tension apparently opposing truths, such as the claim that God is both hidden and revealed, or both transcendent and immanent, or that the kingdom of God has already broken in but is not yet complete, or that we are at the same time sinners and a new creation in Christ in whom our sins are forgiven. The theological movement of the 1920s led especially by Karl Barth and Rudolf Bultmann is often referred to as "dialectical theology."

Docetism   A Christological heresy claiming that Jesus Christ only "appeared" (from the Greek, *dokeo*, "appear") to be human and only appeared to suffer and die on the cross. This effort to protect the divinity of Christ from contact with suffering and death was rejected by the church because it undercut the reality of the Incarnation and the efficacy of Christ's saving work.

doctrine   While the term "doctrine" (derived from the Latin *docere*, "to teach") is sometimes used in the general sense of any church teaching, its more specific reference is to an exposition of an important article of Christian faith, e.g., the doctrine of creation. In the Reformation tradition doctrines are based on the witness of Scripture and are attempts to interpret and summarize its witness in a clear and precise manner. While serving as indispensable guides for the preaching and teaching of the church, doctrinal formulations in the Reformation tradition are not considered infallible but are subject to reexamination in the light of the scriptural witness.

dogma   Meaning "decree," dogma refers to a central doctrine of Christian faith that has been officially recognized by an ecumenical council of the church as normative for a right understanding and confession of Christian faith. The triune nature of God and the union of divine and human natures in the one person of Jesus Christ are the chief examples of "dogma." In Protestant theology, a particular formulation of dogma, like all doctrinal formulations, is provisional and in principle reformable. Some theologians thus speak of true dogma as an "eschatological" (Barth) or "doxological" (Pannenberg) concept because the church must never claim that its dogmatic formulations infallibly or exhaustively express the content of revelation. In Roman Catholic theology, dogmas are truths contained in divine revelation and authoritatively defined by the church's magisterium.

economic Trinity   Refers to the triune God, Father, Son, and Holy Spirit, as related to the world and as evident in the work or "economy" of salvation. It is only on the basis of God's self-revelation and self-communication in the work of Jesus Christ and in the activity of the Holy Spirit (economic Trinity) that we are able, confidently if always inadequately, to speak of real distinctions and relationships within God's one eternal being (immanent Trinity).

ecumenical   The Greek word *oikumene* means "the whole inhabited earth." "Ecumenical movement" refers to the effort throughout much of the twentieth century to bring the Christian churches into closer relationship through common study, worship, and service with the hope of eventual reunion. "Ecumenical theology" refers to theological reflection that draws from all Christian theological traditions rather than seeking only to defend and develop one of those traditions.

ecumenical councils   Refers to church assemblies that represent the whole church and whose decisions are accepted as authoritative and binding. The number of councils recognized as truly ecumenical is disputed in the churches: the Roman Catholic Church counts twenty-one, from Nicea I to Vatican II; the Eastern Orthodox churches recognize the first seven; and many Protestant churches recognize at least the first four.

eschatology   The doctrine of the "last things" or the completion of God's works of creation and redemption. Traditionally, eschatology has dealt with the topics of the second coming of Christ, the resurrection of the dead, the final judgment, and heaven and hell. Because of the importance of the coming reign of God in the message of Jesus, this theme has had special prominence in twentieth-century interpretations of eschatology. The reign of God is not something built by humans but comes as a gift of God. Moreover, it concerns not simply the completion of the life of individuals but also the consummation of God's purposes for the whole creation.

exclusivism/inclusivism/pluralism   These terms are frequently used to designate the most common types of response to questions about the relationship of Christian faith and other religions. "Exclusivism" holds that Christian faith alone is the true religion and only those who explicitly confess Jesus Christ as Lord and Savior will be saved. "Inclusivism" teaches that the grace of God, definitively present and decisively made known in Jesus Christ, is also active among all who are responsive to the divine presence and will in their lives. "Pluralism" holds that all religions mediate knowledge of God and are equally valid ways of salvation, though differing in their symbols and practices.

ex opere operato   A Latin phrase meaning "from the work performed." In Roman Catholic theology of the sacraments, their efficacy does not depend on the faith of the recipient or on the sanctity of the priest but is realized objectively by the sacramental act itself when administered by a duly ordained priest. In Protestant theologies of the sacraments, their efficacy is referred to the work of the Holy Spirit and the importance of the faith of the recipient is underscored.

extra Calvinisticum   A Latin phrase meaning "the Calvinist extra." The phrase was coined by critics of the followers of Calvin because he insisted that God remains transcendent and free in all God's relationships with the world, including the Incarnation. According to Calvin, in assuming human existence, the Word of God does not cease to be active "outside the flesh" *(extra carnem)*. Critics see this doctrine as Nestorian in tendency, while defenders argue that it properly underscores the inseparability of the creative and redemptive activities of the eternal Word of the triune God and that it is in fact the view of the ancient catholic tradition.

extra ecclesiam nulla salus   A Latin phrase translated "outside the church there is no salvation." This controversial claim originated with some of the patristic theologians, especially Cyprian, and is still official teaching of the Roman Catholic Church, although its interpretation has undergone significant modification since Vatican II. Some contemporary theologians, Protestant and Roman Catholic, propose as an alternative: "outside Christ there is no salvation," or "outside communion with God and others made known fully in Christ there is no salvation."

faith   Faith is the personal response of trust and confidence in the gracious God made known in Jesus Christ. As wholehearted dedication of one's life to Christ, faith differs radically from blind submission to church teachings and from routine and unthinking adherence to inherited doctrines and practices. The object of Christian faith is not some thing or idea but the living Lord Jesus Christ who is God with us in the power of the Holy Spirit. Substitution of any other object of faith — whether self, family, church, race, or nation — is idolatry. The subject of faith is the whole person, including mind, will, and affections.

feminist theology   A distinctive vision and method in contemporary theology representing a wide range of concerns including the critique of attitudes and practices of male domination in both church and society (patriarchy); the reclaiming of women's experience as an indispensable theological resource; the rejection of exclusively male images and metaphors of God in liturgy and theology; the recovery of the long-forgotten or suppressed contributions of women in the biblical literature and in church history; and the insistence that women and men be valued and treated fairly and equally in all areas of life.

filioque   A Latin phrase meaning "and from the Son." The phrase was added to the Western text of the Nicene Creed in the sixth century. So altered, the creed affirms that the Holy Spirit proceeds "from the Father and from the Son." This addition to the creed was a major factor in the separation of the Eastern and Western churches in 1054 A.D. While there is universal agreement that the Western church acted imprudently in unilaterally adding the phrase, exegetical and theological arguments continue to be advanced for and against its inclusion. "From the Father through the Son" is among the proposed substitutes to mediate the dispute.

forgiveness   God's free and gracious acceptance of sinners decisively declared in Jesus' teaching, ministry to sinners and outcasts, and death for the salvation of the world. Forgiveness is God's reception of sinners into new communion in advance of and apart from reparations for offenses committed. As an act of divine grace, forgiveness is free, scandalous, and costly. Christians are called by Christ to practice forgiveness in their relationships with others.

freedom   In popular usage as well as in many philosophies ancient and modern, freedom is understood as maximum autonomy and independence from all external constraint. By contrast, Christian theology understands true freedom as the gift of freedom *from* the bondage of sin and death and freedom *for* the new life of reconciliation, communion, and service that God purposes for humanity. This distinctive understanding of human freedom is grounded in God's own exercise of freedom — that is, God's self-determination to be God with and for the world revealed decisively in the life, death, and resurrection of Jesus Christ.

free will   The view that human beings always have the power of choice and that no decisions are necessitated. In Christian theology, debate about the freedom of the will is closely connected with understandings of the doctrines of sin and grace. Theological defenders of free will argue that if sin wholly eradicated human freedom, human beings could not be held responsible for their decisions and actions. Theological critics of free will argue that although human beings make "free choices," under the conditions of sin their choices are determined by desires, motives, and social influences that are inevitably marked by sin. Hence sinners may be said to have a kind of "free will" *(liberum arbitrium)* but apart from God's grace they do not have true human "freedom" *(libertas)* to live in accordance with God's will. The controversy between Erasmus and Luther is a classic in the debate about free will.

gospel   The "good news" of salvation through the free and unmerited grace of God in Jesus Christ. Luther sharply opposed gospel and law as the basis of right relationship to God. Although the law is the good gift of God, it is intended to lead sinners to Christ and not to be a way of establishing one's righteousness before God. For Luther, the distinction between gospel and law contained "the sum of all Christian doctrine," and the person who can rightly distinguish the two is a "right good theologian."

heresy   In the Greek New Testament *hairesis* means "faction" or "sect." In later Christian usage, heresy is teaching that conflicts with the central message of Scripture and the primary doctrines of the church. Schleiermacher identified four major heresies of the Christian faith: the docetic (Christ cannot save us because he is not really human); the ebionitic (Christ cannot save us because he is merely human); the Manichean (humanity is hopelessly evil and cannot be saved); and the Pelagian (humanity is not in need of salvation).

Hispanic theology   The contextual theology that interprets Christian faith in the light of the historical, social, cultural, and religious heritage and experience of Latino/a Christians in North America. Among the emphases of Hispanic theologians are God's solidarity with the poor and the marginalized; the importance of the experience of cultural mixture *(mestizaje)* for understanding God's purpose to establish a community of the different; and Christian life as a summons to struggle *(lucha)* for freedom, justice, and dignity.

historical Jesus   Refers to what can be known of Jesus of Nazareth by modern historical-critical study of early Christian origins in distinction from the portrayals of Jesus in the Gospels and in later church teachings. There have been at least three waves of historical Jesus studies: (1) the liberal nineteenth-century "quest of the historical Jesus" that attempted to write biographies of Jesus (described and critiqued by Albert Schweitzer); (2) the "new quest" of the historical Jesus inaugurated by Ernst Käsemann in the 1950s, whose primary purpose was to show the continuity between the message of Jesus and the New Testament kerygma; and (3) the recent studies of Jesus in his environment, giving special attention to sociological and cultural studies of the first century and emphasizing Jesus' embeddedness in the life and history of the Jewish people.

homoousios   The crucial Greek term used in the Nicene Creed (325 A.D.) to affirm that Jesus Christ the Son of God is "of one substance" with God the Father and hence truly and fully divine. This word contradicted the teaching of the Arians that the Logos-Son, though divine, was "created" and therefore not equal with God the Father.

hope   A gift of God, hope anticipates the fulfillment of God's promises to and purposes for the world. Traditionally considered one of the three "theological virtues" along with faith and love, hope fights against despair and resignation to the way things are and keeps human life open to transformation in personal and social dimensions. At the same time, Christian hope differs from liberal optimism and revolutionary presumption that count on a better future to come as a result of human activity apart from God's grace.

hypostasis   A Greek word used by the Cappadocian theologians in the fourth-century trinitarian debates as a technical term to distinguish the personal distinctions within the one being *(ousia)* of the triune God. In the Latin West *hypostasis* was rendered by the word *persona* ("person"). Neither hypostasis nor persona, as used in the early trinitarian formulations, had the meaning of a "person" in the modern sense of an autonomous agent with an independent self-consciousness and will.

hypostatic union   The technical term for the union of the second "hypostasis" or person of the triune God with a human nature. According to the Formula of Chalcedon, in Jesus Christ divine and human natures are united in one person. Post-Chalcedonian theologians interpreted this to mean that, by virtue of hypostatic union, the single subject of the life of the incarnate Lord is the hypostasis of the eternal Word or the second person of the Trinity who "assumed" or took human nature into union with himself.

idolatry   Meaning literally "worship of idols," idolatry is placing one's ultimate trust in, or giving one's ultimate allegiance to, any creature — whether it be an individual, idea, cause, institution, value system, or nation — rather than in the one and only God. The first of the ten commandments forbids every form of idolatry (Exod. 20:1-5).

imago Dei   This Latin phrase translated "image of God" is one of the basic concepts of the Christian doctrine of human being. The phrase derives from Gen. 1:27: "So God created human beings in God's image; in the image of God he created them." Various answers have been given to the question of what constitutes the image of God in humanity. Among the proposals are self-consciousness, the capacity to reason, freedom of choice, and the unique faculties like reason and imagination that enable humanity to have dominion over the other creatures. Some twentieth-century theologians (e.g.,

Bonhoeffer, Barth) have argued that life in right relationship with God and others constitutes the image of God. For Christian faith and theology, Jesus Christ is the perfect realization of the image of God (Col. 1:15).

immanence From the Latin *immanere,* "remaining within" or "indwelling." God's immanence is God's nearness to and indwelling of all created beings (Ps. 139). Although often understood to be in opposition to the transcendence of God, God's immanence is properly understood as God's intimacy and closeness to all creatures yet without ceasing to be the free and sovereign Lord of all. The various mystical traditions characteristically emphasize the immanence of God over against views of God's otherness as alienated transcendence — mere opposition to and separation from creatures.

immanent Trinity Refers to the internal life and relationships of the triune God in which there is an eternal begetting of the Son by the Father and an eternal breathing forth of the Spirit by the Father and the Son. The "immanent Trinity" and the "economic Trinity" are not two different trinities but one and the same Trinity seen from different perspectives. The "immanent Trinity" is the triune God seen as the free, eternal basis of God's relationship to the world and thus as "God for us in advance" (Barth). The "economic Trinity" is the triune God seen in relationship to the world and particularly in the work of salvation in which the love of God, Father, Son, and Holy Spirit, is made known.

immutability Literally, the capacity to be "unchanging" or "changeless." According to traditional doctrines of God, immutability is one of the most distinguishing attributes of divinity. Unlike all creatures, which are subject to change and corruptibility, God, who is perfect, remains eternally the same and thus is changeless. Much modern theology has challenged this doctrine as being more indebted to ancient Greek philosophy than to Scripture. What characterizes the depiction of God in the scriptural witness is not an abstract notion of changelessness but God's constancy and faithfulness to God's own nature and to God's covenant with the world.

impassibility One of the attributes of God in classical theology, impassibility means God's "immunity to suffering." According to the axioms of ancient Greek metaphysics, to suffer is to change and change is either for the better or for the worse, each being inconsistent with the perfection of God. Hence the being of God must be understood as unmoved and unaffected by events in the world. The doctrine of God's impassibility runs counter to the biblical witness, and it has been thoroughly critiqued by many theologians in recent times (e.g., Bonhoeffer's theology of the "suffering God," Moltmann's theology of the "crucified God").

imputation This technical theological term derives from Paul's argument in Romans 4 that just as God counted or "imputed" righteousness to Abraham on account of his faith, so God counts or imputes righteousness to Christians on account of their faith in Christ. According to the doctrine of imputation, the guilt of Adam is imputed or ascribed by God to all of Adam's descendants because Adam was head of the human race and acted representatively for all, and the righteousness of Christ is imputed or ascribed by God to all who trust in him because Christ is the second Adam and acts as representative of all humanity. Whether righteousness is imputed to believers on account of Christ only in the sense of a legal verdict or whether believers also really become righteous in Christ was vigorously debated in the Reformation period and in subsequent eras of the church.

infallibility   The property of being "incapable of error" ascribed to Scripture by some Protestant churches and to the pope by the Roman Catholic Church. The term "infallible" is used in different ways. For some, the infallibility of Scripture includes every aspect of its teaching, including its historical data, scientific assumptions and statements, and theological and moral teachings. Others employ the term more strictly with reference to Scripture's function in the church as the "infallible rule of faith and life." Still others prefer to speak of the unique and authoritative witness of Scripture to the character, acts, and will of God without using problematic terms like "infallibility" or "inerrancy." The infallibility of the pope, declared a dogma in 1870, means that the pope is guarded from all error when as head of the church he solemnly defines Catholic doctrine concerning matters of faith and morals *ex cathedra*, "from the (papal) chair."

inspiration   That Scripture is "inspired" or composed under the special guidance of the Holy Spirit is a common teaching in classical Christian theology and in the confessions of the church. "All Scripture is inspired by God" (2 Tim. 3:16) is frequently cited in support of this teaching. How to understand the work of the Spirit in inspiring the biblical writers has been a subject of much debate. At one extreme is the claim that the words of Scripture were dictated by God, making Scripture inerrant in every respect. At the opposite extreme, inspiration is equated with religious genius and creative imagination. Between these extremes is the affirmation that the Holy Spirit works in and through the human writers of Scripture to convey God's word, respecting their human limitations and conditioning by historical, social, and cultural contexts.

internal testimony of the Holy Spirit   The doctrine that the Holy Spirit illumines, confirms, and seals the truth of the witness of Scripture in the minds and hearts of believers. For Luther and Calvin, Word and Spirit are inseparable. The Word gives external and objective testimony to the saving acts of God while the Spirit works internally and subjectively to certify and seal the truth of the scriptural writers in the hearts of believers. Calvin writes, "The Word will not find acceptance in human hearts before it is sealed by the inward testimony of the Holy Spirit."

justification   A term drawn from the legal sphere, justification refers to God's gracious pardon and acceptance of sinners not on account of their own virtues or good works but solely because of God's sheer grace embodied in Jesus Christ and received by faith. Believers are accounted just not in themselves but in Christ. As God's free act

414

of forgiveness of sin, justification is the basis of sanctification or the new life in Christ. Luther called the doctrine of justification "the article on which the church stands or falls," and Calvin called it "the hinge on which religion turns."

kenosis   A Greek word meaning "emptying." The verb *ekenosen* is used in Phil. 2:7 where Christ is said to have "emptied" himself and taken the form of a servant for our salvation. Nineteenth-century "kenotic" theologians developed a distinctive interpretation of the Incarnation. Wanting to take the full humanity of Jesus more seriously than traditional Christology, they taught that the incarnate Lord emptied himself of the "metaphysical" attributes of divinity like omnipotence and omniscience while retaining the "moral" attributes like love and holiness. While the concept of kenosis in the sense of self-emptying and self-giving is employed by many theologians today, most would agree that God's act of self-giving does not mean that God ceases in any way to be fully God.

Latin American liberation theology   A theology rooted in the context of the economic deprivation and political oppression of Latin American people. Special emphases of this theology are God's preferential love of the poor, salvation as holistic liberation, and theology as an element in the practice of liberation rather than as mere theory. The concrete settings of Latin American liberation theology are "base Christian communities," local gatherings of lay Christians for worship, Bible study, and strategic planning for social action. Gustavo Gutiérrez is widely recognized as the father of Latin American liberation theology.

law, uses of   In Scripture the law or commandments of God are not burdens but gifts and blessings. Obedience to the law of God serves both human well-being and the glorification of God in the world. Under the conditions of sin, however, the law of God is misused when it becomes an instrument of sinners to justify themselves and to boast before God. Luther spoke of two proper uses of the law: the theological (to unmask human sinfulness and drive sinners to Christ), and the civil (the power of the state to keep order, by force if necessary, and thus restrain evildoers who would otherwise cause chaos). Calvin added a "third use of the law": the use in the life of believers who freely and gladly obey the commandments of God rather than seeing them as a heavy obligation or as a means of salvation.

loci   A Latin term meaning "topics" or "areas," it is used to designate the major subjects of doctrinal or systematic theology. The doctrines of God, creation, providence, humanity, the person and work of Christ, the Holy Spirit, and the church are among the distinct "loci" of theology.

logos   A Greek term meaning "word" but also "reason" and "discourse." The concept of logos played a central role in ancient Greek philosophies like Stoicism. It designated the rationality of the order of nature in which individual human reason participates. In the Old Testament the prophets declare the "word of God" or God's judgment, purpose, and instruction to the people of Israel. Wisdom literature celebrates the eternal "wisdom" of God, sometimes personifying it (Prov. 8). Drawing on some or all of these traditions, the Prologue to the Gospel of John identifies Jesus as the eternal Word of God become flesh (John 1:1-18). This identification formed the basis of the Logos Christology of the early church, according to which Jesus is the perfect expression of the logos (word and wisdom) of God. Logos Christology found in the logos concept a "point of contact" with non-Christian philosophical traditions. It also was important in the development of trinitarian doctrine.

Lord's Supper/eucharist/communion   The Lord's Supper is the central sacrament of the Christian Church. While the churches differ in their theology and practice of the Lord's Supper, there are important points of convergence. In the breaking and eating of the bread and pouring and drinking of the cup with thanksgiving to God, Christ's saving life, death, and resurrection are remembered and proclaimed; his real presence and grace for the forgiveness of sins and the renewal of life are received and celebrated; and the church is strengthened for its mission in the world in the confident hope of Christ's coming again and of the consummation of his saving work. Each of the different names by which this sacrament is known brings out some aspect of its rich meaning. "Lord's Supper" emphasizes that Jesus Christ is the host who invites all to his table and gives himself to all who put their trust in him. "Communion" expresses the fact that in this meal we are repeatedly given new life in communion with God and each other through Christ in the power of the Spirit. The name "eucharist" declares that in this meal the church "gives thanks" in the Spirit to God for God's sacrificial love and great goodness to us in Jesus Christ.

love   Love is the act of seeking and maintaining the good of another. In Scripture the steadfast love of God for Israel *(hesed)* and the self-giving love of God for the world in Jesus Christ *(agape)* define the essential nature of God. The love of God is a free and unconditional gift rather than an act prompted by an internal need or external necessity. Jesus summed up the law in the twofold commandment to love God and neighbor and made the love of enemies the touchstone of genuine love. Following the apostle Paul in 1 Corinthians 13, classical theology has viewed love as the greatest of the three "theological virtues" that include faith and hope.

magisterium   A term that means "teaching office" and refers to designated positions of teaching authority in the church to declare what is sound and binding doctrine. In Roman Catholicism this teaching authority is vested in the bishops, church councils, and ultimately the pope. While the term "magisterium" is not widely used in Protestant churches, there are nevertheless established structures and processes, at the local, national, and international levels, that function as teaching authorities.

marks of the church   According to the Nicene Creed, the distinguishing marks of the church are "one, holy, catholic, and apostolic." Without denying these Nicene marks, the sixteenth-century Reformers insisted that a true Christian church is present whenever there is pure preaching and hearing of the Word of God and right celebration of the sacraments of baptism and the Lord's Supper. In some confessions of the Reformed tradition, discipline is included as a third mark of the church alongside faithful proclamation of the Word and proper observance of the sacraments.

method of correlation Developed by Paul Tillich, the method of correlation connects existential questions arising out of a particular human situation with answers contained in the Christian message. For example, the modern experience of estrangement and alienation is correlated with the Christian message of reconciliation. David Tracy proposes a modification of Tillich's method of correlation by speaking of the need for "mutually critical correlation," where both analysis of a situation and retrieval of the Christian message mutually inform and enrich each other.

ministry The "service" (Latin, *ministerium;* Greek, *diakonia*) of God in the church and through the church to the world. Christian ministry has its basis and model in the ministry of Jesus Christ who as the incarnate Word of God came not to be served but to serve and to give his life as a ransom for many (Mark 10:45). Every baptized Christian is called to share in the ministry of Christ, bearing witness to the gospel and showing compassion to all in need. Particular gifts for ministry are given to all by the Holy Spirit to build up the church and equip it for service in the world (1 Cor. 12–14). Since New Testament times, special ministries of leadership in the church have taken different forms (e.g., bishop, presbyter, and deacon) and are recognized by rites of ordination. In most Protestant churches, the main form of ordained ministry is the pastoral ministry of Word and sacrament in a local congregation.

modalism An interpretation of trinitarian doctrine in which Father, Son, and Holy Spirit are not three distinct, eternal divine persons, as in orthodox trinitarianism, but are simply roles or "modes" of activity of the one, undifferentiated being of God. Thus the Father is God in the role of creator, the Son is God in the role of redeemer, and the Spirit is God in the role of giver of new life. Modalism is also known as Sabellianism after the early third century theologian Sabellius who taught that the modes of God's being were transitory rather than intrinsic and eternal.

modern/postmodern As used in contemporary theology and philosophy, "modern" refers to the worldview dominant in Western society since the period of the Enlightenment. Generally critical of religious traditions, the modern mentality emphasizes autonomous human reason, a closed universe described by Newtonian science, and an optimistic hope about the progress of the human race through education, science, and technology. In distinction, the "postmodern" attitude emphasizes the relativity of all truth claims, the pervasiveness of power interests in all human interaction, and the end of all religious and secular "grand narratives," including the liberal theory of progress and the Marxist theory of the classless state to be achieved through revolution. Some theologians see the emergence of the postmodern era as leading to complete relativism and oppose it as a mortal threat to Christian faith. Other theologians see it as a new opportunity to present the claims of Christian faith in a context where modern prejudices of a closed universe, the supremacy of autonomous reason, and the idea of the absolute self have been superseded.

mujerista theology   The theological work of Hispanic women in the United States. Their goal is to help Latinas to understand the nature of the oppressive forces that control their lives, to struggle against these forces, to develop the Latinas' sense of dignity and moral agency, and to recognize the presence of God in their communities and their everyday life.

natural theology   Refers to a theology based on the natural light of reason, the dictates of conscience, or purported evidences of God in the processes of nature or the events of history. Natural theology is independent of God's revelation attested in Scripture and God's decisive self-communication in Jesus Christ. Karl Barth launched an all-out attack on natural theology as leading to distraction in the faith and life of the church and easily succumbing to idolatry. Barth's opposition is enshrined in the first article of the Barmen Declaration of 1934: "Jesus Christ, as he is attested for us in Scripture, is the one Word of God that we have to hear and that we have to trust and obey in life and in death."

nature and grace   Nature and grace are fundamental categories in Thomistic theology. According to Thomas Aquinas, "Grace does not destroy nature but perfects it." In some scholastic forms of Thomism, this dictum is interpreted to mean that the "nature" of creatures is an independent dynamism and constitutes a kind of substructure to which grace is added from the "outside," e.g., through the use of the sacraments of the church. Twentieth-century Thomists like Karl Rahner reject this model of the relationship of nature and grace as the error of "extrinsicism" and argue that nature is always and everywhere already permeated by grace.

Nicene Creed   A milestone in the development of a fully explicit trinitarian understanding of God, the Nicene Creed, adopted by the first ecumenical council of the church meeting in Nicea in 325 A.D., affirmed the full divinity of Jesus Christ, the Son of God. Against Arius who claimed that the Son, the Logos of God, was not equal to the Father, that he was only the highest of the creatures, and that there was a time when he did not exist, the Nicene Creed confesses Jesus Christ the Son of God to be "of one being" *(homoousios)* with God the Father, not created but "eternally begotten" of the Father. What is commonly called the Nicene Creed today is actually the Nicene-Constantinopolitan Creed. The second ecumenical council meeting in Constantinople in 381 A.D. adopted an expanded version of Nicea including an explicit recognition of the full divinity of the Spirit. The Spirit is called "Lord" and "Life-giver" who is "worshiped and glorified" together with the Father and the Son.

omnipotence   The divine attribute of being "all-powerful," or having "power over all things." Mistakenly construed to mean that God can do everything (including what is self-contradictory) or that God is the direct cause of every event (including what is evil), divine omnipotence is properly understood to mean that God has all the power to accomplish God's creative and redemptive purposes in a manner consistent with God's character. A major concern of Christian theologians, ancient and modern, has been to distinguish God's omnipotence from tyrannical or abusive power. Barth, for example, distinguished God's omnipotence from sheer "almightiness" (which he called the power of the demonic) and spoke of the "omnipotent love" of God. Process theologians distinguish between persuasive and coercive power and ascribe only the former to God.

omniscience   One of the attributes of God in classical Christian theology, omniscience means "knowing all things" or "possessing perfect knowledge." Traditionally, this has been understood to mean that God knows all things past, present, and future in one timeless act of cognition. Some theologians and philosophers have addressed the difficulties this understanding of omniscience presents by saying that God knows the actual as actual and the possible as possible. Others have contended that the Bible does not speak of the omniscience of God in an abstract philosophical sense. Instead, it affirms the wisdom of God, the inner truth, depth, clarity, and purposefulness of God's actions, which remains hidden to us apart from God's self-revelation. According to the apostle Paul, Christ crucified is proclaimed as the hidden wisdom of God, although this proclamation is dismissed as scandalous and foolish by unbelievers (1 Cor. 1:18-25).

ordination   The reception and confirmation of a person into a ministry of leadership in the church. After a period of preparation and examination, the church publicly confirms that God has called a candidate to a special leadership ministry in a service of ordination. The ordination service includes prayers for the empowering grace of the Holy Spirit and the laying on of hands by ordained ministers, symbolizing the gift of the Spirit. In the Roman Catholic and Eastern Orthodox churches, ordination is a sacrament and is held to bestow an "indelible character" *(character indelibilis)* qualifying the ordinand to exclusive exercise of certain leadership practices, such as presiding at the eucharist. Reformation churches also take ordination with great seriousness but characteristically stress the *functional* rather than *ontological* distinction between ordained ministries and the ministry of the whole people of God. No barriers, created by supposed essential differences, should be erected between "clergy" and "laity."

original sin   The condition or state of captivity in which the whole of humanity finds itself after the Fall. Original sin is radical (affecting every aspect of human life) and universal (affecting all human beings). Augustine defended the doctrine of original sin in debate with Pelagius over the possibility of fulfillment of the law apart from grace, and Luther deepened the doctrine in debate with Erasmus over the issue of the freedom of the will. Standing within the Augustinian tradition, Reinhold Niebuhr interpreted the doctrine of original sin as teaching that sin is "inevitable but not necessary": our sinful condition is one from which we cannot escape by our own power, yet we are responsible and without excuse.

panentheism   Literally, the teaching that "everything is in God." Panentheism differs both from pantheism that identifies God with the world and from traditional Christian theism that speaks of God as creator of the world out of nothing. According to panentheism, God and the world, while distinct, are nevertheless parts of a single ontological whole. Some world, if not this world, is necessary to God, and apart from a world God would be only an abstract possibility. For panentheism, God is not only affected by all that happens in the world, but it is through the world that God becomes concrete and reaches full self-actualization.

pantheism   Literally, the teaching that "everything is divine." Pantheism affirms that beyond surface appearances all beings are one with God. Pantheism thus denies the ontological difference between God and creature expressed in the doctrine of creation out of nothing and overlooks the moral difference between the holy God and sinners. It thus loses touch with the radical otherness of the God of the biblical witness and classical Christian faith.

perfection   According to John Wesley, the goal of God's work of sanctification is the perfecting of the saints. Since Jesus calls us to perfect love of God and neighbor (Matt. 5:48), we should direct our lives to this goal and trust in God's power to realize it. Wesley believed that perfection or full sanctification was realized in this life only in relatively few Christians, but that all Christians should at least want to be made perfect in love.

perichoresis   A Greek word translated "mutual indwelling" or "interpenetration." It was first used by patristic theologians to describe the mutual indwelling of the divine and human natures of the incarnate Word. John of Damascus (eighth century) was the first to make extended use of the term to speak also of the mutual indwelling or unique communion of the triune persons. The three persons of the Trinity live in, with, and through each other in ineffable communion. Perichoresis has become a central concept in contemporary trinitarian theology, and theologians make analogous uses of it in other doctrinal loci like theological anthropology and ecclesiology.

person   In modern philosophy a person is a self-conscious individual capable of independent decision and action. In trinitarian theology "person" is a technical term used to refer to Father, Son, and Holy Spirit, who are not three separate beings but are united in essence and distinguished by their relationships with each other. In recent trinitarian theology, relationality is emphasized as a constitutive element of being a person. A major task of trinitarian theology is to avoid the tritheism that hovers over any uncritical use of the modern definition of "person" in trinitarian doctrine and the modalism that reduces the persons of the Trinity to mere modes or manifestations of a solitary being and fails to grasp that the essence of God's being is love and communion.

prayer   A practice, fundamental to Christian faith and life, of calling on God and petitioning God for daily needs. As the lifeline of communion with God, prayer takes many forms, including praise, thanksgiving, confession of sin, lament, petition, and intercession. The model of Christian prayer is the Lord's Prayer taught by Jesus to his disciples. Calvin called prayer "the chief exercise of faith." Barth made prayer central in his depiction of Christian life and spoke of it as a necessary presupposition of all serious theology.

predestination   The doctrine that God has eternally ordained the destiny of human beings. With deep roots in Scripture, this doctrine has been taught in some form by many theologians, including Augustine, Aquinas, Luther, Calvin, Schleiermacher, and Barth. In scholastic Calvinism the doctrine was interpreted to mean God's election of some people to salvation and God's rejection or reprobation of others to damnation. Barth offered a major reinterpretation of the doctrine, centering it on Jesus Christ as both electing God and elected and rejected human being. For Barth election is first and foremost God's self-determination to be God for the world in Jesus Christ. In him all humanity is elect and by him the divine judgment on sin has been borne for all.

process theology   A prominent school of North American theology that emphasizes the "processive" or dynamic character of all reality. In contrast to static views of the world as comprised of inert, unchanging substances, process theology views reality as constituted by "actual occasions" or transient novel events bearing the influence of past events and in turn influencing future events. God is described in process theology as "di-polar," having a "primordial" nature that contains all ideals or possibilities for concrete actualization, and a "consequent" nature that receives, preserves, and harmonizes all that is actualized in the world process. Alfred North Whitehead and Charles Hartshorne are the two chief philosophical sources of American process theology.

proofs of God's existence   Attempts to prove or demonstrate (i.e., provide logically compelling arguments for) God's existence have been perennially debated in philosophy and theology. The most famous formal arguments for God's existence are Anselm's ontological argument (derived from his definition of God as "that than which nothing greater can be conceived") and Thomas Aquinas's five "ways": from motion to an unmoved mover; from causality to a first cause; from contingent being to a necessary being; from value to perfection; and from design to a designer. Many contemporary theologians share Paul Tillich's assessment that these arguments are failures as arguments but that they are significant expressions of the irrepressible human search for God.

providence   The doctrine that God unceasingly cares for the world, that all things are in God's hands, and that God is leading the world to its appointed goal. Abraham's assurance to Isaac that "God will provide" (Gen. 32:8) and Jesus' teaching that not a single sparrow falls without the knowledge of God the Father (Matt. 10:29) are instances of the strong faith in God's providence characteristic of the mainstream of the biblical witness. The doctrine of providence opposes the idea that all things happen by chance. At the same time, divine providence must be distinguished from fatalism or determinism, according to which God directly causes everything that happens.

psychological analogy   One of the two primary analogies for speaking of the mystery of the Trinity, the other being the social analogy. According to the psychological analogy, employed by Augustine, Thomas Aquinas, Karl Rahner, and numerous other theologians, a glimpse of the mystery of the Trinity is found in the differentiated unity of memory, knowledge, and will in an individual human being. This analogy has the advantage of emphasizing the unity of the divine life and the disadvantage of speaking of the three of the Trinity in a way that suggests they are only modes, aspects, or faculties, and hence less than personal.

real presence   A phrase used to designate the real or actual presence of Christ in the Lord's Supper. A doctrine of real presence stands in contrast to views such as Zwingli's that Christ's presence is only figurative or symbolic. While Calvin rejected the doctrine of transubstantiation, he also resisted the idea that the Lord's Supper is a "vain and empty sign," arguing for the real presence of Christ by the power of the Holy Spirit. According to Calvin, in the Lord's Supper, "Christ pours his life into us, as if it penetrated into our bones and marrow." The phrase "real presence" provides common ground to Roman Catholic, Eastern Orthodox, Lutheran, and Reformed theologians whose doctrines of the Lord's Supper may nevertheless differ significantly as to the precise mode of Christ's real presence.

resurrection   Based on the New Testament witness to the resurrection of the crucified Christ, Christians affirm belief in "the resurrection of the dead" (Nicene Creed) and "the resurrection of the body" (Apostles' Creed). Faith and hope in bodily resurrection stand in contrast to the idea of the immortality of the soul. The latter holds immortality to be intrinsic to some aspect of the human creature, whereas resurrection faith presupposes that death is total and the hope for life beyond death rests on the sheer gift of God who brought creation out of nothing and raised the crucified Jesus from the dead. Moreover, resurrection faith affirms the significance of embodied existence in God's sight and by extension the value of the entire material cosmos.

revelation   This word translates the Greek *apocalypsis* and means God's "unveiling" or disclosure of the divine character, purpose, and will. As an event of personal self-disclosure, the revelation of God is God's own free act and must therefore be distinguished from an insight or truth discovered independently by human beings. For Christian faith and theology God's decisive self-revelation is the person and work of Jesus Christ as attested in Scripture. When a distinction is made between special and general revelation, special revelation refers to God's self-disclosure in the covenant history with Israel and supremely in Jesus Christ, and general revelation refers to what can be known of God through observation of nature and by the dictates of universal human conscience.

rule of faith   The expression "rule of faith" *(regula fidei)* is used by patristic theologians like Irenaeus to refer to the brief summary of the faith recognized and confessed in all the churches. It is often appealed to as a rule or standard for the right interpretation of Scripture over against heterodox and heretical interpretations. The rule of faith, as formulated for example in the Apostles' Creed, can be characterized as trinitarian in scope, narrative in form, and centered on the saving work of Jesus Christ.

sacrament   The word derives from the Latin *sacramentum,* which in turn translates the Greek *mysterion,* "mystery." Sacraments are sacred practices of the church based on a scriptural mandate and made effective by the Spirit of God as "means of grace" to confirm the presence and promise of Christ to believers. Augustine defined a sacrament as a "visible sign of an invisible grace," Calvin as a "sign and seal" of God's promise of salvation. Although the definition and number of sacraments varied considerably during the first millennium of the church, the Roman Catholic and Eastern Orthodox churches today recognize seven sacraments: baptism, confirmation, penance, eucharist, holy orders, marriage, and anointing of the sick. In Protestant churches, only baptism and the Lord's Supper are recognized as sacraments, because they alone rest on a direct command of Christ.

salvation   The Greek term *soteria* is translated "salvation" and means rescue from mortal peril, deliverance from sin and death, and the gift of fulfilled life in communion with God. According to the biblical witness, salvation comes from God's mighty acts and above all from the work of Jesus Christ the Savior. The doctrine of the threefold office of Christ and the several theories of atonement are attempts to express the ways in which Christ accomplishes human salvation. It is significant that the New Testament speaks of salvation in past, present, and future tenses: we "have been saved" (Eph. 2:8); we "are being saved" (1 Cor. 15:2); and we "shall be saved" (Rom. 5:10). Paul Tillich rightly notes that "salvation has as many connotations as there are negativities from which salvation is needed." In the early centuries of the church, death and error are the perils from which deliverance is sought, and salvation is the gift of knowledge of God and immortality. In classical Protestantism, salvation is forgiveness of sins and rescue from the condemnation of the law. In pietism and revivalism, salvation is the conquest of specific sins and progress toward moral perfection. In the modern period, the ultimate threat, according to Tillich, is meaninglessness and nihilism, and salvation is the gift of meaning, purpose, and wholeness of life.

sanctification   Sanctification is the process of "being made holy." It is the renewal of life in the power of the Spirit by participation in Christ through membership in the community that is his body. While a deeply personal process, sanctification is cultivated in and for community and involves all the formative practices of Christian life, including worship, prayer, service, and mission. Its basis is justification or forgiveness of sins by God, and its goal is fullness of life in communion with God and others. Calvin spoke of justification and sanctification as the twofold grace *(duplex gratia)* of Christ.

semper reformanda   A Latin phrase meaning "always in need of being reformed." The full motto from which this phrase comes is *ecclesia reformata semper reformanda secundum verbum Dei,* "the church reformed, always in need of being reformed according to the Word of God." This motto expresses the truth that reformation is not a one-time event in the life of the church but is needed again and again. The quest for better understanding and more faithful practice require continuous vigilance and self-criticism in the life of the church in the light of the Word of God.

simul iustus et peccator   A Latin phrase meaning "at the same time justified and sinful." This phrase is related to the Reformers' doctrine of justification by grace through faith alone. While sin continues to be at work in the life of believers, they are graciously forgiven by God for Christ's sake. This doctrine emphasizes the radicality of sin and the gratuity of God's grace and opposes all self-righteousness among believers and all perfectionist doctrines of Christian life.

sin   Sin is all that contravenes the will of God as this is expressed in special revelation (the ten commandments; the life, teaching, death and resurrection of Jesus Christ) or known to some degree by general revelation (conscience, the sense of moral responsibility). An important distinction is made in theology between actual sins (particular transgressions of God's will) and original sin (the radical and universal sinful human condition). Sin is not only manifested in personal life; it is also embedded in social structures. The roots of sin are distrust of God, denial of grace, rejection of life in solidarity with others, and the idolatry of wealth, power, pleasure, or nation. Every Christian doctrine of sin will be explicitly or implicitly correlated with an understanding of the saving work of Jesus Christ.

social analogy   One of the primary analogies for speaking of the mystery of the Trinity, the other being the psychological analogy. According to the social analogy, employed by the Cappadocians (according to some readings), Richard of St. Victor, and contemporary theologians like Jürgen Moltmann and Leonardo Boff, the Trinity is reflected in personal life in relationship. The advantage of the social analogy is that it emphasizes personal relationship and differentiated communion in the triune life, while the disadvantage is that if pressed too hard it verges on tritheism.

sola fide   One of the watchwords of the Reformation, this Latin phrase means "by faith alone." As the apostle Paul teaches in Galatians, Romans 3:21ff., and elsewhere, sinners are justified before God not by their good works, but by God's grace alone received "by faith alone." This teaching does not mean that our faith rather than our works is the way we achieve our salvation. Rather, the grace of God is freely given and is gratefully and trustingly received by faith alone.

sola gratia   A Latin phrase meaning "grace alone." As the free and unmerited mercy and forgiveness of God extended to sinners, God's grace alone is the entirely sufficient basis of the healing of the relationship between God and humanity broken by sin. Grace is not some thing but God's personal self-gift of renewed relationship with us. It includes both God's pardon of our sin (justification) and the power of God's reconciling grace that opens new life in communion with God and others (sanctification).

sola scriptura   According to the sixteenth-century Reformers, the Scriptures of the Old and New Testaments are the only necessary source and sufficient norm of Christian faith and life. The Reformers defended the principle of "scripture alone" against the teaching of the Roman Catholic Church that the tradition of the church is an additional and independent source of revelation and that the magisterium of the church is the ultimate interpreter of Scripture and church tradition. While "scripture alone" has long been seen as an insuperable barrier separating the Roman Catholic and Protestant churches, the difference has been narrowed somewhat in recent decades. On the Roman Catholic side, there is the renewed vitality of biblical studies and the recognition of the primacy of the scriptural witness in post–Vatican II theology, and on the Protestant side there is the acknowledgment that tradition, experience, and reason all play important roles in the interpretation of Scripture.

soteriology   The doctrine of the saving (reconciling, liberating, renewing) work of Jesus Christ and the participation of believers in the new life in Christ by the power of the Holy Spirit. Soteriology thus deals both with the work of Christ "for us" and the transforming work of the Holy Spirit "in us."

spirituality   A term widely used in contemporary theology to refer to the practices that cultivate and strengthen Christian life. The term is a reminder that being a Christian is more than a theory or the acquisition of certain information; it is a practice, a way of life centered in Christ and energized by the power of the Holy Spirit. Some Christian traditions speak of "piety" or "devotional life" or simply "Christian life" instead of spirituality. In all cases the concern is to speak of the importance of such matters as regular worship, prayer, and service in the life of Christians.

subordinationism   An interpretation of trinitarian doctrine in which Son and Spirit are divine persons but "subordinate" or inferior to God the Father. This interpretation differs from orthodox trinitarianism, in which Father, Son, and Spirit are co-equal persons of the one triune God. Subordinationism is driven by the concern to protect true divinity from the suffering and death experienced by the incarnate Word in the economy of salvation.

supersessionism   The teaching that the church "supersedes" or replaces the people of Israel as God's chosen people. Supersessionism is deeply embedded in the Christian tradition and can take a number of different forms. In one form, Israel is seen as preparatory to the coming of the church but is of only historical interest to Christian faith after the establishment of the church. In a still more virulent form, supersessionism teaches that the people of Israel have been rejected and punished by God and replaced by the church as God's chosen. Today most Christian theologians reject supersessionism and acknowledge that it has been a contributing factor in the reprehensible history of anti-Semitism in Western societies. Critics of supersessionism cite Romans 9–11, where Paul argues that Israel remains God's chosen and describes the church as having been "grafted" onto the root of God's elect people.

systematic theology   The name of the area of theological studies whose task is to interpret the major doctrines of Christian faith, explore their interrelationship or "systematic" coherence, and engage in critical and constructive restatement of Christian doctrines in conversation with other theological disciplines and with contemporary culture. "Doctrinal theology," "dogmatic theology," and "constructive theology" are other names for "systematic theology," each name emphasizing one of the aspects of the task.

theodicy   The attempt to defend or justify the goodness, providential care, and wisdom of God in the face of horrendous evil in the world and particularly the suffering of the innocent. The question of theodicy is often stated in the form: If God is both perfectly good and all-powerful, why does evil exist? Whereas in the early modern period natural evils (e.g. earthquakes, floods) were often the occasion of theodicies, in the twentieth and twenty-first centuries the theodicy question is posed more often in relation to the staggering evils and sufferings perpetrated by human beings on each other and on the natural environment.

theologia crucis/theologia gloriae   Latin phrases meaning "theology of the cross/ theology of glory." The phrase "theology of the cross" is associated especially with Martin Luther, who, on the basis of the Pauline proclamation of the cross of Christ, emphasized God's shocking self-revelation and gracious act of redemption through the death of Christ for us. Luther set the "theology of the cross" over against every "theology of glory" that looks for God elsewhere than in Christ and his cross, and that thinks of salvation as other than the free, unmerited gift of God.

theosis   A Greek word meaning "divinization" or "deification." Theosis is a central theme of Eastern Orthodox theology and spirituality, summed up in the familiar statement of Athanasius: "God became human that we might become divine." The closest counterparts to the idea of theosis in the theologies of the Western church are "mystical union" with Christ and "sanctification."

theotokos   A Greek term meaning "bearer of God" and used as a name of Mary, the mother of Jesus. Use of this title in worship was the focus of the fifth-century Christological dispute between Cyril of Alexandria, who supported it, and Nestorius, who rejected it in favor of Christotokos, "bearer of Christ." Since the Councils of Ephesus (431 A.D.) and Chalcedon (451 A.D.), *theotokos* has been recognized as a standard of orthodox Christology in both Eastern and Western churches.

threefold office of Christ   This doctrine articulates the saving work of Christ as his fulfillment of the three divinely appointed vocations or offices of prophet (who proclaims God's Word), priest (who offers redeeming sacrifice to God), and king (who rules in God's name and to God's honor). This way of presenting the work of Christ has the advantage not only of comprehensiveness but also of relating it closely to the Old Testament in which prophet, priest, and king are offices established by God. Calvin was one of the first theologians to develop extensively the doctrine of the threefold office *(munus triplex)* of Christ.

transcendence   From the Latin *transcendere*, "stepping over" or "going beyond." As an attribute of God, transcendence is God's mode of being "beyond" or "above" the world. God's being and power surpass the world and are never identical with, confined to, or exhausted in the world God has freely created and to which God freely relates. The early Barth reclaimed the importance of the transcendence of God by speaking of God as radically free and as "wholly other," while the later Barth spoke of God's transcendence as God's freedom to be "God for us."

transubstantiation   The official Roman Catholic doctrine of the eucharist, according to which, after the consecration by an ordained priest, the "substances" of the bread and wine are changed into the "substances" of the body and blood of Christ, while the "accidents" (external properties or appearances) of the bread and wine remain unchanged. This medieval doctrine, which received formal definition at the Council of Trent in the sixteenth century, was a major point of contention with the Reformers. Some recent Roman Catholic theologians have attempted to reconceptualize the doctrine of transubstantiation by speaking instead of transignification (a change in what the elements signify) or transfinalization (a change in the purpose or use of the elements).

Trinity   The distinctively Christian understanding of God as ineffable mystery of love, distinct in three eternal persons, Father, Son, and Holy Spirit, related to each other as Begetter, Begotten, and Breathed Forth, or as Lover, Beloved, and Love. The three equal persons are united in an eternal movement of mutual self-giving love so intimate as to be an "indwelling" or "in-existing" of each other (perichoresis). The doctrine of the Trinity received formal articulation at the Councils of Nicea (325 A.D.) and Constantinople (381 A.D.), and was further refined in the theologies of Augustine in the West and the Cappadocian theologians in the East.

tritheism   Belief in three gods. Opponents of trinitarian faith charge that it amounts to tritheism, but this is not what is taught by the orthodox doctrine of the Trinity. Trinitarian theologians who emphasize a social analogy and sometimes speak of the Trinity as a "community" or "society" of three persons are said by their critics to risk falling into the heresy of tritheism.

truth   As a quality of the being and activity of God, "truth" means reliability and faithfulness and contrasts with human unfaithfulness and falsehood. For Christian faith and theology, the truth of God and God's will has been personally realized and decisively disclosed in Jesus Christ. Theories of truth discussed by philosophers and theologians include truth as correspondence between language and actual reality, truth as that which is coherent or forms a meaningful pattern, and truth as that which is effective in leading to abundant life. Although one of these theories of truth may be given prominence in the work of a theologian, each must receive appropriate attention.

vestiges of the Trinity   Refers to the "marks" or "traces" of the triune being of God in the creation. A number of theologians have found such traces in the natural world (source, spring, river), in the human mind (memory, understanding, will), in the nuclear family (father, mother, child), and in the epochs of human history (age of the Father, age of the Son, age of the Spirit). A classic treatment of vestiges of the Trinity is found in Augustine's *On the Trinity*. While Barth's rejection of natural theology made him suspicious of efforts to discover vestiges of the Trinity, he nevertheless proposed that the one true vestige of the Trinity is the unity in difference of the revealed, written, and proclaimed Word of God.

via negativa, via eminentiae, via causalitatis   Latin phrases for three "ways" of speaking of God: "the negative way," speaking of God by way of negation: God is infinite, immortal, etc. (see *apophatic theology*); "the way of eminence," speaking of God as the perfect realization of goods and values possessed by creatures: God is all-powerful, all-knowing, etc.; and "the way of causality," speaking of God as the source or origin of all that exists.

visible/invisible church   This distinction is used in two ways. In one use, "visible" church refers to the church on earth here and now (the "church militant"), while "invisible" church refers to all the saints who have died and now live with God in heaven (the "church triumphant"). In a second use, prominent in the Reformed theological tradition, "visible" church refers to the empirical church in which there are both elect and non-elect, and "invisible" church refers to all the elect, living and dead, who are known only to God. The point of the distinction in this second sense is that the church is not self-defining but is defined only by God. However, critics of the second distinction argue that it is at best misleading and at worst denigrates the actual church in favor of a merely ideal church.

womanist theology   The distinctive theological emphases of African American women in the United States. Womanist theology affirms the experience of black women and the deep wisdom formed in the struggle for survival under oppressive conditions. This experience and wisdom are seen as resources for a revitalized faith, a reclaiming of the biblical witness, and a prophetic practice by the church today. Related to both black theology and feminist theology, womanist theology criticizes the former as insufficiently attentive to the reality of sexism in both black and white churches, and criticizes the latter as insufficiently attentive to the realities of racism and classism.

Word of God   Refers to the self-expression or self-communication of God. In the Old Testament the Word of God is spoken through prophets. In the New Testament the Word of God refers at times to what is written in Scripture and proclaimed in the gospel, but primarily it refers to the Word of God that was with God in the beginning (Jn. 1:1) and has been embodied in the person and work of Jesus Christ (John 1:14). Barth developed a highly influential doctrine of the Word of God as event that takes a threefold form: Word of God revealed (incarnate in Jesus Christ), Word of God written (Scripture), and Word of God proclaimed (sermon and sacrament).

Index of Names and Subjects

fallen, 149-54; as renewed in Christ, 160-62

Hume, David, 302

Hunsinger, George, 179n.29

Image of God: different interpretations of, 139-41; as *imago Christi* and *imago Trinitatis*, 141-42

Irenaeus, 59, 194, 233

Isasi-Diaz, Ada Maria, 212n.42

Isherwood, Lisa, 209n.32

Israel: covenant of God with, 24; as elect people of God, 88, 90, 183; irrevocable bond of church to, 323-26; witness of God's judgment and mercy, 56; witness to the Holocaust, 120-21

Jackson, Jesse, 239

Jaki, Stanley L., 115

Jennings, Theodore W., Jr., xiii n.1

Jenson, Robert, 76n.15, 172n.18, 262n.24, 279n.10, 299n.37, 324n.59

Jesus Christ: divinity of, 177-78; greater than every Christology, 169; humanity of, 174-77; resurrection of, 191-96; unity of his person, 178-82; virgin birth of, 176; work of, 182-91. *See also* Christology

Jewett, Paul, 146n.17

Jodock, Darrell, 59n.26

John of Damascus, 79, 173n.19

John Paul II, 299

Johnson, Elizabeth A., 75n.12, 80n.24, 84n.36, 209n.33, 210

Johnson, W. Stacy, 137

Joint Declaration on the Doctrine of Justification, 237-38

Jones, L. Gregory, 243n.47, 295n.33

Jones, Serene, 150n.28, 151n.31

Jones, William, 65n.2

Judgment: on evil and injustice, 133-34; and grace, 90; the last judgment, 345-46

Juergensmeyer, Mark, 65n.3, 334n.8, 335n.12

Jüngel, Eberhard, 81n.29, 101n.12, 157n.43, 158n.46, 237n.31

Justification, 235-39

Kafka, Franz, 238

Kant, Immanuel, 45, 302

Käsemann, Ernst, 325n.60, 334

Kasper, Walter, 181n.33

Kaufman, Gordon, 337n.13

Keck, Leander E., 165n.2, 255n.13

Keifert, Patrick R., 267n.31

Kelly, Anthony, 80n.27

Kelly, J. N. D., 170n.15

Kelsey, David H., 10n.16, 57n.24, 157n.44

Kierkegaard, Søren, 42n.46, 303

Kimball, Charles, 305n.6, 335n.12

King, Martin Luther, Jr., 206, 239

Knitter, Paul F., 166n.6, 307, 313, 315-16

Koyama, Kosuke, 217, 218-19

Kreck, Walter, 54n.19

Kuhn, Thomas, 27n.16

Küng, Hans, 166, 251n.6, 304n.5, 313-14, 347n.36

Kyung, Chung Hyun, 219

LaCugna, Catherine Mowry, 69, 76n.14, 82n.31

Lash, Nicholas, 42n.44, 352n.48

Latin-American Liberation Theology: Christology of, 200-204; context of, 200; emphasis on Christian praxis, 203

Lauber, David, 190n.47

Lee, J. Y., 217

Lee, Sang Hyun, 217-18

Lehmann, Paul, 6n.9, 146, 341n.23, 342

Lessing, G. E., 227

Lewis, Alan, 94n.4

Lifton, Robert Jay, 334n.8

Lindbeck, George, 52n.15, 60n.29, 311-12

Lindsell, Harold, 307n.11

Lindsey, Hal, 335

Lochman, Jan Milič, 76n.15, 242n.44

Lohse, Bernhard, 290n.22

Lois, Julio, 201n.7

Lonergan, Bernard, 115n.38

Long, Thomas G., 277n.5

Lord's Supper: *epiclesis*, 292; and ethics, 294-95; many names of, 292; as meal of thanksgiving, joy, and hope, 291-92;

presence of Christ in, 289-91; as sacrifice, 291-92

Lossky, Vladimir, 26n.11

Love: as concern for the good of others based on God's love for us, 161; definitively expressed in the cross of Christ, 190-91; the triune God as mutual, self-giving, community-forming love, 73

Luther, Martin, 2-3, 7, 26, 41, 46, 57, 102, 104, 156, 173n.21, 205, 223, 236-37, 240-41, 242n.45, 273, 280n.12, 284, 290, 334n.9, 340n.21

McCormack, Bruce, 184n.39

McFadyen, Alistair, 150n.28, 151n.32

McFague, Sallie, 66, 111, 112n.33

McGuckin, John A., 172n.18

McIntyre, John, 226n.7

Mackay, John A. 250

McKelway, Alexander, 147n.19

McKim, Donald K., 242n.44

McLain, F. Michael, 37

Macquarrie, John, 120

Malcolm X, 206

Marcel, Gabriel, 3

Martin, James, 136n.39

Martyn, J. Louis, 161n.50

Marx, Karl, 9, 303, 333

Meeks, M. Douglas, 96n.8

Meier, John P., 165n.2

Melanchthon, Philip, 168

Mesters, Carl, 260n.20

Metz, J. B., 133

Meyendorff, John, 179n.30

Michelangelo, 345

Migliore, Daniel L., 44n.1, 84n.36, 124n.16, 137n.41, 242n.44, 265n.28, 346n.29

Miller, Patrick, D., 242n.42

Minear, Paul, 252

Ministry: of all the people of God, 246-47, 295-96; of word and sacrament, 296-99; ordination of women to, 299-300

Miranda, Jose Porfiro, 190n.48

Mitchell, Basil, 35

Mollenkott, Virginia Ramey, 233n.18

Moltmann, Jürgen, 5n.8, 68, 79n.22, 82n.32, 84n.36, 106, 108-9, 110n.29, 113, 116, 132, 146n.17, 176n.25, 196, 226n.9, 232n.16, 235, 241n.40, 244, 270n.38, 295n.33, 314, 324n.59, 326n.62, 330n.1, 339n.15, 341n.22, 348n.37, 349, 350n.44

Mozart, 112

Munus triplex, 186

Nestorius, 171-72

Newbigin, Lesslie, 265n.28, 311n.23, 320-21

Niebuhr, H. Richard, 28, 32n.24, 33n.25, n.26, 38, 73n.11, 186

Niebuhr, Reinhold, 141n.3, 149, 155, 156, 346

Nietzsche, Friedrich, 250, 303

O'Connor, Flannery, 21

O'Gara, Margaret, 221n.70

Ogden, Schubert, 167n.8

Origen, 321

Otto, Rudolf, 102

Pannenberg, Wolfhart, 84n.36, 143, 148n.21, 157n.43, 159n.48, 289n.20

Paris, Peter J., 207n.24

Park, Andrew Sung, 218

Parousia of Christ, 342-43

Pascal, Blaise, 83

Peacocke, A. R., 113n.35, 116n.42

Pelikan, Jaroslav, 42n.43

Peters, Ted., 150n.28

Phan, Peter C. 219

Pinnock, Clark H., 226n.9, 322n.55

Pittenger, W. Norman, 167n.10

Placher, William C., 53n.18

Plantinga, Cornelius, Jr., 78n.20, 79n.22, 150n.28

Plaskow, Judith, 151n.32

Plato, 100

Polanyi, Michael, 115n.39

Polkinghorne, John, 113n.35, 115n.41, 116n.44, 340n.18, 347

Prayer: the chief exercise of faith, 242; as a mark of mature Christian life, 242; and theology, 15

Primavesi, Anne, 295n.34

Proclamation: based on the biblical text,

Index of Scripture References